Theory and Research
in Abnormal Psychology

Theory and Research in Abnormal Psychology

second edition

Edited by

DAVID L. ROSENHAN
Stanford University

PERRY LONDON
University of Southern California

HOLT, RINEHART AND WINSTON, INC.
New York   Chicago   San Francisco   Atlanta
Dallas   Montreal   Toronto   London   Sydney

Library of Congress Cataloging in Publication Data

Rosenhan, David, comp.
    Theory and research in abnormal psychology.

    Includes bibliographies.
    1. Psychology, Pathological—Addresses, essays, lectures.
I.   London, Perry, joint comp.   II.   Title.
[DNLM: 1.   Psychopathology. WM100 R814t]
RC454.R58   1975   157   74-19495

ISBN: 0-03-084294-8

Preface

The course of any endeavor is marked by constancy and change. And the vitality of abnormal psychology, fortunately, yields no exception. The second edition of *Theory and Research in Abnormal Psychology* reflects that progress and solidity. With regard to constancy, some 25 percent of the papers that were published in the first edition will be found here—a rather high rate of republication which reflects the fact that efforts in this area have a certain durability. Despite all that is new in abnormal psychology, we have not hesitated to reprint old classics, papers that were published more than a decade, and some even five decades, ago. That is as it should be. What Freud wrote as Victorianism was buried; what Mary Cover Jones had to say in 1924, and what Mowrer, Szasz, Zigler, and Phillips wrote in the 1950s and later are as useful today as they were then.

But some things really have changed, and those changes are exciting. The debates that began in the 1950s regarding whether psychological distress was or was not an illness, "mental" or otherwise, have come to a head today and are reflected in a variety of new ideas and approaches, some of which are reprinted here. And the raging acrimonies between the behavior and psychoanalytic therapists, and among the psychoanalytic ones—remember?—have muted considerably, allowing for the emergence of a host of new approaches to the amelioration of psychological distress that simply could not have surfaced a decade ago. Social psychological approaches to treatment, cognitive approaches, issues surrounding self-control—all of these might well have been considered heresies in those days. Today they are seen by most psychologists as holding enormous promise for the treatment of psychological distress.

There has been growing awareness that craziness, like beauty, lies to some extent in the eye of the beholder. Efforts by Erving Goffman and others have strongly implicated the viewer in the process of judging who is mad and how we shall react to them. This important theme is given some further emphasis in the papers by Rosenhan and by Zimbardo et al. The latter paper, which deals with perceptions of and behavior responses towards prisoners, is not, strictly speaking, a paper in abnormal psychology. But the "prisoners" reactions to these perceptions and behaviors are clearly distressing. The processes that seem implicated in that study are also implicated in the perception and treatment of psychiatric patients. Indeed, it may very well be that the contexts in which we find people heavily determine how we judge them, and in particular whether we judge them crazy or sane. The important role of context has already been established by social psychologists for other phenomena. The efforts of Braginsky, Braginsky, and Ring, and of one of us bring them closer to home.

If anything has changed in abnormal psychology over the past few years, it is our view of the roles of cognition and affect in psychological distress and in its amelioration. Feeling states have come to be viewed as more central to psychological functioning than had previously been recognized, and the breadth of their influence can be seen in the papers by Freud and by Schachter. The utility of cognition, its growing influence among both behavior therapies and those therapies that are inspired by research in social psychology, is seen in the papers by Gold-fried and Merbaum, Storms and Nisbett, and Meichenbaum and Goodman, as well as in the ones by Schachter.

The contents of the second edition will, we imagine, hold some surprises for at least some readers. Schachter's paper on obesity, for example, is not likely to be found in a compendium on abnormal psychology. Yet, a moment's consideration reveals that obesity is an important psychological problem. It drastically affects appearance, which, in turn, affects the way we think about ourselves and the ways in which others construe us. It has enormous impact on longevity, such that the appearance of obesity among people who want very much to live is itself an anomaly. From a scientific point of view, the work on obesity derives from a theoretical statement that is very promising, and the research and treatment methods that may derive from it easily allow for validation. All in all, obesity is likely to command much more attention from students of abnormal psychology in the future than it has in the past.

Our selections with regard to treatment have been guided by two considerations: theoretical promise and possibilities for validation. For these reasons, many of the new and innovative possibilities in treatment—the marathons and encounters, the massage therapies, primal therapies, and the like—are simply not represented here. Our concern for validation is, we think, one that every intelligent reader will share. The history of psychotherapy has seen a number of heralded treatments, but very few that have proved effective. However strong our faith in any of the newer treatments, our judgment should stand reserved until effectiveness has been demonstrated. During a period when so much is new in psychotherapy, and so much appears promising, that kind of restraint may be difficult for all of us to come by. Yet, it seems the only responsible course to take at a time when inventions and enthusiasms far exceed validations.

Perhaps the largest change in the substance of abnormal psychology during the past few years concerns the rights of patients. *Wyatt v. Stickney*, which is reprinted here, is but one of a growing number of cases brought against psychiatric institutions and practitioners. Within the next few years, the impact of such cases on psychiatric care is likely to be as great as, and to conflict with, the influences deriving from research and professional policy. The student of abnormal psychology can no longer pretend that his efforts and understandings are limited to those who are psychologically distressed. They go far beyond that to social and communal issues and to public policy. They reach to the heart of law. The broader implications of abnormal psychology need very much to be appreciated.

We have enjoyed putting this book together. The very act of selecting has sharpened our intelligence regarding the substance of abnormal psychology and has increased our confidence regarding the judgments we make about where abnormal psychology is and where it is going. As is always the case in collected works, some of the selections make for difficult reading, and some are relatively easy. The difficult papers are worth mastering. Many of the others are written with enviable grace and clarity, even wit, and should constitute memorable intellectual feasts for any reader.

The revision owes much to many people: To authors and publishers who kindly permitted their efforts to be reprinted here; to Dayna Gutleben, who, while still an undergraduate, helped select, edit, and organize papers with an eye to their educational impact on students; to Carol Westmoreland for executing the administrative chores associated with this book; to Jeanne Kennedy for indexing; and to Pat Nash, Deborah Nichols, Barbara Randall, and Phyllis White for typing and retyping the manuscript.

Stanford, California   D. L. R.
Los Angeles, California   P. L.
November 1974

Contents

Texts in
Abnormal Psychology
Cross-Referenced to
Theory and Research
in Abnormal Psychology,
Second Edition

While *Theory and Research in Abnormal Psychology* can itself be used as a text, it can also serve as a companion reader for other texts. On the following pages, the readings in *Theory and Research in Abnormal Psychology* are correlated to the chapters of major textbooks in abnormal psychology.

Cameron, N., Personality Development and Psychopathology. Boston: Houghton Mifflin, 1963.

CHAPTER 1:   Mowrer (6); Szasz (7); Ausubel (8); APA (13); Zigler and Phillips (14); Ruling on Homosexuality (15); Rosenhan (16); Sarbin and Mancuso (19); Wyatt v. Stickney (20); Minimum Constitutional (21); Wexler (22)
CHAPTER 2:   Freud (2); Campbell and Jaynes (4)
CHAPTER 3:   Freud (2); Campbell and Jaynes (4)
CHAPTER 8:   Jones (24)
CHAPTER 12:   Seligman (11)
CHAPTER 15:   Seligman (11)
CHAPTER 17:   Mosher and Gunderson (12); Braginsky, Braginsky, and Ring (18)
CHAPTER 18:   Seligman (11)

CHAPTER 19: Zimbardo, Haney, Banks, and Jaffe (17)
CHAPTER 22: Goldfried and Merbaum (5); Rosenhan (16); Zimbardo, Haney, Banks, and Jaffe (17); Braginsky, Braginsky, and Ring (18); Wyatt v. Stickney (20); Minimum Constitutional (21); Wexler (22); London (23); Meichenbaum and Goodman (25); Storms and Nisbett (26)

Coleman, J. C., Abnormal Psychology and Modern Life. Fourth Edition. Illinois: Scott, Foresman, 1972.

CHAPTER 1: Mowrer (6); Szasz (7); Ausubel (8); Rosenhan (16); Zimbardo, Haney, Banks, and Jaffe (17); Sarbin and Mancuso (19)
CHAPTER 2: Mowrer (6); Szasz (7); Ausubel (8)
CHAPTER 3: Freud (2); Wyatt v. Stickney (20); Minimum Requirements (21); Wexler (22); Jones (24); London (27)
CHAPTER 4: Mowrer (6); Szasz (7); Ausubel (8)
CHAPTER 5: Freud (2); Campbell and Jaynes (4); Zimbardo, Haney, Banks, and Jaffe (17)
CHAPTER 6: Brain (1); Campbell and Jaynes (4); Mowrer (6); Szasz (7); Ausubel (8)
CHAPTER 7: Goldfried and Merbaum (5); Seligman (11)
CHAPTER 8: Maddi (10); Seligman (11); Jones (24)
CHAPTER 9: Mosher and Gunderson (12); Braginsky, Braginsky, and Ring (18)
CHAPTER 10: Seligman (11)
CHAPTER 11: Zimbardo, Haney, Banks, and Jaffe (17)
CHAPTER 14: Schachter (19)
CHAPTER 17: Mosher and Gunderson (12); Jones (24); Meichenbaum and Goodman (25)
CHAPTER 19: APA (13); Zigler and Phillips (14); Ruling on Homosexuality (15); Rosenhan (16)
CHAPTER 20: Goldfried and Merbaum (5); Szasz (7); Mosher and Gunderson (12); Rosenhan (16); Braginsky, Braginsky, and Ring (18); Wyatt v Stickney (20); Minimum Requirements (21); Wexler (22); London (23); Jones (24); Meichenbaum and Goodman (25); Storms and Nisbett (26); London (27)
CHAPTER 21: Sarbin and Mancuso (19); Wyatt v. Stickney (20); Minimum Requirements (21); Wexler (22)

Abnormal Psychology: Current Perspectives. California: Communications Research Machines, 1972.

CHAPTER 1: Mowrer (6); Szasz (7); Ausubel (8); Sarbin and Mancuso (19); Wyatt v. Stickney (20); Minimum Constitutional (21); Wexler (22); Jones (24)
CHAPTER 2: Mowrer (6); Szasz (7); Ausubel (8); APA (13); Zigler and Phillips (14); Ruling on Homosexuality (15); Rosenhan (16); Zimbardo, Haney, Banks, and Jaffe (17); Sarbin and Mancuso (18)
CHAPTER 3: Maddi (10)
CHAPTER 4: Schachter (3); Campbell and Jaynes (4); Goldfried and Merbaum (5); Storms and Nisbett (26); London (27)
CHAPTER 5: Freud (2); Campbell and Jaynes (4)
CHAPTER 6: Schachter (9); Jones (24); Meichenbaum and Goodman (25)
CHAPTER 7: Mosher and Gunderson (12)

Kleinmuntz, B., Essentials of Abnormal Psychology. New York: Harper & Row, 1974.

London, P., and Rosenhan, D., Foundations of Abnormal Psychology. New York: Holt, Rinehart and Winston, 1968.

CHAPTER 5:   Szasz (7); Ausubel (8); Maddi (10); Rosenhan (16); Zimbardo, Haney, Banks, and Jaffe (17); Sarbin and Mancuso (19)

CHAPTER 8:   Freud (2); Campbell and Jaynes (4); Mowrer (6); Zimbardo, Haney, Banks, and Jaffe (17); London (23)

CHAPTER 9:   Szasz (7); Ausubel (8); Wexler (22); London (27)

CHAPTER 10:   Maddi (10); Seligman (11); APA (13); Zigler and Phillips (14); Ruling on Homosexuality (15); London (23)

CHAPTER 11:   Mowrer (6); Seligman (11); Mosher and Gunderson (12); APA (13); Zigler and Phillips (14); Braginsky, Braginsky, and Ring (18)

CHAPTER 12:   APA (13); Zigler and Phillips (14); Ruling on Homosexuality (15); Rosenhan (16); Sarbin and Mancuso (19)

CHAPTER 13:   Brain (1); Schachter (9)

CHAPTER 15:   Goldfried and Merbaum (5); Mosher and Gunderson (12); Rosenhan (16); Zimbardo, Haney, Banks, and Jaffe (17); Braginsky, Braginsky, and Ring (18); Wyatt v. Stickney (20); Minimum Constitutional (21); Wexler (22); London (23); Jones (24); Meichenbaum and Goodman (25); Storms and Nisbett (26); London (27)

CHAPTER 16:   Freud (2); Campbell and Jaynes (4); Goldfried and Merbaum (5); Wyatt v. Stickney (20); Minimum Constitutional (21); Meichenbaum and Goodman (25); London (27)

Maher, B. A., Principles of Psychopathology: An Experimenal Approach. New York: McGraw-Hill, 1966.

CHAPTER 1:   Rosenhan (16); Zimbardo, Haney, Banks, and Jaffe (17); Sarbin and Mancuso (19)

CHAPTER 2:   Mowrer (6); Szasz (7); Ausubel (8); APA (13); Zigler and Phillips (14); Ruling on Homosexuality (15); Rosenhan (16); Sarbin and Mancuso (19); London (23); London (27)

CHAPTER 3:   Campbell and Jaynes (4)

CHAPTER 5:   London (27)

CHAPTER 8:   Maddi (10)

CHAPTER 9:   Zimbardo, Haney, Banks, and Jaffe (17)

CHAPTER 12:   Mosher and Gunderson (12); Zigler and Phillips (14); Braginsky, Braginsky, and Ring (18)

CHAPTER 13:   Mosher and Gunderson (12)

CHAPTER 14:   Mosher and Gunderson (12)

CHAPTER 15:   Mosher and Gunderson (12)

CHAPTER 16:   Goldfried and Merbaum (5); Rosenhan (16); Zimbardo, Haney, Banks, and Jaffe (17); Braginsky, Braginsky, and Ring (18); Wyatt v. Stickney (20); Minimum Constitutional (21); Wexler (22); London (23); Jones (24); Meichenbaum and Goodman (25); Storms and Nisbett (26); London (27)

CHAPTER 17:   Seligman (11)

Sarason, I. G., Abnormal Psychology: The Problem of Maladaptive Behavior. New York: Appleton-Century-Crofts, 1972.

CHAPTER 1:   Mowrer (6); Szasz (7); Ausubel (8); Rosenhan (16); Zimbardo, Haney, Banks, and Jaffe (17); Sarbin and Mancuso (19); Wyatt v. Stickney (20); Minimum Constitutional (21); Wexler (22)

**Ullmann, L. P., and Krasner, L., A Psychological Approach to Abnormal
Behavior.** New Jersey: Prentice-Hall, 1969.

CHAPTER 20:   Mosher and Gunderson (12); Rosenhan (16); Braginsky, Bragin-
    sky, and Ring (18); Wyatt v. Stickney (20); Minimum Constitutional (21)
CHAPTER 21:   Seligman (11)
CHAPTER 23:   Zimbardo, Haney, Banks, and Jaffe (17)
CHAPTER 26:   Jones (24); Meichenbaum and Goodman (25)
CHAPTER 29:   Goldfried and Merbaum (5); Mowrer (6); Szasz (7); Ausubel
    (8); Wyatt v. Stickney (20); Minimum Constitutional (21); London (23)
APPENDIX: APA (13); Zigler and Phillips (14); Ruling on Homosexuality (15)

White, R. W., and Watt, N. F., The Abnormal Personality. Fourth Edition. New York: Ronald Press, 1973.

CHAPTER 1:   Freud (2); Mowrer (6); Szasz (7); Ausubel (8); APA (13); Zig-
    ler and Phillips (14); Rosenhan (16); Zimbardo, Haney, Banks, and Jaffe
    (17); Sarbin and Mancuso (19); Wyatt v. Stickney (20); Minimum Con-
    stitutional (21); Jones (24)
CHAPTER 2:   Szasz (7); Ausubel (8); Zimbardo, Haney, Banks, and Jaffe (17)
CHAPTER 3.   Freud (2); Campbell and Jaynes (4); Jones (24)
CHAPTER 4:   Campbell and Jaynes (4)
CHAPTER 5:   Campbell and Jaynes (4)
CHAPTER 6:   Maddi (10); Jones (24)
CHAPTER 7:   Goldfried and Merbaum (5); London (23); Jones (24); Meichen-
    baum and Goodman (25); Storms and Nisbett (26); London (27)
CHAPTER 8:   Rosenhan (16); Wyatt v. Stickney (20); Minimum Constitutional
    (21); Wexler (22); London (23)
CHAPTER 9:   Zimbardo, Haney, Banks, and Jaffe (17)
CHAPTER 13:   Mosher and Gunderson (12); Braginsky, Braginsky, and Ring
    (18)
CHAPTER 14:   Seligman (11)
CHAPTER 17:   Rosenhan (16); Braginsky, Braginsky, and Ring (18); Sarbin and
    and Mancuso (19); Wyatt v. Stickney (20); Minimum Constitutional (21);
    Wexler (22)

Zax, M., and Cowen, E. L., Abnormal Psychology: Changing Concepts.
New York: Holt, Rinehart and Winston, 1972.

CHAPTER 1:   Mowrer (6); Szasz (7); Ausubel (8); APA (13); Zigler and Phil-
    lips (14); Ruling on Homosexuality (15); Rosenhan (16); Zimbardo, Haney,
    Banks, and Jaffe (17); Sarbin and Mancuso (19)
CHAPTER 4:   Freud (2); Campbell and Jaynes (4); London (23)
CHAPTER 5:   Mosher and Gunderson (12); Braginsky, Braginsky, and Ring (18)
CHAPTER 6:   Mosher and Gunderson (12)
CHAPTER 7:   Seligman(11)
CHAPTER 8:   Maddi (10); Seligman (11)
CHAPTER 12:   Mowrer (6); Szasz (7); Ausubel (8); Rosenhan (16); Zimbardo,
    Haney, Banks, and Jaffe (17); Braginsky, Braginsky, and Ring (18); Sarbin
    and Mancuso (19); London (23)
CHAPTER 13:   Campbell and Jaynes (4); Goldfried and Merbaum (5); Mowrer
    (6); Szasz (7); Ausubel (8); APA (13); Zigler and Phillips (14); Ruling on
    Homosexuality (15); Rosenhan (16); Zimbardo, Haney, Banks, and Jaffe
    (17); Braginsky, Braginsky, and Ring (18); Sarbin and Mancuso (19);

Theory and Research
in Abnormal Psychology

I

Determinants
of Human Behavior

You can't go very far toward understanding abnormal psychology unless you have a solid foundation in personality processes—processes that apply to all of us, normal or abnormal. The reason for this is simple. Abnormal psychology is not a "different" psychology. Rather, it is the laws of learning, affect, cognition, and experience—laws that hold true for everyone—applied to a particular group: people who are in some way special and, traditionally, people who are especially upset. You have to know something about those laws before you can grasp the meaning of abnormality.

Not only do these laws apply to the abnormal as well as the normal, but the differences between abnormal and normal people may not be quite as great as you imagine. Indeed, we often fail to appreciate how *well* socialized even a "crazy" adult is, how responsive he is to the demands of the culture in which we have all grown up. Consider the psychotic. He strikes you as odd, mad if you will, because in some ways his behavior and thinking deviate grossly from his fellows. But, in fact, only a small segment of his total behavior actually deviates very grossly, and it is that segment to which we are most sensitive. But in other respects, the psychotic is usually very much intact. He may, for example, speak sensibly much of the time, eat his meals as others do, partake of common cultural courtesies, and delight in common joys. He may recognize and respond to many of his responsibilities, pay his bills, observe the regularities of meals, bathing, shaving, and bedtime. It is probably fair to say that, over a 24-hour period, his behavior is overtly disturbed no more than one percent of the time. During ninety-nine percent of the time, his acculturation may be indistinguishable from ours. So great is the impact of learning and of socialization that, even under enormous personal stress, much of what has been acquired remains intact.

Yet he is in distress, often in unbelievable distress. While his overt behavior may seem unimpaired much of the time, his covert thoughts, feelings, and perceptions may be a source of enormous personal anguish to him. To begin to understand that anguish you need to have some insight into man's physiology, especially his brain and nervous system, and into the principles that govern learning and feeling. *Exploring the Frontiers of the Mind* (Reading 1) will give you some idea of the excitement that is part of the explorations of brain, neuroanatomy, and neurochemistry. Indeed, the very connections between the physiology of the brain and the psychology of learning and feeling are being forged here. And in appreciating those connections, you will be able to understand much more of the psychology and physiology of the painful conditions that we call schizophrenia and depression.

You know by now that the psychology of learning is an enormous and complex field. In the long run, our guess is that much of it will be relevant to the understanding of psychological distress. But many of the

3

links remain to be forged. At present, one kind of learning that is patently related to psychological abnormality (as well as, of course, to psychological normality) is the kind that is loosely embraced by the term "identification." You have a sense of what that term means if you can recall trying to behave like one of your parents, or like your best friend, or coming out of a movie and swaggering like the hero. That kind of global learning, which incorporates large segments of behavior and feeling, is technically called *observational learning*. Observational learning is one of the strong buttresses of socialization; and socialization, with all its implications for the expectancy of pleasure and pain and for the acquisition of attractive or obnoxious behavior, lies close to the core of what determines personality, both in the normal and abnormal sense.

Freud was the first to elaborate the role of identification (Reading 2). He suspected that there were several different kinds of identification, each occurring under different conditions and with different consequences. His analysis of identification processes revealed how widespread they were and how potent they were as determiners of a variety of disturbances. Subsequent research has not supported all of Freud's hunches, in part because he was wrong perhaps, and in larger part because we cannot yet measure all that Freud was concerned with. Consequently, a good deal of what Freud was talking about remains speculation—but interesting speculation by a man who was an uncanny observer. Read him closely.

It is not only what you learn and do that determine psychological normality and abnormality, but also how you feel about it. You will therefore want to know as much as you can about the psychology of emotion. Emotions are unquestionably the most difficult area for psychologists to study, largely because they are both subjective and fleeting. The most interesting work on the determinants of emotion has been done by Stanley Schachter (Reading 3). A close and careful analysis of this effort will aid you immeasurably in understanding the emotional aspects of distress and pleasure.

The paper by Byron Campbell and Julian Jaynes (Reading 4) on the reinstatement of trauma, is simply a gem. From it, you should get a sense of the limits of psychological speculation. Moreover, it should clarify for you the role of research in illuminating the processes of learning, and in tempering "common sense." It is still commonplace to hear people speak of an early trauma as a determinant of a person's behavior. Often enough, according to Campbell and Jaynes, they are likely to be wrong. This paper sets forth one of the potential "limiting conditions of trauma" for subsequent psychological functioning. And it also tacitly illuminates the reasons for using animals in the psychological research—you would never try that kind of an experiment on infants!

The final paper in this section deals with a reemerging area in psychology: self-control. It is an area that, some 50 or 60 years ago, occupied a central place in the thinking of leading psychological theorists. But it fell to the side of the road because there were no techniques for researching self-control. Recently, however, some techniques have been developed and it is a fair guess that the issues in self-control will occupy center stage again in our thinking about distressed and nondistressed behavior. A good understanding of the paper by Marvin Goldfried and Michael Merbaum (Reading 5) will enable you to understand a later paper on the psychotherapy of self-control.

1

Exploring the Frontiers of the Mind

The most mysterious, least-known area of man's universe does not lie in the farthest reaches of outer space. Nor is it found in the most remote Amazonian jungle or in the inky blackness of the Mariana Trench. It is located instead inside the human skull, and consists of some 3½ pounds of pinkish-gray material with the consistency of oatmeal. It is, of course, the human brain.

The brain is the most important of the body's organs. The heart, after all, is merely a pump; the lungs are an oxygenation system. But the brain is the master control, the guiding force behind all of man's actions. It is the seat of all human thought and consciousness, the source of the ingenuity that made it possible for man's ancestors to survive and eventually to dominate their physically more powerful adversaries and evolve into the planet's highest form of life. Everything that man has ever been, everything he will be, is the product of his brain. It is the brain that enabled the first humanoid to use tools and that gives his genetic successors the ability to build spacecraft, explore the universe and analyze their discoveries. It is the brain that makes man man.

But it took man centuries to comprehend that there was a miraculous mechanism inside his head and begin to investigate its workings. Aristotle taught his pupils that the brain was merely a radiator or cooling system for the blood; he identified the heart as the organ of thought. Pliny the Elder was one of the first to identify the brain as "the citadel of sense perception." But neither he nor generations of scientists who followed him had the knowledge or techniques to explore it. Investigation was also stymied by philosophical obstacles. The brain was considered the seat of the soul; its nature and its workings were considered not only unfathomable but sacrosanct.

Now man has embarked on a great voyage of discovery. In dozens of laboratories in cities round the world, psychologists, biologists, physicists and chemists, recognizing that what goes on inside the brain cannot be divorced from what goes on outside, in increasing numbers are poking, prodding and analyzing the organ in an attempt to unlock its secrets. Man has split the atom, cracked the genetic code and, in a Promethean step unimaginable less than a quarter-century ago, leaped from his own terrestrial home to the moon. But he has yet to solve the mysteries of memory, learning and consciousness or managed to understand himself.

The brain is the newest and perhaps last frontier in man's exploration of himself. Crossing that frontier could have the same impact on humanity as the discovery that the earth was round. "We are like the Europeans of the 15th century," rhapsodizes one brain researcher. "We're standing on the shores of Spain or Portugal, looking out over the Atlantic. We know that there is something on the other side and that our discovery of exactly what this is will mean that things in our world will never be the same again."

The rapidly growing interest and activity in brain research parallels an energetic, worldwide investigation of genetics that preceded James Watson and Francis Crick's 1953 discovery of the structure of the DNA molecule. Indeed, many outstanding biochemists and microbiologists who helped lay the groundwork for that monumental breakthrough have recognized that the brain now represents science's greatest challenge. Some have announced their conversion to neuroscience, the discipline that deals with the brain and nervous system. The work of the neuroscientists has already produced an exponential increase in man's understanding of the brain—and a good bit of immediately applicable knowledge as well. It has led to a host of new medical and surgical treatments for such disorders as schizophrenia, depression, Parkinson's disease and epilepsy. It has also resulted in improved and promising new techniques for relieving pain and controlling some forms of violence.

Even these accomplishments could seem insignificant once the modern Magellans attain their goal of understanding the brain's functions in thought, memory and in consciousness—the sense of identity that distinguishes man from all other known forms of life. Finding the key to these mysteries of the brain, a discovery that would suddenly explain these functions, could lead to better ways of treating the psychoses and neuroses that plague millions. It could result in identification and correction of the causes of many neurological disorders and, by revealing how the brain works, revolutionize thought, education and communication. It might even help man turn away from what some see as a headlong pursuit of self-destruction. "If man could discover why he is unique, he might not destroy himself," says M.I.T. Professor Francis Schmitt, one of the leading brain researchers (*see box*). "He might respect himself more than he now does."

None of those engaged in neuroscientific research underestimate the difficulty of reaching that understanding, for the brain is an organ of enormous complexity. While a sophisticated electronic computer can store and recall some 100 billion "bits" of information, for example, the capacity of the brain seems infinite. The computer can make out a payroll, compute the trajectory of a spacecraft or figure the odds against drawing a straight flush far faster than any human. But the computer is, after all, a machine, capable of doing only what its human builders tell it to do.

The brain, on the other hand, performs a bewildering variety of far more subtle functions. It regulates man's heart and respiratory rates, controls his body temperature and tells him when to take his hands off hot stoves—all without his really being aware of that control. The brain keeps man in touch with the world around him by constantly sorting out the auditory, visual, olfactory, gustatory and tactile information his senses receive, processing it and enabling him to act upon it. It switches emotions on and off and regulates sexual drives.

Furthermore, the brain, unlike the computer, can repair itself: one area can learn to perform the functions of another in some cases of brain damage. And, unlike the computer, which can be turned off at the flip of a switch, the brain remains continuously active, whether waking or sleeping. It can, like an infinitely

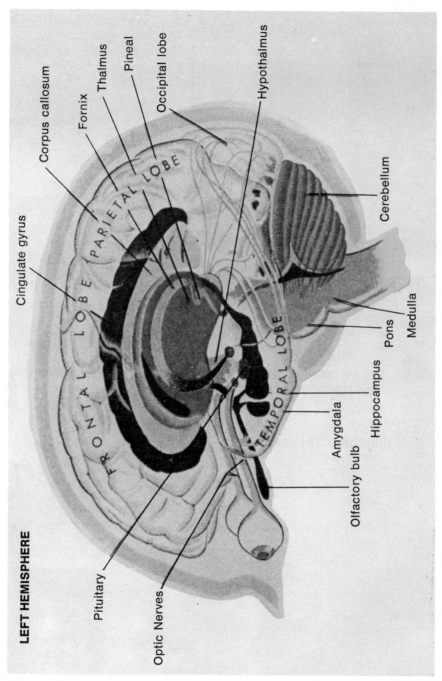

FIG. 1.1   Split from front to rear, the brain reveals its intricate organization. The multilobed cerebrum regulates such functions as speech, hearing and vision. The limbic system, which includes the amygdala, the hippocampus and the hypothalamus, controls the emotions; the pituitary produces hormones linked to growth and development. (Time diagram by W. Hortens.)

FRONTAL VIEW

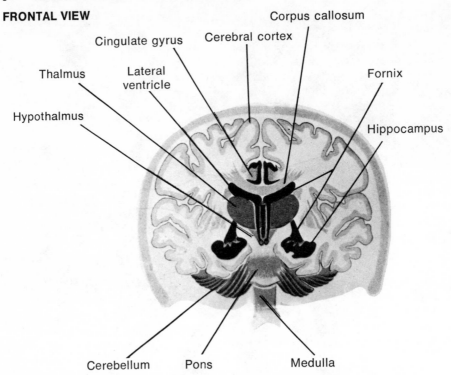

FIG. 1.2   Seen from the front, the brain's hemispheres fill the dome of the skull. The two halves are linked by the corpus callosum. (Time diagram by W. Hortens.)

NEURONAL TRANSMISSION

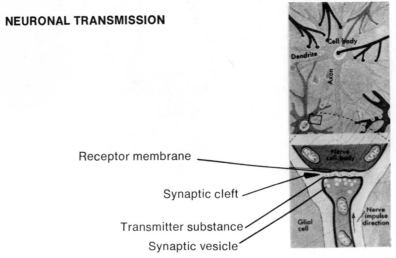

FIG. 1.3   Neurons transmit information by secreting chemicals that cross the synaptic gap and bind to receptor sites on neighboring nerve cells. (Time diagram by W. Hortens.)

repeated image in a hall of mirrors, think about itself as it thinks about itself thinking about itself.

The scientific effort to fathom the miracle of the brain is proceeding on many fronts, often apparently unrelated. Some of the most fascinating yet arcane work in the neurosciences is being done by zoologists like Theodore Bullock, 58, of the Scripps Institution of Oceanography in La Jolla, Calif. He is studying electric fish in order to identify interior pathways of brain communication. That knowledge could lead to an understanding of how a brain communicates within itself. Other apparently tangential but vitally important research is being undertaken by Nobel-Prizewinning Immunologist Gerald Edelman, 44, of New York's Rockefeller University. Edelman notes that the immune system, which enables the body to defend itself against disease, is capable of memory. He has suggested that mechanisms similar to those that enable immunologically active cells to recognize microbes and other foreign material may also play a role in the brain's own memory system. The mechanisms could also conceivably tell cells where they fit into the "wiring diagram" of the brain while the organ is developing.

Most neuroscientists are conducting their research on cellular and subcellular levels, figuring that only by understanding how individual neurons work can they understand how the brain itself functions. "Studying the brain is like looking at a building called a bank and trying to figure out what it's for," says Dr. David Bodian, professor and director of the department of anatomy at Johns Hopkins University School of Medicine in Baltimore. "You can get some idea of its function by watching people go in and out. You can get an even better idea if you go inside and observe more closely."

The most advanced and exciting brain research now being conducted is directed toward discovering how the brain perceives, processes and stores information. Some scientists confine their work to only one area at a time; the brain is too complex and knowledge still too limited to do otherwise. Others, like Professor Hans-Lukas Teuber, 57, who heads M.I.T.'s department of psychology, insist on studying the three aspects together. "The way we perceive patterns, whether through sight, touch or other senses," he says, "is intimately linked to the way we pattern our skilled movements, and both perception and movement inevitably involve problems of memory."

Teuber believes that such knowledge is essential for an understanding of higher brain functions, which intrigue him far more than investigations into so-called psychic phenomena. "The mystery lies where we least expect it: in sensory rather than extrasensory perception," he says. "What fascinates me is the way that you and I are able to sit opposite each other and make sounds that we receive, decode, process and then use as a basis for making more sounds. Now that is a real mystery."

Others, too, are interested in solving that mystery. Robert Galambos, 59, a professor of neurosciences at the University of California at San Diego, is attempting to track auditory impulses from the ear, through the brain stem and into the cortex. He is studying several brain-wave patterns, including what is called the "Aha wave," which the brain generates when it finds what it is looking for.

Hugh Christopher Longuet-Higgins of the University of Edinburgh is trying to make computer models of the way people produce sentences and understand language. Floyd Bloom, 37, chief of the laboratory of neuropharmacology at the National Institute of Mental Health in Bethesda, Md., and Walle Nauta, 57, of M.I.T., are using special staining techniques to trace the brain's neuronal pathways. "We have a long way to go," says Bloom, "but every little piece of information we gather leads us toward a better understanding of the way that the brain reacts to the outside world."

twin mysteries

In their work, all of these researchers are striving toward two major goals: explaining learning and memory. Anatomically, there is no specific learning center in the brain, and there is no explanation for learning. "There is no known basis for learning; it cannot take place," says Teuber. "In fact," he adds jokingly, "as a teacher, I sometimes wonder if it does."

But learning does occur, and most researchers believe that a crucial factor in the process is protein synthesis—the creation of complex molecules. Steven Rose, 35, a professor at Britain's Open University, has found that as chicks were trained to master certain simple skills, certain brain proteins increased.

Sweden's Holger Hydén, 56, director of the Institute of Neurobiology at the University of Göteborg, has found even more convincing evidence that proteins play a role in learning. Hydén (pronounced he-*dayn*) trained rats and then killed them so that their brains could be studied. He found that certain nervous-system proteins were produced in greater amounts during the first part of learning, when the animals were striving to cope with a new problem; over-training the animals produced no higher levels of the substances. Hydén then injected animals with antibodies against the protein, which is called S-100. The injection, which blocked the protein's activity, also caused the animals' learning rate to lessen markedly. Other findings tend to reinforce this conclusion. Protein-deficient rats learn much more slowly than well-fed animals. Also, protein-deficient children from poor families habitually trail better-fed, middle-class children in intellectual development, even when the children receive the same education.

Of equal fascination to researchers is the persistence of memory, the ability not only to store but also to recall information and experiences. In Proust's *Remembrance of Things Past*, Marcel released a flood of memories by tasting a tea-soaked *petite Madeleine*. Others have found that a memory-jogging whiff of perfume, a word, a few notes of music can conjure up similar—and often realistic—recollections of events they experienced many years earlier. A landmark discovery was made by the great Canadian neurosurgeon, Wilder Penfield, when he found that he could stimulate memories electrically. Probing a patient's brain with an electrode in order to locate the source of her epileptic seizures, Penfield was amazed when the young woman recalled an incident from her childhood in vivid detail. Penfield continued his studies and found that touching various parts of his patients' cerebral cortices with an electrode could enable them to remember songs long forgotten and experiences they thought were lost forever.

Subsequent experiments have proved that though the cortex is involved with memory, it does not act like a computer's memory bank, in which each bit of information is stored in a single electronic "cell." Memory, it has been found, is "delocalized" or spread throughout the cortex, and perhaps throughout the higher brain. Removing half the cortex may cause a proportional loss of capacity to remember, but it does not destroy specific memories.

Experiments and observations now support a three-level theory of memory. The lowest level is short-term memory, lasting no more than a few seconds; every moment of life, hundreds of sensory impressions flow into the human brain and are promptly forgotten. On the next level is medium-term memory, which lasts from a few minutes to a few hours, and enables man to remember something like a telephone number just long enough to dial it or to cram for an examination. At the highest level is long-term memory, which is sifted out of all the impressions and information entering the brain and preserved because of its importance, usefulness or vividness.

Long-term memory takes time to register permanently on the brain. If rats are given an electric shock immediately after learning a new skill, memory of the skill is lost. If the shock is delayed for half an hour, the memory is impaired. But if 24 hours elapse between learning and shock, most of the memory remains. Human beings react in the same way.

Most researchers agree that the limbic, or feeling brain plays a key role in long-term memory. The limbic system is concerned with affects—strong emotional experiences, for example—which people obviously remember. One part of the limbic system, the hippocampus, is indisputably vital to memory. Patients whose hippocampi have been destroyed or partially removed cannot recall new information. Dr. Robert Livingston of the University of California at San Diego postulates that the structure plays the same role in memory as the "now store" button does on a computer, determining whether a particular bit of information is to be stored or discarded.

theoretical leap

Many researchers feel that memories are stored and recalled by a combination of macromolecules or large molecules that probably differ considerably from one individual to another. Thus they reject the notion of some science-fiction writers that memory molecules—and thereby memories—may one day be transferred from one brain to another. "The immune response is a learned reaction," says Rockefeller University's Edelman, again citing the parallel between memory and immunology. "There is no Marcel Proust for immunology. I doubt that there's one for the neurosciences."

While focusing down on individual cells in the course of their investigations into the grand scheme of the brain, neuroscientists—like the Persian fairy tale's three princes of Serendip—have been making fortuitous discoveries that have already resulted in improved clinical treatment of several serious illnesses. Among them:

Schizophrenia. Doctors know that two groups of drugs, which include chlorpromazine and haloperidol, are remarkably effective in relieving the thought disorders, hallucinations and extreme withdrawal of schizophrenia, a chronic psychosis that affects one person out of every 100. Both drugs, if administered in excess, can produce symptoms similar to those of Parkinson's disease, a neurological disorder characterized by uncontrollable tremors and lack of coordination. Parkinson's disease is caused by a lack of dopamine, a substance that transmits nerve impulses, in the brain centers that coordinate movement. Biochemical and electrophysiological studies have shown that chlorpromazine and haloperidol block the action of dopamine. Thus brain researchers suspect that schizophrenia results, at least in part, from an excess of dopamine.

Another clue to schizophrenia, says Dr. Seymour Kety, chief of the psychiatric research laboratories at Massachusetts General Hospital, lies in the discovery of an enzyme in the brains of both animals and man that can convert normal brain chemicals like tryptamine to dimethyltryptamine, a well-known hallucinogen. Kety and other scientists speculate that in schizophrenics such a process may be out of control.

Depression. Some severe psychiatric illnesses can now be controlled chemically. Researchers have theorized that depression may result when certain brain substances called monoamines are either lacking or are broken down too quickly. A new class of drugs neutralizes monoamine oxidase (MAO), the enzyme that destroys these substances. The drugs, known as MAO inhibitors, thus prolong the useful life of the monoamines in the brain. The drugs by themselves are not considered a cure for depression, but they can give relief to the victim of acute depression while psychotherapy attempts to get at the root of his problem.

Parkinson's disease, which afflicts over a million Americans, could once be relieved only by severing certain nerve pathways deep in the cerebrum. While the operation relieved the tremors and rigidity of the disease, patients could suffer partial paralysis and loss of speech. Now, most Parkinson's victims can be relieved by a drug known as levodihydroxyphenylalanine, or L-dopa. First used successfully by George Cotzias of the Brookhaven National Laboratory, L-dopa provides a classic example of molecular chemistry at work. Normal movement depends in large part upon the action of dopamine, one of the brain's most important chemical transmitters. Parkinson's disease results from a degeneration of the cells that help produce this chemical. By boosting the level of dopamine in the brain, L-dopa helps to prevent the palsy associated with the disease.

The drug is also enabling doctors to take some tentative yet encouraging steps toward treating Huntington's chorea, a genetically-determined degenerative nerve disease that strikes its victims at about the age of 40 and kills them within 15 years. A group headed by Dr. Leslie Iverson, 36, of the British Medical Research Council's Division of Neurochemical Pharmacology, has been studying the chemical changes in brains of Huntington's victims. The team has found that victims of the disease have lower-than-normal quantities of the transmitter gamma amino butyric acid (GABA) and occasionally-elevated amounts of dopamine. They are now trying to develop drugs that will restore the balance between these chemicals.

Epilepsy, which affects one person out of every 100 is caused by clusters of brain cells, or foci, that discharge electrical impulses paroxysmally. It produces violent seizures resulting in convulsions and unconsciousness, brief staring spells or episodes of uncontrollable rage. Researchers have discovered that most epileptic conditions can be controlled by a drug called Dilantin, which Dr. Frank Morrell, 47, of Chicago's Rush Medical College, believes prevents epileptic discharges from spreading to neighboring neurons.

A technique for relieving cases of epilepsy that resist treatment by drugs has been devised by Dr. Irving Cooper, 51, of St. Barnabas Hospital in New York. Cooper has found that stimulating the cerebellum electrically apparently increases its inhibitory action on the cerebrum. Cooper has implanted electronic "pacemakers" upon the cerebellums of several epileptics, as well as patients suffering from stroke-caused paralysis, cerebral palsy and from dystonia, a neuromuscular defect in which permanently flexed muscles twist and distort the limbs. The device, which stimulates the cerebellum with low-voltage jolts, has produced relief in most of the 70 cases in which it has been used. One muscular 26-year-old man suffered from daily epileptic seizures before he came to Cooper for a pacemaker. Since the machine was implanted a year ago, the man has been free of major seizures.

There are other areas in which neuroscientific research is paying dividends:

Relieving pain. Doctors are still not sure how the brain perceives pain, but some neurosurgeons have found ways of relieving the chronic and acute discomfort associated with terminal cancer and other diseases. Dr. William Sweet, chief of neurosurgery at Massachusetts General Hospital, has found that by destroying small clusters of cells in different parts of the brain, either by freezing or by electric current, he can relieve pain without producing the degrading effects of the old-style prefrontal lobotomy, which often produced antisocial behavior and eventually mental deterioration. He has also found a way of dealing with *tic douloureux,* an excruciatingly painful nervous disorder involving the trigeminal nerve of the face. With his patient sedated but conscious, Sweet places electrodes in the face and destroys certain small nerve fibers that transmit pain without harming those larger fibers involved in perceiving touch. . . .

Biofeedback control. A handful of yoga and Zen masters have known for centuries how to control such autonomic or involuntary nervous functions as heart and respiratory rates. Rockefeller University Psychologist Neal Miller has found ways to help those with a less spiritual outlook to achieve the same kind of control. Using devices that enable patients to monitor various body functions like blood circulation and heartbeat, Miller and other researchers have trained them to raise and lower their blood pressure and hand temperatures. The phenomenon, he explains, is basically no different from other forms of learning. All learning depends on some sort of feedback to the brain—from eyes, hand or other sources—that tells the student whether he is succeeding or failing in what he is trying to do. Biofeedback-monitoring devices simply enable the patient to tell when he is consciously controlling his involuntary functions. Miller's work has been capitalized upon by charlatans and mystics who insist that biofeedback can bring a kind of instant satori to those willing to spend money for lessons and equipment. But many legitimate researchers also believe that biofeedback may prove valuable in controlling moods and dealing with certain illnesses.

While neuroscientists look forward eagerly to the day when they will understand how the brain works, some people feel that they have already gone too far. There are those who fear that new drugs and surgical techniques could be used to impose a form of "mind control" on nonconformists, tranquilize prisoners or inmates of mental hospitals, and tame those whose behavior or ideas society finds troubling. They note that psychosurgery is being widely used in Japan to calm down hyperactive children. They also observe with alarm the tendency of some school physicians to recommend drug treatment for these school children. Others, on a more philosophical level, are concerned lest the neurosciences succeed in erasing the factitious line between "mind" and "brain" and reduce man to a collection of neurons.

Neuroscientists generally appreciate their concern. "It is a measure of the distrust with which science is now viewed that people automatically think first of the evil that scientific knowledge can bring," says M.I.T.'s Teuber. "It's as if we're suffering from some sort of Manhattan Project complex."

Most neuroscientists agree that their science can be abused but doubt that it will be. Schmitt, for example, feels that fear of thought control is unreasonable. "When it comes to thought control," he says, "politicians and journalists do a better job than neuroscientists." Instead, the brain researchers stress that the benefits resulting from their research would far outweigh the dangers. An understanding of how the brain works could lead to treatments for some forms of

The Anatomy of the Brain

Growing out of the spinal cord like the crown of a tree out of its trunk, the brain has several major components (*see* Figs. 1.1, 1.2, and 1.3). The limbic system, an area that surrounds the head of the brain stem and includes such structures as the amygdala, part of the thalamus, hypothalamus and hippocampus, regulates the emotions. The pituitary, which hangs down from the brain stem like an olive from the tree, produces the hormones that influence growth and development. The cerebellum, a fist-sized structure at the rear of the brain that controls movements and coordination, enables man to touch his nose with his finger or throw touchdown passes. But it is the cerebrum that distinguishes man from other animals. Fish have little or no cerebral tissue, nor do birds. Chimpanzees, man's closest animal relatives, have larger cerebrums than most other primates, but man's is the largest.

Consisting largely of gray matter and fissured like a lunar landscape, the cerebrum dominates the human brain, filling the dome of the skull. It also makes man what he is, for it contains the areas that control thought and consciousness, the quality that enables man to remember his past, understand the present and anticipate his future.

Divided down the middle like the two halves of a walnut, the cerebral hemispheres are anatomically separate, but are cross-wired so that each controls the opposite side of the body—the left monitoring the right side, the right regulating the left. One hemisphere—the left in most people—is dominant and contains the areas that are associated with speech and hearing and involved with analytical tasks such as solving an algebra problem. The other governs spatial perception, synthesis of ideas and aesthetic appreciation of art or music. Normally these two hemispheres communicate with each other through a bundle of nerve fibers known as the *corpus callosum*. But if this connection is severed, their autonomy becomes evident. "Split brain" patients lose few of the two-handed skills already learned; they do have great difficulty learning new tasks that require both hands.

The brain is composed of two kinds of cells: neurons, or nerve cells, of which there are some 100 billion, and glia, which outnumber the neurons by a ratio of 10 to 1. Neurons, which are the functional units of the brain (glia, scientists believe, are largely "filler"), are connected to each other by means of long filaments, or dendrites, and form the body's nerve network. These cells receive sensory impulses, process the myriad bits of information pouring into the brain each moment, and transmit the brain's messages out to the various parts of the body, causing such reactions as the contracting and relaxing of muscles.

It has long been known that these messages are transmitted electrically. More recent research has shown that communication between the neurons is also chemical in nature. Neurons have bulbous endings called synapses. These secrete chemicals that cross the submicroscopic gaps between the individual cells, lock onto special sites on the dendrites of neighboring cells and cause these cells to release chemicals of their own. That action allows the passage of current from one cell to another.

The speed with which these cells can carry out their chemical transactions is, quite literally, mind-boggling. Manfred Eigen, 46, director of Germany's noted Max Planck Institute for Biophysical Chemistry in Göttingen, has found that some of the brain's chemical reactions take as little as one-millionth of a second. As many as 100,000 neurons may be involved in transmitting the information that results in as simple an action as stepping back to avoid being struck by an oncoming car. The entire process occurs in less than a second.

mental retardation. A greater knowledge of what takes place during learning could result in improvement in teaching techniques. Even human intelligence might be increased as a result.

A breakthrough could also lead to the kind of social evolution that might help prevent the conflicts that now set man against man and nation against nation. "Most of our evolution has been somatic," says Schmitt. "We've changed our shape. But if we could really understand ourselves and by extension each other, we could evolve socially as well." That kind of evolution, Schmitt contends, may well be necessary for the continuation of the species. "Armies aren't the key to man's survival," he says. "Governments are not enough. Treaties are not enough. Only self-knowledge will help man to survive."

The ocean that separates man from this self-knowledge remains to be charted. Crossing it will require money, dedication, ingenuity and the development of a whole new field of science and technology. The explorers of the brain have embarked on a journey even more significant than the voyage of Columbus in 1492. Columbus discovered a new continent. The explorers of the brain may well discover a new world.

2
Group Psychology and the Analysis of the Ego
Sigmund Freud

Identification is known to psycho-analysis as the earliest expression of an emotional tie with another person. It plays a part in the early history of the Oedipus complex. A little boy will exhibit a special interest in his father; he would like to grow like him and be like him, and take his place everywhere. We may say simply that he takes his father as his ideal. This behaviour has nothing to do with a passive or feminine attitude towards his father (and towards males in general); it is on the contrary typically masculine. It fits in very well with the Oedipus complex, for which it helps to prepare the way.

At the same time as this identification with his father, or a little later, the boy has begun to develop a true object-cathexis towards his mother according to the attachment [anaclitic] type.[1] He then exhibits, therefore, two psychologically distinct ties: a straightforward sexual object-cathexis towards his mother and an identification with his father which takes him as his model. The two subsist side by side for a time without any mutual influence or interference. In consequence of the irresistible advance towards a unification of mental life, they come together

Reprinted from *Group Psychology and the Analysis of the Ego*, Chap. 7, Vol. 23, in *The Complete Psychological Works of Sigmund Freud*, with the permission of Sigmund Freud Copyrights Ltd., The Institute of Psycho-Analysis and Mrs. Alix Strachey, and the Hogarth Press Ltd., and Liveright Publishing Corporation.

at last; and the normal Oedipus complex originates from their confluence. The little boy notices that his father stands in his way with his mother. His identification with his father then takes on a hostile colouring and becomes identical with the wish to replace his father in regard to his mother as well. Identification, in fact, is ambivalent from the very first; it can turn into an expression of tenderness as easily as into a wish for someone's removal. It behaves like a derivative of the first, *oral* phase of the organization of the libido, in which the object that we long for and prize is assimilated by eating and is in that way annihilated as such. The cannibal, as we know, has remained at this standpoint; he has a devouring affection for his enemies and only devours people of whom he is fond.[2]

The subsequent history of this identification with the father may easily be lost sight of. It may happen that the Oedipus complex becomes inverted, and that the father is taken as the object of a feminine attitude, an object from which the directly sexual instincts look for satisfaction; in that event the identification with the father has become the precursor of an object-tie with the father. The same holds good, with the necessary substitutions, of the baby daughter as well.[3]

It is easy to state in a formula the distinction between an identification with the father and the choice of the father as an object. In the first case one's father is what one would like to *be,* and in the second he is what one would like to *have.* The distinction, that is, depends upon whether the tie attaches to the subject or to the object of the ego. The former kind of tie is therefore already possible before any sexual object-choice has been made. It is much more difficult to give a clear metapsychological representation of the distinction. We can only see that identification endeavours to mould a person's own ego after the fashion of the one that has been taken as a model.

Let us disentangle identification as it occurs in the structure of a neurotic symptom from its rather complicated connections. Supposing that a little girl (and we will keep to her for the present) develops the same painful symptom as her mother—for instance, the same tormenting cough. This may come about in various ways. The identification may come from the Oedipus complex; in that case it signifies a hostile desire on the girl's part to take her mother's place, and the symptom expresses her object-love towards her father, and brings about a realization, under the influence of a sense of guilt, of her desire to take her mother's place: 'You wanted to be your mother, and now you *are*—anyhow so far as your sufferings are concerned.' This is the complete mechanism of the structure of a hysterical symptom. Or, on the other hand, the symptom may be the same as that of the person who is loved; so, for instance, Dora[4] imitated her father's cough. In that case we can only describe the state of things by saying *that identification has appeared instead of object-choice, and that object-choice has regressed to identification.* We have heard that identification is the earliest and original form of emotional tie; it often happens that under the conditions in which symptoms are constructed, that is, where there is repression and where the mechanisms of the unconscious are dominant, object-choice is turned back into identification—the ego assumes the characteristics of the object. It is noticeable that in these identifications the ego sometimes copies the person who is not loved and sometimes the one who is loved. It must also strike us that in both cases the identification is a partial and extremely limited one and only borrows a single trait from the person who is its object.

There is a third particularly frequent and important case of symptom formation, in which the identification leaves entirely out of account any object-relation to the person who is being copied. Supposing, for instance, that one of the girls in a boarding school has had a letter from someone with whom she is secretly in love which arouses her jealousy, and that she reacts to it with a fit of hysterics; then some of her friends who know about it will catch the fit, as we say, by mental infection. The mechanism is that of identification based upon the possibility or desire of putting oneself in the same situation. The other girls would like to have a secret love affair too, and under the influence of a sense of guilt they also accept the suffering involved in it. It would be wrong to suppose that they take on the symptom out of sympathy. On the contrary, the sympathy only arises out of the identification, and this is proved by the fact that infection or imitation of this kind takes place in circumstances where even less pre-existing sympathy is to be assumed than usually exists between friends in a girls' school. One ego has perceived a significant analogy with another upon one point—in our example upon openness to a similar emotion; an identification is thereupon constructed on this point, and, under the influence of the pathogenic situation, is displaced on to the symptom which the one ego has produced. The identification by means of the symptom has thus become the mark of a point of coincidence between the two egos which has to be kept repressed.

What we have learned from these three sources may be summarized as follows. First, identification is the original form of emotional tie with an object; secondly, in a regressive way it becomes a substitute for a libidinal object-tie, as it were by means of introjection of the object into the ego; and thirdly, it may arise with any new perception of a common quality shared with some other person who is not an object of the sexual instinct. The more important this common quality is, the more successful may this partial identification become, and it may thus represent the beginning of a new tie.

We already begin to divine that the mutual tie between members of a group is in the nature of an identification of this kind, based upon an important emotional common quality; and we may suspect that this common quality lies in the nature of the tie with the leader. Another suspicion may tell us that we are far from having exhausted the problem of identification, and that we are faced by the process which psychology calls 'empathy [*Einfühlung*]' and which plays the largest part in our understanding of what is inherently foreign to our ego in other people. But we shall here limit ourselves to the immediate emotional effects of identification, and shall leave on one side its significance for our intellectual life.

Psycho-analytic research, which has already occasionally attacked the more difficult problems of the psychoses, has also been able to exhibit identification to us in some other cases which are not immediately comprehensible. I shall treat two of these cases in detail as material for our further consideration.

The genesis of male homosexuality in a large class of cases is as follows.[5] A young man has been unusually long and intensely fixated upon his mother in the sense of the Oedipus complex. But at last, after the end of puberty, the time comes for exchanging his mother for some other sexual object. Things take a sudden turn: the young man does not abandon his mother, but identifies himself with her; he transforms himself into her, and now looks about for objects which can replace his ego for him, and on which he can bestow such love and care as he has experienced from his mother. This is a frequent process, which can be confirmed as often as one likes, and which is naturally quite independent of any hypothesis that may be made as to the organic driving force and the motives of the sudden transformation. A striking thing about this identification is its ample scale; it remoulds the ego in one of its important features—in its sexual character—

upon the model of what has hitherto been the object. In this process the object itself is renounced—whether entirely or in the sense of being preserved only in the unconscious is a question outside the present discussion. Identification with an object that is renounced or lost, as a substitute for that object—introjection of it into the ego—is indeed no longer a novelty to us. A process of the kind may sometimes be directly observed in small children. A short time ago an observation of this sort was published in the *Internationale Zeitschrift für Psychoanalyse*. A child who was unhappy over the loss of a kitten declared straight out that now he himself was the kitten, and accordingly crawled about on all fours, would not eat at table, etc.[6]

Another such instance of introjection of the object has been provided by the analysis of melancholia,[7] an affection which counts among the most notable of its exciting causes the real or emotional loss of a loved object. A leading characteristic of these cases is a cruel self-depreciation of the ego combined with relentless self-criticism and bitter self-reproaches. Analyses have shown that this disparagement and these reproaches apply at bottom to the object and represent the ego's revenge upon it. The shadow of the object has fallen upon the ego, as I have said elsewhere.[8] The introjection of the object is here unmistakably clear.

But these melancholias also show us something else, which may be of importance for our later discussions. They show us the ego divided, fallen apart into two pieces, one of which rages against the second. This second piece is the one which has been altered by introjection and which contains the lost object. But the piece which behaves so cruelly is not unknown to us either. It comprises the conscience, a critical agency within the ego, which even in normal times takes up a critical attitude towards the ego, though never so relentlessly and so unjustifiably. On previous occasions[9] we have been driven to the hypothesis that some such agency develops in our ego which may cut itself off from the rest of the ego and come into conflict with it. We have called it the 'ego ideal', and by way of functions we have ascribed to it self-observation, the moral conscience, the censorship of dreams, and the chief influence in repression. We have said that it is the heir to the original narcissism in which the childish ego enjoyed self-sufficiency; it gradually gathers up from the influences of the environment the demands which that environment makes upon the ego and which the ego cannot always rise to; so that a man, when he cannot be satisfied with his ego itself, may nevertheless be able to find satisfaction in the ego ideal which has been differentiated out of the ego. In delusions of observation, as we have further shown, the disintegration of this agency has become patent, and has thus revealed its origin in the influence of superior powers, and above all of parents.[10] But we have not forgotten to add that the amount of distance between this ego ideal and the real ego is very variable from one individual to another, and that with many people this differentiation within the ego does not go further than with children.

It is now easy to define the difference between identification and such extreme developments of being in love as may be described as "fascination" or "bondage".[11] In the former case the ego has enriched itself with the properties of the object, it has 'introjected' the object into itself, as Ferenczi [1909] expresses it. In the second case it is impoverished, it has surrendered itself to the object, it has substituted the object for its own most important constituent. Closer consideration soon makes it plain, however, that this kind of account creates an illusion of contradistinctions that have no real existence. Economically there is no question of impoverishment or enrichment; it is even possible to describe an extreme case of being in love as a state in which the ego has introjected the object into itself.

Another distinction is perhaps better calculated to meet the essence of the matter. In the case of identification the object has been lost or given up; it is then set up again inside the ego, and the ego makes a partial alteration in itself after the model of the lost object. In the other case the object is retained, and there is a hypercathexis of it by the ego and at the ego's expense. But here again a difficulty presents itself. Is it quite certain that identification presupposes that object-cathexis has been given up? Can there be no identification while the object is retained? And before we embark upon a discussion of this delicate question, the perception may already be beginning to dawn on us that yet another alternative embraces the real essence of the matter, namely, *whether the object is put in the place of the ego or of the ego ideal.*

notes

1. [See Section II of Freud's paper on narcissism (1914c).]
2. See my *Three Essays* (1905d) [*Standard Ed.*, 7, 198] and Abraham (1916).
3. [The 'complete' Oedipus complex, comprising both its 'positive' and its 'negative' forms, is discussed by Freud in Chapter III of *The Ego and the Id* (1923b).]
4. In my 'Fragment of an Analysis of a Case of Hysteria' (1905e) [*Standard Ed.*, 7, 82–3].
5. [See Chapter III of Freud's study on Leonardo (1910c). . . .]
6. Marcuszewicz (1920).
7. [Freud habitually uses the term 'melancholia' for conditions which would now be described as 'depression'.]
8. See 'Mourning and Melancholia' (1917e).
9. In my paper on narcissism (1914c) and in 'Mourning and Melancholia' (1917e).
10. Section III of my paper on narcissism.
11. [The 'bondage' of love had been discussed by Freud in the early part of his paper on 'The Taboo of Virginity' (1918a).]

3

The Interaction of Cognitive and Physiological Determinants of Emotional State

Stanley Schachter

Many years ago, piqued by the disorderly cataloguing of symptoms that characterized the then classic works on emotion, William James offered what was probably the first simple, integrating, theoretical statement on the nature of emotion. This well-known formulation stated simply that "the bodily changes

Reprinted from *Emotion, Obesity, and Crime*, New York: Academic Press, 1971, Chap. 1, pp. 1–23, with the permission of Academic Press and the author.

follow directly the perception of the exciting fact, and that our feeling of the same changes as they occur *is* the emotion (James, 1890, p. 449)." Since James' proposition equates bodily changes and visceral feelings with emotion, it must follow, first, that the different emotions will be accompanied by recognizably different bodily states and, second, that the manipulation of bodily state, by drugs or surgery, will also manipulate emotional state. These implications have, directly or indirectly, guided much of the research on emotion since James' day. The results of this research, on the whole, provided little support for a purely visceral formulation of emotion, and led Cannon (1927, 1929) to his brilliant and devastating critique of the James-Lange theory—a critique based on these points:

1. The total separation of the visceral from the central nervous system does not alter emotional behavior.
2. The same visceral changes occur in very different emotional states and in nonemotional states.
3. The viscera are relatively insensitive structures.
4. Visceral changes are too slow to be a source of emotional feeling.
5. The artificial induction of visceral changes that are typical of strong emotions does not produce the emotions.

   Though new data have weakened the cogency of some of these points, on the whole Cannon's logic and findings make it inescapably clear that a completely peripheral or visceral formulation of emotion, such as the James-Lange theory, is simply inadequate to cope with the facts. In an effort to deal with the obvious inadequacies of a purely visceral or peripheral formulation of emotion, Ruckmick (1936), Hunt, Cole, and Reis (1958), Schachter (1959), and others have suggested that cognitive factors may be major determinants of emotional states. In this [chapter] I shall attempt to spell out the implications of a cognitive-physiological formulation of emotion and to describe a series of experiments designed to test these implications.

   To begin, let us grant, on the basis of much evidence (see Woodworth and Schlosberg, 1954, for example), that a general pattern of sympathetic discharge is characteristic of emotional states. Given such a state of arousal, it is suggested that one labels, interprets, and identifies this state in terms of the characteristics of the precipitating situation and one's apperceptive mass. This suggests, then, that an emotional state may be considered a function of a state of physiological arousal[1] and a cognition appropriate to this state of arousal. The cognition, in a sense, exerts a steering function. Cognitions arising from the immediate situation as interpreted by past experience provide the framework within which one understands and label one's feelings. It is the cognition that determines whether the state of physiological arousal will be labeled "anger," "joy," or whatever.

   In order to examine the implications of this formulation, let us consider how these two elements—a state of physiological arousal and cognitive factors—would interact in a variety of situations. In most emotion-inducing situations, of course, the two factors are completely interrelated. Imagine a man walking alone down a dark alley when a figure with a gun suddenly appears. The perception-cognition "figure with a gun" in some fashion initiates a state of physiological arousal; this state of arousal is interpreted in terms of knowledge about dark alleys and guns, and the state of arousal is labeled "fear." Similarly, a student who unexpectedly learns that he has made Phi Beta Kappa may experience a state of arousal which he will label "joy."

Let us now consider circumstances in which these two elements, the physiological and the cognitive, are, to some extent, independent. First, is the state of physiological arousal alone sufficient to induce an emotion? Best evidence indicates that it is not. Marañon (1924), in a fascinating study, injected 210 of his patients with the sympathomimetic agent adrenaline and then asked them to introspect. Seventy-one percent of his subjects simply reported physical symptoms with no emotional overtone; 29% of the subjects responded in an apparently emotional fashion. Of these, the majority described their feelings in a way that Marañon labeled "cold" or "as if" emotions; that is, they made statements such as "I feel *as if* I were afraid" or "*as if* I were awaiting a great happiness." This is a sort of emotional *déjà vu* experience; these subjects are neither happy nor afraid, but only feel "as if" they were. Finally, a few cases apparently reported a genuine emotional experience. However, in order to produce this reaction in most of these few cases, Marañon points out, "one must suggest a memory with strong affective force but not so strong as to produce an emotion in the normal state. For example, in several cases, we spoke to our patients before the injection about their sick children or dead parents, and they responded calmly to this topic. The same topic presented later, during the adrenal commotion, was sufficient to trigger emotion. This adrenal commotion places the subject in a situation of 'affective imminence' (pp. 307–308)." Apparently, then, to produce a genuinely emotional reaction to adrenaline, Marañon was forced to provide such subjects with an appropriate cognition.

Though Marañon does not explicitly describe his procedure, it is clear that his subjects knew that they were receiving an injection, and in all likelihood they knew that they were receiving adrenaline and probably had some familiarity with its effects. In short, though they underwent the pattern of sympathetic discharge common to strong emotional states, at the same time they had a completely appropriate cognition or explanation of why they felt this way. This, I would suggest, is the reason so few of Marañon's subjects reported any emotional experience.

Consider next a person in a state of physiological arousal for which no immediate explanation or appropriate cognitions are available. Such a state could result were one to inject a subject with adrenaline covertly, or, unknown to him, feed him a sympathomimetic drug such as ephedrine. Under such conditions a subject would be aware of palpitations, tremor, face flushing, and most of the symptoms associated with a discharge of the sympathetic nervous system. In contrast to Marañon's subjects, he would, however, be utterly unaware of why he felt this way. What would be the consequence of such a state?

In other contexts, I (1959) have suggested that just such a state would lead to the arousal of "evaluative needs" (Festinger, 1954); that is, an individual in this state would feel pressures to understand and label his bodily feelings. His bodily state grossly resembles the condition in which it has been at times of emotional excitement. How would he label his present feelings? It is suggested, of course, that he will label his feelings in terms of his knowledge of the immediate situation.[2] Should he at the time be with a beautiful woman he might decide that he was wildly in love or sexually excited. Should he be at a gay party, he might, by comparing himself to others, decide that he was extremely happy and euphoric. Should he be arguing with his wife, he might explode in fury and hatred. Or, should the situation be completely inappropriate, he might decide that he was excited about something that had recently happened to him, or, simply, I suppose, that he was sick. In any case, it is my basic assumption that emotional states are a function of the interaction of such cognitive factors with a state of physiological arousal.

This line of thought, then, leads to the following propositions:

1. Given a state of physiological arousal for which an individual has no immediate explanation, he will "label" this state and describe his feelings in terms of the cognitions available to him. To the extent that cognitive factors are potent determiners of emotional states, one might anticipate that precisely the same state of physiological arousal could be labeled "joy," or "fury," or any of a great number of emotional labels, depending on the cognitive aspects of the situation.
2. Given a state of physiological arousal for which an individual has a completely appropriate explanation (e.g., "I feel this way because I have just received an injection of adrenaline"), no evaluative needs will arise and the individual is unlikely to label his feelings in terms of the alternative cognitions available.

    Now consider a condition in which emotion-inducing cognitions are present but there is no state of physiological arousal. For example, an individual might be completely aware that he is in great danger but for some reason (drug or surgical) remain in a state of physiological quiescence. Does he experience the emotion "fear"? This formulation of emotion as a joint function of a state of physiological arousal and an appropriate cognition, would, of course, suggest that he does not; this leads to my final proposition.
3. Given the same cognitive circumstances, the individual will react emotionally or describe his feelings as emotions only to the extent that he experiences a state of physiological arousal.[3]

The experimental test of these propositions requires, first, the experimental manipulation of a state of physiological arousal, second, the manipulation of the extent to which the subject has an appropriate or proper explanation of his bodily state and, third, the creation of situations from which explanatory cognitions may be derived.

In order to satisfy these experimental requirements, Schachter and Singer (1962) designed an experiment cast in the framework of a study of the effects of vitamin supplements on vision. As soon as a subject arrived, he was taken to a private room and told by the experimenter:

> In this experiment we would like to make various tests of your vision. We are particularly interested in how certain vitamin compounds and vitamin supplements affect the visual skills. In particular, we want to find out how the vitamin compound called "Suproxin" affects your vision.
>
> What we would like to do, with your permission, is to give you a small injection of Suproxin. The injection itself is mild and harmless; however, since some people do object to being injected we don't want to talk you into anything. Would you mind receiving a Suproxin injection?

If the subject agreed to the injection (and all but one of 185 subjects did) the experimenter continued with instructions to be described shortly, then left the room. In a few minutes a physician entered the room, briefly repeated the experimenter's instructions, took the subject's pulse, and then injected him with Suproxin.

Depending upon condition, the subject received one of two forms of Suproxin—epinephrine or a placebo.

Epinephrine or adrenaline is a sympathomimetic drug whose effects, with minor exceptions, compose an almost perfect mimicry of a discharge of the sympathetic nervous system. Shortly after injection systolic blood pressure increases markedly, heart rate increases somewhat, cutaneous blood flow decreases, while muscle and cerebral blood flow increase, blood sugar and lactic acid concentration increase, and respiration rate increases slightly. As far as the subject is concerned, the major subjective symptoms are palpitation, tremor, and sometimes a feeling of flushing and accelerated breathing. With a subcutaneous injection (in the dosage administered to our subjects), such effects usually begin within 3–5 minutes of injection and last anywhere from 10 minutes to an hour. For most subjects these effects are dissipated within 15–20 minutes after injection.

Subjects receiving epinephrine received a subcutaneous injection of ½ cm³ of a 1:1000 solution of Winthrop Laboratory's Suprarenin, a saline solution of epinephrine bitartrate.

Subjects in the placebo condition received a subcutaneous injection of ½ cm³ of saline solution.

manipulating an appropriate explanation

By "appropriate" I refer to the extent to which the subject has an authoritative, unequivocal explanation of his bodily condition. Thus, a subject who had been informed by the physician that as a direct consequence of the injection he would feel palpitations, tremor, etc., would be considered to have a completely appropriate explanation. A subject who had been informed only that the injection would have no side effects would have no explanation of his state. This dimension of appropriateness was manipulated in three experimental conditions called: Epinephrine Informed (Epi Inf), Epinephrine Ignorant (Epi Ign), and Epinephrine Misinformed (Epi Mis).

Immediately after the subject has agreed to the injection and before the physician entered the room, the experimenter's spiel in each of these conditions went as follows:

epinephrine informed

I should tell you that some of our subjects have experienced side effects from the Suproxin. These side effects are transitory and will last only for about 15 or 20 minutes. What will probably happen is that your hand will start to shake, your heart will start to pound, and your face may get warm and flushed. Again, these are side effects lasting about 15 or 20 minutes.

While the physician was giving the injection, she told the subject that the injection was mild and harmless and repeated this description of the symptoms that the subject could expect as a consequence of the shot. In this condition, then, subjects had a completely appropriate explanation of their bodily state. They knew precisely what they would feel and why.

epinephrine ignorant

In this condition, when the subject agreed to the injection the experimenter said nothing else relevant to side effects and simply left the room. While the physician was giving the injection, she told the subject that the injection was mild and harmless and would have no side effects. In this condition the subject had no experimentally provided explanation for his bodily state.

epinephrine misinformed

> I should tell you that some of our subjects have experienced side effects from the Suproxin. These side effects are transitory and will last only for about 15 or 20 minutes. What will probably happen is that your feet will feel numb, you will have an itching sensation over parts of your body, and you may get a slight headache. Again, these are side effects lasting 15 or 20 minutes.

And, again, the physician repeated these symptoms while injecting the subject. None of these symptoms, of course, are consequences of an injection of epinephrine and, in effect, these instructions provide the subject with a completely inappropriate explanation of his bodily feelings. This condition was introduced as a control condition of sorts. It seemed possible that the description of side effects in the Epi Inf condition might turn the subject introspective, self-examining, possibly slightly troubled. Differences on the dependent variable between the Epi Inf and Epi Ign conditions might, then, be due to such factors rather than to differences in appropriateness. The false symptoms in the Epi Mis condition should similarly turn the subject introspective, etc., but the instructions in this condition do not provide an appropriate explanation of the subject's state.

Subjects in all of the above conditions were injected with epinephrine. Finally, there was a placebo condition in which subjects, who were injected with saline solution, were given precisely the same treatment as subjects in the Epi Ign condition.

producing an emotion inducing cognition

My initial hypothesis has suggested that given a state of physiological arousal for which the individual has no adequate explanation, cognitive factors can lead the individual to describe his feelings with any of a diversity of emotional labels. In order to test this hypothesis, it was decided to manipulate emotional states which customarily are considered quite different—euphoria and anger.

There are, of course, many ways to induce such states. In my own research I have concentrated on social determinants of emotional states, and my colleagues and I have been able to demonstrate in other studies that people do evaluate their own feelings by comparing themselves with others around them (Schachter, 1959; Wrightsman, 1960). In this experiment we attempted again to manipulate emotional state by social means. In one set of conditions, the subject is placed together with a stooge who has been trained to act euphorically. In a second set of conditions the subject is with a stooge trained to act in an angry fashion.

euphoria

Immediately[4] after the subject had been injected the physician left the room and the experimenter returned with a stooge whom he introduced as another subject, then said,

> Both of you have had the Suproxin shot and you'll both be taking the same tests of vision. What I ask you to do now is just wait for 20 minutes. The reason for this is that we must allow 20 minutes for the Suproxin to get

from the injection site into the bloodstream. At the end of 20 minutes when we are certain that most of the Suproxin has been absorbed into the bloodstream, we'll begin the tests of vision.

The room in which this was said had been deliberately put into a state of mild disarray. As he was leaving, the experimenter apologetically added,

> The only other thing I should do is to apologize for the condition of the room. I just didn't have time to clean it up. So, if you need any scratch paper or rubber bands or pencils, help yourself. I'll be back in 20 minutes to begin the vision tests.

As soon as the experimenter had left, the stooge introduced himself again, made a series of standard icebreaker comments, and then launched his routine. He reached first for a piece of paper, doodled briefly, crumpled the paper, aimed for a wastebasket, threw, and missed. This led him into a game of "basketball" in which he moved about the room crumpling paper, and trying out fancy basketball shots. Finished with basketball, he said, "This is one of my good days. I feel like a kid again. I think I'll make a plane." He made a paper plane, spent a few minutes flying it around the room, and said, "Even when I was a kid, I was never much good at this." He then tore off the tail of his plane, wadded it up, and making a slingshot of a rubber band, began to shoot the paper. While shooting, he noticed a sloppy pile of manila folders. He built a tower of these folders, then went to the opposite end of the room to shoot at the tower. He knocked down the tower, and while picking up the folders he noticed a pair of hula hoops behind a portable blackboard. He took one of these for himself, put the other within reaching distance of the subject, and began hula hooping. After a few minutes, he replaced the hula hoop and returned to his seat, at which point the experimenter returned to the room.

> This routine was completely standard, though its pace, of course, varied depending upon the subject's reaction, the extent to which he entered into this bedlam and the extent to which he initiated activities of his own. The only variations from this standard routine were those forced by the subject. Should the subject originate some nonsense of his own and request the stooge to join in, he would do so. And he would, of course, respond to any comments initiated by the subject.

> Subjects in each of the three "appropriateness" conditions and in the placebo condition were submitted to this setup. The stooge, of course, never knew in which condition any particular subject fell.

anger

> Immediately after the injection, the experimenter brought a stooge into the subject's room, introduced the two and, after explaining the necessity for a 20 minute delay for "the Suproxin to get from the injection site into the bloodstream," he continued by saying, "We would like you to use these 20 minutes to answer these questionnaires." Then handing out the questionnaires, he concluded with, "I'll be back in 20 minutes to pick up the questionnaires and begin the tests of vision."

> The questionnaires, five pages long, started off innocently by requesting face sheet information and then grew increasingly personal and insulting, asking questions such as, "With how many men (other than your father) has your mother had extra-marital relationships?"

4 and under ———:   5–9 ———:   10 and over ———.

The stooge, sitting directly opposite the subject, paced his own answers so that at all times subject and stooge were working on the same question. At regular points in the questionnaire, the stooge made a series of standardized comments about the questions. His comments started off innocently enough, grew increasingly querulous; finally he ended up in a rage, ripping up his questionnaire, slamming it to the floor, saying "I'm not wasting any more time. I'm getting my books and leaving," and stomping out of the room.

In summary, this is a seven-condition experiment which, for two different emotional states, allows us, first, to evaluate the effects of "appropriateness" on emotional inducibility, and, second, to begin to evaluate the effects of sympathetic activation on emotional inducibility. In schematic form the conditions are the following:

EUPHORIA	ANGER
Epi Inf	Epi Inf
Epi Ign	Epi Ign
Epi Mis	Placebo
Placebo	

The Epi Mis condition was not run in the Anger sequence. This was originally conceived as a control condition and it was felt that its inclusion in the Euphoria conditions alone would suffice as a means of evaluating the possible artifactual effect of the Epi Inf instructions.

measurement

Emotional state was measured in two ways. First, standardized observation, through a one-way mirror, provided a running record of a subject's behavior. To what extent did he act euphoric or angry? Second, on a variety of self-report scales, a subject indicated his moods of the moment.

observation

EUPHORIA

Throughout the stooge's standardized routine an observer kept a running chronicle of what the subject did and said. For each unit of the stooge's behavior the observer coded the subject's behavior in one or more of the following categories.

Category 1: Joins in Activity. If the subject entered into the stooge's activities, i.e., if he made or flew airplanes, threw paper basketballs, hula hooped, etc., his behavior was coded in this category.

Category 2: Initiates New Activity. A subject was so coded if he gave indications of creative euphoria; i.e., if, on his own, he initiated behavior outside of the stooge's routine. Instances of such behavior would be the subject who threw open the window and, laughing, hurled paper basketballs at passersby, or the subject who jumped on a table and spun one hula hoop on his leg and the other on his neck.

Categories 3 and 4: Ignores or Watches Stooge. Subjects who paid flatly no attention to the stooge or who, with or without comment, simply watched the stooge without joining in his activity were coded in these categories.

For any particular unit of behavior, the subject's behavior was coded in one or more of these categories. To test reliability of coding, two observers independently coded two experimental sessions. The observers agreed completely on the coding of 88% of the units.

ANGER

For each of the units of stooge behavior, an observer recorded the subject's responses and coded them according to the following category scheme:

Category 1: Agrees. In response to the stooge the subject makes a comment indicating that he agrees with the stooge's standardized comment or that he, too, is irked by a particular item on the questionnaire. For example, a subject who responded to the stooge's querulous comment on a question about "father's income" by saying, "I don't like that kind of personal question either," would be coded in this category (scored +2).

Category 2: Disagrees. In response to the stooge's comment, the subject makes a comment which indicates that he disagrees with the stooge's meaning or mood; e.g., in response to the stooge's comment on the "father's income" question, such a subject might say, "Take it easy, they probably have a good reason for wanting the information (scored −2)."

Category 3: Neutral. A noncommittal or irrelevant response to the stooge's remark (scored 0).

Category 4: Initiates Agreement or Disagreement. With no instigation by the stooge, a subject, so coded, would have volunteered a remark indicating that he felt the same way or, alternatively, quite differently than the stooge. Examples would be "Boy I hate this kind of thing," or "I'm enjoying this (scored +2 or −2)."

Category 5: Watches. The subject makes no verbal response to the stooge's comment but simply looks directly at him (scored 0).

Category 6: Ignores. The subject makes no verbal response to the stooge's comment, nor does he look at him; the subject, paying no attention at all to the stooge, simply works at his own questionnaire (scored −1).

A subject was scored in one or more of these categories for each unit of stooge behavior. To test reliability, two observers independently coded three experimental sessions. In order to get a behavioral index of anger, observation protocol was scored according to the values presented in parentheses after each of the above definitions of categories. In a unit-by-unit comparison, the two observers agreed completely on the scoring of 71% of the units jointly observed. The scores of the two observers differed by a value of 1 or less for 88% of the units coded, and in not a single case did the two observers differ in the direction of their scoring of a unit.

self-report of mood and physical condition

When the subject's session with the stooge was completed, the experimenter returned to the room, took the pulse of both the subject and the stooge, and said,

Before we proceed with the vision tests, there is one other kind of information which we must have. We have found that there are many things beside Suproxin that affect how well you see in our tests. How hungry you are, how tired you are, and even the mood you're in at the time—whether you feel happy or irritated at the time of testing—will affect how well you see. To understand the data we collect on you, we must be able to figure out which effects are due to causes such as these, and which are caused by Suproxin. The only way we can get such information about your physical and emotional state is to have you tell us. I'll hand out these questionnaires and ask you to answer them as accurately as possible. Obviously, our data on the vision tests will only be as accurate as your description of your mental and physical state.

In keeping with this spiel, the questionnaire that the experimenter passed out contained a number of mock questions about hunger, fatigue, etc., as well as questions of more immediate relevance to the experiment. To measure mood or emotional state the following two were the crucial questions:

1. How irritated, angry or annoyed would you say you feel at present?

I don't feel at all irritated or angry (0)	I feel a little irritated and angry (1)	I feel quite irritated and angry (2)	I feel very irritated and angry (3)	I feel extremely irritated and angry (4)

2. How good or happy would you say that you feel at present?

I don't feel at all happy or good (0)	I feel a little happy and good (1)	I feel quite happy and good (2)	I feel very happy and good (3)	I feel extremely happy and good (4)

To measure the physical effects of epinephrine and determine whether or not the injection had been successful in producing the necessary bodily state, the following questions were asked:

1. Have you experienced any palpitation (consciousness of your own heart beat)?

Not at all (0)	A slight amount (1)	A moderate amount (2)	An intense amount (3)

2. Did you feel any tremor (involuntary shaking of the hands, arms, or legs)?

Not at all (0)	A slight amount (1)	A moderate amount (2)	An intense amount (3)

To measure possible effects of the instructions in the Epi Mis condition, the following questions were asked:

1. Did you feel any numbness in your feet?
2. Did you feel any itching sensation?
3. Did you experience any feeling of headache?

To all three of these questions was attached a four-point scale running from "Not at all" to "An intense amount."

In addition to these scales, the subjects were asked to answer two open-end questions on other physical or emotional sensations they may have experienced during the experimental session. A final measure of bodily state was pulse rate; this was taken by the physician or the experimenter at two times—immediately before the injection and immediately after the session with the stooge.

When the subjects had completed these questionnaires, the experimenter announced that the experiment was over, explained the deception and its necessity in detail, answered any questions, and swore the subjects to secrecy. Finally, the subjects answered a brief questionnaire about their experiences, if any, with adrenaline, and their previous knowledge or suspicion of the experimental setup. There was no indication that any of the subjects had known about the experiment beforehand, but eleven subjects were so extremely suspicious of some crucial feature of the experiment that their data were automatically discarded.

subjects

The subjects were all male college students taking classes in introductory psychology at the University of Minnesota. Some 90% of the students in these classes volunteer for a subject pool for which they receive two extra points on their final exam for every hour that they serve as experimental subjects. For this study the records of all potential subjects were cleared with the Student Health Service in order to insure that no harmful effects would result from the injections.

evaluation of the experimental design

The ideal test of my propositions would require circumstances which this experiment is far from realizing. First, the proposition that, "A state of physiological arousal for which an individual has no immediate explanation will lead him to label this state in terms of the cognitions available to him" obviously requires conditions under which the subject does not and cannot have a proper explanation of his bodily state. Though Singer and I toyed with such fantasies as ventilating the experimental room with vaporized adrenaline, reality forced us to rely on the disguised injection of Suproxin—a technique which was far from ideal, for no matter what the experimenter told them, some subjects inevitably attributed their feelings to the injection. To the extent that subjects did so, differences between the several appropriateness conditions should be attenuated.

Second, the proposition that, "Given the same cognitive circumstances the individual will react emotionally only to the extent that he experiences a state of physiological arousal" requires for its ideal test the manipulation of states of physiological arousal and of physiological quiescence. Though there is no question that epinephrine effectively produces a state of arousal, there is also no question that a placebo does not prevent physiological arousal. To the extent that the experimental situation effectively produces sympathetic stimulation in placebo subjects, the proposition is difficult to test, for such a factor would attenuate differences between epinephrine and placebo subjects.

Both of these factors, then, can be expected to interfere with the test of my propositions. In presenting the results of this study, I shall first present condition by condition results, and then evaluate the effects of these two factors on experimental differences.

results

effects of the injections on bodily state

Let us examine first the success of the injections at producing the bodily state required to examine the propositions at test. Does the injection of epinephrine produce symptoms of sympathetic discharge as compared with the placebo injection? Relevant data are presented in Table 3.1, where it can be immediately seen that, on all items, subjects who were in epinephrine conditions showed considerably more evidence of sympathetic activation than did subjects in placebo conditions. In all epinephrine conditions pulse rate increased significantly when compared with the decrease characteristics of the placebo conditions.[5] On the scales it is clear that epinephrine subjects experience considerably more palpitation and tremor than do placebo subjects. In all possible comparisons on these symptoms, the mean scores of subjects in any of the epinephrine conditions are greater than the corresponding scores in the placebo conditions at better than the .001 level of significance. Examination of the absolute values of these scores makes it quite clear that subjects in epinephrine conditions were, indeed, in a state of physiological arousal, while most subjects in placebo conditions were in a relative state of physiological quiescence.

TABLE 3.1   THE EFFECTS OF THE INJECTIONS ON BODILY STATE

		PULSE		SELF-RATING OF				
CONDITION	N	PRE	POST	PALPI-TATION	TREMOR	NUMB-NESS	ITCH-ING	HEAD-ACHE
Euphoria								
Epi Inf	27	85.7	88.6	1.20	1.43	0	0.16	0.32
Epi Ign	26	84.6	85.6	1.83	1.76	0.15	0	0.55
Epi Mis	26	82.9	86.0	1.27	2.00	0.06	0.08	0.23
Placebo	26	80.4	77.1	0.29	0.21	0.09	0	0.27
Anger								
Epi Inf	23	85.9	92.4	1.26	1.41	0.17	0	0.11
Epi Ign	23	85.0	96.8	1.44	1.78	0	0.06	0.21
Placebo	23	84.5	79.6	0.59	0.24	0.14	0.06	0.06

The epinephrine injection, of course, did not work with equal effectiveness for all subjects; indeed for a few subjects it did not work at all. Such subjects reported almost no palpitation or tremor, showed no increase in pulse, and described no other relevant physical symptoms. Since, for such subjects, the necessary experimental conditions were not established, they were automatically excluded from the data and all further tabular presentations will not include them. Table 3.1, however, does include the data of these subjects. There were four in euphoria conditions, and one in anger conditions.

In order to evaluate further data on Epi Mis subjects it is necessary to note the results of the "numbness," "itching," and "headache" scales also presented in Table 3.1. Clearly the subjects in the Epi Mis condition do not differ on these scales from subjects in any of the other experimental conditions.

effects of the manipulations on emotional state

EUPHORIA:

Self-Report. The effects of the several manipulations on emotional state in the euphoria conditions are presented in Table 3.2. The scores recorded in this table are derived for each subject by subtracting the value of the point he checked on the irritation scale from the value of the point he checked on the happiness scale. Thus, if a subject were to check the point "I feel a little irritated and angry" on the irritation scale and the point "I feel very happy and good" on the happiness scale, his score would be +2. The higher the positive value, the happier and better the subject reports himself as feeling. Even though, for expositional simplicity, an index is employed, it should be noted that the two components of the index each yield results completely consistent with those obtained by use of this index.

TABLE 3.2   SELF-REPORT OF EMOTIONAL STATE IN THE EUPHORIA CONDITIONS

CONDITION	N	SELF-REPORT SCALES
Epi Inf	25	0.98
Epi Ign	25	1.78
Epi Mis	25	1.90
Placebo	26	1.61

COMPARISON	p^a
Epi Inf vs. Epi Mis	$<.01$
Epi Inf vs. Epi Ign	.02
Placebo vs. Epi Mis, Ign, or Inf	n.s.

[a] All p values reported throughout this [chapter] are two-tailed.

Let us examine first the effects of the appropriateness instructions. Comparison of the scores for the Epi Mis and Epi Inf conditions makes it immediately clear that the experimental differences are not due to artifacts resulting from the informed instructions. In both conditions the subject was warned to expect a variety of symptoms as a consequence of the injection. In the Epi Mis condition, where the symptoms were inappropriate to the subject's bodily state, the self-report score is almost twice that in the Epi Inf condition, where the symptoms were completely appropriate to the subject's bodily state. It is reasonable, then, to attribute differences between informed subjects and those in other conditions to differences in manipulated appropriateness rather than to artifacts such as introspectiveness or self-examination.

It is clear that, consistent with expectations, subjects were more susceptible to the stooge's mood and, consequently, more euphoric when they had no explanation of their own bodily states than when they did. The means of both the Epi Ign and Epi Mis conditions are considerably greater than the mean of the Epi Inf condition.

Comparing the placebo to the epinephrine conditions, we note a pattern which will repeat itself throughout the data. Placebo subjects are less euphoric than either Epi Mis or Epi Ign subjects, but somewhat more euphoric than Epi

Inf subjects. These differences are not, however, statistically significant. We shall consider the epinephrine-placebo comparisons in detail in a later section of this chapter following the presentation of additional relevant data. For the moment, it is clear only that manipulating appropriateness has had a very strong effect on euphoria.

Behavior. Let us next examine the extent to which the subject's behavior was affected by the experimental manipulations. To the extent that his mood has been affected, one should expect that the subject will join in the stooge's whirl of manic activity and initiate similar activities of his own. The relevant data are presented in Table 3.3. The column labeled "Activity index" presents summary figures on the extent to which the subject joined in the stooge's activity. This is a weighted index which reflects both the nature of the activities in which the subject engaged and the amount of time he was active. The index was devised by assigning the following weights to the subject's activities: 5, hula hooping; 4, shooting with slingshot; 3, paper airplanes; 2, paper basketballs; 1, doodling; 0, does nothing. Pretest scaling on 15 college students ordered these activities with respect to the degree of euphoria they represented. Weights were assigned in accordance with this order so that the wilder the activity, the heavier the weight. These weights are multiplied by an estimate of the amount of time the subject spent in each activity and the summed products make up the activity index for each subject. This index may be considered a measure of behavioral euphoria. It should be noted that the same between-condition relationships hold for the two components of this index as for the index itself.

The column labeled "Mean number of acts initiated" presents data on what might be called "creative euphoria"—the extent to which the subject deviates from the stooge's routine and initiates euphoric activities of his own.

On both behavioral indices, we find precisely the same pattern of relationships as those obtained with self-reports. Epi Mis subjects behave somewhat more

TABLE 3.3   BEHAVIORAL INDICATIONS OF EMOTIONAL STATE IN THE EUPHORIA CONDITIONS

CONDITION	N	ACTIVITY INDEX	MEAN NUMBER OF ACTS INITIATED
Epi Inf	25	12.72	.20
Epi Ign	25	18.28	.56
Epi Mis	25	22.56	.84
Placebo	26	16.00	.54

	p VALUE	
COMPARISON	ACTIVITY INDEX	INITIATES[a]
Epi Inf vs. Epi Mis	.05	.03
Epi Inf vs. Epi Ign	n.s.	.08
Placebo vs. Epi Mis, Ign, or Inf	n.s.	n.s.

[a] Tested by X^2 comparison of the proportion of subjects in each condition initiating new acts.

euphorically than do Epi Ign subjects, who in turn behave more euphorically than do Epi Inf subjects. On all measures, then, there is consistent evidence that a subject will take over the stooge's euphoric mood to the extent that he has no other explanation of his bodily state.

Again, it should be noted that on these behavioral indices, Epi Ign and Epi Mis subjects are somewhat more euphoric than placebo subjects, but, troublingly, not significantly so.

ANGER:

Self-report. Before presenting data for the anger conditions, one point must be made about the anger manipulation. In the situation devised, anger, if manifested, is most likely to be directed at the experimenter and his annoyingly personal questionnaire. As we subsequently discovered, this was rather unfortunate, for the subjects, who had volunteered for the experiment in order to obtain extra points on their final exam, simply refused to endanger these points by publicly blowing up, admitting their irritation to the experimenter's face, or spoiling the questionnaire. Though, as the reader will see, the subjects were quite willing to manifest anger when they were alone with the stooge, they hesitated to do so on material (self-ratings of mood and questionnaire) that the experimenter might see, and only after the purposes of the experiment had been revealed did these subjects admit to the experimenter that they had been irked or irritated.

This experimentally unfortunate situation pretty much forces us to rely on the behavioral indices derived from observation of the subject's presumably private interaction with the stooge. We do, however, present data on the self-report scales in Table 3.4. These figures are derived in the same way as the figures presented in Table 3.2 for the euphoria conditions; i.e., the value checked on the irritation scale is subtracted from the value checked on the happiness scale. Though, for the reasons stated above, the absolute magnitude of these figures (all positive) is relatively meaningless, we can, of course, anticipate precisely the reverse results from those obtained in the euphoria conditions; i.e., the Epi Inf subjects in the anger conditions should again be less susceptible to the stooge's mood and should, therefore, describe themselves as in a somewhat happier frame of mind than subjects in the Epi Ign condition. This is the case; the Epi Inf subjects average 1.91 on the self-report scales, while the Epi Ign subjects average 1.39.

Evaluating the effects of the injections, we note again that, as anticipated,

TABLE 3.4   SELF-REPORT OF EMOTIONAL STATE IN THE ANGER CONDITIONS

CONDITION	N	SELF-REPORT SCALES
Epi Inf	22	1.91
Epi Ign	23	1.39
Placebo	23	1.63

COMPARISON	p
Epi Inf vs. Epi Ign	.08
Placebo vs. Epi Ign or Inf	n.s.

Epi Ign subjects are somewhat less happy than Placebo subjects but, once more, this is not a significant difference.

Behavior. The subject's responses to the stooge, during the period when both were filling out their questionnaires, were systematically coded to provide a behavioral index of anger. The coding scheme and the numerical values attached to each of the categories have been described in the methodology section. To arrive at an "Anger index" the numerical value assigned to a subject's responses to the stooge is summed together for the several units of stooge behavior. With the coding scheme used, a positive value for this index indicates that the subject agrees with the stooge's comment and is growing angry. A negative value indicates that the subject either disagrees with the stooge or ignores him.

It is anticipated, of course, that subjects in the Epi Ign condition will be angrier than subjects in the Epi Inf condition. As can be seen in Table 3.5, this is indeed the case. The Anger index for the Epi Ign condition is positive and large, indicating that these subjects have become angry, while in the Epi Inf condition the Anger index is slightly negative in value, indicating that these subjects have failed to catch the stooge's mood at all. It seems clear that providing the subject with an appropriate explanation of his bodily state greatly reduces his tendency to interpret his state in terms of the cognitions provided by the stooge's angry behavior.

TABLE 3.5 BEHAVIORAL INDICATIONS OF EMOTIONAL STATE IN THE ANGER CONDITIONS

CONDITION	N	ANGER INDEX
Epi Inf	22	−0.18
Epi Ign	23	+2.28
Placebo	22[a]	+0.79

COMPARISON	p
Epi Inf vs. Epi Ign	<.01
Epi Ign vs. Placebo	<.05
Placebo vs. Epi Inf	n.s.

[a] For one subject in this condition the sound system went dead and the observer could not code his reactions.

Finally, on this behavioral index it can be seen that subjects in the Epi Ign condition are significantly angrier than subjects in the Placebo condition. Behaviorally, at least, the injection of epinephrine appears to have led subjects to an angrier state than comparable subjects who received placebo shots.

conformation of data to theoretical expectations

Now that the basic data of this study have been presented, let us examine closely the extent to which they conform to theoretical expectations. If our hypotheses are correct and if this experimental design provided a perfect test for these hypotheses, it should be anticipated that in the euphoria conditions the degree of experimentally produced euphoria should vary in the following fashion:

$$\text{Epi Mis} \geqq \text{Epi Ign} > \text{Epi Inf} = \text{Placebo}$$

And in the anger conditions, anger should conform to the following pattern:

$$\text{Epi Ign} > \text{Epi Inf} = \text{Placebo}$$

In both sets of conditions, it is the case that emotional level in the Epi Mis and Epi Ign conditions is considerably greater than that achieved in the corresponding Epi Inf conditions. The results for the Placebo condition, however, are ambiguous, for consistently the Placebo subjects fall between the Epi Ign and the Epi Inf subjects. This is a particularly troubling pattern, for it makes it impossible to evaluate unequivocally the effects of the state of physiological arousal, and indeed raises serious questions about our entire theoretical structure. Though the emotional level is consistently greater in the Epi Mis and Epi Ign conditions than in the Placebo condition, this difference is significant at acceptable probability levels only in the anger conditions.

In order to explore the problem further, let us examine the experimental factors identified earlier, which might have acted to restrain the emotional level in the Epi Ign and Epi Mis conditions. As pointed out earlier, the ideal test of the first two hypotheses requires an experimental setup in which the subject flatly has no way of evaluating his state of physiological arousal other than by means of the experimentally provided cognitions. Had it been possible to physiologically produce a state of sympathetic activation by means other than injection, one could have approached this experimental ideal more closely than in the present setup. As it stands, however, there is always a reasonable alternative cognition available to the aroused subject—he feels the way he does because of the injection. To the extent that the subject seizes on such an explanation of his bodily state, we should expect that he will be uninfluenced by the stooge. Evidence presented in Table 3.6 for the anger condition and in Table 3.7 for the euphoria conditions indicates that this is, indeed, the case.

As mentioned earlier, some of the Epi Ign and Epi Mis subjects in their answers to the open-end questions clearly attributed their physical state to the injection, e.g., "The shot gave me the shivers." In Tables 3.6 and 3.7 such subjects are labeled "Self-informed." In Table 3.6 it can be seen that the self-informed subjects are considerably less angry than are the remaining subjects; indeed, they are not angry at all. With these self-informed subjects eliminated, the difference between the Epi Ign and the Placebo conditions is significant at the .01 level.

Precisely the same pattern is evident in Table 3.7 for the euphoria conditions. In both the Epi Mis and the Epi Ign conditions, the self-informed subjects have considerably lower activity indices than do the remaining subjects. Elim-

TABLE 3.6   THE EFFECTS OF ATTRIBUTING BODILY STATE TO THE INJECTION ON ANGER IN THE ANGER EPI IGN CONDITION

CONDITION	N	ANGER INDEX[a]
Self-informed subjects	3	−1.67
Others	20	+2.88

[a] Self-informed vs. Others: $p = .05$.

TABLE 3.7 THE EFFECTS OF ATTRIBUTING BODILY STATE TO THE INJECTION ON EUPHORIA IN THE EUPHORIA EPI IGN AND EPI MIS CONDITIONS

	EPI IGN	
	N	ACTIVITY INDEX[a]
Self-informed subjects	8	11.63
Others	17	21.14
	EPI MIS	
	N	ACTIVITY INDEX[b]
Self-informed subjects	5	12.40
Others	20	25.10

[a] Self-informed vs. Others, $p = .05$.
[b] Self-informed vs. Others, $p = .10$.

inating self-informed subjects, comparison of both of these conditions with the Placebo condition yields a difference significant at the .03 level. It should be noted, too, that the self-informed subjects have much the same score on the activity index as do the experimental Epi Inf subjects (Table 3.3).

It would appear, then, that the experimental procedure of injecting the subjects, by providing an alternative cognition, has, to some extent, obscured the effects of epinephrine. When account is taken of this artifact, the evidence is good that the state of physiological arousal is a necessary component of an emotional experience, for when self-informed subjects are removed, epinephrine subjects give consistent indications of greater emotionality than do placebo subjects.

Let us examine next the fact that consistently the emotional level, both reported and behavioral, in Placebo conditions is greater than that in the Epi Inf conditions. Theoretically, of course, it should be expected that the two conditions will be equally low, for by assuming that emotional state is a joint function of a state of physiological arousal and of the appropriateness of a cognition we are, in effect, assuming a multiplicative function, so that if either component is at zero, emotional level is at zero. As noted earlier, this expectation should hold if we can be sure that there is no sympathetic activation in the Placebo conditions. Such an assumption, of course, is completely unrealistic, for the injection of placebo does not prevent sympathetic activation. The experimental situations were fairly dramatic, and certainly some of the placebo subjects gave indications of physiological arousal. If our general line of reasoning is correct, it should be anticipated that the emotional level of subjects who gave indications of sympathetic activity will be greater than that of subjects who do not. The relevant evidence is presented in Tables 3.8 and 3.9.

As an index of sympathetic activation, Singer and I used the most direct and unequivocal measure available—change in pulse rate. It can be seen in Table 3.1 that the predominant pattern in the Placebo condition is a decrease in pulse rate. We assumed, therefore, that those subjects whose pulse increased or remained the same gave indications of sympathetic activity, while those subjects whose pulse decreased did not. In Table 3.8, for the euphoria condition, it is immediately

TABLE 3.8 SYMPATHETIC ACTIVATION AND EUPHORIA IN THE EUPHORIA PLACEBO CONDITION

SUBJECTS WHOSE:	N	ACTIVITY INDEX[a]
Pulse decreased	14	10.67
Pulse increased or remained same	12	23.17

[a] Pulse decrease vs. pulse increase or same, $p = .02$.

TABLE 3.9 SYMPATHETIC ACTIVATION AND ANGER IN ANGER PLACEBO CONDITION

SUBJECTS WHOSE:	N[a]	ANGER INDEX[b]
Pulse decreased	13	+0.15
Pulse increased or remained same	8	+1.69

[a] N reduced by two cases owing to failure of sound system in one case and experimenter's failure to take pulse in another.

[b] Pulse decrease vs. pulse increase or same, $p = .01$.

clear that subjects who gave indications of sympathetic activity are considerably more euphoric than are subjects who show no sympathetic activity. This relationship is, of course, confounded by the fact that euphoric subjects are considerably more active than noneuphoric subjects—a factor which, independent of mood, could elevate pulse rate. However, no such factor operates in the anger condition where angry subjects are neither more active nor talkative than calm subjects. It can be seen in Table 3.9 that Placebo subjects who show signs of sympathetic activation give indications of considerably more anger than do subjects who show no such signs. Conforming to expectations, sympathetic activation accompanies an increase in emotional level.

It should be noted, too, that the emotional levels of subjects showing no signs of sympathetic activity are quite comparable to the emotional levels of subjects in the parallel Epi Inf conditions (see Tables 3.3 and 3.5). The similarity of these sets of scores and their uniformly low level of indicated emotionality would certainly make it appear that both factors are essential to an emotional state. When either the level of sympathetic arousal is low, or a completely appropriate cognition is available, the level of emotionality is low.

discussion

Let us summarize the major findings of this experiment and examine the extent to which they support the propositions offered in the introduction of this chapter: It has been suggested, first, that given a state of physiological arousal for which an individual has no explanation, he will label this state in terms of the cognitions available to him. This implies, of course, that by manipulating the cognitions of an individual in such a state we can manipulate his feelings in diverse directions. Experimental results support this proposition for, following the injection of epinephrine, those subjects who had no explanation for the bodily state thus produced gave behavioral and self-report indications that they had been readily manipulable into the disparate feeling states of euphoria and anger.

From this first proposition, it must follow that given a state of physiological arousal for which the individual has a completely satisfactory explanation, he will not label this state in terms of the alternative cognitions available. Experimental evidence strongly supports this expectation. In those conditions in which subjects were injected with epinephrine and told precisely what they would feel and why, they proved relatively immune to any effects of the manipulated cognitions. In the anger condition, such subjects did not report or show anger; in the euphoria condition such subjects reported themselves as far less happy than subjects with an identical bodily state but no adequate knowledge of why they felt the way they did.

Finally, it has been suggested that given constant cognitive circumstances, an individual will react emotionally only to the extent that he experiences a state of physiological arousal. Without taking account of experimental artifacts, the evidence in support of this proposition is consistent but tentative. When the effects of "self-informing" tendencies in epinephrine subjects and of "self-arousing" tendencies in placebo subjects are partialed out, the evidence strongly supports the proposition.

notes

1. Though the first experiments to be described are concerned largely with the physiological changes produced by the injection of adrenaline, which appear to be primarily the result of sympathetic excitation, the term physiological arousal is used in preference to the more specific "excitement of the sympathetic nervous system" because there are indications, to be discussed later, that this formulation is applicable to a variety of bodily states.

2. This suggestion is not new. Several psychologists have suggested that situational factors should be considered the chief differentiators of the emotions. Hunt, Cole, and Reis (1958) probably make this point most explicitly in their study distinguishing among fear, anger, and sorrow in terms of situational characteristics.

3. In his critique of the James-Lange theory of emotion, Cannon (1929) makes the point that sympathectomized animals and patients do seem to manifest emotional behavior. This criticism is, of course, as applicable to the above proposition as it was to the James-Lange formulation. . . .

4. It was, of course, imperative that the sequence with the stooge begin before the subject felt his first symptoms, for otherwise the subject would be virtually forced to interpret his feelings in terms of events preceding the stooge's entrance. Pretests had indicated that, for most subjects, epinephrine-caused symptoms began within 3-5 minutes after injection. A deliberate attempt was made then to bring in the stooge within one minute after the subject's injection.

5. It can be seen in Table 3.1 that the rise in the pulse rate of subjects injected with epinephrine is greater in the anger than in the euphoria conditions. This finding, which has been the subject of fairly exotic interpretations in critical discussions of this experiment (Plutchik and Ax, 1967; Stein, 1967), is undoubtedly most simply explained by the fact that the anger manipulation took somewhat less time than the euphoria manipulation, and the second pulse reading was, therefore, taken sooner on the average in the anger than in the euphoria condition. The typical reaction to an injection of adrenaline in the dosage used is a very rapid rise in heart rate, and then a steady and gradual decline.

references

Cannon, W. B. The James-Lange theory of emotions: A critical examination and an alternative theory. *American Journal of Psychology*, 1927, *39*, 106–124.

Cannon, W. B. *Bodily changes in pain, hunger, fear, and rage*. (2nd ed.) New York: Appleton, 1929.

Festinger, L. A theory of social comparison processes. *Human Relations*, 1954, *7*, 114–140.

Hunt, J. McV., Cole, M. W., & Reis, E. S. Situational cues distinguishing anger, fear, and sorrow. *American Journal of Psychology*, 1958, *71*, 136–151.

James, W. *The principles of psychology*. New York: Henry Holt, 1890, 449.

Marañon, G. Contribution à l'étude de l'action émotive de l'adrénaline. *Revue Francaise d'Endocrinologie*, 1924, *2*, 301–325.

Plutchik, R., & Ax, A. F. A Critique of "determinants of emotional state" by Schachter and Singer, 1962, *Psychophysiology*, 1967, *4*, 79–82.

Ruckmick, C. A. *The psychology of feeling and emotion*. New York: McGraw-Hill, 1936.

Schachter, S. *The psychology of affiliation*. Stanford, Ca: Stanford University Press, 1959.

Schachter, S., & Singer, J. E. Cognitive, social, and physiological determinants of emotional state. *Psychological Review*, 1962, *69*, 379–399.

Stein, M. Some physiological considerations of the relationship between the autonomic nervous system and behavior. In D. C. Glass (Ed.), *Neurophysiology and Emotion*. New York: Rockefeller University Press, 1967.

Woodworth, R. S., & Schlosberg, H. *Experimental psychology*. New York: Holt, 1954.

Wrightsman, L. S. Effects of waiting with others on changes in level of felt anxiety. *Journal of Abnormal and Social Psychology*, 1960, *61*, 216–220.

4

Reinstatement

Byron A. Campbell and Julian Jaynes

In most of the phyla from arthropods to man early experience exerts a multiplicity of effects on adult behavior (Beach & Jaynes, 1954; Scott, 1962). Sometimes such effects are the simple persistence in adult behavior of habits formed early in life. In other instances it may be that early experience influences later behavior by structuring the individual's perceptual or response capacities. And in still others, there is a critical period of development during which some aspect of behavior, on which later behaviors depend, is learned and molded for life.

In this paper we suggest yet another mechanism. Although obvious and disarmingly simple, it yet seems to the authors of such neglected importance as

Reprinted from *Psychological Review*, 1966, Vol. 73, No. 5, pp. 478–480. Copyright 1966 by the American Psychological Association. Reprinted by permission.

to warrant this note and the coining of a term for it. By *reinstatement* we denote a small amount of partial practice or repetition of an experience over the developmental period which is enough to maintain an early learned response at a high level, but is not enough to produce any effect in animals which have not had the early experience. The following experiment is meant as a demonstration of this phenomenon in a commonly studied instance of learning.

method

The subjects were 30 albino rats of the Wistar strain born and raised in the Princeton colony. They were divided into three groups of 10 each, with an equal number of males and females in each. The apparatus used was one commonly used in fear experiments (Campbell & Campbell, 1961). It consisted of two compartments separated by a door, a black one with a grid floor, and a white compartment with a solid metal floor. Shock could be administered to the grid of the black compartment. To two of the three groups an early fear-arousing experience was given in the black compartment. This consisted of placing the rat just after weaning, when approximately 25 days old, on the grid side of the apparatus with the door fixed so that the rat could not escape, then giving the rat 15 2-second 170-volt shocks on a 20-second variable interval schedule, taking approximately 5 minutes, then removing the animal and placing him on the nonshock side for 5 minutes, and then repeating this entire procedure once. Thus each animal received a total of 30 shocks. At the end of this period the rat was removed and placed in a home cage. A third control group was run through this procedure without any shock being administered to the grid. During the next month a total of three shocks—the reinstatements—were given to one of the early experience groups and to the control group. These shocks were administered 7, 14, and 21 days after the original training session. The procedure was to administer, at some random number of seconds up to a minute after the animal was placed on the grid side of the apparatus, a single 2-second shock of the same intensity as before. The rat was then placed in the white compartment for an identical period of time and then returned to its home cage. On alternate weeks the animal was placed first on the nonshock side of the cage and then on the shock side, with half of the animals being placed on the shock side for the first reinstatement procedure and half on the safe side. Otherwise this procedure was precisely the same as the training procedure except that only 1 instead of 30 shocks was administered. The second pretrained group was given the same procedure except that no shock was administered. One week after the third reinstatement procedure, when the animals were 53 days of age, they were all tested for the effects of their early experience. This was done by placing them individually in the black compartment (where all of them had been shocked at one time or another) with the door removed so that the animal could run freely into the white compartment. The time spent in the white compartment over the ensuing hour was then recorded.

results and discussion

The results were unequivocal. As seen in Figure 4.1, the group that had received the early fearful experience followed by three 2-second shocks administered at weekly intervals, spent an increasing percentage of its time in the white compartment during the 1-hour test period, thus showing the effects of the early fearful experience with the black compartment. In contrast, the group that had had a similar early experience just after weaning, but no reinstatement of it in the intervening month, failed to show any significant fear of the black compartment, spending on the average all but about 10 minutes of the hour on that side. Similarly the group which had not had any early traumatic experience, but had received the three brief shocks over the month, failed to acquire any significant fear of the black compartment. The difference between the first group and the other two groups is, as it appears on the graph, highly reliable statistically $(p < .01$, Mann-Whitney U test).

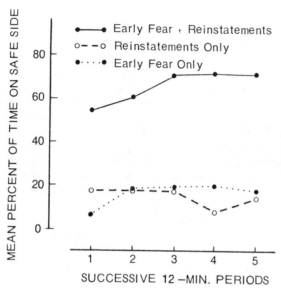

FIG. 4.1   The effect of reinstatement of early fear on later behavior.

There is nothing dramatically surprising about this finding. It is indeed what anyone thinking carefully about learning and practice would expect, namely, that there is some small amount of practice over certain time intervals which could maintain a previously learned response and yet not be enough to train naïve animals to perform that response. The possibility that this mechanism of reinstatement has wide and important applicability in the ontogeny of behavior in many vertebrate species seems beyond question.

In theoretical analyses of human growth and development traumatic events in infancy and childhood have long occupied a central, if controversial, role. In Freud's early analyses, traumatic events in childhood were considered a major cause of adult behavior disorders. With time, this view was gradually modified such that White writing in 1956 summed up current opinion by stating:

> Undoubtedly it is true that some adult neuroses have their origin in violently frightening events. . . . The theory has long since been abandoned, however, that all neuroses, or even a majority of neuroses, take their start from traumatic events [1956, p. 238].

The early trauma theory has inconsistencies with certain facts of memory and learning as well. First, on a mere phenomenological level, we know that memory becomes more and more dim the further back into our childhood we try to remember. Second, in rats, the earlier in life that a fearful experience is given the animal, the more likely it is to be forgotten in adulthood (Campbell & Campbell, 1962). Third, in chickens, the earlier in the critical period that the chick is imprinted, the more likely it is to be forgotten when the animal reaches the juvenile stages (Jaynes, 1957). This evidence seems to indicate that the organism is constantly forgetting, time or neurological maturation or perhaps other processes constantly changing the mnemonic traces of events and feelings. And all the evidence suggests that the earlier the experience has occurred, the more profound and the faster the forgetting.

In this context reinstatement is proposed as a major mechanism by which the effects of early experiences can be perpetuated and incorporated into adult personality. Following an early experience, either pleasant or unpleasant, three developments may occur. First, the experience may be gradually forgotten as described above. Second, it may be remembered and persist indefinitely if it is occasionally reinstated. The language-based cultures of human societies are particularly rich in methods of such reinstatement, including ones so simple as occasionally reminding a child of a previous event or feeling. Even the child may occasionally reinstate the experience himself under the prompting of his ethical value system. A third possibility is the active repression of the experience, and we suggest here that the repression itself—as well as the experience—may undergo either forgetting or maintenance by reinstatement in exactly the same way. Again, the language-based cultures of man contain many reinstatement-of-repression mechanisms such as parental conversational taboos, etc., which determine what repressions are maintained into adult life. In a general sense, we propose that any learned response, whether acquired in infancy or adulthood, conscious or unconscious, instrumental or autonomic, joyful or traumatic, can be maintained at a high level by an occasional reinstatement.

Moreover, reinstatement as a principle has considerable adaptive significance, particularly in the learning of fear. Young organisms, at least after a short initial period of apparent fearlessness in some species, become highly vulnerable to the acquisition of fears. These fears have, of course, great survival value in keeping the young organism away from danger. But if they all persisted and could not be forgotten, they would imprison the animal in his own prior experience, making adult adaptive behavior impossible. It is thus essential to adult activity that most early experiences be forgotten, and that only those experiences which are periodically reinstated by a particular habitat or culture be retained.

references

Beach, F. A., & Jaynes, J. Effects of early experience upon the behavior of animals. *Psychological Bulletin*, 1954, *51*, 239–263.

Campbell, B. A., & Campbell, E. H. Retention and extinction of learned fear in infant and adult rats. *Journal of Comparative and Physiological Psychology*, 1962, *55*, 1–8.

Jaynes, J. Imprinting: The interaction of learned and innate behavior: II. The critical period. *Journal of Comparative and Physiological Psychology*, 1957, *50*, 6–7.

Scott, J. P. Critical periods in behavioral development. *Science*, 1962, *138*, 949–958.

White, R. W. *The Abnormal Personality*. (2nd ed.) New York: The Ronald Press, 1956.

5

A Perspective on Self-Control

Marvin R. Goldfried and Michael Merbaum

Perhaps more openly than any other psychotherapeutic approach, behavior therapy has directly confronted the broad moral and therapeutic issue of control as it exists within the therapeutic relationship. A working assumption in behavior therapy is that the client enters therapy because of behavior problems which he is unable to solve by himself, and, therefore, seeks the assistance and direction of the therapist in order to eliminate these difficulties. This orientation provides a therapeutic atmosphere that endorses the overt manipulation of client behavior and promotes deliberate attempts to create appropriate environments for the purpose of behavior change. As a consequence, behavior therapy has frequently been criticized on the grounds that only minimal attention is given to the role of the client in creating his own conditions and guidelines for self-improvement. It seemed to many that undue emphasis was placed on the therapist as the absolute controller who directly manipulated the conditions he assumed were necessary for personal growth to take place.

Despite these criticisms, however, behavior therapists, like therapists from other orientations, have always recognized that the ultimate goal of therapy is to provide the client with the resources to cope independently with his own life. For example, this recognition may be noted in the writings of Dollard and Miller (1950), who suggest: "It is desirable that the patient have some skill at the deliberate solution of emotional problems which we call self-study. In the ordinary case, this skill is a by-product of the original therapeutic training" (p. 436). In more recent years, behavior therapists have paid greater recognition to this ultimate goal at the outset of treatment, and have begun to develop therapeutic procedures which might more directly facilitate self-control.

In their now classic debate on the control of human behavior, Rogers and Skinner (1956) raise certain questions which are relevant to this issue. Although this debate is usually cited as illustrating the differences between Rogers' and Skinner's orientations, there are certain important points on which they happen to agree. Both acknowledge that the dangers associated with the control of human behavior can indeed be frightening, and both recognize the importance of providing the client with a certain measure of self-direction. The point at which the essential difference occurs between the client-centered and behavioral approaches is with respect to the *means* by which this goal may be achieved. Rather than viewing the client's inner direction as an outcome of some natural, though undefined growth process, the behavior therapist has staunchly maintained that the ultimate achievement of self-control, like any other ability, can be learned through the systematic application of various principles of behavior change. Thus, just as one must provide external control and direction in the initial stages of teaching a child to ride a bicycle, the eventual achievement of self-control may require the active and deliberate efforts of the therapist.

In recent years, the importance of self-control has gained momentum as both therapy and research have helped to illuminate the crucial variables that have been involved. The purpose of this paper is to provide an overview of the work that has been done in this area. We shall begin by discussing at greater length previous interest in the topic of self-control, as it has existed both within the psychoanalytically oriented and behavioral traditions. After providing a working definition of self-control, the remainder of the paper reviews and evaluates the work which has been done on the various mechanisms of self-control.

the psychoanalytic tradition

The ingenuity man has developed to consciously regulate his own behavior has fascinated virtually all scholars at one time or another. The philosophical notion of *will* or *willpower* was invented as a conceptual explanation to account for the ability of rational man to assert himself and thereby sustain his integrity with relative immunity from external coercion. For most western philosophers *will* was guided by reason, conscious volition, and the conviction that man is endowed with the capacity to voluntarily suppress base impulses and desires that would otherwise subvert the exercise of wise choice.

A classic version of this position is provided by John Stuart Mill, who reflected:

> He who lets the world, or his own portion of it, choose his plan of life for him, has no need of any other faculty than the ape-like one of imitation. He who chooses his plan for himself, employs all of his faculties. He must use observation to see, reasoning and judgment to foresee, activity to gather materials for decision, discrimination to decide and when he has decided, firmness and self-control to hold to his deliberate decision.

This glorification of reason as a cornerstone of *will* in nineteenth-century Victorian philosophy was seriously challenged by Freud's insights into the irrational forces influencing man's behavior.

The ingenious psychic system which Freud devised comprised an assortment of motivational systems operating in simultaneous conflict and harmony with one another. The maturing of the individual required the harnessing of these forces in order to achieve a balance in personal functioning. Perhaps the most important concept distinguishing psychoanalytic theory from other views was the role of the unconscious in determining behavior. Conscious, willful action was relegated to a subordinate position and the power of reason was dismissed as a deceptive veneer for man's instinctual satisfaction.

At the core of the psyche was the Id, where innate biological drives pressed for immediate and mindless gratification. This was a self-contained world of instinctual strivings that were completely autonomous from environmental control. Within this section of the mind, repressed anxieties and fears were also developmentally superimposed over these intrinsic motivational states. Basically, the Id was thought to serve its own affective self-interest, without any cognitive checks to moderate its consequences on the working of the total organism.

Arising out of the Id, through a process of maturational differentiation, emerged the Ego. The aim of the Ego was to provide a balance between unreasonable affective expression and the demands of external reality. As the antithesis of the Id, the Superego was hypothesized as a specialized division of the Ego. Among other functions, the role of the Superego was to oversee the Id's intentions and to encourage the Ego to suppress, usually because of guilt, all impulse expressions violating moral norms of conduct.

The external environment, society and culture, play a rather ambiguous role in influencing behavior in psychoanalytic theory. Rapaport (1960) points out, for example, that Freud's theoretical views of reality underwent at least three revisions and elaborations. At first Freud considered reality, or actually the mental representation of reality, to be the target of ego defense. It was assumed that early traumatic experiences were the source of pathological disturbance, and the object of ego defense operations was to neutralize their catastrophic effect. Freud's revision of this early theory succeeded in expanding the influence of reality in determining the course of normal development. He went on to postulate a secondary thought process which established a direct and veridical connection between the person and his environment. The "secondary process" has a "broad access to reality over which it exercises selective judgment and choices" (Rapaport, 1960, p. 59). In his final revision, Freud conceived of reality as a real threat to security. Id drive states were conceived of as being the true focus of defense because their free expression had the potential for creating disastrous conflict with the external world. As Rapaport states, "defense against drives came to represent reality and, as constituents of Ego and Superego structure, they became internalized regulators of behavior" (p. 59). Despite some theoretical concessions in recognizing the impact of environmental reality, the external world was viewed by Freud as an antagonist to be feared rather than an ally to be courted.

This sketch of the enormously complicated topology of Freud's psychic system is obviously incomplete. However, insofar as the issue of self-control is concerned, it is the Ego which develops as the clearest internal representative of reality and the coordinator of coherent mental processes from which reason and sanity unfold. The Ego is endowed with energy which is used to achieve psychological equilibrium by neutralizing the force of the Id, Superego, and external reality when their conflicts tend to jeopardize the smooth functioning of the system. This is normally accomplished through defense mechanisms whose function is to delay, subvert, compromise, or block the return of repressed material into conscious control of the person's psychological life. Since most of the Ego is itself unconscious, however, psychic battles usually occur without conscious awareness and without voluntary control.

A creative extension of Freud's Ego concept was offered by Hartmann (1958), who suggested that the Ego does not simply develop out of the Id, but can be conceived of as a separately developing potential readiness for psychological adaptation. This conflict-free Ego apparatus is not directly involved with defensive operations, but is responsive to maturational and learning experiences essential to the acquisition of social competence skills. According to Hartmann, certain important functions such as visual perception, object comprehension, language development, various forms of thinking, as well as important phases of motor development, are not necessarily bound up with aggressive or sexual urges. The Ego, as conceived by Hartmann, is purposive and autonomous from the pressures of internal drive states and from the coercive impact of environmental stimulation. As stated by Hartmann (1958): "in addition to controlling internal impulses, the Ego also functions in assisting the individual to control his behavior so as to adapt to the demands of the real world."

Rapaport (1958) extended Hartmann's observations by attempting to define the balance of psychological ingredients which sustain the autonomy of the Ego. Rapaport assumes that, "while the ultimate guarantees of the Ego's autonomy from the Id are man's constitutionally given apparatuses of reality relatedness, the ultimate guarantees of the Ego's autonomy from the environment are man's constitutionally given drives." Thus, Rapaport insisted on two essential autonomies which provide an intrapsychic balance and which serve to protect the organism against inner or outer violations of personal integrity.

The theorizing by Hartmann, Rapaport, and other contemporary Ego psychoanalytic theorists extended Freud's ideas by emphasizing the value of Ego resources as a prerequisite for healthy psychological growth. This change in focus also produced certain radical revisions in psychoanalytic therapeutic technique. Rather than therapeutic attention exclusively directed toward the control of irrational drive states or repressed conflicts, greater interest developed in areas of reality adaptation and the rearrangement of cognitions that regulate behavior. Nevertheless, even with provocative alterations in some areas of psychoanalytic thinking, the organism is still seen as a closed system, where the behavioral pathologies are usually screens for some underlying inner cause residing exclusively within the person. It follows theoretically that if those causes could be identified and subjected to successful emotional and intellectual scrutiny, the pathology would disappear. Attempts at more direct facilitation of purposeful action are generally dismissed as superficial, or at best supportive.

One additional point is worth noting. The goal of most psychoanalytic therapy is personality change in a global sense. Specific changes in behavior are part of a more general personality change package. Thus, ego control or self-control will in most instances have to be bolstered generally, rather than specifically, to correct a particular problem area. While this overall goal is certainly an admirable one, particularly when self-control is at stake, the path is often too time-consuming and financially costly to cope with the urgent and practical demand for treatment currently existing in society. Fortunately, recent clinical theory and practice in behavior therapy have created a rapidly developing alternative to psychoanalytic therapies, especially within the broad area of cognitive reorganization.

the behavioral tradition

In the latter part of the nineteenth century, experimental psychology emerged from the shadows of philosophy and established itself as a separate scientific discipline. Many psychologists, particularly those interested in the process of learning, gravitated toward the natural sciences as a major source of guidance and direction. In keeping with this orientation, the subject matter of psychology became overt behavior rather than subjective private experience, and a rigorous attempt was made to discover methods for generating data that could be observed, recorded, and reliably reproduced by other scientists.

In America, a new psychology found its inspiration through the radical influence of John B. Watson, a young psychologist from the University of Chicago. In 1913, Watson boldly proclaimed that "psychology as the behaviorist views it is a purely objective branch of natural science. Its theoretical goal is the prediction and control of behavior." The term "conditioning" became the rallying ground for those psychologists committed to an experimental psychology based upon objective stimulus-response relationships.

One important feature of this theoretical revolution was a decided preference for subject populations that would yield data to meet stringent standards for scientific purity. For this purpose, animals were much more appropriate than human beings. The reasons for the selection of infrahuman subjects are not difficult to understand. Animals, unlike humans, could be placed in research environments with genetic, early experience and experimental conditions highly controlled. Furthermore, the ethical quandary of subjecting humans to many aversive deprivations could be conveniently bypassed. While most of the learning research was conducted on animals, a general assumption of most learning theorists was that they could eventually extrapolate from the apparent regularities in animal behavior to the realm of human experience.

Despite the interest in extending its findings to human behavior, learning theory has had difficulty in incorporating "private events" such as thoughts, fantasy, imagination and the like within its theoretical framework. Indeed, there was a noticeable reluctance of theorists to speculate in this area, in large part due to the difficulty in specifying and quantifying the physical properties of the internal environment. In recent years, however, with a shift in importance from infrahuman to human experimentation, the relevance of symbolic activity has been revived in behavior theories. This change can be attributed to the kinds of issues being approached, as well as to the evolution of an improved psychological technology. Particularly relevant to understanding some of the unique properties of human learning are studies dealing with the areas of self-control, self-regulation, and self-reinforcement. Bandura (1969) provides a salient restatement of this problem.

> Unlike humans, who continually engage in self-evaluative and self-reinforcing behavior, rats or chimpanzees are disinclined to pat themselves on the back for commendable performances, or to berate themselves for getting lost in culs-de-sac. By contrast, people typically set themselves certain standards of behavior and self-administer rewarding or punishing consequences depending on whether their performances fall short of, match, or exceed their self-prescribed demands. (p. 32)

The concept of self-control as applied to human learning is, for the most part, a contemporary theoretical problem in learning. Many current notions about self-control phenomena, however, are extensions of issues learning theorists have been studying for years. For example, the way in which well-entrenched habits become extinguished, unlearned, or counter-conditioned has always been a popular topic in the learning literature, and the solution to this problem is directly associated with the ultimate purpose of self-control. A variety of learning theorists have approached these provocative problems from their own special vantage points.

Guthrie (1935), for example, was convinced that the breaking of habits could be achieved by learning new responses to the same stimulus situation which previously elicited the old habit. He assumed that this new learning would interfere with the execution of the old habit and the latter would eventually decay as new behavior became tied to the same situational cues. Thus, in order to effectively substitute new responses, the cues which were contiguous to the old habit would have to be carefully identified, and the new behavior inserted at the appropriate point in the sequence. What Guthrie was advocating was a method of treatment based on a program of stimulus control. By continually repeating the maladaptive habit sequence and by introducing adaptive responses at appropriate intervals, a new stimulus complex could be arranged. The crucial feature of what Guthrie was advocating, then, is that the person become more attentive to the stimuli controlling his response. With this information, the individual can learn to manage his own behavior more effectively.

A serious attempt to define theoretically the operation of the higher mental processes in the solution of emotional problems was outlined by Miller and Dollard (1941) and Dollard and Miller (1950) in their classic works *Social Learning and Imitation* and *Personality and Psychotherapy.* In building their system, a distinction was made between two levels of habitual and automatic reflexive behavior. The next level was composed of responses mediated by symbolic internal activity, and represented the "higher mental processes." In the symbolic sphere two forms of behavior were noted. One, labeled "instrumental behavior," included all voluntary motor action functionally intended to produce changes in the relationship between the organism and its environment. This behavior is similar to operant responses described by Skinner. The most complex problem-solving role, however, was reserved for the "cue-producing responses." These are defined as mental operations such as language, thinking, images, and the like, which mediate socially complex behavior. The temporal and spatial patterning of these mediating responses and the inherent flexibility of ideational cues facilitate the deliberate and rational use of mental faculties in the solution of a wide range of intellectual and emotional problems. Reason, foresight, insight, and logic are mental attributes characteristically associated with the effective utilization of cue-producing responses.

Dollard and Miller were very much impressed with man's potential for the creative use of higher mental faculties. In many ways, their work laid the foundation for subsequent work in the area of self-control by Bandura (1969). Bandura conceptualizes self-control phenomena within what he refers to as a reciprocal-interaction framework. This general theory combines both mediational (cognitive) and nonmediational (observable instrumental behavior) concepts in accounting for learning and performance change. Bandura assumes, for example, that reinforcement contingencies can significantly influence behavior without the benefit of cognitive awareness to mediate this action. However, through extensive self-monitoring, individuals are usually capable of identifying the contingency rules which govern their behavior. With this information, they can learn to control subsequent behavior more effectively than if awareness were nonexistent. While giving ample coverage to the obvious significance of operant and classical conditioning in learning, Bandura leans toward a formulation that emphasizes symbolic activity as a special human phenomenon which cannot be duplicated in animal research. This is particularly true of the concept of self-reinforcement, an essential component of the self-control process. Bandura suggests that patterns of self-reinforcement are the product of early childhood learning, powerfully transmitted through contact with parents and other social agents. To a great extent this learning is symbolically acquired through vicarious observational methods. Self-control represents the blending of these previously internalized standards of conduct with current environmental contingencies to produce complex social behavior.

Although frequently regarded as an uncompromising environmentalist, Skinner (1953) has never dismissed the significance of private events in the analysis of behavior. In *Science and Human Behavior* he notes:

> Yet to a considerable extent an individual does appear to shape his own destiny. He is often able to do something about the variables affecting

him. Some degree of "self-determination" of conduct is usually recognized in the creative behavior of the artist and scientist, in the self-exploratory behavior of the writer, and in the self-discipline of the ascetic. Humbler versions of self-determination are more familiar. The individual "chooses" between alternative courses of action, "thinks through" a problem while isolated from the relevant environment, and guards his health or his position in society through the exercise of "self-control." (p. 228)

Skinner's theoretical analysis of self-control is essentially an extension of general principles of operant behavior. An individual is said to have exercised self-control when he can effectively influence the variables of which his behavior is a function. Whether the process requires arranging environmental conditions to increase the possibility of receiving positive reinforcement, or manipulating inner emotional states to discipline the emergence of certain desired instrumental behaviors, the purposes and principles involved are generally the same. Skinner regards self-control as behavior like any other behavior. Thus, self-control is a function of personal history variables interacting with current environmental influences to create the conditions for individual action.

Kanfer and Phillips (1970) detail the dimensions of self-control and offer concrete suggestions as to how undesirable response sequences can be disrupted or replaced. Their theoretical and empirical analysis is heavily influenced by Skinner. In reviewing the literature they propose a series of instrumental steps which, if taken properly, appear to facilitate the emergence of successful self-control. Of prime value is the initiation of self-control operations *early* in the response sequence. A further suggestion is the liberal use of environmental support systems designed to restrict the possibility of the emission of the maladaptive target behavior, and the simultaneous encouragement of alternate responses, particularly alternate behavior which will be socially reinforced. Extremely vital is a clear specification of the desired end product of the self-control effort. Finally, they stress the importance of obtaining clear feedback, so that self-corrective measures can be introduced if the program begins to lose momentum.

It is readily apparent from the summaries of different behavior theory approaches to the issues of self-control that both mediational and non-mediational views are represented. From our point of view, a comprehensive theory should account for both components.

a working definition of self-control

Self-control can be viewed as a process through which an individual becomes the principal agent in guiding, directing, and regulating those features of his own behavior that might eventually lead to desired positive consequences. Typically, the emphasis in self-control is placed on those variables *beneath the skin* which determine the motivation for change. It is equally important to realize, however, that environmental influences have played a vital role in developing the unique behavioral properties of the self-control sequence. Thus, we assume that self-control is a skill learned through various social contacts, and the repertoire of effective self-control responses is gradually built up through increased experimentation with a complex environment. Once the basic self-control information and techniques have been acquired, however, the environment does not automatically release the form or content of the self-control behavior. Rather, a certain degree of judgmental direction is required, whereby the individual himself must formulate a plan of action, test the efficiency of the personal control operation used, and appraise whether the performance and its outcome have met internalized standards of competence. One might best characterize this aspect of self-control as an exercise in discrimination and problem solving.

In distilling the various approaches to the problem of self-control, we suggest the following definition: *Self-control represents a personal decision arrived at through conscious deliberation for the purpose of integrating action which is designed to achieve certain desired outcomes or goals as determined by the individual himself.* A number of points in this orientation require further clarification.

According to our orientation, we conceive of the act of self-control as being mediated by cognitive processes which are available to conscious recognition. Miller and Dollard (1941) and Dollard and Miller (1950) have labeled these intermediary internal behaviors as "cue-producing responses." Bandura (1969) and Kanfer (1970) have similarly stressed the importance of mediating variables in dealing with the process of self-control. All of these conceptions lean heavily on the importance of thought and language in delaying impulsive action. . . .

It is crucial to point out that attempts at self-management usually appear when the smooth execution of normal response chains are inadequate to cope with current internal or external demands. In many ways this reality poses a particularly difficult task for most people because the behavior to be controlled is often one that results in immediate positive reinforcement, but adverse future consequences. Examples of this phenomenon are legion—smoking, overeating, deviant sexual behavior, unrestrained aggression, and the like. Kanfer and Phillips (1970) suggest:

> The process of self-control always involves the change of the probability of executing a response that has both rewarding and aversive consequences, and the selective initiation of a controlling response by a person even though the tempting response is available and more immediately rewarding. (p. 414)

Realistically, the demand for self-regulation may not initially stem from the individual himself. Social agencies may instigate the process by threatening retaliation if the unacceptable behavior is not brought under appropriate control. Or, due to the availability of new information from an external source, the decision to attempt self-control is initiated. A good example of an external source producing a massive self-controlling response from many was the Surgeon General's report on the relationship between cigarettes and cancer. Another familiar example is the feedback typically gotten from friends about how unattractively obese one is becoming because of poor eating habits. Internal experience may also set the self-control process in motion; guilt, embarrassment, and shame over habitual but irrational acts are powerful incentives for change. The violation of internalized norms of conduct generates exceedingly powerful emotional reactions which can be relieved only when the maladaptive behavior is absolutely controlled, or at least sharply reduced in frequency. For an excellent theoretical analysis of those variables associated with committing oneself to behavior change, the reader is referred to Marston and Feldman (1971) and Kopel (1972).

In summary, our definition of self-control includes the following points:

1. A prerequisite of self-control is that it is the individual himself who determines his own special goal or outcome to be achieved. This is not to say that

he may be uninfluenced to adopt a particular goal. In the final analysis, however, the choice remains an individual matter.

2. We assume that the strategies for self-control must be deliberately and consciously arranged to reduce the frequency of the unacceptable target behavior.
These strategies may include various degrees of personal self-regulation, or
may involve the enlisting of environmental support to enhance the attempts
at self-control. Regardless of which strategy is employed, a necessary condition is that the person must both be able to verbalize his goal, and to specify
each of the several steps he will take to alter his problematic behavior.

3. We view self-control as a functionally defined concept. That is, whether or
not one has demonstrated self-control is determined not so much upon procedures employed as it is on the consequences of the action taken.

4. It is our contention that self-control cannot be regarded as a global personality
construct. Instead, self-control may more appropriately be viewed as referring
to a specific response, or perhaps class of responses, relevant to the alteration of certain maladaptive behaviors.

5. Finally, it is assumed that self-control does not emerge from any innate potential within the individual, but is acquired through experience, whether it
be trial-and-error or more systematic learning.

mechanisms of self-control

In the section which follows, we shall describe some of the self-control
procedures which have been used for the modification of various forms of problematic behavior, including maladaptive *emotional-physiological* reactions as
well as problematic *instrumental* responses.

While it seems almost like a contradiction in terms to discuss the means
by which one can gain control over "involuntary" behaviors, the modification of
emotional-physiological reactions has been approached by training the individual
to manipulate those voluntary responses which serve as elicitory stimuli for such
involuntary reactions (Bijou and Baer, 1961). The control of maladaptive emotional-physiological reactions has involved autosuggestion and self-administered
relaxation techniques, cognitive relabeling, and self-administered aversive conditioning procedures. In the case of maladaptive instrumental behaviors, the
self-control procedures have included the manipulation of those environmental
stimuli which set the occasion for the behavior, the use of self-verbalizations to
initiate and direct more adaptive behaviors, and the employment of self-reinforcement techniques to establish favorable consequences for competing adaptive
responses.

self-control of maladaptive
emotional-physiological reactions

There are several forms of maladaptive emotional-physiological reactions—
such as anxiety, deviant sexual attractions, low pain thresholds, epileptic seizures—
which have been the target of self-control procedures. Rather than focusing our
discussion on each of these reactions per se, we shall describe the various self-
control mechanisms used in dealing with these difficulties—i.e., such procedures
as autosuggestion and self-administered relaxation, cognitive relabeling, and self-
administered aversive conditioning—illustrating each with the type of maladaptive
behavior toward which it typically has been directed.

AUTOSUGGESTION AND SELF-ADMINISTERED RELAXATION

The use of autosuggestive techniques has received widespread attention over the years, with one of the objectives being the attainment of direct control over *physiological* reactions. Within the area of behavior modification, the most popular of these procedures involves Jacobson's (1938) method for training in deep muscular relaxation. Used as one of the essential components of systematic desensitization, Jacobson's procedure, or its abbreviated variations (e.g., Paul, 1966), involves training the individual in alternately tensing and relaxing various muscle groups, until he is capable of voluntarily arriving at a state of deep muscular relaxation. Accompanying this muscular relaxation are various autonomic concomitants, including decrease in pulse rate, blood pressure, and skin conductance (Jacobson, 1938; Paul, 1969a).

Another procedure which has been used for the control of physiological reactions has been Schultz and Luthe's (1959) method for "autogenic training." Bearing some similarities to both Jacobson's method and yoga exercises, autogenic training is a form of autosuggestion in which the individual is given practice in attending to both his physiological sensations and his immediate state of consciousness. The procedure involves daily practice of certain exercises, including complete muscular relaxation, and concentration on subjective sensations of warmth and heaviness. As is the case with Jacobson's procedure, autogenic training has been found to be an effective method for learning to gain control over various aspects of physiological reactivity (Schultz & Luthe, 1959).

A somewhat different approach to the control of autonomic responsivity has been described by Lang (1968). Rather than training the individual in any particular exercises along the lines described by Jacobson or Schultz and Luthe, Lang and his associates found that by providing subjects with continual feedback regarding their cardiac activity, together with instructions to maintain a steady rate, it was possible to get subjects to the point where they could voluntarily control their own heart rate.

The attempt to train individuals to obtain direct control over autonomic activity has also been illustrated in a fascinating case study reported by Efron (1957). After training an epileptic patient to inhibit the onset of seizures by having her inhale an unpleasant odor during the early phases of the aura, Efron conditioned these olfactory stimuli to the *sight* of a specific object (i.e., the patient's bracelet). With repeated practice, the physical presence of the bracelet alone was sufficient for blocking the onset of the fits. Carrying this higher order conditioning procedure one step further, the patient eventually reached the point where by merely *thinking* of the bracelet, she was successfully able to inhibit the seizures.

Closely related to the control of physiological reactivity have been attempts to modify *negative emotional reactions*, particularly anxiety. According to Jacobson (1938), the state achieved through deep muscular relaxation is such that it *directly* (i.e., physiologically) inhibits anxiety reactions. As yet, there has been no empirical confirmation of this hypothesis (Lang, 1969), and competing explanations for the relationship between physiological and emotional responses have been proposed by others (e.g., Schachter & Singer, 1962). Regardless of what the underlying process might entail, training in relaxation—typically, although not necessarily within the context of systematic desensitization—has nonetheless been found to serve as an effective procedure for the reduction of anxiety.

Some attempts have been made to conduct systematic desensitization in such a way so that most of the procedure could be carried out directly by the client himself (e.g., Kahn & Baker, 1968; Migler & Wolpe, 1967). The purpose of most of these reports has been to demonstrate that self-administered desensitization may be used as a way of freeing professional therapeutic time, rather than a means by which the client might be provided with a more general coping technique. By contrast, the use of systematic desensitization as a procedure for training in self-control has been described by Goldfried (1971). On the basis of various research findings, systematic desensitization is presented as a means for providing the individual with an active skill for coping with anxiety-producing situations in general, rather than as a passive desensitization of specific fears. Within this model of desensitization, Goldfried has outlined specific procedural modifications, each of which is likely to facilitate the learning of this self-regulating skill.

Several case studies have been reported in which the attempt was made to instruct the client in anxiety-reducing techniques, the goal of which was training in self-control. Goldfried (1973) has described a case of generalized anxiety, where a multidimensional hierarchy was used to provide the client with the skill of "relaxing away" her anxieties in a multitude of situations. Similarly, Lazarus (1958) has reported the case of a client who was able to prevent severe anxiety attacks by use of autohypnotic techniques. The procedure described by Lazarus was, in essence, very similar to the use of relaxation *in vivo*. Weil and Goldfried (1972) have described the successful use of self-administered relaxation procedures with an eleven-year-old suffering from insomnia. In a deliberate attempt to train a client in self-control procedures for reducing heterosexual anxiety, D'Zurilla (1969) employed one of the procedural modifications outlined by Goldfried (1971). Thus, the client was asked to *maintain* the anxiety-producing image during systematic desensitization while relaxing away this tension, so as to provide a "behavioral rehearsal" for relaxing *in vivo* whenever experiencing feelings of anxiety. Arkowitz (1969) has reported the results of a case in which he trained a client in the technique of self-desensitization to alleviate a problem involving heterosexual anxiety, but where the client was successful in employing the same procedures at a later time in other, unrelated situations (e.g., examination anxiety).

In addition to the control of physiological and emotional responses, autosuggestive procedures have also been employed to increase *tolerance for noxious stimuli*. Salter (1941) has described a self-hypnotic procedure which may be used to raise pain threshold. For each of the training procedures described—which in many ways are similar to the exercises outlined by Schultz and Luthe (1959)—the emphasis is on providing the individual with the ability to be in control of his own physiological and cognitive state.

One area in particular which has received considerable attention by those interested in the application of self-control procedures for tolerance of noxious stimulation has been that of obstetrics. Based on the assumption that the pain associated with labor is due to muscular tension resulting from fear, Read (1944) developed procedures for training in "natural childbirth." The training technique makes use of rapid breathing exercises as well as practice in muscular relaxation, all of which is directed toward breaking the presumed vicious cycle between fear, muscular tension, and pain. A variation of these procedures was developed by Lamaze (1958) and Velvovski and his associates (Velvovski, Platonov, Ploticher, & Csougom, 1960). This technique, which has been referred to as the "psychoprophylactic method," does not accept Read's assumption of the intrinsic relationship between fear, muscular tension, and pain. Instead, the training technique focuses on the attempt to directly raise the pain threshold by having uterine contractions serve as a signal for rapid breathing, which is accompanied by intense concentration on the sensations of breathing, and not the pain. The psychoprophylactic method also incorporates various other principles which are directed at reducing the noxious components of childbirth (e.g., the term "pain" is replaced by "contraction").

The effectiveness of the natural childbirth and psychoprophylactic techniques has been attested to by various clinical studies which, because of the fact that subjects were self-selected and controls were absent, have more the status of a series of case reports than they do controlled investigation (Goodrich & Thomas, 1948; Kline & Guze, 1955; Yahia & Ulin, 1965). The findings of these several reports indicate that women who underwent a training program prior to childbirth typically required less medication or anesthesia during the delivery.

We may note a study by Kanfer and Goldfoot (1966) on the tolerance of noxious stimulation as having direct relevance to self-control training for childbirth—particularly the psychoprophylactic method. In order to determine effective procedures by which an individual might raise his pain threshold, Kanfer and Goldfoot had subjects attend to various stimuli while one hand was immersed in ice water. The results of the study revealed that pain tolerance could be increased by focusing one's attention on non-pain-related stimuli (e.g., slides, a clock). These findings are interpreted by the authors as indicating that the self-control mechanism involved here may entail attending to "cues which compete with the response-produced cues associated with noxious events" (Kanfer & Goldfoot, 1966, p. 84). A follow-up study by Kanfer and Seidner (1972) has indicated that pain tolerance could be increased still further if the subject had direct responsibility for *producing* the competing cues.

Within the context of one of his investigations on hypnosis, Orne (1959) has also reported some findings relevant to self-directed tolerance for noxious events. Orne's working model of hypnosis incorporates not only an altered state of consciousness, but also the person's role-conception of the hypnotized subject, as well as his increased motivation to react in given ways. Orne's study on the motivational component of hypnosis is most relevant here. The noxious task employed by Orne was one which required subjects to hold a heavy weight at arm's length until it became intolerable. Male subjects in a waking state who were motivated to continue as long as possible were able to persist longer on this same task than they could while under the influence of hypnotic suggestion. Within the context of self-control, the important finding in this study is the fact that the individual's motivational state per se can greatly influence his ability to tolerate noxious stimulation.

In summary, it would appear that the use of autosuggestive and self-administered relaxation procedures has an important potential for attaining self-control over physiological reactions, the reduction of anxiety, and increasing one's tolerance for noxious stimulation. However, work in this area is still in its infancy, and a greater refinement of theory and technique may bring about revolutionary changes in clinical practice.

COGNITIVE RELABELING

The behavioral approach has often been criticized on the grounds that it neglects the existence of the individual's cognitive processes. Except perhaps for the most "radical" of behavior therapists, however, the judicious reference to mediational processes in conceptualizing human functioning may be seen as completely consistent with a behavioral viewpoint (cf. Davison, Goldfried, & Krasner, 1970). The two major theoretical sources for the use of cognitive relabeling as a self-control process consist of Miller and Dollard's (1941) and Dollard and Miller's (1950) discussion of labeling and the "higher mental processes," and Schachter and Singer's (1962) description of the interaction between cognitive and physiological factors in determining emotional state.

Although Dollard and Miller (1950) have typically been faulted by behavior therapists for simply translating traditional psychoanalytic procedures into learning theory terminology, rather than suggesting innovative techniques which might stem directly from behavioral principles, they nonetheless have provided one of the most significant theoretical platforms on which certain behavioral techniques have subsequently been based. In particular, their discussion of "cue-producing responses"—whether involving the overt use of language or covert self-statements—as a means of facilitating or inhibiting other responses is highly relevant to the question of self-control.

In describing their mediational view of emotional arousal, Dollard and Miller point out that fear reactions may often be elicited by the individual's cue-producing response (i.e., label) to a given situation, rather than the objective stimulus properties of the situation itself. They argue that by modifying the label one attaches to the situation, it should be possible to alter the individual's maladaptive emotional reaction. Rational psychotherapy (Ellis, 1958), or as it has more recently been called, rational-emotive therapy (Ellis, 1962), is based on a proposition very much like that described by Dollard and Miller. As Ellis states it:

> It would appear, then, that positive human emotions, such as feelings of love or elation, are often associated with or result from thoughts, or internalized sentences, stated in some form or variation of the phrase "This is good!" and that negative human emotions, such as feelings of anger or depression, are frequently associated with or result from thoughts or sentences which are stated in some form or variation of the phrase "This is bad!" (p. 37)

An experimental test of the effects of self-verbalization on mood states has been carried out by Velten (1968). Subjects were asked to read self-referent statements which reflected elation ("This is great—I really do feel good—I *am* elated about things"), depression ("I have too many bad things in my life"), or neutral feelings ("Utah is the Beehive State"). Consistent with his hypothesis, Velten found that mood changed as a function of the statements read. These changes were measured by the subject's verbal report, as well as by such indirect indicators as writing speed, decision time, reaction time on a word-association task, and spontaneous verbalizations. Rimm and Litvak (1969) similarly tested the effects of self-verbalizations on emotional arousal, and found that a significantly greater emotional reaction (as indicated by breathing rate and depth) was elicited by affect-related statements than by neutral ones. Consequently, the basic assumption that self-statements are capable of eliciting maladaptive emotional responses appears to have empirical support.

In addition to maintaining that a person's internal sentences determine his emotional state, Ellis (1958) additionally assumes that maladaptive emotional reactions stem from self-statements which are, in fact, *irrational* (e.g., "Everyone must love me," "I must be perfect," etc.). The primary goal of therapy from his orientation is to have the client modify these unrealistic internal sentences. Included among the various ways in which an attempt is made to modify these self-verbalizations are instructions given to the client that, whenever he experiences emotional upset in some life situation, he should stop to ask himself whether some irrational internal sentences may be at the root of this feeling (e.g., "I *must* do extremely well on this task"). If so, he is encouraged to replace the irrational statement with a more appropriate one (e.g., "It would be *nice* if I could do very well on this task"). Thus, instead of engaging in what is essentially self-defeating (i.e., emotionally-arousing) labeling activities, the client is trained to understand and control these cue-producing responses.

Although the research findings of Velten (1968) and Rimm and Litvak (1969) corroborate one of the basic assumptions underlying rational-emotive therapy, much of the support comes from case reports. On the basis of uncontrolled case studies with a variety of different problems (e.g., Ellis, 1957b, 1959, 1961), the therapeutic effectiveness of this approach would appear to be promising. In addition, some data based on controlled outcome research, which are just beginning to appear in the literature (e.g., Karst & Trexler, 1970; Meichenbaum, Gilmore, & Fedoravicius, 1971), similarly offer support for the effectiveness of the procedure.

Homme's (1965b) description of the self-generated nature of emotional reactions, while employing Skinnerian terminology, is very much within the spirit of Miller and Dollard. Instead of maintaining that emotional responses may be mediated by "cue-producing responses," Homme discusses the role of "coverants"—a contraction of "covert operant"—in the control of maladaptive emotional reactions. He suggests that the frequency of adaptive coverants may be increased by emitting them immediately prior to some high probability behavior (cf. Premack, 1959). According to Homme, if brushing one's teeth can be made contingent upon telling oneself "I feel great," for example, it should be possible to bring about a more positive mood state. Although the successful use of this technique has been reported in a case study (Johnson, 1971), this approach has not yet been tested by means of controlled outcome studies.

In Schachter and Singer's (1962) discussion of the determinants of emotional state, they maintain that the specific emotion experienced by an individual depends not only upon his state of physiological arousal, but also on the way in which he *interprets* or *labels* this state. They further suggest that this labeling process itself is influenced by what the individual attributes as being at the origin of this arousal. This view has been tested empirically by several studies, some of which have direct implications for providing an individual with control over his maladaptive emotional states, and increasing his tolerance for noxious stimulation.

In Schachter and Singer's (1962) classic study in this area, they began by injecting a number of subjects with epinephrine. Some of the subjects were informed that they would experience certain physiological effects as a result of the drug, while others were left uninformed as to the origin of their state of arousal. Although all subjects were exposed to a confederate displaying considerable anger, the group which was informed as to the effects of the drug reacted with significantly less anger than did the uninformed group. According to Schachter and Singer, the informed subjects had attributed their arousal state to the drug and not the emotional nature of the social situation, and consequently were less influenced by the cues associated with the confederate's emotional state. Essentially the same findings were obtained with subjects exposed to a euphoric confederate, thus supporting the notion that emotional state is greatly influenced by the individual's covert labeling.

The effect of cognitive evaluation of arousal states was also studied by Valins (1966), where male subjects were presented slides of seminude females and were given the opportunity to concomitantly monitor their heart rate. The changes in heart rate fed back to the subjects were in fact bogus, and were provided as a basis by which subjects might attribute certain emotional reactions as resulting from the slides. In comparison to subjects who monitored these same sound changes, but who were led to believe they had nothing to do with their internal reactions, experimental subjects subsequently reported greater attraction to the pictures.

In applying this attribution paradigm to the modification of a maladaptive emotional response, Valins and Ray (1967) have interpreted the anxiety-reduction which occurs during systematic desensitization as being based on the individual having learned to control his physiological state, which he then labels as indicating "I am no longer afraid." To test this hypothesis, Valins and Ray provided snake phobics with false feedback as to their physiological state as they viewed pictures of snakes. To enhance the credibility of the feedback, signs of reactivity were provided when subjects were given the signal they were about to receive a shock. The results of the Valins and Ray study indicated that subjects who were "cognitively desensitized" to fear of snakes showed less avoidance behavior than subjects who were instructed that what they had heard while viewing pictures of snakes consisted of meaningless sounds.

In commenting on the study by Valins and Ray, Bandura (1969) has cautioned against drawing any far-reaching extrapolations which might be based on these findings, primarily because of the fact that no adequate preassessment was obtained on the subjects' initial fear of snakes. In light of a replication of this study by Sushinsky and Bootzin (1970), in which a more stringent preassessment for fear level was employed, this caution was well taken. Using subjects whose avoidance behavior appeared to be stronger than those in the Valins and Ray study, Sushinsky and Bootzin were *unable* to demonstrate the effects of cognitive desensitization.

In a study on the cognitive manipulation of pain, Nisbett and Schachter (1966) gave subjects a placebo and then subjected them to a mild electric shock. Those subjects who were led to believe that the physiological arousal experienced during the shock was due to the *drug*, rather than the shock, were able to tolerate significantly more pain stimulation. These findings failed to hold up in another condition, however, where the shock provided was strong.

The implications of differential attribution, as it directly relates to the self-control of tolerance for noxious stimulation, was investigated by Davison and Valins (1969). In an attempt to manipulate pain tolerance, they administered shock to a group of subjects and then provided them with a drug (actually a placebo) which would presumably increase pain tolerance. So as to reinforce the subjects' expectations regarding the effectiveness of the drug, the shock levels were surreptitiously reduced once the drug had "taken effect." Shortly thereafter, the experimental treatment was introduced, which consisted of telling half of the subjects that the drug had worn off, and informing the remainder of the subjects that it really was a placebo. Subjects who were led to believe that the drug had *no effect* reported having more confidence in their ability to withstand shock on a subsequent trial and, in fact, were found to tolerate more shock in a subsequent experiment. These findings are interpreted as providing a method for facilitating self-control by attributing changes to one's own efforts.

Although the work by Schachter and Singer, as well as subsequent investigators, appears to have relevance for the control of maladaptive emotional reactions and ability to tolerate noxious stimulation, there are certain conflicting findings which suggest limitations to this approach. Sushinsky and Bootzin's (1970) failure to replicate Valins and Ray (1967), as well as Nisbett and Schachter's (1966) finding that cognitive manipulation of pain was successful for mild, but not strong, levels of shock would suggest that a key question which remains unanswered is the effectiveness with which such cognitive manipulations are capable of modifying emotional states at various levels of intensity. In essence, the issue may involve the question of how effectively an individual can "delude" himself into maintaining cognitively that he is no longer afraid, or that he is better able to tolerate noxious stimulation, when so many other aspects of his reaction inform him that he indeed is anxious, or that the shock does indeed hurt.

SELF-ADMINISTERED AVERSIVE CONDITIONING

The use of self-administered aversive conditioning for the modification of maladaptive emotional responses has typically been employed in those instances where there exists a maladaptive positive reaction to certain stimuli. The aversive counterconditioning procedures entail the pairing of an aversive stimulus with those stimuli which serve as attractions for the deviant reactions, the objective of which is to establish a conditioned aversion to these tempting situations.

The typical approach which has been employed in self-administered aversive counterconditioning has involved the implementation of these procedures by means of an *imaginal* pairing of positive and aversive stimuli (Anant, 1967; Cautela, 1967; Davison, 1968a; Gold & Neufeld, 1965; Miller, 1959). Although there have been slight variations in the way in which the technique is implemented, the basic procedure may be exemplified by Cautela's (1967) description of *covert sensitization*. Cautela suggests that the client first be trained in techniques of deep muscular relaxation, the purpose of which is not entirely clear. Once in a relaxed state, the individual is instructed to visualize the situation with which the pleasurable, but maladaptive activity (e.g., drinking, deviant sexual behavior) is typically associated. As the person imagines himself getting closer to actually engaging in the maladaptive behavior, he is asked to imagine himself getting more and more nauseous, until, immediately prior to the behavior itself, he begins to vomit. Upon withdrawing from the situation, the feeling of nausea disappears. The client is instructed to practice covert sensitization at home between sessions, and perhaps most important of all, to *use* the technique when actually tempted to engage in these behaviors in actual life situations.

The use of self-administered, imaginal aversive conditioning has been employed in the treatment of alcoholism (Anant, 1967; Ashem & Donner, 1968; Cautela, 1966; Miller, 1959), obesity (Cautela, 1966b; Harris, 1969; Stuart, 1967), cigarette-smoking (Keutzer, 1968; Tooley & Pratt, 1967), deviant sexual behavior (Barlow, Leitenberg, & Agras, 1969; Cautela, 1967; Davison, 1968a; Gold & Neufeld, 1965), and maladaptive interactions with a parent (Davison, 1969b).

In addition to the success reported in those uncontrolled case reports in which self-administered aversive procedures were employed, the technique has received empirical confirmation in controlled investigations as well. Thus, Ashem and Donner (1968) employed covert sensitization with alcoholics, all of whom had a history of unsuccessfully having undergone various forms of treatment. In comparison with a no-contact group, those clients who were treated with covert sensitization showed significantly higher abstinence rates after a six-month follow-up. Barlow et al. (1969) studied the effectiveness of covert sensitization in two cases of sexual deviation (homosexuality and pedophilia), in which the acquisition phase of the training was followed by an extinction period and then again by a reacquisition phase. In comparison with base-line data, they found a decline in reported sexual arousal to previously tempting scenes when presented in imagination, as well as a decrease in maladaptive sexual urges experienced *in vivo*. During the extinction phase, in which only the scenes were presented, the clients again reported sexual arousal, but these feelings disappeared again during reacquisition.

The fact that the subjects in Barlow et al.'s study reverted back to their pretreatment state during extinction would suggest that (a) clients should continue employing the self-administered aversive conditioning even though behavior change has presumably taken place, or (b) some attempt should be made to establish more sexually appropriate stimuli as sources of arousal. In this regard, we may note Bandura's (1969) description of conditioned aversion:

> The major value of aversion procedures is that they provide a means of achieving control over injurious behavior for a period of time during which alternative, and more rewarding, modes of response can be established and strengthened. Used by itself, this method may bring about only temporary suppression of deviant tendencies. (p. 509)

The success achieved by Ashem and Donner (1966) and Davison (1968a) who, in addition to employing aversive counterconditioning, made an attempt to build in more adaptive responses, would seem to confirm Bandura's recommendation.

Along these lines, we might note the approach to self-administered aversive conditioning suggested by Homme (1965b). Homme suggests that an individual can learn to gain control by emitting aversive self-statements or "covert operants" (e.g., "Cigarettes cause cancer.") in the presence of stimuli which typically elicit the maladaptive reaction (e.g., desire to smoke). Following this, the person is encouraged to substitute some statement antithetical to the maladaptive behavior (e.g., "I will feel better.") and then engage in some reinforcing activity (e.g., drinking coffee).

In a criticism of Homme's procedures, Mahoney (1970) cautions that by emitting the self-verbalization (e.g., "Cigarettes cause cancer.") for the suppression of some maladaptive behavior, the technique may paradoxically serve to remind the person of the behavior he is trying to eliminate, thereby making self-control more difficult. Another problem noted by Mahoney is that the "aversive" self-statement may lose its noxious quality after a period of time, especially when it is paired with reinforcing activities. These criticisms are well-taken, although there is little data currently available as yet to back them up. In one study on the effectiveness of Homme's suggested treatment procedures, the technique was found to be successful in modifying smoking behavior, but no more effective than treatment with a placebo (Keutzer, 1968). In many respects, Homme's suggested approach may represent only a weak version of the other procedures for self-administered aversive conditioning.

One more point might be made regarding the use of aversive counterconditioning procedures. Very much within the context of self-control, Bandura (1969) suggests that rather than viewing aversion procedures as resulting in a passive modification of the valence of certain stimuli, it could more appropriately be construed as a means for providing the individual with the technique of aversive self-stimulation, which he may then actively use to counteract the tempting quality of the addictive stimuli. According to this view, then, the training procedure can be construed as a "behavioral rehearsal" for what the individual is to do in the real-life situation, much the same way as systematic desensitization can be interpreted as a means for providing the individual with a strategy for coping with anxiety-producing events (cf. Goldfried, 1971).

self-control of maladaptive instrumental responses

Although there is probably no limit to the variety of maladaptive instrumental responses which would be amenable to self-control procedures, the problems which have received most of the attention in the literature consist of overeating and smoking, with a few reports appearing on marital problems and poor study habits. The procedures which have been employed in training individuals to gain control over maladaptive instrumental responses include techniques involving stimulus control, the use of verbal self-directions, and the institution of self-reinforcement following the occurrence of more adaptive, competing behaviors. Although we shall discuss each of these procedures separately in the section which follows, they clearly may be used in combination. Indeed, the combined use of each of these techniques is likely to be most effective in obtaining self-control.

STIMULUS CONTROL

Although instrumental behavior is typically thought of as being maintained primarily by reinforcing consequences, it is also controlled by discriminative stimuli which have been associated with the reinforced behavior. Thus, the pigeon learns to peck at a disk only when the light is on, and the first cup of coffee in the morning serves as a cue for an individual to light up a cigarette. The relevance of stimulus control for self-regulation stems primarily from the fact that an individual is capable of modifying certain maladaptive behaviors by altering the discriminative stimuli associated with these behaviors. Skinner (1953) has described self-directed stimulus control as a means by which the individual can either avoid some temptation by removing discriminative stimuli, or facilitate the occurrence of certain adaptive responses by exposing himself to certain stimuli which will increase its likelihood.

A problem area toward which much of the work on stimulus control has been directed is that of obesity. The attempt to gain control over eating habits by manipulating the discriminative stimuli associated with such behaviors is particularly relevant in light of the findings by Schachter and his associates (Goldman, Jaffa, & Schachter, 1968; Schachter, 1967; Schachter & Gross, 1968) that, in comparison to individuals of normal weight, the eating habits of obese individuals are more likely to be controlled by external factors than by the internal sensations of hunger. Self-directed weight-control programs using techniques of stimulus control have been described by Ferster, Nurnberger, and Levitt (1962), Harris (1969), and Stuart (1967). The procedure used in these programs is similar, and typically involves narrowing the range of situations and times during which eating can occur. In addition, the individual is instructed to avoid eating while engaging in other activities, such as reading or watching TV, the general purpose of which is to have these situations no longer function as discriminative stimuli for eating. Although these programs have typically been shown to be effective in bringing about weight loss, the inclusion of a variety of self-control techniques (e.g., covert sensitization) makes it difficult to isolate the relative effectiveness of this procedure alone.

Other problems to which stimulus control has been applied include the modification of smoking behavior (Nolan, 1968; Ober, 1968; Upper & Meredith, 1970), inefficient study habits (Goldiamond, 1965c), and marital problems (Goldiamond, 1965c). As has been the case with the work done on weight control, the use of stimulus control in each of these other instances involves the narrowing of those discriminative stimuli which are associated with the maladaptive responses.

The use of stimulus control for the elimination of smoking behavior may be illustrated with a case study reported by Nolan (1968). The procedure was implemented by having the individual—Nolan's wife—agree to smoke only when sitting in a certain chair. In addition, things were arranged so that no other activities, such as reading, watching TV, or holding a conversation, could be carried out while sitting in this chair. As a result of following this procedure, she was able to abstain from smoking after a period of one month.

The successful use of stimulus control procedures for the modification of smoking has also been reported by Upper and Meredith (1970). The treatment program consisted of having subjects use a portable timer which was set according to their typical interval between cigarettes. The buzzer which sounded at the end of the interval served as a signal for their smoking. Once their smoking behavior was under control of the buzzer, subjects gradually increased the time between signals. The results of the study indicated that when compared to subjects in attention-placebo and no-contact control groups, those participating in the stimulus control program showed significantly greater decrements in smoking behavior.

Goldiamond (1965c) has described other problematic behaviors for which a stimulus control approach was employed. In the case of a student unable to maintain efficient study behavior, for example, it was recommended that the student's desk be used for study only, and that other activities be carried out elsewhere. Goldiamond also describes a marital problem in which he recommended rearranging the household furniture so as to provide a stimulus situation which had less of an association with the marital arguments. Also associated with this case was the husband's tendency to sulk. Although the individual's privilege to sulk was acknowledged, he was instructed to do so only in a certain place. The fact that sulking decreased after a regime of engaging in this activity while sitting on a "sulking stool" in the garage, however, may be better illustrative of aversive, rather than stimulus control.

For some reason, the range of problems described in the literature toward which stimulus-control has been applied seems to be fairly narrow. Considering the fact that external stimuli mark the occasion for so much of our everyday behavior, principals of stimulus control would seem to have the potential for providing an individual with the means by which he might modify a wide variety of maladaptive behaviors.

VERBAL SELF-DIRECTION

In addition to the external stimulus control of behavior, man's use of language provides him with the ability to generate his own stimuli, which in turn, are capable of directing his actions. This may consist either of simple self-generated verbal commands which instigate certain behaviors (Skinner, 1953), or more complex planning and reasoning which can influence the decision to emit certain behaviors and not others (Dollard & Miller, 1950; Miller & Dollard, 1941).

The role of self-instruction for the control of overt behavior has been studied developmentally by Luria (1961), who concludes that prior to age four, children are typically unable to use self-verbalizations as a means for regulating their behavior. The likelihood that this finding is tied to the specific nature of previous learning history, rather than any innate developmental sequence, is suggested by recent work in this area. For example, in a study by S. L. Bem (1967), it was found that under conditions of specialized training, three-year-olds were brought to the point where they eventually were capable of utilizing self-instruction to control their behavior. Similar findings have been reported by Meichenbaum and Goodman (1971) with impulsive grade-school children.

The use of self-instruction as a means of self-control among children has also been studied by O'Leary (1968), who found it to be effective in providing subjects with the ability to resist the temptation to cheat. In this study, grade-school boys were allowed to work on a task in which the probability of obtaining a prize could be increased by cheating. The cheating consisted of pressing a key at the "wrong" time to obtain marbles which later could be exchanged for a prize. Although all children were aware of what was "right" and "wrong," the frequency of transgressions was significantly less for those boys who were instructed to tell themselves whether they should press or not prior to actually responding.

In conjunction with a description of the way in which an individual can learn to manage his own contingencies, Homme (1965b) describes the use of "coverants" or self-administered verbal contracts, to increase the likelihood that certain behaviors will occur. According to Homme, the individual who wants to facilitate study behavior should tell himself something like: "As soon as I complete this reading assignment, I can reinforce myself by watching TV." In a case report described by Johnson (1971), Homme's coverant technique was successfully employed by a client as an aid in directing adaptive interpersonal behaviors. The likelihood of emitting the appropriate coverant at any given time was insured by having the client carry in his possession index cards containing these verbal statements. This use of the index card procedure may be viewed as a way of gaining some stimulus control over the likelihood of utilizing these self-verbalizations.

In dealing with situations requiring more than simple self-directed statements, Miller and Dollard (1941) and Dollard and Miller (1950) describe the use of cue-producing responses in the process of coping with various situations where the most appropriate response is not apparent. The use of "higher mental processes," argue Miller and Dollard, can eliminate many of the negative consequences which are likely to accompany overt trial and error. Man's ability to reason and plan, particularly when faced with a problematic situation requiring some decision on his part, plays a significant role in the likelihood of his controlling his own fate.

Based in part on some of the suggestions outlined by Miller and Dollard, D'Zurilla and Goldfried (1971; 1973) have outlined procedures for training in problem-solving. Within the context of facilitating self-control, these procedures are directed toward enabling the individual to become better able to decide upon the most effective course of action when confronted with a problematic situation. The training procedures are directed toward providing the individual with the ability to utilize each of the following steps in coping with difficult life situations: (a) being able to recognize problematic situations when they occur and making an attempt to resist the temptation to act impulsively or do nothing to deal with the situation; (b) defining the situation in concrete or operational terms, and then formulating the major issues with which he must cope; (c) generating a number of possible behaviors which might be pursued in this situation; (d) deciding on the course(s) of action most likely to result in positive consequences; and finally (e) acting upon the final decision and verifying the effectiveness of the behavior in resolving the problematic situation.

The effectiveness of some of the techniques outlined by D'Zurilla and Goldfried (1971; 1973) may be illustrated by the work of Parnes and Meadow (1959) and Meadow and Parnes (1959). In an attempt to facilitate creative problem-solving, Parnes and Meadow tested the effectiveness of "brainstorming" instructions. The brainstorming technique emphasizes that the individual generate as many ideas as possible in a given situation, inhibiting any premature evaluation as to their value. When compared with a group who was told to produce only "good" ideas, subjects using brain-storming instructions were able to produce not only more ideas, but also ideas of good quality. Further, subjects ·who had previously taken part in a course on creative problem-solving (Meadows & Parnes) were better able to generate good ideas under brainstorming conditions than those subjects who had no prior formal training in this procedure.

Although the use of self-verbalized instructions would appear to be an effective way of modifying behavior—whether it consists of relatively simple self-verbalized prods for emitting a given response, or more complex problem-solving processes involved in arriving at an effective course of action—the necessity for a behavior being followed by positive consequences nonetheless exists. This is nicely demonstrated in a token economy program by Ayllon and Azrin (1964), where it was found that instructions, when *combined* with reinforcement, were more effective in modifying behavior than either of the two employed alone. Although the use of self-directions would appear to be particularly useful in instigating certain adaptive behaviors which might otherwise be less likely to occur, once emitted, these responses must be maintained by reinforcing consequences.

SELF-REINFORCEMENT

In its traditional usage the concept of reinforcement has been defined in terms of events which originate outside the person, typically involving the physical act of administering reinforcing consequences by agents other than the person himself. Under these conditions, the behavioral criteria for obtaining reinforcement are determined by a community in which the individual has only marginal control. In contrast, the phenomenon of self-reinforcement highlights the responsibility of each individual in the evaluation of his own behavior and by the presentation of self-initiated reinforcement in symbolic or actual terms.

One of the major hurdles in self-reinforcement research involves devising ways of objectifying and recording the self-reinforcement response itself. It may be sufficient theoretically to assume that self-reinforcement is a viable concept, but it is another matter to demonstrate the actual occurrence of the event, let alone calculate the effect it may have on subsequent behavior. Kanfer and Marston (1963a) have dealt with this problem by first requiring a person to make a judgmental assessment of his personal performance (a cognitive component) and then to link this covert response to an instrumental motor response which produces a specific object (a token) as a material reward. In this study the authors found they could influence self-reinforcement by varying the attitude (positive or negative) of the experimenter who initially dispensed the reward tokens. Their interpretation of this study is that self-reinforcement can be categorically objectified as a response that is subject to the intervention of social reinforcement.

As we have seen by the Kanfer and Marston research, self-reinforcement can be considered a response with properties that are amenable to shaping by behavioral principles common to the maintenance of most operants. In a different line of research, Bandura and his associates (Bandura & Kupers, 1964; Bandura & Perloff, 1967) have examined the growth of self-reinforcement under conditions where no immediate external reinforcement is involved. Their position, which has received considerable support in a number of studies, demonstrates that the matching of a person's standards for self-reinforcement to the observed behavior of a model is a powerful determiner of one's style of self-reinforcement. In the vicarious learning paradigm, the subject observes rather than acts in the presence of a model. Thus, the necessary data for complex social behavior are symbolically absorbed, collated, and assigned appropriate response weights without ever having been actually performed during the acquisition process. Bandura believes that much of our social behavior is generated through such observational learning, and is then externally reinforced at a later date. In terms of economy, if Bandura and Walters (1963) are correct, the vicarious learning paradigm spares an organism the tediousness of learning through stages of successive approximation typically assumed to be necessary in operant conditioning theory.

In an experimental investigation of the origins of varying standards for self-reinforcement, Bandura and Kupers (1964) had grade-school children observe models who displayed varying criteria for self-reinforcement. In one condition, the model rewarded himself with candy and self-approving statements for only high-level performance on a particular game; in the second condition, a low performance standard was sufficient for self-reinforcement. The results of this study clearly indicated that on subsequent performance trials, the standards for self-reinforcement displayed by the children reflected those standards they had observed in the model. Bandura and Kupers also found certain characteristics of the model himself to be important, in that adults constituted more powerful models that did peers.

A later study by Liebert and Allen (1967) demonstrated that the development of self-reinforcement standards may be facilitated by having the model verbalize the particular "rule structure." That is, the child who observed the self-reinforcing pattern of the model, and additionally heard the model verbalize rule structure (e.g., *"That's* a good score . . . that *deserves* a chip.") was more likely to assume the model's self-reinforcement standards than was the child for whom no rule structure was provided.

Although the observational learning and direct reinforcement paradigms have been employed in the investigation of the developmental origins of self-reinforcement, the actual process of socialization typically involves each of these social learning principles. Recognizing this joint influence, Mischel and Liebert (1966) investigated the effect of modeling and direct reinforcement, both when they were consistent and when they were contradictory. The results of their study indicate that children who observed a model displaying a high standard for self-reinforcement, and who additionally were directly rewarded only for their high level of performance, were most consistent in their adoption of this self-reinforcement pattern. This was true in their own subsequent performance, as well as in the transmission of this pattern of self-reinforcement to other children when asked to "demonstrate" how the game worked. Those children who were subjected to inconsistent training procedures—where the model set high standards for himself, but used low standards for rewarding the child, or vice versa—were more likely to adopt the lower standards for self-reinforcement. The results of this study demonstrate quite nicely that the socialization agent who attempts to train children in self-control by having them "do as I say, not as I do," is more likely to be unsuccessful than one who utilizes a more systematic approach based on relevant social learning principles.

In the typical real-life situation, self-reinforcement and external reinforcement are events which exist concurrently, often making it difficult to completely isolate their independent action. Nonetheless, in order to affirm the effect of self-reinforcement, it has been essential to devise "pure" self-reinforcement conditions that are not contaminated by external reinforcement. Thus, Bandura and Perloff (1967) compared children who were given the opportunity to be self-rewarding with children who received externally administered reinforcement, and with a control group who received no apparent reinforcement from either source. The results of this study indicated that the self and external reinforcement treatments were equally effective, and that the children in both of these conditions were more highly productive than those children in the control condition. Subsequent work by Johnson (1970) on self-reinforcement has confirmed these findings.

A prime working assumption underlying self-reinforcement is that internal standards provide the criteria by which behavior is judged to be eligible for reinforcement. If, for example, behavior is simple and habitual, it is rare to find these responses self-reinforced. Kanfer (1968) suggests, on the other hand, that when skills are being formed, or when creative work is being carried out, self-rewards or criticisms are frequently introduced. Under these conditions, self-surveillance probably aids in maintaining an optimum motivational level and in addition provides an ongoing monitoring system to insure that a particular level of competence is being attained. Kanfer and Marston (1963b) found, for example, that self-rewarding responses were more frequent when high competence behavior was emitted on difficult as compared with easy tasks. In addition, the clearer the performance standards were on a specific task, the easier it was for the subject to provide himself with accurate feedback.

From a clinical perspective, Kanfer and Marston suggest that the shaping of self-reinforcement is somewhat analogous to self-confidence training. Following this research direction, Rehm and Marston (1968) initiated a therapy procedure based on a self-reinforcement program for male students who were inhibited in dating. An elaborate procedure was developed in which each client specified for himself a series of interpersonal tasks in which he would like to feel more comfortable. After arranging these tasks in order of increasing difficulty, the client was encouraged to perform them *in vivo* and then to evaluate his own behavior along a prearranged scale of approach or avoidance. Sessions with the therapist reviewed the week's work, and self-administered points were given for success or failure in a given task. For exemplary achievements, the therapist offered positive verbal reinforcement. When the clients rated their performance in the low categories, the therapist asked them "how they might have changed their behavior to increase their self-evaluation." Under no circumstances did the therapist actually suggest alternative behaviors. This therapeutic procedure was compared with a nonspecific therapy group and a no-therapy control composed of individuals with similar social problems. It was found that compared with the nonspecific therapy and control conditions, the self-reinforcement therapy group showed significantly more improvement on measures dealing with self-reports of anxiety as well as overt behavior. The authors contend that self-reinforcement therapy is valuable because the person not only acts as his own therapist, but also because the rearrangement of his own cognitive self-evaluative systems is motivationally self-induced.

In a recent paper, Cautela (1970) has offered a therapeutic procedure based upon principles of self-reinforcement. Unlike most research methods, which generally require a physically palpable self-reinforcement response (acquiring tokens, points, etc.), Cautela's reinforcement response is exclusively mediated and executed in imagination. According to Cautela, "covert reinforcement," as the therapeutic procedure is called, is also inferentially capable of explaining behavior change and maintenance in nonpathological contexts. The first step in the self-reinforcement program is the identification of those mental images representing objects or situations which, if visualized, create a positive emotional reaction. While the client is in a relaxed state, he is asked to imagine current social situations with which he is experiencing difficulties. He is instructed to visualize these situations and imagine himself behaving in a socially effective and non-anxious manner. At various points in the imaginal sequence, the client administers to himself the prearranged reinforcement images, provided he feels he is eligible for the delivery of reinforcement. The client is also instructed to practice the procedure at home.

An important practical approach to the use of self-reinforcement in producing greater self-control was advanced by Homme (1965b, 1966). Homme, theorizing from a Skinnerian frame of reference, has devised an imaginative operant conditioning paradigm that incorporates Premack's differential probability hypothesis (Premack, 1965). Homme assumes that people can be trained to effectively manage their own covert and overt behavior through what he terms "contingency management." Drawing on the Premack principle, "for any pair of responses, the more probable one will reinforce the less probable one," (Premack, 1965, p. 132); Homme has evolved a self-reinforcement paradigm that may be useful in the modification of various troublesome behavior. The sequence of events outlined by Homme requires (a) the identification of stimuli which precede the unwanted act, (b) the interposition of a thought antithetical to the target stimuli, (c) a thought supporting the virtues of an alternative course of action, and (d) a self-induced maneuver which provides reinforcement as a consequence of refraining from the habitual behavior.

In summary, the reality of self-reinforcement as an integral feature of self-control is currently assuming a focal position in theories of behavior. While in no way underestimating the powerful impact of environmental contingencies, the emphasis on covert processes has merely enlarged the picture. Interestingly enough, the shift in emphasis now being introduced by behavioral theorists is anything but original to the dynamicist who has always considered internal states as his primary targets for treatment. What is original, we believe, is the concerted effort to integrate, objectify, and specify the antecedents of self-regulatory processes in scientifically meaningful terms. This demands, among other things, a close connection between theory and research. The extensive research program by Bandura and his co-workers is an excellent case in point. Through his research, the critical influence of models in vicariously transmitting social information without the intervention of immediate environmental consequences has been vividly demonstrated. In addition, Kanfer and his colleagues have begun to conceptualize theoretically the environmental origins and internal determinants associated with self-rewarding and self-critical response styles. Further work in this area has incalculable clinical significance.

summary and conclusions

In contrast to most other views of self-control, the behavioral orientation stresses the belief that self-control may be facilitated through the process of learning, much the same as any other aspect of human functioning. According to this view, it makes little sense to describe an individual as having "good" or "poor" self-control. Rather than being viewed as a general trait, the behavioral approach to the study of self-control has focused on the different procedures which might be employed in allowing the individual to gain greater control over various forms of problematic behaviors. In the case of deviant emotional-physiological reactions—including anxiety, deviant sexual attractions, low pain threshold, epileptic seizures, and attraction to such potentially maladapted sources of gratification as alcohol and cigarettes—the methods for obtaining greater self-control have involved autosuggestion and self-administered relaxation techniques, cognitive relabeling, and the use of self-administered aversive conditioning procedures. Although there is probably no limit to the various types of maladaptive instrumental responses for which self-control procedures would be relevant, most of the work which has been done in this area has been concerned with overeating, smoking, marital problems, and poor work habits. The procedures which have been typically employed in training individuals to gain control over maladaptive instrumental responses include techniques involving stimulus control, the use of verbal self-directions, and the institution of self-reinforcement following the occurrence of more adaptive, competing behaviors.

Thus, the concept of self-control may best be viewed as a generic term encompassing a variety of different procedures which may be employed to modify various types of maladaptive behaviors. The same is true of the term "behavior modification." When viewed as the therapeutic application of general principles of psychology to individuals manifesting deviant behavior, behavior modification similarly encompasses a number of therapeutic procedures for dealing with a large array of behavior problems. These similarities should not come as too much of a surprise, particularly when one views self-control as involving these same principles of behavior change. However, within the self-control framework, the individual is explicitly taught to function as his own therapist. As is the case with behavior modification procedures in general, the question of which self-control procedure or procedures to use in any given instance may be determined only after a careful assessment of those variables maintaining the maladaptive behavior (cf. Goldfried and Pomeranz, 1968; Mischel, 1968; Peterson, 1968).

The work which has been done up until this point on self-control and behavior modification is clearly in its formative state. Many of the techniques employed have been based on a tenuous extrapolation from behavior theory and research. Although the several procedures have shown to be successful in individual cases, the greatest need at present is for more controlled outcome studies. In much of the research work done in this area, the method employed has typically involved a "treatment package," in which a number of different self-control techniques were included. What is ultimately needed, then, is outcome research to determine the effectiveness of each technique when used alone, as well as their interaction with other self-control procedures (cf. Mahoney, 1972).

One final point before concluding. The increased interest in very recent years on the importance of self-control appears to have paralleled the situation where man is becoming more and more concerned about the dangers of external control (cf. Skinner, 1971). The potential of external control has become more frightening of late, perhaps because we are more aware of its existence, but also because the number of ways in which we can be controlled by others is becoming more pervasive and effective. While acknowledging the crucial need for effective behavior technology, London (1969) has called attention to the moral and ethical questions associated with being controlled. As a means of counteracting this danger, he notes the following:

> In order to defend individual freedom, it is necessary to enhance the power of individuals. If behavior technology endangers freedom by giving refined powers to controllers, then the antidote which promotes freedom is to give more refined power over their own behavior to those who are endangered. Since everyone is endangered, this means facilitating self-control in every one. (pp. 213–214)

Because of the importance of this issue, one of the major contributions the behavioral sciences can make to society is to help convert the promise of self-control into a reality. Our personal and group integrity is likely to depend on this.

references

Anant, S. S. A note on the treatment of alcoholics by a verbal aversion technique. *Canadian Psychologist*, 1967, 8A, 19–22.

Arkowitz, H. Desensitizations as a self-control procedure: A case report. Unpublished manuscript, University of Oregon, 1969.

Ashem, B., & Donner, L. Covert sensitization with alcoholics: A controlled replication. *Behaviour Research and Therapy*, 1968, 6, 7–12.

Ayllon, T., & Azrin, N. H. Reinforcement and instructions with mental patients. *Journal of the Experimental Analysis of Behavior*, 1964, 7, 327–331.

Bandura, A. *Principles of behavior modification*. New York: Holt, Rinehart and Winston, 1969.

Bandura, A., & Kupers, C. J. Transmission of patterns of self-reinforcement through modeling. *Journal of Abnormal and Social Psychology*, 1964, 69, 1–9.

Bandura, A., & Perloff, B. Relative efficacy of self-monitored and externally imposed reinforcement systems. *Journal of Personality and Social Psychology*, 1967, 7, 111–116.

Bandura, A., & Walters, R. H. *Social learning and personality development*. New York: Holt, Rinehart and Winston, 1963.

Barlow, D. H., Leitenberg, H., & Agras, W. S. Experimental control of sexual deviation through manipulation of the noxious scene in covert sensitization. *Journal of Abnormal Psychology*, 1969, 74, 596–601.

Bem, S. L. Verbal Self-control: The establishment of effective self-instruction. *Journal of Experimental Psychology*, 1967, 74, 485–491.

Bijou, S. W., & Baer, D. M. *Child development I: A systematic and empirical theory*. New York: Appleton, 1961.

Cautela, J. R. A behavior therapy approach to pervasive anxiety. *Behaviour Research and Therapy*, 1966, 4, 99–109. (a)

Cautela, J. R. Treatment of compulsive behavior by covert sensitization. *Psychological Record*, 1966, *16*, 33–41. (b)

Cautela, J. R. Covert sensitization. *Psychological Reports*, 1967, *20*, 459–468.

Cautela, J. R. Covert reinforcement. *Behavior Therapy*, 1970, *1*, 33–50.

Davison, G. C. Elimination of a sadistic fantasy by a client-controlled counter-conditioning technique: A case study. *Journal of Abnormal Psychology*, 1968, *73*, 84–90. (a)

Davison, G. C. Self-control through "imaginal aversive contingency" and "one-downmanship": Enabling the powerless to accommodate unreasonableness. In J. D. Krumboltz & C. E. Thoresen (Eds.), *Behavioral counseling: Cases and techniques*. New York: Holt, Rinehart and Winston, 1969. (b)

Davison, G. C., Goldfried, M. R., & Krasner, L. A postdoctoral program in behavior modification: Theory and practice. *American Psychologist*, 1970, *25*, 767–772.

Davison, G. C., & Valins, S. Maintenance of self-attributed and drug-attributed behavior change. *Journal of Personality and Social Psychology*, 1969, *11*, 25–33.

Dollard, J., & Miller, N. E. *Personality and psychotherapy*. New York: McGraw-Hill, 1950.

D'Zurilla, T. J. Reducing heterosexual anxiety. In J. D. Krumboltz and C. E. Thoresen (Eds.), *Behavioral counseling: Cases and techniques*. New York: Holt, Rinehart and Winston, 1969.

D'Zurilla, T. J., & Goldfried, M. R. Problem solving and behavior modification. *Journal of Abnormal Psychology*, 1971, *78*, 107–126.

D'Zurilla, T. J., & Goldfried, M. R. Cognitive processes, problem-solving, and effective behavior. In M. R. Goldfried & M. Merbaum (Eds.), *Behavior change through self-control*. New York: Holt, Rinehart and Winston, 1973.

Efron, R. The unconditioned inhibition of uncinate fits. *Brain*, 1957, *80*, 251–262.

Ellis, A. Outcome of employing three techniques of psychotherapy. *Journal of Clinical Psychology*, 1957, *13*, 344–350. (b)

Ellis, A. Rational psychotherapy. *Journal of General Psychology*, 1958, *59*, 35–49.

Ellis, A. A homosexual treated with rational psychotherapy. *Journal of Clinical Psychology*, 1959, *15*, 338–343.

Ellis, A. The treatment of a psychopath with rational psychotherapy. *Journal of Psychology*, 1961, *51*, 141–150.

Ellis, A. *Reason and emotion in psychotherapy*. New York: Lyle Stuart, 1962.

Ferster, C. B., Nurnberger, J. I., & Levitt, E. E. The control of eating. *Journal of Mathetics*, 1962, *1*, 87–109.

Freud, S. *Collected Papers*. London: Hogarth Press, 1924–1950.

Freud, S. *Basic Writing*. New York: Modern Library, 1938.

Gold, S., & Neufeld, I. L. A learning approach to the treatment of homosexuality. *Behaviour Research and Therapy*, 1965, *2*, 201–204.

Goldfried, M. R. Systematic desensitization as training in self-control. *Journal of Consulting and Clinical Psychology*, 1971, *37*, 228–235.

Goldfried, M. R. Reduction of generalized anxiety through a variant of systematic desensitization. In M. R. Goldfried & M. Merbaum (Eds.), *Behavior change through self-control*. New York: Holt, Rinehart and Winston, 1973.

Goldfried, M. R., & Pomeranz, D. M. Role of assessment in behavior modification. *Psychological Reports*, 1968, *23*, 75–87.

Goldiamond, I. Self-control procedures in personal behavior problems. *Psychological Reports*, 1965, *17*, 851–868. (c)

Goldman, R., Jaffa, M., & Schachter, S. Yom Kippur, Air France, dormitory food, and the eating behavior of obese and normal persons. *Journal of Personality and Social Psychology*, 1968, *10*, 117–123.

Goodrich, F. W., Jr., and Thomas, H. A clinical study of natural childbirth. *American Journal of Obstetrics and Gynecology*, 1948, *56*, 875–883.

Guthrie, E. R. *The psychology of learning.* New York: Harper & Row, 1935.

Harris, M. B. Self-directed program for weight control: A pilot study. *Journal of Abnormal Psychology,* 1969, *74,* 263–270.

Hartmann, H. *Ego Psychology and the problem of adaptation.* (Trans. by D. Rapaport) New York: International University Press, 1958.

Homme, L. E. Control of coverants: The operants of the mind. *Psychological Record,* 1965, *15,* 501–511. (b)

Homme, L. E. Contiguity theory and contingency management. *Psychological Record,* 1966, *16,* 233–241.

Jacobson, E. *Progressive Relaxation.* Chicago: University of Chicago Press, 1938.

Johnson, S. B. Self-reinforcement vs. external reinforcement in behavior modification with children. *Developmental Psychology,* 1970, *3,* 147–148.

Johnson, W. G. Some applications of Homme's coverant control therapy: Two case reports. *Behavior Therapy,* 1971, *2,* 240–248.

Kahn, M., & Baker, B. Desensitization with minimal therapist contact. *Journal of Abnormal Psychology,* 1968, *73,* 198–200.

Kanfer, F. H. Verbal conditioning: A review of its current status. In T. R. Dixon & D. L. Horton (Eds.), *Verbal behavior and its relation to general S-R theory.* Englewood Cliffs, N.J.: Prentice-Hall, 1968.

Kanfer, F. H. Self-regulation: Research, issues, and speculations. In C. Neuringer & J. L. Michael (Eds.), *Behavior modification in clinical psychology.* New York: Appleton, 1970.

Kanfer, F. H., & Goldfoot, D. A. Self-control and tolerance of noxious stimulation. *Psychological Reports,* 1966, *18,* 79–85.

Kanfer, F. H., & Marston, A. R. Conditioning of self-reinforcing responses: An analogue to self-confidence training. *Psychological Reports,* 1963, *13,* 63–70. (a)

Kanfer, F. H., & Marston, A. R. Determinants of self-reinforcement in human learning. *Journal of Experimental Psychology,* 1963, *66,* 245–254. (b)

Kanfer, F. H., & Phillips, J. S. *Learning foundations of behavior therapy.* New York: Wiley, 1970.

Kanfer, F. H., & Seidner, M. L. Self-control: Factors enhancing tolerance of noxious stimulation. *Journal of Personality and Social Psychology,* 1972, in press.

Karst, T. O., & Trexler, L. D. Initial study using fixed-role and rational-emotive therapy in treating public-speaking anxiety. *Journal of Consulting and Clinical Psychology,* 1970, *34,* 360–366.

Keutzer, C. S. Behavior modification of smoking: The experimental investigation of diverse techniques. *Behaviour Research and Therapy,* 1968, *6,* 137–157.

Kline, M. V., & Guze, H. Self-hypnosis in childbirth: A clinical evaluation of a patient conditioning program. *Journal of Clinical and Experimental Hypnosis,* 1955, *3,* 142–147.

Kopel, S. Self-control: Some new perspectives. Unpublished manuscript, University of Oregon, 1972.

Lamaze, F. *Painless childbirth: Psychoprophylactic method.* London: Burke Publishing Co., 1958.

Lang, P. J. Fear reduction and fear behavior: Problems in treating a construct. In J. M. Shlien (Ed.), *Research in Psychotherapy.* Vol. III. Washington, D.C.: American Psychological Association, 1968.

Lang, P. J. The mechanics of desensitization and the laboratory study of human fear. In C. M. Franks (Ed.), *Behavior therapy: Assessment and status.* New York: McGraw-Hill, 1969.

Lazarus, A. A. Some clinical applications of autohypnosis. *Medical Proceedings, South Africa,* 1958, *4,* 848–850.

Liebert, R. M., & Allen, M. K. The effects of rule structure and reward magnitude on the acquisition and adoption of self-reward criteria. *Psychological Reports*, 1967, *21*, 445–452.

London, P. *Behavior control.* New York: Harper & Row, 1969.

Luria, A. R. *The role of speech in the regulation of normal and abnormal behavior.* New York: Pergamon, 1961.

Mahoney, M. J. Toward an experimental analysis of coverant control. *Behavior Therapy*, 1970, *1*, 510–521.

Mahoney, M. J. Research issues in self-management. *Behavior Therapy*, 1972, *3*, 45–63.

Marston, A. R., & Feldman, S. E. Toward use of self-control in behavior modification. Unpublished manuscript, University of Southern California, 1971.

Meadow, A., & Parnes, S. J. Evaluation of training in creative problem-solving. *Journal of Applied Psychology*, 1959, *43*, 189–194.

Meichenbaum, D. H., Gilmore, J. B., & Fedoravicius, A. Group insight versus group desensitization in treating speech anxiety. *Journal of Consulting and Clinical Psychology*, 1971, *36*, 410–421.

Meichenbaum, D. H., & Goodman, J. Training impulsive children to talk to themselves: A means of developing self-control. *Journal of Abnormal Psychology*, 1971, *77*, 115–126.

Migler, B., & Wolpe, J. Automated self-desensitization: A case report. *Behaviour Research and Therapy*, 1967, *5*, 133–135.

Miller, M. M. Treatment of chronic alcoholism by hypnotic aversion. *Journal of the American Medical Association*, 1959, *171*, 1492–1495.

Miller, N. E., & Dollard, J. *Social learning and imitation.* New Haven: Yale University Press, 1941.

Mischel, W. *Personality and assessment.* New York: Wiley, 1968.

Mischel, W., & Liebert, R. M. Effects of discrepancies between observed and imposed reward criteria on their acquisition and transmission. *Journal of Personality and Social Psychology*, 1966, *3*, 45–53.

Nisbett, R. E., & Schachter, S. Cognitive manipulation of pain. *Journal of Experimental Social Psychology*, 1966, *2*, 227–236.

Nolan, J. D. Self-control and procedures in the modification of smoking behavior. *Journal of Consulting and Clinical Psychology*, 1968, *32*, 92–93.

Ober, D. C. Modification of smoking behavior. *Journal of Consulting and Clinical Psychology*, 1968, *32*, 543–549.

O'Leary, K. D. The effects of self-instruction on immoral behavior. *Journal of Experimental Child Psychology*, 1968, *6*, 297–301.

Orne, M. T. The nature of hypnosis: Artifact and essence. *Journal of Abnormal and Social Psychology*, 1959, *58*, 277–299.

Parnes, S. J., & Meadow, A. Effects of "brainstorming" instructions on creative problem solving by trained and untrained subjects. *Journal of Educational Psychology*, 1959, *50*, 171–176.

Paul, G. L. *Insight versus desensitization in psychotherapy.* Stanford: Stanford University Press, 1966.

Paul, G. L. Outcome of systematic desensitization II: Controlled investigations of individual treatment, technique variations, and current status. In C. M. Franks (Ed.), *Behavior therapy: Assessment and status.* New York: McGraw-Hill, 1969. (a)

Peterson, D. R. *The clinical study of social behavior.* New York: Appleton, 1968.

Premack, D. Toward empirical behavior laws: I. Positive reinforcement. *Psychological Review*, 1959, *66*, 219–233.

Premack, D. Reinforcement theory. In David Levine (Ed.), *Nebraska symposium on motivation.* Lincoln: University of Nebraska Press, 1965.

Rapaport, D. The theory of ego autonomy: A generalization. *Bulletin of the Menninger Clinic*, 1958, *22*, 13–35.

Rapaport, D. The structure of psychoanalytic theory. *Psychological Issues*, 1960, *2*, No. 6.

Read, G. D. *Childbirth without fear*. New York: Harper & Row, 1944.

Rehm, L. P., & Marston, A. R. Reduction of social anxiety through modification of self-reinforcement: An instigation therapy technique. *Journal of Consulting and Clinical Psychology*, 1968, *32*, 565–574.

Rimm, D. C., & Litvak, S. B. Self-verbalization and emotional arousal. *Journal of Abnormal Psychology*, 1969, *74*, 181–187.

Rogers, C. R., & Skinner, B. F. Some issues concerning the control of human behavior. *Science*, 1956, *124*, 1057–1066.

Salter, A. Three techniques of autohypnosis. *Journal of General Psychology*, 1941, *24*, 423–438.

Schachter, S. Cognitive effects on bodily functioning: Studies of obesity and eating. In D. C. Glass (Ed.), *Neurophysiology and emotion*. New York: Rockefeller University Press and Russell Sage Foundation, 1967.

Schachter, S., & Gross, L. P. Manipulated time and eating behavior. *Journal of Personality and Social Psychology*, 1968, *10*, 98–106.

Schachter, S., & Singer, J. E. Cognitive, social, and physiological determinants of emotional state. *Psychological Review*, 1962, *69*, 379–399.

Schultz, J. H., & Luthe, W. *Autogenic training*. New York: Grune & Stratton, 1959.

Skinner, B. F. *Science and human behavior*. New York: Macmillan, 1953.

Skinner, B. F. *Beyond freedom and dignity*. New York: Knopf, 1971.

Stuart, R. B. Behavioral control of overeating. *Behaviour Research and Therapy*, 1967, *5*, 357–365.

Sushinsky, L. W., & Bootzin, R. R. Cognitive desensitization as a model of systematic desensitization. *Behaviour Research and Therapy*, 1970, *8*, 29–33.

Tooley, J. T., & Pratt, S. An experimental procedure for the extinction of smoking behavior. *Psychological Record*, 1967, *17*, 209–218.

Upper, D., & Meredith, L. A stimulus control approach to the modification of smoking behavior. Paper presented at the meeting of the American Psychological Association, Miami, September 1970.

Valins, S. Cognitive effects of false heart-rate feedback. *Journal of Personality and Social Psychology*, 1966, *4*, 400–408.

Valins, S., & Ray, A. A. Effects of cognitive desensitization on avoidance behavior. *Journal of Personality and Social Psychology*, 1967, *7*, 345–350.

Velten, E., Jr. A laboratory task for induction of mood states. *Behaviour Research and Therapy*, 1968, *6*, 473–482.

Velvovski, I. Z., Platonov, K. I., Ploticher, V. A., & Csougom, E. A. *Painless childbirth through psychoprophylaxis*. Moscow: Foreign Languages Publication House, 1960.

Watson, J. B. Psychology as a behaviorist views it. *Psychological Review*, 1913, *20*, 158–177.

Weil, G., & Goldfried, M. R. Treatment of insomnia in an eleven-year-old child through self-relaxation. Unpublished manuscript. SUNY at Stony Brook, 1972.

Yahia, C., & Ulin, P. R. Preliminary experience with a psycho-physical program of preparation for childbirth. *American Journal of Obstetrics and Gynecology*, 1965, *93*, 942–949.

THINK

1. Here is a case study:

   > A middle-aged man grew a beard for the first time a few months after his father died in a distant part of the country. The son had been told that his father had gone unshaved for several days just before he died, and one relative had emphasized to him the shock she had felt when she had beheld the father's helpless, whiskered face instead of his usual robust, cleanly shaved cheeks and chin. Hearing this, the son pictured clearly how his father must have looked. Then the image vanished. A few weeks after this experience he decided to let his beard grow—"just for kicks." But for days, each time he washed and saw his whiskery image in the mirror, a vision of his dying father's unshaved face flashed before his eyes and he experienced a welling-up of grief. After more than two years he shaved the beard off, ostensibly because he "had his kicks." Actually, it was because his most intense period of mourning had ended. . . . He felt comfortable only when he had his beard very short—to match his memory image of his dying father's unshaved face. (George Mahl, *Psychological Conflict and Defense*, New York: Harcourt Brace Jovanovich, 1971, p. 166.)

   Try to be as precise as you can in describing the processes that, according to Freud, led to the growth of the beard and its shearing.
2. If, according to Schachter, an emotion is a joint function of physiological arousal and of cognitions appropriate to that arousal, how might you explain an emotion like love, which seems to persist for a long time?
3. Freud argued that psychological trauma in infancy affected one throughout life, such that a vigorous childhood beating could precipitate adult mental distress. What implications does Campbell's and Jaynes' experiment have for Freud's position? For child-rearing practices in general? How might adulthood experiences obliterate the effects of earlier experience?
4. Now consider that one difference between children and rats is that children can, and often do, remember and mentally rehearse a traumatic experience. If this is so, might they not require *actual* reinstatement in order to maintain the effects of trauma?
5. Try to find a behavior that you (or a friend) recently tried unsuccessfully to self-control, such as eating, tantrums, study habits, or smoking.

   In light of the paper by Goldfried and Merbaum, what strategies of control would you now attempt to implement? And are there any that Goldfried and Merbaum neglected to mention?
6. Recent advances in understanding the brain have not been uniformly greeted with enthusiasm. Some people are concerned that those understandings might be the first step in achieving all kinds of unwarranted and unwanted political control over individuals. The same brain implantation techniques that might cure rage could also be used to induce political conformity. How do you feel about these arguments? Are there ways to avoid the side effects of understanding the brain?
7. In the light of present knowledge, which holds that memories are stored in protein molecules, is it possible that in the future, memories, and perhaps entire personalities, could be transferred from one individual to another?

II

The Meaning of
Mental Health and Illness

What is mental illness?

What do normality and abnormality mean?

What do we mean by mental health?

These are not academic questions. Increasingly, the answers to them have become significant for the kinds of anguishes we treat, and the ways in which we treat them. A few examples will give you the flavor of the issues here:

—A young man inadvertently hurts someone's feelings, and experiences considerable guilt about it. Is the guilt "neurotic"? Is guilt always irrational? Would it be more "normal" not to experience guilt?

—Because she wants very much to get into medical school, a young woman cheats on an examination. She feels badly about cheating. But she would also feel badly about failing to get into medical school. Is the cheating "abnormal"? Is the concern about beating out the competition for medical school admission abnormal?

—A man is married to someone whom he truly dislikes. As a result, it seems that he has become sexually impotent with her. At the same time, he neither believes in divorce nor extramarital sex. What do you recommend? Should he abstain? Or should he change his beliefs? Is his a neurotic problem?

—Socialized to modesty in dress and behavior, a woman experiences considerable conflict on coming to college. "Mixed" dormitories upset her. So too, do tight-fitting clothes and "short shorts." To wear longsleeved dresses with hemlines below the knee would mark her as a deviant (even if she could find an "acceptable" place to live). But to abandon her background and the religious beliefs that support it would mark her as a conformist, if not worse. What do you recommend?

There are at least two questions here, and it is to these questions that the three papers in this section are addressed. First, which values are consistent with mental health, and which are not? Is guilt always "bad" in the sense that it clearly implies neurosis, or is guilt sometimes evidence *for* mental health. O. Hobart Mowrer, for example, strongly believes that a powerful sense of guilt is a good guide for man, away from neurosis, even away from psychological distress and towards mental health (Reading 6). Other theorists, it seems to him, have so implicated guilt in neurosis, that the alternative to neurosis involves the abolition of guilt—and therefore, psychopathy, which is defined as the absence of guilt. The first issue then, is: When is guilt necessary for mental health, and when is it not? And more generally, which values are necessary for mental health, and which are deleterious?

The second question is: Does mental illness exist? Should we be calling people mentally ill, in the same sense that we call them physically ill? Does the metaphor mean anything? Does it facilitate our understanding of these people, or our treatment of them?

Thomas Szasz has advocated that mental illness is a myth, and that the term and those associated with it ought to be abolished (Reading 7). There are problems in living, he argues, but those are not illnesses, in any sense of that term. The argument is a compelling one, but it does not go unchallenged. In the third essay in this section, David Ausubel (Reading

8) examines the need for, and utility of, the phrase mental illness. His, too, is a compelling argument. Szasz and Ausubel also deal with the role of values in mental health, which is the problem that Mowrer is mainly concerned with. Together, you will find that these three papers neatly package the issues in this area.

6

"Sin," the Lesser of Two Evils

O. Hobart Mowrer

Following the presentation of a paper on "Constructive Aspects of the Concept of Sin in Psychotherapy" at the 1959 APA convention in Cincinnati, I have repeatedly been asked by psychologists and psychiatrists: "But *why* must you use that awful word 'sin,' instead of some more neutral term such as 'wrongdoing,' 'irresponsibility,' or 'immorality'?" And even a religious layman has reproached me on the grounds that "Sin is such a *strong* word." Its *strength*, surely, is an asset, not a liability; for in the face of failure which has resulted from our erstwhile use of feebler concepts, we have very heavy work for it to do. Besides, sin (in contrast to its more neutral equivalents) is such a handy *little* word that it would be a pity to let it entirely disappear from usage. With Humpty-Dumpty, we ought to expect words to be "well-behaved" and to mean what *we* want them to!

A few years ago I was invited to teach in the summer session at one of our great Pacific Coast universities; and toward the end of the term, a student in my class on Personality Theory said to me one day: "Did you know that near the beginning of this course you created a kind of scandal on this campus?" Then he explained that I had once used the word "sin" without saying "so-called" or making a joke about it. This, the student said, was virtually unheard-of in a psychology professor and had occasioned considerable dismay and perplexity. I did not even recall the incident; but the more I have thought about the reaction it produced, the more frequently I have found myself using the term—with, I hope, something more than mere perversity.

Traditionally, sin has been thought of as whatever causes one to go to Hell; and since Hell, as a place of otherworldly retribution and torment, has conveniently dropped out of most religious as well as secular thought, the concept of sin might indeed seem antiquated and absurd. But, as I observed in the Cincinnati paper, Hell is still very much with us in those states of mind and being which we call neurosis and psychosis; and I have come increasingly, at least in my own mind, to identify anything that carries us toward these forms of perdition as *sin*. Irresponsibility, wrongdoing, immorality, sin: what do the terms matter if we can thus understand more accurately the nature of psychopathology and gain greater practical control over its ramified forms and manifestations?

Reprinted from *American Psychologist*, 1960, Vol. 15, No. 5, pp. 301–304.

But now the fat is in the fire! Have we not been taught on high authority that personality disorder is not one's own "fault," that the neurotic is *not* "responsible" for his suffering, that he has done nothing wrong, committed no "sin"? "Mental illness," according to a poster which was widely circulated a few years ago, "is no disgrace. It might happen to anyone." And behind all this, of course, was the Freudian hypothesis that neurosis stems from a "too severe superego," which is the product of a too strenuous socialization of the individual at the hands of harsh, unloving parents and an irrational society. The trouble lay, supposedly, not in anything wrong or "sinful" which the individual has himself *done,* but in things he merely *wants* to do but cannot, because of *repression.*

The neurotic was thus not sinful but *sick,* the helpless, innocent victim of "the sins of the fathers," and could be rescued only by a specialized, esoteric form of *treatment.* Anna Russell catches the spirit of this doctrine well when she sings, in "Psychiatric Folksong,"

> At three I had a feeling of
>   Ambivalence toward my brothers,
> And so it follows naturally
>   I poisoned all my lovers.
> But now I'm happy; I have learned
>   The lesson this has taught;
> That everything I do that's wrong
>   Is someone else's fault.

Freud saw all this not only as a great scientific discovery but also as a strategic gain for the profession which had thus far treated him so indifferently. It was, one may conjecture, a sort of gift, an offering or service which would place medicine in such debt to him that it could no longer ignore or reject him. In his *Autobiography* Freud (1935) puts it thus:

> My medical conscience felt pleased at my having arrived at this conclusion [that neurosis has a sexual basis]. I hoped that I had filled up a gap in medical science, which, in dealing with a function of such great biological importance, had failed to take into account any injuries beyond those caused by infection or by gross anatomical lesions. The medical aspect of the matter was, moreover, supported by the fact that sexuality was not something purely mental. It had a somatic side as well . . . (p. 45).

In his book on *The Problem of Lay Analysis,* Freud (1927) later took a somewhat different position (see also Chapter 9 of the third volume of Jones' biography of Freud, 1957); but by this time his Big Idea had been let loose in the world and was no longer entirely under his control.

Psychologists were, as we know, among the first of the outlying professional groups to "take up" psychoanalysis. By being analyzed, we not only learned— in an intimate, personal way—about this new and revolutionary science; we also (or so we imagined) were qualifying ourselves for the practice of analysis as a form of therapy. Now we are beginning to see how illusory this all was. We accepted psychoanalytic theory long before it had been adequately tested and thus embraced as "science" a set of presuppositions which we are now painfully having to repudiate. But, more than this, in accepting the premise that the neurotically disturbed person is basically *sick,* we surrendered our professional independence and authenticity. Now, to the extent that we have subscribed to the doctrine of mental *illness* (and tried to take part in its "treatment"), we have laid ourselves open to some really very embarrassing charges from our friends in psychiatry.

In 1954 the American Psychiatric Association, with the approval of the American Medical Association and the American Psychoanalytic Association, published a resolution on "relations between medicine and psychology," which it reissued (during the supposed "moratorium") in 1957. This document needs no extensive review in these pages; but a few sentences may be quoted to indicate what a powerful fulcrum the sickness conception of neurosis provides for the aggrandizement of medicine.

> For centuries the Western world has placed on the medical profession responsibility for the diagnosis and treatment of illness. Medical practice acts have been designed to protect the public from unqualified practitioners and to define the special responsibilities assumed by those who practice the heal-ing art. . . . Psychiatry is the medical speciality concerned with illness that has chiefly mental symptoms. . . . Psychotherapy is a form of medical treat-ment and does not form the basis for a separate profession. . . . When mem-bers of these [other] professions contribute to the diagnosis and treatment of illness, their professional contributions must be coordinated under medical responsibility (pp. 1–2).

So long as we subscribe to the view that neurosis is a bona fide "illness," without moral implications or dimensions, our position will, of necessity, continue to be an awkward one. And it is here I suggest that, as between the concept of sin (however unsatisfactory it may in some ways be) and that of sickness, sin is indeed the lesser of two evils. We have tried the sickness horn of this dilemma and impaled ourselves upon it. Perhaps, despite our erstwhile protestations, we shall yet find sin more congenial.

We psychologists do not, I believe, object *in principle* to the type of authority which psychiatrists wish to exercise, or to our being subject to other medical controls, if they were truly functional. But authority and power ought to go with demonstrated competence, which medicine clearly has in the phys-ical realm but, equally clearly, does not have in "psychiatry." Despite some pretentious affirmations to the contrary, the fact is that psychoanalysis, on which modern "dynamic" psychiatry is largely based, is in a state of virtual collapse and imminent demise. And the tranquilizers and other forms of so-called chemotherapy are admittedly only ameliorative, not basically curative. So now, to the extent that we have accepted the "illness" postulate and thus been lured under the penumbra of medicine, we are in the ungraceful maneuver of "getting out."[1]

But the question remains: Where do we *go*, what do we *do*, now? Some believe that our best policy is to become frankly agnostic for the time being, to admit that we know next to nothing about either the cause or correction of psychopathology and therefore ought to concentrate on *research*. This is certainly a safe policy, and it may also be the wisest one. But since this matter of man's total adjustment and psychosocial survival does not quickly yield up its innermost secrets to conventional types of scientific inquiry, I believe it will do no harm for us at the same time to be thinking about some frankly ideological matters.

For several decades we psychologists looked upon the whole matter of sin and moral accountability as a great incubus and acclaimed our liberation from it as epoch-making. But at length we have discovered that to be "free" in this sense, i.e., to have the excuse of being "sick" rather than *sinful,* is to court the danger of also becoming *lost.* This danger is, I believe, betokened by the wide-spread interest in Existentialism which we are presently witnessing. In becoming amoral, ethically neutral, and "free," we have cut the very roots of our being; lost our deepest sense of self-hood and identity; and, with neurotics themselves, find ourselves asking: Who *am* I? What is my *destiny?* What does living (existence) *mean?*

In reaction to the state of near-limbo into which we have drifted, we have become suddenly aware, once again, of the problem of *values* and of their centrality in the human enterprise. This trend is clearly apparent in the programs at our recent professional meetings, in journal articles, and, to some extent already, in our elementary textbooks. Something very basic is obviously happening to psychologists and their "self-image."

In this process of moving away from our erstwhile medical "entanglements," it would be a very natural thing for us to form a closer and friendlier relationship than we have previously had with religion and theology. And something of this sort is unquestionably occurring. At the APA Annual Convention in 1956 there was, for the first time in our history I believe, a symposium on religion and mental health; and each ensuing year has seen other clear indications of a developing rapprochement.

However, here too there is a difficulty—of a most surprising kind. At the very time that psychologists are becoming distrustful of the sickness approach to personality disturbance and are beginning to look with more benign interest and respect toward certain moral and religious precepts, religionists themselves are being caught up in and bedazzled by the same preposterous system of thought as that from which we psychologists are just recovering. It would be possible to document this development at length; but reference to such recent "theological" works as Richard V. McCann's *Delinquency—Sickness or Sin?* (1957) and Carl Michalson's *Faith for Personal Crises* (1958, see especially Chapter 3) will suffice.

We have already alluded to Anna Russell's "Psychiatric Folksong" and, in addition, should call attention to Katie Lee's 12-inch LP recording "Songs of Couch and Consultation." That entertainment and literary people are broadly rejecting psychoanalytic froth for the more solid substance of moral accountability is indicated by many current novels and plays. It is not without significance that Arthur Miller's *Death of a Salesman,* written in the philosophical vein of Hawthorne's great novel *The Scarlet Letter,* has, for example, been received so well.

How very strange and inverted our present situation therefore is! Traditionally clergymen have worried about the world's entertainments and entertainers and, for a time at least, about psychology and psychologists. Now, ironically, the entertainers and psychologists are *worrying about the clergymen.* Eventually, of course, clergymen will return to a sounder, less fantastic position; but in the meantime, we psychologists can perhaps play a socially useful and, also, scientifically productive role if we pursue, with all seriousness and candor, our discovery of the essentially moral nature of human existence and of that "living death" which we call psychopathology. This, of course, is not the place to go deeply into the substantive aspects of the problem; but one illustration of the fruitfulness of such exploration may be cited.

In reconsidering the possibility that sin must, after all, be taken seriously, many psychologists seem perplexed as to what attitude one should take *toward the sinner.* "Nonjudgmental," "nonpunitive," "nondirective," "warm," "accepting," "ethically neutral": these words have been so very generally used to form the supposedly proper therapeutic imago that reintroduction of the concept of sin throws us badly off balance. *Our* attitudes, as would-be therapists or helping persons, toward the neurotic (sinner) are apparently less important than his attitude *toward himself;* and, as we know, it is usually—in the most general sense—a rejecting one. Therefore, we have reasoned, the way to get the neurotic to accept and love himself is for us to love and accept *him,* an inference which flows equally from the Freudian assumption that the patient is not really guilty or sinful but only fancies himself so and from the view of Rogers that we are all inherently good and are corrupted by our experiences with the external, everyday world.

But what is here generally overlooked, it seems, is that recovery (constructive change, redemption) is most assuredly attained, not by helping a person reject and rise above his sins, but by helping him *accept them.* This is the paradox which we have not at all understood and which is the very crux of the problem. Just so long as a person lives under the shadow of real, unacknowledged, and unexpiated guilt, he *cannot* (if he has any character at all) "accept himself"; and all *our efforts* to reassure and accept him will avail nothing. He will continue to hate himself and to suffer the inevitable consequences of self-hatred. But the moment he (with or without "assistance") begins to accept his guilt and his sinfulness, the possibility of radical reformation opens up; and with this, the individual may legitimately, though not without pain and effort, pass from deep, pervasive self-rejection and self-torture to a new freedom, of self-respect and peace.

Thus we arrive, not only at a new (really very old) conception of the nature of "neurosis" which may change our entire approach to this problem, but also at an understanding of one of the most fundamental fallacies of Freudian psychoanalysis and many kindred efforts at psychotherapy. Freud observed, quite accurately, that the neurotic tortures himself; and he conjectured that this type of suffering arose from the irrationality and overseverity of the superego. But at once there was an empirical as well as logical difficulty which Freud (unlike some of his followers) faithfully acknowledged. In the *New Introductory Lectures on Psychoanalysis* (1933), he said:

> The superego [paradoxically] seems to have made a one-sided selection [as between the loving and the punitive attitudes of the parents], and to have chosen only the harshness and severity of the parents, their preventive and punitive functions, while their loving care is not taken up and continued by it. If the parents have really ruled with a rod of iron, we easily understand the child developing a severe superego, but, contrary to our expectations, experience shows that the superego may reflect the same relentless harshness even when the up-bringing has been gentle and kind (p. 90).

• And then Freud adds, candidly: "We ourselves do not feel that we have fully understood it." In this we can fully agree. For the only way to resolve the paradox of self-hatred and self-punishment is to assume, not that it represents merely an "introjection" of the attitudes of others, but that the self-hatred is realistically justified and will persist until the individual, by radically altered attitude *and action,* honestly and realistically comes to feel that he now deserves something better. As long as one remains, in old-fashioned religious phraseology, hard-of-heart and unrepentant, just so long will one's conscience hold him in the vise-like grip of "neurotic" rigidity and suffering. But if, at length, an individual confesses his past stupidities and errors and makes what poor attempts he can at restitution, then the superego (like the parents of an earlier day—and society in general) forgives and relaxes its stern hold; and the individual once again is free, "well" (Mowrer, 1959).

But here we too, like Freud, encounter a difficulty. There is some evidence that human beings do not change radically unless they first acknowledge their sins; but we also know how hard it is for one to make such an acknowledgment unless he has *already changed*. In other words, the full realization of deep worth-lessness is a severe ego "insult"; and one must have some new source of strength, it seems, to endure it. This is a mystery (or is it only a mistaken observation?) which traditional theology has tried to resolve in various ways—without complete success. Can we psychologists do better?

note

1. Thoughtful psychiatrists are also beginning to question the legitimacy of the disease concept in this area. In an article entitled "The Myth of Mental Illness" which appeared after this paper went to press, Thomas S. Szasz (1960) is particularly outspoken on this score. He says: ". . . the notion of mental illness has outlived whatever usefulness it might have had and . . . now functions merely as a convenient myth. . . . mental illness is a myth, whose function it is to disguise and thus render more palatable the bitter pill of moral conflicts in human relations" (p. 118). Szasz' entire article deserves careful attention.

references

American Psychiatric Association, Committee on Relations between Psychiatry and Psychology. Resolution on relations of medicine and psychology. *Amer. Psychiat. Ass. Mail Pouch*, 1954, October.
Freud, S. *The problem of lay analysis*. New York: Brentano, 1927.
Freud, S. *New introductory lectures on psychoanalysis*. New York: Norton, 1933.
Freud, S. *Autobiography*. New York: Norton, 1935.
Jones, E. *The life and work of Sigmund Freud*. Vol. 3. New York: Basic Books, 1957.
McCann, R. V. *Delinquency: Sickness or sin?* New York: Harper, 1957.
Michalson, C. *Faith for personal crises*. London: Epworth, 1958.
Mowrer, O. H. Changing conceptions of the unconscious. *J. nerv. ment. Dis.*, 1959, *129*, 222–234.
Szasz, T. S. The myth of mental illness. *Amer. Psychologist*, 1960, *15*, 113–118.

7
The Myth of Mental Illness

Thomas S. Szasz

My aim in this essay is to raise the question "Is there such a thing as mental illness?" and to argue that there is not. Since the notion of mental illness is extremely widely used nowadays, inquiry into the ways in which this term is employed would seem to be especially indicated. Mental illness, of course, is not

Reprinted from *American Psychologist*, 1960, Vol. 15, No. 2, pp. 113–118.
Copyright 1960 by the American Psychological Association. Reprinted by permission.

literally a "thing"—or physical object—and hence it can "exist" only in the same sort of way in which other theoretical concepts exist. Yet, familiar theories are in the habit of posing, sooner or later—at least to those who come to believe in them —as "objective truths" (or "facts"). During certain historical periods, explanatory conceptions such as deities, witches, and microorganisms appeared not only as theories but as self-evident *causes* of a vast number of events. I submit that today mental illness is widely regarded in a somewhat similar fashion, that is, as the cause of innumerable diverse happenings. As an antidote to the complacent use of the notion of mental illness—whether as a self-evident phenomenon, theory, or cause—let us ask this question: What is meant when it is asserted that someone is mentally ill?

In what follows I shall describe briefly the main uses to which the concept of mental illness has been put. I shall argue that this notion has outlived whatever usefulness it might have had and that it now functions merely as a convenient myth.

mental illness as a sign of brain disease

The notion of mental illness derives its main support from such phenomena as syphilis of the brain or delirious conditions—intoxications, for instance—in which persons are known to manifest various peculiarities or disorders of thinking and behavior. Correctly speaking, however, these are diseases of the brain, not of the mind. According to one school of thought, *all* so-called mental illness is of this type. The assumption is made that some neurological defect, perhaps a very subtle one, will ultimately be found for all the disorders of thinking and behavior. Many contemporary psychiatrists, physicians, and other scientists hold this view. This position implies that people *cannot* have troubles—expressed in what are *now called* "mental illnesses"—because of differences in personal needs, opinions, social aspirations, values, and so on. *All problems in living* are attributed to physico-chemical processes which in due time will be discovered by medical research.

"Mental illnesses" are thus regarded as basically no different than all other diseases (that is, of the body). The only difference, in this view, between mental and bodily diseases is that the former, affecting the brain, manifest themselves by means of mental symptoms; whereas the latter, affecting other organ systems (for example, the skin, liver, etc.), manifest themselves by means of symptoms referable to those parts of the body. This view rests on and expresses what are, in my opinion, two fundamental errors.

In the first place, what central nervous system symptoms would correspond to a skin eruption or a fracture? It would *not* be some emotion or complex bit of behavior. Rather, it would be blindness or a paralysis of some part of the body. The crux of the matter is that a disease of the brain, analogous to a disease of the skin or bone, is a neurological defect, and not a problem in living. For example, a *defect* in a person's visual field may be satisfactorily explained by correlating it with certain definite lesions in the nervous system. On the other hand, a person's *belief*—whether this be a belief in Christianity, in Communism, or in the idea that his internal organs are "rotting" and that his body is, in fact, already "dead"— cannot be explained by a defect or disease of the nervous system. Explanations of this sort of occurrence—assuming that one is interested in the belief itself and does not regard it simply as a "symptom" or expression of something else that is *more interesting*—must be sought along different lines.

The second error in regarding complex psychosocial behavior, consisting of communications about ourselves and the world about us, as mere symptoms of neurological functioning is *epistemological*. In other words, it is an error pertaining not to any mistakes in observation or reasoning, as such, but rather to the way in which we organize and express our knowledge. In the present case, the error lies in making a symmetrical dualism between mental and physical (or bodily) symptoms, a dualism which is merely a habit of speech and to which no known observations can be found to correspond. Let us see if this is so. In medical practice, when we speak of physical disturbances, we mean either signs (for example, a fever) or symptoms (for example, pain). We speak of mental symptoms, on the other hand, when we refer to a patient's *communications about himself, others, and the world about him.* He might state that he is Napoleon or that he is being persecuted by the Communists. These would be considered mental symptoms *only* if the observer believed that the patient was *not* Napoleon or that he was *not* being persecuted by the Communists. This makes it apparent that the statement that "X is a mental symptom" involves rendering a judgment. The judgment entails, moreover, a covert comparison or matching of the patient's ideas, concepts, or beliefs with those of the observer and the society in which they live. The notion of mental symptom is therefore inextricably tied to the *social* (including *ethical*) *context* in which it is made in much the same way as the notion of bodily symptom is tied to an *anatomical* and *genetic context* (Szasz, 1957a, 1957b).

To sum up what has been said thus far: I have tried to show that for those who regard mental symptoms as signs of brain disease, the concept of mental illness is unnecessary and misleading. For what they mean is that people so labeled suffer from diseases of the brain; and, if that is what they mean, it would seem better for the sake of clarity to say that and not something else.

mental illness as a name for problems in living

The term "mental illness" is widely used to describe something which is very different than a disease of the brain. Many people today take it for granted that living is an arduous process. Its hardship for modern man, moreover, derives not so much from a struggle for biological survival as from the stresses and strains inherent in the social intercourse of complex human personalities. In this context, the notion of mental illness is used to identify or describe some feature of an individual's so-called personality. Mental illness—as a deformity of the personality, so to speak—is then regarded as the *cause* of the human disharmony. It is implicit in this view that social intercourse between people is regarded as something *inherently harmonious*, its disturbance being due solely to the presence of "mental illness" in many people. This is obviously fallacious reasoning, for it makes the abstraction "mental illness" into a *cause*, even though this abstraction was created in the first place to serve only as a shorthand expression for certain types of human behavior. It now becomes necessary to ask: "What kinds of behavior are regarded as indicative of mental illness, and by whom?"

The concept of illness, whether bodily or mental, implies *deviation from some clearly defined norm.* In the case of physical illness, the norm is the structural and functional integrity of the human body. Thus, although the desirability of physical health, as such, is an ethical value, what health *is* can be stated in anatomical and physiological terms. What is the norm deviation from which is regarded as mental illness? This question cannot be easily answered. But whatever this norm might be, we can be certain of only one thing: namely, that it is a norm that must be stated in terms of *psychosocial, ethical,* and *legal* concepts. For example, notions such as "excessive repression" or "acting out an unconscious impulse" illustrate the use of psychological concepts for judging (so-called) mental health and illness. The idea that chronic hostility, vengefulness, or divorce are indicative of mental illness would be illustrations of the use of ethical norms (that is, the desirability of love, kindness, and a stable marriage relationship). Finally, the widespread psychiatric opinion that only a mentally ill person would commit homicide illustrates the use of a legal concept as a norm of mental health. The norm from which deviation is measured whenever one speaks of a mental illness is a *psychosocial and ethical one.* Yet, the remedy is sought in terms of *medical* measures which—it is hoped and assumed—are free from wide differences of ethical value. The definition of the disorder and the terms in which its remedy are sought are therefore at serious odds with one another. The practical significance of this covert conflict between the alleged nature of the defect and the remedy can hardly be exaggerated.

Having identified the norms used to measure deviations in cases of mental illness, we will now turn to the question: "Who defines the norms and hence the deviation?" Two basic answers may be offered: (*a*) It may be the person himself (that is, the patient) who decides that he deviates from a norm. For example, an artist may believe that he suffers from a work inhibition; and he may implement this conclusion by seeking help *for* himself from a psychotherapist. (*b*) It may be someone other than the patient who decides that the latter is deviant (for example, relatives, physicians, legal authorities, society generally, etc.). In such a case a psychiatrist may be hired by others to do something *to* the patient in order to correct the deviation.

These considerations underscore the importance of asking the question "Whose agent is the psychiatrist?" and of giving a candid answer to it (Szasz, 1956, 1958). The psychiatrist (psychologist or nonmedical psychotherapist), it now develops, may be the agent of the patient, of the relatives, of the school, of the military services, of a business organization, of a court of law, and so forth. In speaking of the psychiatrist as the agent of these persons or organizations, it is not implied that his values concerning norms, or his ideas and aims concerning the proper nature of remedial action, need to coincide exactly with those of his employer. For example, a patient in individual psychotherapy may believe that his salvation lies in a new marriage; his psychotherapist need not share this hypothesis. As the patient's agent, however, he must abstain from bringing social or legal force to bear on the patient which would prevent him from putting his beliefs into action. If his *contract* is with the patient, the psychiatrist (psychotherapist) may disagree with him or stop his treatment; but he cannot engage others to obstruct the patient's aspirations. Similarly, if a psychiatrist is engaged by a court to determine the sanity of a criminal, he need not fully share the legal authorities' values and intentions in regard to the criminal and the means available for dealing with him. But the psychiatrist is expressly barred from stating, for example, that it is not the criminal who is "insane" but the men who wrote the law on the basis of which the very actions that are being judged are regarded as "criminal." Such an opinion could be voiced, of course, but not in a courtroom, and not by a psychiatrist who makes it his practice to assist the court in performing its daily work.

To recapitulate: In actual contemporary social usage, the finding of a mental illness is made by establishing a deviance in behavior from certain psychosocial, ethical, or legal norms. The judgment may be made, as in medicine, by the patient, the physician (psychiatrist), or others. Remedial action, finally, tends to be sought in a therapeutic—or covertly medical—framework, thus creating a situation in which *psychosocial, ethical,* and/or *legal deviations* are claimed to be correctible by (so-called) *medical action.* Since medical action is designed to correct only medical deviations, it seems logically absurd to expect that it will help solve problems whose very existence had been defined and established on nonmedical grounds. I think that these considerations may be fruitfully applied to the present use of tranquilizers and, more generally, to what might be expected of drugs of whatever type in regard to the amelioration or solution of problems in human living.

the role of ethics in psychiatry

Anything that people *do*—in contrast to things that *happen* to them (Peters, 1958)—takes place in a context of value. In this broad sense, no human activity is devoid of ethical implications. When the values underlying certain activities are widely shared, those who participate in their pursuit may lose sight of them altogether. The discipline of medicine, both as a pure science (for example, research) and as a technology (for example, therapy), contains many ethical considerations and judgments. Unfortunately, these are often denied, minimized, or merely kept out of focus; for the ideal of the medical profession as well as of the people whom it serves seems to be having a system of medicine (allegedly) free of ethical value. This sentimental notion is expressed by such things as the doctor's willingness to treat and help patients irrespective of their religious or political beliefs, whether they are rich or poor, etc. While there may be some grounds for this belief—albeit it is a view that is not impressively true even in these regards—the fact remains that ethical considerations encompass a vast range of human affairs. By making the practice of medicine neutral in regard to some specific issues of value need not, and cannot, mean that it can be kept free from all such values. The practice of medicine is intimately tied to ethics; and the first thing that we must do, it seems to me, is to try to make this clear and explicit. I shall let this matter rest here, for it does not concern us specifically in this essay. Lest there be any vagueness, however, about how or where ethics and medicine meet, let me remind the reader of such issues as birth control, abortion, suicide, and euthanasia as only a few of the major areas of current ethicomedical controversy.

Psychiatry, I submit, is very much more intimately tied to problems of ethics than is medicine. I use the word "psychiatry" here to refer to that contemporary discipline which is concerned with *problems in living* (and not with diseases of the brain, which are problems for neurology). Problems in human relations can be analyzed, interpreted, and given meaning only within given social and ethical contexts. Accordingly, it *does* make a difference—arguments to the contrary notwithstanding—what the psychiatrist's socioethical orientations happen to be; for these will influence his ideas on what is wrong with the patient, what deserves comment or interpretation, in what possible directions change might be desirable, and so forth. Even in medicine proper, these factors play a role, as for instance, in the divergent orientations which physicians, depending on their religious affiliations, have toward such things as birth control and therapeutic abortion. Can anyone really believe that a psychotherapist's ideas concerning religious belief, slavery, or other similar issues play no role in his practical work? If they do make a difference, what are we to infer from it? Does it not seem reasonable that we ought to have different psychiatric therapies—each expressly recognized for the ethical positions which they embody—for, say, Catholics and Jews, religious persons and agnostics, democrats and communists, white suprema-cists and Negroes, and so on? Indeed, if we look at how psychiatry is actually practiced today (especially in the United States), we find that people do seek psychiatric help in accordance with their social status and ethical beliefs (Hollingshead & Redlich, 1958). This should really not surprise us more than being told that practicing Catholics rarely frequent birth control clinics.

The foregoing position which holds that contemporary psychotherapists deal with problems in living, rather than with mental illnesses and their cures, stands in opposition to a currently prevalent claim, according to which mental illness is just as "real" and "objective" as bodily illness. This is a confusing claim since it is never known exactly what is meant by such words as "real" and "objective." I suspect, however, that what is intended by the proponents of this view is to create the idea in the popular mind that mental illness is some sort of disease entity, like an infection or a malignancy. If this were true, one could *catch* or *get* a "mental illness," one might *have* or *harbor* it, one might *transmit* it to others, and finally one could get *rid* of it. In my opinion, there is not a shred of evidence to support this idea. To the contrary, all the evidence is the other way and supports the view that what people now call mental illnesses are for the most part *communications* expressing unacceptable ideas, often framed, moreover, in an unusual idiom. The scope of this essay allows me to do no more than mention this alternative theoretical approach to this problem (Szasz, 1957c).

This is not the place to consider in detail the similarities and differences between bodily and mental illnesses. It shall suffice for us here to emphasize only one important difference between them: namely, that whereas bodily disease refers to public, physicochemical occurrences, the notion of mental illness is used to codify relatively more private, sociopsychological happenings of which the observer (diagnostician) forms a part. In other words, the psychiatrist does not stand *apart* from what he observes, but is, in Harry Stack Sullivan's apt words, a "participant observer." This means that he is *committed* to some picture of what he considers reality—and to what he thinks society considers reality—and he observes and judges the patient's behavior in the light of these considerations. This touches on our earlier observation that the notion of mental symptom itself implies a comparison between observer and observed, psychiatrist and patient. This is so obvious that I may be charged with belaboring trivialities. Let me therefore say once more that my aim in presenting this argument was expressly to criticize and counter a prevailing contemporary tendency to deny the moral aspects of psychiatry (and psychotherapy) and to substitute for them allegedly value-free medical considerations. Psychotherapy, for example, is being widely practiced as though it entailed nothing other than restoring the patient from a state of mental sickness to one of mental health. While it is generally accepted that mental illness has something to do with man's social (or interpersonal) relations, it is paradoxically maintained that problems of values (that is, of ethics) do not arise in this process.[1] Yet, in one sense, much of psychotherapy may revolve around nothing other than the elucidation and weighing of goals and values— many of which may be mutually contradictory—and the means whereby they might best be harmonized, realized, or relinquished.

The diversity of human values and the methods by means of which they may be realized is so vast, and many of them remain so unacknowledged, that they cannot fail but lead to conflicts in human relations. Indeed, to say that human relations at all levels—from mother to child, through husband and wife, to nation and nation—are fraught with stress, strain, and disharmony is, once again, making the obvious explicit. Yet, what may be obvious may be also poorly understood. This I think is the case here. For it seems to me that—at least in our scientific theories of behavior—we have failed to *accept* the simple fact that human relations are inherently fraught with difficulties and that to make them even relatively harmonious requires much patience and hard work. I submit that the idea of mental illness is now being put to work to obscure certain difficulties which at present may be inherent—not that they need be unmodifiable—in the social intercourse of persons. If this is true, the concept functions as a disguise; for instead of calling attention to conflicting human needs, aspirations, and values, the notion of mental illness provides an amoral and impersonal "thing" (an "illness") as an explanation for *problems in living* (Szasz, 1959). We may recall in this connection that not so long ago it was devils and witches who were held responsible for men's problems in social living. The belief in mental illness, as something other than man's trouble in getting along with his fellow man, is the proper heir to the belief in demonology and witchcraft. Mental illness exists or is "real" in exactly the same sense in which witches existed or were "real."

choice, responsibility, and psychiatry

While I have argued that mental illnesses do not exist, I obviously did not imply that the social and psychological occurrences to which this label is currently being attached also do not exist. Like the personal and social troubles which people had in the Middle Ages, they are real enough. It is the labels we give them that concerns us and, having labelled them, what we do about them. While I cannot go into the ramified implications of this problem here, it is worth noting that a demonologic conception of problems in living gave rise to therapy along theological lines. Today, a belief in mental illness implies—nay, requires—therapy along medical or psychotherapeutic lines.

What is implied in the line of thought set forth here is something quite different. I do not intend to offer a new conception of "psychiatric illness" nor a new form of "therapy." My aim is more modest and yet also more ambitious. It is to suggest that the phenomena now called mental illnesses be looked at afresh and more simply, that they be removed from the category of illnesses, and that they be regarded as the expressions of man's struggle with the problem of *how* he should live. The last mentioned problem is obviously a vast one, its enormity reflecting not only man's inability to cope with his environment, but even more his increasing self-reflectiveness.

By problems in living, then, I refer to that truly explosive chain reaction which began with man's fall from divine grace by partaking of the fruit of the tree of knowledge. Man's awareness of himself and of the world about him seems to be a steadily expanding one, bringing in its wake an ever larger *burden of understanding* (an expression borrowed from Susanne Langer, 1953). *This burden, then, is to be expected and must not be misinterpreted.* Our only *rational* means for lightening it is *more understanding*, and appropriate *action* based on such understanding. The main alternative lies in acting as though the burden were not what in fact we perceive it to be and taking refuge in an outmoded theological view of man. In the latter view, man does not fashion his life and much of his world about him, but merely lives out his fate in a world created by superior beings. This may logically lead to pleading nonresponsibility in the face of seemingly unfathomable problems and difficulties. Yet, if man fails to take increasing responsibility for his actions, individually as well as collectively, it seems unlikely that some higher power or being would assume this task and carry this burden for him. Moreover, this seems hardly the proper time in human history for obscuring the issue of man's responsibility for his actions by hiding it behind the skirt of an all-explaining conception of mental illness.

conclusions

I have tried to show that the notion of mental illness has outlived whatever usefulness it might have had and that it now functions merely as a convenient myth. As such, it is a true heir to religious myths in general, and to the belief in witchcraft in particular; the role of all these belief-systems was to act as *social tranquilizers*, thus encouraging the hope that mastery of certain specific problems may be achieved by means of substitutive (symbolic-magical) operations. The notion of mental illness thus serves mainly to obscure the everyday fact that life for most people is a continuous struggle, not for biological survival, but for a "place in the sun," "peace of mind," or some other human value. For man aware of himself and of the world about him, once the needs for preserving the body (and perhaps the race) are more or less satisfied, the problem arises as to what he should do with himself. Sustained adherence to the myth of mental illness allows people to avoid facing this problem, believing that mental health, conceived as the absence of mental illness, automatically insures the making of right and safe choices in one's conduct of life. But the facts are all the other way. It is the making of good choices in life that others regard, retrospectively, as good mental health!

The myth of mental illness encourages us, moreover, to believe in its logical corollary: that social intercourse would be harmonious, satisfying, and the secure basis of a "good life" were it not for the disrupting influences of mental illness or "psychopathology." The potentiality for universal human happiness, in this form at least, seems to me but another example of the I-wish-it-were-true type of fantasy. I do believe that human happiness or well-being on a hitherto unimaginably large scale, and not just for a select few, is possible. This goal could be achieved, however, only at the cost of many men, and not just a few being willing and able to tackle their personal, social, and ethical conflicts. This means having the courage and integrity to forego waging battles on false fronts, finding solutions for substitute problems—for instance, fighting the battle of stomach acid and chronic fatigue instead of facing up to a marital conflict.

Our adversaries are not demons, witches, fate, or mental illness. We have no enemy whom we can fight, exorcise, or dispel by "cure." What we do have are *problems in living*—whether these be biologic, economic, political, or sociopsychological. In this essay I was concerned only with problems belonging in the last mentioned category, and within this group mainly with those pertaining to moral values. The field to which modern psychiatry addresses itself is vast, and I made no effort to encompass it all. My argument was limited to the proposition that mental illness is a myth, whose function it is to disguise and thus render more palatable the bitter pill of moral conflicts in human relations.

note

1. Freud went so far as to say that: "I consider ethics to be taken for granted. Actually I have never done a mean thing" (Jones, 1957, p. 247). This surely is a strange thing to say for someone who has studied man as a social being as closely as did Freud. I mention it here to show how the notion of "illness" (in the case of psychoanalysis, "psychopathology," or "mental illness") was used by Freud—and by most of his followers—as a means for classifying certain forms of human behavior as falling within the scope of medicine, and hence (by *fiat*) outside that of ethics!

references

Hollingshead, A. B., & Redlich, F. C. *Social class and mental illness*. New York: Wiley, 1958.

Jones, E. *The life and work of Sigmund Freud*. Vol. III. New York: Basic Books, 1959.

Langer, S. K. *Philosophy in a new key*. New York: Mentor Books, 1953.

Peters, R. S. *The concept of motivation*. London: Routledge & Kegan Paul, 1958.

Szasz, T. S. Malingering: "Diagnosis" or social condemnation? *AMA Arch Neurol. Psychiat.*, 1956, 76, 432–443.

Szasz, T. S. *Pain and pleasure: A study of bodily feelings*. New York: Basic Books, 1957. (a)

Szasz, T. S. The problem of psychiatric nosology: A contribution to a situational analysis of psychiatric operations. *Amer. J. Psychiat.*, 1957, *114*, 405–413. (b)

Szasz, T. S. On the theory of psychoanalytic treatment. *Int. J. Psycho-Anal.*, 1957, 38, 166–182. (c)

Szasz, T. S. Psychiatry, ethics and the criminal law. *Columbia Law Rev.*, 1958, 58, 183–198.

Szasz, T. S. Moral conflict and psychiatry, *Yale Rev.*, 1959.

8

Personality Disorder Is Disease

David P. Ausubel

In two recent articles in the *American Psychologist*, Szasz (1960) and Mowrer (1960) have argued the case for discarding the concept of mental illness. The essence of Mowrer's position is that since medical science lacks "demonstrated competence . . . in psychiatry," psychology would be wise to "get out" from "under the penumbra of medicine," and to regard the behavior disorders as manifestations of sin rather than of disease (p. 302). Szasz' position, as

Reprinted from *American Psychologist*, 1961, Vol. 16, No. 2, pp. 69–74. Copyright 1961 by the American Psychological Association. Reprinted by permission.

we shall see shortly, is somewhat more complex than Mowrer's, but agrees with the latter in emphasizing the moral as opposed to the psychopathological basis of abnormal behavior.

For a long time now, clinical psychology has both repudiated the relevance of moral judgment and accountability for assessing behavioral acts and choices, and has chafed under medical (psychiatric) control and authority in diagnosing and treating the personality disorders. One can readily appreciate, therefore, Mowrer's eagerness to sever the historical and professional ties that bind clinical psychology to medicine, even if this means denying that psychological disturbances constitute a form of illness, and even if psychology's close working relationship with psychiatry must be replaced by a new rapprochement with sin and theology, as "the lesser of two evils" (pp. 302–303). One can also sympathize with Mowrer's and Szasz' dissatisfaction with prevailing amoral and nonjudgmental trends in clinical psychology and with their entirely commendable efforts to restore moral judgment and accountability to a respectable place among the criteria used in evaluating human behavior, both normal and abnormal.

Opposition to these two trends in the handling of the behavior disorders (i.e., to medical control and to nonjudgmental therapeutic attitudes), however, does not necessarily imply abandonment of the concept of mental illness. There is no inconsistency whatsoever in maintaining, on the one hand, that most purposeful human activity has a moral aspect the reality of which psychologists cannot afford to ignore (Ausubel, 1952, p. 462), that man is morally accountable for the majority of his misdeeds (Ausubel, 1952, p. 469), and that psychological rather than medical training and sophistication are basic to competence in the personality disorders (Ausubel, 1956, p. 101), and affirming, on the other hand, that the latter disorders are genuine manifestations of illness. In recent years psychology has been steadily moving away from the formerly fashionable stance of ethical neutrality in the behavioral sciences; and in spite of strident medical claims regarding superior professional qualifications and preclusive legal responsibility for treating psychiatric patients, and notwithstanding the nominally restrictive provisions of medical practice acts, clinical psychologists have been assuming an increasingly more important, independent, and responsible role in treating the mentally ill population of the United States.

It would be instructive at this point to examine the tactics of certain other medically allied professions in freeing themselves from medical control and in acquiring independent, legally recognized professional status. In no instance have they resorted to the devious stratagem of denying that they were treating diseases, in the hope of mollifying medical opposition and legitimizing their own professional activities. They took the position instead that simply because a given condition is defined as a disease, its treatment need not necessarily be turned over to doctors of medicine if other equally competent professional specialists were available. That this position is legally and politically tenable is demonstrated by the fact that an impressively large number of recognized diseases are legally treated today by both medical *and* nonmedical specialists (e.g., diseases of the mouth, face, jaws, teeth, eyes, and feet). And there are few convincing reasons for believing that psychiatrists wield that much more political power than physicians, maxillofacial surgeons, ophthalmologists, and orthopedic surgeons, that they could be successful where these latter specialists have failed, in legally restricting practice in their particular area of competence to holders of the medical degree. Hence, even if psychologists were not currently managing to hold their own vis-à-vis psychiatrists, it would be far less dangerous and much more forthright to press for the necessary ameliorative legislation than to seek cover behind an outmoded and thoroughly discredited conception of the behavior disorders.

the Szasz-Mowrer position

Szasz' (1960) contention that the concept of mental illness "now functions merely as a convenient myth" (p. 118) is grounded on four unsubstantiated and logically untenable propositions, which can be fairly summarized as follows:

1. Only symptoms resulting from demonstrable physical lesions qualify as legitimate manifestations of disease. Brain pathology is a type of physical lesion, but its symptoms properly speaking, are neurological rather than psychological in nature. Under no circumstances, therefore, can mental symptoms be considered a form of illness.
2. A basic dichotomy exists between *mental* symptoms, on the one hand, which are subjective in nature, dependent on subjective judgment and personal involvement of the observer, and referable to cultural-ethical norms, and *physical* symptoms, on the other hand, which are allegedly objective in nature, ascertainable without personal involvement of the observer, and independent of cultural norms and ethical standards. Only symptoms possessing the latter set of characteristics are genuinely reflective of illness and amenable to medical treatment.
3. Mental symptoms are merely expressions of problems of living and, hence, cannot be regarded as manifestations of a pathological condition. The concept of mental illness is misleading and demonological because it seeks to explain psychological disturbance in particular and human disharmony in general in terms of a metaphorical but nonexistent disease entity, instead of attributing them to inherent difficulties in coming to grips with elusive problems of choice and responsibility.
4. Personality disorders, therefore, can be most fruitfully conceptualized as products of moral conflict, confusion, and aberration. Mowrer (1960) extends this latter proposition to include the dictum that psychiatric symptoms are primarily reflective of unacknowledged sin, and that individuals manifesting these symptoms are responsible for and deserve their suffering, both because of their original transgressions and because they refuse to avow and expiate their guilt (pp. 301, 304).

Widespread adoption of the Szasz-Mowrer view of the personality disorders would, in my opinion, turn back the psychiatric clock twenty-five hundred years. The most significant and perhaps the only real advance registered by mankind in evolving a rational and humane method of handling behavioral aberrations has been in substituting a concept of disease for the demonological and retributional doctrines regarding their nature and etiology that flourished until comparatively recent times. Conceptualized as illness, the symptoms of personality disorders can be interpreted in the light of underlying stresses and resistances, both genic and environmental, and can be evaluated in relation to *specifiable* quantitative and qualitative norms of appropriately adaptive behavior, both cross-culturally and within a particular cultural context. It would behoove us, therefore, before we abandon the concept of mental illness and return to the medieval doctrine of unexpiated sin or adopt Szasz' ambiguous criterion of difficulty in ethical choice and responsibility, to subject the foregoing propositions to careful and detailed study.

mental symptoms and brain pathology

Although I agree with Szasz in rejecting the doctrine that ultimately some neuroanatomic or neurophysiologic defect will be discovered in *all* cases of personality disorder, I disagree with his reasons for not accepting this proposition. Notwithstanding Szasz' straw man presentation of their position, the proponents of the extreme somatic view do not really assert that the *particular nature* of a patient's disordered beliefs can be correlated with "certain definite lesions in the nervous system" (Szasz, 1960, p. 113). They hold rather that normal cognitive and behavioral functioning depends on the anatomic and physiologic integrity of certain key areas of the brain, and that impairment of this substrate integrity, therefore, provides a physical basis for disturbed ideation and behavior, but does not explain, except in a very gross way, the particular kinds of symptoms involved. In fact, they are generally inclined to attribute the *specific* character of the patient's symptoms to the nature of his pre-illness personality structure, the substrate integrity of which is impaired by the lesion or metabolic defect in question.

Nevertheless, even though this type of reasoning plausibly accounts for the psychological symptoms found in general paresis, various toxic deleria, and other comparable conditions, it is an extremely improbable explanation of *all* instances of personality disorder. Unlike the tissues of any other organ, brain tissue possesses the unique property of making possible awareness of and adjustment to the world of sensory, social, and symbolic stimulation. Hence by virtue of this unique relationship of the nervous system to the environment, diseases of behavior and personality may reflect abnormalities in personal and social adjustment, quite apart from any structural or metabolic disturbance in the underlying neural substrate. I would conclude, therefore, that although brain pathology is probably not the most important cause of behavior disorder, it is undoubtedly responsible for the incidence of *some* psychological abnormalities *as well as* for various neurological signs and symptoms.

But even if we completely accepted Szasz' view that brain pathology does not account for any symptoms of personality disorder, it would still be unnecessary to accept his assertion that to qualify as a genuine manifestation of disease a given symptom must be caused by a physical lesion. Adoption of such a criterion would be arbitrary and inconsistent both with medical and lay connotations of the term "disease," which in current usage is generally regarded as including any marked deviation, physical, mental, or behavioral, from normally desirable standards of structural and functional integrity.

mental versus physical symptoms

Szasz contends that since the analogy between physical and mental symptoms is patently fallacious, the postulated parallelism between physical and mental disease is logically untenable. This line of reasoning is based on the assumption that the two categories of symptoms can be sharply dichotomized with respect to such basic dimensions as objectivity-subjectivity, the relevance of cultural norms, and the need for personal involvement of the observer. In my opinion, the existence of such a dichotomy cannot be empirically demonstrated in convincing fashion.

Practically all symptoms of bodily disease involve some elements of subjective judgment—both on the part of the patient and of the physician. Pain is perhaps the most important and commonly used criterion of physical illness. Yet, any evaluation of its reported locus, intensity, character, and duration is dependent upon the patient's subjective appraisal of his own sensations and on the physician's assessment of the latter's pain threshold, intelligence, and personality structure. It is also a medical commonplace that the severity of pain in most instances of bodily illness may be mitigated by the administration of a placebo. Furthermore, in taking a meaningful history the physician must not only serve as a participant observer but also as a skilled interpreter of human behavior. It is the rare patient who does not react psychologically to the signs of physical illness; and hence physicians are constantly called upon to decide, for example, to what extent precordial pain and reported tightness in the chest are manifestations of coronary insufficiency, of fear of cardiac disease and impending death, or of combinations of both conditions. Even such allegedly objective signs as pulse rate, BMR, blood pressure, and blood cholesterol have their subjective and relativistic aspects. Pulse rate and blood pressure are notoriously susceptible to emotional influences, and BMR and blood cholesterol fluctuate widely from one cultural environment to another (Dreyfuss & Czaczkes, 1959). And anyone who believes that ethical norms have no relevance for physical illness has obviously failed to consider the problems confronting Catholic patients and/or physicians when issues of contraception, abortion, and preferential saving of the mother's as against the fetus' life must be faced in the context of various obstetrical emergencies and medical contraindications to pregnancy.

It should now be clear, therefore, that symptoms not only do not need a physical basis to qualify as manifestations of illness, but also that the evaluation of *all* symptoms, physical as well as mental, is dependent in large measure on subjective judgment, emotional factors, cultural-ethical norms, and personal involvement on the part of the observer. These considerations alone render no longer tenable Szasz' contention (1960, p. 114) that there is an inherent contradiction between using cultural and ethical norms as criteria of mental disease, on the one hand, and of employing medical measures of treatment on the other. But even if the postulated dichotomy between mental and physical symptoms were valid, the use of physical measures in treating subjective and relativisitic psychological symptoms would still be warranted. Once we accept the proposition that impairment of the neural substrate of personality can result in behavior disorder, it is logically consistent to accept the corollary proposition that other kinds of manipulation of the same neural substrate can conceivably have therapeutic effects, irrespective of whether the underlying cause of the mental symptoms is physical or psychological.

mental illness and problems of living

"The phenomena now called mental illness," argues Szasz (1960), can be regarded more forthrightly and simply as "expressions of man's struggle with the problem of how he should live" (p. 117). This statement undoubtedly oversimplifies the nature of personality disorders; but even if it were adequately inclusive it would not be inconsistent with the position that these disorders are a manifestation of illness. There is no valid reason why a particular symptom cannot both reflect a problem in living *and* constitute a manifestation of disease. The notion of mental illness, conceived in this way, would not "obscure the everyday fact that life for most people is a continuous struggle . . . for a 'place in the sun', 'peace of mind,' or some other human value" (p. 118). It is quite true, as Szasz points out, that "human relations are inherently fraught with difficulties" (p. 117), and that most people manage to cope with such difficulties without becoming mentally ill. But conceding this fact hardly precludes the possibility that some individuals, either because of the magnitude of the stress involved, or because of genically or environmentally induced susceptibility to ordinary degrees of stress, respond to the problems of living with behavior that is either seriously distorted or sufficiently unadaptive to prevent normal interpersonal relations and vocational functioning. The latter outcome—gross deviation from a designated range of desirable behavioral variability—conforms to the generally understood meaning of mental illness.

The plausibility of subsuming abnormal behavioral reactions to stress under the general rubric of disease is further enhanced by the fact that these reactions include the same three principal categories of symptoms found in physical illness. Depression and catastrophic impairment of self-esteem, for example, are manifestations of personality disorder which are symptomologically comparable to edema in cardiac failure or to heart murmurs in valvular disease. They are indicative of underlying pathology but are neither adaptive nor adjustive. Symptoms such as hypomanic overactivity and compulsive striving toward unrealistically high achievement goals, on the other hand, are both adaptive and adjustive, and constitute a type of compensatory response to basic feelings of inadequacy, which is not unlike cardiac hypertrophy in hypertensive heart disease or elevated white blood cell count in acute infections. And finally, distortive psychological defenses that have some adjustive value but are generally maladaptive (e.g., phobias, delusions, autistic fantasies) are analogous to the pathological situation found in conditions like pneumonia, in which the excessive outpouring of serum and phagocytes in defensive response to pathogenic bacteria literally causes the patient to drown in his own fluids.

Within the context of this same general proposition, Szasz repudiates the concept of mental illness as demonological in nature, i.e., as the "true heir to religious myths in general and to the belief in witchcraft in particular" (p. 118) because it allegedly employs a reified abstraction ("a deformity of personality") to account in causal terms both for "human disharmony" and for symptoms of behavior disorder (p. 114). But again he appears to be demolishing a straw man. Modern students of personality disorder do not regard mental illness as a cause of human disharmony, but as a co-manifestation with it of inherent difficulties in personal adjustment and interpersonal relations; and in so far as I can accurately interpret the literature, psychopathologists do not conceive of mental illness as a cause of particular behavioral symptoms but as a generic term under which these symptoms can be subsumed.

mental illness and moral responsibility

Szasz' final reason for regarding mental illness as a myth is really a corollary of his previously considered more general proposition that mental symptoms are essentially reflective of problems of living and hence do not legitimately qualify as manifestations of disease. It focuses on difficulties of ethical choice and responsibility as the particular life problems most likely to be productive of personality disorder. Mowrer (1960) further extends this corollary by asserting that neurotic and psychotic individuals are responsible for their suffering (p. 301), and that unacknowledged and unexpiated sin, in turn, is the basic cause of this suffering (p. 304). As previously suggested, however, one can plausibly accept the proposition that psychiatrists and clinical psychologists have erred in trying to divorce behavioral evaluation from ethical considerations, in conducting psychotherapy in an amoral setting, and in confusing the psychological explanation of unethical behavior with absolution from accountability for same, *without* necessarily endorsing the view that personality disorders are basically a reflection of sin, and that victims of these disorders are less ill than responsible for their symptoms (Ausubel, 1952, pp. 392–397, 465–471).

In the first place, it is possible in most instances (although admittedly difficult in some) to distinguish quite unambiguously between mental illness and ordinary cases of immorality. The vast majority of persons who are guilty of moral lapses knowingly violate their own ethical precepts for expediential reasons— despite being volitionally capable at the time, both of choosing the more moral alternative and of exercising the necessary inhibitory control (Ausubel, 1952, pp. 465–471). Such persons, also, usually do not exhibit any signs of behavior disorder. At crucial choice points in facing the problems of living they simply choose the opportunistic instead of the moral alternative. They are not mentally ill, but they are clearly accountable for their misconduct. Hence, since personality disorder and immorality are neither coextensive nor mutually exclusive conditions, the concept of mental illness need not necessarily obscure the issue of moral accountability.

Second, guilt may be a contributory factor in behavior disorder, but is by no means the only or principal cause thereof. Feelings of guilt may give rise to anxiety and depression; but in the absence of catastrophic impairment of self-esteem induced by *other* factors, these symptoms tend to be transitory and peripheral in nature (Ausubel, 1952, pp. 362–363). Repression of guilt, is more a consequence than a cause of anxiety. Guilt is repressed in order to avoid the anxiety producing trauma to self-esteem that would otherwise result if it were acknowledged. Repression per se enters the causal picture in anxiety only secondarily—by obviating "the possibility of punishment, confession, expiation, and other guilt reduction mechanisms" (Ausubel, 1952, p. 456). Furthermore, in most types of personality disorder other than anxiety, depression, and various complications of anxiety such as phobias, obsessions, and compulsion, guilt feelings are either not particularly prominent (schizophrenic reactions), or are conspicuously absent (e.g., classical cases of inadequate or aggressive, antisocial psychopathy).

Third, it is just as unreasonable to hold an individual responsible for symptoms of behavior disorder as to deem him accountable for symptoms of physical illness. He is no more culpable for his inability to cope with sociopsychological stress than he would be for his inability to resist the spread of infectious organisms. In those instances where warranted guilt feelings *do* contribute to personality disorder, the patient is accountable for the misdeeds underlying his guilt, but is hardly responsible for the symptoms brought on by the guilt feelings or for unlawful acts committed during his illness. Acknowledgment of guilt may be therapeutically beneficial under these circumstances, but punishment for the original misconduct should obviously be deferred until after recovery.

Lastly, even if it were true that all personality disorder is a reflection of sin and that people are accountable for their behavioral symptoms, it would still be unnecessary to deny that these symptoms are manifestations of disease. Illness is no less real because the victim happens to be culpable for his illness. A glutton with hypertensive heart disease undoubtedly aggravates his condition by over-eating, and is culpable in part for the often fatal symptoms of his disease, but what reasonable person would claim that for this reason he is not really ill?

conclusions

Four propositions in support of the argument for discarding the concept of mental illness were carefully examined, and the following conclusions were reached:

First, although brain pathology is probably not the major cause of personality disorder, it does account for *some* psychological symptoms by impairing the neural substrate of personality. In any case, however, a symptom need not reflect a physical lesion in order to qualify as a genuine manifestation of disease.

Second, Szasz' postulated dichotomy between mental and physical symptoms is untenable because the assessment of *all* symptoms is dependent to some extent on subjective judgment, emotional factors, cultural-ethical norms, and personal involvement of the observer. Furthermore, the use of medical measures in treating behavior disorders—irrespective of whether the underlying causes are neural or psychological—is defensible on the grounds that if inadvertent impairment of the neural substrate of personality can have distortive effects on behavior, directed manipulation of the same substrate may have therapeutic effects.

Third, there is no inherent contradiction in regarding mental symptoms both as expressions of problems in living *and* as manifestations of illness. The latter situation results when individuals are for various reasons unable to cope with such problems, and react with seriously distorted or maladaptive behavior. The three principal categories of behavioral symptoms—manifestations of impaired functioning, adaptive compensation, and defensive overreaction—are also found in bodily disease. The concept of mental illness has never been advanced as a demonological cause of human disharmony, but only as a co-manifestation with it of certain inescapable difficulties and hazards in personal and social adjustment. The same concept is also generally accepted as a generic term for all behavioral symptoms rather than as a reified cause of these symptoms.

Fourth, the view that personality disorder is less a manifestation of illness than of sin, i.e., of culpable inadequacy in meeting problems of ethical choice and responsibility, and that victims of behavior disorder are therefore morally accountable for their symptoms, is neither logically nor empirically tenable. In most instances immoral behavior and mental illness are clearly distinguishable conditions. Guilt is only a secondary etiological factor in anxiety and depression, and in other personality disorders is either not prominent or conspicuously absent. The issue of culpability for symptoms is largely irrelevant in handling the behavior disorders, and in any case does not detract from the reality of the illness.

In general, it is both unnecessary and potentially dangerous to discard the concept of mental illness on the grounds that only in this way can clinical psychology escape from the professional domination of medicine. Dentists, podiatrists, optometrists, and osteopaths have managed to acquire an independent professional status without rejecting the concept of disease. It is equally unnecessary and dangerous to substitute the doctrine of sin for illness in order to counteract prevailing amoral and nonjudgmental trends in psychotherapy. The hypothesis of repressed guilt does not adequately explain most kinds and instances of personality disorder, and the concept of mental illness does not preclude judgments of moral accountability where warranted. Definition of behavior disorder in terms of sin or of difficulties associated with ethical choice and responsibility would substitute theological disputation and philosophical wrangling about values for specifiable quantitative and qualitative criteria of disease.

references

Ausubel, D. P. *Ego development and the personality disorders.* New York: Grune & Stratton, 1952.

Ausubel, D. P. Relationships between psychology and psychiatry: The hidden issues. *Amer. Psychologist,* 1956, *11,* 99–105.

Dreyfuss, F., & Czaczkes, J. W. Blood cholesterol and uric acid of healthy medical students under the stress of an examination. *AMA Arch. Intern. Med.,* 1959, *103,* 708.

Mowrer, O. H. "Sin," the lesser of two evils. *Amer. Psychologist,* 1960, *15,* 301–304.

Szasz, T. S. The myth of mental illness. *Amer. Psychologist,* 1960, *15,* 113–118.

THINK

1. Thomas Szasz contends that mental illness has not been defined and independently established on medical grounds. Rather, the notion is the product of subjective observations and beliefs made by the patient, the psychiatrist, or others. Consequently, he advocates the end of medical therapies for the mentally distressed, entirely because it is absurd to expect medicine to solve problems that arise from, and are defined within, a nonmedical framework. But what about the fact that some drugs can relieve symptoms of anxiety, and even psychotic depression and delusions? How do you reconcile that fact with Szasz's position? Does the effectiveness of these tranquilizers discredit his theory, or would Szasz consider symptoms relieved by tranquilizers comparable to physical lesions?

2. Szasz has argued that "the notion of mental illness has outlived whatever usefulness it might have had and that it now functions merely as a . . . social tranquilizer, thus encouraging the hope that mastery of certain specific problems may be achieved by means of certain substitutive (symbolic-magical) operations." What do you think of this position? What improvements in the treatment of the mentally distressed might occur if Szasz's ideas were wholeheartedly adopted? And, conversely, are there any real dangers in his views? What might happen, for good and for bad, if we abolish the notion of mental illness?

3. Szasz: "The notion of mental illness . . . serves mainly to obscure the everyday fact that life for most people is a continuous struggle, not for biological survival, but for . . . some . . . human value."

    Ausubel: "Widespread adoptions of the Szasz-Mowrer view of the personality disorder would . . . turn back the psychiatric clock 2,500 years."

    Who is right?
    Why?

4. Guilt is real, according to Mowrer. "So long as a person lives under the shadow of real, unacknowledged, and unexpiated guilt, he cannot accept himself. . . ." How do you feel about the argument? Is all guilt real? Might there possibly be guilt that is "unreal"? And, if you find that you are unhappy with Mowrer's position, how do you handle the issues he raises? When is guilt real, and when is it unreal?

III

The Nature
of Psychological Distress

There is no easy way, much less a short way, to capture the nature of psychological distress. Psychologists and psychiatrists have written endlessly about it. So, too, have writers and poets. To presume to sample the nature of psychological distress in four readings is, from the viewpoint of all that has been written, a galling insouciance. And yet, choices need to be made. The papers that are presented here were chosen both because they were exciting and also because they illuminate the breadth of psychological dysfunction.

Take obesity as an example of psychological dysfunction (Reading 9). Perhaps you are surprised to find it considered in this context, since obesity is so clearly, so visibly a *physical* symptom. We consider it here because beneath that physical exterior lies a wealth of interesting psychology. Obesity is, first of all, one of the foremost killers in Western civilization. Fat people have shorter lives and greater illnesses while they live than do cigarette smokers (who also suffer an interesting set of psychological symptoms). And while fat kills, fat people don't want to die any sooner than the rest of us. Nor do they want to be sick or ugly. Why then, do they eat so much? Overeating seems to be guided by a fascinating set of psychological principles, principles that are implicated in the experience of affect (Reading 3) as well as sleeplessness (Reading 26). Stanley Schachter's efforts, then, are seminal to a cognitive psychology of abnormality, of which obesity is a striking exemplar.

Among the host of symptoms that characterize psychological distress, one of the newer ones is a sense of meaninglessness in life. For a variety of reasons, that symptom is likely to become even more common than it is now. Many of the values that our parents and grandparents took for granted, seem now to have fallen away. And meaningful values to replace those old ones are not yet widely available or accepted. Therefore, many people seem to go through long periods in their lives of not knowing what they stand for. Moreover, because there is more leisure time today than there was 30 years ago, people have more time to examine their lives and to ask what it is all about. Thus, it may very well be the case that the problem of finding suitable values to live by is as old as mankind is, but it seems that, right now, mankind has more time to look at those problems than he ever did before. These issues are taken up by Salvatore Maddi in the context of neurosis (Reading 10). But you will want to consider whether they are truly neurotic, or simply reflective of current conditions of living.

The problem of persistent depression—why it occurs and how it can be alleviated—has concerned psychological theorists for decades. Depression is puzzling. It often persists long after the disappearance of any visible reason for being sad. Moreover, it seems occasionally to be initiated for no good reason. Depression is sometimes profound and enduring, occasionally culminating in self-mutilation or suicide. Very early, Freud remarked on the relationship between identification and depression (Reading 2), thus launching psychoanalytic concern for this phenomenon. Learning theorists, too, have addressed themselves to depression. And no theory of learning has been as powerful in its data and speculativeness about depression as the effort that links depression to learned-helplessness (Reading 11). Martin E. P. Seligman's paper merges experimental and clinical psychology, and tacitly makes clear the role of experimentation in illuminating clinical problems.

The final paper in this section deals with schizophrenia—the most baffling and anguishing of the psychological disorders. *Schizophrenia, 1972* (Reading 12) summarizes the current state of knowledge in this area. It is a difficult reading, one that will tax and occasionally exceed your background in psychology and in allied sciences. But it is worth mastering, worth every bit of effort you can put into it. It will give you a sense of the complexity of the disorder, how much we already know, and how much remains to be learned. The study of schizophrenia embraces psychology in its broadest sense, including physiology, biochemistry, and genetics. In no other area do you get so strong a sense of interdisciplinary scientific ferment as you do in the study of schizophrenia.

9

Some Extraordinary Facts about Obese Humans and Rats

Stanley Schachter

Several years ago, when I was working on the problem of the labeling of bodily states, I first became aware of Stunkard's (Stunkard & Koch, 1964) work on obesity and gastric motility. At that time, my students and I had been working on a series of studies concerned with the interaction of cognitive and physiological determinants of emotional state (Schachter, 1964). Our experiments had all involved manipulating bodily state by injections of adrenaline or placebo and simultaneously manipulating cognitive and situational variables that were presumed to affect a subject's interpretation of his bodily state. In essence, these experiments had demonstrated that cognitive factors play a major role in determining how a subject interprets his bodily feelings. Precisely the same set of physiological symptoms—an adrenaline-induced state of sympathetic arousal—could be interpreted as euphoria, or anger, or anxiety, or indeed as no emotional state at all, depending very largely on our cognitive and situational manipulations. In short, there is not an invariant, one-to-one relationship between a set of physiological symptoms and a psychological state.

This conclusion was based entirely on studies that manipulated bodily state

Reprinted from *American Psychologist*, 1971, Vol. 26, No. 2, pp. 129–144. Copyright 1971 by the American Psychological Association. Reprinted by permission.

by the exogenous administration of adrenaline or some other agent. My interest in Stunkard's research was generated by the fact that his work suggested that the same conclusion might be valid for endogenous physiological states. In his study, Stunkard had his subjects do without breakfast and come to his laboratory at 9:00 A.M. They swallowed a gastric balloon, and for the next four hours, Stunkard continuously recorded stomach contractions. Every 15 minutes, he asked his subjects, "Do you feel hungry?" They answered "Yes" or "No," and that is all there was to the study. He has then a record of the extent to which stomach contractions coincide with self-reports of hunger. For normally sized subjects, the two coincide closely. When the stomach contracts, the normal subject is likely to report hunger; when the stomach is quiescent, the normal subject is likely to say that he does not feel hungry. For the obese, on the other hand, there is little correspondence between gastric motility and self-reports of hunger. Whether or not the obese subject describes himself as hungry seems to have almost nothing to do with the state of his gut. There are, then, major individual differences in the extent to which this particular bodily activity—gastric motility—is associated with the feeling state labeled "hunger."

To pursue this lead, we (Schachter, Goldman, & Gordon, 1968) designed an experiment in which we attempted to manipulate gastric motility and the other physiological correlates of food deprivation by the obvious technique of manipulating food deprivation so that some subjects had empty stomachs and others full stomachs before entering an experimental eating situation. The experiment was disguised as a study of taste, and subjects had been asked to do without the meal (lunch or dinner) that preceded the experiment.

When a subject arrived, he was, depending on condition, either fed roast beef sandwiches or fed nothing. He was then seated in front of five bowls of crackers, presented with a long set of rating scales and told, "We want you to judge each cracker on the dimensions (salty, cheesy, garlicky, etc.) listed on these sheets. Taste as many or as few of the crackers of each type as you want in making your judgments; the important thing is that your ratings be as accurate as possible."

The subject then tasted and rated crackers for 15 minutes, under the impression that this was a taste test, and we simply counted the number of crackers that he ate. There were, of course, two types of subjects: obese subjects (from 14% to 75% overweight) and normal subjects (from 8% underweight to 9% overweight).

To review expectations: If it is correct that the obese do not label as hunger the bodily states associated with food deprivation, then this manipulation should have no effect on the amount eaten by obese subjects; on the other hand, the eating behavior of normal subjects should directly parallel the effects of the manipulation on bodily state.

It will be a surprise to no one to learn, from Figure 9.1, that normal subjects ate considerably fewer crackers when their stomachs were full of roast beef sandwiches than when their stomachs were empty. The results for obese subjects stand in fascinating contrast. They ate as much—in fact slightly more—when their stomachs were full as when they were empty. Obviously, the actual state of the stomach has nothing to do with the eating behavior of the obese.[1]

In similar studies (Schachter, 1967; Schachter et al., 1968), we have attempted to manipulate bodily state by manipulating fear and by injecting subjects with epinephrine. Both manipulations are based on Cannon's (1915) and Carlson's (1916) demonstrations that both the state of fear and the injection of

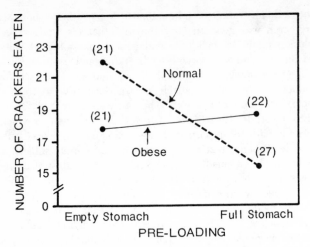

FIG. 9.1   The effects of preloading on eating.

epinephrine will inhibit gastric motility and increase blood sugar—both peripheral physiological changes associated with low hunger. These manipulations have no effects at all on obese subjects, but do affect the amounts eaten by normal subjects.

It seems clear that the set of bodily symptoms the subject labels "hunger" differs for obese and normal subjects. Whether one measures gastric motility as Stunkard did, or manipulates motility and the other physiological correlates of food deprivation, as I assume my students and I have done, one finds, for normal subjects, a high degree of correspondence between the state of the gut and eating behavior and, for obese subjects, virtually no correspondence.

Whether or not they are responsive to these particular visceral cues, the obese *do* eat, and the search for the cues that trigger obese eating occupied my students' and my attention for a number of years. Since the experimental details of this search have been published (Schachter, 1967, 1968, 1971), and I believe are fairly well known, I will take time now only to summarize our conclusions— eating by the obese seems unrelated to any internal, visceral state, but is determined by external, food-relevant cues such as the sight, smell, and taste of food. Now, obviously, such external cues to some extent affect anyone's eating behavior. However, for normals these external factors clearly interact with internal state. They may affect what, where, and how much the normal eats, but chiefly when he is in a state of physiological hunger. For the obese, I suggest, internal state is irrelevant, and eating is determined largely by external cues.

As you may know, there have been a number of experiments. testing this hypothesis about the external sensitivity of the obese. To convey some feeling for the nature of the supporting data, I will describe two typical experiments. In one of these, Nisbett (1968a) examined the effects of the sight of food. He reasoned that if the sight of food is a potent cue, the externally sensitive, obese person should eat just as long as food is in sight, and when, in effect, he has consumed all of the available cues, he should stop and make no further attempt to eat. In contrast, the amounts eaten by a normal subject should depend on his physiological needs, not on the quantity of food in sight. Thus, if only a small amount of food is in sight but the subject is given the opportunity to forage for more, the normal subject should eat more than the obese subject. In contrast, if a large amount of food is in sight, the obese should eat more than the normal subject.

To test these expectations, Nisbett provided subjects, who had not eaten lunch, with either one or three roast beef sandwiches. He told them to help themselves and, as he was leaving, pointed to a refrigerator across the room and said, "There are dozens more sandwiches in the refrigerator. Have as many as you want." His results are presented in Table 9.1. As you can see, obese subjects ate significantly more than normals when presented with three sandwiches, but ate significantly less than normals when presented with only one sandwich.

TABLE 9.1   EFFECT OF QUANTITY OF VISIBLE FOOD ON AMOUNTS EATEN

	NO. SANDWICHES	
SUBJECTS	One	Three
Normal	1.96	1.88
Obese	1.48	2.32

Note.—From Nisbett (1968a).

In another study, Decke (1971) examined the effects of taste on eating. She reasoned that taste, like the sight or smell of food, is essentially an external cue. Good taste, then, should stimulate the obese to eat more than normals, and bad taste, of course, should have the reverse effect.

In a taste test context, Decke provided her subjects with either a decent vanilla milk shake or with a vanilla milk shake plus quinine. The effects of this taste manipulation are conveyed in Table 9.2 where, as you can see, obese subjects drank more than normals when the milk shake was good and drank considerably less when the milk shake had been laced with quinine.

TABLE 9.2   EFFECT OF TASTE ON EATING

	OUNCES CONSUMED IN	
SUBJECTS	Good taste	Bad taste
Normal	10.6	6.4
Obese	13.9	2.6

Note.—From Decke (1971).

Now, anyone who sees Decke's milk shake data and who is familiar with physiological psychology will note that this is precisely what Miller, Bailey, and Stevenson (1950) found and what Teitelbaum (1955) found in the lesioned hyperphagic rat. For those of you who are unfamiliar with this preparation, let me review the facts about this animal. If you make bilateral lesions in the ventro-medial nuclei of the hypothalamus, you are likely to get an animal that will eat prodigious amounts of food and will eventually achieve monumental weight—a creature of nightmares. This has been demonstrated for rats, cats, mice, monkeys, rabbits, goats, dogs, and sparrows. Classic descriptions of these preparations portray an animal that immediately after the operation staggers over to its food hopper and shovels in food. For several weeks, this voracious eating continues, and there is, of course, very rapid weight gain. This is called the dynamic phase of hyperphagia. Finally, a plateau is reached, at which point the animal's weight levels off, and its food intake drops to a level only slightly above that of the normal animal. This is called the static phase. During both the static and the dynamic stages, the lesioned animal is also characterized as markedly inactive, and as irascible, emotional, and generally bitchy.

Now it turns out that though the lesioned animal is normally a heavy eater, if you add quinine to its food it drastically decreases its intake to levels far below that of a normal animal's whose food has been similarly tainted. On the other hand, if to its normal food you add dextrose, or lard, or something that is apparently tasty to a rat, the lesioned animal increases its intake to levels considerably above its regular intake and above the intake of a control rat whose food has also been enriched.

The similarity of these facts about the finickiness of the lesioned rat to Decke's findings in her milk shake experiment is, of course, striking, and many people (notably Nisbett, 1968a, 1970) have pointed to this and other similarities between our data on obese humans and the physiologist's data on the obese rat. In order to determine if there was anything more to this than an engaging, occasional resemblance between two otherwise remotely connected sets of data, Judith Rodin and I decided to treat the matter dead seriously and, where possible, to make a point-for-point comparison of every fact we could learn about the hypothalamic, obese rat with every fact we could learn about the obese human. Before describing the results of our work, I would like, however, to be sure that you are aware of the areas of my expertise. I am not a physiological psychologist. Though I am pretty sure that I've eaten a hypothalamus, I doubt that I've ever seen one. When I say something like "bilateral lesions of the ventromedial nuclei of the hypothalamus," you can be sure that I've memorized it. I make this personal confession because of the dilemma that Rodin, also a physiological innocent, and I faced in our work. Though we couldn't have succeeded, we attempted to read *everything* about the ventromedial lesioned rat. If you've ever made this sort of attempt, you may have been seized by the same despair as were we when it sometimes seemed as if there were no such thing as a fact that *someone* had not failed to confirm. (I include in this sweeping generalization, by the way, the apparent fact that a ventromedial lesion produces a hyperphagic, obese animal—see Reynolds, 1963, and Rabin and Smith, 1968.) And it sometimes seemed as if there were no such thing as an experiment which *someone* had not failed to replicate. Since I happen to have spent my college physics lab course personally disproving most of the laws of physics, I cannot say that I find this particularly surprising, but if one is trying to decide what is the fact, it is a depressing state of affairs. In our own areas of expertise, this probably isn't too serious a problem. Each of us in our specialities knows how to evaluate a piece of work. In a field in which you are not expert, you simply cannot, except in the crudest of cases, evaluate. If several experimenters have different results, you just don't know which to believe. In order to cope with this dilemma, Rodin and I decided to treat each of our facts in batting average terms. For each fact, I will inform you of the number of studies that have been concerned with the fact and the proportion of these studies that work out in a given direction. To be included in the batting average, we required only that a study present all or a substantial portion of its data, rather than report the author's impressions or present only the data of one or two presumably representative cases. I should also note that in all cases we have relied on the data and not on what the experimenter said about the data. It may seem silly to make this point explicit, but it is the case that in a few studies, for some perverse reason, the experimenter's conclusions simply have nothing to do with his data. Finally, I should note that in all comparisons of animal and human data, I will consider the data only for animals in the static phase of obesity, animals who, like our human subjects, are already fat. In general, however, the results for dynamic and static animals are quite similar.

As a shorthand method of making comparisons between studies and species, I shall throughout the rest of this article employ what we can call a Fat to Normal (F/N) ratio in which we simply get an index by dividing the magnitude of the effect for fat subjects by the magnitude of the effect for normal control subjects. Thus, if in a particular study the fat rats ate an average of 15 grams of food and normal rats ate 10 grams, the F/N ratio would be 1.50, indicating that the fat rats ate 50% more food than normal rats.

To begin our comparisons, let us return to the effects of taste on eating behavior. We know that fat human beings eat more of a good-tasting food than do normal human beings and that they eat less of bad-tasting food than do normals. The physiologists have done almost identical experiments to ours, and in Line 1 of Table 9.3 we can compare the effects of good-tasting food on lesioned animals and on men. You will notice on the left that Rodin and I found six studies on lesioned animals, in this case largely rats. Batting average: five of the six studies indicate that lesioned, static, obese animals eat more of a good-tasting food than do their normal controls. The average F/N ratio for these six studies is 1.45, indicating that fat rats on the average eat 45% more of good-tasting food than do normal rats. On the right side of the table, you can see that there have been two human studies, and that both of these studies indicate that fat humans eat more of good-tasting food than do normal humans. The average F/N ratio for humans is 1.42, indicating that fat human eat 42% more of good-tasting food than do normally sized humans.[2]

Incidentally, please keep in mind throughout this exercise that the left side of each table will always contain the data for lesioned animals, very largely rats, that have been abused by a variety of people named Epstein, and Teitlebaum, and Stellar, and Miller, and so on. The right side of each table will always contain the data for humans, mostly Columbia College students, nice boys who go home every Friday night, where, I suppose, they too are abused by a variety of people named Epstein, and Teitelbaum, and Stellar, and Miller.

In Line 2 of Table 9.3, we have the effects of bad taste on consumption. For both animals and men, in all of these studies bad taste was manipulated by the addition of quinine to the food. There are four animal studies; three of the four indicate that fat animals eat less than normal animals, and the average F/N ratio is .76. There are two human studies: one of the two indicates that fats eat considerably less bad food than normals; the other indicates no significant difference between the two groups, and the mean F/N ratio for these two studies .84. For this particular fact, the data are more fragile than one would like, but the trends for the two species are certainly parallel.

To continue this examination of parallel facts: the eating habits of the lesioned rats have been thoroughly studied, particularly by Teitelbaum and Campbell (1958). It turns out that static obese rats eat on the average slightly, not considerably, more than normal rats. They also eat fewer meals per day, eat more

TABLE 9.3 EFFECTS OF TASTE ON EATING

	ANIMALS		HUMANS	
CONDITION	Batting average	Mean F/N	Mean F/N	Batting average
Good food	5/6	1.45	1.42	2/2
Bad food	3/4	.76	.84	1/2

Note.—F/N = Fat to normal ratio.

per meal, and eat more rapidly than do normal animals. For each of these facts, we have parallel data for humans. Before presenting these data, I should note that for humans, I have, wherever possible, restricted myself to behavioral studies, studies in which the investigators have actually measured how much their subjects eat. I hope no one will be offended, I assume no one will be surprised, if I say that I am skeptical of the self-reports of fat people about how much they eat or exercise.[3] For those of you who feel that this is high-handed selection of studies, may I remind you of Stunkard's famous chronic fat patients who were fed everything that, in interviews, they admitted to eating daily, and who all steadily lost weight on this diet.

Considering first the average amount eaten per day when on ad-lib feeding of ordinary lab chow or pellets, you will note in Line 1 of Table 9.4 that consistently static obese rats eat somewhat (19%) more than do their normal counterparts. The data for humans are derived from all of the studies I know of in which eating is placed in a noshing, or ad-lib, context; that is, a bowl of ordinary food, usually nuts or crackers, is placed in the room, the experiment presumably has nothing to do with eating, and the subject is free to eat or not, as he chooses, just as is a rat in its cage. In two of the three experiments conducted in this context, obese subjects eat slightly more than do normals; in the third experiment, the two groups eat precisely the same number of crackers. For both humans and rats, then, the fat subject eats only slightly more than the normal subject.

Turning next to the number of meals per day, we note on Line 2 of Table 9.4 that for both rats and humans, fatter subjects consistently eat fewer meals per day. (A rat meal is defined by Teitelbaum and Campbell, 1958, as "any burst of

TABLE 9.4 EATING HABITS

	ANIMALS		HUMANS	
VARIABLE	Batting average	Mean F/N	Mean F/N	Batting average
Amount of food eaten ad lib	9/9	1.19	1.16	2/3
No. meals per day	4/4	.85	.92	3/3
Amount eaten per meal	2/2	1.34	1.29	5/5
Speed of eating	1/1	1.28	1.26	1/1

Note.—F/N = Fat to normal ratio.

food intake of at least five pellets separated by at least 5 min. from any other burst [p. 138].") For humans, these particular data are based on self-report or interview studies, for I know of no relevant behavioral data. In any case, again the data for the lesioned rat and the obese human correspond very closely indeed.

From the previous two facts, it should, of course, follow that obese subjects will eat more per meal than normal subjects, and, as can be seen in Line 3 of Table 9.4, this is the case for both lesioned rats and obese humans. The data for rats are based on two experiments that simply recorded the amount of food eaten per eating burst. The data for humans are based on all experiments in which a plate of food, usually sandwiches, is placed before a subject, and he is told to help himself to lunch or dinner.

Our final datum on eating habits is the speed of eating. Teitelbaum and Campbell (1958) simply recorded the number of pellets their animals ate per minute. Since there is nothing else to do when you are sitting behind a one-way screen watching a subject eat, Nisbett (1968b—data not reported in paper) recorded the number of spoonfuls of ice cream his subjects ate per minute. The comparison of the two studies is drawn in Line 4 of Table 9.4, where you will note an unsettling similarity in the rate at which lesioned rats and obese humans outspeed their normal counterparts.[4]

All told, then, in the existing literature, Rodin and I found a total of six items of behavior on which it is possible to make rather precise comparisons between lesioned rats and obese humans. These are mostly nonobvious facts, and the comparisons drawn between the two sets of experiments do not attempt to push the analogies beyond the point of common sense. I do not think there can be much debate about pellets versus spoonfuls of ice cream consumed per minute as equivalent measures of eating rate. For all six facts in the existing literature, the parallels between the species are striking. What the lesioned, fat rat does, the obese human does.

In addition to these facts, we identified two other areas of behavior in which it is possible to draw somewhat more fanciful, though still not ridiculous, comparisons between the species. These are the areas of emotionality and of activity. Though there has been little systematic study of emotionality, virtually everyone who has worked with these animals agrees that the lesioned animals are hyperexcitable, easily startled, overemotional, and generally bitchy to handle. In addition, work by Singh (1969) and research on active avoidance learning do generally support this characterization of the lesioned animal as an emotional beast.

For humans, we have two experiments from which it is possible to draw conclusions about emotionality. In one of these (Schachter et al., 1968), we manipulated fear by threat of painful electric shock. On a variety of rating scales, fat subjects acknowledged that they were somewhat more frightened and anxious than did normal subjects. In a second experiment, Rodin (1970) had her subjects listen to an audio tape while they were working at either a monitoring or a proofreading task. The tapes were either neutral (requiring the subject to think about either rain or seashells) or emotionally charged (requiring the subject to think about his own death or about the bombing of Hiroshima). The emotionally charged tapes produced dramatic differences between subjects. On a variety of rating scales, the obese described themselves as considerably more upset and disturbed than did normal subjects; they reported more palpitations and changes in breathing rate than did normals; and performance, at either the proofreading or monitoring tasks, deteriorated dramatically more for obese than for normal subjects.

Again, then, the data are consistent, for both the lesioned animal and the obese human seem to react more emotionally than their normal counterparts.

Finally, on activity, numerous studies using stabilimeter cages or activity wheels have demonstrated that the lesioned animal is markedly less active than the normal animal. This is not, I should add, a totally trivial fact indicating only that the lesioned animal has trouble shlepping his immense bulk around the cage, for the dynamic hyperphagic rat—who though not yet fat, will be—is quite as lethargic as his obese counterpart. On the human side, Bullen, Reed, and Mayer (1964) have taken movies of girls at camp during their scheduled periods of swimming, tennis, and volleyball. They categorize each camper for her degree of activity or exertion during these periods, and do find that the normal campers are more active than are the obese girls.

All told, then, Rodin and I found a total of eight facts, indicating a perfect parallel between the behavior of the lesioned rat and the obese human. We have, so far, found no fact on which the two species differ. Now all of this has proved such an engaging exercise that my students and I decided to play "real" scientist, and we constructed a matrix. We simply listed every fact we could find about the lesioned animals and every fact we could find about obese humans. I have told you about those facts for which parallel data exist. There are, however, numerous holes in the matrix—facts for rats for which no parallel human data have yet been collected, and vice versa. For the past year, we have been engaged in filling in these holes—designing for humans, experiments that have no particular rhyme or reason except that someone once did such an expriment on lesioned rats. For example, it is a fact that though lesioned rats will outeat normal rats when food is easily available, they will not lift a paw if they have to work to get food. In a Skinner box setup, Teitelbaum (1957) finds that at FR1, when one press yields one pellet, fat lesioned rats outpress normal. As the payoff decreases, however, fat rats press less and less until at FR256, they do not manage to get a single pellet during a 12-hour experimental session, whereas normal rats are still industriously pressing away. Similarly, Miller et al. (1950) found that though lesioned rats ate more than normal controls when an unweighted lid covered the food dish, they ate less than did the controls when a 75-gram weight was fastened to the lid. They also found that the lesioned rats ran more slowly down an alley to food than controls did and pulled less hard when temporarily restrained by a harness. In short, fat rats will not work to get food.

Since there was no human parallel to these studies, Lucy Friedman and I designed a study in which, when a subject arrived, he was asked simply to sit at the experimenter's desk and fill out a variety of personality tests and questionnaires. Besides the usual student litter, there was a bag of almonds on the desk. The experimenter helped herself to a nut, invited the subject to do the same, and then left him alone with his questionnaires and nuts for 15 minutes. There were two sets of conditions. In one, the nuts had shells on them; in the other, the nuts had no shells. I assume we agree that eating nuts with shells is considerably more work than eating nuts with no shells.

The top half of Table 9.5 presents for normal subjects the numbers who do and do not eat nuts in the two conditions. As you can see, shells or no shells has virtually no impact on normal subjects. Fifty-five percent of normals eat nuts without shells, and 50% eat nuts with shells. I am a little self-conscious about the data for obese subjects, for it looks as if I were too stupid to know how to fake data. I know how to fake data, and were I to do so, the bottom half of Table 9.5

TABLE 9.5 EFFECTS OF WORK ON THE EATING BEHAVIOR OF NORMAL AND FAT SUBJECTS

Nuts have	Number who	
	Eat	Don't eat
NORMAL SUBJECTS		
Shells	10	10
No shells	11	9
FAT SUBJECTS		
Shells	1	19
No shells	19	1

certainly would not look the way it does. When the nuts have no shells, 19 of 20 fat subjects eat nuts. When the nuts have shells on them, 1 out of 20 fat subjects eats. Obviously, the parallel to Miller's and to Teitelbaum's rats is perfect. When the food is easy to get at, fat subjects, rat or human, eat more than normals; when the food is hard to get at, fat subjects eat less than normals.

Incidentally, as a casual corollary of these and other findings, one could expect that, given acceptable food, fat eaters would be more likely than normals to choose the easiest way of eating. In order to check on this, Lucy Friedman, Joel Handler, and I went to a large number of Chinese and Japanese restaurants, categorized each patron as he entered the restaurant as obese or normal, and then simply noted whether he ate with chopsticks or with silverware. Among Occidentals, for whom chopsticks can be an ordeal, we found that almost five times the proportion of normal eaters ate with chopsticks as did obese eaters—22.4% of normals and 4.7% of the obese ate with chopsticks.

In another matrix-hole-filling experiment, Patricia Pliner (1970) has demonstrated that obese humans, like lesioned rats, do not regulate food consumption when they are preloaded with solids but, again like the rats, do regulate when they are preloaded with liquids.

In addition to these experiments, we are currently conducting studies on pain sensitivity and on passive versus active avoidance learning—all designed to fill in more holes in our human-lesioned rat matrix. To date, we have a total of 12 nonobvious facts in which the behaviors of lesioned rats parallel perfectly the behaviors of obese humans. Though I cannot believe that as our matrix-hole-filling experiments continue, this perfect parallelism will continue, I submit that even now these are mind-boggling data. I would also submit, however, that we have played this enchanting game just about long enough. This is, after all, science through analogy—a sport I recommend with the same qualifications and enthusiasms with which I recommend skiing—and it is time that we asked what on earth does it all mean? To which at this point I can only answer ruefully that I wish to God I really knew.

On its most primitive level, I suppose that I would love to play doctor and issue pronouncements such as, "Madam, you have a very sick hypothalamus." And, indeed, I do know of one case of human obesity (Reeves & Plum, 1969) accompanied by a precisely localized neoplasm that destroyed the ventromedial hypothalamus. This is an astonishing case study, for the lady reads like a lesioned rat—she ate immense amounts of food, as much as 10,000 calories a day, grew impressively fat and was apparently a wildly emotional creature given to frequent outbursts of laughing, crying, and rage. Now I am not, of course, going to suggest that this lady is anything but a pathological extreme. The only vaguely relevant study I know of is a morphological study (Maren, 1955) of the hypothalami of genetically obese mice, an animal whose behavior also resembles the lesioned rat's, which found no structural differences between obese and normal mice.

Mrosovsky (1971) has been developing a more sober hypothesis. Comparing the hibernator and the ventromedial lesioned rat, Mrosovsky has been playing much the same analogical game as have I, and he, too, has noted the marked behavioral similarities of his two species to the obese human. He hypothesizes that the unlesioned, obese animal, rodent or human, has a ventromedial hypothalamus that is functionally quiescent. Though I would be willing to bet that when the appropriate biochemical and electrophysiological studies are done, Mrosovsky will be proven correct, I do not believe that this is a fact which is of fundamental interest to psychologists. Most of us, I suspect, have long been convinced, psychodynamics notwithstanding, that there is *something* biologically responsible for human obesity, and to be able suddenly to point a finger at an offending structure would not really put us much ahead. After all, we've known about the adrenal medulla and emotion for more than 50 years, and I doubt that this particular bit of knowledge has been of much help in our understanding of aggression, or fear, or virtually any other emotional state.

If it is true that the ventromedial hypothalamus is functionally quiescent, for us the question must be, for what function, psychologically speaking, is it quiescent? What processes, or inputs, or outputs are mediated by this particular structure? Speculation and theorizing about the functions of this area have tended to be cautious and modest. Essentially, two suggestions have been made—one that the area is a satiety center, and the other that the area is an emotionality center. Both Miller (1964) and Stellar (1954) have tentatively suggested that the ventromedial area is a satiety center—that in some fashion it monitors the signals indicating a sufficiency of food and inhibits the excitatory (Eat! Eat!) impulses initiated in the lateral hypothalamus. This inhibitory-satiety mechanism can account for the hyperphagia of the lesioned animals and, consequently, for their obesity. It can also account for most of the facts that I outlined earlier about the daily eating habits of these animals. It cannot by itself, however, account for the finickiness of these animals, nor can it, as I believe I can show, account for the apparent unwillingness of these animals to work for food. Finally, this hypothesis is simply irrelevant to the demonstrated inactivity and hyperemotionality of these animals. This irrelevance, however, is not critical if one assumes, as does Stellar, that discrete neural centers, also located in the ventromedial area, control activity and emotionality. The satiety theory, then, can account for some, but by no means all, of the critical facts about eating, and it has nothing to say about activity or emotionality.

As a theoretically more ambitious alternative, Grossman (1966, 1967) has proposed that the ventromedial area be considered the emotionality center and that the facts about eating be derived from this assumption. By definition, Grossman's hypothesis accounts for the emotionality of these animals, and his own work on active avoidance learning certainly supports the emotionality hypothesis. I must confess, however, that I have difficulty in understanding just why these emotional animals become fat. In essence, Grossman (1966) assumes that "lesions in or near the VMH sharply increase an animal's affective responsiveness to apparently all sensory stimuli [p. 1]." On the basis of this general statement, he suggests that "the 'finickiness' of the ventromedial animal might then reflect a change in its affective response to taste." This could, of course, account for the fact that lesioned animals eat more very good- and less very bad-tasting food than do normals. However, I simply find it hard to believe that this affective hypothesis can account for the basic fact about these animals—that for weeks on end, the lesioned animals eat grossly more of ordinary, freely available lab chow.

Grossman (1967) attributes the fact that lesioned animals will not work for food to their "exaggerated response to handling, the test situation, the deprivation regimen, and the requirement of having to work for their daily bread [p. 358]." I suppose all of this is possible, I simply find it farfetched. At the very least, the response to handling and to the deprivation regime should be just as exaggerated whether the reinforcement schedule is FR1 or FR256 and the lesioned animals do press more than the normals at FR1.

My skepticism, however, is irrelevant, and Grossman may be correct. There are, however, at least two facts with which, it seems to me, Grossman's hypothesis cannot cope. First, it would seem to me that an animal with an affective response to food would be likely to eat more rather than less often per day, as is the fact. Second, it is simply common sense to expect that an animal with strong "affective responsiveness to all sensory stimuli" will be a very active animal indeed, but the lesioned animal is presumably hypoactive.

None of the existing theories, then, can cope with all of the currently available facts. For the remainder of this article, I am going to try my hand at developing a hypothesis that I believe can cope with more of the facts than can the available alternatives. It is a hypothesis that derives entirely from our work on human obesity. I believe, however, that it can explain as many of the facts about ventromedial-lesioned rats as it can about the human obese. If future experimental work on animals proves this correct, it would certainly suggest that science by analogy has merits other than its entertainment value.

The gist of our findings on humans is this—the eating behavior of the obese is under external, rather than internal, control. In effect, the obese seem stimulus-bound. When a food-relevant cue is present, the obese are more likely to eat and to eat a great deal than are normals. When such a cue is absent, the obese are less likely to try to eat or to complain about hunger. Though I have not, in this article, developed this latter point, there is evidence that, in the absence of food-relevant cues, the obese have a far easier time fasting than do normals, while in the presence of such cues, they have a harder time fasting (Goldman, Jaffa, & Schachter, 1968).

Since it is a little hard to believe that such stimulus-binding is limited to food-relevant cues, for some time now my students and I have been concerned with the generalizability of these facts. Given our starting point, this concern has led to some rather odd little experiments. For example, Judith Rodin, Peter Herman, and I have asked subjects to look at slides on which are portrayed 13 objects or words. Each slide is exposed for five seconds, and the subject is then asked to recall what he saw. Fat subjects recall more objects than do normal subjects. The experiment has been replicated, and this appears to be a reliable phenomenon.

In another study, Rodin, Herman, and I compared fat and normal subjects on simple and on complex or disjunctive reaction time. For simple reaction time, they are instructed to lift their finger from a telegraph key as soon as the stimulus light comes on. On this task, there are no differences between obese and normal subjects. For complex reaction time, there are two stimulus lights and two tele-graph keys, and subjects are instructed to lift their left finger when the right light comes on and lift their right finger when the left light comes on. Obese subjects respond more rapidly and make fewer errors. Since this was a little hard to be-lieve, this study was repeated three times—each time with the same results—the obese are simply better at complex reaction time than are normals. I do not pre-tend to understand these results, but they do seem to indicate that, for some reason, the obese are more efficient stimulus or information processors.

At this stage, obviously, this is shotgun research which, in coordination with the results of our eating experiments, seems to indicate that it may be useful to more generally characterize the obese as stimulus-bound and to hypothesize that any stimulus, above a given intensity level, is more likely to evoke an appro-priate response from an obese than from a normal subject.

Our first test of implications of this hypothesis in a noneating setting is Rodin's (1970) experiment on the effects of distraction on performance. She rea-soned that if the stimulus-binding hypothesis is correct, distracting, irrelevant stimuli should be more disruptive for obese than for normal subjects when they are performing a task requiring concentration. Presumably, the impinging stimu-lus is more likely to grip the attention of the stimulus-bound obese subject. To test this guess, she had her subjects work at a simple proofreading task. In one condition, the subjects corrected proof with no distractions at all. In the three other conditions, they corrected proof while listening to recorded tapes that varied in the degree to which they were likely to grip a subject's attention, and there-fore distract him. The results are presented in Figure 9.2, where, as you can see, the obese are better at proofreading when undistracted but their performance

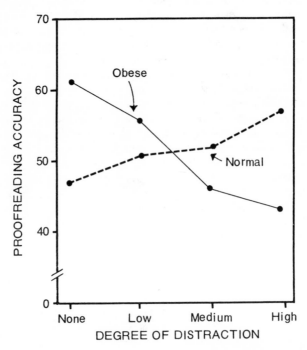

FIG. 9.2 The effects of distraction on performance (from Rodin, 1970).

seriously deteriorates as they are distracted until, at extreme distraction, they are considerably worse than normals. Rodin finds precisely the same pattern of results, by the way, in a similar study in which she uses the complex reaction time task I have already described rather than the proofreading task. For humans, then, there is evidence, outside of the eating context, to support the hypothesis.

Let us return to consideration of the ventromedial lesioned animal and examine the implications of the hypothesis that any stimulus, above a given intensity level, is more likely to evoke an appropriate response from a lesioned than from an intact animal. This is a hypothesis which is, in many ways, similar to Grossman's hypothesis and, on the face of it, would appear to be vulnerable to exactly the same criticisms as I have leveled at his theory. There are, however, crucial differences that will become evident as I elaborate this notion. I assume it is self-evident that my hypothesis can explain the emotionality of the lesioned animals and, with the exception of meal frequency—a fact to which I will return —can account for virtually all of our facts about the daily eating habits of these animals. I will, therefore, begin consideration of the hypothesis by examining its implications for those facts that have been most troubling for alternative formulations and by examining those facts that seem to most clearly contradict my own hypothesis.

Let us turn first to the perverse and fascinating fact that though lesioned animals will outeat normals when food is easily available, they simply will not work for food. In my terms, this is an incomplete fact which may prove only that a remote food stimulus will not evoke a food-acquiring response. It is the case that in the experiments concerned with this fact, virtually every manipulation of work has covaried the remoteness or prominence of the food cue. Food at the end of a long alleyway is obviously a more remote cue than food in the animal's food dish. Pellets available only after 256 presses of a lever are certainly more remote food stimuli than pellets available after each press of a lever. If the stimulus-binding hypothesis is correct, it should be anticipated that, in contrast to the results when the food cue is remote, the lesioned animal will work harder than the normal animal when the food stimulus is prominent and compelling. Though the appropriate experiment has not yet been done on rats, to my delight I have learned recently that such an experiment has been done on humans by William Johnson (1970), who independently has been pursuing a line of thought similar to mine.

Johnson seated his subject at a table, fastened his hand in a harness, and, to get food, required the subject for 12 minutes to pull, with his index finger, on a ringer that was attached by wire to a seven-pound weight. He received food on a VR50 schedule—that is, on the average, a subject received a quarter of a sandwich for every 50 pulls of the ring. Obviously, this was moderately hard work.

To vary stimulus prominence, Johnson manipulated food visibility and prior taste of food. In "food visible" conditions, he placed beside the subject one desirable sandwich covered in a transparent wrap. In addition, as the subject satisfied the VR requirements, he placed beside him quarter sandwiches similarly wrapped. In "food invisible" conditions, Johnson followed exactly the same procedures, but wrapped the sandwiches in white, nontransparent shelf paper. Subjects, of course, did not eat until they had completed their 12 minutes of labor.

As a second means of varying cue prominence, half of the subjects ate a quarter of a very good sandwich immediately before they began work. The remaining subjects ate a roughly equivalent portion of plain white bread.

In Figure 9.3, you can see the effects of these manipulations on effort. I

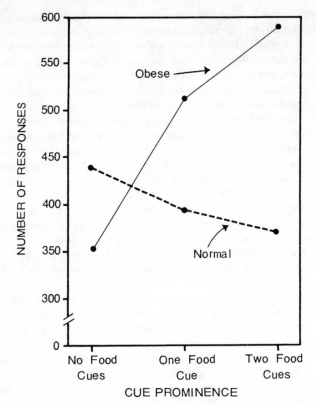

FIG. 9.3   The effect of food cue prominence on effort (from Johnson, 1970).

have arranged the conditions along the dimension of food cue prominence—ranging from no prominent food cues to two prominent food cues—that is, the subjects
ate a quarter sandwich and the food was visible. As you can see, the stimulus
prominence manipulations have a marked effect on the obese, for they work far
harder when the food cues are prominent and compelling than when they are in-
conspicuous. In contrast, cue prominence has relatively little effect on normal
subjects.

Please note also that these results parallel Miller's and Teitelbaum's results
with lesioned rats. When the food cues are remote, the obese human work less
hard for food than the normally sized human. The fact that this relationship flips
when the cues are prominent is, of course, a delight to me, and wouldn't it be
absorbing to replicate this experiment on lesioned rats?

Let us turn next to the fact that lesioned rats are hypoactive. If ever a
fact were incompatible with a hypothesis, this one is it. Surely an animal that is
more responsive to any stimulus should be hyper-, not hypoactive. Yet this is a
most peculiar fact—for it remains a fact only because one rather crucial finding
in the literature has been generally overlooked and because the definition of activity seems restricted to measures obtained in running wheels or in stabilimeter-type
living cages.

Studies of activity have with fair consistency reported dramatically less
activity for lesioned than for normal rats. With one exception, these studies report
data in terms of total activity per unit time, making no distinction between periods

when the animal room was quiet and undisturbed and periods involving the mild ferment of animal-tending activities. Gladfelter and Brobeck (1962), however, report activity data separately for the "43-hour period when the constant-temperature room was dark and quiet and the rats were undisturbed" and for the "five-hour period when the room was lighted and the rats were cared for [p. 811]." During the quiet time, these investigators find precisely what almost everyone else does—lesioned rats are markedly less active. During the animal-tending period, however, lesioned animals are just about as active as normal animals. In short, when the stimulus field is relatively barren and there is little to react to, the ventromedial animal is inactive; when the field is made up of the routine noises, stirrings, and disturbances involved in tending an animal laboratory, the lesioned animal is just about as active as the normal animal.

Though this is an instructive fact, it hardly proves my hypothesis, which specifies that above a given stimulus intensity the lesioned animal should be *more* reactive than the normal animal. Let us, then, ask—is there any evidence that lesioned animals are more active than normal animals? There is, if you are willing to grant that specific activities such as lever pressing or avoidance behavior are as much "activity" as the gross, overall measures obtained in stabilimeter-mounted living cages.

In his study of activity, Teitelbaum (1957) has distinguished between random and food-directed activity. As do most other investigators, he finds that in their cages, lesioned rats are much less active than are normals. During a 12-hour stint in a Skinner box, however, when on a FR1 schedule, the lesioned animals are more active; that is, they press more than do normals. Thus, when the food cue is salient and prominent, as it is on an FR1 schedule, the lesioned animal is very active indeed. And, as you know, when the food cue is remote, as it is on an FR64 or FR256 schedule, the lesioned animal is inactive.

Since lever pressing is activity in pursuit of food, I suppose one should be cautious in accepting these data as support for my argument. Let us turn, then, to avoidance learning where most of the experiments are unrelated to food.

In overall batting average terms,[5] no area could be messier than this one, for in three of six studies, lesioned animals are better and in three worse at avoidance than normals. However, if one distinguishes between passive and active avoidance, things become considerably more coherent.

In active avoidance studies, a conditioned stimulus, such as a light or buzzer, precedes a noxious event such as electrifying the floor grid. To avoid the shock, the animal must perform some action such as jumping into the nonelectrified compartment of a shuttle box. In three of four such studies, the lesioned animals learn considerably more rapidly than do normal animals. By this criterion, at least, lesioned animals are more reactive than normal animals.[6] Parenthetically, it is amusing to note that the response latencies of the lesioned animal are smaller (Grossman, 1966) than those of the normal animal, just as in our studies of complex reaction time, obese humans are faster than normal humans.

In contrast to these results, lesioned animals do considerably worse than normal animals in passive avoidance studies. In these studies, the animal's water dish or the lever of a Skinner box are electrified so that if, during the experimental period, the animal touches these objects he receives a shock. In both of the studies we have so far found on passive learning, the lesioned animals do considerably worse than normal animals. They either press the lever or touch the water dish more than do normals and accordingly are shocked far more often. Thus, when the situation requires a response if the animal is to avoid shock, the lesioned animal does better than the normal animal. Conversely, if the situation requires response quiescence if the animal is to avoid shock, the lesioned animal does far worse than the normal animal. This pair of facts, I suggest, provides strong support for the hypothesis that beyond a given stimulus intensity, the lesioned animal is more reactive than the normal animal. I would also suggest that without some variant of this hypothesis, the overall pattern of results on avoidance learning is incoherent.

All in all, then, one can make a case of sorts for the suggestion that there are specifiable circumstances in which lesioned animals will be more active. It is hardly an ideal case, and only an experiment that measures the effects of systematically varied stimulus field richness on gross activity can test the point.

These ruminations on activity do suggest a refinement of the general hypothesis and also, I trust, make clear why I have insisted on inserting that awkward phrase "above a given intensity level" in all statements of the hypothesis. For activity, it appears to be the case that the lesioned animal is less active when the stimulus is remote and more active when the stimulus is prominent. This interaction between reactivity and stimulus prominence is presented graphically in Figure 9.4. This is a formulation which I believe fits almost all of the available data, on both animals and men, remarkably well. It is also a formulation which for good ad-hoc reasons bears a striking resemblance to almost every relevant set of data I have discussed.

For human eating behavior, virtually every fact we have supports the assertion that the obese eat more than normals when the food cue is prominent and less when the cue is remote. In Johnson's study of work and cue prominence, the obese do not work as hard as normals when there are no prominent food cues, but work much harder when the food cues are highly salient. In Nisbett's one- and three-sandwich experiment, the obese subjects eat just as long as food cues are prominent—that is, the sandwiches are directly in front of the subject—but when these immediate cues have been consumed, they stop eating. Thus, they eat more than normals in the three-sandwich condition and less in the one-sandwich condition. We also know that the obese have an easy time fasting in the absence of food cues and a hard time in the presence of such cues, and so on.

About eating habits we know that the obese eat larger meals (what could be a more prominent cue than food on the plate?), but eat fewer meals (as they should if it requires a particularly potent food cue to trigger an eating response).

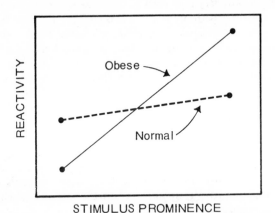

STIMULUS PROMINENCE

FIG. 9.4 Theoretical curves of relationship of reactivity to stimulus prominence.

Even the fact that the obese eat more rapidly can be easily derived from this formulation.

For rats, this formulation in general fits what we know about eating habits, but can be considered a good explanation of the various experimental facts only if you are willing to accept my reinterpretation, in terms of cue prominence, of such experiments as Miller et al.'s (1950) study of the effects of work on eating. If, as would I, you would rather suspend judgment until the appropriate experiments have been done on lesioned rats, mark it down as an engaging possibility.

Given the rough state of what we know about emotionality, this formulation seems to fit the data for humans and rats about equally well. The lesioned rats are vicious when handled and lethargic when left alone. In the Rodin (1970) experiment which required subjects to listen to either neutral or emotionally disturbing tapes, obese subjects described themselves (and behaved accordingly) as less emotional than normals when the tapes were neutral and much more emotional than normals when the tapes were disturbing.

All in all, given the variety of species and behaviors involved, it is not a bad ad-hoc hypothesis. So far there has been only one study deliberately designed to test some of the ideas implicit in this formulation. This is Lee Ross's (1969) study of the effects of cue salience on eating. Ross formulated this experiment in the days when we were struggling with some of the data inconsistent with our external-internal theory of eating behavior (see Schachter, 1967). Since the world is full of food cues, it was particularly embarrassing to discover that obese subjects ate less frequently than normals. Short of invoking denial mechanisms, such a fact could be reconciled with the theory only if we assumed that a food cue must be potent in order to trigger an eating response in an obese subject—the difference between a hot dog stand two blocks away and a hot dog under your nose, savory with mustard and steaming with sauerkraut.

To test the effects of cue prominence, Ross simply had subjects sit at a table covered with a variety of objects among which was a large tin of shelled cashew nuts. Presumably, the subjects were there to take part in a study of thinking. There were two sets of experimental conditions. In high-cue-saliency conditions, the table and the nuts were illuminated by an unshaded table lamp containing a 40-watt bulb. In low-saliency conditions, the lamp was shaded and contained a 7½-watt red bulb. The measure of eating was simply the difference in the weight of the tin of nuts before and after the subject thought his experimentally required thoughts. The results are presented in Figure 9.5, which, needless to say, though I will say it, bears a marked resemblance to our theoretical curves.

So much for small triumphs. Let us turn now to some of the problems of this formulation. Though I do not intend to detail a catalog of failings, I would like to make explicit some of my discomforts.

1. Though there has been no direct experimental study of the problem, it seems to be generally thought that the lesioned rat is hyposexual, which, if true, is one hell of a note for a theory which postulates superreactivity. It is the case, however, that gonadal atrophy is frequently a consequence of this operation (Brooks & Lambert, 1946; Hetherington & Ransom, 1940). Possibly, then, we should consider sexual activity as artifactually quite distinct from either gross activity or stimulus-bound activity such as avoidance behavior.

2. I am made uncomfortable by the fact that the obese, both human and rat, eat less bad food than do normals. I simply find it difficult to conceive of nonresponsiveness as a response. I suppose I could conceptually pussyfoot around

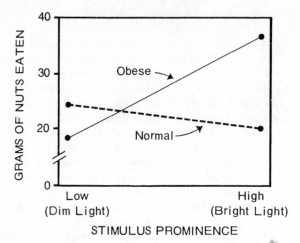

STIMULUS PROMINENCE

FIG. 9.5   The effects of stimulus intensity on amount eaten (from Ross, 1969).

this difficulty, but I cannot imagine the definition of response that would allow me to cope with both this fact and with the facts about passive avoidance. I take some comfort from the observation that of all of the facts about animals and humans, the fact about bad taste has the weakest batting average. It may yet turn out not to be a fact.

3. Though the fact that obese humans eat less often is no problem, the fact that obese rats also eat less often is awkward, for it is a bit difficult to see how food stimulus intensity can vary for a caged rat on an ad-lib schedule. This may seem farfetched, but there is some experimental evidence that this may be due to the staleness of the food. Brooks, Lockwood, and Wiggins (1946), using mash for food, demonstrated that lesioned rats do not outeat normals when the food is even slightly stale. Only when the food was absolutely fresh and newly placed in the cage did lesioned rats eat conspicuously more than normal rats. It seems doubtful, however, that this could be the explanation for results obtained with pellets.

4. As with food, one should expect from this formulation that the animal's water intake would increase following the lesion. There does not appear to have been much systematic study of the problem, but what data exist are inconsistent from one study to the next. Several studies indicate decreased water intake; at least one study (Krasne, 1964) indicates no change following the operation; and there are even rare occasional case reports of polydipsia. Possibly my interactional hypothesis can cope with this chaos, and systematically varying the salience of the water cue will systematically affect the water intake of the ventromedial animal. It is also possible that under any circumstance, water, smell-less and taste-less, is a remote cue.

There are, then, difficulties with this formulation. These may be the kinds of difficulties that will ultimately damn the theory, or at least establish its limits. Alternatively, these may mostly be apparent difficulties, and this view of matters may help us clarify inconsistent sets of data, for I suspect that by systematically varying cue prominence we can systematically vary the lesioned animal's reactivity on many dimensions. We shall see. Granting the difficulties, for the moment this view of matters does manage to subsume a surprisingly diverse set of facts about animals and men under one quite simple theoretical scheme.

Since I have presented this article as a more or less personal history of the development of a set of ideas, I would like to conclude by taking a more formal look at this body of data, theory, and speculation, by examining what I believe we now know, what seems to be good guesswork, and what is still out-and-out speculation.

1. With some confidence, we can say that obese humans are externally controlled or stimulus-bound. There is little question that this is true of their eating behavior, and evidence is rapidly accumulating that eating is a special case of the more general state.

I have suggested that stimulus prominence and reactivity are key variables in understanding the realms of behavior with which I have been concerned, and Figure 9.4 represents a first guess as to the nature of the differential functions involved for obese and normal humans. The specific shapes of the curves are, of course, pure guesswork, and the only absolute requirement that I believe the data impose on the theory is that there be an interaction such that at low levels of stimulus prominence, the obese are less reactive, and at high levels of prominence more reactive, than normals.

2. With considerably less confidence, I believe we can say that this same set of hypotheses may explain many of the differences between the ventromedial lesioned rat and his intact counterpart. This conclusion is based on the fact that so much of the existing data either fit or can be plausibly reinterpreted to fit these ideas. Obviously, the crucial experiments have yet to be done.

3. Finally, and most tentatively, one may guess that the obesity of rats and men has a common physiological locus in the ventromedial hypothalamus. I must emphasize that this guess is based *entirely* on the persistent and tantalizing analogies between lesioned rats and obese humans. There is absolutely no relevant independent evidence. However, should future work support this speculation, I suspect, in light of the evidence already supporting the stimulus-binding hypotheses, that we are in for a radical revision of our notions about the hypothalamus.

notes

1. The obese subject's failure to regulate when preloaded with sandwiches or some other solid food has now been replicated three times. Pliner's (1970) recent work, however, indicates that the obese will regulate, though not as well as normals, when preloaded with liquid food.

2. The technically informed reader undoubtedly will wish to know precisely which studies and what data are included in Tables 9.3 and 9.4. There are so many studies involved that, within the context of this paper, it is impossible to supply this information. Dr. Rodin and I are preparing a monograph on this work which will, of course, provide full details on such matters.

3. In three of four such self-report studies, fat people report eating considerably less food than do normals.

4. Fat rats do not drink more rapidly than do normals. There are no comparable data for humans.

5. Of all the behavioral areas so far considered, avoidance learning is probably the one for which it makes least sense either to adopt a batting average approach or to attempt to treat the research as a conceptually equivalent set of studies. Except in this area, the great majority of experiments have used, as subjects, rats with electrolytically produced lesions. In the avoidance learning area, the subjects have been mice, rats, and cats; the lesions are variously electrolytically produced, produced by gold thioglucose

injections, or are "functional" lesions produced by topical application of atropine or some other agent.

6. Reactive, yes, but what about activity in the more primitive sense of simply moving or scrambling about the experimental box? Even in this respect, the lesioned animals appear to outmove the normals, for Turner, Sechzer, and Liebelt (1967) report that,

> The experimental groups, both mice and rats, emitted strong escape tendencies prior to the onset of shock and in response to shock. Repeated attempts were made to climb out of the test apparatus. This group showed much more vocalization than the control group. . . . In contrast to the behavior of the experimental animals, the control animals appeared to become immobilized or to "freeze" both before and during the shock period. Thus, there was little attempt to escape and little vocalization [p. 242].

references

Brooks, C. McC., & Lambert, E. F. A study of the effect of limitation of food intake and the method of feeding on the rate of weight gain during hypothalamic obesity in the albino rat. *American Journal of Physiology*, 1946, *147*, 695–707.

Brooks, C. McC., Lockwood, R. A., & Wiggins, M. L. A study of the effect of hypothalamic lesions on the eating habits of the albino rat. *American Journal of Physiology*, 1946, *147*, 735–741.

Bullen, B. A., Reed, R. B., & Mayer, J. Physical activity of obese and nonobese adolescent girls appraised by motion picture sampling. *American Journal of Clinical Nutrition*, 1964, *14*, 211–223.

Cannon, W. B. *Bodily changes in pain, hunger, fear and rage.* (2nd ed.) New York: Appleton, 1915.

Carlson, A. J. *The control of hunger in health and disease.* Chicago: University of Chicago Press, 1916.

Decke, E. Effects of taste on the eating behavior of obese and normal persons. Cited in S. Schachter, *Emotion, obesity, and crime.* New York: Academic Press, 1971.

Gladfelter, W. E., & Brobeck, J. R. Decreased spontaneous locomotor activity in the rat induced by hopothalamic lesions. *American Journal of Physiology*, 1962, *203*, 811–817.

Goldman, R., Jaffa, M., & Schachter, S. Yom Kippur, Air France, dormitory food, and the eating behavior of obese and normal persons. *Journal of Personality and Social Psychology*, 1968, *10*, 117–123.

Grossman, S. P. The VMH: A center for affective reactions, satiety, or both? *International Journal of Physiology and Behavior*, 1966, *1*, 1–10.

Grossman, S. P. *A textbook of physiological psychology.* New York: Wiley, 1967.

Hetherington, A. W., & Ransom, S. W. Hypothalamic lesions and adiposity in the rat. *Anatomical Record*, 1940, *78*, 149–172.

Johnson, W. G. The effect of prior-taste and food visibility on the food-directed instrumental performance of obese individuals. Unpublished doctoral dissertation, Catholic University of America, 1970.

Krasne, F. B. Unpublished study cited in N. E. Miller, Some psycho-physiological studies of motivation and of the behavioural effects of illness. *Bulletin of the British Psychological Society*, 1964, *17*, 1–20.

Maren, T. H. Cited in J. L. Fuller & G. A. Jacoby, Central and sensory control of food intake in genetically obese mice. *American Journal of Physiology*, 1955, *183*, 279–283.

Miller, N. E. Some psycho-physiological studies of motivation and of the behavioural effects of illness. *Bulletin of the British Psychological Society*, 1964, *17*, 1–20.

Miller, N. E., Bailey, C. J., & Stevenson, J. A. F. Decreased "hunger" but increased food intake resulting from hypothalamic lesions. *Science*, 1950, *112*, 256–259.

Mrosovsky, N. *Hibernation and the hypothalamus.* New York: Appleton-Century-Crofts, 1971.

Nisbett, R. E. Determinants of food intake in human obesity. *Science*, 1968, *159*, 1254–1255. (a)

Nisbett, R. E. Taste, deprivation, and weight determinants of eating behavior. *Journal of Personality and Social Psychology*, 1968, *10*, 107–116. (b)

Nisbett, R. E. Eating and obesity in men and animals. In press, 1971.

Pliner, P. Effects of liquid and solid preloads on the eating behavior of obese and normal persons. Unpublished doctoral dissertation, Columbia University, 1970.

Rabin, B. M., & Smith, C. J. Behavioral comparison of the effectiveness of irritative and non-irritative lesions in producing hypothalamic hyperphagia. *Physiology and Behavior*, 1968, *3*, 417–420.

Reeves, A. G., & Plum, F. Hyperphagia, rage, and dementia accompanying a ventromedial hypothalamic neoplasm. *Archives of Neurology*, 1969, *20*, 616–624.

Reynolds, R. W. Ventromedial hypothalamic lesions with hyperphagia. *American Journal of Physiology*, 1963, *204*, 60–62.

Rodin, J. Effects of distraction on performance of obese and normal subjects. Unpublished doctoral dissertation, Columbia University, 1970.

Ross, L. D. Cue- and cognition-controlled eating among obese and normal subjects. Unpublished doctoral dissertation, Columbia University, 1969.

Schachter, S. The interaction of cognitive and physiological determinants of emotional state. In L. Berkowitz (Ed.), *Advances in experimental social psychology.* Vol. 1. New York: Academic Press, 1964.

Schachter, S. Cognitive effects on bodily functioning: Studies of obesity and eating. In D. C. Glass (Ed.), *Neurophysiology and emotion.* New York: Rockefeller University Press and Russell Sage Foundation, 1967.

Schachter, S. Obesity and eating. *Science*, 1968, *161*, 751–756.

Schachter, S. *Emotion, obesity, and crime.* New York: Academic Press, 1971.

Schachter, S., Goldman, R., & Gordon, A. Effects of fear, food deprivation, and obesity on eating. *Journal of Personality and Social Psychology*, 1968, *10*, 91–97.

Singh, D. Comparison of hyperemotionality caused by lesions in the septal and ventromedial hypothalamic areas in the rat. *Psychonomic Science*, 1969, *16*, 3–4.

Stellar, E. The physiology of motivation. *Psychological Review*, 1954, *61*, 5–22.

Stunkard, A., & Koch, C. The interpretation of gastric motility: I. Apparent bias in the reports of hunger by obese persons. *Archives of General Psychiatry*, 1964, *11*, 74–82.

Teitelbaum, P. Sensory control of hypothalamic hyperphagia. *Journal of Comparative and Physiological Psychology*, 1955, *48*, 156–163.

Teitelbaum, P. Random and food-directed activity in hyperphagic and normal rats. *Journal of Comparative and Physiological Psychology*, 1957, *50*, 486–490.

Teitelbaum, P., & Campbell, B. A. Ingestion patterns in hyperphagic and normal rats. *Journal of Comparative and Physiological Psychology*, 1958, *51*, 135–141.

Turner, S. G., Sechzer, J. A., & Liebelt, R. A. Sensitivity to electric shock after ventromedial hypothalamic lesions. *Experimental Neurology*, 1967, *19*, 236–244.

10

The Existential Neurosis

Salavatore R. Maddi

Social critics, philosophers, sociologists, and psychotherapists are raising the cry that alienation and the problems of existence form the sickness of our times. Even though a significant proportion of the statements has been vague and polemical, more and more people are hanging on every word. I do not think this is merely the new fad. There is too much insistence and desperation in people's attempts to understand the commentaries that have been made in some terms that will make a difference in their lives. It is too hard to overlook the evidence that people seeking psychotherapy do so in ever increasing numbers because they are deeply dissatisfied with the nature and bases of their living. It is too obvious that even those who do not seek psychotherapy often feel alone and empty.

Under the circumstances, the best thing serious students of the human condition can do is try for clarity and precision in thinking about alienation and the problems of existence. My task in this paper falls within this category of endeavor. What I will do is offer a model for the understanding of psychopathology and then use the model in ordering the various themes common in existential writings. Sometimes I will agree with writers in this field, and sometimes I will be reinterpreting their views. My basic aim in all this is to attempt to bring order and structure to an amorphous and complex literature in a way that clarifies the parts of it bearing on psychopathology and on mental health.

a model for neurosis

At the outset we need a model for neurosis that can serve as a heuristic device, a thread of Ariadne, lest we lose our way in the labyrinth of words that has been created. The model I suggest we adopt represents fairly standard thinking in the area, happily enough. It starts with the notion of a neurosis as a set of symptoms that can be distinguished not only from mental health but also from other psychopathological states. So the hysterical neurosis, for example, can be described as a set of cognitive and motor symptoms that are absent not only in the healthy state, but also in other classes of illness, like psychosis, and other neuroses, like obsessive-compulsiveness. When we discuss the existential neurosis, then, we will be searching for a set of relevant symptoms that are clearly different both from whatever we consider to be mental health and from other forms of psychopathology.

Reprinted from the *Journal of Abnormal Psychology*, 1967, Vol. 72, No. 4, pp. 311–325. Copyright 1967 by the American Psychological Association. Reprinted by permission.

Further, the model distinguishes between the neurosis itself and the premorbid personality out of which the neurosis may come through a process of breakdown. For example, if you are working within a psychoanalytic framework, you would say that the obsessive-compulsive neurosis represents the breakdown of the anal character type. While the anal character type bears some strong resemblances to the obsessive-compulsive neurosis (e.g., the reliance upon defense mechanisms of intellectualization, isolation, and undoing), the latter includes symptoms (e.g., obsessions and compulsions) that are considered pathological and that appear in only minimal form in the former. The premorbid personality is within the category of normality, though like the neurosis it can be distinguished from other types of premorbid personality. As there is an anal character type, so also are there phallic and oral character types. The differences between the premorbid personalities define predispositions to different kinds of neuroses. The significance of all this for discussion of the existential neurosis is that we will want to define a premorbid personality for which the neurosis itself is a believable breakdown product.

Premorbid personalities define predispositions to particular neurotic manifestations because they incorporate vulnerabilities to particular kinds of stress. The next aspect of the model, stress, is best considered to be something objectively describable, whether originating inside or outside the person, that represents a comprehensive enough threat to the personality to disrupt the premorbid balance or adjustment. Obviously, stress has to be defined with the characteristics of premorbid personality in mind. Loss of a strong loved one may be especially stressful to the person with an oral character, because in that character satisfaction of dependency is especially important for adequate functioning. Stress can be a sudden occurrence, or an accumulation of undermining events, as long as what is called stress is reasonably specifiable.

The model states that neurosis is some joint function of premorbidity and stress. Without attempting to state the exact nature of the function, some facets of the relationship are apparent. If there is zero stress, there should be no neurosis. Further, the amount of stress necessary to precipitate a neurosis should depend upon the intensity of the vulnerability constituted by the premorbid characteristics. But it should be kept in mind that the stress must match the nature of the vulnerability if undermining of the premorbid adjustment is to be possible. In considering the existential neurosis, I will try to identify the kinds of stress that are relevant, though it will be very difficult to make any qualitative statements about how much stress is too much.

Any model which involves the notion of premorbidity, or that which predisposes to illness, also involves the notion of what the ideal personality would be. What I am saying is not very mysterious or new. In psychoanalytic thinking, the ideal is genital personality, whereas in Rogerian thinking, the ideal is the fully functioning person. The ideal personality is usually a null class, which nonetheless has the very important theoretical function of permitting specification of what it is about the premorbid personality that predisposes to illness. In discussing the existential neurosis, we should expect to understand at least those aspects of the ideal personality that insure against the likelihood of that disorder. It may, in addition, be possible to gain an even more comprehensive sense than that of what is ideal.

The rest of the model refers to development. There is first ideal development, or that series of early life experiences that culminate in the ideal personality. Second, there is what might be called deviant development—a series of life experiences leading to premorbidity. It should be possible to specify the particular developmental deviancy that accounts for particular premorbid personalities. It will be important in this article to consider the developmental vicissitudes producing the premorbid state out of which the existential neurosis may come, and, in this consideration, a sense of what would be developmentally more ideal will necessarily be gained.

Without a doubt there are vexing questions that can be raised concerning this model. But rather than raise them here, let me encourage you to consider the general outlines of the model as no more than an interesting and plausible heuristic device. In that spirit, let us plunge in.

the symptoms called existential neurosis

Like all neuroses, we should expect the existential neurosis to have cognitive, affective, and actional components. Once we have accepted the heuristic notion that there are existential manifestations some of which are neurotic and some of which are not, we have already begun to find the road to clarity. The cognitive component of the existential neurosis is meaninglessness, or chronic inability to believe in the truth, importance, usefulness, or interest value of any of the things one is engaged in or can imagine doing. The most characteristic features of affective tone are blandness and boredom, punctuated by periods of depression which become less frequent as the disorder is prolonged. As to the realm of action, activity level may be low to moderate, but more important than amount of activity is the introspective and objectively observable fact that activities are not chosen. There is little selectivity, it being immaterial to the person what if any activities he pursues. If there is any selectivity shown, it is in the direction of ensuring minimal expenditure of effort and decision making.

It is important to recognize that the syndrome described above refers to a chronic state of the organism. I do not refer to stabs of doubt, in the cognitive domain, or occasional indifference and passivity, in the affective and actional domains. Rather, I refer to the settled state of meaninglessness, apathy, and aimlessness, such that contradictory states of commitment, enthusiasm, and activeness are the exception rather than the rule. The temporary state of doubt, though an existential manifestation, is not here defined as part of the existential neurosis. Indeed, doubt is a by-product of vigorous mental health, I shall argue later, no matter how painful it may be.

If my model is to be served, the existential neurosis must be distinguished from other forms of illness. I take it that the obviousness of its difference from such psychotic states as schizophrenia and senile psychosis, such character disorders as homosexuality and psychopathy, and such neuroses as obsessive-compulsiveness and hysteria, is clear without further attention. Of the traditional states of psychopathology, the existential neurosis probably most nearly resembles neuraesthenia and depression. It is from these two disorders that distinctions are important. The major difference between neuraesthenia and the existential neurosis is that the dreadful lack of energy and somatic decreptitude of the former is not present in the latter. There is certainly listlessness in existential neurosis, but it is not experienced as a primarily somatic disability. In addition, the cognitive state of meaninglessness is virtually absent in neuraesthenia.

The distinction between depression and the existential neurosis is harder to make, specifically because the latter state sometimes includes sadness, and usually includes low activity level. But in existential neurosis, depressive affect is the exception rather than the rule, with apathy—an actual absence of strong emotion—being the usual state. Apathy is not typical of depression, though it may occur occasionally in that disorder. In traditional terms, what I am calling the existential neurosis might actually be called depression, but this would involve an unwarranted stretching of the latter concept, taking some such form as inferring depressive affect hidden by defenses such that apathy was the visible resultant. But once we have decided that traditional terminology is not necessarily exhaustive in describing psychopathology, the syndrome I have called the existential neurosis is very likely to emerge as discriminably different from depression.

The way I have defined it, the existential neurosis is characterized by the belief that one's life is meaningless, by the affective tone of apathy and boredom, and by the absence of selectivity in actions. This symptom cluster is, to judge from the writing of many psychotherapists, sociologists, and social critics (e.g., Fromm, 1955; Josephson & Josephson, 1962; May, Angel, & Ellenberger, 1958; Sykes, 1964), rampant in contemporary life. It may seem as if what I am talking about as existential neurosis is much closer to alienation from self, than it is to alienation from society. But on reflection, it should be clear that the existential neurotic would be separated from deep interaction with others as well as from his own personal vitality. Therefore, I find the existential neurotic to be alienated both from self and from society. Indeed, the notions of self-alienation and societal alienation represent little more to me than biases reflecting whether the theorist considers the individual or the group to be the most important unit of analysis.

Nonetheless, it is true that traits sometimes considered under the rubric of alienation are not covered by my definition of the existential neurosis. Such things as anguish, rebelliousness, acute dissatisfaction, and civil disobedience are sometimes considered evidence of alienation. Alienation in such cases is usually taken to be from society and not at all from self. First, I should affirm that such traits are not to be considered part of the existential neurosis. The symptoms of the neurosis all point to a rather comprehensive psychological death, where there is no longer even anguish or anger to remind the person that he is a person, and a very dissatisfied one at that. But what can be said in understanding these traits that I have excluded? Sometimes, what is meant is doubt of the kind that I will later argue is quite healthy. Even when this is not the case, I have difficulty understanding why the traits are considered evidence of alienation in the first place. After all, a person acutely dissatisfied with society, and actively trying to change it through his own actions, is hardly alienated in any important sense. He is accepting the importance of society by the stance that it is worth changing, and feeling perhaps even more powerfully than most of us that he can produce a change. There is little here of the meaninglessness and powerlessness that are supposed to characterize alienation. The person with these traits may well have some psychological malady, but unless his social protest masks an underlying tendency toward meaninglessness, apathy, and aimlessness, the malady bears little relationship to either existential neurosis or what has been called alienation.

The character of Meursault in Camus' (1946) *The Stranger* is a perfect example of the existential neurotic. He frequently says, and even more frequently implies, that he believes life to be meaningless and his activities to be arbitrary. He is virtually always bored and apathetic. He never imagines or daydreams. He has no goals. He makes only the most minimal decisions, doing little more than is necessary to keep a simple job as a clerk. He walks in his mother's funeral cortege and makes love to a woman with the same apathy and indifference. He frequently says, "It's all the same to me." His perceptions are banal and colorless. The most difference anything makes is to be mildly irritating. He has this reaction, for example, to the heat of the sun, but then does nothing about it. Although it might seem remarkable that a novel about such a person could have any literary power at all, it is precisely because of the omnipresence of the symptom cluster we have been calling existential neurosis that the reader is intrigued and shocked. When Meursault finally murders a man without any emotional provocation or reaction, without any premeditation or reason, without any greater decision than is involved in resolving to take a walk, the reader is not even surprised. Anything is possible for Meursault, specifically because nothing is anything of importance. His is a vegetative existence that amounts to psychological death. Some writers have called this a state of nonbeing (e.g., May et al., 1958; Sartre, 1956).

the premorbid personality

Turning to the premorbid personality out of which the existential neurosis can come through a process of breakdown precipitated by appropriate stress, I find that the concept of central importance is that of *identity*. I define identity in phenomenological terms, as that which you consider yourself to be. Although a person's identity is not necessarily expressed in verbal terms at any given time, it can be so stated if the person reflects upon the question of what he thinks he is. In focusing upon identity, therefore, I am not implying something that is barred from awareness.

Theorists having recourse to this kind of concept of identity or self have frequently considered of importance the discrepancy between one's sense of identity and one's natural potentialities as a human being. In following that lead, I would say that the premorbid personality corresponding to the existential neurosis is one in which the identity includes only some of the things that express the true nature of man. I will not discuss the true nature of man until the section of this paper on the ideal personality. It will suffice for initial purposes to say that the premorbid identity can be considered overly *concrete* and *fragmentary*. These are certainly ideas that are, in one form or another, common enough in the existential literature (e.g., Fromm, 1955; Kierkegaard, 1954; May et al., 1958). But to say this and nothing more is to fall short of the precision really necessary for adequate understanding of the etiology of existential neurosis. We must ask in what ways is the premorbid identity overly concrete and fragmentary?

The best way to summarize the problem is that the premorbid identity stresses qualities of man that are, among those he has, the ones least unique to him both as opposed to other species and to other men. In other words, the identity is insufficiently humanistic. For our society at this point in time, it is easy to say what an insufficiently humanistic identity looks like. Such an identity leads the person to consider himself to be nothing more than *a player of social roles and an embodiment of biological needs*. I must stress that the difficulty is not so much that man is not these two things, but that what he is in addition to them finds little representation in identity. Considering yourself to be an embodiment of biological needs certainly does not set you apart from other species. Neither does the view of yourself as a player of social roles, for most subhuman species have social differentiation of at least a rudimentary sort. And there is little in either of the two components of identity that permits much sense of difference between individual men, except in the trivial sense that the particular social roles played this moment may be different for me than for you, and the biological needs that I have right now may happen to be different than those you have. But tomorrow, or an hour from now, the situation may change, and we may not even have that small basis for distinguishing ourselves from one another. The overarching fact of life for a person with the premorbid personality I have described is that all men play a small number of social roles and all men embody a few biological needs, and that is that.

Consider what it means to view yourself as a player of social roles. First, you accept the idea that the social system—a set of interrelated institutions operating according to a different group of laws than those that govern individual existence—is a terribly real and important force in living. Second, you believe that the way you presently perceive the social system and have been taught it to be is its real and unchangeable nature. Finally, you consider it not only inevitable, but proper, that you conform to the pressures of the social system. A major aim in life becomes playing the roles that are necessarily yours as well as you can.

Also imagine what it means to consider yourself an embodiment of biological needs. First, you believe that such needs as that for food, water, and sex are terribly important and real forces in living. Second, you are convinced that an important gauge of the adequacy of the life is the degree to which these needs are satisfied. Finally, you believe that any alternative to direct expression of these needs, if an alternative were possible, would be unwise because it would constitute a violation of the true nature of man. All this means that a major aim in life becomes biological survival and satisfaction.

A person who has only these two themes represented in his identity would feel powerless in the face of social pressures from without, and powerless in the face of biological pressures from within. Both social and biological pressures would be considered independent variables, that is, variables that influence the behavior of the person without themselves being influenced by him. Naturally he tries to play his social roles well and to insure physical satisfaction and survival. Indeed, he *is* his social roles and biological needs. In other words, his identity is overly concrete. The goals of serving social roles and biological needs often lead in different, if not incompatible, directions. Generally speaking, the person will try to serve social and biological pressures at different times, or in different places, keeping possible incompatibilities from the eyes of others and from direct confrontation in his own awareness. In other words, this kind of identity is overly fragmentary.

For vividness, consider further the cognitive and affective state of the person with the premorbid personality under discussion. In the cognitive realm, the person would be rather consistently pragmatic and materialistic in his outlook on life. The pragmatism would come primarily from accepting the necessity of playing certain social roles. How often one hears that the world is the way it is, so one might as well be practical about it! The materialism would come primarily from the view that man is an embodiment of biological needs. The pursuit of material things is given the status of a natural process. How often one hears that narrow self-interest is the only real motivating force outside of society! Superimposed upon the fairly consistent pragmatism and materialism would be more transitory states of fatalism, cynicism, and pessimism. These transitory cognitive states would presumably mirror the moment-to-moment economy of social system and biological rewards and punishments. There is a final implication contained in the premorbid personality that is extremely important. If you consider yourself bound by certain rules of social interaction, on the one hand, and in need of certain material goods for satisfaction and survival, on the other hand, relationships between yourself and other people will be made on contractual grounds, rather than on the grounds of tradition or intimacy. The person with a premorbid personality will tend to look upon relationships as serving some specific social or biological end. His view of relationship will be rather cold-blooded.

Turning to the affective realm, the person with a premorbid identity would tend to worry about such things as whether he is considered by others to be conscientious, whether he is seen to be a nice person, whether he is admired, whether people can guess the animal lusts within him, whether he can satisfy his needs without interfering too much with social role playing. His predominant affective states would be fear and anxiety, and these would be only aggravated by the frequent incompatibility between serving other-directed social aims and self-interested biological aims. The other affective states typical of the premorbid state stem from the continual emphasis upon contractual relationships. Since relationships are defined in terms of limited, specific goals, and in terms of the economic considerations of who is getting what out of interaction, social life will be rather structured and superficial. Contractual relationships are devoid of intimacy, commitment, and spontaneity because of the preemptiveness of role playing and need expression. Thus, important affective states associated with premorbidity would be loneliness and disappointment. On the one hand, the person feels anxious and afraid a good deal of the time, while on the other hand, he feels alone and as if something were missing from his life.

You will have recognized in the discussion of the premorbid personality many of the features common in writings on alienation. There is much in what I have said that is reminiscent of Fromm's (1955) marketing personality and Sartre's (1956) idea of bad faith, to name only two sources. I want to encourage you to think of the premorbid personality not as a sickness in itself, but rather as a predisposition to sickness of an existential sort. What I have described as premorbidity is simply too common and livable to be considered frank neurosis, though it is a state with its own characteristic sufferings and limitations. The premorbid person is still too much enmeshed in the problems of his living, still too much concerned with having a successful life, to be considered existentially neurotic, given the implications of detachment from life included in that idea.

precipitating stress

For the person with a premorbid identity, life may go on in a rather empty, though superficially adequate, way for a long time. He may even be reasonably successful in objective terms, keeping his vague dissatisfactions and anxieties to himself. But he may also be precipitated into an existential neurosis if he encounters stress of the right content and sufficient intensity to be undermining.

The stresses that will be effective are those that have content that strikes at the vulnerabilities inherent in defining yourself as nothing more than a player of social roles and an embodiment of biological needs. The stronger this self-definition the weaker can the stress be and still produce breakdown. In speaking of precipitating stress, I do not mean the things that merely make the person worry. The threats of social censure or biological deprivation are potent sources of concern for the premorbid personality we are discussing, but these things do not ordinarily cause the kind of comprehensive breakdown involved in the existential neurosis. *The stresses that can produce the neurosis are ones that disconfirm the premorbid identity by forcing recognition of its overly concrete, fragmentary, and nonhumanistic nature.*

Three stresses come readily to mind, though there are bound to be others as well. Perhaps the most effective of them is the concrete threat of imminent death. It is my impression that this threat must be to your own life in order to be very effective. Even the threatened death of someone reasonably close to you may not have the force I am about to describe. Perhaps those of you who have faced the threat of death to yourself and to others will know what I mean. If the threat of death actually does lead to death, people with the premorbid identity tend to die *The Death of Ivan Ilych*, in the great novella by Tolstoi (1960). Ilych knows he is dying of a horrible disorder, and this colors all his perceptions and judgments. Most of the visitors to his bedside are business associates who, he comes to realize, are only performing what they experience as a distasteful obligation of their social role. Then he realizes that the same thing is true of his own family! None of these people is deeply touched by his drift toward death, for theirs is a contractual rather than intimate relationship to him. And even more horrible, he realizes the appropriateness of their behavior because he too has thought of and experienced them only in contractual, superficial terms. The triviality and superficiality of their materialism and social conformity—and his own —are thrown into sharp relief by the threat of death. He becomes acutely aware of his wasted life and can tell himself nothing that will permit a peaceful death. He realizes that he has always felt deprived of intimacy, love, spontaneity, and enthusiasm. By renouncing himself and the people around him, he is finally able to feel truly human and alive just at the point where he dies physically. This story is didactically and literarily powerful because this is a tragic way to die. What bankruptcy when it is death that frees us from the impoverishing shackles of social conformity and biological needs!

If the person with a premorbid identity who is faced with the threat of imminent death should actually recover rather than die he is likely to experience an existential neurosis. Before he dies, Ilych is certainly a good example of this. If the threat of death disconfirms your previous identity, then you have no identity to work with, and in an adult this is virtually the same as psychological death. The adequacy of recovery from the existential neurosis will be determined by whether the person can use, or be helped to use, the knowledge gained through facing death to build a more comprehensive, abstract, humanistic identity.

The second stress that can precipitate existential neurosis is gross disruption of the social order, through such things as war, conquest, and economic depression, leading to disintegration of social roles and even of the institutionalized mechanisms for satisfying biological needs. Such catastrophe has two effects on people with the premorbid identity. First, it makes it difficult to continue to obtain the usual rewards for playing social roles and expressing biological needs. Second, and more important, disruption of the social order demonstrates the relativity of society to someone who has been treating it as absolute reality. The premorbid person is left without much basis for living and an existential neurosis may well ensue. Thinking along very similar channels, Durkheim (1951) saw social upheaval, or anomie, as a factor increasing suicide rates.

The final stress is difficult to describe because it is less dramatic than threat of death and social upheaval. Not only is this stress less dramatic, but it is usually an accumulation of events rather than something that need happen only once. And yet, this final stress is probably the most usual precipitating factor in the existential neurosis. The stress I mean is the repeated confrontation with the limitation on deep and comprehensive experiencing produced by the premorbid identity. These confrontations usually come about through other people's insistence on pointing out the person's existential failures. The aggressive action of other people is more or less necessary because the person with the premorbid identity usually avoids self-confrontation. But let there be a close relative who is suffering because of the person's premorbidity and confrontations will be forced.

A good example of this kind of stress and its effects is to be found in Arthur Miller's (1964) *After the Fall*. During the first two-thirds of the play, Quentin discovers that his is what I would call a premorbid identity. The discovery is a terribly painful stress. It begins when his first wife, working up the courage for a separation and divorce, tries, after a long period of docility, to force him to recognize the limitations in their relationship and her deep dissatisfaction with him. In listening to his own attempts to answer her charges, and in considering her attacks, he begins to recognize that his has been little more than a contractual commitment to her. He has been merely conforming to social roles in being husband and father. Under her scrutiny, he begins to recognize his superficial sexuality—a biological need—as well. He feels at fault for his limitations, but can do little about them, instead asking pathetically for understanding. His wife is also important in forcing recognition that his offer to defend his old law professor in court is not out of deep affection, or intimacy, or even loyalty, but rather out of an attempt to convince people that he feels these ways toward this man. Frightened and distraught by what he is learning about himself, Quentin finally begins to envy his wife for her ability to experience deeply and know what she wants.

After the breakup of his first marriage, Quentin moves impulsively into a second. His second wife, Maggie, idealizes him, and he feels reassured about himself, though he has not really changed much. It is only after they have been married for some time that Quentin begins to appreciate Maggie's extraordinary neediness and lack of differentiation as a person. Her adulation of him can no longer serve to reassure him, and to make matters worse, he has new evidence of his superficiality in his inability to reach her in any significant way. He must stand by and let her commit suicide, having decided that the most he can do is to save his own life! Whatever depth of personality could have saved her in a husband, he simply did not have.

After Maggie's death, Quentin spends 2 years or so in a state of meaninglessness, apathy, and aimlessness. He does not work, he does not relate to people, he merely drifts. This period is clearly one of existential neurosis, and can be seen as precipitated by a person's being forced repeatedly to confront the limitations on living produced by social conformity and expression of biological need.

the ideal personality

From the discussion of the premorbid personality, it will come as no surprise that the ideal identity from my point of view is abstract, unified, and humanistic. I would remind you of Emerson's (Atkinson, 1940) elegant plea for such an identity at the beginning of *The American Scholar*:

It is one of those fables which out of an unknown antiquity convey an unlooked-for wisdom, that the gods, in the beginning, divided Man into men, that he might be more helpful to himself; just as the hand was divided into fingers, the better to answer its end.

The old fable covers a doctrine ever new and sublime; that there is One Man—present to all particular men only partially, or through one faculty; and that you must take the whole society to find the whole man. Man is not a farmer, or a professor, or an engineer, but he is all. Man is priest, and scholar, and statesman, and producer, and soldier. In the *divided* or social state these functions are parcelled out to individuals, each of whom aims to do his stint of the joint work, whilst each other performs his. The fable implies that the individual, to possess himself, must sometimes return from his own labor to embrace all the other laborers. But, unfortunately, this original unit, this fountain of power, has been so distributed to multitudes, has been so minutely subdivided and peddled out, that it is spilled into drops, and cannot be gathered. The state of society is one in which the members have suffered amputation from the trunk, and strut about so many walking monsters—a good finger, a neck, a stomach, an elbow, but never a man.

Man is thus metamorphosed into a thing, into many things. The planter, who is Man sent out into the field to gather food, is seldom cheered by any idea of the true dignity of his ministry. He sees his bushel and his cart, and nothing beyond, and sinks into the farmer, instead of Man on the farm. The tradesman scarcely ever gives an ideal worth to his work, but is ridden by the routine of his craft, and the soul is subject to dollars. The priest becomes a form; the attorney a statute-book; the mechanic a machine; the sailor a rope of the ship.

In this distribution of functions the scholar is the delegated intellect. In the right state he is *Man Thinking*. In the degenerate state, when the victim of society, he tends to become a mere thinker, or still worse, the parrot of other men's thinking [pp. 45–46].

This quote criticizes concretizations (e.g., when a man is a farmer, instead of man on the farm) and fragmentation (e.g., one can find a good finger, neck, etc., but never a man), and implies that the antidote to this ill is humanistic in nature (e.g., note the capitalization of man). Rousing and emotionally convincing though Emerson is, he does not give us a theory of man that makes this ideal identity rationally understandable. I shall try to present the rough outlines of such a theory, which is based on Emerson's intuitive lead and the writings of many other people concerned with the problems of existence.

First, let us assume that there are three sides to man's nature—social, biological, and psychological. The social side refers to interpersonal relationships, the biological side to physical survival and satisfaction, and the psychological side to mental processes, primarily symbolization, imagination, and judgment. Assume further that all three sides are of equal importance for successful living, and that curtailment of expression of any of them sets up some kind of premorbidity.

When you express your psychological side fully and vigorously, you generate symbols that represent concrete experiences in the general form that makes clear their similarities to and differences from other experiences. You also have an active and uninhibited imagination, which you use as a guide rather than substitute for action. In other words, you let your imagination reveal what you want your life to be, and then attempt to act on that knowledge. The psychological faculty of judgment functions as a check upon the validity of your imagination. When you act upon imagination, you can evaluate the nature of your ensuing experience in order to determine whether it is really what you seem to want. Does the action lead to satisfaction, or is it frightening or boring? Hence the knowledge gained through exercising judgment is also used as a guide to living.

Of the psychological, biological, and social sides of man, it is the psychological side that is most human. All subhuman species have biological requirements for survival and satisfaction, and these requirements are generally acted upon in a straightforward and simple manner. Most subhuman species have patterned social relationships. Indeed, sometimes subhuman society is quite complex and extensive. But even then it tends to be rigidly organized and characterized by social roleship. Only in man is it reasonable to consider the psychological side of life to be of much importance. Indeed, when social and biological behavior is unusually subtle and complex in man it is because of his most human, or psychological, side.

Let me make my position more vivid by contrasting the lives of people with premorbid and ideal identities. Whereas both premorbid and ideal identities involve expression of the social and biological sides of man, only the ideal identity shows much representation of the psychological side. Because the premorbid person does not have available to him the generalizing, unifying, humanizing effect of psychological expression, encompassing as it does symbolization, imagination, and judgment, he achieves only the most obvious, common, superficial forms of social and biological expression. He accepts social roles as given, tries to play them as well as he can, and sees himself quite literally as the roles he plays. He accepts biological needs as given and acts on them in a way that is isolated and unreflective, however straightforward it may be. The best example of such biological expression is with regard to the sexual need. The premorbid person considers sexuality to be no more than an animalistic urge, and satisfies it as simply as possible, with little consideration of relationship, affection, or even comprehensiveness of attraction. Little wonder that though he seems very social, he frequently feels insecure, lonely, and without intimacy, and that though he seems very active in expressing biological needs, he frequently feels incompletely satisfied. The loneliness and incomplete satisfaction are signs that he is deprived of psychological expression.

As the premorbid person does not rely upon the processes of symbolization, imagination, and judgment, favoring instead the view that life is determined by social and biological considerations, he not only feels powerless to influence his actions, but also does indeed lead an existence that is rather stereotyped and unchanging. As no human being is completely without psychological expression, the premorbid person often has a glimmer of awareness that his life is not what it might be. This accumulated sense of missed opportunity is what May et al. (1958, pp. 37-91) have called ontological guilt.

With vigorous psychological expression, would come social and biological living that is more unified, subtle, deep, and rewarding than that I have described above. The person with the ideal identity would not feel powerless in the face of social and biological pressures, because he puts heavy reliance in living on his own processes of symbolization, imagination, and judgment. He would perceive many alternatives to simple role playing and isolated biological satisfaction. Because he seems himself to be the "fountain of power," to use Emerson's excellent phrase, his social and biological living transcend the concrete instance and involve anything that he can imagine and anything that is evaluated by him as worthwhile.

So, if contractual relationships leave him unsatisfied, he can choose to relate otherwise, such as on the basis of shared personal experience. He can even make a start on this by talking with others about his dissatisfaction with merely playing social roles. Once he does this, he will undoubtedly find some people who will be encouraged to share their own feelings of loneliness with him, and the road to more subtle, myriadly rewarding social relations has already been found. If simple, unreflective expression of biological urges leaves him unsatisfied, he can choose to explore other forms of expression. For example, instead of merely seeking food, he can make hunger the basis for more comprehensive satisfaction by cooking especially tasty dishes, or by eating in the company of people with whom he feels intimate. And the same with sex. He can make sexual expression a subtle, complex, changing thing, indulged in with people toward whom he feels intimate and affectionate on other than simply sexual grounds. There will be many more parts to the life of the person with an ideal identity, and the parts will achieve much closer integration than is true for the premorbid person.

One important consequence of reliance upon his imagination and judgment as guides to living is that the ideal person is not a conformist. Some critics of my position would argue that it amounts to advocating the unleashing of monsters on the world. What is to stop a person from murdering, or robbing, if he feels so free to put his imagination into operation? Psychologists like Rogers (1961) would answer this criticism by contending that there is nothing basic to the organism that would lead in the direction of such monstrosities. As the individual is oriented toward survival, so too does his natural functioning support the survival of his species. One can easily develop an evolutionary argument for this position. Rogers would believe that only an imagination already perverted by psychopathogenic social pressures would lead the person in the direction of terrible aggressions toward his fellow men. I have considerable sympathy for this position, but would like to add to it the notion that judgment is a maturing supplement to imagination. Your imagination might even include the bases for catastrophic action, perhaps at a time when someone has hurt you badly, and still you might not act on the imagination if judgment provided some balance. I sincerely feel that although the ideal person might well make mistakes in life, he will not be a monster simply because he does not conform to the most obvious societal pressures.

It should be remembered that Emerson's (Atkinson, 1940, p. 148) conclusion that "whosoever would be a man must be a nonconformist" is echoed by many of the world's finest thinkers. If a critic responds by claiming that this kind of thinking permits such abominations as Hitler, I would suggest that he was a badly twisted man who showed less imagination than repetitive, compulsive preoccupations, and less judgment than megalomanic overconfidence. It is only by losing the usual standards of what is meant by imagination and judgment that Hitler and the ideal identity can be discussed in the same breath! But a secondary argument could be made that the position I am taking makes it at least possible for some twisted person like Hitler to gain dangerous power because those around him believe enough in imagination and judgment as guides to living that they may not see that he is only a pseudo-example of this in time to do anything about it. This is a terribly weak argument. Indeed, it is much more likely that people who define themselves as social role players and embodiments of biological needs will not recognize or be able to stop a man like Hitler. It is to the point that Hannah Arendt (1964) subtitled her treatise on the enacting of the final solution to the "Jewish problem" *a report on the banality of evil*. To judge from reports, the rank-and-file Germans were simply following rules when they gassed people!

Another consequence of relying upon imagination and judgment as guides to action is that the life of the ideal person will be a frequently changing, unfolding thing. New possibilities will be constantly developing, though it is unlikely that the process of change will be without pattern or continuity. The reliance upon judgment insures that there will be values and principles represented in the personality, and these would be slow to change. But more concrete experiential possibilities would change, presumably in an orderly fashion, due to the abstract view of experience and the play of imagination. The person with an ideal identity would not, then, be beset by boredom or by ontological guilt. Indeed, he would feel emotions deeply and spontaneously, be they pleasant or unpleasant. He would be enthusiastic and committed.

But his life would not be quite that rosy. When you are in a rather continual process of change, you cannot predict what existential outcomes will be. Interestingly enough, we find that doubt (Frankl, 1955) or existential anxiety (May et al., 1958, pp. 37-91) is a necessary concomitant of the ideal identity. When you stop to think about it, it is quite understandable that someone who is his own standard of meaning would be unsure and anxious at times when he was changing.

Looked at in this way, doubt (existential anxiety) is actually a sign of strength, rather than illness. This is precisely what was meant by Camus (1955) when he said, "I cherish my nights of despair," and Tillich (1952) when he designated doubt to be the "god above God." Powerful expression to doubt as an aspect of humanism, and therefore strength, is given by Frankl (1955) when he says:

> Challenging the meaning of life can . . . never be taken as a manifestation of morbidity or abnormality; it is rather the truest expression of the state of being human, the mark of the most human nature in man. For we can easily imagine highly developed animals or insects—say ants or bees—which in many aspects of their social organization are actually superior to man. But we can never imagine any such creature raising the question of the meaning of its own existence, and thus challenging this existence. It is reserved for man alone to find his very existence questionable, to experience the whole dubiousness of being. More than such faculties as power of speech, conceptual thinking, or walking erect, this factor of doubting the significance of his own existence is what sets man apart from animal [p. 30].

On logical grounds alone, nothing so basic to man's nature as doubt could ever be defined as psychopathological, for to do so would be to call everyone sick by virtue of his true nature. This logical argument is made more psychologically compelling by recognizing that when one is one's own standard of meaning, that will entail accepting and even valuing doubt because it is the necessary concomitant of the uncertainty produced by personal change. To avoid doubt is to avoid change and to give over the power in living to social and biological considerations. This is too big a price to pay for comfort alone. In avoiding the tragedies, you also lose the potentiality of triumphs.

precipitating stress and the ideal personality

If the ideal identity is truly an improvement over the premorbid identity, then the stresses that precipitate breakdown in the latter should be ineffective in the former. You will recall that the three stresses mentioned earlier are the threat of imminent death, social upheaval, and the accumulated sense of failure in living deeply and commitedly.

The ideal person would be so actively and enthusiastically enmeshed in living socially, biologically, and psychologically that the therapeutic effect of threat of imminent death would be markedly diminished. You simply do not need the threat of death to remind you to take life seriously and live in the immediate moment, if you are already doing these things. To the ideal person, such a threat could be frightening to some degree, but it would not be helpful. A definite implication of my saying this is the belief that the emphasis on death as what makes life important, which appears in one form or another in so much existential writing, is only of relative importance. Only when you think in terms of premorbidity as the true nature of man and the world, do you celebrate the purifying effects of threat of imminent death.

If the ideal person actually does come to the point of death, he will die a much more graceful death than that of Ivan Ilych. Death for the ideal person will be no more than a very unfortunate interruption of an intense and gratifying life process. I contend that someone who is living well will more easily face death than someone who senses that he has not even lived at all. In any event, it seems clear that the threat of imminent death will hardly precipitate an existential neurosis in a person with the ideal identity.

As to social upheaval, it is interesting to note in detail Durkheim's (1955) point of view on anomic suicide:

> It is not true . . . that human activity can be released from all restraint. Nothing in the world can enjoy such a privilege. All existence being a part of the universe is relative to the remainder; its nature and method of manifestation accordingly depend not only on itself but on other beings, who consequently restrain and regulate it. Here there are only differences of degree and form between the mineral realm and the thinking person. Man's characteristic privilege is that the bond he accepts is not physical but moral; that is, social. He is governed not by a material environment brutally imposed on him, but by a conscience superior to his own, the superiority of what he feels. Because the greater, better part of his existence transcends the body, he escapes the body's yoke, but is subject to that of society.
>
> But when society is disturbed by some painful crisis . . . it is momentarily incapable of exercising this influence; thence come the sudden rises in the curve of suicides which we have pointed out [p. 252].

Durkheim clearly believes that man's animalistic, self-interested urges must be held in check by societal regulation of life. Naturally, then, social upheaval would lead to a rise in suicide and, incidentally, in existential neurosis. But it is also likely that times of social upheaval involve intense creativity. While some people are committing suicide, others are using to good advantage the freedom achieved by the breakdown of monolithic social institutions. We should remember that the Italian Renaissance was a time of extraordinary social upheaval, and while suicide must have been high, so too was creativity. That the increase in creativity might have been due to the existence of ideal persons, for whom freedom from social pressures was helpful, is suggested by the following quote from the *Oration on the Dignity of Man*, written by Pico della Mirandola (1956), a most Renaissance man:

> Neither heavenly nor earthly, neither mortal nor immortal have we created thee, so that thou mightest be free according to thy own will and honor, to thy own creator and builder. To thee alone we gave growth and development depending on thy own free will. Thou bearest in thee the germs of a universal life [p. 17].

Rather than constituting a stress, social upheaval may well be a boon for the person with the real identity.

Finally, there is the matter of an accumulated sense that your life is a failure in terms of depth and committedness of experience. Actually, I am speechless here. It is simply incomprehensible that a person with an ideal identity would ever experience the painful course of self-revelation leading to existential neurosis seen in Arthur Miller's Quentin. The person with an ideal identity will certainly make mistakes, and suffer for them, but will not go for as long as Quentin with no cognizance for his superficiality and attendant frustration, and, hence, will not be in the position of condemning his life.

ideal and deviant development

It is natural at this point to raise the question of how ideal and premorbid identities develop. But before launching into considerations of early experience and their effects on later personality, one obviously relevant and thorny problem should be raised. It is the problem of free will.

Some of you may have long since decided that I have left the scientific fold with all this emphasis upon the person himself as the "fountain of power." Does this not mean, you will ask, that according to me man's actions are not determined by anything but his own will? And is this not a view antithetical to science? Let me try to explain why I think what I am saying is quite scientific. *I am explicating the way in which a particular set of beliefs about oneself and the nature of the world can lead to actions that are more varied, active, and changeable than is true when that set of beliefs is absent.* In the psychologist's terms, I am focusing upon proactive and reactive behavior, and attempting to explain the differences between them on the basis of differences in sense of identity. The functioning of the ideal person is well summarized by the concept of proactive behavior, with its emphasis on the person as an influence on his environment. In contrast, reactive behavior, which is influenced by the environment, is very descriptive of the premorbid person. But just because proactive behavior is more varied, flexible, and original is no reason to presume it is not caused in a scientifically specifiable way. In my view, proactive behavior is caused by the characteristics of the ideal personality, namely, the humanistic belief in oneself as the fountain of power, and the associated preparedness to exercise fully the psychological as well as social and biological sides of man. Further, the ideal personality is not a mysterious implant of God, like the concept of soul. The ideal personality, like the premorbid personality, is formed out of early life experiences. I propose to sketch these experiences in the paragraphs that follow. Clearly, my position assumes that all action is determined in a specifiable scientific way. My approach amounts to availing oneself of the value in recognizing that some behavior is active while some is passive without assuming anything about a soul, or divine inspiration, or mysterious freedom.

In developing an ideal identity it certainly helps to start out with a minimum of average intelligence, but once having this, the rest depends upon the parent-child relationship, and the supplementation of this in later relationships that are significant. Even relationship of child to teacher needs to be considered. One route to ideal development is for the person to experience in his relationships with significant people in his life what Rogers (1959) has called unconditional positive regard. This means that the person is appreciated as a human being and knows it. With such appreciation, the person comes to value his own humanness, and is able to act without fear and inhibition from all three sides of himself. But unconditional positive regard is not enough. There must be something better suited to point the young person in particular directions rather than others. The people around him must value symbolization, imagination, and judgment and encourage and support the child when he shows evidence of these psychological processes. But in this, the emphasis must be upon the child's own psychological processes, rather than on his parroting those of others. In addition, the child's range of experience must be broad, so that the generalizing function of symbolization, and the ordering function of judgment will have raw material with which to work. A broad range of experience may also have the secondary value of firing the imagination. Finally, it is crucial that the significant people in the child's life recognize the importance of social and biological functioning as well, so that they can encourage him in such expression. Their encouragement, however, should not be in the service of accepting social roles and animalistic urges, so much as in the conviction that social and biological living is what you make it, and, in the final analysis, these two sides of man are not so separate from each other and from the life of the mind.

From this brief statement, it is easy to see what would be deviant development leading to premorbidity. All you need to develop a premorbid identity is to grow up around people in significant relationship to you who value only some aspects of you, who believe in social roles and biological needs as the only defining pressures of life, and who are either afraid of active symbolization, imagination, and judgment, or see no particular relevance of these processes to living. Have these significant people act on their views in interactions with the child, and he will develop a premorbid identity.

While my brief remarks may seem somewhat flippant, I urge you to recognize that the two kinds of identity are almost that simply caused.

concluding remarks

If I have succeeded in my purpose, you should have a clearer, potentially research-oriented sense of existential disorder, its precursors, and its opposite, than you did before. In addition, you should have found documented here aspects of your own life and those of the people you know well.

If I have drawn the outlines of premorbid identity at all well, you will have recognized its great frequency in our contemporary Western world. While one can point to a set of early experiences in explaining the development of premorbidity, this does not help very much in understanding why this type of personality should be so prevalent these days. Inevitably, the question is raised of why so many parents and significant people in the life of modern-day youngsters instill in them the seeds of premorbidity. This question requires an answer concerning the general cultural milieu in which both adult and child exist. It is as products of their culture that adults influence the young.

Much has been written about the cultural causes of conformity, materialism, and shallow living, and I do not intend to review that literature here. But I would like to point to three broad views, of special interest to psychologists, that have gone far toward creating a cultural climate congenial to premorbidity. The men usually associated with these views are Darwin, Weber, and Freud.

Darwin argued a kinship between all animals, and this view has been sloppily interpreted by many to mean that man is very little different from lower animals. Any characteristics of man that do not seem amply represented in lower animals must be epiphenomenal, or reducible to simpler, animalistic things. Inevitably, such a view undercuts the importance of psychological processes and humanistic doctrines. And that is just what happened. I would like to point out, however, that there is nothing in the concept of a phylogenetic scale that justifies overlooking the importance of characteristics that seem to emerge at one level, having appeared in what may be only minimal prototypical form at lower levels. Add this to the reasonable view that man is really quite far on the scale from his next lower kin, and you have a form of Darwinism that is not so incompatible with my view of the ideal identity, and that would not be a cultural seed for the existential neurosis. To those psychologists who have rashly made what Murray (1954, p. 435) calls "the audacious assumption of species equivalence" between man and white rat I would say that a meaningful comparative psychology is as much interested in the differences as the similarities between species.

The sociologist Weber was certainly among the first to formally specify that modern, industrial society is necessarily bureaucratic in nature. This view has been considered to mean that the social roles a person is delegated are the most important things about him. Indeed, many a modern sociologist will define personality as the sum total of the social roles played by a person. Anyone who accepts such a view of himself without looking more deeply into the matter will very likely either be on the road to premorbidity himself, or be the kind of parent that breeds premorbidity in his children. In trying to show that there is an alternative to this view, let me agree that all behavior can be analyzed as social role playing, but point out that this does not necessarily mean that the social system is unchangeable and an irresistible shaper of individual living. The first step in convincing yourself of this is recognizing that there are different types of social roles. Social roles differ in their rigidity, preemptiveness, status, initiative requirements, and even in the degree to which they involve the person changing existing social roles. The import of all this is that some social roles encourage the expression of symbolization, imagination, and judgment. Clear examples are roles of leadership, power, and aestheticism. The second step in convincing yourself that the social system is not necessarily the prime mover of individual life is to ask yourself the question of how any person comes to play certain types of roles as opposed to others. In any society that does not restrict competition for roles, the roles that a person actually does come to play will be determined in part by his view of the good life and his sense of personal identity. The person with the ideal identity will gravitate toward roles involving symbolization, imagination, and judgment, while the person with the premorbid identity will avoid these roles. Indeed, the sense of powerlessness and despair pointed to by Marx in people playing social roles that are inhuman may be a psychological problem as much as a sociological one.

Finally, we come to Freud. It may not have escaped your recognition that Freud, in classical libido theory, gives expression to the belief that life represents a compromise between the necessity of playing social roles and of expressing biological needs. He makes what I have called premorbidity the ideal! Further, for Freud the psychological processes are defensive in nature, reflecting at most no more than a pale shadow of the truth. It is not hard to believe that our current-day outlook that thought processes are not to be trusted and that man's self-interested sexual nature needs to be checked by society was given great impetus by Freud's theory. Interestingly enough, his theory may well have served as a necessary corrective in his day, when thought had become arid through neglect of the biological side of man and too heavy in emphasis upon judgment to the detriment of imagination. But because his theory was a corrective rather than something more comprehensively adequate, its acceptance into the general culture has contributed to setting the stage for a new emphasis in psychopathology, namely, the existential neurosis.

references

Arendt, H. *Eichmann in Jerusalem—a report on the banality of evil*. New York: Viking, 1964.

Atkinson, B. (Ed.) *The selected writings of Ralph Waldo Emerson*. New York: Modern Library, 1940.

Camus, A. *The stranger*. New York: Knopf, 1946.

Camus, A. *The myth of Sisyphus and other essays*. (Trans. by J. O'Brien) New York: Knopf, 1955.

della Mirandola, P. *Oration on the dignity of man*. (Trans. by A. A. Caponigri) Chicago: Gateway, 1956.

Durkheim, E. *Suicide*. Glencoe, Ill.: Free Press, 1951.

Frankl, V. *The doctor and the soul*. (Trans. by R. Winston & C. Winston) New York: Knopf, 1955.

Fromm, E. *The sane society*. New York: Rinehart, 1955.

Josephson, E., & Josephson, M. (Eds.) *Man alone*. New York: Dell, 1962.

Kierkegaard, S. *The sickness unto death*. (Trans. by W. Lowrie) New York: Doubleday, 1954.

May, R., Angel, E., & Ellenberger, H. F. (Eds.) *Existence*. New York: Basic Books, 1958.

Miller, A. *After the fall*. New York: Viking, 1964.

Murray, H. A. Toward a classification of interaction. In T. Parsons & E. A. Shils (Eds.), *Toward a general theory of action*. Cambridge, Mass.: Harvard University Press, 1954. Pp. 435 ff.

Rogers, C. R. A theory of therapy, personality, and interpersonal relationships, as developed in the client-centered framework. In S. Koch (Ed.), *Psychology: A study of a science*. Vol. 3. New York: McGrall-Hill, 1959. Pp. 184–256.

Rogers, C. R. *On becoming a person*. Boston: Houghton Mifflin, 1961.

Sartre, J. P. *Being and nothingness*. (Trans. by H. Barnes) New York: Philosophical Library, 1956.

Sykes, G. (Ed.) *Alienation*. New York: Braziller, 1964.

Tillich, P *.The courage to be*. New Haven: Yale University Press, 1952.

Tolstoi, L. *The death of Ivan Illych*. New York: Signet, 1960.

11

Depression and Learned Helplessness

Martin E. P. Seligman

Two fairly substantial literatures dealing with maladaptive behavior appear to be converging. This paper highlights some commonalities between the phenomenon of learned helplessness in animals and depression in man, and it suggests

From R. J. Friedman and M. Katz (Eds.), *The Psychology of Depression: Contemporary Theory and Research*. By permission of Hemisphere Publishing Corporation, Washington, D.C.

tentatively that learned helplessness may provide a model for the understanding of reactive depression.

It has happened more than once that investigators have discovered and analyzed dramatic bits of maladaptive behavior in their animals and suggested that they illuminated some form of psychopathology in man. Pavlov (1) found that conditioned reflexes of dogs disintegrated when the experimenter made discrimination problems increasingly difficult. Liddell (2) found that restrained sheep given very many conditioning trials, stopped making conditioned flexion responses to the signals paired with shock. Both Pavlov and Liddell claimed they had demonstrated "experimental neuroses." Masserman (3) and Wolpe (4) found that hungry cats would not eat in compartments in which they had been shocked, and claimed that they had brought phobias into the laboratory. Maier (5) found that rats formed response fixations when confronted with insoluble discrimination problems and explained the findings as frustration. The experimental analyses of these phenomena was reasonably thorough, but the argument that they analyzed human psychopathology was usually saltatory, and occasionally downright unconvincing. Worse, the arguments were usually plausibility arguments that did not lend themselves readily to disconfirmation. How would one *test* whether Masserman's cats had phobias, anyway? Let us try to state some rules of argument for claiming that an animal phenomenon provides a model of a form of psychopathology in man.

ground rules

Four lines of evidence that two phenomena are similar seem relevant to this question: 1) symptoms: behavioral and physiological; 2) etiology; 3) cure; 4) prevention. It is not to be expected that any actual experimental phenomenon will meet all these criteria for any actual form of psychopathology in one fell swoop, but making the form of the argument explicit has two virtues: it makes similarity claims more testable and it can help us to narrow the definition of the clinical phenomenon. As two phenomena converge on one or two of the criteria, investigators can then test the model by looking for similarities predicted along the other criteria. So, for example, if learned helplessness in dogs presents similar behavior to reactive depression in man and the etiology of the two is similar, as we shall argue, and it turns out that the only way to cure learned helplessness is to forcibly expose dogs to responding that produces relief, one has a prediction about cure of depression in man: the recognition that responding is effective in producing reinforcement should be the central issue in successful therapy. If this is tested and confirmed, the model is strengthened. Strengthening such a model empirically is not only a matter of the animal phenomenon suggesting what to look for in the human phenomenon, but is a two-way street: so, if imipramine (a tricyclic drug) helps reactive depression, does it also relieve learned helplessness in animals? (See also McKinney and Bunney (6) for a discussion of the need for an animal model of depression.)

⁻ In addition to enhanced testability, a model can help sharpen the definition of the clinical phenomenon since the laboratory phenomenon is often well defined, while the phenomenon to be modelled is poorly defined. Consider, for example, the question of whether learned helplessness and depression show similar behavioral symptoms. Because it is a laboratory phenomenon helplessness has necessary behaviors which define its presence or absence. Depression, on the other hand, does not have a necessary condition which defines it. Rather, it is a convenient diagnostic label which denotes a constellation of symptoms, no one of which is necessary. The relationship among phenomena called depression is perhaps best described as a family resemblance (see Wittgenstein (7), paragraphs 66–77 for a general statement of this argument). Thus depressives often report feeling very sad, but this is not necessary for the diagnosis to be depression. If a patient doesn't feel sad, but is verbally and motorically retarded, cries a lot, is anorexic, and the onset of symptoms can be traced to his wife's death, depression is still the appropriate clinical label. But the retardation is also not necessary, as in agitated depression, and both feelings of sadness and retardation together are not necessary; for "depressive equivalents" may show neither, but only disturbed sleep, anorexia, weight loss and crying. Clinical labels can best be seen as denoting a family, "a complicated network of similarities overlapping and crisscrossing." A well-defined laboratory model does not mirror the openendedness of the clinical label, rather it clips it off at the edges by imposing necessary conditions on it. Thus if a particular model of depression is valid, some phenomena, formerly classified as depression may be excluded. The label "depression" denotes passive individuals with negative cognitive sets about the effects of their own actions, who become depressed upon the loss of an important source of gratification—the perfect case for learned helplessness to model; but it also denotes agitated patients who readily initiate active responses, and who become depressed with no obvious external cause. As we shall see, learned helplessness does not capture the whole spectrum of depressions, but it is rather an attempt to understand depressions in which the individual is slow to initiate responses, believes himself to be powerless and hopeless, has a negative outlook on the future, and which began as a reaction to having lost his control over relief of suffering and gratification.

Let us now turn to an examination of learned helplessness in animals and depression in man in terms of similarity along the four criteria outlined.

behavioral manifestations

learned helplessness

When an experimentally naive dog receives escape-avoidance training in a shuttle box, the following behavior typically occurs: at the onset of the first traumatic electric shock, the dog runs frantically about, defecating, urinating, and howling, until it accidentally scrambles over the barrier and so escapes the shock. On the next trial, the dog, running and howling, crosses the barrier more quickly than on the preceding trial. This pattern continues until the dog learns to avoid shock altogether. Overmier and Seligman (8), and Seligman and Maier (9) found a striking difference between this pattern of behavior and that exhibited by dogs first given inescapable electric shocks in a Pavlovian hammock. Such a dog's first reactions to shock in the shuttle box are much the same as those of a naive dog. However, in dramatic contrast to a naive dog, a typical dog which has experienced uncontrollable shocks before avoidance training soon stops running and howling and sits or lies, quietly whining, until shock terminates. The dog does not cross the barrier and escape from shock. Rather, it seems to give up and passively accepts the shock. On succeeding trials, the dog continues to fail to make escape movements and takes as much shock as the experimenter chooses to give.

There is another peculiar characteristic of the behavior of dogs which have first experienced inescapable shock. Such dogs occasionally jump the barrier early in training and escape, but then revert to taking the shock; they fail to profit from exposure to the barrier-jumping-shock-termination contingency. In naive dogs a successful escape response is a reliable predictor of future, short-latency escape responses.

The escape-avoidance behavior of over 150 dogs which had received prior inescapable shocks has been studied. Two-thirds of these dogs did not escape; the other third escaped and avoided in normal fashion. It is obvious that failure to escape is highly maladaptive since it means that the dog takes 50 seconds of severe, pulsating shock on each trial. In contrast, only 6 percent of experimentally naive dogs failed to escape in the shuttle box. So any given dog either fails to escape on almost every trial or learns normally. An intermediate outcome is rare.

A typical experimental procedure which produces failures to escape shock is as follows. On the first day, the subject is strapped into a hammock and given 64 unsignalled, inescapable electric shocks, each 5.0 seconds long and 6.0ma intensity. The shocks occur randomly in time. Twenty-four hours later, the dog is given 10 trials of signalized escape-avoidance training in the shuttle box. The onset of the CS (dimmed illumination) begins each trial, and the CS remains on until the trial ends. The CS-US interval is 10 seconds. If the dog jumps the barrier (set at shoulder height) during this interval, the CS terminates and no shock occurs. Failure to jump during the CS-US interval leads to a 4.5ma shock which remains until the subject jumps the barrier. If the subject fails to jump the barrier within 60 seconds after the CS onset, the trial automatically terminates and the shuttle box performance which typically results is that the group pretreated with inescapable shocks responds much more slowly than does the group not so pretreated.

We use the term "learned helplessness" to describe the interference with adaptive responding produced by inescapable shock and also as a shorthand to describe the process which we believe underlies the behavior (see *Etiology*). So, learned helplessness in the dog is defined by two behaviors: 1) dogs which have had experience with uncontrollable shock *fail to initiate responses* to escape shock or are slower to make responses than naive dogs, and 2) if the dog does make a response which turns off shock it has *more trouble learning that responding is effective* than a naive dog.

Learned helplessness is not an isolated phenomenon. Aside from the studies of Overmier and Seligman (8), and Seligman and Maier (9), such interference was also reported in dogs by Carlson and Black (10), Leaf (11), Seligman, Maier, and Geer (12), Overmier (13), Maier (14), and Seligman and Groves (15). Nor is it restricted to dogs: deficits in escaping or avoiding shock after experience with uncontrollable shock has been shown in rats, cats, dogs, fish, mice and men. Using rats, at least 16 studies have shown interference as a consequence of inescapable shock. For example, Mowrer (16), Dinsmoor and Campbell (17, 18), and Dinsmoor (19), all found that rats which had received inescapable shock were retarded in initiating their first barpress-escape response and were slower to acquire the response once it had been emitted. Brown and Jacobs (20), Mullin and Mogenson (21), and Weiss, Krieckhaus, and Conte (22), all found that fear conditioning that is carried out with inescapable shocks resulted in escape and avoidance decrements. In addition, the more trials of inescapable shock there are, the poorer is the subsequent escape and avoidance performance (Cohen and Looney (23)). Inescapable shocks imposed on weanling rats produce escape (and sometimes avoidance) decrements when the rats are adults (Brookshire, Littman and Stewart (24); Levine, Chevalier and Korchin (25); Denenberg and Bell (26); Denenberg (27)). Unlike the dog, however, the rat shows small interference with escape responding. Only Cohen and Looney (23) find rats who will sit and take shock, as opposed to being merely slower to escape.

Using cats, Seward and Humphrey (28) reported interference in escape resulting from previous inescapable shocks. Behrend and Bitterman (29) found that inescapable shocks retarded later Sidman avoidance learning by fish in an aquatic shuttle box, and Pinckney (30) and Padilla, Padilla, Ketterer, and Giacalone (31) found that uncontrollable shock retarded later shuttle box avoidance learning in goldfish. Using humans, MacDonald (32) found that inescapable shocks delivered to the finger retarded the later acquisition of finger-withdrawal avoidance. Thornton and Jacobs (33) found that after exposure to inescapable shock human subjects 1) failed to escape for shock and 2) failed to associate responding and reinforcement even after they made successful responses. Hiroto (34) found that students who had received inescapable loud noise were highly debilitated in learning to shuttle to escape noise, whereas escapable noise and no noise groups were not debilitated. Interestingly this effect was larger when subjects were given chance vs. skill instruction, and in subjects who perceived reinforcers as determined by outside forces (externals) as opposed to being caused by their own actions (internals). Rascinskas (35) has also reported such debilitation in humans following inescapable electric shock.

Inability to control trauma not only disrupts shock escape in a variety of species, but also interferes with a range of adaptive behaviors. Powell and Creer (36) found that rats that had received inescapable shocks initiated less pain-elicited aggression toward other rats. McCulloch and Bruner (37) reported that rats given inescapable shocks were slower to learn to swim out of a water maze, and Braud, Wepmann, and Russo (38) reported similar findings in mice. Brookshire, Littman and Stewart (24) (experiment 6) reported that inescapable shocks given to weanling rats disrupted food-getting behavior in adulthood when the rats were very hungry.

Situations involving uncontrollable USs other than shock can produce effects which may be related to failure to escape shock. Escape deficits can be produced by inescapable tumbling (Anderson & Paden (39)) and by loud noise (Hiroto (34)); passivity from defeat in fighting (Kahn (40)), and sudden death from defeat (Ewing (41)) or restraint (Richter (42)). Harlow, Harlow, and Suomi (43) reported that 45-day-old monkeys made helpless by 45 days of confinement to a narrow pit showed deficits later in locomotion, exploration, and social behavior. Maier, Seligman and Solomon (44), and Seligman, Maier, and Solomon (45) have reviewed and discussed the generality of the effects of inescapable USs across species and situations at greater length.

Besides passivity and retarded response-relief learning, there are four other characteristics associated with learned helplessness which are relevant to depressive symptomatology in man: the first is that helplessness has a time course. In dogs, inescapable shock produces transient as well as nontransient interference with escape (Overmier and Seligman (8)) and avoidance (Overmier (13)): 24 hours after *one* session of inescapable shock, dogs are helpless; but if intervals longer than 48 hours elapse, responding is normal. This is also true of goldfish (Padilla, et al. (31)). With multiple sessions of inescapable shock, helplessness is not transient (Seligman and Groves (15), Seligman, Maier, and Geer (12)). Weiss (46) found a parallel time course for weight loss in rats given uncontrollable shock, but other than this no such time course has been found in the rat or other species (e.g., Anderson, Cole and McVaugh (47)). In spite of the fact that nontransient learned helplessness occurs, one session of inescapable shocks may produce a physiological depletion which is restored with time. Weiss, Stone and Harrell (48), and Miller and Weiss (49) speculated that some physiological depletion such as norepinephrine may be partially responsible for the transient form of helplessness.

Three other findings exhaust what little knowledge we now have about the physiology of learned helplessness. As for gross physiology, Weiss (46) reported that uncontrollable shock retarded weight gain more than controllable shock in rats. Mowrer and Viek (50), and Lindner (51) reported more anorexia in rats given inescapable shock than in rats given escapable shock. Weiss, Stone and Harrell (48) reported that whole-brain norepinephrine was depleted in the brains of rats who could not control shocks, while rats who could control shocks showed elevated NE. It is unknown at the present time whether such NE depletion is either a necessary or a sufficient condition for learned helplessness, but it seems to be concomitant in rats. It is of interest, however, that Weiss, Stone and Harrell (48) undertook these studies because NE depletion has been hypothesized as the cause of depression in man.

In summary, experience with uncontrollable trauma produces six effects related to depression. The two basic effects are: 1) animals become passive in the face of trauma; i.e., they are slower to initiate responses to alleviate trauma and may not respond at all, and 2) animals are retarded at learning that their responses control trauma; i.e., if the animal makes a response which produces relief, he may have trouble "catching on" to the response-relief contingency. This maladaptive behavior appears in a variety of species including man, and over a range of tasks which require voluntary responding. In addition, this phenomenon 3) dissipates in time, and has 4) anorexia, 5) weight loss and 6) whole brain norephinephrine depletion associated with it at least in the rat.

depression

Depression is not well-defined and indeed, this is one reason why it needs a model. The clinical "entity" has multifarious symptoms, and for our purposes, I shall focus on those which seem central to the diagnosis *and* which may be related to learned helplessness. We shall concentrate on manifestations of depression:

a) Passivity: the slower response initiation, retardation, and lowered amplitude of behavior seen in depression.
b) Negative expectations: the readiness with which depressed patients construe their actions, even if they succeed, as having failed or being futile.
c) The sense of helplessness, hopelessness, and powerlessness which depressed patients frequently voice.

a) PASSIVITY.

The word "depressed" as a behavioral description denotes a reduction or depression in responding. It is, therefore, not surprising that diagnoses of depression often centrally involve the failure or the slowness of the patient to initiate responses. In a systematic study of the symptoms of depression, Grinker, Miller, Sabshin, Nunn, Nunnally (52) describe this in a number of ways:

Isolated and withdrawn, prefers to remain by himself, stays in bed much of the time (p. 169).

Gait and general behavior slow and retarded. Volume of voice decreased, sits alone very quietly (p. 170).
Feels unable to act, feels unable to make decisions (p. 166).
(They) give the appearance of an "empty" person who has "given up" (p. 166).

Mendels (53) describes the slowdown in responding associated with depression:

> Loss of interest, decrease in energy, inability to accomplish tasks, difficulty in concentration, and the erosion of motivation and ambition all combine to impair efficient functioning. For many depressives the first signs of the illness are in the area of their increasing inability to cope with their work and responsibilities. (p. 7).

Beck (54) describes "paralysis of the will" as a striking feature of depression:

> In severe cases, there often is complete paralysis of the will. The patient has no desire to do anything, even those things which are essential to life. Consequently, he may be relatively immobile unless prodded or pushed into activity by others. It is sometimes necessary to pull the patient out of bed, wash, dress, and feed him.

Bleuler (55) included inhibition of action as one of the three traits composing "melancholia." (p. 209).

Two recent studies document the lowered voluntary response initiation of depressives. Lewinsohn (56) found that depressed patients initiated fewer verbal social actions, and were slower to respond to social initiatives of others. Ekman (57) examined non-verbal communication in depressed patients. He reported that "illustrators," a class of voluntary hand motions which cohere with the intent of the conversation, were depleted in depressed patients. In contrast, "adaptors," involuntary adjustive hand motions like hand-rubbing, were not depleted. As improvement in depression occurred, the number of illustrators increased and adaptors decreased.

So, descriptions of the symptoms of depression include—often centrally—passivity, a failure of the patient to initiate responses.

b) NEGATIVE EXPECTATIONS.

Depressed patients are "set" to interpret their own responses when they do make them, as failures or as doomed to failure. Beck (54) construes this as the first member of the primary triad of depression.

> The depressed patient is peculiarly sensitive to any impediments to his goal-directed activity. An obstacle is regarded as an impossible barrier, difficulty in dealing with a problem is interpreted as a total failure. His cognitive response to a problem or difficulty is likely to be an idea such as "I'm licked," "I'll never be able to do this," or "I'm blocked no matter what I do". . . . In achievement-oriented situations depressed patients are particularly prone to react with a sense of failure. As shown in controlled experiments (Loeb, Beck, Diggory, & Tuthill (58)) they tend to underestimate their actual performances (Beck (54), pp. 256–257). (See also Mendels (53), p. 8.)

Indeed, Beck views the passive and retarded behavior of depressed patients as stemming from their negative expectations of their own effectiveness:

> The loss of spontaneous motivation, or paralysis of the will, has been considered a symptom *par excellence* of depression in the classical literature. The loss of motivation may be viewed as the result of the patient's hopelessness and pessimism: as long as he expects a negative outcome from any course

of action, he is stripped of any internal stimulation to do anything (Beck (54), p. 263).

Friedman (59) found that depressed patients performed more poorly than normals in reaction to a light signal and recognition time for common objects, but even more striking was their subjective estimate of how poorly they thought they would do: "When the examiner would bring the patient into the testing room, the patient would immediately protest that her or she could not possibly take the tests, was unable to do anything, or felt too bad or too tired, was incapable, hopeless, etc. . . . While performing adequately the patient would occasionally and less frequently reiterate the original protest, saying 'I can't do it,' 'I don't know how,' etc." This is a very common experience of experimenters testing depressed patients.

c) FEELINGS OF HELPLESSNESS, HOPELESSNESS AND POWERLESSNESS.

Although this is a discussion of the behavioral and physiological symptoms of depression, we cannot avoid mentioning the subjective content which is a concomitant of passivity and negative expectations in man. Depressed people say they feel helpless, hopeless, and powerless, and by this they mean that they believe that they are unable to control or influence those aspects of their lives which are significant to them.

Grinker et al. (52) conclude their book by describing the "factor describing characteristics of hopelessness, helplessness, failure, sadness, unworthiness, guilt and internal suffering" as the "essence of depression."

Melges and Bowlby (60) also characterize depressed patients in this way and Bibring (61) *defines* depression "as the emotional expression (indicative) of a state of helplessness and powerlessness of the ego."

There are several other characteristics of depression in man which parallel learned helplessness. Depression seems to have its time courses: Wallace (62), in discussing the "disaster syndrome," reported that following sudden catastrophes depression occurs for about a day or so and then functioning returns to normal. It seems possible that multiple traumatic events intervening between the initial disaster and recovery might potentiate depression considerably, as we have found with dogs. We should also note that endogenous or process depression is characterized by cyclic fluctuations, between depression and mania, usually on the order of weeks or months. Moreover, it is commonly thought that almost all depressions dissipate in time, although whether the period is more commonly measurable in days, weeks, months, or years is a mattter of some dispute (e.g., Paskind (63, 64), Lundquist (65), and Kraines (66)).

Aside from time course, both weight loss and anorexia are common gross physiological signs of depression. As for pharmacology, there is some evidence that imipramine, a drug which increases the NE available in the central nervous system possibly by blocking its uptake, breaks up depression. Klerman and Cole (67), and Cole (68) reported positive results of imipramine over placebos. Monoamineoxidase (MAO) inhibitors, which prevent the breakdown of NE, may be useful in relieving depression (Davis (69) and Cole (68)). Reserpine, a drug which depletes NE, produces depression in man. The catecholamine hypothesis of affective disorders proposed by Schildkraut (70) claims that depression in man is associated with the deficiency of NE at receptor sites in the brain, while elation may be associated with its excess.

commonalities

So there are considerable parallels between the behaviors which define learned helplessness and major symptoms of depression. Helpless animals become passive in the face of later trauma; they do not initiate responses to control trauma and the amplitude of responding is lowered. Depressed patients are characterized by diminished response initiation; their behavioral repertoire is impoverished and in severe cases, almost stuporous (Hoch (71)). Helpless animals do not benefit from exposure to experiences in which responding now produces relief; rather they often revert to passively accepting shock. Depressed patients have strong negative expectations about the effectiveness of their own responding. They construe even actions that succeed as having failed and underestimate and devalue their own performance. In addition, evidence exists which suggests that both learned helplessness and depression dissipate in time, are associated with weight loss and anorexia, or loss of libido, and norepinephrine depletion.

Finally, it is not an accident that we have used the word "helplessness" to describe the behavior of dogs in our laboratory. Animals that lie down in traumatic shock that could be removed simply by jumping to the other side, and who fail even to make escape movements are readily seen as helpless. Moreover we should not forget that depressed patients commonly describe themselves as helpless, hopeless and powerless.

differences

Unfortunately for model-building there are always a large number of differences between any two phenomena and only a limited number of similarities. Let us focus on those differences which loom large. The biggest single difference is that people talk and can tell you about what they're thinking and feeling, but animals don't. Because people talk about their feelings and thoughts, many of the symptoms which go into a clinical diagnosis of depression are couched in subjective terms: sadness, loss of self-esteem, feeling blue, apathy, feeling of being at the end of the rope, loneliness, and feeling worthless. Human-based theorizing readily incorporates such verbal reports. For example, Schmale (72), and Engel and Schmale (73) have drawn an important and useful distinction between helplessness and hopelessness among human patients: helplessness is a belief that no one will do anything to aid you and hopelessness a belief that neither you nor anyone else can do anything. It is a limitation of our model that such a distinction cannot be made with animals, and that we must use these terms interchangeably. It should not go unsaid, however, that our helpless dogs look different from normal dogs to us. We do not know the dimension, facial, vocal, or whatever, which leads to our impression, but these dogs look "sad" and "morose" to us. In principle this is a quantifiable impression.

In addition to subjective symptoms, there are behavioral manifestations of depressions which do not have clear infra-human equivalents: Two such are suicide and sobbing. One behavioral manifestation of depression which has parallels in animals is sleep disturbance, but there is no evidence one way or another of its occurring in learned helplessness.

What occurs in learned helplessness that does not occur in depression? Stomach ulcers (Weiss (46, 74); Miller and Weiss (49)) occur more during uncontrollable than controllable shock, but we know of no data correlating ulcers and depression in man. Uncontrollable trauma also produces more stress than controllable shock as measured by behavioral suppression (Mowrer and Viek, (50), Hoffman and Fleshler (75), and Hearst (76)), by defecation and conditioned fear (Weiss (47)), and by subjective report (Lepanto, Moroney, and Zenhausern (77)). The question of whether depressed people are more anxious than others does not have a clear answer. Beck (54) reported that while both depression and "anxiety" can be observed in some individuals, only a small positive correlation exists over a population of 606 in-patients. We can speculate that anxiety and depression are related in the following way: When a man or animal is confronted with a threat or a loss, he will respond with fear or anxiety initially. If he learns that it is wholly controllable, anxiety, having served its function, disappears. If he learns or is convinced that the event is utterly uncontrollable, depression replaces anxiety.

Finally, the asymmetry between the sets of evidence should be pointed out. The evidence on learned helplessness is experimental and unselected, while the evidence on the behavioral and physiological manifestations of depression is clinical, anecdotal, and selected. Few experiments have *tested* whether depressed people are slower to initiate voluntary responses to obtain relief or slower to learn that responding produces relief. Such experiments would help test the model.

In summary, there seems to be strong similarity of the defining behaviors of learned helplessness and the most salient manifestations of depression. On the other hand, the subjective attributes of depression while not inconsistent with learned helplessness, are also not deduced from the theory.

etiology

learned helplessness

The causes of learned helplessness are reasonably well understood. It is not trauma *per se* that produces interference with later adaptive responding, *but not having control over trauma*. The distinction between controllable and uncontrollable reinforcement is central to the phenomenon and theory of helplessness, so let us now examine it.

Learning theorists have usually viewed the relations between instrumental responding and outcomes that organisms could learn about as described by a line depicting the conditional probability of a reinforcement following a response $p(RFT/R)$. This line varies from zero to 1. At 1, every response produces a reinforcement (continuous reinforcement). At zero, a response never produces reinforcement (extinction). Intermediate points on the line represent various degrees of partial reinforcement. A simple line, however, does not exhaust relations between response and outcomes to which organisms are sensitive. Rewards or punishments sometimes occur when no specific response has been made. It would be a woefully maladaptive S that could not learn about such a contingency. Rather than representing instrumental learning as occurring along a single dimension, we can better describe it using the 2-dimensional space shown in Figure 11.1. The x-axis $(p(RFT/R))$ represents the traditional dimension, conditional-probability of reinforcement, following a response.

Orthogonal to the conditional probability of reinforcement, given a response, is the conditional probability of reinforcement, given the absence of *that* response. This dimension is represented along the y-axis. We believe that Ss learn about variations along *both* dimensions conjointly. Thus, S may learn the

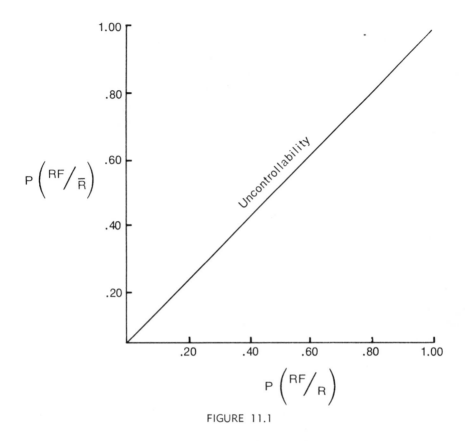

FIGURE 11.1

extent to which relief occurs when it does not make a specific response at the same time as it learns the extent to which relief occurs when it does make a specific response. Systematic changes in behavior occur with systematic changes along both dimensions.

There is considerable convergence of opinion and evidence among learning theorists today that organisms can learn about the contingencies within this instrumental training space, including the crucial 45° line (e.g., Church (78); Gibbon (79); Maier, Seligman & Solomon (44); Poresky (80); Premack (81); Rescorla (82, 83); Seligman, Maier & Solomon (45); Wagner (84); Watson (85); and Weiss (46)).

The traditional training line has been thoroughly explored (e.g., Ferster and Skinner (86), and Honig (87)). The points in the training space which are of special concern for helplessness are those that lie along the 45° line, (x, y, where x=7). Whether or not the organism responds, it still gets the same density of reinforcement. The conditional probability of reinforcement, given a specific response, *does not differ* from the conditional probability of reinforcement in the absence of that response. Responding and reinforcement are independent.

The concept of control is defined within this instrumental training space. Any time there is something the organism can do or refrain from doing that changes what it gets, it has control. Specifically, a response stands in control of a reinforcer *if and only if*:

$$p(RFT/R \neq p(RFT/\bar{R}).$$

That is, the probability of reinforcement given a response is different from the probability of reinforcement in the absence of that response. Furthermore, when a response will not change what S gets, the response and reinforcement are independent. Specifically, when a response is independent of a reinforcer, $p(RFT/R)$ $=p(RFT/\overline{R})$. When this is true of all responses S *cannot control* the reinforcer, the outcome is uncontrollable and nothing the organism does matters.

The passivity of dogs in the face of trauma and their difficulty in benefitting from response-relief contingencies results, we believe, from their having learned that responding and trauma are independent—that trauma is uncontrollable. This is the heart of the learned helplessness hypothesis. The hypothesis states that when shock is inescapable, the organism learns that responding and shock termination are independent (the probability of shock termination given any response doesn't differ from its probability in the absence of that response). Learning that trauma is uncontrollable has three effects: 1) a motivational one: it reduces the probability that the subject will initiate responses to escape, because part of the incentive for making such responses is the expectation that they will bring relief. If the subject has previously learned that its responses have no effect on trauma, this contravenes the expectation. Thus the organism's motivation to respond is undermined by experience with reinforcers it cannot control. It should be obvious to the reader that this motivational effect is what we believe underlies passivity in learned helplessness, and if the model is valid, in depression. 2) a cognitive effect: learning that responding and shock are independent makes it more difficult to learn that responding *does* produce relief, when the organism makes a response which actually terminates shock. In general, if one has acquired a cognitive set in which A's are irrelevant to B's, it will be harder for one to learn that A's produce B's when they do. By the helplessness hypothesis, this mechanism is responsible for the difficulty that helpless dogs have in learning that responding produces relief, even after they respond and successfully turn off shock. Further, if the model is valid, it is this mechanism which produces the "negative expectations" of depression. 3) an emotional effect: although it does not follow directly from the helplessness hypothesis, we have mentioned that uncontrollable shock also has an emotional impact on animals. Uncontrollable shock produces more conditioned fear, ulcers, weight loss, defecation, and pain than controllable shock. (See Maier, Seligman, and Solomon (44), and Seligman, Maier, and Solomon (45) for a more rigorous statement of the helplessness hypothesis and the relevant evidence.)

We have tested and confirmed this hypothesis in several ways. We began by ruling out alternative hypotheses: It is unlikely that our dogs have either become adapted (and therefore not motivated enough to escape shock) or sensitized (and therefore too disorganized to escape shock) by pretreatment with shock; for making the shock very intense or very mild in the shuttle box does not attenuate the phenomenon. Further, it is unlikely that the dogs have learned during inescapable shock by explicit or superstitious reinforcement or punishment, some motor response pattern which competes with barrier jumping in the shuttle box; for interference occurs even if the dogs are paralyzed by curare and can make no overt motor responses during shock. Seligman and Maier (9) performed a direct test of the hypothesis that learning that shock was uncontrollable, and not shock *per se*, causes helplessness. Three groups of eight dogs were used. An Escape Group was trained in the hammock to press a panel with their nose or head in order to turn off shock. A Yoked Group received shocks identical to the shocks delivered to the Escape Group. The Yoked Group differed from the Escape

Group only with respect to the degree of instrumental control which it had over shock; for pressing the panel in the Yoked Group did not affect the programmed shocks. A Naive Control Group received no shock in the hammock.

Twenty-four hours following the hammock treatment, all three groups received escape/avoidance training in the shuttle box. The Escape Group and the Naive Control Group suffered no impairment in shuttle box performance. In contrast, the Yoked Group showed significantly slower latencies than the Naive Control Group. Six of the eight Ss in the Yoked Group failed to escape shock. Thus the helplessness hypothesis was supported. It was *not the shock itself*, but not controlling shock, that produced failure to escape.

Maier (14) provided more dramatic confirmation of the hypothesis. In response to the criticism that what gets learned during uncontrollable trauma is not a cognitive set as we have proposed, but some motor response which has been reinforced by shock termination which antagonizes barrier jumping, Maier (14) reinforced the most antagonistic response he could find. One group of ten dogs (Passive-Escape) was tied down in the harness and had panels pushed to ¼" of the sides and top of their heads. Only by *not* moving their heads, by remaining passive and still, could these dogs terminate shock. Another group of ten (Yoked) received the same shock in the hammock, but it was independent of a responding. A third group received no shock. A response-learning source of helplessness predicts that when the dogs were later tested in the shuttle box, the Passive-Escape Group should be the most helpless since they had been explicitly reinforced for not moving during shock. The cognitive-set view makes a different prediction: These dogs could control shock, even though it took a passive response to do it. Some response, even one which competes with barrier jumping, produced relief, and they should not learn response-reinforcement independence. As predicted, the dogs in the Yoked Group were predominantly helpless in the shuttle box escape, and the naive controls escaped normally. The Passive-Escape Group at first looked for "still" ways of minimizing shock in the shuttle box. Failing to find these, they all began to escape and avoid. Thus it was not trauma *per se*, nor interfering motor habits that produced failure to escape, but having learned that no response at all can control trauma.

So learning that responding and reinforcement are independent causes retarded response initiation, but does it also cause a negative cognitive set which interferes with forming later associations? Evidence from four different areas in the recent animal learning literature supports the prediction that independence between events retards later learning that events are correlated: 1) Seligman (88) reported that when stimulus and shock were presented independently, rats later were retarded at learning that a second stimulus predicted shock. 2) Bresnahan (89), and Thomas, Freeman, Svinicki, Burr, and Lyons (90) reported that experience with the value of one stimulus dimension presented independently of food retarded rats' ability to discriminate along other dimensions. 3) MacKintosh (91) reviewed a substantial discrimination learning literature which points to the conclusion that when values along a stimulus dimension are independent of reinforcement, animals are retarded at discrimination learning when values along this dimension are later correlated with reinforcement (see also Kemler and Shepp (92)). Maier (5) reviewed a set of related results. 4) Gamzu and Williams (93) reported that pigeons exposed to independence between a lighted key and grain are retarded at acquiring "autoshaping" when the lighted key later signals grain.

In summary, one cause of laboratory-produced helplessness seems to be learning that one cannot control important events. Learning that responding and reinforcement are independent results in a cognitive set which has two basic effects: Fewer responses to control reinforcement are initiated, and associating successful responding with reinforcement becomes more difficult.

depression

The etiology of depression is less clear than its behavioral manifestations. A dichotomy between kinds of depression has been made and will be useful for our purposes: The "exogenous-endogenous" or "process-reactive" distinction (e.g., Kiloh and Garside (94); Kraepelin (95); and Partridge (96). Without endorsing the claim that a dividing line can be well drawn, it appears that depression sometimes occurs cyclically and with no identifiable external event precipitating it (e.g., Kraines (66)), and that it may cycle regularly between mania and depression. These so-called "endogenous" or "process" depressions and their immediate etiology are presumably biochemical and/or genetic. On the other hand, depression is also sometimes clearly precipitated by environmental events. This form of depression—"reactive" or "exogenous"—is the primary concern of this paper. It is heuristic to regard the process-reactive distinction as a continuum rather than dichotomy: On the extreme of the reactive side, strong events of the kind discussed below are necessary. In between may lie a continuum of preparedness to become depressed when faced with helplessness-inducing external events, with the most mild events setting off depression at the extreme process end.

Let us enumerate some of the events which typically precipitate depression: Failure in work or school; death, loss, rejection or separation from loved ones; physical disease and growing old. There are a host of others, but these capture the flavor of the kinds of events which often precipitate depression. What do all these have in common?

Four recent theorists of depression seem to be largely in agreement about the etiology of depression, and what they agree on is the centrality of helplessness and hopelessness. Bibring (61), arguing from a dynamic viewpoint, sees helplessness as the cause of depression.

> What has been described as the basic mechanism of depression, the ego's shocking awareness of its helplessness in regard to its aspirations, is assumed to represent the core of normal, neurotic, and probably also psychotic depression (p. 39).

Melges and Bowlby (60) see a similar cause of depression:

> Our thesis is that while a depressed patient's goals remain relatively unchanged his estimate of the likelihood of achieving them and his confidence in the efficacy of his own skilled actions are both diminished . . . the depressed person believes that his plans of action are no longer effective in reaching his continuing and long range goals. . . . From this state of mind is derived, we believe, much depressive symptomology, including indecisiveness, inability to act, making increased demands on others and feelings of worthlessness and of guilt about not discharging duties.

Beck (54, 97, 98) sees depression as resulting primarily from a negative cognitive set, largely about the patient's abilities to change his situation.

> A primary factor appears to be the activation of idiosyncratic cognitive patterns which divert the thinking into specific channels that deviate from reality. As a result, the patient perseverates in making negative judgments

and misinterpretations. These distortions may be categorized within the triad of negative interpretations of experience; negative evaluations of the self; and negative expectations of the future (Beck (54), p. 27).

Lichtenberg (99) sees hopelessness as the defining characteristic of depression:

> Depression is defined as a manifestation of felt hopelessness regarding the attainment of goals when responsibility for the hopelessness is attributed to one's personal defects. In this context hope is conceived to be a function of the perceived probability of success with respect to goal attainment.

I believe what joins these views and lies at the heart of depression is unitary: The depressed patient has learned or believes that he cannot control those elements of his life which relieve suffering or bring him gratification. In short, he believes that he is helpless. Consider a few of the common precipitating events: What is the meaning of job failure or incompetence at school? Frequently it means that all of a person's efforts have been in vain, his responses have failed to bring about the gratification he desires: He cannot find responses which control reinforcement. When an individual is rejected by someone he loves, he can no longer control this significant source of gratification and support. When a parent or lover dies, the bereaved is in a situation in which he is powerless to produce or influ- ence love from the dead person. Physical disease and growing old are helplessness situations *par excellence*. In these conditions, the person finds his own responses ineffective and is often thrown onto the care of others. Supporting this, Abramo- witz (100) reported a significant correlation between depression and lack of belief in the efficacy of one's own responding as measured by the Rotter Internal-Ex- ternal locus of control scale (Rotter (101)).

It should be remarked that situations like this often may lead to anxiety as well as depression. Anxiety may occur while the person still hopes and is search- ing for a way out, and it may give way to depression when he finally believes that there is nothing he can do. In summary, I suggest that what depressing situ- ations have in common is that the patient finds himself no longer in control of those aspects of his life which are important to him.

differences

So both learned helplessness and depression may be caused by learning that responding and reinforcement are independent. But this view runs into sev- eral problems. It is apparent that depression sometimes results from experiences in which relief is independent of responding. For the aged person forced into an old people's home, no response can relieve the situation. But true independence of responding and reinforcement does not seem to capture other common precipi- tants of depression. Consider the accountant who is fired from his job because he is incompetent. Here, there are response contingencies: His *own* incompetence results in his being fired and he becomes depressed. This is not response-inde- pendence because incompetent responses produced firing, and refraining from in- competent responses would have salvaged the job. So here is a situation in which the person is helpless and becomes depressed but responding and reinforcement are not independent.

This example is difficult for the model and suggests that our operational definition of helplessness may be too restrictive. At one level the patient had control, but at another level he did not. That is, *if he had been able* to make competent responses and refrain from incompetent ones he would not have been fired. But he was not able to and in this sense he was helpless. Mandler (102), and Mandler and Watson (103) have discussed helplessness in terms of response unavailability: Rats that are placed satiated in a maze where they learned to get food while hungry show highly disrupted behavior. They suggest that the lack of appropriate responses to deal with the new situation is the cause. Obviously if responses and reinforcement are independent, the organism is helpless in this sense of response unavailability, as well as if there are dependencies but the organism cannot make the response. Broadening helplessness to response unavailability, while making the concept somewhat less precise, may help to explain the depression of our incompetent accountant.

Ferster (104); Kaufman and Rosenblum (105); McKinney and Bunney (6); and Liberman and Raskin (106), have suggested that depression is caused by extinction procedures or the *loss* of reinforcers. There is no contradiction between the learned helplessness and extinction views of depression; helplessness, however, is more general. This is a subtle point and needs some elucidation. Extinction commonly denotes a set of contingencies in which reinforcement is withdrawn from the situation, so that the subjects' responses (as well as lack of responding) no longer produce reinforcement. Loss of reinforcers, as in the case of the death of a loved one, can be viewed as an extinction procedure. In conventional extinction procedures the probability of the reinforcer occurring is zero whether or not the subject responds. It is important to realize that such extinction is a special case of independence between responding and reinforcement. Reinforcement, however, may also be presented with a probability greater than zero, and still be presented independent of responding. This is the typical helplessness paradigm, and such procedures cause responding to decrease in probability (Rescorla and Skucy (107)). A view, therefore, which talks about independence between responding and reinforcement subsumes the extinction view and in addition suggests that situations in which reinforcers still occur, but independent of responding, also will cause depression.

Can depression actually be caused by situations other than extinction, in which reinforcements still occur, but they are not under the individual's control? To put it another way, "Is a net loss of reinforcers necessary for depression, or can depression occur when there is only loss of control without loss of reinforcers?" Would a Casanova who slept with seven new girls every week become depressed if he found out that it was not because of his amatory prowess, but because of his wealth or his fairy godmother? This is a theoretically interesting case, and we can only speculate about what would happen. It is appropriate to mention "success" depression in this context. When people finally reach a goal such as becoming APA president or getting a Ph.D. after years of striving, depression often ensues when the goal is reached. This puzzling phenomenon is clearly a problem for a loss view of depression. From a helplessness view, success depression may occur because reinforcers are no longer contingent on present responding: After years of goal directed instrumental activity, one now gets his reinforcers because of who he is rather than what he is doing. The common clinical impression that beautiful women get depressed and attempt suicide frequently also seems relevant: Positive reinforcers abound but not because of what she *does* but because of how she looks. Would a generation of children raised with abundant positive reinforcers which they got independently of what they did become clinically depressed?

In the last paragraph, we slipped into talking about uncontrollable "positive" reinforcers as a possible cause of depression, while the laboratory evidence for learned helplessness comes from uncontrollable "aversive" reinforcers. How do organisms react to noncontingent positive reinforcers? Carder and Berkowitz (108), Jensen (109), and Neuringer (110), all reported that animals choose response-contingent food over response-ingredient food. Receiving positive reinforcers free is not as positive as working for them. Watson (111) reported that human infants whose own pillow pressing produced the movement of a mobile hung over their cribs began smiling and cooing earlier than a group in which stimulation was response independent. These studies indicate that response contingent positive stimulation is more positive than the same stimulation when it is response independent. We do not know if such response independent stimulation is actually negative or worse than nothing, and as yet we do not know if noncontingent positive reinforcement retards response initiation and learning of response-reward contingency as does noncontingent aversive stimulation. It seems possible that while response independent trauma may produce depression and helplessness, response independent positive reinforcers may merely produce boredom or apathy. To summarize, uncontrollable aversive events produce helplessness in animals and probably depression in man. Uncontrollable positive events are less preferred than controllable ones, and this may be related to success depression in man. But whether uncontrollable positive reinforcement is depressing or helplessness engendering is unknown.

One final difference concerns the course of acquisition of learned helplessness. Helplessness in the laboratory takes a number of trials to produce: We commonly present 64 electric shocks, and it takes quite a few trials for dogs to learn that responding and relief are independent. Depression, on the other hand, can be produced in one "trial" as when a child dies. There are two responses to this objection: 1) Beck (54) noted that a series of blows is more effective than one event in producing depression, and 2) the fact that people have language greatly compresses the number of "trials" needed to produce learning. What would take an animal many exposures to learn can be learned by a person when only a few words are spoken. The death of a child literally *tells* a person that its love is now beyond his control.

cure

learned helplessness

We have found only one treatment that cures helplessness in dogs. By the helplessness hypothesis, the dog does not try to escape because he expects that no instrumental response will produce shock termination. By forcibly exposing the dog to the fact that responding produces reinforcement this expectation should be changed. Seligman, Maier, and Geer (12), however, found that forcibly dragging the dog from side to side in the shuttle box, so that the dog's changing compartments terminated shock, cured helplessness. The experimenters pulled three chronically helpless dogs back and forth across the shuttle box with long leashes. This was done during CS and shock, with the barrier removed. After being pulled across the center of the shuttle box (thus terminating shock and CS) 20, 35, and 50 times, respectively, each dog began to respond on his own. Then the barrier was replaced, and the subject continued to escape and avoid. The recovery from helplessness was complete and lasting, and this finding has been replicated with over two dozen helpless dogs.

The behavior of animals during "leash pulling " was noteworthy. At the beginning of the procedure, a good deal of force had to be exerted to pull the dog across the center of the shuttle box. Less and less force was needed as training progressed. A stage was typically reached in which a slight nudge of the leash would drive the dog into action. Finally, each dog initiated its own response, and thereafter failure to escape was very rare. The initial problem seemed to be one of "getting going."

We first tried other procedures with little success. Merely removing the barrier, our calling to the dog from the safe side, dropping food into the safe side, kicking the dangerous side of the box—all failed. Until the correct response occurred repeatedly, the dog was not effectively exposed to the response-relief contingency. It is significant that so many forced exposures were required before the dogs responded on their own. This observation supported the twofold interpretation of the effects of inescapable shock: 1) the motivation to initiate responses during shock was low, and 2) the ability to associate successful responses with relief was impaired.

depression

We do not know how to cure depression. Left alone, it sometimes dissipates over weeks or months. But there are therapies which are reported to alleviate depression and which are consonant with a learned helplessness model. It is important to note that the success of a therapy often has little to do with its theoretical underpinnings, and the following "evidence" should not be regarded as a test of the model. These are merely a set of examples that seem to have exposure to response-produced success as a curative factor for depression. According to the helplessness view the central theme in successful therapy should be having the patient find out and come to believe that his responses produce the gratifications he desires—that he is, in short, an effective human being. Bibring (61) saw the matter similarly:

> The same conditions which bring about depression (helplessness) in reverse serve frequently the restitution from depression. Generally one can say that depression subsides either (a) when the narcissistically important goals and objects appear to be again within reach (which is frequently followed by a temporary elation) or (b) when they become sufficiently modified or reduced to become realizable, or (c) when they are altogether relinquished, or (d) when the ego recovers the narcissistic shock by regaining its self-esteem with the help of various recovery mechanisms (with or without any change of objective or goal) (p. 43).

Beck's (98) recently developed cognitive therapy for depression is aimed at similar goals. Beck sees success manipulations as changing the negative cognitive set (I'm an ineffective person) of the depressed person to a more positive set, and argues that the primary task of the therapist is to change the negative expectational schema of the depressed patient to a more optimistic one.

Melges and Bowlby (60) also see mitigation of helplessness as the central theme in the treatment of depression:

> If the argument that hopelessness in one or another of its forms is a central dynamic in certain kinds of psychopathology turns out to be valid, treatment measures would need to be evaluated in terms of the degree to which they help the patients to change their attitude toward the future. . . . A principal

aim of insight-oriented therapy is to help a patient recognize some of the archaic and unreachable goals towards which he may still be striving, and some also of the impracticable plans to which he may still be wedded, aims that are especially clear when a patient is suffering from a pathological form of mourning. By psychoanalytic techniques, it is believed, a patient can sometimes be freed from the conditions that led him to become hopeless, and given opportunity both to set himself more reachable goals and to adopt more effective plans. Behavioral techniques also are being explored to see how successful they can be in setting up more positive attitudes in the future.

Other forms of therapy which are reported effective against depression seem to involve inducing the patient to see that he can control important reinforcers by his own actions. The "Tuscaloosa Plan" (Taulbee and Wright (112)), involves putting severely depressed patients in an "anti-depression room." In this room the patient is abused: He is told to sand a block of wood, and then reprimanded because he sanded against the grain. He then sands with the grain and is reprimanded for sanding with the grain. This mistreatment continues until the depressed patient expresses an appropriate amount of hostility. He is then let out of the room. This breaks up depression. From a helplessness view, the patient is *forced* to emit one of the most powerful responses people have for controlling others—anger—and when this response is dragged out of his depleted repertoire, he is powerfully reinforced. Such depressed patients may see that they can be more effective in controlling their environment.

Lazarus (113) discussed three methods of treatment effective in depression, all of which seem to involve the patient's relearning that he controls reinforcers: 1) Assertive training, (Wolpe and Lazarus (114)) in which the patient rehearses and then puts into practice social responses which assert himself and bring about social reinforcers. 2) Affective expression in which the patient merely expresses anger. When this succeeds, it might result from displacement or counterconditioning, but it should not be overlooked that the expression of affect is a response which often has strong effects on the social environment. 3) Morita therapy (Kora (115)) puts patients in bed for about a week to "sensitize them to reinforcement" and progresses from light work to heavy work to complicated work. Such gradual exposure to the response-reinforcement contingencies of work resembles Burgess' (116) therapy aimed at reinforcing active behaviors in depressives. In a graded task treatment of depression, Burgess first had her patients emit some minimal bit of behavior like making a telephone call. She emphasized that it is crucial that the patient succeed, rather than just start it and give up. The task requirements were then increased, and the patient was reinforced by the attention and interest of the therapist for successfully completing the tasks. Concomitantly, Burgess reduced the secondary gain of the depressed behaviors, by ignoring them. Such a treatment may be successful because it exposes the patient to the contingencies between his own actions and significant rewards and punishments.

Some comment is in order on the role of "secondary gain" in depression. In order to explain depression, Burgess (116) and others have relied heavily on the reinforcement which the patient gets for his depressed behaviors. It is tempting to seek to remove their reinforcers during therapy, but caution is in order here. Secondary gain may explain the persistence or maintenance of *some* depressive behaviors, but it does not explain how they began. Helplessness suggests that failure to initiate active responding originates in the perception that the patient cannot control reinforcers. Thus a depressed patient's passivity probably can have two sources: 1) Patients who are passive for instrumental reasons, since staying depressed brings them sympathy, love and attention, and 2) Patients who are passive because they believe that *no* responses at all will be effective in controlling their environment. In this sense, secondary gain, while a practical hindrance to therapy, may be a hopeful sign in depression: It means that there is at least some response (albeit passive) that the patient believes he can effectively perform. Maier (14) found that dogs who were reinforced by shock termination for being passive were not nearly as debilitated as dogs for whom all responding was independent of shock termination. Similarly, patients who use their depression as a way of controlling reinforcers are less helpless than those who have given up.

Finally, individuals often adopt their own strategies for dealing with their minor depressions. Mine is to force myself to work: Sit down and write a paper, read a difficult text, or an article from a technical journal, or do a math problem. What better way is there for an intellectual to see that his responses still are effective and bring gratification than to plunge into writing, heavy reading, or problem solving? The problem is getting started.

commonalities

Learned helplessness can be broken up by forcing the passive dog to see that his responses produce reinforcement. A variety of techniques and theories suggest that therapy aimed at breaking up depression should center on the patient's sense of efficacy: Depression may be directly antagonized when patients come to see that their own responses are effective in alleviating their suffering and producing gratification.

difficulties

Many therapies, from psychoanalysis to T-groups, claim to be able to cure depression. The evidence presented above is selective: Only those treatments which seem compatible with helplessness were discussed. It is barely possible that when other therapies work it is because they reinstate the patient's sense of efficacy. Less anecdotal and selected evidence, however, is sorely needed on the effective elements of therapy in depression.

prevention

learned helplessness

Dramatic successes in medicine have come more frequently from prevention than from treatment, and I would hazard a guess that inoculation and immunization have saved many more lives than cure. Surprisingly, psychotherapy is almost exclusively limited to curative procedures, and preventative procedures rarely play an explicit role. In our studies of dogs we found that behavioral immunization provided an easy and effective means of preventing learned helplessness.

The helplessness viewpoint suggested a way to immunize dogs against inescapable shocks. Initial experience with escapable shocks should do two things:

1) interfere with learning that responding and shock termination are independent, and 2) allow the dog to discriminate between the situation where shocks are escapable and where they are inescapable. The relevant experiment was done by Seligman and Maier (9). One group of dogs was given ten escape-avoidance trials in the shuttle box before they received inescapable shocks in the hammock. Interference with subsequent escape-avoidance behavior was eliminated. That is, immunized dogs continued to respond normally when placed in the shuttle box 24 hours after inescapable shock treatment in the hammock. Another interesting finding emerged: The dogs which began by learning to escape shock in the shuttle box pressed the panels four times as often in the hammock during the inescapable shocks as did naive dogs, even though pressing panels had no effect on shock. Such panel pressing probably measures the attempts of the dog to control shock. Seligman, Marques, and Radford (117) extended these findings by first letting the dogs escape shock by panel pressing in the hammock. This was followed by inescapable shock in the same place. The experience with control over shock termination prevented the dogs from becoming helpless when they were later tested in a new apparatus, the shuttle box.

Other findings from our laboratory support the idea that experience controlling trauma may protect organisms from the helplessness caused by inescapable trauma. Recall that among dogs of unknown history, helplessness is a statistical effect: Approximately ⅔ of dogs given inescapable shock become helpless, while ⅓ respond normally. About 5 percent of naive dogs are helpless in the shuttle box without any prior experience with inescapable shock. Why do some dogs become helpless and others not? Could it be possible that those dogs who do not become helpless even after inescapable shock have had a pre-laboratory history of uncontrollable trauma? Seligman and Groves (15) tested this hypothesis by raising dogs singly in cages in the laboratory. Relative to dogs of variegated history, these dogs had very limited experience controlling anything. Cage-reared dogs proved to be more susceptible to helplessness: While it took four sessions of inescapable shock to produce helplessness one week later in dogs of unknown history, only two sessions of inescapable shock in the hammock were needed to cause helplessness in the cage-reared dogs. Lessac and Solomon (118) also reported that dogs reared in isolation seem prone to interference with escape. Thus dogs who are deprived of natural opportunities to master reinforcers in their developmental history may be more vulnerable to helplessness than naturally immunized dogs.

In this regard, we should mention the dramatic findings of Richter (42) on sudden death in wild rats. Richter discovered that when wild rats were squeezed in his hand until they stopped struggling, they drowned suddenly when placed in a water tank from which there was no escape. Unlike non-squeezed rats who swam for 60 hours before drowning, these rats died within 30 minutes. This phenomenon may be related to the findings of Engel and Ader (119) on enhanced susceptibility to death among hopeless and helpless humans, of Spitz (120) on the death of children following "anaclitic depression," the common reports of zookeepers on the high mortality rate of captured wild animals, to animal "hypnosis" (Chertok (121)), and to the findings of Ewing (41) that submissive cockroaches die mysteriously after defeat by dominant ones. Richter (42) reported that he could prevent sudden death by a technique which resembles our immunization procedure: If he held the rat, then let it go, held it again and let it go, sudden death did not occur. Further, if, after holding it, he put the rat in the water, took it out, put it in again and rescued it again, sudden death was prevented. These procedures, like our own, may provide the rat with a sense of control over trauma and thereby immunize against sudden death caused by inescapable trauma. Richter (42) speculated that the critical variable in sudden death was "hopelessness": Being held and squeezed in the hands of a predator seems a dramatic instance of loss of control over its environment for a wild animal.

depression

Even less is known about the prevention of depression than about its physiology or cure. Almost everyone sometimes loses control over the reinforcements that are significant to them: Parents die, loved ones reject you. Everyone also becomes at least mildly and transiently depressed in the wake of such events. But why are some people hospitalized for long periods and others resilient? We can only speculate about this, but the data on immunization against helplessness guide our speculations in a definite direction. The life histories of those individuals who are particularly resistant to depression or resilient from depression may have been filled with mastery. These people may have had extensive experience controlling and manipulating the sources of reinforcement in their lives, and may therefore perceive the future optimistically. Those people who are particularly susceptible to depression may have had lives relatively devoid of mastery. Their lives may have been full of situations in which they were helpless to influence their sources of suffering and gratification.

The relationship of depression in adults to loss of parents when young seems relevant: It seems likely that children who lose their parents experience helplessness and might be more vulnerable to later depression. The findings on this topic are mixed but lean toward establishing parental death as a predisposing factor in depression. Birtchnell (122, 123) reported that severely depressed patients had more parental, particularly maternal, deaths than less depressed patients. He also reported greater early parental death or absence in suicide attemptors. Similar findings have been reported by Brown, Epps, and McGlashan (124); Beck, Sethi, and Tuthill (125); Forrest, Fraser, and Priest (126); Dennehy (127); and Hill and Price (128), but they conflict as to whether loss of father or mother is the predisposing factor. In addition, the early studies are open to the criticism that the effect is not specific to depression, but may merely reflect a higher incidence of psychiatric disorders. Finally, Munro (129) did not find a significant difference between depressed patients and controls on early parental loss. So, it is possible, although not established, that losing a parent when young may make one more vulnerable to depression.

A caveat is in order here, however. While it seems reasonable that extensive experience controlling reinforcement might make one more resilient from depression, how about the person who has met *only* with success? Is an individual whose responses have always succeeded more susceptible to depression when confronted with situations beyond his control? It seems reasonable that too much experience controlling reinforcers might not allow the development and use of coping responses against failure, just as too little control might prevent the development of coping.

One can also look at successful therapy as preventative. After all, therapy is usually not focused just on undoing past problems. It also should arm the patient against future depressions. Would therapy for depression be more successful if it was explicitly aimed at providing the patient with a wide repertoire of coping responses that he could use in future situations in which he finds he cannot control reinforcement by his usual responses?

Finally, we can speculate about child rearing. What kind of experiences can best protect our children against the debilitating effects of helplessness and depression? A tentative answer follows from the learned helplessness view of depression: A childhood of experiences in which one's own actions are instrumental in bringing about gratification and removing annoyances. To see oneself as an effective human being may require a childhood filled with powerful synchronies between responding and its consequences.

references

1. Pavlov, I. P. *Conditioned Reflexes.* New York, Dover, 1927.
2. Liddell, H. *Emotional Hazards in Animals and Man.* Springfield, Ill., The Free Press of Glencoe, 1953.
3. Masserman, J. H. *Behavior and Neurosis.* Chicago, University of Chicago Press, 1943.
4. Wolpe, J. *Psychotherapy by Reciprocal Inhibition.* Stanford, Stanford University Press, 1958.
5. Maier, N. R. F. *Frustration.* Ann Arbor, University of Michigan Press, 1949.
6. McKinney, W. T., & Bunney, W. E. Animal model of depression. Review of evidence: Implications for research. *Arch. Gen. Psychiat., 21,* 240–248, 1969.
7. Wittgenstein, L. *Philosophical Investigations.* New York, The Macmillan Company, 1953.
8. Overmier, J. B., & Seligman, M. E. P. Effects of inescapable shock upon subsequent escape and avoidance learning. *J. Comp. Physiol. Psychol., 63,* 23–33, 1967.
9. Seligman, M. E. P., & Maier, S. F. Failure to escape traumatic shock. *J. Exp. Psychol., 74,* 1–9, 1967.
10. Carlson, N. J., & Black, A. H. Traumatic avoidance learning: The effects of preventing escape responses. *Canad. J. Psychol., 14,* 21–28, 1957.
11. Leaf, R. C. Avoidance response evocation as a function of prior discriminative fear conditioning under curare. *J. Comp. Physiol. Psychol., 58,* 446–449, 1964.
12. Seligman, M. E. P., Maier, S. F., & Geer, J. The alleviation of learned helplessness in the dog. *J. Abnorm. Soc. Psychol., 73,* 256–262, 1968.
13. Overmier, J. B. Interference with avoidance behavior: failure to avoid traumatic shock. *J. Exp. Psychol., 78,* 340–343, 1968.
14. Maier, S. F. Failure to escape traumatic shock: incompatible skeletal motor responses or learned helplessness? *Learn. & Motiv., 1,* 157–170, 1970.
15. Seligman, M. E. P., & Groves, D. Non-transient learned helplessness. *Psychonomic Sci., 19,* 191–192, 1970
16. Mowrer, O. H. An experimental analysis of "regression" with incidental observations on "reaction formation." *J. Abnor. Soc. Psychol., 35,* 56–87, 1940.
17. Dinsmoor, J., & Campbell, S. L. Escape-from-shock training following exposure to inescapable shock. *Psychol. Reports, 2,* 34–49, 1956.
18. Dinsmoor, J., & Campbell, S. L. Level of current and time between sessions as factors in adaptation to shock. *Psychol. Reports, 2,* 441–444, 1956.
19. Dinsmoor, J. Pulse duration and food deprivation in escape from shock training. *Psychol. Reports, 4,* 531–534, 1958.
20. Brown, J., & Jacobs, A. The role of fear in the motivation and acquisition of responses. *J. Exp. Psychol., 39,* 747–759, 1949.

21. Mullin, A. D., & Mogenson, G. J. Effects of fear conditioning on avoidance learning. *Psychol. Reports, 13*, 707–710, 1963.
22. Weiss, J. M., Krieckhaus, E. E., & Conte, R. Effects of fear conditioning on subsequent avoidance behavior. *J. Comp. Physiol. Psychol., 65*, 413–421, 1968.
23. Cohen, P. S., & Looney, T. A. Interference effects of noncontingent shocks upon subsequent acquisition of escape responding in a jump-up box. Paper presented at Eastern Psychological Assoc., New York, 1971.
24. Brookshire, K. H., Littman, R. A., & Stewart, C. N. Residue of shock trauma in the white rat: a three factor theory. *Psychol. Monogr., 75* (10, whole number 514), 1961.
25. Levine, S., Chevalier, J., & Korchin, S. The effects of early shock and handling on later avoidance learning. *J. Pers., 24*, 475–493, 1956.
26. Dennenberg, V. H., & Bell, R. Critical periods for the effects of infantile experience on adult learning. *Sci., 131*, 227–228, 1960.
27. Dennenberg, V. H. Effects of avoidable and unavoidable shock upon mortality in the rat. *Psychol. Reports, 14*, 43–46, 1964.
28. Seward, J., & Humphrey, G. L. Avoidance learning as a function of pre-training in the cat. *J. Comp. Physiol. Psychol., 63*, 338–341, 1967.
29. Behrend, E. R., & Bitterman, M. E. Sidman avoidance in the fish. *J. Exp. Analysis Behav., 13*, 229–242, 1963.
30. Pinckney, G. Avoidance learning in fish as a function of prior fear conditioning. *Psychol. Reports, 20*, 71–74, 1967.
31. Padilla, A. M., Padilla, C., Ketterer, T., & Giacalone, D. Inescapable shocks and subsequent avoidance conditioning in goldfish, Carrasius Avratus. *Psychonomic Sci., 20*, 295–296, 1970.
32. MacDonald, A. Effects of adaptation to the unconditioned stimulus upon the formation of conditioned avoidance responses. *J. Exp. Psychol., 36*, 1–12, 1946.
33. Thornton, J. W., & Jacobs, P. D. Learned helplessness in human subjects. *J. Exp. Psychol., 87*, 369–372, 1971.
34. Hiroto, D. S. The relationship between learned helplessness and locus of control. Unpublished doctoral dissertation, University of Portland, 1971.
35. Racinskas, John R. Maladaptive consequences of loss or lack of control over aversive events. Unpublished doctoral dissertation, Waterloo University, Ontario, Canada, 1971.
36. Powell, P. A., & Creer, T. L. Interaction of developmental and environmental variables in shock-elicited aggression. *J. Comp. Physiol. Psychol., 69*, 219–225, 1969.
37. McCulloch, T. L., & Bruner, J. S. The effect of electric shock upon subsequent learning in the rat. *J. Psychol., 7*, 333–336, 1939.
38. Braud, W., Wepmann, B., & Russo, D. Task and species generality of the "helplessness" phenomenon. *Psychonomic Sci., 16*, 154–155, 1969.
39. Anderson, D. C., & Paden, P. Passive avoidance response learning as a function of prior tumbling trauma. *Psychonomic Sci., 4*, 129–130, 1966.
40. Kahn, M. W. The effect of severe defeat at various age levels on the aggressive behavior of mice. *J. Genet. Psychol., 79*, 117–130, 1951.
41. Ewing, L. S. Fighting and death from stress in a cockroach. *Sci., 155*, 1035–1036, 1967.
42. Richter, C. On the phenomenon of sudden death in animals and man. *Psychosom. Med., 19*, 191–198, 1957.
43. Harlow, H. F., Harlow, M. K., & Suomi, S. J. From thought to therapy: Lessons from a primate laboratory. *Amer. Sci., 59*, 538–549, 1971.
44. Maier, S. F., Seligman, M. E. P., & Solomon, R. L. Pavlovian fear conditioning and learned helplessness. In Campbell, B. A., & Church, R. M., *Punishment*. New York, Appleton-Century-Crofts, 1969, 299–343.

45. Seligman, M. E. P., Maier, S. F., & Solomon, R. L. Unpredictable and uncontrollable aversive events. In Brush, F. R., *Aversive Conditioning and Learning.* New York, Academic Press, 1971, 347–400.
46. Weiss, J. M. Effects of coping response on stress. *J. Comp. Physiol. Psychol., 65,* 251–260, 1968.
47. Anderson, D. C., Cole, J., & McVaugh, W. Variations in unsignaled inescapable preshock as determinants of responses to punishment. *J. Comp. Physiol. Psychol., 65,* Monograph supplement 1–17, 1968.
48. Weiss, J. M., Stone, E. A., & Harrell, N. Coping behavior and brain norepinephrine level in rats. *J. Comp. Physiol. Psychol., 72,* 153–160, 1970.
49. Miller, N., & Weiss, J. M. Effects of somatic or visceral responses to punishment. In Campbell, B. A., & Church, R. M., (Eds.) *Punishment and Aversive Behavior.* New York, Appleton-Century-Crofts, 1969, 343–372.
50. Mowrer, O. H., & Viek, P. An experimental analogue of fear from a sense of helplessness. *J. Abnorm. Soc. Psychol., 43,* 193–200, 1948.
51. Lindner, M. Hereditary and environmental influences upon resistance to stress. Unpublished doctoral dissertation, University of Pennsylvania, 1968.
52. Grinker, R., Miller, J., Sabshin, M., Nunn, R., & Nunnally, J. *The Phenomena of Depressions.* New York, Hoeber, 1961.
53. Mendels, J. *Concepts of Depression.* New York, Wiley, 1970.
54. Beck, A. T. *Depression.* New York, Hoeber, 1967.
55. Bleuler, E. *Dementia Praecox or the Group of Schizophrenia,* trans. by Zinken, J. New York International University Press, 1953 (1911).
56. Lewinsohn, P. Paper presented at NIMH conference on depression. Airlie, Virginia, October 1971.
57. Ekman, P. Paper presented at NIMH conference on depression, Airlie, Virginia, October 1971.
58. Loeb, A., Beck, A. T., Diggory, J. C., & Tuthill, R. Expectancy, level of aspiration, performance and self evaluation in depression. Proceedings of the annual convention, *Amer. Psychol. Assoc., 2,* 193–194, 1967.
59. Friedman, A. S., Minimal effects of severe depression on cognitive functioning. *J. Abnorm. Soc. Psychol., 69,* 237–243, 1964.
60. Melges, F. T., & Bowlby, J. Types of hopelessness in psychopathological process. *Arch. Gen. Psychiat., 20,* 690–699, 1969.
61. Bibring, E. The mechanism of depression. In *Affective Disorders,* by Greenacre, P., (ed.). New York International University Press, 1953, 13–48.
62. Wallace, A. F. C. Mazeway disintegration: The individual's perception of socio-cultural disorganization. *Human Organization, 16,* 23–27, 1957.
63. Paskind, H. A. Brief attacks of manic-depressive depression. *Arch. Neurol. Psychiat., 22,* 123–124, 1929.
64. Paskind, H. A. Manic-depressive psychosis in private practice: Length of attack and length of interval. *Arch. Neurol. Psychiat., 23,* 789–794, 1930.
65. Lundquist, G. Prognosis and course in manic depressive psychosis. *Acta. Psychiat. Neurol. Suppl., 35,* 1945.
66. Kraines, S. H. *Mental Depressions and Their Treatment.* New York, Macmillan, 1957.
67. Klerman, G. L., & Cole, J. O. Clinical and pharmacology of imipramine and related antidepressant compounds. *Pharmacol. Rev., 17,* 101–141, 1965.
68. Cole, J. O. Therapeutic efficacy of antidepressant drugs. *J. Amer. Med. Assn., 190,* 448–455, 1964.
69. Davis, J. Efficacy of tranquilizing and antidepressant drugs. *Arch. Gen., Psychiat., 13,* 552–572, 1965.
70. Schildkraut, J. J. The catecholamine hypothesis of affective disorders: A review of supporting evidence. *Amer. J. Psychiat., 122,* 509–522, 1965.
71. Hoch, A. *Benign Stupors: A Study of a New Manic-Depressive Reaction Type.* New York, Macmillan, 1921.

72. Schmale, A. A genetic view of affects. *The Psychoanal. Stud. of the Child,* 19, 287–310, 1964.
73. Engel, G., & Schmale, A. Psychoanalytic theory of somatic disorder. *J. Amer. Psychoanal. Assn.,* 15, 344–365, 1967.
74. Weiss, J. M. Effects of coping behavior in different warning signal combinations on stress pathology in rats. *J. Comp. Physiol. Psychol.,* 77, 1–13, 1971.
75. Hoffman, H. S., & Fleshler, M. Stimulus aspects of aversive controls: The effects of response contingent shock. *J. Exp. Analy. Behav.,* 8, 89–96, 1965.
76. Hearst, E. Stress induced breakdown of an appetitive discrimination. *J. Exper. Analy. Behav.,* 8, 135–146, 1965.
77. Lepanto, R., Moroney, W., & Zenhausern, R. The contribution of anxiety to the laboratory investigation of pain. *Psychonomic Sci.,* 3, 475–476, 1965.
78. Church, R. M. Response suppression. In Campbell, B. A., & Church, R. M. (eds.) *Punishment and Aversive Behavior.* New York, Appleton-Century-Crofts, 1969, 111–156.
79. Gibbon, J. Contingency spaces and random controls in classical and instrumental conditioning. Paper presented at Eastern Psychological Association, Atlantic City, April, 1970.
80. Poresky, R. Noncontingency detection and its effects. Paper presented at Eastern Psychological Assoc., Atlantic City, April, 1970.
81. Premack, D. Reinforcement theory. In Jones, M. (ed.) *Nebraska Symposium on Motivation,* 1965.
82. Rescorla, R. A. Pavlovian conditioning and its proper control procedures. *Psychol. Rev.,* 74, 71–80, 1967.
83. Rescorla, R. A. Probability of shock in the presence and absence of the CS in fear conditioning. *J. Comp. Physiol. Psychol.,* 66, 1–5, 1968.
84. Wagner, A. R. Stimulus selection and a "Modified Continuity Theory." In G. H. Bower and J. T. Spence (eds.), *The Psychology of Learning and Motivation,* vol. 3. New York, Academic Press, 1969.
85. Watson, J. S. Memory and "contingency analysis" in infant learning. *Merrill-Palmer Quart. Behav. Develpm.,* 13, 55–76, 1967.
86. Ferster, C. B., & Skinner, B. F. *Schedules of Reinforcement.* New York, Appleton-Century-Crofts, 1957.
87. Honig, W. H. (ed.) *Operant Behavior: Theory and Research.* New York, Appleton-Century-Crofts, 1966.
88. Seligman, M. E. P. Chronic fear produced by unpredictable shock. *J. Comp. Physiol. Psychol.,* 65, 402–411, 1968.
89. Bresnahan, E. L. Effects of intradimensional and extradimensional equivalence training, and extradimensional discrimination training upon stimulus control. Paper presented at American Psychological Association, Washington, September 1969.
90. Thomas, D. R., Freeman, F., Svinicki, J. G., Burr, D. E., & Lyons, J. Effects of extradimensional training on stimulus generalization. *J. Exp. Psychol.,* 83, # 2, part 2, 1–22, 1970.
91. MacKintosh, N. J. Selective attention in animal learning. *Psychol. Bull.,* 64, 124–150, 1965.
92. Kemler, D., & Shepp, B. The learning and transfer of dimensional relevance and irrelevance in children. *J. Exp. Psychol.,* 90, 120–127, 1971.
93. Gamzu, E., & Williams, D. A. Classical conditioning of a complex skeletal response. *Sci.,* 171, 923–925, 1971.
94. Kiloh, L. G., & Garside, R. F. The independence of neurotic depression and endogenous depression. *Brit. J. Psychiat.,* 109, 451–463, 1963.
95. Kraepelin, E. Manic-depressive insanity and paranoia. In *Textbook of Psychiatry,* translated by Barclay, R. M. Edinburgh, Livingstone, 1913.
96. Partridge, M. Some reflections on the nature of affective disorders arising from the results of prefrontal leucotomy. *J. Ment. Sci.,* 95, 795–825, 1949.

97. Beck, A. T. The phenomena of depression: A synthesis. In Offer, D., & Freedman, D. X. (eds.), *Clinical Research in Perspective: Essays in Honor of Roy R. Grinker, Sr.* New York, Basic Books, 1970.

98. Beck, A. T. Cognitive therapy: Nature and relation to behavior therapy. *Behav. Ther., 1,* 184–200, 1970.

99. Lichtenberg, P. A definition and analysis of depression. *Arch. Neurol. Psychiat., 77,* 516–527, 1957.

100. Abramowitz, S. I. Locus of control and self reported depression among college students. *Psychol. Rep., 25,* 149–150, 1969.

101. Rotter, J. Generalized expectancies for internal vs. external control of reinforcement. *Psychol. Monogr.,* whole number 609, 966.

102. Mandler, G. The interruption of behavior. In D. Levine (ed.) *Nebraska Symposium on Motivation.* Lincoln, Nebraska, University of Nebraska Press, 1964, 163–219.

103. Mandler, G., & Watson, D. L. Anxiety and the interruption of behavior. In Spielberger, C. D. (ed) *Anxiety and Behavior.* New York, Academic Press, 1966.

104. Ferster, C. B. Animal behavior and mental illness. *Psychol. Rec., 16,* 345–346, 1966.

105. Kaufman, I. C., & Rosenblum, L. A. The reaction to separation in infant monkeys: Anaclitic depression and conservation-withdrawal. *Psychosom. Med., 29,* 648–675, 1967.

106. Liberman, R. P., & Raskin, D. E. Depression: A behavioral formulation. *Arch. Gen. Psychiat., 24,* 515–523, 1971.

107. Rescorla, R. A., & Skucy, J. Effect of response independent reinforcers during extinction. *J. Comp. Physiol. Psychol., 67,* 381–389, 1969.

108. Carder, B., & Berkowitz, K. Rats preference for earned in comparison with free food. *Sci., 167,* 1273–1274, 1970.

109. Jensen, G. D. Preference for bar pressing over "freeloading" as a function of the number of rewarded presses. *J. Exp. Psychol., 65,* 451–454, 1963.

110. Neuringer, A. J. Animals respond for food in the presence of free food. *Sci., 166,* 399–400, 1969.

111. Watson, J. S. Smiling, cooing, and "the game." Read at American Psychological Association meeting, Miami Beach, Florida, 1970.

112. Taulbee, E. S., & Wright, H. W. A psychosocial-behavioral model for therapeutic intervention. In C. D. Spielberger (ed.), *Current Topics in Clinical and Community Psychology,* III. New York, Academic Press, 1971.

113. Lazarus, A. A. Learning theory and the treatment of depression. *Behav. Res. Ther., 6,* 83–89, 1968.

114. Wolpe, J., & Larzarus, A. A. *Behavior Therapy Techniques.* Oxford, Pergamon Press, 1969.

115. Kora, T. Morita therapy. *Int. J. Psychiat., 1,* 611–645, 1965.

116. Burgess, E. The modification of depressive behavior. In Rubin, R., & Franks, C. (eds.), *Advances in Behavior Therapy.* New York, Academic Press, 1968.

117. Seligman, M. E. P., Marques, D., & Radford, R. Dominance and helplessness in rats. In preparation.

118. Lessac, M., & Solomon, R. L. Effects of early isolation on the later adaptive behavior of beagles: A methodological demonstration. *Develpm. Psychol., 1,* 14–25, 1969.

119. Engel, G., & Ader, R. Psychological factors in organic disease. *Mental Health Program Reports.* Public Health Service Publication #1568, NIMH, 1967, 1–23.

120. Spitz, R. Anaclitic depression. In: *The Psychoanalytic Study of the Child.* New York International University Press, 1946, 2, 313–342.

121. Chertok, L. Animal hypnosis. In Fox, M. W. (ed.), *Abnormal Behavior in Animals.* Philadelphia, Saunders, 1968.

122. Birtchnell, J. Depression in relation to early and recent parent death. *Brit. J. Psychiat.*, *11*, 299–306, 1970.
123. Birtchnell, J. The relationship between attempted suicide, depression, and parent death. *Brit. J. Psychiat.*, *116*, 307–313, 1970.
124. Brown, F., Epps, P., & McGlashan, A. The remote and immediate effects of orphanhood. *Proc. Third World Congr. Psychiat.*, Montreal, 1961.
125. Beck, A. T., Sethi, B., & Tuthill, R. Childhood bereavement and adult depression. *Arch. Gen. Psychiat.*, *9*, 295–302, 1963.
126. Forrest, C., Fraser, R., & Priest, R. Environmental factors in depressive illness. *Brit. J. Psychiat.*, *111*, 243–253, 1965.
127. Dennehy, C. Childhood bereavement and psychiatric illness. *Brit. J. Psychiat.*, *112*, 1049–1069, 1966.
128. Hill, O., & Price, J. Childhood bereavement and adult depression. *Brit. J. Psychiat.*, *113*, 743–751, 1967.
129. Munro, A. Parental deprivation in depressive patients. *Brit. J. Psychiat.*, *112*, 433–457, 1966.

12

Special Report: Schizophrenia, 1972

Loren R. Mosher and John G. Gunderson
with Sherry Buchsbaum

The number of resident schizophrenic patients in State and county mental hospitals fell to 180,000 in 1969 (the latest year for which data are available). This continues a dramatic downward trend which first became evident in 1963. The 15,000 drop from the preceding year's total of 195,000 reflects not only a reduction in the absolute number of resident schizophrenic patients but an accelerating *rate* of decline—from 7.1 percent in 1967–1968 to 7.7 percent in 1968–1969. Overall, between 1962 and 1969, there was a 31 percent decrease in resident schizophrenic patients paralleled by a concurrent 10 percent decrease in schizophrenic patients admitted for the first time to State and county mental hospitals. Thus, schizophrenics, who accounted for 21 percent of first admissions to these institutions in 1962, made up only 15 percent of the total in 1969. Over the same 7-year period, first admissions for diagnostic categories other than schizophrenia *increased* by 36 percent, and the census of nonschizophrenic resident patients declined by only 26 percent. Despite the *overall* decrease in the number of first admissions diagnosed as schizophrenic, the number admitted in the under-25 age group between 1962 and 1969 increased by nearly 19 percent (Taube 1971).

Although the statistics reported above are, on the whole, encouraging, schizophrenia remains a problem of enormous magnitude. In 1969, there were 474,000 additions (new admissions, readmissions, and returns from leave) of

Reprinted from *Schizophrenia Bulletin*, No. 7:12–52, Winter 1973, with the permission of the first author.

schizophrenic patients to all types of facilities. This figure represents only a crude approximation of the annual incidence of schizophrenia, since it is a duplicated count of persons admitted more than once to the same or to another facility and does not include an estimate of untreated cases.

Perhaps the most disquieting aspect of the schizophrenic disorder is its tendency to *recur*—a tendency that remains unchecked. In 1969, for example, fully 69 percent of total admissions to State and county mental hospitals had received previous care in such facilities. Multiple readmissions obviously contributed to the startlingly high number of reported patient-care episodes for schizophrenia—nearly 840,000. This figure approximates a 1-year interval prevalence of schizophrenia, since it includes the number of schizophrenics on the rolls of facilities at the beginning of 1969, plus all additions to these facilities in the succeeding 12 months. Thus, it is clear that, in terms of resource utilization, schizophrenia remains a grippingly serious problem that can be assuaged temporarily but cannot yet be prevented from recurring.

Declines in the number of schizophrenic patients resident in, or first admitted to, State and county mental hospitals are related to such factors as the growth of psychiatric units in general hospitals, widespread use of tranquilizers, increased availability of outpatient care, development of day-care facilities, and establishment of community mental health centers. While in 1969 the majority (63 percent) of schizophrenic patients were still cared for as hospital inpatients, a growing number were treated in outpatient clinics (35 percent) and day-care centers (2 percent). It is interesting to note that the number of schizophrenic patients treated in outpatient clinics nearly doubled between 1966 and 1969. . . .

the NIMH effort

We cite figures with great facility; yet what schizophrenia is, the process by which it develops, and the means for treatment elude adequate solution. Questions are deceptively easy to frame, but exceedingly difficult to answer. The study of schizophrenia remains a vast and complex problem involving the knowledge of a number of disciplines and the implementation of a variety of research approaches. Nonetheless, current investigative and therapeutic efforts may be roughly categorized in three broad areas.

The first focuses on identification and delineation of deficits in schizophrenia—in effect, an examination of what is "wrong" with schizophrenic patients. Prominent among the symptoms found in individual patients have been an inability to use language logically and effectively, disturbed patterns of learning and performance, decreased motivation or apathy in many situations, distorted sensory acuity and perception, and disturbed conceptual processes. The range of symptoms is such that research in this area demands knowledge of language and communication, emotion, motivation, perception, cognition, and personality, as well as the neural and endocrine bases of behavior.

Such knowledge, which can in part be obtained through basic behavior research, is important but nonetheless is insufficient to answer questions concerned with the second major area of interest—the development of the schizophrenic disorder. In contrast to basic behavioral research, etiological investigations must rely on the study of patients. A broad array of methods from the behavioral and biological sciences are being applied to the search for possible causative factors in the schizophrenic syndrome. Among the potentially significant factors are alterations in body chemistry, genetic abnormalities, upsetting family relations or faulty interpersonal communication, emotional stress resulting from traumatic events, and unsupportive community social structures. These examples, far from exhausting the range of possibilities, merely indicate the breadth of research necessary for the ultimate solution of the problem of etiology.

A third aspect of the problem deals with the development of effective treatments for those persons already diagnosed as schizophrenic. At one end of the research spectrum, scientists are attempting to determine the mechanisms by which psychoactive drugs have their effect; at the other, studies of family interaction, personality, and group dynamics are being undertaken to explore those social processes that may aggravate or ameliorate the disorder. . . .

diagnosis, description, and psychological function

A reliable diagnostic system has eluded psychiatry since the time of Kraepelin's first systematic efforts. Psychiatrists using a given diagnostic system still find themselves in disagreement, both about *how* to label a particular patient and *what* the label signifies. Traditionally, diagnostic systems have depended on the patient's presenting signs and symptoms; yet their significance to his past life or eventual outcome has been difficult to establish. Moreover, the reported signs and symptoms often vary according to the observer's theoretical stance and depth of knowledge. Further complicating the diagnostician's task is the fact that "presenting" signs and symptoms are changeable; a patient who was initially seen as a simple schizophrenic, for example, may look paranoid or hebephrenic after more intensive scrutiny. These and other frustrations have given rise to efforts to classify patients according to other criteria—notably past history or prognosis. While past history is useful in differentiating extreme types (e.g., good from poor premorbid patients), it fails to characterize adequately the majority of schizophrenic patients who fall midway along the process-reactive continuum. As a diagnostic tool, prognosis, too, seems inadequate—affected as it is by the uncertain influences of intervention efforts. Some nosologists claim that basic psychological, neurological, metabolic, or genetic indices are the most useful ways of classifying the schizophrenias. In the midst of all this disagreement, one thing is clear: there is not yet any universally accepted or consistent way of integrating the concepts of past history, prognosis, symptomatology, and neurobiological groupings into one diagnostic system. No doubt this difficulty reflects the very complexities of human nature which are so confusingly intertwined in schizophrenia.

cross-national studies

Past efforts to understand cross-national variations in the reported incidence of schizophrenia have revealed that disparities relate more to the diagnostic biases of psychiatrists in various parts of the world than to actual differences in patient populations. As part of the nine-nation collaborative International Pilot Study of Schizophrenia (IPSS) sponsored by the World Health Organization, the U.S. field center's investigative team has begun an attempt to standardize and revise prevailing diagnostic classifications (Strauss and Carpenter). In the first stage of this effort, the following diagnostic systems were compared for prognostic value in a group of 110 American patients: 1) Standard American clinical diagnoses based on the American Psychiatric Association's diagnostic manual. 2) Computer-derived diagnoses developed by J. K. Wing in London. 3) Lorr's psychotic types, based on the inpatient Multidimensional Psychiatric Scale. 4) Symptom clusters characteristic of the schizophrenic patients in this pilot study. Initial results indicated that none of the four systems can significantly predict 2-year followup status; on the other hand, use of multiple regression techniques demonstrates that certain prognostic items selected from these systems correlate highly with followup status. These preliminary findings replicate results of other studies relating past history to future outcome, and also suggest the lack of predictive validity of commonly used diagnostic systems.

Another large cross-national study of diagnostic practices utilized factor-analytic techniques on 700 items contained in a structured interview administered to 500 patients in the United States and England (Fleiss, Gurland, and Cooper, 1971). One result was the separation of retarded speech and movement from flat affect. The investigators then examined clinical subgroupings of schizophrenia to determine how they differed on these two dimensions. With respect to retardation, catatonic schizophrenics scored significantly higher than hebephrenics, who in turn scored significantly higher than paranoids. Flat affect was more characteristic of hebephrenics than of either catatonic or paranoid schizophrenics.

In another phase of this study focusing on national diagnostic biases, psychiatrists in New York and London were shown identical video tapes of diagnostic interviews (Zubin). Patients tended to be diagnosed schizophrenic by American psychiatrists if they showed some disorganization of thought, despite the presence of marked mood disturbance as well; British psychiatrists, on the other hand, weighted affective disturbances more heavily and diagnosed the same patients as suffering from mania or depression. These video-taped exercises have now been extended to audiences across the United States and parts of Canada. Interestingly, American psychiatrists practicing in western states were fairly similar to British psychiatrists in their diagnostic tendencies and perception of psychopathology; Canadian psychiatrists appeared to have diagnostic habits midway between the British and New York extremes.

To determine whether culturally derived diagnostic biases might influence concordance rates for schizophrenia in twins, six clinicians from Britain, the United States, and Japan used historical summaries to diagnose each of 114 twins as "schizophrenic," "questionably schizophrenic," "other diagnoses," or "normal" (Shields and Gottesman 1971). While varying considerably in the breadth or narrowness of their conceptions of schizophrenia, the clinicians reached high (80 percent) agreement in their diagnoses. The concordance rate, based on a consensual diagnosis, was similar to that previously reported by British psychiatrists. Interestingly, the two judges who had used the broadest and narrowest diagnostic criteria *both* found a lower concordance rate than that arrived at by the combined consensual diagnosis. The relatively high reliability in the evaluation of written material (rather than live interviews) in this study is in accord with work previously reported by other workers.

the schizophrenias—methods of classification

The system of computer-derived diagnoses developed by Spitzer and Endicott (1971) has been further refined, resulting in still higher agreement with traditional clinical diagnoses. The computer-derived diagnoses are likely to be helpful in establishing more consistent diagnostic labeling according to the traditional American Psychiatric Association classificatory system; but there might be better criteria for classifying schizophrenia than symptomatology. . . .

Another method for categorizing schizophrenic patients is based on a life-crisis model; patients are divided according to the nature of the crisis they underwent and their characteristic mode of handling it. In an effort to sort out clinical subtypes according to the course of decompensation and recompensation, Grinker, Holzman, and Kayton are collecting a bank of interview tapes on schizophrenic patients. Thus far, they have reviewed interviews with 60 young schizophrenics whose entrance into college had precipitated states of turmoil, confusion, and withdrawal. Most of these patients had experienced depression and loneliness, and felt irretrievably isolated despite some attempts to deal with environmental challenges.

Because of their confused thinking, many had severe anxieties about "going to pieces" or "going crazy," and under this pressure a few developed hallucinations. Once hospitalized, these subjects reconstituted quickly and were able to reconstruct the details of their disturbances during their second interview. The investigators hope that out of this interview program will ultimately emerge several subgroups of schizophrenic patients with discrete histories, clinical presentations, and responses to treatment.

Other efforts to find a meaningful diagnostic scheme have grouped schizophrenic patients according to their prognosis after hospitalization. Rosen, Klein, and Gittelman-Klein (1971), for example, studied the 3-year incidence of rehospitalization in a group of 81 patients. The results indicate that, if either age of first psychiatric contact or premorbid asocial adjustment is controlled, then marital status has no prognostic utility. This finding calls into question the central significance marital status is given on many prognostic scales. The results also suggest that the presence of premorbid asocial adjustment is an almost certain indicator of rehospitalization (87.2 percent), regardless of the patient's age when first treated for psychiatric problems. Among patients with some history of adequate social adjustment, however, the younger the age at which they first came to psychiatric attention, the greater their chances of being rehospitalized.

Another longitudinal effort to elucidate prognostic determinants was made by Yarden and Discipio (1971) in a 3-year followup of 18 young schizophrenics who exhibited abnormal movements of choreiform or athetoid type (with grimacing, tics, stereotypes, and mannerisms independent of drug side effects) and 36 consecutively admitted schizophrenic controls free of movement disorders. The patients with movement abnormalities were younger at first hospitalization than the controls, and their disease had progressed more steadily, with early and profound mental deterioration. The majority of the experimental group remained in the hospital for the entire observation period despite intensive treatment efforts, while members of the control group were hospitalized for shorter periods and showed better treatment response. With their obvious neurological deficits, the experimental subjects may represent a "neurological" subgroup within classic Bleulerian process schizophrenia.[1]

psychological function

A number of investigators have sought evidence of a basic psychological deficiency specific and pathognomonic for schizophrenia. While peculiarities in such functions as attention, cognition, and perception have been demonstrated in many schizophrenic patients, no one deficit characterizes *all* schizophrenics or is found *only* in schizophrenics. This persistent problem raises a double question:

Should the concept of schizophrenia be narrowed or, conversely, broadened? Of course, the failure to find a specific deficit in all schizophrenics might simply mean that the deficit is secondary to something more basic to the condition.

One deficit which has been found in young schizophrenics involves the memory system. Koh and Kayton describe these patients as inconsistent in organizing material and idiosyncratic in making associations. Their immediate memory span was narrow compared with that of both nonschizophrenic psychiatric patients and normal controls. When the words to be remembered were ranked according to whether they were pleasant or unpleasant, both control groups recalled the pleasant words significantly better than the unpleasant words, while schizophrenics did not. This finding may reflect, in the test situation, the anhedonia, or defective capacity for experiencing pleasure, so often found among schizophrenics. Further studies indicated that the schizophrenic's impaired short-term memory probably adversely affected his performance in these experiments. In a comparison of nonverbal perceptual memory, subjects were asked to compare their estimates of the number of dots in two slides. Only the schizophrenics failed to exhibit much improvement over repeated trials. This finding suggests that the schizophrenic's perceptual memory trace may decay rapidly or be particularly vulnerable to interference.

The above-mentioned apparent deficit in memory might also be explained by the attentional problems so often demonstrated in schizophrenics. Interested in learning whether attentional deficits persist beyond the period of psychotic disorganization, Wohlberg studied 16 first-admission female schizophrenic patients who were discharged after a rapid remission. At the time of study, these female patients had been discharged for more than a year, were off medication, and were functioning at their premorbid level. To the untrained observer, none appeared to be mentally ill, although one of two "blind" independent judges was able to distinguish them from 20 control subjects in a post-testing interview. Subjects were given the Continuous Performance Test, which required them to depress a lever whenever an X preceded by an A flashed on a screen. A distraction condition was interposed to disrupt attention. The remitted schizophrenic women made significantly more errors of omission (missing the X-A sequence) and commission (depressing the lever in the absence of the X-A sequence) than did the control subjects. They also had a longer correct-response latency time as testing progressed. These results indicate that, even after clinical recovery, there may remain a residual attentional defect in schizophrenic patients. Its presence at a time when the individual is clinically "well" supports the hypothesis that attentional problems could antecede the development of overt psychosis.

Although it has frequently been alleged that paranoid schizophrenics have better preserved mental functioning than other schizophrenic patients, a number of recent studies cast some doubt upon the validity of this notion. Intrigued by provocative results in a small sample of schizophrenics, Jerome and Young (1972) studied a larger number of subjects and confirmed their initial finding that chronic undifferentiated schizophrenics consistently obtained higher scores on problem-solving tasks than paranoid schizophrenics. The paranoids' performance was particularly disrupted by increases in problem size or objective uncertainty and when a change of set was necessitated by a reversal of the information cue. The chronic undifferentiated patients, on the other hand, showed losses in scores only when problem size was increased. The low scores of the paranoid schizophrenics were attributed to a deficiency in a basic heuristic quality—the ability to deal with sets of objects.

Since the original observations of Bleuler, who stressed the primary role of associative disturbances in schizophrenia and noted the frequent disruption of word meanings, many experiments have related the poor performance of schizophrenic patients on abstraction tasks to associative disturbances in word meaning. Willner and Struve (1970), for example, have attempted to devise tests of abstraction and word association which pinpoint the relationship between associative dysfunction and impaired abstraction. They have reported evidence for the simultaneous occurrence of severe associative disturbance and impaired abstraction in the same patients. In further studies, Willner found that poor scores on abstraction tests (based on interpreting analogies) consistently predicted EEG abnormalities in over 200 hospitalized psychiatric patients, regardless of whether they were on drugs.

In studying the learning problems of schizophrenic patients, Hannes has addressed an issue which is central to the interpretation of studies like those described above: Do deficits found in schizophrenics represent real differences or merely poor motivation relative to controls? Hannes compared the ability of schizophrenic patients and normals to learn alternating patterns of lights (L) and sounds (S). On a single alternating pattern (S,L,S,L, etc.) the patients learned as quickly as the normals. When these same groups were later compared on a double alternating pattern (S–S, L–L, S–S, etc.), the patients once again learned as quickly as the normals. This indicated that prior exposure to the single alternating pattern improved the ability of the patients to learn, since in a previous test of the double alternating pattern (without prior introduction of the single alternating one) Hannes had found schizophrenics less able to learn than normals. The fact that the second group of patients learned the double alternating pattern as well as normals suggested to the investigator that the observed impairment of the schizophrenics on double alternating learning in the initial experiment may have been attributable to motivation. The investigator hypothesized that the single alternating task was a simple task requiring little motivation for its learning which, once absorbed, made the learning of a double alternating task relatively simple, again requiring little motivation. Although other explanations for the data could be made, this study at least suggests the danger in too readily interpreting the results of tests which depend upon subjects' performance.

Summing up the diverse series of studies described above is difficult, perhaps impossible. It does appear, though, that looking at the schizophrenic person from a variety of points of view allows for his more adequate characterization— rather than such an oversimplified one as, "schizophrenia is a disorder of perception"—and may reflect more accurately the intricacies and complexities of his personality, which is affected in so many ways by this disorder. After all, in schizophrenia the person *is* the disorder; he does not carry it as an organ lesion, and therefore his entire person—not one facet of it—must be described.

genetics

twin studies

Recent twin studies have tended to diminish previously estimated concordance rates for schizophrenia (the frequency of the disorder's occurrence in both twins). The improved methodology of these genetic studies and the consistency of their results, however, suggest a genetic factor in at least some types of schizophrenia. Most geneticists now believe that schizophrenia, per se, is not inherited. Rather it is a *predisposition* to schizophrenia (or, perhaps, to psychopathology in general) which is transmitted genetically.

An analysis of the nearly 16,000 pairs of male twins born from 1917 to 1927 who served in the U.S. Armed Services found 420 pairs in which one or both twins were diagnosed as schizophrenic (Allen et al. 1971). The data show that 26 of 95 monozygotic pairs (27.4 percent) and six of 125 dizygotic pairs (5.7 percent) were concordant for schizophrenia. This is consistent with the results of other recent studies of twins based on birth-record ascertainment and in contrast to those of earlier studies based on hospitalized cases, which generally found concordance rates as high as 75 percent. An interesting sidelight of this study was the discovery of a comparatively greater genetic influence in the development of affective psychosis as compared to schizophrenia. For affective disorders five of 13 monozygotic pairs (38.5 percent) and none of 27 dizygotic twin pairs were concordant. It is interesting to note that schizo-affective cases followed a pattern more similar to affective than to schizophrenic psychoses; seven of 14 monozygotic pairs (50 percent) and none of 12 dizygotic pairs in the schizo-affective category were concordant. These data suggest to the investigators that, if genetically determined biochemical factors are found in schizophrenia, they are likely to be more subtle and more environmentally entwined than those associated with the affective psychoses.

Although the study of twins is most often thought of as a genetic tool, this type of investigation can also elucidate environmental factors when identical twins *discordant* with respect to a particular characteristic (i.e., one twin has it and his co-twin does not) are compared; we include studies of this type here because the genetic factor is controlled in the comparison between twins. Using the discordant twin method, Pollin and his group have attempted to define the environmental influences which lead one member of a pair of identical twins to become schizophrenic while the other does not. By comparing the very different life courses of two genetically identical individuals, the investigators attempt to examine the role of specific environmental variables on the development of schizophrenia. Efforts have been made to evaluate the twins biochemically, neurologically, and diagnostically.

An early report suggested that a possible genetically determined catecholamine elevation might be present in twin pairs which included a schizophrenic. Further investigation has shown, however, that 3-methoxy, 4-hydroxy-phenyl-glycol (MHPG), the catecholamine which is believed to be the best measure of central nervous system (rather than peripheral) catecholamine release, is not elevated in the twins studied (Pollin 1971).

In the past year, neurological findings in 22 identical twin pairs (15 discordant for schizophrenia, three concordant, and four psychologically normal) were reported (Mosher, Pollin, and Stabenau 1971b). Two careful independent neurological examinations and two EEG's were done on each twin. Eleven of 15 schizophrenic index cases in the discordant pairs, two of six schizophrenics in the concordant pairs, and two of eight normal twins were judged as "probably" or "definitely" neurologically abnormal. In the discordant pairs, significantly more abnormal signs were found in the schizophrenic index twins than in their non-schizophrenic co-twins. In addition, significant correlations were found between high neuropathology scores and both low intelligence and high levels of psychopathology. Although the EEG data revealed few clear abnormalities and striking intrapair concordance, half the sample had some minor deviation from normal on at least one of their EEG's. The authors conclude that, based on these findings, it is not possible to decide whether the neurological abnormalities preceded the development of schizophrenia or were a consequence of it. They emphasize the care that must be exercised in interpreting differences between schizophrenics and normals as etiologically significant, since the schizophrenic has been subject to the incalculable effects of such correlates of psychiatric care as prolonged hospitalization, electroshock therapy, and tranquilizing drugs.

In another study of the same sample of discordant twin pairs, Mosher, Stabenau, and Pollin (1971) addressed a genetic, rather than an environmental, issue. If schizophrenia is transmitted as a single dominant gene—a theory advanced by a number of investigators—then most of the nonpsychotic co-twins of schizophrenics should manifest "schizoid" characteristics (indicative of the schizophrenic genotype in the absence of its phenotypic expression as clinically identifiable schizophrenia). Based on careful assessments of clinical interview material, however, Mosher and his colleagues found no greater evidence of schizoid characteristics in 15 nonpsychotic co-twins of schizophrenics than in eight normal controls. While no firm conclusions can be drawn on the basis of this small sample, the study casts doubt upon the concept of schizoid personality as an expression of a genetic predisposition to schizophrenia.

relatives of schizophrenics

In Norway, Kringlen has studied the psychiatric status of 70 adult offspring of 22 pairs of parents who were both psychotic. Although previous studies have demonstrated that individuals reared in such families have a 30 to 60 percent risk of developing schizophrenia, only 19 percent of the offspring in the present sample developed a psychosis, usually schizophrenia. (Even with age correction, the maximal incidence of psychosis in this sample would be less than 25 percent, according to Kringlen.) Thirty-eight percent of the offspring had a diagnosis of neurosis, psychopathy, or alcoholism, and the remaining 41 percent were classified as normal.[2] The last group is a particularly interesting one: How did 41 percent of these high risk offspring manage to grow up normal despite the extremely unfavorable genetic and environmental odds against them? What were the skills which enabled them to cope with seemingly very pathological environments? How were these coping skills learned? These as yet unanswerable questions point up a regrettably neglected area of schizophrenia research—the identification of those strengths which hold pathology at bay. Knowledge of these coping skills and their antecedents would be a most important aid in developing preventive measures and treatment.

A number of investigators are now attempting to determine how a genetic predisposition interacts with environmental factors in order to predict which "susceptible" individuals will and will not succumb to schizophrenia. The importance of the environmental contribution to psychosis has been highlighted by ongoing collaborative studies in Denmark. Based on a study of adopted-away offspring of schizophrenic parents, Rosenthal et al. (1971) reported that the likelihood of schizophrenia occurring is reduced if the child is adopted and raised by nonschizophrenic parents.

In a separate but related study, Kety et al. (1971) compared the prevalence of schizophrenic spectrum (chronic, acute, borderline) disorders among biological relatives of 33 adopted schizophrenics with their occurrence in relatives of the schizophrenics' adoptive parents. Preliminary results showed a greater number (13 out of 150) of schizophrenia-related disorders in the biological relatives than in the adoptive relatives (two of 74). These results were then compared to the prevalence of schizophrenia-related disorders among relatives of a control group comprised of 33 matched adopted individuals who had no recorded history of mental illness. For this group of adoptees, three of 156 biological relatives and two of 83 adoptive relatives had schizophrenia-related disorders. Thus, the prevalence of schizophrenia among biological relatives of the adopted children who ultimately became schizophrenic is significantly elevated. Based on findings to date, Kety et al. have concluded that genetic factors are important in the development of schizophrenia.

Genetic studies presently underway reflect a shift from concentration on the dilemma of genetics vs. environment to more productive attempts to define the specific ways in which a genetic predisposition interacts with the environment to produce schizophrenia. Many important questions remain to be answered. For example, can an individual develop schizophrenia without a genetic predisposition? Is it possible to define precisely the predisposition to schizophrenia? Which environmental influences are most schizophrenogenic when interacting with a genetic predisposition? The high risk and family studies, in particular, offer logical extensions to the geneticists' vulnerability determinations in seeking answers to these perplexing questions.

the family

As genetic studies clarify the importance of environmental conditions in precipitating schizophrenia, studies of families assume even greater importance. Despite advances in our understanding of the schizophrenic's family since the time of Frieda Fromm-Reichmann's first discussion of "schizophrenogenic" mothers, we are still a long way from showing that the repeatedly observed patterns of pathological interaction in these families have etiological significance. Two major questions remain to be answered: Do differences between parents of schizophrenics and other groups of parents precede, or are they a consequence of, their child's development of psychosis? This crucial question can best be addressed by high risk studies conducted *prior* to manifest illness (recent developments in this area are discussed in another section of this report). A second important question to be answered by family studies relates to the "selection" of a child to develop psychopathology. That is, why does only *one* of several children in a family become schizophrenic? Two studies which address this important question have recently been reported.

In a sample of 11 identical twin pairs discordant for schizophrenia, Mosher, Pollin, and Stabenau (1971a) employed clinical assessments and objective tests to interpret different outcomes in a given family. Measures of identification, cognitive style, thought disorder, dominance-submissiveness, and global psychopathology in the twins and in their parents showed that:

- The schizophrenic index twins tended to be identified with the parent who was psychologically less healthy (usually the mother); objective tests (the Minnesota Multiphasic Personality Inventory ego strength and masculinity-femininity scales) which were used to parallel clinical assessments of psychopathology and identification, respectively, were equivocal in their documentation of these findings.

- Clinically, the index twins were judged to be more "global" in their cognitive styles than their nonschizophrenic co-twins, and were rated as identified with the more "global" member of the parental pair; the related objective measure (the Embedded Figures Test) supported this finding strongly.
- The schizophrenic indexes were generally the most submissive members of the twin pairs.
- The mothers in these families were rated as less healthy and, contrary to their culturally ascribed submissive-expressive role, tended to be dominant.

Based on these findings, Mosher, Pollin, and Stabenau suggest that the index twin, as a result of an initial constitutional difference from his co-twin (e.g., lower birth weight), may have been given more attention by the parent who was less healthy psychologically and who had less clear cognitive processes. This early established pattern of identification with the more "psychopathological" parent, the authors postulate, led to the differential development of unclear thought patterns in the index twin.

Waxler and Mishler (1971) also addressed the question of how one family member could be "singled out" to develop schizophrenia, but their approach to this issue was different from that taken by Mosher, Pollin, and Stebenau. Parents who had one normal and one schizophrenic adolescent or young adult offspring were asked to participate in a two-part experimental situation, once with the schizophrenic child and again with a well sibling (who was of the same sex as the patient and close to him in age). While these three-person groups—the two parents and one of their children—discussed items on which they disagreed, their interactions were recorded and then analyzed. A number of variables were examined, including interpersonal control strategies, expressiveness, responsiveness, each parent's behavior, their combined behavior as a parental pair, and the relative amount of behavior directed towards the child. When the sessions with the schizophrenic offspring and their parents were compared to sessions involving a control group of matched normal parents and their offspring, the patients' families proved more pathological on almost all measures of interaction. Interaction in the normal control sessions was then compared to interaction in the sessions involving the schizophrenic's parents and a well sibling. In this experimental condition, significant differences between the groups were rare, suggesting that family interactions vary according to the presence or absence of the schizophrenic child. But in apparent contradiction of this finding, a direct comparison of the parents' interaction with the schizophrenic offspring to their interaction with the well sibling revealed *no* significant differences on any variable! Because of the seeming incompatibility of these findings (which may reflect a sample too small to generate significant results with any consistency) Waxler and Mishler were hesitant to defer to the hypothesis that the pathology observed in parents of schizophrenics is a response to their offspring's illness, but did point out that the alternative hypothesis—implicating a systematically different parental interaction with the sick and well child—received no positive empirical support. One other aspect of this study is worthy of note. When the sample of families of schizophrenics was subdivided according to the offspring's premorbid status, measures of expressiveness and interruptions showed that families with poor premorbid schizophrenic children were closer to normal than families whose schizophrenic offspring had good premorbid histories.

Wynne and Singer are well known for their development of measures of communication deviance (e.g., peculiar language, overexactness, or blurred meanings) which distinguish among the parents of schizophrenics, other psychiatric patients, and normals. Recently, these investigators established that the frequency of communication deviances shown by parents is highly predictive of the severity of illness found in their most disturbed offspring. This variable is significant even when the effects of other variables, such as clinical diagnosis of the parents, social class of the family, age, education of various family members, and sex of the offspring, are taken into account or held constant. Wynne and Singer have also found that severity of parental illness is a valuable predictor of diagnosis in the offspring. The clinical diagnosis of the parents and their communication deviance scores include components which are statistically independent of one another and which each separately predict the offspring's diagnosis with accuracy. A diagnosis of borderline syndrome in the parents is especially valuable for predicting a subdiagnosis of process schizophrenia in the offspring. The parents of reactive schizophrenics, in contrast to those of process schizophrenics, show relatively little pathology by clinical diagnosis; they do, however, show high communication deviance scores—albeit somewhat lower than those of parents of process patients. Data analyses of 41 subcategories of communication deviance have now reached a stage at which it is possible to specify and confirm that the communication behavior of the parents of schizophrenics, though different from that of the schizophrenics themselves, is highly predictive of the occurrence and severity of schizophrenic illness in the offspring.

After comparing the interactional patterns in families of disturbed (borderline psychotic) 8- to 12-year-olds to those in families with less-disturbed (character-disordered and neurotic) or normal children, Schuham concluded that the nonverbal dimensions of observed interactions are able discriminators of disturbed families. In a preliminary report on 25 family groups, families with a borderline psychotic offspring tended to manifest shorter discussion times, to disagree more, and to be less able to maintain coalitions than normal families. The degree of pathology in the child could be accurately discriminated using the following variables: 1) Number of discussions in which consensus took place; 2) amount of family talking time; 3) number of mother/father coalitions sustained when the child disagreed; and 4) number of interruptions. The fact that two of these discriminating variables (talking time and number of interruptions) are unrelated to content confirms the importance attributed to noncontent measures in other studies. The finding of consistent differences among three types of family groups is particularly impressive in view of the relatively small sample size and the fact that subjects were drawn from a heretofore rarely studied age group.

Sojit (1971), an investigator working in South America, carried out an interesting study of the reaction of parents of schizophrenics to a *double bind*. Briefly, the double bind is a situation in which a subject is asked to respond to a communication which has an overt and covert message requiring mutually exclusive or incongruent responses. This study modifies the original concept (which was applied to the families of schizophrenics exclusively) by proposing that double binds are present in all families and in a number of social contexts. In the double-bind situation used by Sojit, subjects were told to interpret a proverb in a way that suggested it had only *one* meaning when, in fact, it had two equally possible but opposite interpretations. Responses of eight pairs of parents of schizophrenics were compared to responses made by parents of delinquents, parents of patients with ulcerative colitis, and parents of normals. Out of a total sample of 54 parental pairs, the parents of schizophrenics gave the most invalid interpretations and disaffirmed their own or their spouses' interpretations most frequently. Even when not placed in a double-bind situation, the parents of schizophrenics still tended to give invalid interpretations; thus, only the disaffirmative or contradictory quality of their responses was specific to the double bind. Because each of the four groups of parents showed different patterns of response to the experimental situation, the double bind might be described as a particular type of conflict which may be related to various disorders; its pathogenicity lies in the differing models of response parents present to their child. What is specific to schizophrenia, therefore, may not be the double bind itself but, rather, a contradictory, disaffirming response pattern to it.

One of the most important questions which remains to be answered by family studies involves "selection" of one family member to be schizophrenic. Although the results of the two studies which attempted to explore this issue seem contradictory, they do provide a useful starting point for future investigations of this important question. They also highlight the problems and complexities which continue to haunt the field of family research in schizophrenia.

studies of populations at "high risk"

Because it is not possible to conclude whether findings in studies of already manifest, diagnosed schizophrenics reflect a cause or result of the subjects' illness, many frustrated investigators are now turning to the "high risk" research approach. In brief, this investigative strategy entails the prospective study of persons who, for some reason (e.g., the fact that they have a schizophrenic parent) are thought to be vulnerable to breakdown. By studying the preschizophrenic from earliest childhood, investigators hope to identify biochemical, physiological, psychological, or life-history characteristics which distinguish him—even before his disorder becomes manifest—from normal controls and other individuals "at risk" who do not develop psychiatric illness. The predisposing signs and symptoms identified in initial studies will be used to refine and expand the criteria used (now largely genetic) for selecting individuals at risk. Eventually, of course, the accumulated findings of high risk studies will be a major aid in the development of preventive intervention programs. In the past year a number of investigators began to report early results of their long-term studies; to provide a profile of the preschizophrenic from gestation to adolescence, findings will be summarized here in order of the increasing age of the sample at risk.

complications of pregnancy and birth

The earliest application of the high risk technique was a longitudinal study of 207 Danish schoolchildren aged 10-20. Recently, Mednick (1970) reported on the first 20 subjects in this group to develop a "mental disorder." Perhaps the most interesting distinguishing characteristic of these 20 individuals is the fact that 70 percent of their mothers experienced serious complications of pregnancy or childbirth. This finding is considered particularly suggestive because another of Mednick's studies demonstrated that schizophrenic women tend to have more difficulties in childbirth than nonschizophrenic expectant mothers.

Intrigued by Mednick's findings, Sameroff compared 12 pregnant schizophrenic women to 12 pregnant women with other psychiatric diagnoses (mainly neurotic depressions) and 12 matched normal controls. Both psychiatric groups had significantly more delivery complications than the controls, and the EEG's of their newborn babies showed frequent abnormalities. This study confirms the impression that disturbed mothers have considerable difficulty in childbirth, but indicates that these complications are not a risk factor specific to schizophrenia.

newborns

Schachter has studied the physiological functioning of newborn offspring of schizophrenic mothers; he hoped by this method to isolate differential functioning at a time when it could be attributed to genetic and pregnancy risk factors. Several days after birth, 13 infants were exposed to clicking noises of several intensities and at various intervals. The heart rate of these infants was more variable and showed a greater rise in level during the experimental sessions than did the heart rate of 32 neonates of normal mothers. It would seem, therefore, that an early physiological difference may be present in the children of schizophrenics, but no firm conclusions can be drawn until this finding's specificity and independence of such factors as birth weight and maternal birth medication have been established.

preschool-aged children

Grunebaum and his group have compared the preschool children of 47 recently discharged psychotic mothers with a matched group of children of non-psychotic mothers. In the course of testing, the high risk children (who ranged in age from 4 months to 6 years at the initial testing) demonstrated as much negative affect as the controls but significantly less positive affect. Unlike the children of normal mothers, they tended to be passively compliant in problem-solving situations, interacted little with examiners, were reluctant to ask questions, and frequently failed to meet task requirements. Within the high risk group, the children of schizophrenic mothers exhibited even less positive affect and greater attentional deficits than the offspring of other types of psychiatric patients. They also formed the least appropriate relationships to the examiners, tending to be either overinhibited or uncontrolled in expressing their feelings. In general, then, these tentative findings (based on relatively small numbers of children) portray the preschool child whose mother has had a recent schizophrenic episode as inattentive, withdrawn, and showing little positive affect.

school-aged children

Miller has described a sample of 108 school-aged children with schizophrenic mothers from a sociological point of view by comparing their records of contact with community facilities (legal, medical, or educational) to the records of 57 children of welfare recipients and of 50 children matched for social class. Despite a tendency for the schizophrenic mothers to have more divorces, separations, and open conflicts in the home than the controls, their children were less likely to engage in socially deviant behavior than either the children of welfare mothers or the matched controls. Children with schizophrenic mothers were even somewhat *less* likely to be referred for psychiatric evaluation; of the eight who *were* referred, however, four were diagnosed as schizophrenic. None of the 15 psychiatric referrals from the other two groups were so diagnosed.

Watt et al. (1970) attempted to identify characteristics predictive of schizophrenia by retrospectively comparing the childhood public school records of 30 hospitalized adult schizophrenics with those of 90 matched classroom controls. They found that the preschizophrenic boys had exhibited unsocialized aggression, while the girls had been overinhibited, introverted hyperconformists. Because these results are consistent with those found in Mednick's (1970) longitudinal study in Denmark, it was concluded that such behavior patterns in school children are significant predictors of schizophrenic outcome. The depiction of the preschizophrenic boy as aggressive is in marked contrast to the long-held view of him as withdrawn and inhibited.

In a similar retrospective study, Kreisman (1970) focused on the quality of adolescent friendships formed by a group of young, hospitalized, male schizophrenics and a matched group of unhospitalized normal controls. Kreisman's hypothesis that schizophrenics would recall greater difficulty in their friendships was confirmed. The few peer relationships the patients had succeeded in establishing were notable for their lack of intimacy.

Marcus has made psychological and neurological assessments of 100 Israeli children (aged 8–14), half of whom had a schizophrenic parent and half of whom did not. Based on "blind" clinical interviews, index cases (i.e., children with a schizophrenic parent) could be distinguished from controls on the following traits: peer relations, suspicion of peers, feelings of not belonging, group activity, mental activity, energy, initiative, oral habits, humor, lisping, fluency of speech, and preschizophrenic trends. Examined by a neurologist who did not know which children had schizophrenic parents, the groups were distinguishable when subdivided by age: Index cases under 11 years of age consistently had higher neuropathology scores than controls, while older indexes did not differ from controls. The investigator hypothesized that there may be a neurological predisposition in the indexes which either disappears at adolescence or moves the individual toward a schizophrenic denouement. Three of the children in this study who have now entered adolescence have become schizophrenic; all were index cases. Because of the suggestive findings in this and other studies, most new research protocols involving children at risk include intensive neurological evaluations.

adolescents

Most high risk studies have used genetic relationships (i.e., having a schizophrenic parent) to identify vulnerable individuals. Yet, the majority of people who develop schizophrenia do *not* have a schizophrenic parent. Thus, findings in groups selected on this genetic basis may not be generalizable to the rest of the universe (about 90 percent) of schizophrenics. In an effort to circumvent this limitation, Rodnick and Goldstein have used referral for psychological treatment during adolescence as a criterion of vulnerability and have evaluated patterns of interaction in 50 families whose adolescent children had been seen in a local outpatient clinic. The teenaged subjects were divided into four types based on their presenting problem: 1) aggressive, antisocial; 2) active family conflict; 3) passive, negative; and 4) withdrawn, socially isolated. A 5-year followup of 25 subjects disclosed that only a few had achieved even average social competence and most were just "struggling along" with marginal success. Three (or possibly four) of this group had had a psychotic break during the followup period, and preliminary evidence suggests that subjects of types 2 and 4 are most vulnerable to breakdown. In a retrospective survey of a group of acute schizophrenics, the same investigators found that patients thought to have good prognoses (as determined by the Phillips Scale of Premorbid Adjustment) had family relationships and social competence similar to type 2 adolescents, while those judged to have poor prognoses had backgrounds similar to those classified as type 4. Thus, Rodnick and Goldstein's combined prospective-retrospective approach has validated the importance of the poor premorbid/good premorbid (or process-reactive) dimension—a dichotomy which researchers have long found useful in dealing with the problem of diagnostic heterogeneity in hospitalized schizophrenics (Goldstein 1971). This prospective evidence confirms that at least two indicators of premorbid adjustment—adolescent social competence and family interactional style—are useful in predicting the occurrence of schizophrenia.

As a group, the studies discussed above provide a rough, preillness description of the individual who is destined to develop schizophrenia. His birth process is likely to have been disturbed, and as an infant, he may have shown neurological abnormalities and possibly some unusual stimulus responsivity. By several years of age, he probably was rather withdrawn and inattentive, and his feelings had begun to seem overly inhibited or poorly controlled. He was not likely to have been a serious behavior problem in school, but may have been somewhat aggressive (or, if a girl, inhibited). Guarded in his interaction with peers, he probably complained of feeling like an outsider. Neurological examination may have shown nonspecific signs of neuropathology which tended to disappear after age 11. In adolescence, his difficulties with peers may have grown more severe; very likely, he complained of loneliness and a lack of intimate friendships.

Until this sketchy picture of the preschizophrenic is more conclusively drawn, a determined effort must be made to avoid prematurely "labeling" children who manifest some or all of these characteristics or planning intervention programs for them. Some of the important questions to be asked are: Who should determine whether a child is to be treated preventively? What treatments should be offered, and what is their potential long-term harm? In what context should such intervention be undertaken—psychiatric, educational, or familial? It does not seem that our ability to identify truly preschizophrenic children is yet well enough developed for us to plan a comprehensive program of preventive intervention.

childhood schizophrenia and autism

Although far less prevalent than schizophrenia of adolescence and adulthood, the severe functional disorders of childhood are equally perplexing. The two major childhood psychoses were identified as diagnostic categories only recently—childhood schizophrenia in 1933 and autism a decade later. Because distinctions between these categories remain blurred, prevalence rates vary widely (estimates range from 2 to 6 per 10,000 population), and disagreement among clinicians diagnosing the same child is common. It is now generally agreed that children with functional psychoses are characterized by difficulties in four major areas:

- Receptor behavior or perception;
- Language;
- Social attachments; and
- Sense of self, or identity.

But controversy still exists over more specific characteristics: *Which* and *how many* signs and symptoms within these broad functional categories are necessary or sufficient to make a diagnosis (DeMyer et al. 1971)? Explanations of *how* and *why* the disorders occur at all are even more speculative.

Understandably, the parents who must live with, care for, and raise seriously disturbed children want to know why their child is deviant; they search—sometimes in desperation—for a means of "curing" him. The disappointing truth is that investigators do not now have adequate answers to offer parents; no specific etiological factors have been isolated, and no treatment is curative. This is not to say, however, that neither causal hypotheses nor helpful treatments are available. Rather it means that no *simple* or *completely satisfactory* explanation of etiology or treatment program has yet been found.

learning deficits

Several scientists have described a learning deficit in autistic children which they characterize as failure to transfer information across modes. Lovaas, for example, has found that autistic children react to the simultaneous presence of two or more sensory inputs by "overselecting," or responding to only one of the inputs. Thus, he observed that autistic children who were simultaneously presented visual, auditory, and tactile cues could respond to only one cue at a time. It was as if, when the autistic child listened, he could not see or feel, or vice versa. Lovaas believes that this finding has implications which might aid in the understanding of autism. Since most learning involves the simultaneous presentation of cues, an inability to process compound input would prevent learning—possibly explaining the autistic child's characteristic failure to acquire new behaviors. Also, since speech (an auditory stimulus) has meaning in association with a *context* (often visual), an inability to handle *both* auditory and visual components would tend to preclude the development of meaningful speech—another typical feature of the autistic child. Therefore, Lovaas' finding of stimulus overselectivity in these children indicates a need to revise the methods now used to train them. Often, a "prompt," or extra cue, is thought to aid the child in making correct responses in a learning task. But given the autistic child's difficulty in handling more than *one* type of stimulus at a time, this extra "helpful" stimulus may actually make it still more difficult for him to learn.

An ongoing study by the same investigator illustrates another peculiar attentional deficit associated with autism. When Lovaas attempted to train a group of autistic children to discriminate between a boy and a girl doll, he found that they seemed to base their distinction on a single, often inappropriate, piece of clothing. For example, some children failed to recognize the boy doll when its *shoes* had been removed by the experimenter. Normal children, on the other hand, responded primarily to the dolls' heads and thus were able to answer appropriately, regardless of any clothing switches—even if the experimenter put the skirt on the boy doll and the pants on the girl. Thus, it appears that autistic children have abnormal difficulty, not only in handling different *types* of stimuli (i.e., visual, auditory, and tactile), but in identifying *relevant* stimuli of one (e.g., visual) type.

DeMyer and her colleagues at the Indiana University Medical School have found that the autistic child often suffers from what they term a "failure of symbolic transformation," or a marked difficulty in transferring learning from one mode to another. The fact that a child can be taught to *write* a letter of the alphabet, for example, does not necessarily mean that he will simultaneously be able to *say* its sound (and vice versa). The particular modalities involved in transfer problems (e.g., audio to visual, visual to vocal, or visual to motor) vary from child to child but are stable within an individual and can be reliably reproduced.

This investigative team has also been interested in comparing psychotic and brain-damaged children. The chief differences, they find, relate to visual memory and understanding of abstract language. Young psychotics have even more difficulty than brain-damaged children in understanding and reproducing both verbal and nonverbal communication. . . .

family studies

Parents of psychotic children have been the focus of investigation since Kanner originally characterized them as "refrigerator parents." Allen et al. (1971) recently attempted to determine whether they are really, as Kanner implied, colder, more intellectual people who stimulate their children less than parents of normal or nonpsychotic brain-damaged children. Allen et al. found that parents of autistic children were, in fact, no more intellectually oriented than other parents and that, as measured by a total parental stimulation index, they had stimulated their children as much as normal parents and more than parents of nonpsychotic, brain-damaged children. Both the mothers of normal and autistic children were rated as having been warmer and more verbal during their children's infancy than the mothers of brain-damaged children. Based on their parents' recollections, the three groups of children had differed in their alertness during infancy; autistic and brain-damaged children were described as having been less alert than normal infants. There was no relationship between the presence or absence of overt signs of brain damage in the children and the warmth and responsiveness of the parents to their children as infants. It should be pointed out that these conclusions are based on parents' retrospective accounts and, as such, are subject to possible distortion. Nonetheless, this systematic study casts doubt upon the sweeping generalizations sometimes made, based on fragmentary anecdotal reports, about parents "causing" autism.

Reports of communicational difficulties in the parents of adult schizophrenic patients have stimulated a search for comparable deficits in the parents of autistic children. To this end, Schopler and Loftin (1969) recently employed the Object Sorting Test, a measure often used to differentiate parents of adult schizophrenics from those of normals, to study the parents of psychotic, retarded, or normal children. In an attempt to control for the effects of the testing situation, Schopler and Loftin tested one group of parents in the context of their autistic or retarded child and another group in the context of a normal sibling of the afflicted child. When tested in the context of a normal child, the parents of normal, retarded, and autistic children performed about the same. In the context of an afflicted child, however, the parents of autistic children evidenced more thought disorder than either the parents of retarded or normal children. Schopler and Loftin suggest that the relatively poorer performance of parents of autistic children may reflect a sense of guilt and uneasiness; unlike the parents of retarded children, they frequently have been made to feel that their behavior is "responsible" for their child's problem.

In a study of the same genre, William Goldfarb and his colleagues at the Henry Ittleson Center for Child Research compared the clarity of communication in mothers of schizophrenic children with that of mothers of children hospitalized for chronic orthopedic conditions. Based on video-taped recordings of surprise visits, mothers of the "orthopedic" children were found to be superior in verbal clarity to mothers of schizophrenic children. When the schizophrenic children were subclassified according to evidence of neurological dysfunction, mothers of "organic" schizophrenic children showed greater verbal clarity than mothers of "nonorganic" schizophrenic children, though their performance was still inferior to that of the mothers of nonpsychotic control children.

The two family studies summarized above present results which seem somewhat at variance. This might be attributable to differences in the groups of children whose parents were investigated. Were the children's ages, symptom patterns, and verbal behaviors similar? A second factor that may have influenced results is the differing methodologies used; Schopler and Loftin employed a relatively structured test-taking situation while the Ittleson group used a more naturalistic, unstructured mother-child encounter. A third factor could be the different control groups used, since the borderline between autism and retardation is more difficult to draw than that between autism and orthopedic handicaps. Yet another factor may be heterogeneity within the sample of children designated autistic; if Schopler and Loftin had subclassified their subjects according to probability of brain damage, for example, might they have found more evidence of thought disorder in the parents of nonneurologically impaired autistic children than in parents of autistic children with some apparent neurological dysfunction? A final problem is statistical; because of the relatively small number of autistic children studied, only very large differences between groups could achieve statistical significance. This analysis by no means exhausts the possible reasons for the seemingly divergent finds, but it does indicate the possible sources of differences (other than the parents themselves) which make any simplistic interpretation of the two studies hazardous. It is not yet possible to conclude whether parents of autistic children have thinking and communicational deviances.

treatment

The treatment of childhood schizophrenia remains as perplexing as its etiology. For the most part, the tranquilizing drugs, so useful with adult patients, have not been particularly effective with these children. Various nonsomatic treatments are currently employed, including behavior therapy, psychotherapy, and psychoeducational therapy. Results achieved seem to be dictated more by the original degree of severity of illness than by the specifics of the therapeutic procedure employed. DeMyer and her associates at Indiana University recently reviewed their treatment results in 67 children and concluded that the type of treatment was not related to outcome. In their experience, the most accurate predictors of outcome were IQ and estimated amount of brain damage. No child with an initial measured IQ of less than 60 and a high score on a brain-damage index had a good outcome. As employed by the Indiana group, operant conditioning therapy seemed to be the most effective approach to treatment. While failing to enhance the psychotic child's ability to make an acceptable social and school adjustment, this form of treatment, and the training of parents in its use, did seem to enable more children to remain in the parental home than traditional treatment modes or no therapy at all. Of the 67 children followed, 58 percent had poor, and 33 percent had fair, outcomes. Only 9 percent, or six of these 67 children, were considered to have achieved a level of functioning equal to that of their normal counterparts in school, home, and community. A discouraging conclusion reached by the Indiana group was that, even when the psychotic symptoms which had originally led to the diagnosis of autism disappeared, significant, if less dramatic, problems remained. Although such symptoms of autism as withdrawal and negativism and ritualistic behavior became less prominent after treatment, the learning of language and other precision skills remained virtually impossible for these children.

In an attempt to understand why learning disabilities prove so persistent in psychotic children, Churchill (1971) designed a series of experiments which measured "pathological" behaviors (avoidance, tantrums, self-stimulation) and normal behaviors (eye contact, social responsiveness) under conditions of high success and of high failure on the same task. It was found that the pathological behaviors and the amount of looking increased significantly when the children were working under a condition of high and sustained failure. This study was repeated, with essentially the same results, using a variety of subjects including nonpsychotic and mentally retarded children. It would seem, therefore, that some of the more conspicuous symptoms of autism and childhood schizophrenia might better be thought of as "normal" responses to sustained and unrelieved frustration; the underlying problem of psychotic children, supported by the evidence cited above, may actually be a severe learning disability.

William Goldfarb and his group at the Ittleson Center recently examined changes which took place in 40 schizophrenic children over a 3-year period of intensive inpatient treatment. Tests and observations covered general adaptive status, response to schooling, social maturity, perception, conceptual response, intelligence, speech and language, and psychomotor capacity. A dramatic range of individual differences was found among the 40 children in adaptive levels and in curves of growth or change, but impressive growth was evident in most areas of function; only receptor behavior (perception) seemed relatively unaffected by treatment. Goldfarb and his colleagues have also designed a treatment program to provide their patients with the kind of clear communication they see as lacking (based on their findings noted earlier) in the children's mothers. This program utilizes an auditory feedback model to describe the development and treatment of defective communication. On the assumption that normal language behavior requires a self-regulating auditory monitoring system, the Goldfarb group attempts to open the closed auditory channel and to build effective auditory monitoring. In other words, they confront the child with the differences between his communications and acceptable standards of communication. As he develops sensitivity to errors, the child learns to correct his patterns of communication. Recordings of the treatment of four children, seen four times a week—in some cases for as long as 2 years—confirm improvement in auditory and more general behavior. Instances have been noted of generalization of auditory awareness to awareness of other types of error, with linked improvements in attentional and discriminative response.

Schopler et al. (1971) have reported that psychotic children learn better in a structured than an unstructured situation. Variation in capacity to tolerate lack of structure was associated with the individual child's level of development. Children at lower levels of development required more structure for maintaining a learning set than did children at higher levels of development. These findings suggest that, because of its lack of structure, traditional play therapy is inappropriate for most psychotic children. But because the required degree of structure varies according to the characteristics of the individual child, more highly structured therapies—e.g., operant conditioning—may not offer maximum help for every psychotic child either, if rates and levels of development are disregarded.

Schopler and Reichler (1971) have described the use of parents as the main therapeutic agents or teachers for their own psychotic child. This approach has been effective in preventing elaboration of psychosis, promoting recovery where possible, and increasing adaptation between child and family. Perhaps the most dramatic evidence of this program's impact is the fact that participating parents formed the North Carolina Chapter of the National Society for Autistic Children and pressed for legislation to provide education for their children in the public schools. This bill, which emphasized parent participation, was passed and funded, making North Carolina the first State in the nation to have an educational program for psychotic children which integrates school and family. The action of Schopler and others at the University of North Carolina in bringing interested laymen into active participation in their program is noteworthy; its beneficial effects for all parties are obvious in the action taken by the State legislature.

some conclusions

The major orientation of the studies reported here has been phenomenological—an effort to describe what the children we label as psychotic are really like and, in particular, to characterize their perception, speech, social relations, and sense of self. The careful, refined description of a series of behaviors under each of these four areas seems far preferable to preoccupation with a summary label like childhood schizophrenia—which tells us little about the child as a developing person with a variety of deficits, problems, and competencies. The ability to compare groups across studies, which can only result from careful description, is especially important for a disorder as uncommon as childhood psychosis. In this way, each researcher can collect relatively few cases in his own region, but can expand his sample greatly by being able to compare his children with those reported by other workers. Also, because children grow and develop so rapidly, independent of the presence of psychosis, only by using very refined descriptors will it be possible to take into account these normal developmental processes in comparing children. Finally, this emphasis on careful description will help prevent the field from too readily applying diagnostic labels to children—a process which, if too highly valued for its own sake, can have adverse effects. When the individuality, heterogeneity, and complexity of each child are subsumed under a too-summary term, the child may ultimately be thought of as the embodiment of a label rather than as an individual; and in a child with pervasive difficulties in social attachment, such a process can only reinforce detachment.

Some investigators consider infantile autism to be qualitatively different from childhood schizophrenia, using severity of illness as the major differentiating feature. Such a stand has its dangers. By prematurely separating the two categories, we might design research to test a hypothesis about autism and fail to substantiate it; but had childhood schizophrenia been included in the study, we might have found that it was true for a subgroup which included the less ill autistics and more ill schizophrenics. Ideally, a research design should allow data to be analyzed with subjects pooled and separated into more homogeneous subgroups. Thus, great care must be exercised in labeling to prevent misuse and consequent harm, not only to the child, but to the advancement of knowledge.

In view of the strong emphasis placed by the NIMH on problems of childhood, it seems likely that resources will be made increasingly available for research on childhood disorders, including schizophrenia. As we have seen, new

State-sponsored treatment programs for autism have been established in North Carolina; and the Community Mental Health Centers Act now provides special funds to develop services for children. A new publication, *The Journal of Childhood Autism and Schizophrenia*, devoted exclusively to this problem, appeared in 1971. These developments portend hope for the psychotic child, his parents, and investigators. Through greater collaboration among those working to solve this important and difficult problem, we will eventually be able to deal more adequately with those children whose normal growth and development is so impaired by the occurrence of psychosis.

biology

biochemical studies

The biochemical investigation of schizophrenia has largely been based on the belief that an abnormal substance may be causally related to schizophrenia's occurrence. A recent comprehensive review of work carried out in this area during the 1960's concludes: "To date, no biochemical abnormalities have been consistently and exclusively associated with schizophrenia" (Wyatt, Termini, and Davis 1971, p. 44). There remain, however, a number of biochemical hypotheses about which the evidence is either contradictory or incomplete or both. Recent genetic studies suggest that, if a specific biological vulnerability to schizophrenia does exist, it may be highly sensitive to environmental influence. While this suggestion will hardly come as a surprise to the scores of researchers who have been frustrated in their efforts to find such an elusive and transient biochemical abnormality, it highlights the extremely complex problems of research in this area. One particularly perplexing problem which continually confronts biological researchers is the fact that the diagnosis of schizophrenia is based on signs and symptoms which may bear little relationship to biological abnormalities or even to clinically significant entities.

In a promising research effort, which is relevant to psychosis in general as well as to schizophrenia, Meltzer (1970) continues to investigate muscle abnormalities and serum muscle enzyme (creatine phosphokinase) elevations. Elevated serum enzymes characterize about two-thirds of acute psychotics, and there have been abnormal and unique muscle biopsy findings in over half of these. The relationship of serum enzyme changes to the psychotic process is uncertain, but these changes do tend to be specific to acute decompensations (i.e., the enzyme levels decline on recovery). Findings are unrelated to physical activity, muscle tension, stress, corticosteroids, catecholamines, thyroid conditions, weight loss, or oral medications. Intramuscular medications, on the other hand, have been shown to produce similar, though short-lived, serum enzyme changes. Other studies show a high correlation between creatine phosphokinase (CPK) elevations and decreases in REM sleep. A sizable minority (about one-fourth) of the first-degree relatives of acutely psychotic patients show small, persistent baseline elevations in CPK activity and a hyperactive enzyme response to exercise. Further studies are required to define the clinical, prognostic, or genetic significance of these abnormalities and to explain their occasional occurrence in nonpsychotic controls. At the present time, the findings are intriguing but inexplicable, and of unknown practical relevance.

The well-known transmethylation hypothesis suggests that schizophrenia is caused by endogenously produced methylated amines which act as hallucinogens, thereby producing psychotic symptoms. Because of the similarity in chemical structure between mescaline and some of the catecholamines, many scientists have theorized that catecholamines could be abnormally methylated into a mescaline-like compound. The enzymes needed for methylating either derivatives of catecholamines or indoleamines have now been demonstrated to be present in human brain.

With this established, a new hypothesis has been advanced that schizophrenics do not produce an abnormal methylated amine but, rather, are unable to *demethylate* (as nonpsychotics can) a normally occurring but hallucinogenic methylated amine. Testing this hypothesis, Friedhoff administered an extremely powerful dimethoxy (doubly methylated) hallucinogen, N-acetyl-dimethoxyphenethylamine (NADMPEA), and found that it could be demethylated to an inactive derivative in both schizophrenics and normals. Although these data appear to argue against the hypothesized demethylating abnormality, further evidence suggests that, compared to control subjects, acute schizophrenics may demethylate unusually quickly, and chronic schizophrenics unusually slowly. Thus, the hypothesis remains viable. Friedhoff has also demonstrated that man is able to synthesize from dopamine (known to be concentrated in the extrapyramidal system of the brain) compounds that are structurally and pharmacollogically similar to the dimethoxy hallucinogens (like mescaline or NADMPEA). This is important because it provides a possible link between the methylation hypotheses and the effect of the major tranquilizers, which are known to reduce the activity of the dopamine substances in the extrapyramidal system. Before such a link can be established, however, it remains to be shown that those dopamine substances affected by tranquilizers actually *do* produce abnormal dimethoxy hallucinogens which give rise to schizophrenic symptomatology.

In a series of animal studies on a variant of the transmethylation hypothesis, Barchas has shown that, when S-adenosylmethionine, the prime methyl donor in the body, transfers its methyl group to the amines, the remaining portion of the S-adenosylmethionine molecule inhibits further methylation. He has also shown that this inhibition can be overcome by an enzyme contained in the brains of rats. In projected studies of human subjects, Barchas hopes to confirm the hypothesis suggested by his findings—that overly large quantities of an enzyme, such as that found in the rat, might exist in schizophrenia and thereby cause an abnormally large production of pathogenic methylated amines.

The role of histamine in schizophrenia has been under study for 20 years. Its possible importance in this disorder's etiology is suggested by the repeated demonstration of low histamine sensitivity among schizophrenic patients. Although schizophrenics have previously been reported to have generally higher serum histamine levels than nonschizophrenics, Pfeiffer et al. (1970) more recently reported that, when more sophisticated laboratory techniques were applied to a group of 20 chronic schizophrenics, many actually had lower than normal blood histamine levels; a few, however, did have elevated levels. In a followup study of 138 outpatient schizophrenics and 31 nonpsychiatric controls, the investigator confirmed his previous findings and also showed that histamine blood levels correlated highly with the more easily obtainable basophil count. Members of the low-histamine group showed more paranoia and hallucinations, while members of the high-histamine group had serious depressions. Despite these findings, it is difficult to foresee now how a substance like histamine, with no known physiological function, could directly influence the occurrence of schizophrenia. In related work on trace metals (copper and zinc), Pfeiffer has found that about 11 percent of patients studied have low zincs, while approximately 20 percent have high copper. The role of trace metals in mental states is an interesting new avenue of exploration, both because of isolated past reports of their deviance and because of recent advances in the general understanding of the metabolism of these elements. . . .

treatment

The major tranquilizers are generally credited for the dramatic decline in the number of resident schizophrenic patients, even though this downward trend did not become evident nationwide until 1963—8 years after the phenothiazines first came into use. Recently, there has been an acceleration in the *rate* of decline of resident schizophrenic patients. This development is somewhat surprising, since the effects of the phenothiazines might logically have been expected to "plateau," leaving a hard core of unresponsive, therefore undischargeable, patients. For this reason, some authorities believe that the recent, accelerated decreases in patient populations do not stem directly from the use of antipsychotic drugs but, rather, from the development of new psychosocial treatment programs and from changes in administrative policies. These new programs and policies are themselves the result of a resurgence of interest in schizophrenia largely brought about by the phenothiazines' effectiveness. Thus, the introduction of antipsychotic drugs has been instrumental, both directly and indirectly, in the release of ever greater numbers of schizophrenic patients to the community.

Despite the importance of psychosocial treatment programs in any long-range efforts on behalf of the schizophrenic person, few adequate studies of the various forms of psychological treatment have ever been carried out. This is probably due, in part, to the fact that some psychosocial approaches are of relatively recent vintage (e.g., milieu and group therapy); individual psychotherapy has had a long history, however, so the failure to accumulate adequate evidence for its efficacy is more difficult to fathom. It would seem that we should be able to say, with some certainty by now, what treatments should be given to what patients, in what sequence, in what combination, and for how long. At the moment, however, we are unable even to answer such relatively simple questions as whether longer-term treatment in a well-staffed intensive care facility is more valuable to newly admitted schizophrenics than very short-term treatment in the same type of facility. Thus, short-term treatment programs (the most common model in psychiatric wards of general hospitals) are based more on faith than scientific evidence.

psychopharmacological studies

The proliferation of antipsychotic agents which occurred in the late 1950's and early 1960's has now abated, and it is generally agreed that few striking psychopharmacological advances have been made in the last several years. This has been a period of consolidation of knowledge, a period during which the usefulness of the tranquilizing drugs has been put into clear perspective as their advantages, disadvantages, and limitations have become more widely known.

Investigative interest is currently focused on such questions as: What are the differential response patterns of various types of patients to various drugs?

What are reliable predictors of response? What are the nature and frequency of undesirable side effects? How can such side effects be treated or prevented? What is the relationship of drug absorption, distribution, and metabolism to therapeutic and side effects? What are the effects of combining drugs? What are the relative advantages and disadvantages of the long-acting neuroleptic medications in the management of schizophrenic patients in the community? Are the salutary effects of drugs enhanced when administered in conjunction with psychosocial therapies?

During the past few years, several attempts have been made to discover a rationale for selecting the "right drug for the right patient." All have had only limited success. Hollister et al. (1971) used a computer profile classificatory system to assign schizophrenic patients, on the basis of their presenting symptoms and signs, to one of three prototypical groups: *paranoid, depressed,* and *"core."* A series of controlled and uncontrolled studies have demonstrated that each of the major classes of antipsychotic agents was effective in all three types of patients, particularly paranoids. Thus, Hollister et al. concluded that, although the differential response of patients to some types of drugs may provide clues to specificity of action based on chemical structural differences, the choice of a particular drug for a particular patient must still be a largely empirical judgment.

A newer approach to this problem is the attempt to relate levels of phenothiazines in the blood to ingested dose and clinical responsiveness. Simpson has reported large differences in blood levels among patients on a similar dosage of drugs, but precisely how the dose, route of administration, and response interact with degree of illness remains to be elucidated. This approach may eventually explain why some patients are very sensitive to small amounts of drugs, while others are unaffected by exceedingly large doses.

Goldstein (1970) reported some rather provocative findings in a psychopharmacological study. After dividing a sample of newly admitted schizophrenics into good premorbid and poor premorbid groups, he assigned patients randomly to drug (thioridazine, 100 mg. Q.I.D.) or placebo and studied their psychophysiological and behavioral responsiveness over a 21-day period. Data indicated that poor premorbid patients responded to thioridazine administration with autonomic attenuation, reduced schizophrenic thinking, less avoidance behavior, and less anxiety; poor premorbid patients on placebo showed deterioration in these areas. Good premorbid patients receiving medication showed greater autonomic responsivity, greater avoidance behavior, and more remote associations than those on placebo. When the good premorbid patients were further divided into paranoid and nonparanoid subgroups, paranoids on placebo were found to show decreased cognitive adequacy and greater vigilance for threat in the environment than was apparent in paranoids receiving active medication. Nonparanoid/good premorbid patients, on the other hand, showed *no* deterioration on placebo and little positive drug response. Goldstein's findings confirm the importance of drugs in poor premorbid schizophrenics. Among the good premorbid patients, a paranoid subgroup appeared to benefit from drugs, while good premorbid/nonparanoid patients seemed actually to be adversely affected by drug treatment.

Davis and Janowski (see Bass) at the Tennessee Neuropsychiatric Institute have addressed the failure of some patients to respond to drugs from a slightly different point of view. They speculate that nonresponders may fall into two categories: 1) patients who are given overly high doses of phenothiazines and hence develop a toxic psychosis; and 2) patients who are given only moderate doses of phenothiazines but who nonetheless accumulate toxic levels in the blood because they cannot metabolize the drugs properly. To explore this problem, these investigators are admitting poor drug responders and measuring their metabolism of chlorpromazine. One intriguing finding, thus far, is that the administration of pharmacological antagonists to the antipsychotic drugs can produce a dramatic clearing of psychosis in many nonresponders.

In other studies of the toxicity of phenothiazine derivatives, these same investigators surveyed hospitals in their area for the presence of tardive dyskinesia, an extrapyramidal disorder which occurs in patients who have been receiving high doses of phenothiazines for prolonged periods. Approximately 30 percent of patients in these hospitals showed some degree of dyskinesia, and 5 to 10 percent had quite severe tardive dyskinesia. As disturbances of this type are not helped by antiparkinsonian medication, they may represent a serious, previously little-noticed hazard in long-term use of phenothiazines.

To understand better the relationship of dose to clinical response, Clark et al. (1970) studied the response of female chronic schizophrenics to fixed daily dosages of chlorpromazine ranging from 0 to 150 to 300 to 600 mg. per day. They found that dosages of 300 mg. per day produced a response equivalent to that of 600 mg. per day, but with fewer side effects. The lower dose of 150 mg. per day was found to be more effective than nothing at all but not so effective as the higher doses. Clark et al. also studied the influence of age and duration of hospitalization on dose responsiveness. Like many other investigators, they found that the younger and more briefly hospitalized (less than 10 years) patients responded to the high dosage, while the older and longer hospitalized patients achieved maximum clinical response to 300 mg. of chlorpromazine per day or less.

Knowledge of the mechanisms of action of centrally active psychopharmacological agents is crucial to an eventual understanding of the fundamental processes affected by these agents. Working toward this end, Gallant is presently studying the neurophysiological effects of various psychopharmacological compounds on cats with permanently implanted subcortical and cortical electrodes. He finds that antipsychotic agents are associated with an inhibition of the mesencephalic reticular formation and with decreases in the amplitude of local evoked potentials (LEP's); the same agents appear to facilitate the electrical activity and LEP's in the median forebrain bundle, septal area, hippocampus, and cortex. Anti-anxiety agents cause neurophysiological changes similar to those outlined above, except in having no significant effect upon the cortex. The LEP effects of both antidepressant and hallucinogenic agents are approximately the opposite of those produced by the antipsychotic drugs. Gallant is hopeful that these findings will lead to a more adequate understanding of the basic neurophysiology of currently used psychopharmacological agents.

The controversy about the possible therapeutic value of nicotinic acid and nicotinamide (substances which have been advanced as extremely helpful adjuncts to the "usual" treatment of schizophrenia) has been partially resolved. Over the past year, three well-controlled studies have been reported. The largest of these, conducted by McGrath et al. (1972) in four Irish mental hospitals, assigned 265 consecutively admitted schizophrenic patients to usual treatment plus 3 g. a day of nicotinamide or placebo. They found no significant effect at either 30 days or 1 year from the addition of nicotinamide; in fact, there was a slight trend in favor of the placebo group at 1 year. The results of two smaller Canadian studies (Ban and Lehmann 1970 and Ramsey et al. 1970), which examined the efficacy of both nicotinic acid and nicotinamide, were in essential agreement with those of McGrath's group. Thus, it would appear that neither nicotinamide nor nicotinic acid adds much, if anything, to the "usual" treatment of schizophrenia (i.e., with phenothiazines). Responding to these disappointing results, some clinicians have asserted that the efficacy of nicotinic acid (or nicotinamide) only becomes apparent over the long term, in reduced rehospitalization rates. This aspect of the hypothesis is presently being investigated, but no definitive conclusions are yet available. Nonetheless, the negative results obtained by McGrath et al. and the Canadian collaborative group, taken in conjunction with the reports of side effects (e.g., flushing) and toxicity (e.g., liver damage or hyperglycemia) associated with high doses of nicotinamide and nicotinic acid suggest a need for caution in its use.

"Orthomolecular" treatment is an approach which takes its name from a theoretical paper by Linus Pauling which was published in *Science* in 1967. The basic tenet of this theory is that schizophrenia and other functional mental illnesses may be the result of vitamin deficiencies. The treatment program which was developed, based on this theory, includes high doses of niacin, vitamin C, vitamin B_6, and occasionally other vitamins and hormones as well. At the moment, neither the validity of the orthomolecular theory nor the efficacy of the related treatment program has been substantiated. Until the indications for their use are more clear cut, vitamins should only be used as adjuncts to other better established forms of treatment.

behavior therapy

Over the last few years, behavior therapy has come into vogue as an important treatment modality for schizophrenic patients, especially chronically hospitalized ones. A large number of studies have found this approach effective in decreasing symptoms and increasing levels of social functioning within the hospital. A token-economy program in Indiana (Small), for example, found that, after an average stay of 6 months, nearly two-thirds of schizophrenic patients who had been chronically hospitalized for many years could be rehabilitated. These results are in essential agreement with those of others and validate further the importance of this mode of treatment for many schizophrenics. Unfortunately, the effectiveness of even this relatively well-defined treatment procedure derived from experimental psychology is still open to question; it is not yet possible to conclude, based on available data, how much of its effectiveness is due to the specifics of a treatment program and how much can be attributed to the revitalized interest and enthusiasm generated by an exciting new approach; even more importantly, it is still impossible to determine what subgroup of patients profits most from this type of program.

aftercare

In the past year, three studies have examined the effectiveness of drugs and other treatment approaches in keeping discharged patients out of mental hospitals. Claghorn and Kinross-Wright (1971) studied an aftercare program in which every fifth patient who came to an outpatient clinic after discharge was designated as a control and given no further treatment in the clinic; the remaining four patients were seen regularly, usually once a month. When appointments were missed, patients were called and given a later appointment or, if necessary, visited at home. At 2-year followup, Claghorn and Kinross-Wright found that 37 percent of the control patients, as compared with 8 percent of the experimental patients, had been rehospitalized. Interestingly, the rehospitalization rates found in the two groups were so constant that the control group proved unnecessary. This allowed the investigators to institute brief psychotherapy, group therapy, and other re-socialization and educative efforts aimed at raising the level of functioning of patients maintained at home.

Hogarty and Goldberg (1973) recently reported on a study in which a sample of 374 recently discharged schizophrenic patients was divided into four treatment groups: chlorpromazine alone, placebo alone, chlorpromazine plus a combination of intensive social case work and vocational rehabilitation counseling (called by this group, major role therapy), and placebo plus major role therapy. At the end of 1 year, 72.5 percent of the placebo alone group, 63 percent of the placebo plus major role therapy group, 33 percent of the chlorpromazine alone group, and 26 percent of the chlorpromazine plus major role therapy group had been rehospitalized. Hogarty and Goldberg conclude that, although the chlor-promazine was clearly most important in determining outcome, the major role therapy also significantly reduced relapse rates in the groups. It is possible that the real contribution of major role therapy was in encouraging the discharged patients to continue taking their medications regularly. Hogarty and Goldberg plan further studies to determine to what extent major role therapy is associated with more reliable drug usage and whether its effectiveness, which only became apparent during the second 6 months of the study, will continue during the 2nd year after discharge. This last point is an important one in all studies of psychological treatment of schizophrenia: That is, it is crucial to continue treatment long enough to allow its effects to become apparent. Had these investigators only studied major role therapy for 6 months, they would have prematurely, and incorrectly, concluded that it added nothing to drug treatment alone.

The 5-year followup of an experimental program which attempted to maintain patients at home by means of drugs and public health nursing care has recently been reported by Davis, Dinitz, and Pasamanick (1972). In the original study, newly admitted schizophrenics were randomly assigned to one of three groups: an experimental group living at home and receiving drugs and public health nursing care, and two control groups, one receiving placebo and public health nursing care and the other, State hospital care ("usual" care). Over a 30-month period, this study demonstrated that 75 percent of the experimental group could be successfully maintained at home. Results of a longer-term followup, however, revealed a gradual erosion of the original significant differences, when only usual clinic and aftercare services were available. By the end of 5 years, no differences in social or psychological functioning could be found among the three groups. The investigators see in these findings a need for more intensive and long-term aftercare than is now available in the community.

Taken together, the three studies reviewed above provide strong evidence for the usefulness of aftercare in maintaining schizophrenics in the community. While most often focused upon the continuation of drugs, the experimental aftercare programs all demanded human concern and helpfulness on the part of staff members. The importance of these qualities is illustrated by the significant effect of major role therapy in the Hogarty and Goldberg study. Still, we need much more research on the effects of family, work, and recreation on community functioning of discharged patients. Moreover, if appropriate aftercare facilities are to be developed, the effects of patients returning to live with their families must be assessed; it would be valuable to know if adverse consequences can be avoided by the use of alternative nonhospital residential facilities.

In a study of the community treatment of hospitalized chronic patients, Weinman attempted to answer the following questions:

- Are community programs more effective than hospital programs for chronic patients?
- What is the best focus of professional staff services—working directly with patients in modifying behavior, or training community members for treatment roles?
- Which is the most effective setting for discharged patients—living in homes with enablers (specially trained paraprofessionals) or in apartments with other patients and receiving supervision from visiting enablers?

Preliminary results indicate that community treatment is more effective than both socioenvironmental (intensive milieu therapy) and traditional hospital treatment. Community treatment was associated with significantly lower readmission rates and greater independence than either socioenvironmental or traditional hospital treatment. Both professional staff and trained enablers were equally effective in working directly with patients. Readmission rates were not affected by whether patients lived in the homes of enablers or in apartments with other patients, although the latter group, perhaps by necessity, assumed greater independence. This study illustrates very well the emerging role of the paraprofessional in the treatment of schizophrenia. Many believe that a paraprofessional whose background is similar to his patient's might be better able than the mental health professional to see the other person's point of view, and regard him as a peer with "problems" rather than as a patient with a "disease." Because he is familiar with the patient's culture, the paraprofessional may be especially well suited to after-care, helping the discharged patient deal with the down-to-earth, day-to-day problems of living.

day hospitals

Day hospitals have been used increasingly over the last decade and a half, and recently studies of their relative effectiveness have been reported. Herz et al. (1971) compared day hospital and inpatient treatment in 90 patients (45 assigned to each condition). Both day patients and inpatients were treated on the same ward by the same staff and participated in the same activities during the day. On the average, daycare patients spent 48.5 days in the hospital, as compared with 38.8 days for the inpatients. At 30 days, 58 percent of the day patients, as compared with 33 percent of the inpatients, had left the hospital; at 60 days, the corresponding figures were 78 and 42 percent, respectively. On virtually every measure of outcome, there was clear evidence of the superiority of day-care treatment. Not only did day patients return to full-time life in the community and resume their occupational roles sooner, but they were more apt to remain in the community without subsequent readmission to the hospital. In addition, measures of psychopathology revealed that, at 4 weeks, the day patients had made more improvement on several dimensions of manifest psychopathology. As only half of the patients in this study were schizophrenics and a large number of schizophrenics were excluded from the sample as being too ill to participate, the generalizability of the results for schizophrenia is somewhat limited. It would seem, though, that day care is an important and feasible alternative for the less ill schizophrenic.

In another study of day care versus inpatient hospitalization, Washburn found that patients admitted to day care showed a slight decrease in pathology after 1 month but that, in the subsequent 4 months, no further reductions in pathology seemed to occur. Indeed, there was a trend toward increasing pathology through 5 months of treatment. He also found that patients who were considered well enough to come to the day center but who were instead assigned to inpatient care showed significantly greater improvement during the 1st month than patients in the day-care program. By the 5th month, however, levels of pathology were slightly higher than in patients assigned to day care. Washburn urges caution in interpreting these preliminary data because of the relatively small number of patients involved in his study.

Guy et al. (1969) randomly assigned schizophrenics to aftercare in a day center or to an outpatient program using chemotherapy alone. They found that patients admitted to the day hospital subsequently showed significantly greater reduction in hostility, emotional withdrawal, suspiciousness, unusual thought content, and uncooperativeness as compared with patients who received only outpatient care.

closing of a state hospital

The role of the State mental hospital in the treatment of mental illness has been the subject of much debate over the last 20 years, and arguments, pro and con, have intensified since the passage of the community mental health center legislation in 1963. One faction determinedly asserts that the State mental hospital system should be abolished, while another recommends, with equal conviction, that these hospitals be integrated into the community and their research and training efforts be expanded. Still others maintain that the State mental hospital should play a role in the network of mental health services on a regional basis, providing at a tertiary level those specialized services which often are unavailable at the primary or secondary level.

The closing of Modesto State Hospital [in California] was accomplished over an 18-month period and involved the disposition of 1,300 patients and about 900 employees. Two investigators (Bird 1970 and Keenan 1971) who studied this process and its effects on patients, employees, and the town of Modesto report the following interesting developments: First, the initial reaction of the employees and the townspeople to the closing of the hospital was negative. It was felt that patients would be hurt by the transfer and that their care would be less adequate in other facilities. These initial fears proved largely unfounded, however, as all patients were given complete physical and psychiatric assessments prior to transfer and individual plans were worked out in each case. Of the 1,300 patients in the hospital when its impending closing was announced, 300 returned home, about 500 were placed in other community facilities (e.g., boarding care or family care), and 500 were transferred to other State hospitals. The process of evaluation, planning, and transfer went more quickly than had been anticipated, so that the hospital was closed a month prior to the date initially anticipated. Employees were all guaranteed a chance to obtain equivalent employment in other State facilities—an option which, for many, involved moving. Sixty-six percent of the employees accepted transfers, 24 percent resigned, and 10 percent retired. Of the resignations, slightly more than half had found other employment by the time the closing took place. Thus, only about 10 percent of the hospital's employees were unemployed (because they could not, or would not, move to obtain work) as a result of the hospital's closing. The serious economic setback which the local business community initially feared also does not appear to have occurred, since no direct damage to the economy could be pinpointed. Townspeople interviewed felt that the closing represented a significant economic loss, but one which the economy had been able to absorb without serious hardship.

The lack of serious economic impact on the community may reflect a number of factors:

- Many employees who accepted transfer did not actually change their places of residence but, instead, commuted to their new employment in a State hospital 50 miles away; thus, their income remained in the original community.
- Much of the purchasing for the State hospital had been done on a statewide basis by the Department of Mental Hygiene and was not then a direct loss to the community.
- The relatively gradual nature of the long-anticipated closing made it easier for the town to absorb the accompanying loss of income.
- The land and buildings were given to the town and were to be put to use as a junior college; thus the town gained a potential source of employment and revenue, as well as a needed campus site.

Although the closing of the hospital was well planned in most respects, community leaders seem not to have anticipated one extremely important issue—impact of the closing on the community mental health program and welfare services. In retrospect, the hospital's loss would have been cause for little concern had the city fathers more energetically insisted that the county and State first meet all their responsibilities to existing community mental health programs. These programs might have adequately handled most problems presented by the hospital's closing had they been promptly allocated the additional resources necessary to their assumption of newly enlarged responsibilities. The county was also remiss in failing to enlarge its welfare services in anticipation of the closing. Although very few of the former hospital employees needed unemployment benefits, patients relocated in nursing homes, foster homes, or in relatives' homes often needed welfare benefits or services. This demand severely burdened social workers' case loads. Perhaps the greatest lesson to be learned from the Modesto experience is the importance of expanding aftercare and welfare services in conjunction with the closing process so that their availability to ex-hospital patients is assured.

present forms of treatment—an assessment

In summary, what can be said about the adequacy of present-day efforts to treat schizophrenia? The major tranquilizers are, of course, widely recognized as the single most economical and effective treatment for most schizophrenics. It is becoming increasingly apparent, however, that drugs alone are not sufficiently powerful to dispel the difficulties schizophrenics continually confront. Recent research findings confirm the long-held belief of many clinicians that psychological intervention—at the minimum, some form of continuing human contact and support—is an important addition to drug treatment. Indeed, intensified programs of psychosocial treatment seem to be the best method of reducing readmission rates and enhancing levels of community functioning of schizophrenic individuals. Some clinicians maintain that the provision of adequate psychosocial treatment would obviate the necessity for drug treatment in many schizophrenic patients.

In time, it may be possible to specify which patients, receiving what type of psychological treatment, should not receive drugs. This kind of specification takes on increasing importance as evidence of the serious hazards of long-term drug treatment, such as tardive dyskinesia, accumulates.

At present, however, it is only possible to say that drugs, plus some form of continuing interpersonal care, offer our best hope of successful outcomes in the treatment of schizophrenic patients.

problems and the future

This report, like its predecessors, has attempted to illuminate the issues currently confronting those involved in the study of schizophrenia. Some of the major unresolved questions in this research area are:

- Is schizophrenia a single disease or a heterogeneous syndrome?
- Is something inherited which predisposes an individual to develop schizophrenia? If so, what is it? and how does it operate?
- Do the peculiar behavior patterns found in the parents of schizophrenics cause the disorder, or are they responses to the offspring's schizophrenic behavior?
- What differentiates the offspring who becomes schizophrenic from his siblings who do not?
- What are the important variables to be studied in psychotic children?
- What aspects of community life ameliorate or exacerbate schizophrenia?
- Which psychosocial treatments, delivered in what context, should be utilized with which patients?

Clearly, we have much to learn about schizophrenia, since the questions which appear above represent only a smattering of the gaps in our knowledge of this baffling disorder. But, to strike a more hopeful note, we do seem to be making notable progress in a few areas of schizophrenia research.

diagnosis: new methods

Over the past decade, impressive strides have been made in the refinement of diagnostic systems—long the subject of heated debate. There have recently been developed reliable, cross-culturally valid interview instruments which focus more on behavioral descriptors than on summary labels. Thus, it is now increasingly possible to make meaningful comparisons across studies of "schizophrenia." By using the newly available interview instruments, researchers will be better able to categorize subjects along a *variety* of parameters; this will facilitate the efforts of other investigators to replicate findings on a truly similar group of patients—rather than, as too often happened in the past, on an obviously heterogeneous and dissimilar group of patients who share with the original samples of patients little more than an arbitrary diagnosis of "schizophrenia." Improved methods of diagnostic assessment will also make it more feasible to undertake large collaborative research projects addressing problems which must be investigated in more than one setting.

The new diagnostic techniques remain principally research instruments, despite the obvious benefits to be derived from their application (perhaps in modified form) to clinical practice. This is just one example of the unfortunate gulf which continues to exist between researchers and clinicians. If the gulf is ever to be closed, a determined effort must be made to reawaken these two groups to their common interests. Perhaps the most practical setting for such an effort is the university hospital, where both researchers and clinicians serve in the same capacity—as teachers. A genuine mutual exchange seems most likely to occur on this common ground; and it is here, too, that improved communication among members of the next generation of researchers and clinicians can be most easily effected.

heredity vs. environment: a false argument

With the increasing sophistication of research methodology has come a more realistic, less doctrinaire view of the role of either genetics or environment in schizophrenia's etiology. The interaction of both genetic and environmental factors in producing this disorder is now widely recognized. Nonetheless, a minority of mental health workers still see heredity—or, conversely, environment—as the *only* cause of schizophrenia. This unnecessary polarization seems to be based on personal bias, since the available scientific evidence does not support a simplistic heredity-*or*-environment explanation. Furthermore, either of the two extreme positions has negative implications for treatment. An unresponsive patient may be viewed by the "genetic" faction as suffering from an inevitable, progressive, and untreatable hereditary disease—a belief which tends to discourage vigorous treatment efforts. Those who hold that environmental factors are all-important, on the other hand, may explain away a treatment failure by blaming "interfering parents" or a "rotten society" for causing and perpetuating the patient's disturbance.

Surely, if the history of schizophrenia research and treatment has anything to teach us, it is the importance of maintaining an open mind when dealing with this complex disorder.

schizophrenia—a biochemical disorder?

The hypothesis that abnormal methylation processes are related to schizophrenia is now two decades old and, despite tremendous investigative efforts, has been neither substantiated nor refuted. Thus, the role of methylation in causing schizophrenia is a controversial, unresolved problem of long standing. Interestingly, the failure to resolve this issue is due not to lack of investigative interest but to inadequate technology. The issue is raised here because there now have been developed clinical and biochemical methods which may allow us to obtain a more definitive answer. Indeed, it appears that we will be able to report significant new findings in this particularly difficult area over the next several years.

treatment: involving the family

The families of schizophrenic patients have been a major focus of investigative interest since the early 1950's. Although research on the family has not provided conclusive evidence that the schizophrenic's parents either cause or maintain his phychosis, this work has had an important impact on the conceptual framework of many mental health workers. In light of the repeated demonstration of abnormal behavior patterns in the families of schizophrenics, it is difficult to view the individual patient as the sole victim of schizophrenia; the severe problems of one family member will almost inevitably reverberate throughout his whole family, and any or all of the family members may play a role in perpetuating these problems. Reflecting this growing awareness of the family's involvement, most treatment programs continue to focus on the patient but are also directed, to some extent, toward his family. Indeed, there is a school of therapy which views the entire family as "the patient." But whether a treatment program actually deals directly with the family is less important than that its conceptual focus at least includes them. With the nationwide trend toward treating schizophrenic patients in the community, growing numbers of patients are now receiving care in outpatient clinics or in day hospitals. Very often, these patients (who in the past would have been housed in remote State hospitals) live with their families. In these circumstances, the patient's relationships with other family members are a legitimate and useful concern of those who seek to treat him. Moreover, members of the mental health professions have a clear responsibility to assist the families of schizophrenics in assuming the enlarged responsibilities which we, by our espousal of community treatment, have thrust upon them.

individuals at risk—a broader definition?

Investigative interest in individuals at relatively high risk for the development of schizophrenia has mushroomed in the past 5 years. No other area of schizophrenia research has grown so rapidly over this period. One troubling aspect of ongoing applications of this research strategy is their almost exclusive dependence upon the offspring of schizophrenic parents as a pool of "vulnerable" individuals. Although there are advantages to be derived from defining a sample by this genetic method, the fact that samples derived in other ways are not being widely studied may betray stereotypic thinking in this young field. While not unusual in a new and growing area of interest, this type of overly narrow focus can lead investigators to miss very important opportunities. Clearly, there is a need to pay careful attention to nongenetically defined groups vulnerable to schizophrenia (e.g., urban slum dwellers and persons in cultural transition). It must be remembered, after all, that approximately 90 percent of adult schizophrenics do *not* have a schizophrenic parent.

The importance of high risk studies as a possible means of documenting the development of schizophrenia has been widely recognized. One contribution of these studies which has not been sufficiently highlighted, however, is the provision of data about *normal* development and *invulnerability* to psychiatric disorder.

disorders of childhood

The study of childhood psychoses is another area which has seen a tremendous upsurge of interest in recent years. While this evidence of increased commitment has provided a measure of relief to the families of psychotic children, their ordeal, though perhaps a little less lonely now, remains a formidable one. Because their children's problems are so special and so severe, programs for dealing with them are often either unavailable or exorbitantly expensive. The two institutions to which parents most frequently appeal for help—Medicine and Education—sometimes seem to be trying to outdo each other in their attempts to disclaim responsibility for the care of these children. "Your child has a *medical* problem," say the schools. "He needs special *education*," respond the hospitals and clinics. Parents begin to feel that they are doomed to hear an ever-recurring dialogue in which only one message is clear: "There is nothing we can do for your child." In the end, parents whose children are rejected by existing special classes or special treatment centers are left with a choice of keeping the child at home or relegating him to custodial care in a State institution; both choices seem unreasonable. To alleviate this situation, a better coordination of educational and medical services is mandatory. If shared responsibility is ultimately considered unrealistic, it would seem preferable that the child's care be the primary responsibility (with medical backup, of course) of the educational systems so that he can stay as nearly within the usual school- and family-based life of most children as is feasible. This is the course which has been followed in Great Britain and which was recently adopted in North Carolina. Perhaps the program developed in North Carolina will serve as a pilot program in which problems can be worked out before the system is introduced elsewhere.

some recommendations

The closing of Modesto State Hospital (discussed earlier) throws into bold relief the revolution in psychiatric care which is presently underway—namely, the shift away from large, distant, usually poorly staffed, basically custodial institutions to small, local, relatively well-staffed, active treatment facilities. Illustrating this trend is the fact that, between 1967 and 1969, the proportion of all patient-care episodes handled by community mental health centers rose from 4 to 10 percent.

Although this shift is generally considered a laudable development, we should attend to several factors which, if ignored, could lead to the failure of humanitarian goals. First, it must be recognized that most people would rather not be confronted on a day-to-day basis with behavior that is defined as socially deviant; and one result of the community orientation of mental health care will certainly be increased contact with deviance. Furthermore, the patient's deviant behavior is likely to adversely affect his family's functioning and may cause considerable embarrassment. If we demand that families assume primary responsibility for the care of an ill relative, without provision for *their* needs, we can expect a backlash against our community-oriented efforts; and the voice of the average man in the street, who has also been discomfited by the deviant behavior of patients, will be added to the families' chorus unless we provide for *his* needs. For families, it would appear we need a continuum of nonfamily, nonhospital, residential facilities where patients can live for varying lengths of time. For example, some of these facilities could handle acute disturbance, while others would provide indefinite, minimally supportive living arrangements. Thus, both patient and family would be offered a broader choice than home *or* hospital care. The former is very often too burdensome for the family, while the latter is expensive and may be too intensive for the patient's needs. Our present treatment system is grossly inadequate in this regard. It is estimated, for example, that we have only one-fifth as many halfway houses as are needed. In addition, the concept of continuity of care, while often cited, is seldom put into practice. Rehabilitation services specifically designed for psychiatric patients are almost nonexistent. If we are to decrease the tremendous readmission rates and enhance levels of community functioning in discharged patients, measures must be taken to provide a continuum of facilities, continuity of care, and specific rehabilitation programs.

If you believe the solution to schizophrenia will be a biochemical one and that little effort should be expended on the treatment measures noted above, consider the following apocryphal story:

> Imagine . . . a man of 40 whose mother has been surreptitiously spiking his orange juice with LSD for the past 25 years. (We've all heard of the schizophrenogenic mother, but this poor man has an hallucinogenic mother.) Suddenly, the mother dies, and the morning of her funeral her bereaved son's biochemical peculiarity is suddenly corrected. Could we really expect this man to pick up a hat and briefcase and head downtown for his first day on the job? One suspects that psychological therapy and retraining would be vital in helping this poor fellow match his behavior pattern to his newfound biochemical normality. [Mosher 1971, p. 93.]

Imagine, further, that this former "acidhead" *did* receive the benefits of an intensive program of therapy and job training. He would still have difficulty finding a job if a stigma were attached to his former psychotic state. Would his family be able to accept the "new" him, especially if, for years, they had felt burdened by and ashamed of him? Clearly, even after his miraculous cure, the formerly psychotic person would still confront significant social problems.

Just as clearly, these are problems now faced by the discharged schizophrenic patient. To obviate them will require a vigorous effort to educate the public about schizophrenia and other forms of mental illness. We are returning more and more psychiatric patients to the community; we must also take steps to insure that their reception will not be a hostile one. Only in this way will we be able to assure the continued humanization of the treatment of schizophrenia —a disorder which is, after all, unique to human kind.

notes

1. In a personal communication, Manfred Bleuler recently characterized classic Bleulerian process schizophrenia as a term "invented in America" and not truly representative of his father's views of schizophrenia. Eugen Bleuler did "consider the possibility of a 'primary disease' of somatic origin," but this was not more than a possibility, and the primary disease was not a psychosis. What formed the psychosis—the psychosis in itself—was in his mind neither primary nor a process nor somatic but was what we today would call a 'psychodynamically intelligible psychological development.'"

2. Two percent of the sample are not accounted for.

references

Allen, J.; DeMyer, M.K.; Norton, J.A.; Pontius, W.; and Yang, E. Intellectuality in parents of psychotic, subnormal, and normal children. *Journal of Autism and Childhood Schizophrenia*, 1(3):311–326, 1971.

Allen, M.; Cohen, S.; and Pollin, W. Schizophrenia in veteran twins: A diagnostic review. *American Journal of Psychiatry*, 128(8):939–945, 1972.

Ban, T.A., and Lehmann, H.E. *Nicotinic Acid in the Treatment of Schizophrenias. Progress Report I.* Toronto: Canadian Mental Health Association, 1970.

Barchas, J. "Melatonin and Central Nervous System." (MH 13259) Stanford University, Stanford, Calif.

Bass, A.D. "Psychopharmacology Research Center." (MH 11468) Vanderbilt University, Nashville, Tenn.

Bellak, L. "Patterns of Ego Functions in Schizophrenia." (MH 14260) New York University, New York, N.Y.

Bird, B.J. "A Preliminary Study of the Closing of Modesto State Hospital." Unpublished manuscript, National Institute of Mental Health, Rockville, Md., 1970.

Churchill, D.W. Effects of success and failure in psychotic children. *Archives of General Psychiatry,* 25:208–214, 1971.

Claghorn, J.L., and Kinross-Wright, J. Reduction in hospitalization of schizophrenics. *American Journal of Psychiatry,* 128(3):344–347, 1971.

Clark, M.L.; Ramsey, H.R.; Ragland, R.E.; Rahhal, D.K.; Serafetinides, E.A.; and Costiloe, J.P. Chlorpromazine in chronic schizophrenia: Behavioral dose-response relationships. *Psychopharmacologia,* 18(3):260–270, 1970.

Collins, P. "Reaction Time Measures in Time Intensity Reciprocity Between Psychiatric Patients and Normals." Presented at the meetings of the Eastern Psychological Association, New York, N.Y., 1971.

Davis, A.E.; Dinitz, S.; and Pasamanick, B. The prevention of hospitalization in schizophrenia: Five years after an experimental program. *American Journal of Orthopsychiatry,* 42(3):375–388, 1972.

DeMyer, M.K. "Research Center for Early Childhood Schizophrenia." (MH 5154) Indiana University, Indianapolis, Ind.

DeMyer, M.K.; Churchill, D.W.; Pontius, W.; and Gilkey, K.M. A comparison of five diagnostic systems for childhood schizophrenia and infantile autism. *Journal of Autism and Childhood Schizophrenia,* 1(2):175–189, 1971.

Fleiss, J.L.; Gurland, B.J.; and Cooper, J.E. Some contributions to the measurement of psychopathology. *British Journal of Psychiatry,* 119(553):647–656, 1971.

Friedhoff, A. "Biological Studies of Psychotic Disorders." (MH 8618) New York University Medical Center, New York, N.Y.

Gallant, D.M. "Clinical Evaluation of New Chemotherapeutic Agents." (MH 3701) Tulane University, New Orleans, La.

Goldfarb, W. "Growth and Family Patterns in Childhood Schizophrenia." (MH 5753) Henry Ittleson Center for Child Research, Bronx, N.Y.

Goldstein, M.J. "A Follow-Up Study of Disturbed Adolescents." Presented at the 79th annual meeting of the American Psychological Association, 1971.

Goldstein, M.J. Premorbid adjustment, paranoid status, and patterns of response to phenothiazine in acute schizophrenia. *Schizophrenia Bulletin,* No. 3:24–37, Winter 1970.

Grinker, R.R.; Holzman, P.; and Kayton, L.A. "Psychosomatic Clinical Research Center." (MH 5519) Michael Reese Hospital and Medical Center, Chicago, Ill.

Grunebaum, H. "Intensive Nursing Aftercare for Psychotic Mothers." (MH 13946) Massachusetts Mental Health Center, Boston, Mass.

Guy, W.; Gross, M.; Hogarty, G.E.; and Dennis, H. A controlled evaluation of day hospital effectiveness. *Archives of General Psychiatry,* 20(3):329–338, 1969.

Hannes, M. "Reaction Time in Schizophrenia." (MH 14412) Biometrics Research, New York, N.Y.

Herz, M.I.; Endicott, J.; Spitzer, R.L.; and Mesnikoff, A. Day versus inpatient hospitalization: A controlled study. *American Journal of Psychiatry,* 127 (10):1371–1382, 1971.

Hogarty, G.E.; Goldberg, S.C.; and the Collaborative Study Group. Drug and sociotherapy in the aftercare of schizophrenic patients: One-year relapse rates. *Archives of General Psychiatry*, 28(1):54–64, 1973.

Hollister, L.E.; Overall, J.E.; Katz, G.; Higginbotham, W.E.; and Kimbell, I. Oxypertine and thiothixene in newly admitted schizophrenic patients: A further search for specific indications of antipsychotic drugs. *Clinical Pharmacology and Therapeutics*, 12(3):531–538, 1971.

Jordan, K., and Prugh, D.G. Schizophreniform psychosis of childhood. *American Journal of Psychiatry*, 128(3):323–331, 1971.

Keenan, B. "Modesto State Hospital Closing: A Case Study of the Impacted Employees and the Community." Unpublished manuscript, National Institute of Mental Health, Rockville, Md., 1971.

Kety, S.S.; Rosenthal, D.; Wender, P.H.; and Schulsinger, F. Mental illness in the biological and adoptive families of adopted schizophrenics. *American Journal of Psychiatry*, 128(3):302–306, 1971.

Koh, S.D., and Kayton, L.A. "Short-term Memory Processes in Schizophrenia." (MH 18991) Michael Reese Hospital, Chicago, Ill.

Kreisman, D. Social interaction and intimacy in preschizophrenic adolescence. In: Zubin, J., ed. *The Psychopathology of Adolescence*. New York: Grune and Stratton, Inc., 1970. pp. 299–318.

Kriegel, J.; Sutton, S.; and Kerr, J. Effect of modality shift on reaction time in schizophrenia. In: Kietzman et al., eds. *Objective Indicators of Psychopathology*. New York: Academic Press, Inc., in press.

Kringlen, E. "Twin and Family Studies in the Functional Psychoses." (MH 15758) Institute of Psychiatry, Bergen, Norway.

Lifshitz, K. "Evoked Brain Information Processing and Schizophrenia." (MH 16957) Rockland State Hospital, Orangeburg, N.Y.

Lovaas, O.I. "Studies of Childhood Schizophrenia." (MH 11440) University of California, Los Angeles, Calif.

McGrath, S.D.; O'Brien, P.F.; Power, P.J.; and Shea, J.R. Nicotinamide treatment of schizophrenia. *Schizophrenia Bulletin*, No. 5:74–76, Spring 1972.

Marcus, J. "Schizophrenic Offspring—Infant Studies." (PL 480, No. 06-278-2) Hebrew University Medical School, Jerusalem, Israel.

Mednick, S. Breakdown in individuals at high risk for schizophrenia: Possible predispositional perinatal factors. *Mental Hygiene*, 54(1):50–63, 1970.

Mednick, S. "Perinatal Complications Related to Social Pathology." (MH 19630) New School for Social Research, New York, N.Y.

Meltzer, H.Y. Muscle abnormalities in acute psychoses. *Archives of General Psychiatry*, 23:481–491, 1970.

Miller, D. "Mental Patients as Parents—Their Children's Fate." (MH 16337) Scientific Analysis Corporation, San Francisco, Calif.

Mosher, L.R. New treatment systems for schizophrenia. *Schizophrenia*, 3(2):87–93, 1971.

Mosher, L.R., and Feinsilver, D. *Special Report: Schizophrenia*. Rockville, Md.: National Institute of Mental Health, Publication No. (HSM) 72-9042, 1971.

Mosher, L.R.; Pollin, W.; and Stabenau, J.R. Families with identical twins discordant for schizophrenia: Some relationships between identification, thinking styles, psychopathology and dominance-submissiveness. *British Journal of Psychiatry*, 118:29–42, 1917a.

Mosher, L.R.; Pollin, W.; and Stabenau, J.R. Identical twins discordant for schizophrenia: Neurologic findings. *Archives of General Psychiatry*, 24:422–430, 1971b.

Mosher, L.R.; Stabenau, J.R.; and Pollin, W. "Schizoidness in the Non-Schizophrenic Identical Co-twins of Schizophrenics." Presented at the Vth World Congress of Psychiatry, Mexico City, Dec. 1971.

Ornitz, E. "Neurophysiologic Correlates of Autistic Behavior." (MH 13517) University of California, Los Angeles, Calif.

Pauling, L. Orthomolecular psychiatry. *Science,* 160(3825):265–271, 1967.

Pfeiffer, C.C. "Cerebral Neurohumors and Behavior." (MH 4229) New Jersey Neuropsychiatric Institute, Princeton, N.J.

Pfeiffer, C.C.; Iliev, V.; Jenney, E.H.; and Cawley, J. "Histamine, Polyamines and Trace Metals in the Schizophrenias." Presented at the International Congress of Neuropharmacology, 1970.

Pollin, W. A possible genetic factor related to psychosis. *American Journal of Psychiatry,* 128(3):311–316, 1971.

Ramsey, R.A.; Ban, T.A.; Lehmann, H.E.; Saxena, B.M.; and Bennett, J. Nicotinic acid as adjuvant therapy in newly admitted schizophrenic patients. *Canadian Medical Association Journal,* 102:939–942, 1970.

Rodnick, E.H., and Goldstein, M.J. "Coping Behavior in Schizophrenia." (MH 8744) University of California, Los Angeles, Calif.

Rosen, B.; Klein, D.F.; and Gittelman-Klein, R. The prediction of rehospitalization: The relationship between age of first psychiatric treatment contact, marital status, and premorbid asocial adjustment. *Journal of Nervous and Mental Disease,* 152(1):17–22, 1971.

Rosenthal, D.; Wender, P.; Kety, S.S.; Welner, J.; and Schulsinger, F. The adopted-away offspring of schizophrenics. *American Journal of Psychiatry,* 128(3):307–311, 1971.

Saletu, B.; Itil, T.M.; and Saletu, M. Auditory evoked response, EEG, and thought process in schizophrenics. *American Journal of Psychiatry,* 128(3):336–343, 1971.

Sameroff, A. "Neonatal Factors in Serious Mental Disorders." (MH 16544) University of Rochester, Rochester, N.Y.

Schachter, J. "Reactivity of Neonates of Schizophrenic Patients." (MH 19677) Pittsburgh Child Guidance Center, University of Pittsburgh School of Medicine, Pittsburgh, Pa.

Schopler, E.; Brehm, S.S.; Kinsbourne, M.; and Reichler, R.J. Effect of treatment structure on development in autistic children. *Archives of General Psychiatry,* 24:415–421, 1971.

Schopler, E., and Loftin, J. Thought disorders in parents of psychotic children: A function of test anxiety. *Archives of General Psychiatry,* 20:174–181, 1969.

Schopler, E., and Reichler, R.J. Parents as cotherapists in the treatment of psychotic children. *Journal of Autism and Childhood Schizophrenia,* 1(1):87–102, 1971.

Schuham, A. "Coalition Formation in Family Interaction." (MH 17258) University of Oklahoma Medical Center, Oklahoma City, Okla.

Shagass, C. "Electrophysiological Studies of Psychiatric Disorders." (MH 12507) Temple University, Philadelphia, Pa.

Shields, J., and Gottesman, I.I. "Cross-National Diagnosis and the Heritability of Schizophrenia." Presented at the Vth World Congress of Psychiatry, Mexico City, 1971.

Simpson, G.M. "Drug Screening Program for Drug Resistant Schizophrenics." (MH 8240) Rockland State Hospital, Orangeburg, N.Y.

Small, J.G. "EEG and Clinical Variables in Affective Psychosis." (MH 14638) LaRue D. Carter Memorial Hospital, Indianapolis, Ind.

Sojit, C.M. The double bind hypothesis and the parents of schizophrenics. *Family Process,* 110(1):53–74, 1971.

Spitzer, R.L., and Endicott, J. An integrated group of forms for automated psychiatric case records: A progress report. *Archives of General Psychiatry,* 24(5):448–453, 1971.

Strauss, J., and Carpenter, W. Cited in *Annual Report, Mental Health Intramural Research Program, Division of Clinical and Behavioral Research, and Division of Biological and Biochemical Research.* National Institute of Mental Health, Bethesda, Md., 1970–1971. p. 62.

Taube, C.A. *Statistical Note 55. Changes in the Age-Sex-Diagnostic Composition of First Admissions to State and County Mental Hospitals—1962–1969.* Rockville, Md.: National Institute of Mental Health, DHEW Publication No. (HSM) 72-9012, 1971.

Washburn, S.L. "Controlled Evaluation of Psychiatric Day Care." (MH 17464) McLean Hospital, Belmont, Mass.

Watt, N.F.; Stolorow, R.D.; Lubensky, A.W.; and McClelland, D.C. School adjustment and behavior of children hospitalized for schizophrenia as adults. *American Journal of Orthopsychiatry,* 40(4):637–657, 1970.

Waxler, N.E., and Mishler, E.G. Parental interaction with schizophrenic children and well siblings. An experimental test of some etiological theories. *Archives of General Psychiatry,* 25:223–231, 1971.

Weinman, B. "Treatment Deployment for Chronics." (MH 15008) Philadelphia State Hospital, Philadelphia, Pa.

Willner, A.E. "Analogical Reasoning in Normals and Schizophrenics." (MH 15933) Hillside Hospital, Glen Oaks, N.Y.

Willner, A.E., and Struve, F.A. An analogy test that predicts EEG abnormality: Use with hospitalized psychiatric patients. *Archives of General Psychiatry,* 23(5):428–437, 1970.

Wohlberg, G. "Sustained Attention in Remitted Schizophrenics." (MH 18920) Boston University School of Medicine, Boston, Mass.

Wyatt, R.J.; Termini, B.A.; and Davis, J. Biochemical and sleep studies of schizophrenia: A review of the literature—1960–1970. *Schizophrenia Bulletin,* No. 4:10–66, Fall 1971.

Wynne, L., and Singer, M. "Communication Deviance Scores in Families of Schizophrenics." Intramural Research Program, NIMH, Bethesda, Md.

Yarden, P.E., and Discipio, W.J. Abnormal movements and prognosis in schizophrenia. *American Journal of Psychiatry,* 128(3):317–323, 1971.

Young, M.L., and Jerome, E.A. Problem solving performance of paranoid and nonparanoid schizophrenics. *Archives of General Psychiatry,* 26(5):442–444, 1972.

Zahn, T.P. Cited in *Annual Report, Mental Health Intramural Research Program, Division of Clinical and Behavioral Research, and Division of Biological and Biochemical Research.* National Institute of Mental Health, Bethesda, Md., 1970–1971. p. 62.

Zubin, J. "Diagnosis of Mental Disorder in the U.S. and U.K." (MH 9191) New York State Psychiatric Institute, New York, N.Y.

THINK

1. The existential neurosis, according to Maddi, implicates depression. And depression often brings with it a sense of meaninglessness. How would you tell the existential neurosis from neurotic depression?

2. It is clear that fat people are much less sensitive than thin ones to their internal hunger state. What effects would teaching fat people to discriminate their internal states have? Would they generally become less stimulus-bound? Would they begin to think like "skinnies"?

   Perhaps it is not possible to teach obese people to discriminate their internal states. That would certainly be the case if their inability to discriminate those states was due to a hypothalmic lesion, as Schachter speculates. If that were the case, short of "repairing" the lesion, how might one help an obese person to lose weight, and to remain thin?

3. Schachter's paper on the possible relationship between obesity and hypothalmic lesions, and Seligman's speculations on the relationship between learned helplessness and depression, proceed mainly by analogy. Schachter openly admits that he has never seen a hypothalmus, and Seligman's animals have never actually said that they were depressed. Those are pretty far-out hunches, yet they are often the stuff out of which science is made. You might just want to go back and read those papers again to get a further sense of the analogies on which they are based.

4. In Seligman's learned helplessness research, exposure to an uncontrollable trauma has several effects on dogs and other animals. It reduces the ability to learn, it causes anorexis or loss of appetite, and it seems to reduce the amount of norepinephrine that circulates in the central nervous system. Seligman believes these effects are analogous to the causes and symptoms of depression in humans. If he is right, for the alleviation of depression does it matter whether we train individuals to overcome the "learned helplessness" by psychological means, or if we administer a drug that, say, increases the amount of norepinephrine in the central nervous system? Similarly, if the parallel that Seligman is arguing holds, should one be able to cure learned helplessness in dogs by administering to them the same medications that are effective with human depressions?

5. How do you account for the decline in hospital admissions for schizophrenia? Are people being diagnosed differently, or better? Is outpatient treatment improving? Are people simply avoiding hospitals? And why has the number of admissions of people under 25 *increased* some 19 percent between 1962 and 1969?

6. Why does schizophrenia recur?

7. It has been observed by some theorists that schizophrenia involves learning deficits. Other theorists believe that schizophrenics can learn as well as normals, but the reason that they seem to do poorly on tests is that they are not as motivated as normals to succeed on those tests. These competing hypotheses are neither trivial nor academic, since much of what we do in treatment depends on whether we consider schizophrenics to be suffering a learning or a motivational disability. How might one decide between these hypotheses? Can you think of an experiment, or an argument, that might shift the balance in one direction or the other?

8. What difference does it make whether we believe that schizophrenia itself is inherited, or that the *predisposition* to schizophrenia is inherited? Is that a question that merely plays with words? If not, is there any evidence that one or the other position is correct?

9. Almost without exception, patients who are discharged from the hospital are discharged because they are thought to be able to conduct their lives ef-

fectively outside that setting. Yet the readmission rate is extraordinarily high, *except* for patients receiving postdischarge aftercare; they have a considerably lower rate of readmission. Why should aftercare be so necessary? And why should it be so effective? What implications do these studies have for the nature of schizophrenia, and the usefulness of psychiatric hospitals?

IV

The Problems
of Psychological Diagnosis

To read the *Diagnostic and Statistical Manual* of the American Psychiatric Association (Reading 13) is to read a very orderly description of various kinds of psychological disturbances. There will be a few disturbances that possibly surprise you, and perhaps one or two that you thought would be described, but are not. On the whole, however, if your impressions match our own, you will feel that these descriptions are pretty lucid characterizations of known psychological disorders. You will feel that people like those described in the *Manual* exist and can be differentiated from each other, and from the rest of us.

It is therefore distressing to find that, however clear those differences appear to be in theory, in fact they are quite blurred. There is considerable overlap between the categories described in the *Manual*. So much is this the case that Edward Zigler and Leslie Phillips (Reading 14) find that the similarities among the symptoms that comprise the various diagnostic characterizations far outweigh their differences. No diagnosis appears to have a unique set of symptoms, and nearly all symptoms are to be found across all diagnoses. Some of the reasons for this diagnostic morass are discussed by Zigler and Phillips, and you may find other interesting reasons. All in all, however, the differences between what the *Psychiatric Manual* prescribes and what the researchers find are painfully large; and they raise some thorny questions about the role of diagnosis in psychological assessment.

The problems with the *Diagnostic and Statistical Manual* are not limited to the apparent difficulty in verifying its crisp definitions in reality, but appear to extend also to social definitions of abnormality. Nowhere is this matter clearer at the present time than with the issues that surround homosexual behavior. On the one hand, psychiatric and psychological literature is dense with descriptions of the dynamics, antecedents, and correlates of homosexuality. Freud, for example, was deeply concerned with the vicissitudes of homosexual impulses and so, too, were the generations of his successors. On the other hand, homosexuals have long felt themselves unjustly labeled and maligned by psychiatric diagnoses. For them, homosexual behaviors are as freely chosen and as "normal" as heterosexual ones. They have argued with increasing vigor over the past few years that psychiatric labels *create* rather than ameliorate problems for homosexuals, that those labels define an imaginary disorder.

On December 15, 1973, the Board of Trustees of the American Psychiatric Association, apparently in response to the claims of homosexual groups, voted that homosexuality per se, was no longer a psychiatric disorder. Some of the flavor of the issues surrounding that decision is captured in an interview conducted by *The New York Times* shortly after the vote was announced. Dr. Irving Bieber, one of the foremost students of homosexuality, and Dr. Robert Spitzer, a leading diagnostic researcher, debate the implications of that decision in Reading 15.

The question of whether homosexuality is or is not a psychiatric disorder is not an academic one. Many psychiatrists were distressed by the

Board's decision, and the vote was put before the entire membership of the American Psychiatric Association (—as if the question of a psychiatric disorder can be resolved by a vote!). Early in 1974, the membership sustained the Board. But the vote was hardly unanimous—the battle was quite acrimonious, reflecting the deeply held views of many psychiatrists with regard to this kind of behavior.

13

Descriptions of Psychological Distress

III. psychoses not attributed to physical conditions listed previously (295–298)

This major category is for patients whose psychosis is not caused by physical conditions listed previously. Nevertheless, some of these patients may show additional signs of an organic condition. If these organic signs are prominent the patient should receive the appropriate additional diagnosis.

295 schizophrenia

This large category includes a group of disorders manifested by characteristic disturbances of thinking, mood and behavior. Disturbances in thinking are marked by alterations of concept formation which may lead to misinterpretation of reality and sometimes to delusions and hallucinations, which frequently appear psychologically self-protective. Corollary mood changes include ambivalent, constricted and inappropriate emotional responsiveness and loss of empathy with others. Behavior may be withdrawn, regressive and bizarre. The schizophrenias, in which the mental status is attributable primarily to a *thought* disorder, are to be distinguished from the *Major affective illnesses* (q.v.) which are dominated by a *mood* disorder. The *Paranoid states* (q.v.) are distinguished from schizophrenia by the narrowness of their distortions of reality and by the absence of other psychotic symptoms.

295.0 SCHIZOPHRENIA, SIMPLE TYPE

This psychosis is characterized chiefly by a slow and insidious reduction of external attachments and interests and by apathy and indifference leading to impoverishment of interpersonal relations, mental deterioration, and adjustment on a lower level of functioning. In general, the condition is less dramatically psy-

From the *Diagnostic and Statistical Manual of Mental Disorders,* Second Edition, Washington, D.C.: American Psychiatric Association, 1968, pp. 32–52 with the permission of the American Psychiatric Association.

chotic than are the hebephrenic, catatonic, and paranoid types of schizophrenia. Also, it contrasts with schizoid personality, in which there is little or no progression of the disorder.

295.1 SCHIZOPHRENIA, HEBEPHRENIC TYPE

This psychosis is characterized by disorganized thinking, shallow and inappropriate affect, unpredictable giggling, silly and regressive behavior and mannerisms, and frequent hypochondriacal complaints. Delusions and hallucinations, if present, are transient and not well organized.

295.2 SCHIZOPHRENIA, CATATONIC TYPE

295.23° Schizophrenia, catatonic type, excited°
295.24° Schizophrenia, catatonic type, withdrawn°

It is frequently possible and useful to distinguish two subtypes of catatonic schizophrenia. One is marked by excessive and sometimes violent motor activity and excitement and the other by generalized inhibition manifested by stupor, mutism, negativism, or waxy flexibility. In time, some cases deteriorate to a vegetative state.

295.3 SCHIZOPHRENIA, PARANOID TYPE

This type of schizophrenia is characterized primarily by the presence of persecutory or grandiose delusions, often associated with hallucinations. Excessive religiosity is sometimes seen. The patient's attitude is frequently hostile and aggressive, and his behavior tends to be consistent with his delusions. In general the disorder does not manifest the gross personality disorganization of the hebephrenic and catatonic types, perhaps because the patient uses the mechanism of projection, which ascribes to others characteristics he cannot accept in himself. Three subtypes of the disorder may sometimes be differentiated, depending on the predominant symptoms: hostile, grandiose, and hallucinatory.

295.4 ACUTE SCHIZOPHRENIC EPISODE

This diagnosis does not apply to acute episodes of schizophrenic disorders described elsewhere. This condition is distinguished by the acute onset of schizophrenic symptoms, often associated with confusion, perplexity, ideas of reference, emotional turmoil, dreamlike dissociation, and excitement, depression, or fear. The acute onset distinguishes this condition from simple schizophrenia. In time these patients may take on the characteristics of catatonic, hebephrenic or paranoid schizophrenia, in which case their diagnosis should be changed accordingly. In many cases the patient recovers within weeks, but sometimes his disorganization becomes progressive. More frequently remission is followed by recurrence. (In DSM-I this condition was listed as "Schizophrenia, acute undifferentiated type.")

295.5 SCHIZOPHRENIA, LATENT TYPE

This category is for patients having clear symptoms of schizophrenia but no history of a psychotic schizophrenic episode. Disorders sometimes designated as incipient, pre-psychotic, pseudoneurotic, pseudo-psychopathic, or borderline schizophrenia are categorized here. (This category includes some patients who were diagnosed in DSM-I under "Schizophrenic reaction, chronic undifferentiated

---

°—Asterisk indicates categories added to ICD-8 for use in the United States only.

type." Others formerly included in that DSM-I category are now classified under *Schizophrenia, other [and unspecified] types* (q.v.).)

295.6 SCHIZOPHRENIA, RESIDUAL TYPE

This category is for patients showing signs of schizophrenia but who, following a psychotic schizophrenic episode, are no longer psychotic.

295.7 SCHIZOPHRENIA, SCHIZO-AFFECTIVE TYPE

This category is for patients showing a mixture of schizophrenic symptoms and pronounced elation or depression. Within this category it may be useful to distinguish excited from depressed types as follows:

295.73* *Schizophrenia, schizo-affective type, excited**

295.74* *Schizophrenia, schizo-affective type, depressed**

295.8* SCHIZOPHRENIA, CHILDHOOD TYPE*

This category is for cases in which schizophrenic symptoms appear before puberty. The condition may be manifested by autistic, atypical, and withdrawn behavior; failure to develop indentity separate from the mother's; and general unevenness, gross immaturity and inadequacy in development. These developmental defects may result in mental retardation, which should also be diagnosed. (This category is for use in the United States and does not appear in ICD-8. It is equivalent to "Schizophrenic reaction, childhood type" in DSM-I.)

295.90 Schizophrenia, chronic undifferentiated type** This category is for patients who show mixed schizophrenic symptoms and who present definite schizophrenic thought, affect and behavior not classifiable under the other types of schizophrenia. It is distinguished from *Schizoid personality* (q.v.). (This category is equivalent to "Schizophrenic reaction, chronic undifferentiated type" in DSM-I except that it does not include cases now diagnosed as *Schizophrenia, latent type* and *Schizophrenia, other [and unspecified] types.*)

295.99 Schizophrenia, other [and unspecified] types** This category is for any type of schizophrenia not previously described. (In DSM-I "Schizophrenic reaction, chronic undifferentiated type" included this category and also what is now called *Schizophrenia, latent type* and *Schizophrenia, chronic undifferentiated type.*)

296 major affective disorders ((affective psychoses))

This group of psychoses is characterized by a single disorder of mood, either extreme depression or elation, that dominates the mental life of the patient and is responsible for whatever loss of contact he has with his environment. The onset of the mood does not seem to be related directly to a precipitating life experience and therefore is distinguishable from *Psychotic depressive reaction* and *Depressive neurosis*. (This category is not equivalent to the DSM-I heading "Affective reactions," which included "Psychotic depressive reaction.")

296.0 INVOLUTIONAL MELANCHOLIA

This is a disorder occurring in the involutional period and characterized by worry, anxiety, agitation, and severe insomnia. Feelings of guilt and somatic preoccupations are frequently present and may be of delusional proportions. This disorder is distinguishable from *Manic-depressive illness* (q.v.) by the absence of previous episodes; it is distinguished from *Schizophrenia* (q.v.) in that impaired reality testing is due to a disorder of mood; and it is distinguished from *Psychotic depressive reaction* (q.v.) in that the depression is not due to some life experience. Opinion is divided as to whether this psychosis can be distinguished from the other affective disorders. It is, therefore, recommended that involutional patients not be given this diagnosis unless all other affective disorders have been ruled out. (In DSM-I this disorder was considered one of two subtypes of "Involutional Psychotic Reaction.")

MANIC-DEPRESSIVE ILLNESSES (MANIC-DEPRESSIVE PSYCHOSES)

These disorders are marked by severe mood swings and a tendency to remission and recurrence. Patients may be given this diagnosis in the absence of a previous history of affective psychosis if there is no obvious precipitating event. This disorder is divided into three major subtypes: manic type, depressed type, and circular type.

296.1 MANIC-DEPRESSIVE ILLNESS, MANIC TYPE ((MANIC-DEPRESSIVE PSYCHOSIS, MANIC TYPE))

This disorder consists exclusively of manic episodes. These episodes are characterized by excessive elation, irritability, talkativeness, flight of ideas, and accelerated speech and motor activity. Brief periods of depression sometimes occur, but they are never true depressive episodes.

296.2 MANIC-DEPRESSIVE ILLNESS, DEPRESSED TYPE ((MANIC-DEPRESSIVE PSYCHOSIS, DEPRESSED TYPE))

This disorder consists exclusively of depressive episodes. These episodes are characterized by severely depressed mood and by mental and motor retardation progressing occasionally to stupor. Uneasiness, apprehension, perplexity and agitation may also be present. When illusions, hallucinations, and delusions (usually of guilt or of hypochondriacal or paranoid ideas) occur, they are attributable to the dominant mood disorder. Because it is a primary mood disorder, this psychosis differs from the *Psychotic depressive reaction*, which is more easily attributable to precipitating stress. Cases incompletely labelled as "psychotic depression" should be classified here rather than under *Psychotic depressive reaction*.

296.3 MANIC-DEPRESSIVE ILLNESS, CIRCULAR TYPE ((MANIC-DEPRESSIVE PSYCHOSIS, CIRCULAR TYPE))

This disorder is distinguished by at least one attack of both a depressive episode *and* a manic episode. This phenomenon makes clear why manic and depressed types are combined into a single category. (In DSM-I these cases were diagnosed under "Manic depressive reaction, other.") The current episode should be specified and coded as one of the following:

296.33° *Manic-depressive illness, circular type, manic°*
296.34° *Manic-depressive illness, circular type, depressed°*

296.8 OTHER MAJOR AFFECTIVE DISORDER ((AFFECTIVE PSYCHOSIS, OTHER))

Major affective disorders for which a more specific diagnosis has not been made are included here. It is also for "mixed" manic-depressive illness, in which manic and depressive symptoms appear almost simultaneously. It does not include

Psychotic depressive reaction (q.v.) or *Depressive neurosis* (q.v.). (In DSM-I this category was included under "Manic depressive reaction, other.")

[296.9 UNSPECIFIED MAJOR AFFECTIVE DISORDER]
> *[Affective disorder not otherwise specified]*
> *[Manic-depressive illness not otherwise specified]*

297 paranoid states

These are psychotic disorders in which a delusion, generally persecutory or grandiose, is the essential abnormality. Disturbances in mood, behavior and thinking (including hallucinations) are derived from this delusion. This distinguishes paranoid states from the affective psychoses and schizophrenias, in which mood and thought disorders, respectively, are the central abnormalities. Most authorities, however, question whether disorders in this group are distinct clinical entities and not merely variants of schizophrenia or paranoid personality.

297.0 PARANOIA
This extremely rare condition is characterized by gradual development of an intricate, complex, and elaborate paranoid system based on and often proceeding logically from misinterpretation of an actual event. Frequently the patient considers himself endowed with unique and superior ability. In spite of a chronic course the condition does not seem to interfere with the rest of the patient's thinking and personality.

297.1 INVOLUTIONAL PARANOID STATE ((INVOLUTIONAL PARAPHRENIA))
This paranoid psychosis is characterized by delusion formation with onset in the involutional period. Formerly it was classified as a paranoid variety of involutional psychotic reaction. The absence of conspicuous thought disorders typical of schizophrenia distinguishes it from that group.

297.9 OTHER PARANOID STATE
This is a residual category for paranoid psychotic reactions not classified earlier.

298 other psychoses

298.0 PSYCHOTIC DEPRESSIVE REACTION ((REACTIVE DEPRESSIVE PSYCHOSIS))
This psychosis is distinguished by a depressive mood attributable to some experience. Ordinarily the individual has no history of repeated depressions or cyclothymic mood swings. The differentiation between this condition and *Depressive neurosis* (q.v.) depends on whether the reaction impairs reality testing or functional adequacy enough to be considered a psychosis. (In DSM-I this condition was included with the affective psychoses.)

[298.1 REACTIVE EXCITATION]

[298.2 REACTIVE CONFUSION]
> *[Acute or subacute confusional state]*

[298.3 ACUTE PARANOID REACTION]

[298.9 REACTIVE PSYCHOSIS, UNSPECIFIED]

[299 unspecified psychosis]

[Dementia, insanity or psychosis not otherwise specified] This is not a diagnosis but is listed here for librarians and statisticians to use in coding incomplete diagnoses. Clinicians are expected to complete a differential diagnosis for patients who manifest features of several psychoses.

IV. neuroses (300)

300 neuroses

Anxiety is the chief characteristic of the neuroses. It may be felt and expressed directly, or it may be controlled unconsciously and automatically by conversion, displacement and various other psychological mechanisms. Generally, these mechanisms produce symptoms experienced as subjective distress from which the patient desires relief.

The neuroses, as contrasted to the psychoses, manifest neither gross distortion or misinterpretation of external reality, nor gross personality disorganization. A possible exception to this is hysterial neurosis, which some believe may occasionally be accompanied by hallucinations and other symptoms encountered in psychoses.

Traditionally, neurotic patients, however severely handicapped by their symptoms, are not classified as psychotic because they are aware that their mental functioning is disturbed.

300.0 ANXIETY NEUROSIS

This neurosis is characterized by anxious over-concern extending to panic and frequently associated with somatic symptoms. Unlike *Phobic neurosis* (q.v.), anxiety may occur under any circumstances and is not restricted to specific situations or objects. This disorder must be distinguished from normal apprehension or fear, which occurs in realistically dangerous situations.

300.1 HYSTERICAL NEUROSIS

This neurosis is characterized by an involuntary psychogenic loss or disorder of function. Symptoms characteristically begin and end suddenly in emotionally charged situations and are symbolic of the underlying conflicts. Often they can be modified by suggestion alone. This is a new diagnosis that encompasses the former diagnoses "Conversion reaction" and "Dissociative reaction" in DSM-I. This distinction between conversion and dissociative reactions should be preserved by using one of the following diagnoses whenever possible.

300.13 Hysterical neurosis, conversion type* In the conversion type, the special senses or voluntary nervous system are affected, causing such symptoms as blindness, deafness, anosmia, anaesthesias, paraesthesias, paralyses, ataxias, akinesias, and dyskinesias. Often the patient shows an inappropirate lack of concern or *belle indifférence* about these symptoms, which may actually provide secondary gains by winning him sympathy or relieving him of unpleasant responsibilities.

This type of hysterical neurosis must be distinguished from psychophysiologic disorders, which are mediated by the autonomic nervous system; from malingering, which is done consciously; and from neurological lesions, which cause anatomically circumscribed symptoms.

300.14° Hysterical neurosis, dissociative type°   In the dissociative type, alterations may occur in the patient's state of consciousness or in his identity, to produce such symptoms as amnesia, somnambulism, fugue, and multiple personality.

300.2 PHOBIC NEUROSIS

This condition is characterized by intense fear of an object or situation which the patient consciously recognizes as no real danger to him. His apprehension may be experienced as faintness, fatigue, palpitations, nausea, tremor, and even panic. Phobias are generally attributed to fears displaced to the phobic object or situation from some other object of which the patient is unaware. A wide range of phobias has been described.

300.3 OBSESSIVE COMPULSIVE NEUROSIS

This disorder is characterized by the persistent intrusion of unwanted thoughts, urges, or actions that the patient is unable to stop. The thoughts may consist of single words or ideas, ruminations, or trains of thought often perceived by the patient as nonsensical. The actions vary from simple movements to complex rituals such as repeated handwashing. Anxiety and distress are often present either if the patient is prevented from completing his compulsive ritual or if he is concerned about being unable to control it himself.

300.4 DEPRESSIVE NEUROSIS

This disorder is manifested by an excessive reaction of depression due to an internal conflict or to an identifiable event such as the loss of a love object or cherished possession. It is to be distinguished from *Involutional melancholia* (q.v.) and *Manic-depressive illness* (q.v.). *Reactive depressions* or *Depressive reactions* are to be classified here.

300.5 NEURASTHENIC NEUROSIS ((NEURASTHENIA))

This condition is characterized by complaints of chronic weakness, easy fatigability, and sometimes exhaustion. Unlike hysterical neurosis the patient's complaints are genuinely distressing to him and there is no evidence of secondary gain. It differs from *Anxiety neurosis* (q.v.) and from the *Psychophysiologic disorders* (q.v.) in the nature of the predominant complaint. It differs from *Depressive neurosis* (q.v.) in the moderateness of the depression and in the chronicity of its course. (In DSM-I this condition was called "Psychophysiologic nervous system reaction.")

300.6 DEPERSONALIZATION NEUROSIS ((DEPERSONALIZATION SYNDROME))

This syndrome is dominated by a feeling of unreality and of estrangement from the self, body, or surroundings. This diagnosis should not be used if the condition is part of some other mental disorder, such as an acute situational reaction. A brief experience of depersonalization is not necessarily a symptom of illness.

300.7 HYPOCHONDRIACAL NEUROSIS

This condition is dominated by preoccupation with the body and with fear of presumed diseases of various organs. Though the fears are not of delusional quality as in psychotic depressions, they persist despite reassurance. The condition differs from hysterical neurosis in that there are no actual losses or distortions of function.

300.8 OTHER NEUROSIS

This classification includes specific psychoneurotic disorders not classified elsewhere such as "writer's cramp" and other occupational neuroses. Clinicians should not use this category for patients with "mixed" neuroses, which should be diagnosed according to the predominant symptom.

[300.9 UNSPECIFIED NEUROSIS]

This category is not a diagnosis. It is for the use of record librarians and statisticians to code incomplete diagnoses.

V. personality disorders and certain other non-psychotic mental disorders (301–304)

301 personality disorders

This group of disorders is characterized by deeply ingrained maladaptive patterns of behavior that are perceptibly different in quality from psychotic and neurotic symptoms. Generally, these are life-long patterns, often recognizable by the time of adolescence or earlier. Sometimes the pattern is determined primarily by malfunctioning of the brain, but such cases should be classified under one of the non-psychotic organic brain syndromes rather than here. (In DSM-I "Personality Disorders" also included disorders now classified under *Sexual deviation, Alcoholism,* and *Drug dependence.*)

301.0 PARANOID PERSONALITY

This behavioral pattern is characterized by hypersensitivity, rigidity, unwarranted suspicion, jealousy, envy, excessive self-importance, and a tendency to blame others and ascribe evil motives to them. These characteristics often interfere with the patient's ability to maintain satisfactory interpersonal relations. Of course, the presence of suspicion of itself does not justify this diagnosis, since the suspicion may be warranted in some instances.

301.1 CYCLOTHYMIC PERSONALITY ((AFFECTIVE PERSONALITY))

This behavior pattern is manifested by recurring and alternating periods of depression and elation. Periods of elation may be marked by ambition, warmth, enthusiasm, optimism, and high energy. Periods of depression may be marked by worry, pessimism, low energy, and a sense of futility. These mood variations are not readily attributable to external circumstances. If possible, the diagnosis should specify whether the mood is characteristically depressed, hypomanic, or alternating.

301.2 SCHIZOID PERSONALITY

This behavior pattern manifests shyness, over-sensitivity, seclusiveness, avoidance of close or competitive relationships, and often eccentricity. Autistic thinking without loss of capacity to recognize reality is common, as is daydreaming and the inability to express hostility and ordinary aggressive feelings. These patients react to disturbing experiences and conflicts with apparent detachment.

301.3 EXPLOSIVE PERSONALITY (EPILEPTOID PERSONALITY DISORDER)

This behavior pattern is characterized by gross outbursts of rage or of verbal or physical aggressiveness. These outbursts are strikingly different from the patient's usual behavior, and he may be regretful and repentant for them. These patients are generally considered excitable, aggressive and over-responsive to environmental pressures. It is the intensity of the outbursts and the individual's inability to control them which distinguishes this group. Cases diagnosed as "aggressive personality" are classified here. If the patient is amnesic for the outbursts, the diagnosis of *Hysterical neurosis, Non-psychotic OBS with epilepsy* or *Psychosis with epilepsy* should be considered.

301.4 OBSESSIVE COMPULSIVE PERSONALITY ((ANANKASTIC PERSONALITY))

This behavior pattern is characterized by excessive concern with conformity and adherence to standards of conscience. Consequently, individuals in this group may be rigid, over-inhibited, over-conscientious, over-dutiful, and unable to relax easily. This disorder may lead to an *Obsessive compulsive neurosis* (q.v.), from which it must be distinguished.

301.5 HYSTERICAL PERSONALITY (HISTRIONIC PERSONALITY DISORDER)

These behavior patterns are characterized by excitability, emotional instability, over-reactivity, and self-dramatization. This self-dramatization is always attention-seeking and often seductive, whether or not the patient is aware of its purpose. These personalities are also immature, self-centered, often vain, and usually dependent on others. This disorder must be differentiated from *Hysterical neurosis* (q.v.).

301.6 ASTHENIC PERSONALITY

This behavior pattern is characterized by easy fatigability, low energy level, lack of enthusiasm, marked incapacity for enjoyment, and oversensitivity to physical and emotional stress. This disorder must be differentiated from *Neurasthenic neurosis* (q.v.).

301.7 ANTISOCIAL PERSONALITY

This term is reserved for individuals who are basically unsocialized and whose behavior pattern brings them repeatedly into conflict with society. They are incapable of significant loyalty to individuals, groups, or social values. They are grossly selfish, callous, irresponsible, impulsive, and unable to feel guilt or to learn from experience and punishment. Frustration tolerance is low. They tend to blame others or offer plausible rationalizations for their behavior. A mere history of repeated legal or social offenses is not sufficient to justify this diagnosis. *Group delinquent reaction of childhood (or adolescence)* (q.v.), and *Social maladjustment without manifest psychiatric disorder* (q.v.) should be ruled out before making this diagnosis.

301.81° Passive-aggressive personality° This behavior pattern is characterized by both passivity and aggressiveness. The aggressiveness may be expressed passively, for example by obstructionism, pouting, procrastination, intentional inefficiency, or stubbornness. This behavior commonly reflects hostility which the individual feels he dare not express openly. Often the behavior is one expression of the patient's resentment at failing to find gratification in a relationship with an individual or institution upon which he is over-dependent.

301.82° Inadequate personality° This behavior pattern is characterized by ineffectual responses to emotional, social, intellectual and physical demands. While the patient seems neither physically nor mentally deficient, he does manifest inadaptability, ineptness, poor judgment, social instability, and lack of physical and emotional stamina.

301.89° Other personality disorders of specified types (Immature personality, Passive-dependent personality, etc.)°

301.9 [UNSPECIFIED PERSONALITY DISORDER]

302 sexual deviations

This category is for individuals whose sexual interests are directed primarily toward objects other than people of the opposite sex, toward sexual acts not usually associated with coitus, or toward coitus performed under bizarre circumstances as in necrophilia, pedophilia, sexual sadism, and fetishism. Even though many find their practices distasteful, they remain unable to substitute normal sexual behavior for them. This diagnosis is not appropriate for individuals who perform deviant sexual acts because normal sexual objects are not available to them.

302.0 HOMOSEXUALITY

302.1 FETISHISM

302.2 PEDOPHILIA

302.3 TRANSVESTITISM

302.4 EXHIBITIONISM

302.5° VOYEURISM°

302.6° SADISM°

302.7° MASOCHISM°

302.8 OTHER SEXUAL DEVIATION

[302.9 UNSPECIFIED SEXUAL DEVIATION]

303 alcoholism

This category is for patients whose alcohol intake is great enough to damage their physical health, or their personal or social functioning, or when it has become a prerequisite to normal functioning. If the alcoholism is due to another mental disorder, both diagnoses should be made. The following types of alcoholism are recognized:

303.0 EPISODIC EXCESSIVE DRINKING

If alcoholism is present and the individual becomes intoxicated as frequently as four times a year, the condition should be classified here. Intoxication is defined as a state in which the individual's coordination or speech is definitely impaired or his behavior is clearly altered.

303.1 HABITUAL EXCESSIVE DRINKING

This diagnosis is given to persons who are alcoholic and who either become intoxicated more than 12 times a year or are recognizably under the influence of alcohol more than once a week, even though not intoxicated.

303.2 ALCOHOL ADDICTION

This condition should be diagnosed when there is direct or strong presumptive evidence that the patient is dependent on alcohol. If available, the best direct evidence of such dependence is the appearance of withdrawal symptoms. The inability of the patient to go one day without drinking is presumptive evidence. When heavy drinking continues for three months or more it is reasonable to presume addiction to alcohol has been established.

303.9 OTHER [AND UNSPECIFIED] ALCOHOLISM

304 drug dependence

This category is for patients who are addicted to or dependent on drugs other than alcohol, tobacco, and ordinary caffeine-containing beverages. Dependence on medically prescribed drugs is also excluded so long as the drug is medically indicated and the intake is proportionate to the medical need. The diagnosis requires evidence of habitual use or a clear sense of need for the drug. Withdrawal symptoms are not the only evidence of dependence; while always present when opium derivatives are withdrawn, they may be entirely absent when cocaine or marihuana are withdrawn. The diagnosis may stand alone or be coupled with any other diagnosis.

304.0 DRUG DEPENDENCE, OPIUM, OPIUM ALKALOIDS AND THEIR DERIVATIVES

304.1 DRUG DEPENDENCE, SYNTHETIC ANALGESICS WITH MORPHINELIKE EFFECTS

304.2 DRUG DEPENDENCE, BARBITURATES

304.3 DRUG DEPENDENCE, OTHER HYPNOTICS AND SEDATIVES OR "TRANQUILIZERS"

304.4 DRUG DEPENDENCE, COCAINE

304.5 DRUG DEPENDENCE, CANNABIS SATIVA (HASHISH, MARIHUANA)

304.6 DRUG DEPENDENCE, OTHER PSYCHO-STIMULANTS (AMPHETAMINES, ETC.)

304.7 DRUG DEPENDENCE, HALLUCINOGENS

304.8 OTHER DRUG DEPENDENCE

[304.9 UNSPECIFIED DRUG DEPENDENCE]

VI. psychophysiologic disorders (305)

305 psychophysiologic disorders ((physical disorders
of presumably psychogenic orgin))

This group of disorders is characterized by physical symptoms that are caused by emotional factors and involve a single organ system, usually under autonomic nervous system innervation. The physiological changes involved are those that normally accompany certain emotional states, but in these disorders the changes are more intense and sustained. The individual may not be consciously aware of his emotional state. If there is an additional psychiatric disorder, it should be diagnosed separately, whether or not it is presumed to contribute to the physical disorder. The specific physical disorder should be named and classified in one of the following categories.

305.0 PSYCHOPHYSIOLOGIC SKIN DISORDER
This diagnosis applies to skin reactions such as neurodermatosis, pruritis, atopic dematitis, and hyperhydrosis in which emotional factors play a causative role.

305.1 PSYCHOPHYSIOLOGIC MUSCULOSKELETAL DISORDER
This diagnosis applies to musculoskeletal disorders such as backache, muscle cramps, and myalgias, and tension headaches in which emotional factors play a causative role. Differentiation from hysterical neurosis is of prime importance and at times extremely difficult.

305.2 PSYCHOPHYSIOLOGIC RESPIRATORY DISORDER
This diagnosis applies to respiratory disorders such as bronchial asthma, hyperventilation syndromes, sighing, and hiccoughs in which emotional factors play a causative role.

305.3 PSYCHOPHYSIOLOGIC CARDIOVASCULAR DISORDER
This diagnosis applies to cardiovascular disorders such as paroxysmal tachycardia, hypertension, vascular spasms, and migraine in which emotional factors play a causative role.

305.4 PSYCHOPHYSIOLOGIC HEMIC AND LYMPHATIC DISORDER
Here may be included any disturbances in the hemic and lymphatic system in which emotional factors are found to play a causative role. ICD-8 has included this category so that all organ systems will be covered.

305.5 PSYCHOPHYSIOLOGIC GASTRO-INTESTINAL DISORDER

This diagnosis applies to specific types of gastrointestinal disorders such as peptic ulcer, chronic gastritis, ulcerative or mucous colitis, constipation, hyperacidity, pylorospasm, "heartburn," and "irritable colon" in which emotional factors play a causative role.

305.6 PSYCHOPHYSIOLOGIC GENITO-URINARY DISORDER

This diagnosis applies to genito-urinary disorders such as disturbances in menstruation and micturition, dyspareunia, and impotence in which emotional factors play a causative role.

305.7 PSYCHOPHYSIOLOGIC ENDOCRINE DISORDER

This diagnosis applies to endocrine disorders in which emotional factors play a causative role. The disturbance should be specified.

305.8 PSYCHOPHYSIOLOGIC DISORDER OF ORGAN OF SPECIAL SENSE

This diagnosis applies to any disturbance in the organs of special sense in which emotional factors play a causative role. Conversion reactions are excluded.

305.9 PSYCHOPHYSIOLOGIC DISORDER OF OTHER TYPE

VII. special symptoms (306)

306 special symptoms not elsewhere classified

This category is for the occasional patient whose psychopathology is manifested by a single specific symptom. An example might be anorexia nervosa under *Feeding disturbance* as listed below. It does not apply, however, if the symptom is the result of an organic illness or defect or other mental disorder. For example, anorexia nervosa due to schizophrenia would not be included here.

306.0 SPEECH DISTURBANCE

306.1 SPECIFIC LEARNING DISTURBANCE

306.2 TIC

306.3 OTHER PSYCHOMOTOR DISORDER

306.4 DISORDER OF SLEEP

306.5 FEEDING DISTURBANCE

306.6 ENURESIS

306.7 ENCOPRESIS

306.8 CEPHALALGIA

306.9 OTHER SPECIAL SYMPTOM

VIII. transient situational disturbances (307)

307* transient situational disturbances[1]

This major category is reserved for more or less transient disorders of any severity (including those of psychotic proportions) that occur in individuals without any apparent underlying mental disorders and that represent an acute reaction to overwhelming environmental stress. A diagnosis in this category should specify the cause and manifestations of the disturbance so far as possible. If the patient has good adaptive capacity his symptoms usually recede as the stress diminishes. If, however, the symptoms persist after the stress is removed, the diagnosis of another mental disorder is indicated. Disorders in this category are classified according to the patient's developmental stage as follows:

307.0* ADJUSTMENT REACTION OF INFANCY*
Example: A grief reaction associated with separation from patient's mother, manifested by crying spells, loss of appetite and severe social withdrawal.

307.1* ADJUSTMENT REACTION OF CHILDHOOD*
Example: Jealousy associated with birth of patient's younger brother and manifested by nocturnal enuresis, attention-getting behavior, and fear of being abandoned.

307.2* ADJUSTMENT REACTION OF ADOLESCENCE*
Example: Irritability and depression associated with school failure and manifested by temper outbursts, brooding and discouragement.

307.3* ADJUSTMENT REACTION OF ADULT LIFE*
Example: Resentment with depressive tone associated with an unwanted pregnancy and manifested by hostile complaints and suicidal gestures.
Example: Fear associated with military combat and manifested by trembling, running and hiding.
Example: A Ganser syndrome associated with death sentence and manifested by incorrect but approximate answers to questions.

307.4* ADJUSTMENT REACTION OF LATE LIFE*
Example: Feelings of rejection associated with forced retirement and manifested by social withdrawal.

IX. behavior disorders of childhood and adolescence (308)

308* behavior disorders of childhood and adolescence
((behavior disorders of childhood))[2]

This major category is reserved for disorders occurring in childhood and adolescence that are more stable, internalized, and resistant to treatment than *Transient situational disturbances* (q.v.) but less so than *Psychoses, Neuroses,* and *Personality disorders* (q.v.). This intermediate stability is attributed to the greater fluidity of all behavior at this age. Characteristic manifestations include such symptoms as overactivity, inattentiveness, shyness, feeling of rejection, over-aggressiveness, timidity, and delinquency.

308.0° HYPERKINETIC REACTION OF CHILDHOOD (OR ADOLESCENCE)°

This disorder is characterized by overactivity, restlessness, distractibility, and short attention span, especially in young children; the behavior usually diminishes in adolescence.

If this behavior is caused by organic brain damage, it should be diagnosed under the appropriate non-psychotic *organic brain syndrome* (q.v.).

308.1° WITHDRAWING REACTION OF CHILDHOOD (OR ADOLESCENCE)°

This disorder is characterized by seclusiveness, detachment, sensitivity, shyness, timidity, and general inability to form close interpersonal relationships. This diagnosis should be reserved for those who cannot be classified as having *Schizophrenia* (q.v.) and whose tendencies toward withdrawal have not yet stabilized enough to justify the diagnosis of *Schizoid personality* (q.v.).

308.2° OVERANXIOUS REACTION OF CHILDHOOD (OR ADOLESCENCE)°

This disorder is characterized by chronic anxiety, excessive and unrealistic fears, sleeplessness, nightmares, and exaggerated autonomic responses. The patient tends to be immature, self-conscious, grossly lacking in self-confidence, conforming, inhibited, dutiful, approval-seeking, and apprehensive in new situations and unfamiliar surroundings. It is to be distinguished from *Neuroses* (q.v.).

308.3° RUNAWAY REACTION OF CHILDHOOD (OR ADOLESCENCE)°

Individuals with this disorder characteristically escape from threatening situations by running away from home for a day or more without permission. Typically they are immature and timid, and feel rejected at home, inadequate, and friendless. They often steal furtively.

308.4° UNSOCIALIZED AGGRESSIVE REACTION OF CHILDHOOD (OR ADOLESCENCE)°

This disorder is characterized by overt or covert hostile disobedience, quarrelsomeness, physical and verbal aggressiveness, vengefulness, and destructiveness. Temper tantrums, solitary stealing, lying, and hostile teasing of other children are common. These patients usually have no consistent parental acceptance and discipline. This diagnosis should be distinguished from *Antisocial personality* (q.v.), *Runaway reaction of childhood (or adolescence)* (q.v.), and *Group delinquent reaction of childhood (or adolescence)* (q.v.).

308.5° GROUP DELINQUENT REACTION OF CHILDHOOD (OR ADOLESCENCE)°

Individuals with this disorder have acquired the values, behavior, and skills of a delinquent peer group or gang to whom they are loyal and with whom they characteristically steal, skip school, and stay out late at night. The condition is more common in boys than girls. When group delinquency occurs with girls it usually involves sexual delinquency, although shoplifting is also common.

308.9* OTHER REACTION OF CHILDHOOD (OR ADOLESCENCE)*

Here are to be classified children and adolescents having disorders not described in this group but which are nevertheless more serious than transient situational disturbances and less serious than psychoses, neuroses, and personality disorders. The particular disorder should be specified.

X. conditions without manifest psychiatric disorder and non-specific conditions (316*–318*)

316* social maladjustments without manifest psychiatric disorder

This category is for recording the conditions of individuals who are psychiatrically normal but who nevertheless have severe enough problems to warrant examination by a psychiatrist. These conditions may either become or precipitate a diagnosable mental disorder.

316.0* MARITAL MALADJUSTMENT*

This category is for individuals who are psychiatrically normal but who have significant conflicts or maladjustments in marriage.

316.1* SOCIAL MALADJUSTMENT*

This category is for individuals thrown into an unfamiliar culture (culture shock) or into a conflict arising from divided loyalties to two cultures.

316.2* OCCUPATIONAL MALADJUSTMENT*

This category is for psychiatrically normal individuals who are grossly maladjusted in their work.

316.3* DYSSOCIAL BEHAVIOR*

This category is for individuals who are not classifiable as anti-social personalities, but who are predatory and follow more or less criminal pursuits, such as racketeers, dishonest gamblers, prostitutes, and dope peddlers. (DSM-I classified this condition as "Sociopathic personality disorder, dyssocial type.")

316.9* OTHER SOCIAL MALADJUSTMENT*

317* non-specific conditions*

This category is for conditions that cannot be classified under any of the previous categories, even after all facts bearing on the case have been investigated. This category is not for "Diagnosis deferred" (q.v.).

318* no mental disorder*

This term is used when, following psychiatric examination, none of the previous disorders is found. It is not to be used for patients whose disorders are in remission.

notes

1. The terms included under DSM-II Category 307*, "Transient situational disturbances," differ from those in Category 307 of the ICD. DSM-II Category 307*, "Transient situational disturbances," contains adjustment reactions of infancy (307.0*), childhood (307.1*), adolescence (307.2*), adult life (307.3*), and late life (307.4*). ICD Category 307, "Transient situational disturbances," includes only the adjustment reactions of adolescence, adult life and late life. ICD 308, "Behavioral disorders of children," contains the reactions of infancy and childhood. These differences must be taken into account in preparing statistical tabulations to conform to ICD categories.

2. The terms included under DSM-II Category 308*, "Behavioral disorders of childhood and adolescence," differ from those in Category 308 of the ICD. DSM-II Category 308* includes "Behavioral disorders of childhood and adolescence," whereas ICD Category 308 includes only "Behavioral disorders of childhood." DSM-II Category 308* *does not* include "Adjustment reactions of infancy and childhood," whereas ICD Category 308 does. In the DSM-II classification, "Adjustment reactions of infancy and childhood" are allocated to 307* (Transitional situational disturbances). These differences should be taken into account in preparing statistical tabulations to conform to the ICD categories.

references

American Psychiatric Association. *Diagnostic and statistical manual, mental disorders.* (1st ed.) Washington, D.C.: 1952.
World Health Organization. *International Classification of Diseases.* (8th rev.) Geneva: 1968.

14

Psychiatric Diagnosis and Symptomatology

Edward Zigler and Leslie Phillips

Zigler and Phillips (1961b) recently reviewed and evaluated the myriad criticisms which have been leveled against the conventional system of psychiatric diagnosis (e.g., Harrower, 1950; Hoch & Zubin, 1953; Menninger, 1955; Noyes,

Reprinted from the *Journal of Abnormal and Social Psychology,* 1961, Vol. 63, No. 1, pp. 69–75. Copyright 1961 by the American Psychological Association. Reprinted by permission.

1953; Roe, 1949; Rogers, 1951; Rotter, 1954). Two frequently recurring arguments have been that this classificatory schema lacks reliability (Ash, 1949; Bosien, 1938; Eysenck, 1952; Mehlman, 1952; Roe, 1949; Rotter, 1954; Scott, 1958) and that many of its categories encompass individuals who are heterogeneous with respect to various criteria (King, 1954; Rotter, 1954; Wittenborn, 1952; Wittenborn & Bailey, 1952; Wittenborn & Weiss, 1952).

Several investigators have noted the conceptual and methodological weaknesses of those studies which have emphasized the unreliability of psychiatric diagnosis and have offered evidence that the present system is reliable (Foulds, 1955; Hunt, Wittson, & Hunt, 1953; Schmidt & Fonda, 1956; Seeman, 1953). The studies concerned with the reliability of psychiatric diagnosis suggest that so long as diagnosis is confined to broad categories it is reasonably reliable, with reliability diminishing as one proceeds from broad inclusive class categories to narrower, more specific ones (Zigler & Phillips, 1961b).

The present status of the heterogeneity criticism is much less clear. The confusion surrounding this issue appears to stem from the inherent ambiguity of the heterogeneity parameter (Zigler & Phillips, 1961b) as well as from the failure of certain investigators (Rotter, 1954) to differentiate homogeneity from reliability. As King (1954) has noted, reliability refers to the agreement in assigning individuals to diagnostic categories, whereas homogeneity refers to the uniformity of behavior subsumed within categories. The failure to differentiate adequately between these concepts can in part be ascribed to their inherent overlap.

The demarcation of this area of commonality can be sharpened by noting that what defines any diagnostic category is a particular symptom configuration. As the reliability of the categories decreases, their heterogeneity must increase. This can best be exemplified by the extreme case in which individuals are indiscriminately assigned to the various classifications. In this instance, each category would include every possible symptom pattern. But although a decrease in the reliability of a category is invariably accompanied by an increase in its heterogeneity, categories which subsume quite heterogeneous phenomena are not necessarily unreliable. There are many categories throughout science which, though reliable, subsume quite diverse phenomena—e.g., organic vs. inorganic matter. Thus, the reliability of psychiatric diagnosis is not determined by the number or diversity of symptoms which any diagnostic category encompasses, but is determined rather by the extent to which the same symptoms appear in more than one category of the system.

On the basis of the studies noted, it appears reasonable to assume that each of the broad diagnostic categories in common psychiatric use is both heterogeneous (subsumes a large number of diverse symptoms) and reasonably reliable (any particular symptom will tend to occur in only one category). One of the major purposes of this study is to evaluate empirically the validity of this position. Although the defense of the present diagnostic system tends to rest almost exclusively on the merits of its descriptive and nondynamic aspects (Caveny, Wittson, Hunt, & Herman, 1955; Eysenck, 1952; Hunt et al., 1953; Jellinek, 1939), surprisingly little evidence is available that membership in a diagnostic category conveys accurate information about the gross symptomatology of the patient. The findings of studies that have examined this issue (Freudenberg & Robertson, 1956; Wittenborn, Holzberg, & Simon, 1953) suggest that although the occurrence of certain symptoms tends to be associated with particular diagnostic categories, many symptoms are related to more than one category. These findings also indicate that even in those cases where a statistically significant relationship exists between the occurrence of a symptom and a diagnostic category, the symptom also occurs in a remarkably high proportion of individuals assigned to other diagnostic categories.

That further investigations of this type are needed can be emphasized by pointing out certain ambiguities of the two studies just noted. One of these (Wittenborn et al., 1953) employed narrow diagnostic categories rather than broad, inclusive ones. As pointed out earlier, this reduces the reliability of the categories and affects both the number of symptoms appearing in a category and the overlap of symptoms from category to category. Neither study employed a sample of patients in which all of the major functional diagnostic groups were represented. Nor did either study make use of the spontaneously noted symptoms of the patient. Instead, each patient in both studies was rated on each of the 55 symptoms which compose the Wittenborn symptom scales. Thus, the upper limit of the number of symptoms which appear in any category is arbitrarily established.

Use of the Wittenborn scales raises the issue of the pathognomonic vs. nonpathognomonic symptom, a distinction advanced by Thorne (1953). In view of the manner in which symptoms were chosen for inclusion in the Wittenborn (1950) scales, it is quite possible that many of these symptoms are not those characteristically employed to define membership in a particular diagnostic class, but are nonpathognomonic symptoms, characteristic of virtually any hospitalized individual. If such were the case, use of the Wittenborn scales would artificially increase the number of symptoms occurring in any diagnostic category while also making it more likely that a symptom would appear in more than one category.

In addition to a further clarification of the homogeneity and reliability issues, the second major objective of this study is a comparison of the present diagnostic system with the system of psychiatric classification recently advanced by Phillips and Rabinovitch (1958). These investigators, after empirically identifying three symptom clusters, conceptualized one of the three groups of symptoms as being indicative of "self-deprivation and turning against the self," another as "self-indulgence and turning against others," and a third as indicative of "avoidance of others." In a second study (Zigler & Phillips, 1960), it was found that these three symptom categories were related to the level of premorbid social effectiveness attained by the patient. After a cursory examination of the symptoms in each of the three categories, it was suggested that these three symptom categories correspond to the manic-depressive, character disorder, and schizophrenic syndromes, respectively. In view of this suggestion and the findings of Hollingshead and Redlich (1958) that conventional psychiatric categories are also related to premorbid social adequacy, it is of interest to investigate the degree of correspondence or overlap between the Phillips and Rabinovitch symptom categories and conventional psychiatric categories.

method

subjects

The study was based on an examination of the case histories of 793 patients admitted to Worcester State Hospital during a 12-year period (1945-1957). The particular case histories used were those of patients who were referred to the psychology department for psychological appraisal and who were eventually diagnosed as suffering from a functional disorder. While this sample includes a wide variety of cases, extremely deteriorated or very agitated patients are seldom referred for psychological evaluation and are not adequately represented here. These patients differed from those used in earlier studies (Freudenberg & Robertson, 1956; Wittenborn et al., 1953) in that they included individuals who varied widely in their degree of diagnostic difficulty, rather than presenting little or no diagnostic problem.

diagnosis

The diagnosis ascribed to each patient in the study was that psychiatric classification agreed upon at a diagnostic staff conference and noted on the patient's hospital record as his primary diagnosis. The diagnostic classification of mental illness used by Worcester State Hospital during this period was based on the *Standard Classified Nomenclature of Disease* (1945-1952) and *Diagnostic and Statistical Manual of Mental Disorder* (1953-1957).

The patients in the present study were categorized into four major diagnostic groups: manic-depressive, schizophrenic, psychoneurotic, and character disorder. The composition of each of these groups was as follows:

1. Manic-depressive here was defined to include the diagnoses of involutional psychotic reaction; manic-depressive, manic; manic-depressive, depressive; manic-depressive, other; and psychotic depressive reaction ($N = 75$).
2. The schizophrenic group included those with diagnoses of the following types of schizophrenic reactions: simple, hebephrenic, catatonic, paranoid, undifferentiated, and schizo-affective ($N = 287$).
3. Psychoneurotic patients carried diagnoses of the following types of psychoneurotic reactions: anxiety, dissociative, conversion, phobic, obsessive-compulsive, depressive, and other similar reactions ($N = 152$).
4. Character disorder was defined to include diagnoses of personality pattern disturbance—inadequate, schizoid, cyclothymic, or paranoid type; personality trait disturbance—emotionally unstable, passive-aggressive, compulsive personality, or other type; and, such sociopathic disturbances as antisocial, dyssocial, sexual deviation, alcoholism, and drug addiction ($N = 279$).

symptoms

A symptom in the present study, as in early studies (Philips & Rabinovitch, 1958; Zigler & Phillips, 1960), refers to the description of a patient's behavior by a psychiatrist at the time of initial institutional contact or the description of behavior presented by referring physicians as the primary reason for hospitalization. The symptoms include specific actions (assault), general behavior patterns (irresponsible behavior), thoughts (sexual preoccupations), somatic reactions (headaches), and general affect states (being tense). Examination of the 793 case records resulted in the tabulation of 48 discrete presenting symptoms. Symptoms which did not occur in at least 5% of the individuals included in any one of the four diagnostic categories were eliminated from further consideration; their low frequency of occurrence made them unsuitable for the type of statistical treatment employed. Employment of this criterion resulted in the following 13 symptoms being excluded from consideration: addictions other than drinking, delirium tremens, fearful, memory impairment, amnesia, blackouts, convulsions, eats a lot, charged with murder, fire setting, feels going crazy, feeling of sexual inadequacy, and compulsions.

Of the 35 symptoms employed in the present study, 31 had previously (Phillips & Rabinovitch, 1958; Zigler & Phillips, 1960) been placed in the category of self-deprivation and turning against the self, self-indulgence and turning against others, or avoidance of others. Prior to the analyses conducted in this study, the four remaining symptoms were classified in the following manner: Psychosomatic disorders, phobias, and obsessions were placed in the self-deprivation and turning against the self category, and depersonalization was placed into the avoidance of others category. This categorization of the four symptoms appears to be most in accord with the conceptual framework underlying the symptom categories.

results

In order to assess the number of symptoms appearing in each of the four diagnostic categories and the frequency with which the various symptoms appeared in each of these, the percentage of individuals in each category who manifested each symptom was computed. These percentages, as well as the percentage of the total sample manifesting each symptom, are presented in Table 14.1. Symptoms in this table are arranged in the order of their frequency of occurrence in the total sample.

As can be seen in Table 14.1, of the 35 symptoms, 30 appear in the manic-depressive, 34 in the character disorder, and all 35 in both the psychoneurotic and schizophrenic categories.

The chi square test of independence was employed to evaluate the tendency of each of the 35 symptoms either to occur or not to occur in each of the four diagnostic categories. Thus, 140 comparisons were made. The frequencies entered into the cells of each of these 2×2 contingency tables were the number of individuals in a particular diagnostic category who exhibited or did not exhibit a particular symptom vs. the number of individuals who did or did not exhibit that symptom in the other three diagnostic categories combined. Since the .05 level of significance was selected, 7 statistically significant relationships would be expected due to chance alone. Actually, 67 such relationships were found. These findings are summarized in Table 14.2, which lists those symptoms whose frequency of occurrence in a particular diagnostic group differed significantly from the frequency of occurrence of the symptoms in the other three diagnostic groups combined.

While this last analysis discloses which symptoms are significantly related to the particular diagnostic categories, it does not reveal the extent of the relationships. Furthermore, this analysis tends to be misleading in that in many instances where a significant relationship exists between a symptom and a diagnostic category, that symptom appears with surprisingly high frequency in the other diagnostic categories. In order to assess the degree of relationship between the symptoms and the diagnostic categories, contingency coefficients were computed for each of those contingency tables which resulted in a significant chi square.[1] The results of this analysis are presented in Table 14.3, in which symptoms are grouped according to the three symptom categories discussed earlier.

In addition to indicating the degree of relationship which obtains between each symptom and each diagnostic category, Table 14.3 shows the nature and

TABLE 14.1 PERCENTAGE OF INDIVIDUALS IN TOTAL SAMPLE AND IN EACH DIAGNOSTIC CATEGORY MANIFESTING EACH SYMPTOM

SYMPTOM	TOTAL HOS-PITAL (N = 793)	MANIC-DEPRES-SIVE (N = 75)	PSYCHO-NEU-ROTIC (N = 152)	CHAR-ACTER DIS-ORDER (N = 279)	SCHIZO-PHRENIC (N = 287)
Depressed	38	64	58	31	28
Tense	37	32	46	33	36
Suspiciousness	35	25	16	17	65
Drinking	19	17	14	32	8
Hallucinations	19	11	4	12	35
Suicidal attempt	16	24	19	15	12
Suicidal ideas	15	29	23	15	8
Bodily complaints	15	21	21	5	19
Emotional outburst	14	17	12	18	9
Withdrawn	14	4	12	7	25
Perplexed	14	9	9	8	24
Assaultive	12	5	6	18	5
Self-depreciatory	12	16	16	8	13
Threatens assault	10	4	11	14	7
Sexual preoccupation	10	9	9	6	14
Maniacal outburst	9	11	6	7	12
Bizarre ideas	9	11	1	2	20
Robbery	8	0	3	18	3
Apathetic	8	8	8	4	11
Irresponsible behavior	7	3	7	9	7
Headaches	6	7	10	4	5
Perversions (except homosexuality)	5	0	5	10	2
Euphoria	5	17	2	2	5
Fears own hostile impulses	5	4	9	5	2
Mood swings	5	9	5	4	4
Insomnia	5	11	7	3	5
Psychosomatic disorders	4	7	6	3	5
Does not eat	4	9	4	2	4
Lying	3	0	1	7	0
Homosexuality	3	3	3	8	2
Rape	3	0	3	8	1
Obsessions	3	8	3	1	4
Depersonalization	3	4	1	0	6
Feels perverted	3	0	3	1	5
Phobias	2	4	5	0	2

extent of the relationships between the symptom categories and the major diagnostic groups. In those instances where a significant relationship holds between a symptom and a diagnosis, the degree of relationship, as estimated by the contingency coefficient, tends to be quite small. In 33 of the 67 instances where a significant relationship occurs, the absolute magnitude of the contingency coefficient is .10 or less. In only one instance is there a coefficient greater than .30.

TABLE 14.2   SYMPTOMS TENDING TO JOINTLY OCCUR OR NOT TO OCCUR WITH EACH OF THE DIAGNOSTIC CATEGORIES

	MANIC-DEPRESSIVE	PSYCHO-NEUROTIC	CHARACTER DISORDER	SCHIZOPHRENIC
Symptoms which tend to occur	Suicidal attempt Suicidal ideas Euphoria Depressed Insomnia Obsessions Does not eat	Suicidal ideas Bodily complaints Tense Headaches Depressed Fears own hostile impulses Phobias	Perversions (except homosexuality) Drinking Robbery Assaultive Threatens assault Emotional outburst Lying Homosexuality Rape	Suspiciousness Perplexed Bizarre ideas Hallucinations Sexual preoccupation Apathetic Withdrawn Depersonalization Feels perverted Maniacal outbursts Bodily complaints
Symptoms which tend not to occur	Withdrawn Robbery	Suspiciousness Perplexed Bizarre ideas Hallucinations Robbery Assaultive	Suspiciousness Perplexed Bizarre ideas Hallucinations Sexual preoccupation Apathetic Withdrawn Depersonalization Feels perverted Euphoria Bodily complaints Self-depreciatory Depressed Phobias Obsessions	Perversions (except homosexuality) Drinking Threatens assault Emotional outbursts Lying Rape Suicidal attempt Suicidal ideas Depressed Fears own hostile impulses

These significant but relatively small contingency coefficients indicate that while there is a *relationship* between the two sets of categories, both category systems retain a considerable amount of independent variance. The nature of the relationship here seems quite clear. The self-deprivation and turning against the self category is positively related to both the manic-depressive and psychoneurotic categories but negatively related to the other two. Self-indulgence and turning against others is positively related to the character disorders but negatively related to the other three diagnostic groups. Avoidance of others is positively related to the schizophrenic category but negatively related to the other three.

discussion

A certain degree of relationship has been discovered between symptom manifestation and diagnosis. However, the most striking finding of the present study is that the magnitude of these relationships is generally so small that mem-

TABLE 14.3   MAGNITUDE OF THE RELATIONSHIP BETWEEN SYMPTOMS AND DIAGNOSES

SYMPTOM	MANIC-DEPRESSIVE	PSYCHO-NEUROTIC	CHARACTER DISORDER	SCHIZO-PHRENIC
Category 1				
Self-deprivation and turning against the self:				
Suicidal attempt	.07			−.07
Suicidal ideas	.13	.10		−.16
Euphoria	.19		−.08	
Bodily complaints		.09	−.20	.10
Tense		.09		
Headaches		.09		
Self-depreciatory			−.09	
Depressed	.17	.19	−.11	−.16
Fears own hostile impulses		.10		−.08
Mood swings				
Insomnia	.08			
Psychosomatic disorder				
Phobias		.10	−.09	
Obsessions	.09		−.10	
Does not eat	.09			
Category 2				
Self-indulgence and turning against others:				
Maniacal outbursts				.08
Perversions (except homosexuality)			.16	−.11
Drinking			.24	−.20
Robbery	−.08	−.09	.27	
Irresponsible behavior				
Assaultive		−.09	.12	
Threatens assault			.11	−.08
Emotional outburst			.10	−.10
Lying			.19	−.11
Homosexuality			.08	
Rape			.18	−.09
Category 3				
Avoidance of others:				
Suspiciousness		−.19	−.27	.42
Perplexed		−.07	−.13	.21
Bizarre ideas		−.13	−.18	.27
Hallucinations		−.18	−.13	.30
Sexual preoccupation			−.09	.11
Apathetic			−.09	.09
Withdrawn	−.09		−.15	.24
Depersonalization			−.11	.15
Feels perverted			−.08	.10

bership in a particular diagnostic group conveys only minimal information about the symptomatology of the patient. One is faced with the perplexing finding that the occurrence of a wide variety of symptoms may be related to more than one diagnostic category. These data are essentially in agreement with those of earlier studies (Freudenberg & Robertson, 1956; Wittenborn et al., 1953). Since the basis for diagnostic classification is ostensibly symptom manifestation, the question arises as to why such classification has been found to be reliable in spite of the fact that symptoms tend to occur with surprisingly comparable frequency across diagnostic groupings.

One possible answer is that although single symptoms may not grossly differentiate diagnoses, configurations of symptoms do so discriminate. In opposition to this view is the finding of Freudenberg and Robertson (1956) that complex combinations of symptoms do not lead to greater differentiation between diagnoses. Another possibility is that symptoms are not sufficiently unitary indices. It is open to question whether "withdrawal" in the depressive is qualitatively of the same nature as "withdrawal" in the schizophrenic, or whether the "suicidal attempt" of the depressive is the equivalent of the histrionics of the psychopath. While certain investigators (Wittenborn et al., 1953) have attempted to meet this deficiency by dimensionalizing symptoms, the criticism advanced above has nevertheless been leveled at even these efforts (Freudenberg & Robertson, 1956).

In relation to this problem, one is reminded of the position taken by Thorne (1953) that the experienced clinician diagnoses not on the basis of textbook symptoms but primarily on the basis of "the feel of the case." It may be that the diagnostician is responding to finer gradations of those discernible behaviors which are labeled symptoms than are defined by the classical indices of particular diagnoses. In addition to this, the clinician may be responding to some global configuration which transcends symptomatology or to criteria which lie beyond the domain of psychiatry proper. This possibility receives some support from the finding of Hollingshead and Redlich (1958) that diagnosis is related to social class membership. It receives further support from the finding of Zigler and Phillips (1961a) that diagnosis is related to premorbid social competence as measured by variables which both include and go beyond those typically employed to define social class membership. To the extent that such factors influence the diagnostic process, it suggests that psychiatric classification is based not on pathological manifestations alone but on the clinician's evaluation of the over-all maturity level of the patient. This view is supported by both the clinical folklore and the systematic evidence which characterize the manic-depressive and the psychoneurotic as mature, of higher socioeconomic class, phallic, etc. In contrast, schizophrenics and character disorders are typically conceived as immature, regressed, of lower socioeconomic class, oral, etc.

Another finding of the present study is that there is a positive relationship between the symptom clusters proposed by Phillips and Rabinovitch (1958) and psychiatric diagnosis. Thus, the self-deprivation and turning against the self symptom cluster is related to both the manic-depressive and psychoneurotic categories. The self-indulgence and turning against others and the avoidance of others clusters are positively related to the character disorder and schizophrenia categories, respectively. Since psychiatric classification is related to these global role orientations also, it may be that we have here another basis for diagnosis which is independent of the specific pathological behaviors manifested.

The finding of a relationship between the Phillips and Rabinovitch (1958) symptom clusters and conventional psychiatric diagnoses is also relevant to the heterogeneity issue raised here earlier. It has been asserted (Rotter, 1954) that symptoms are completely chance occurrences, unrelated to the "deeper" or more "dynamic" aspects of individual functioning. To find this view in an area which so heavily emphasizes determinism is somewhat surprising, and it has been refuted at some length (Eysenck, 1953; Jenkins, 1953; Phillips & Rabinovitch, 1958; Wittenborn et al., 1953). Nevertheless, if heterogeneity is defined simply as the number of symptoms which appear in any diagnostic category, the findings of the present study would support the view that our present diagnostic categories are heterogeneous in native phenomena. An alternative solution to the heterogeneity-homogeneity problem is, however, possible. Homogeneity may be defined in terms of the imposition of some organizing principle on otherwise discrete and apparently random pathological events. This is merely to assert that homogeneity is a construction of the observer or classifier rather than a quality which inheres in symptomatic behaviors. The Phillips and Rabinovitch symptom clusters represent just such an attempt at conceptual classification, and they, thus, provide a means for viewing diverse pathological behaviors as basically homogeneous in nature.

summary

This study was directed towards an examination of the relationship between symptom manifestation and inclusion in a particular diagnostic category. The study also investigated the nature of the relationship between the present diagnostic system and the system of psychiatric classification recently advanced by Phillips and Rabinovitch (1958). The most striking finding of the present study is that although relationships exist between symptoms and diagnoses, the magnitude of these relationships is generally so small that membership in a particular diagnostic group conveys only minimal information about the symptomatology of the patient. A relationship was also found between the Phillips and Rabinovitch symptom categories and the conventional psychiatric classification. These findings were discussed in relation to the issues of reliability and heterogeneity.

note

1. The contingency coefficient was chosen in preference to the phi coefficient because of the extremely uneven split which prevailed between occurrence and nonoccurrence for almost all of the symptoms. Since a contingency coefficient based on 2×2 tables has a maximum value of approximately .70, the coefficients reported in this study represent a conservative estimate of the relationships obtaining between symptoms and diagnostic categories. It should further be noted that the contingency coefficient is significant at the same level reached by the chi square from which it was computed. Thus, all contingency coefficients reported are significant at least at the .05 level. The contingency coefficient can only be positive in value. Nevertheless, they are reported here as negative in the instances where the relationship between symptom and diagnosis is such that the symptom tends not to occur with that diagnosis.

references

Ash, P. The reliability of psychiatric diagnosis. *J. abnorm. soc. Psychol.*, 1949, *44*, 272–277.

Boisen, A. Types of dementia praecox:—A study in psychiatric classification. *Psychiatry*, 1938, *1*, 233–236.

Caveny, E., Wittson, C., Hunt, W., & Herman, R. Psychiatric diagnosis, its nature and function. *J. nerv. ment. Dis.*, 1955, *121*, 367–380.

Eysenck, H. *The scientific study of personality.* London: Routledge & Kegan Paul, 1952.

Eysenck, H. The logical basis of factor analysis. *Amer. Psychologist*, 1953, *8*, 105–113.

Foulds, G. The reliability of psychiatric, and the validity of psychological diagnosis. *J. ment. Sci.*, 1955, *101*, 851–862.

Freudenberg, R., & Robertson, J. Symptoms in relation to psychiatric diagnosis and treatment. *Arch. neurol. Psychiat.*, 1956, *76*, 14–22.

Harrower, M. (Ed.) *Diagnostic psychological testing.* Springfield, Ill.: Charles C Thomas, 1950.

Hoch, P., & Zubin, J. (Eds.) *Current problems in psychiatric diagnosis.* New York: Grune & Stratton, 1953.

Hollingshead, A. B., & Redlich, F. C. *Social class and mental illness; A community study.* New York: Wiley, 1958.

Hunt, W., Wittson, C., & Hunt, E. A theoretical and practical analysis of the diagnostic process. In P. Hoch & J. Zubin (Eds.), *Current problems in psychiatric diagnosis.* New York: Grune & Stratton, 1953. Pp. 53–65.

Jellinek, E. Some principles of psychiatric classification. *Psychiatry*, 1939, *2*, 161–165.

Jenkins, R. Symptomatology and dynamics in diagnosis: A medical perspective. *J. clin. Psychol.*, 1953, *9*, 149–150.

King, G. Research with neuropsychiatric samples. *J. Psychol.*, 1954, *38*, 383–387.

Mehlman, B. The reliability of psychiatric diagnosis. *J. abnorm. soc. Psychol.*, 1952, *47*, 577–578.

Menninger, K. The practice of psychiatry. *Dig. Neurol. Psychiat.*, 1955, *23*, 101.

Noyes, A. *Modern clinical psychiatry.* Philadelphia: Saunders, 1953.

Phillips, L., & Rabinovitch, M. Social role and patterns of symptomatic behaviors. *J. abnorm. soc. Psychol.*, 1958, *57*, 181–186.

Roe, A. Integration of personality theory and clinical practice. *J. abnorm. soc. Psychol.*, 1949, *44*, 36–41.

Rogers, C. *Client-centered therapy.* Boston: Houghton Mifflin, 1951.

Rotter, J. *Social learning and clinical psychology.* New York: Prentice-Hall, 1954.

Schmidt, H., & Fonda, C. The reliability of psychiatric diagnosis: A new look. *J. abnorm. soc. Psychol.*, 1956. *52*, 262–267.

Scott, W. Research definitions of mental health and mental illness. *Psychol. Bull.*, 1958, *55*, 1–45.

Seeman, W. Psychiatric diagnosis: An investigation of interperson-reliability after didactic instruction. *J. nerv. ment. Dis.*, 1953, *118*, 541–544.

Thorne, F. Back to fundamentals. *J. clin. Psychol.*, 1953, *9*, 89–91.

Wittenborn, J. A new procedure for evaluating mental hospital patients. *J. consult. Psychol.*, 1950, *14*, 500–501.

Wittenborn, J. The behavioral symptoms for certain organic psychoses. *J. consult. Psychol.*, 1952, *16*, 104–106.

Wittenborn, J., & Bailey, C. The symptoms of involutional psychosis. *J. consult. Psychol.*, 1952, *16*, 13–17.

Wittenborn, J., Holzberg, J., & Simon, B. Symptom correlates for descriptive diagnosis. *Genet. psychol. Monogr.*, 1953, *47*, 237–301.

Wittenborn, J., & Weiss, W. Patients diagnosed manic depressive psychosis-manic state. *J. consult. Psychol.*, 1952, *16*, 193–198.

Zigler, E., & Phillips, L. Social effectiveness and symptomatic behaviors. *J. abnorm. soc. Psychol.*, 1960, *61*, 231–238.

Zigler, E., & Phillips, L. Case history data and psychiatric diagnosis. *J. consult. Psychol.*, 1961, *25*, 458. (a)

Zigler, E., & Phillips, L. Psychiatric diagnosis: A critique. *J. abnorm. soc. Psychol.*, 1961, in press. (b)

15

The APA Ruling on Homosexuality

On December 15, 1973, the Board of Trustees of the American Psychiatric Association approved a change in its official manual of psychiatric disorders. "Homosexuality per se," the trustees voted, should no longer be considered a "psychiatric disorder"; it should be defined instead as a "sexual orientation disturbance." The editors of The New York Times asked two psychiatrists, Robert L. Spitzer, M.D., associate professor of clinical psychiatry at Columbia, and member of the nomenclature committee of the APA, and Irving Bieber, M.D., clinical professor of psychiatry at the New York Medical College and chairman of the research committee on male homosexuality, to discuss the APA decision. An edited version of their discussion follows.

At the outset, they were asked to state their positions on the question: "Is homosexuality a psychiatric disorder?"

DR. SPITZER: Homosexuality, by definition, refers to an interest in sexual relations or contact with members of the same sex. Now, when we come to the question of whether or not homosexuality is a psychiatric illness, we have to have some criteria for what a psychiatric illness or disorder is. The criteria I propose applies to almost all of the conditions that are generally considered psychiatric disorders: The condition must either regularly cause subjective distress or regularly be associated with some generalized impairment in social effectiveness or functioning.

Clearly homosexuality per se does not meet these requirements: Many homosexuals are satisfied with their sexual orientation and demonstrate no generalized impairment.

If homosexuality does not meet the criteria for psychiatric disorder, what is it? Descriptively, we can say that it is one form of sexual behavior. However, in no longer considering it a psychiatric disorder, we are not saying that it is normal, or that it is as valuable as heterosexuality. We must recognize that for those homosexuals who are troubled, or dissatisfied with their homosexual feel-

Excerpted from *The New York Times*, December 23, 1973. © 1973 by The New York Times Company. Reprinted by permission.

ings, that we are then dealing with a psychiatric disorder because we then have subjective distress.

DR. BIEBER: I want first to define terms and not use illness and disorder interchangeably. The popular connotation of mental illness is psychotic illness. Now I don't believe homosexuality is a mental illness in that connotation.

As far as civil rights go, I am in complete favor of all civil rights for homosexuals: No matter how a particular sexual adaptation is arrived at in an adult, sexual behavior between consenting adults is a private matter.

The central question is: Is homosexuality a normal sexual variant, that develops like left-handedness does in some people, or does it represent some kind of disturbance in sexual development? There is no question in my mind: Every male homosexual goes through an initial stage of heterosexual development, and in all homosexuals, there has been a disturbance of normal heterosexual development, as a result of fears which produce anxieties and inhibitions of sexual function. His sexual adaptation is a substitutive adaptation.

I'd like to give you an analogy. In polio, you get a range of reactions of injuries. Some kids are totally paralyzed. Their walking function is gone. Others are able to walk with braces, others have enough muscle left so that they can be rehabilitated and can actually get to walk by themselves. The analogy falls down only in that the injury of polio is irreversible. But what you have in a homosexual adult is a person whose heterosexual function is crippled like the legs of a polio victim.

What are we going to call this? Are you going to say this is normal? That a person who has legs that have been actually paralyzed by polio is a normal person even though the polio is no longer active? The fears that have created the homosexuality, and the psychological inhibitions, belong in some kind of psychiatric representation.

DR. SPITZER: It now appears that although Dr. Bieber doesn't believe homosexuality is a mental illness, he would like to categorize it some place in between. If that is the case, why is he upset about the recent decision? It doesn't say homosexuality is normal. It only says it doesn't meet the criteria for psychiatric illness or disorder.

But before Dr. Bieber answers this question—Much of the language that Dr. Bieber uses (homosexuals are crippled, there is an injury) represents precisely the definitions that homosexuals now refuse to accept. Homosexuals are insisting they no longer want to view themselves this way.

the redefinition

And the reason that this new proposal was unanimously passed by the three committees of the APA and finally by the Board of Trustees, is not that the American Psychiatric Association has been taken over by some wild revolutionaries or latent homosexuals. It is that we feel that we have to keep step with the times. Psychiatry, which once was regarded as in the vanguard of the movement to liberate people from their troubles, is now viewed by many, and with some justification, as being an agent of social control. So it makes absolute sense to me not to list as a mental disorder those individuals who are satisfied and not in conflict with their sexual orientation.

DR. BIEBER: I didn't say homosexuality was a mental illness. And the Diagnostic and Statistical Manual of Psychiatric Disorder (DSM) contains other conditions [that do not satisfy Dr. Spitzer's definition] that I don't consider mental disorders either, such as voyeurism and fetishism.

DR. SPITZER: I haven't given as much thought [as Dr. Bieber] to the problems of voyeurism and fetishism, and perhaps that's because the voyeurs and fetishists have not yet organized themselves and forced us to do that. But it is true that there probably are some other conditions, and perhaps they include voyeurism and fetishism, which do not meet the criteria [of mental disorders]. I would be for reviewing those conditions as well.

I would like to ask you: Would you be in favor of adding the condition of asexuality, or celibacy, to the DSM?

DR. BIEBER: In individuals who have no operational sexuality, apart from those in certain professions, like the clergy, where it is demanded? Yes, I would.

DR. SPITZER: Well, you see, that exactly illustrates our difficulty here. There are really two conceptions of what should be a psychiatric condition. There are those who, with me, believe there should be a limited conception, which is close to a medical model, and there are those who believe that all psychological behavior which does not meet some general standard of optimal behavior, such as fanaticism, racism, male chauvinism, vegetarianism, asexuality should be added to the nomenclature.

By removing homosexuality from the nomenclature we are not saying it is abnormal but we are not saying it is normal. And I also believe that normal and abnormal are, strictly speaking, not psychiatric terms.

DR. BIEBER: These are questions now of definition.

DR. SPITZER: They are. That is the whole issue.

science and civil rights

DR. BIEBER: I am talking as a scientist. I think I made it clear that as a civil rights person, I was in the vanguard for civil rights for homosexuals.

This is a completely different issue. We are psychiatrists. I am a scientist primarily. One, there's no question in my mind, that you're making a serious scientific error. Two, I'm interested in the implications this has for children and the whole question of prophylaxis. I can pick out the entire population at risk in male homosexuality at the age of five, six, seven, eight. If these children are treated, and their parents are treated, they will not become homosexuals.

DR. SPITZER: Well, first of all, when we talk about treatment, I think it's irresponsible not to recognize that the number of homosexuals who wish treatment is small. The real problem is that the number of psychiatrists available to treat these individuals is small. Treatment is lengthy.

DR. BIEBER: That's irrelevant.

DR. SPITZER: No, it is not irrelevant.

DR. BIEBER: Do you think frigidity should be in the DSM?

DR. SPITZER: I would have to say that when it is a symptom of distress, yes.

DR. BIEBER: You mean a woman who is frigid and is not distressed by it—

DR. SPITZER: She does not have a mental disorder.

DR. BIEBER: So you're going to make two classifications for frigidity too. Frigidity that causes distress is the only one that remains. Is that correct?

DR. SPITZER: No, I'm not sure if that's correct. I think there is a distinction. Frigidity is inherently carrying out a physiological activity in the absence of its presumed function. That is different from homosexuality.

DR. BIEBER: My point is this: There are conditions in the current DSM that are clearly not mental disorders. Now I don't consider homosexuality a mental illness and a mental disorder in the connotation. Yet I consider it an injury to function caused by psychological fear. It belongs in the DSM the way frigidity does because frigidity is also an injury to a sexual function caused by fear.

EDITOR: What difference does it make whether homosexuality is designated as a mental illness in the DSM?

DR. SPITZER: It certainly has a real effect on psychiatric practice. I think there's no doubt that many psychiatrists have had difficulty treating homosexuals who came in wishing help for conditions other than their homosexuality.

Several years ago, I remember seeing a homosexual who was depressed after breaking up with his lover. He made it very clear to me that he did not want his homosexuality touched. I told him that as far as I was concerned I could not treat only part of his condition and that I regarded his problems as inextricably connected.

I don't think that my behavior was that unusual. I think that many homosexuals have avoided seeking psychiatric treatment because they believed their homosexuality would be attacked. This change will make it easier for homosexuals to get treatment when they want treatment but they don't want their homosexuality disturbed.

DR. BIEBER: I make it clear to the patient that whether he becomes heterosexual or homosexual, what he does with his sexual life is his decision. My job is to help him resolve as much of his problem as I can.

So, again, we must distinguish a scientific attitude from utilitarian uses, whether they're social, political or are going to get more patients into treatment.

DR. SPITZER: I wondered if I could quote Freud, who in 1935, answering a letter from a mother of a homosexual, said the following: "I gather from your letter that your son is a homosexual. Homosexuality is assuredly no advantage but it is nothing to be ashamed of. No vice, no degradation. It cannot be classified as an illness. We consider it to be a variation of the sexual function produced by a certain arrest of sexual development." On what basis do you disagree with Freud's view that homosexuality is not an illness. Or you are now saying that you don't regard it as an illness?

DR. BIEBER: I never said it was an illness.

Let me define homosexuality. It's an operational definition. Homosexuality, in an adult, is repetitive or preferential sexual behavior between same sex members [caused by fear].

DR. SPITZER: I think many members of our profession would agree that Dr. Bieber's formulation might apply to some homosexuals. We find it difficult to believe it applies to all homosexuals, now, or in other cultures, such as Ancient Greece, in which there was an institutionalized form of homosexuality.

DR. BIEBER: I will only claim expertise in the current Western culture. Everything I say applies only to our current culture. I can give you a group of cultures in which no homosexuality exists. One in which it's almost totally absent is the Israeli kibbutz.

DR. SPITZER: This discussion was supposed to be about whether homosexuality is an illness.

DR. BIEBER: It's not.

DR. SPITZER: Dr. Bieber wants to define homosexuality. Now what the APA has done is to agree with him that it is not an illness. But it has not said what it is.

DR. BIEBER: The APA has not agreed with me. [The inference from the APA reclassification] is that homosexuality is a normal variant, just like heterosexuality.

I say homosexuality is a psychiatric injury to function and belongs in any psychiatric manual. Now that doesn't mean I consider it an illness any more than I consider frigidity an illness. As long as something like frigidity will be in the manual, disorders of sexual functioning and homosexuality belong there. And to differentiate two types, to take what is really the most injured homosexual and say he shouldn't be in the DSM, and that the least injured, the one who has the potential left for restoring his heterosexuality, should be diagnosed as a sexual orientation disorder, to me seems wild.

value judgements?

DR. SPITZER: It seems wild to you because you have as your value system that everybody should be heterosexual.

DR. BIEBER: You think it's a value system? Do I think all homosexuals today should become heterosexuals? Definitely not. There are many homosexuals, maybe two-thirds of them, for whom heterosexuality is no longer possible.

DR. SPITZER: But should they feel that their heterosexuality is injured or crippled?

DR. BIEBER: If they want to be accurate, they can view that their heterosexuality has been irreparably injured.

DR. SPITZER: Injury is already a value.

DR. BIEBER: Injury is not a value. A broken leg is not a value.

DR. SPITZER: I cannot function homosexually but I would not regard it as an injury. You wouldn't either.

DR. BIEBER: That is not a counterpart.

DR. SPITZER: Well I believe it is. We come into this world, according to psychoanalytic notions, with a polymorphous perverse sexuality.

DR. BIEBER: I don't accept that.

DR. SPITZER: The animal kingdom suggests that we do come in with an undifferentiated sexual response. As a result of experience, although there may be some genetic factors involved, most of us become heterosexual and some of us become homosexual.

DR. BIEBER: I'm surprised that you, as a biologist, could talk that way. Every mammalian, every animal, whose reproduction depends on heterosexual mating, has inborn biological mechanisms to guarantee heterosexuality.

DR. SPITZER: But the capacity for homosexual response is universal in the animal kingdom.

DR. BIEBER: You'd have to define homosexual response.

But before we go, let's say this. We both agree that homosexuality is not a mental illness.

EDITOR: On this you agree. On what then do you disagree?

DR. SPITZER: Well, we disagree on how it should be characterized, and I have to say that is it easier for me to say how it should not be characterized than how it should be. I don't regard homosexuality as optimal as heterosexual development. I would agree with Freud that something has happened in the development of the sexual instinct that leads one to be incapable of or not interested in heterosexual functioning. I am loath, however, to apply the word disorder because of its many implications.

EDITOR: Can I ask one last question? What is your distinction between a disorder and a sexual orientation disturbance?

DR. SPITZER: I make no distinction. The category sexual orientation disturbance was designed for those homosexuals who were in conflict with their homosexuality. Some of them may wish treatment. Some of them may wish to become heterosexual, some of them may wish to learn to live with their homosexuality and to get rid of the guilt feelings that they may have about it.

DR. BIEBER: If a homosexual's function can't be restored, I don't want him to function guilitily about homosexuality. I want him to be happy.

THINK

1. Why is the existential neurosis not separately listed in the *Manual*? More generally, what does it "take" to get a syndrome listed, and why might certain symptoms or syndromes be excluded or overlooked?
2. Imagine that someone appeared in your office with the symptoms that Maddi wrote about. How might you diagnose him if you limited yourself to the categories that are included in the manual?
3. Zigler and Phillips find enormous overlap between the symptoms that are used to justify a diagnosis. Why should that be? How can you have different diagnoses, which presumably reflect different symptoms, and yet get such overlap? How is it that these observations were not made sooner? And most important, if the data in the Zigler and Phillips paper really describe the present state of psychological diagnosis (and there is considerable evidence that they do), how is it that we continue to diagnose? Why don't we give up the entire diagnostic enterprise?
4. It seems to have been the politics of homosexuality, and particularly the plight and pressure of gay liberation groups, that compelled the Board of Trustees of the American Psychiatric Association to change their view regarding homosexuality. How do you feel about that decision? If you feel that homosexuality is not a psychiatric problem, would you feel the same way about say, pedophilia (an adult sexual preference for children) or voyeurism? And if you feel that the Association was wrong (as many psychiatrists continue to feel), where do you draw the line between preferences that merely reflect "tastes" and those that are abnormal? These are awfully difficult questions. They go to the very heart of what is meant by abnormality and "normality."
5. The evidence in support of current diagnostic practices is nowhere near as substantial as it might be, thus leading some writers, such as T.S. Szasz, to suggest that diagnosis should be abandoned entirely. But the major function of diagnosis is classification, and classification is necessary for the progress of science. Can one legitimately argue that diagnosis should be abandoned altogether? Or rather does only proper classification, not poor classification, facilitate science? Is there any point in distinguishing diagnoses for scientific purposes, from diagnoses that go into the patient's record and become part of his personal social history?

The Contexts
of Psychopathology

"Craziness" is not merely a matter of personality. It is also a matter of context. Where you find a person determines your impression of him quite as much as his behavior does. And your impression of him determines how you will treat him.

However much you may resist this idea, the fact of the matter is that we all respond to people according to their contextual characteristics. The son of a senator, for example, strikes you differently—perhaps better, perhaps worse, but certainly differently—than the son of a carpenter. A wealthy girl seems different than a poor one. You would probably rather be called an administrative assistant than a secretary, a supplies manager than a stock clerk—even though the work is the same, regardless of the title. Titles, wealth, social status, and such are what we mean by contextual characteristics. It is no surprise then that many people strive for status and wealth. They have the feeling that others will react better to them, even though their own personal characteristics remain the same.

The reverse holds true, too. Much as we try to achieve a high status, we try desperately to avoid a low one, and for the same reasons: If status partly determines the reaction of others, then low status is likely to evoke bad reactions.

People who suffer psychological distress are among the lowest status people you can find. And they evoke very negative reactions. Of course, those reactions have a lot to do with the way psychiatric patients behave. But that's not the whole story, by any means. D. L. Rosenhan (Reading 16) demonstrates that the context of the psychiatric hospital is so powerful that even genuine sanity goes undetected there. It is not merely because of their behavior that the distressed are treated badly. Even when their behavior is perfectly "normal," so long as they are found in low status contexts, they will be considered low status people and treated accordingly. For the true psychiatric patient, the combination of having low status characteristics (that is, psychological distress) and being in a low status place is nearly unbeatable for its capacity to evoke negative reactions from others.

No wonder, then, that Theodore Sarbin and James Mancuso (Reading 19), in reviewing the massive attempt across decades to evoke sympathy for the psychologically distressed, call that attempt "the failure of a moral enterprise." For we are really of two minds with regard to the psychologically distressed. Clearly they need and deserve our sympathy and help. But clearly also, their station (in addition to their behavior) makes them aversive, regardless of how much we wish that that were not the case. That ambivalance produces a stalemate of enormous proportion. Over time, little change has occurred in peoples' attitudes toward the distressed.

On reading these words, any decent person is likely to feel that he or she is the exception who would treat psychiatric patients quite well, regardless of what others do. And perhaps you *are* the exception. But forgive us if we seem pessimistic on the matter. Changing one's attitudes is very likely *not* a matter of mere good intentions, as Philip Zimbardo and his colleagues point out (Reading 17). They worked with another group of low status people—prisoners, in a specially designed prison. These prisoners were experimental subjects who had, in fact, never committed a crime. Indeed, they were not distinguishably different from the people who were their guards. Nevertheless, the roles of prisoner and guard, and the context in which both groups found themselves, were very powerful ingredients. It was a study that was supposed to last for two weeks, but broke up in six days. Read why, and then ask yourself whether you could have withstood the pressures of either role—prisoner or guard.

If there is any hope of treating psychiatric patients decently, that hope probably lies in efforts to understand them, rather than in attempts to compel sympathy for them. In Reading 18, Benjamin Braginsky, Dorothea Braginsky, and Kenneth Ring demonstrate, in a set of exciting experiments, that in some crucial respects psychiatric patients are like the rest of us. Not only are their needs identical to our own, but they gratify them in precisely the ways that we do. That sounds absurdly simplistic, but we often forget that "crazy" people are not crazy all the time or in all ways. Indeed, it is much more likely that their craziness is quite specific and focal, but that *we*, through processes of selective perception, tend to imagine that craziness to be greatly magnified. *We* often see *them* as crazier than they really are.

Craziness, as you will see, lies not only in the distressed person. Like beauty, it is much in the eye of the beholder. And the eye of the beholder is itself easily influenced by the status of the beheld and the context in which he is found.

16

On Being Sane in Insane Places

D. L. Rosenhan

If sanity and insanity exist, how shall we know them?

The question is neither capricious nor itself insane. However much we may be personally convinced that we can tell the normal from the abnormal, the evidence is simply not compelling. It is commonplace, for example, to read about murder trials wherein eminent psychiatrists for the defense are contradicted by equally eminent psychiatrists for the prosecution on the matter of the defendant's sanity. More generally, there are a great deal of conflicting data on the reliability,

Reprinted from *Science*, 1973, Vol. 179, pp. 250–258. Copyright 1973 by the *American Association for the Advancement of Science.*

utility, and meaning of such terms as "sanity," "insanity," "mental illness," and "schizophrenia" (1). Finally, as early as 1934, Benedict suggested that normality and abnormality are not universal (2). What is viewed as normal in one culture may be seen as quite aberrant in another. Thus, notions of normality and abnormality may not be quite as accurate as people believe they are.

To raise questions regarding normality and abnormality is in no way to question the fact that some behaviors are deviant or odd. Murder is deviant. So, too, are hallucinations. Nor does raising such questions deny the existence of the personal anguish that is often associated with "mental illness." Anxiety and depression exist. Psychological suffering exists. But normality and abnormality, sanity and insanity, and the diagnoses that flow from them may be less substantive than many believe them to be.

At its heart, the question of whether the sane can be distinguished from the insane (and whether degrees of insanity can be distinguished from each other) is a simple matter: do the salient characteristics that lead to diagnoses reside in the patients themselves or in the environments and contexts in which observers find them? From Bleuler, through Kretchmer, through the formulators of the recently revised *Diagnostic and Statistical Manual* of the American Psychiatric Association, the belief has been strong that patients present symptoms, that those symptoms can be categorized, and, implicitly, that the sane are distinguishable from the insane. More recently, however, this belief has been questioned. Based in part on theoretical and anthropological considerations, but also on philosophical, legal, and therapeutic ones, the view has grown that psychological categorization of mental illness is useless at best and downright harmful, misleading, and pejorative at worst. Psychiatric diagnoses, in this view, are in the minds of the observers and are not valid summaries of characteristics displayed by the observed (3–5).

Gains can be made in deciding which of these is more nearly accurate by getting normal people (that is, people who do not have, and have never suffered, symptoms of serious psychiatric disorders) admitted to psychiatric hospitals and then determining whether they were discovered to be sane and, if so, how. If the sanity of such pseudopatients were always detected, there would be prima facie evidence that a sane individual can be distinguished from the insane context in which he is found. Normality (and presumably abnormality) is distinct enough that it can be recognized wherever it occurs, for it is carried within the person. If, on the other hand, the sanity of the pseudopatients were never discovered, serious difficulties would arise for those who support traditional modes of psychiatric diagnosis. Given that the hospital staff was not incompetent, that the pseudopatient had been behaving as sanely as he had been outside of the hospital, and that it had never been previously suggested that he belonged in a psychiatric hospital, such an unlikely outcome would support the view that psychiatric diagnosis betrays little about the patient but much about the environment in which an observer finds him.

This article describes such an experiment. Eight sane people gained secret admission to 12 different hospitals (6). Their diagnostic experiences constitute the data of the first part of this article; the remainder is devoted to a description of their experiences in psychiatric institutions. Too few psychiatrists and psychologists, even those who have worked in such hospitals, know what the experience is like. They rarely talk about it with former patients, perhaps because they distrust information coming from the previously insane. Those who have worked in psychiatric hospitals are likely to have adapted so thoroughly to the settings that they are insensitive to the impact of that experience. And while there have been occasional reports of researchers who submitted themselves to psychiatric hospitalization (7), these researchers have commonly remained in the hospitals for short periods of time, often with the knowledge of the hospital staff. It is difficult to know the extent to which they were treated like patients or like research colleagues. Nevertheless, their reports about the inside of the psychiatric hospital have been valuable. This article extends those efforts.

pseudopatients and their settings

The eight pseudopatients were a varied group. One was a psychology graduate student in his 20's. The remaining seven were older and "established." Among them were three psychologists, a pediatrician, a psychiatrist, a painter, and a housewife. Three pseudopatients were women, five were men. All of them employed pseudonyms, lest their alleged diagnoses embarrass them later. Those who were in mental health professions alleged another occupation in order to avoid the special attentions that might be accorded by staff, as a matter of courtesy or caution, to ailing colleagues (8). With the exception of myself (I was the first pseudopatient and my presence was known to the hospital administrator and chief psychologist and, so far as I can tell, to them alone), the presence of pseudopatients and the nature of the research program was not known to the hospital staffs (9).

The settings were similarly varied. In order to generalize the findings, admission into a variety of hospitals was sought. The 12 hospitals in the sample were located in five different states on the East and West coasts. Some were old and shabby, some were quite new. Some were research-oriented, others not. Some had good staff-patient ratios, others were quite understaffed. Only one was a strictly private hospital. All of the others were supported by state or federal funds or, in one instance, by university funds.

After calling the hospital for an appointment, the pseudopatient arrived at the admissions office complaining that he had been hearing voices. Asked what the voices said, he replied that they were often unclear, but as far as he could tell they said "empty," "hollow," and "thud." The voices were unfamiliar and were of the same sex as the pseudopatient. The choice of these symptoms was occasioned by their apparent similarity to existential symptoms. Such symptoms are alleged to arise from painful concerns about the perceived meaninglessness of one's life. It is as if the hallucinating person were saying, "My life is empty and hollow." The choice of these symptoms was also determined by the *absence* of a single report of existential psychoses in the literature.

Beyond alleging the symptoms and falsifying name, vocation, and employment, no further alterations of person, history, or circumstances were made. The significant events of the pseudopatient's life history were presented as they had actually occurred. Relationships with parents and siblings, with spouse and children, with people at work and in school, consistent with the aforementioned exceptions, were described as they were or had been. Frustrations and upsets were described along with joys and satisfactions. These facts are important to remember. If anything, they strongly biased the subsequent results in favor of detecting sanity, since none of their histories or current behaviors were seriously pathological in any way.

Immediately upon admission to the psychiatric ward, the pseudopatient ceased simulating *any* symptoms of abnormality. In some cases, there was a brief period of mild nervousness and anxiety, since none of the pseudopatients really believed that they would be admitted so easily. Indeed, their shared fear was that they would be immediately exposed as frauds and greatly embarrassed. Moreover, many of them had never visited a psychiatric ward; even those who had, nevertheless had some genuine fears about what might happen to them. Their nervousness, then, was quite appropriate to the novelty of the hospital setting, and it abated rapidly.

Apart from that short-lived nervousness, the pseudopatient behaved on the ward as he "normally" behaved. The pseudopatient spoke to patients and staff as he might ordinarily. Because there is uncommonly little to do on a psychiatric ward, he attempted to engage others in conversation. When asked by staff how he was feeling, he indicated that he was fine, that he no longer experienced symptoms. He responded to instructions from attendants, to calls for medication (which was not swallowed), and to dining-hall instructions. Beyond such activities as were available to him on the admissions ward, he spent his time writing down his observations about the ward, its patients, and the staff. Initially these notes were written "secretly," but as it soon became clear that no one much cared, they were subsequently written on standard tables of paper in such public places as the dayroom. No secret was made of these activities.

The pseudopatient, very much as a true psychiatric patient, entered a hospital with no foreknowledge of when he would be discharged. Each was told that he would have to get out by his own devices, essentially by convincing the staff that he was sane. The psychological stresses associated with hospitalization were considerable, and all but one of the pseudopatients desired to be discharged almost immediately after being admitted. They were, therefore, motivated not only to behave sanely, but to be paragons of cooperation. That their behavior was in no way disruptive is confirmed by nursing reports, which have been obtained on most of the patients. These reports uniformly indicate that the patients were "friendly," "cooperative," and "exhibited no abnormal indications."

the normal are not detectably sane

Despite their public "show" of sanity, the pseudopatients were never detected. Admitted, except in one case, with a diagnosis of schizophrenia (10), each was discharged with a diagnosis of schizophrenia "in remission." The label "in remission" should in no way be dismissed as a formality, for at no time during any hospitalization had any question been raised about any pseudopatient's simulation. Nor are there any indications in the hospital records that the pseudopatient's status was suspect. Rather, the evidence is strong that, once labeled schizophrenic, the pseudopatient was stuck with that label. If the pseudopatient was to be discharged, he must naturally be "in remission"; but he was not sane, nor, in the institution's view, had he ever been sane.

The uniform failure to recognize sanity cannot be attributed to the quality of the hospitals, for, although there were considerable variations among them, several are considered excellent. Nor can it be alleged that there was simply not enough time to observe the pseudopatients. Length of hospitalization ranged from 7 to 52 days, with an average of 19 days. The pseudopatients were not, in fact, carefully observed, but this failure clearly speaks more to traditions within psychiatric hospitals than to lack of opportunity.

Finally, it cannot be said that the failure to recognize the pseudopatients' sanity was due to the fact that they were not behaving sanely. While there was clearly some tension present in all of them, their daily visitors could detect no serious behavioral consequences—nor, indeed, could other patients. It was quite common for the patients to "detect" the pseudopatients' sanity. During the first three hospitalizations, when accurate counts were kept, 35 of a total of 118 patients on the admissions ward voiced their suspicions, some vigorously. "You're not crazy. You're a journalist, or a professor [referring to the continual note-taking]. You're checking up on the hospital." While most of the patients were reassured by the pseudopatient's insistence that he had been sick before he came in but was fine now, some continued to believe that the pseudopatient was sane throughout his hospitalization (11). The fact that the patients often recognized normality when staff did not raises important questions.

Failure to detect sanity during the course of hospitalization may be due to the fact that physicians operate with a strong bias toward what statisticians call the type 2 error (5). This is to say that physicians are more inclined to call a healthy person sick (a false positive, type 2) than a sick person healthy (a false negative, type 1). The reasons for this are not hard to find: it is clearly more dangerous to misdiagnose illness than health. Better to err on the side of caution, to suspect illness even among the healthy.

But what holds for medicine does not hold equally well for psychiatry. Medical illnesses, while unfortunate, are not commonly pejorative. Psychiatric diagnoses, on the contrary, carry with them personal, legal, and social stigmas (12). It was therefore important to see whether the tendency toward diagnosing the sane insane could be reversed. The following experiment was arranged at a research and teaching hospital whose staff had heard these findings but doubted that such an error could occur in their hospital. The staff was informed that at some time during the following 3 months, one or more pseudopatients would attempt to be admitted into the psychiatric hospital. Each staff member was asked to rate each patient who presented himself at admissions or on the ward according to the likelihood that the patient was a pseudopatient. A 10-point scale was used, with a 1 and 2 reflecting high confidence that the patient was a pseudopatient.

Judgments were obtained on 193 patients who were admitted for psychiatric treatment. All staff who had had sustained contact with or primary responsibility for the patient—attendants, nurses, psychiatrists, physicians, and psychologists—were asked to make judgments. Forty-one patients were alleged, with high confidence, to be pseudopatients by at least one member of the staff. Twenty-three were considered suspect by at least one psychiatrist. Nineteen were suspected by one psychiatrist and one other staff member. Actually, no genuine pseudopatient (at least from my group) presented himself during this period.

The experiment is instructive. It indicates that the tendency to designate sane people as insane can be reversed when the stakes (in this case, prestige and diagnostic acumen) are high. But what can be said of the 19 people who were suspected of being "sane" by one psychiatrist and another staff member? Were these people truly "sane," or was it rather the case that in the course of avoiding the type 2 error the staff tended to make more errors of the first sort—calling the crazy "sane"? There is no way of knowing. But one thing is certain: any diagnostic process that lends itself so readily to massive errors of this sort cannot be a very reliable one.

the stickiness of psychodiagnostic labels

Beyond the tendency to call the healthy sick—a tendency that accounts better for diagnostic behavior on admission than it does for such behavior after a lengthy period of exposure—the data speak to the massive role of labeling in psychiatric assessment. Having once been labeled schizophrenic, there is nothing the pseudopatient can do to overcome the tag. The tag profoundly colors others' perceptions of him and his behavior.

From one viewpoint, these data are hardly surprising, for it has long been known that elements are given meaning by the context in which they occur. Gestalt psychology made this point vigorously, and Asch (13) demonstrated that there are "central" personality traits (such as "warm" versus "cold") which are so powerful that they markedly color the meaning of other information in forming an impression of a given personality (14). "Insane," "schizophrenic," "manic-depressive," and "crazy" are probably among the most powerful of such central traits. Once a person is designated abnormal, all of his other behaviors and characteristics are colored by that label. Indeed, that label is so powerful that many of the pseudopatients' normal behaviors were overlooked entirely or profoundly misinterpreted. Some examples may clarify this issue.

Earlier I indicated that there were no changes in the pseudopatient's personal history and current status beyond those of name, employment, and, where necessary, vocation. Otherwise, a veridical description of personal history and circumstances was offered. Those circumstances were not psychotic. How were they made consonant with the diagnosis of psychosis? Or were those diagnoses modified in such a way as to bring them into accord with the circumstances of the pseudopatient's life, as described by him?

As far as I can determine, diagnoses were in no way affected by the relative health of the circumstances of a pseudopatient's life. Rather, the reverse occurred: the perception of his circumstances was shaped entirely by the diagnosis. A clear example of such translation is found in the case of a pseudopatient who had had a close relationship with his mother but was rather remote from his father during his early childhood. During adolescence and beyond, however, his father became a close friend, while his relationship with his mother cooled. His present relationship with his wife was characteristically close and warm. Apart from occasional angry exchanges, friction was minimal. The children had rarely been spanked. Surely there is nothing especially pathological about such a history. Indeed, many readers may see a similar pattern in their own experiences, with no markedly deleterious consequences. Observe, however, how such a history was translated in the psychopathological context, this from the case summary prepared after the patient was discharged.

> This white 39-year-old male . . . manifests a long history of considerable ambivalence in close relationships, which begins in early childhood. A warm relationship with his mother cools during his adolescence. A distant relationship to his father is described as becoming very intense. Affective stability is absent. His attempts to control emotionality with his wife and children are punctuated by angry outbursts and, in the case of the children, spankings. And while he says that he has several good friends, one senses considerable ambivalence embedded in those relationships also. . . .

The facts of the case were unintentionally distorted by the staff to achieve consistency with a popular theory of the dynamics of a schizophrenic reaction (15).

Nothing of an ambivalent nature had been described in relations with parents, spouse, or friends. To the extent that ambivalence could be inferred, it was probably not greater than is found in all human relationships. It is true the pseudo-patient's relationships with his parents changed over time, but in the ordinary context that would hardly be remarkable—indeed, it might very well be expected. Clearly, the meaning ascribed to his verbalizations (that is, ambivalence, affective instability) was determined by the diagnosis: schizophrenia. An entirely different meaning would have been ascribed if it were known that the man was "normal."

All pseudopatients took extensive notes publicly. Under ordinary circumstances, such behavior would have raised questions in the minds of observers, as, in fact, it did among patients. Indeed, it seemed so certain that the notes would elicit suspicion that elaborate precautions were taken to remove them from the ward each day. But the precautions proved needless. The closest any staff member came to questioning these notes occurred when one pseudopatient asked his physician what kind of medication he was receiving and began to write down the response. "You needn't write it," he was told gently. "If you have trouble remembering, just ask me again."

If no questions were asked of the pseudopatients, how was their writing interpreted? Nursing records for three patients indicate that the writing was seen as an aspect of their pathological behavior. "Patient engages in writing behavior" was the daily nursing comment on one of the pseudopatients who was never questioned about his writing. Given that the patient is in the hospital, he must be psychologically disturbed. And given that he is disturbed, continuous writing must be a behavioral manifestation of that disturbance, perhaps a subset of the compulsive behaviors that are sometimes correlated with schizophrenia.

One tacit characteristic of psychiatric diagnosis is that it locates the sources of aberration within the individual and rarely within the complex of stimuli that surrounds him. Consequently, behaviors that are stimulated by the environment are commonly misattributed to the patient's disorder. For example, one kindly nurse found a pseudopatient pacing the long hospital corridors. "Nervous, Mr. X?" she asked. "No, bored," he said.

The notes kept by pseudopatients are full of patient behaviors that were misinterpreted by well-intentioned staff. Often enough, a patient would go "berserk" because he had, wittingly or unwittingly, been mistreated by, say, an attendant. A nurse coming upon the scene would rarely inquire even cursorily into the environmental stimuli of the patient's behavior. Rather, she assumed that his upset derived from his pathology, not from his present interactions with other staff members. Occasionally, the staff might assume that the patient's family (especially when they had recently visited) or other patients had stimulated the outburst. But never were the staff found to assume that one of themselves or the structure of the hospital had anything to do with a patient's behavior. One psychiatrist pointed to a group of patients who were sitting outside the cafeteria entrance half an hour before lunchtime. To a group of young residents he indicated that such behavior was characteristic of the oral-acquisitive nature of the syndrome. It seemed not to occur to him that there were very few things to anticipate in a psychiatric hospital besides eating.

A psychiatric label has a life and an influence of its own. Once the impression has been formed that the patient is schizophrenic, the expectation is that he will continue to be schizophrenic. When a sufficient amount of time has passed, during which the patient has done nothing bizarre, he is considered to be in remission and available for discharge. But the label endures beyond discharge, with the unconfirmed expectation that he will behave as a schizophrenic again. Such labels, conferred by mental health professionals, are as influential on the patient as they are on his relatives and friends, and it should not surprise anyone that the diagnosis acts on all of them as a self-fulfilling prophecy. Eventually, the patient himself accepts the diagnosis, with all of its surplus meanings and expectations, and behaves accordingly (5).

The inferences to be made from these matters are quite simple. Much as Zigler and Phillips have demonstrated that there is enormous overlap in the symptoms presented by patients who have been variously diagnosed (16), so there is enormous overlap in the behaviors of the sane and the insane. The sane are not "sane" all of the time. We lose our tempers "for no good reason." We are occasionally depressed or anxious, again for no good reason. And we may find it difficult to get along with one or another person—again for no reason that we can specify. Similarly, the insane are not always insane. Indeed, it was the impression of the pseudopatients while living with them that they were sane for long periods of time—that the bizarre behaviors upon which their diagnoses were allegedly predicated constituted only a small fraction of their total behavior. If it makes no sense to label ourselves permanently depressed on the basis of an occasional depression, then it takes better evidence than is presently available to label all patients insane or schizophrenic on the basis of bizarre behaviors or cognitions. It seems more useful, as Mischel (17) has pointed out, to limit our discussions to *behaviors*, the stimuli that provoke them, and their correlates.

It is not known why powerful impressions of personality traits, such as "crazy" or "insane," arise. Conceivably, when the origins of and stimuli that give rise to a behavior are remote or unknown, or when the behavior strikes us as immutable, trait labels regarding the *behaver* arise. When, on the other hand, the origins and stimuli are known and available, discourse is limited to the behavior itself. Thus, I may hallucinate because I am sleeping, or I may hallucinate because I have ingested a peculiar drug. These are termed sleep-induced hallucinations, or dreams, and drug-induced hallucinations, respectively. But when the stimuli to my hallucinations are unknown, that is called craziness, or schizophrenia—as if that inference were somehow as illuminating as the others.

the experience of psychiatric hospitalization

The term "mental illness" is of recent origin. It was coined by people who were humane in their inclinations and who wanted very much to raise the station of (and the public's sympathies toward) the psychologically disturbed from that of witches and "crazies" to one that was akin to the physically ill. And they were at least partially successful, for the treatment of the mentally ill *has* improved considerably over the years. But while treatment has improved, it is doubtful that people really regard the mentally ill in the same way that they view the physically ill. A broken leg is something one recovers from, but mental illness allegedly endures forever (18). A broken leg does not threaten the observer, but a crazy schizophrenic? There is by now a host of evidence that attitudes toward the mentally ill are characterized by fear, hostility, aloofness, suspicion, and dread (19). The mentally ill are society's lepers.

That such attitudes infect the general population is perhaps not surprising, only upsetting. But that they affect the professionals—attendants, nurses, physicians, psychologists, and social workers—who treat and deal with the mentally ill is more disconcerting, both because such attitudes are self-evidently pernicious and because they are unwitting. Most mental health professionals would insist that they are sympathetic toward the mentally ill, that they are neither avoidant nor hostile. But it is more likely that an exquisite ambivalence characterizes their relations with psychiatric patients, such that their avowed impulses are only part of their entire attitude. Negative attitudes are there too and can easily be detected. Such attitudes should not surprise us. They are the natural offspring of the labels patients wear and the places in which they are found.

Consider the structure of the typical psychiatric hospital. Staff and patients are strictly segregated. Staff have their own living space, including their dining facilities, bathrooms, and assembly places. The glassed quarters that contain the professional staff, which the pseudopatients came to call "the cage," sit out on every dayroom. The staff emerge primarily for caretaking purposes—to give medication, to conduct a therapy or group meeting, to instruct or reprimand a patient. Otherwise, staff keep to themselves, almost as if the disorder that afflicts their charges is somehow catching.

So much is patient-staff segregation the rule that, for four public hospitals in which an attempt was made to measure the degree to which staff and patients mingle, it was necessary to use "time out of the staff cage" as the operational measure. While it was not the case that all time spent out of the cage was spent mingling with patients (attendants, for example, would occasionally emerge to watch television in the dayroom), it was the only way in which one could gather reliable data on time for measuring.

The average amount of time spent by attendants outside of the cage was 11.3 percent (range, 3 to 52 percent). This figure does not represent only time spent mingling with patients, but also includes time spent on such chores as folding laundry, supervising patients while they shave, directing ward cleanup, and sending patients to off-ward activities. It was the relatively rare attendant who spent time talking with patients or playing games with them. It proved impossible to obtain a "percent mingling time" for nurses, since the amount of time they spent out of the cage was too brief. Rather, we counted instances of emergence from the cage. On the average, daytime nurses emerged from the cage 11.5 times per shift, including instances when they left the ward entirely (range, 4 to 39 times). Late afternoon and night nurses were even less available, emerging on the average 9.4 times per shift (range, 4 to 41 times). Data on early morning nurses, who arrived usually after midnight and departed at 8 a.m., are not available because patients were asleep during most of this period.

Physicians, especially psychiatrists, were even less available. They were rarely seen on the wards. Quite commonly, they would be seen only when they arrived and departed, with the remaining time being spent in their offices or in the cage. On the average, physicians emerged on the ward 6.7 times per day (range, 1 to 17 times). It proved difficult to make an accurate estimate in this regard, since physicians often maintained hours that allowed them to come and go at different times.

The hierarchical organization of the psychiatric hospital has been commented on before (20), but the latent meaning of that kind of organization is worth noting again. Those with the most power have least to do with patients, and those with the least power are most involved with them. Recall, however, that the acquisition of role-appropriate behaviors occurs mainly through the observation of others, with the most powerful having the most influence. Consequently, it is understandable that attendants not only spend more time with patients than do any other members of the staff—that is required by their station in the hierarchy—but also, insofar as they learn from their superiors' behavior, spend as little time with patients as they can. Attendants are seen mainly in the cage, which is where the models, the action, and the power are.

I turn now to a different set of studies, these dealing with staff response to patient-initiated contact. It has long been known that the amount of time a person spends with you can be an index of your significance to him. If he initiates and maintains eye contact, there is reason to believe that he is considering your requests and needs. If he pauses to chat or actually stops and talks, there is added reason to infer that he is individuating you. In four hospitals, the pseudo-patient approached the staff member with a request which took the following form: "Pardon me, Mr. [or Dr. or Mrs.] X, could you tell me when I will be eligible for grounds privileges?" (or ". . . when I will be presented at the staff meeting?" or ". . . when I am likely to be discharged?"). While the content of the question varied according to the appropriateness of the target and the pseudo-patient's (apparent) current needs the form was always a courteous and relevant request for information. Care was taken never to approach a particular member of the staff more than once a day, lest the staff member become suspicious or irritated. In examining these data, remember that the behavior of the pseudo-patients was neither bizarre nor disruptive. One could indeed engage in good conversation with them.

The data for these experiments are shown in Table 16.1, separately for physicians (column 1) and for nurses and attendants (column 2). Minor differences between these four institutions were overwhelmed by the degree to which staff avoided continuing contacts that patients had initiated. By far, their most common response consisted of either a brief response to the question, offered while they were "on the move" and with head averted, or no response at all.

The encounter frequently took the following bizarre form: (pseudopatient) "Pardon me, Dr. X. Could you tell me when I am eligible for grounds privileges?" (physician) "Good morning, Dave. How are you today?" (Moves off without waiting for a response.)

It is instructive to compare these data with data recently obtained at Stanford University. It has been alleged that large and eminent universities are characterized by faculty who are so busy that they have no time for students. For this comparison, a young lady approached individual faculty members who seemed to be walking purposefully to some meeting or teaching engagement and asked them the following six questions.

1. "Pardon me, could you direct me to Encina Hall?" (at the medical school: ". . . to the Clinical Research Center?").
2. "Do you know where Fish Annex is?" (there is no Fish Annex at Stanford).
3. "Do you teach here?"
4. "How does one apply for admission to the college?" (at the medical school: ". . . to the medical school?").
5. "Is it difficult to get in?"
6. "Is there financial aid?"

Without exception, as can be seen in Table 16.1 (column 3), all of the questions were answered. No matter how rushed they were, all respondents not only maintained eye contact, but stopped to talk. Indeed, many of the respondents went out of their way to direct or take the questioner to the office she was seeking,

TABLE 16.1   SELF-INITIATED CONTACT BY PSEUDOPATIENTS WITH PSYCHIATRISTS AND NURSES AND ATTENDANTS, COMPARED TO CONTACT WITH OTHER GROUPS.

| | PSYCHIATRIC HOSPITALS | | UNIVERSITY CAMPUS (NONMEDICAL) | UNIVERSITY MEDICAL CENTER PHYSICIANS | | |
| | (1) | (2) | (3) | (4) | (5) | (6) |
CONTACT	Psychiatrists	Nurses and attendants	Faculty	"Looking for a psychiatrist"	"Looking for an internist"	No additional comment
Responses						
Moves on, head averted (%)	71	88	0	0	0	0
Makes eye contact (%)	23	10	0	11	0	0
Pauses and chats (%)	2	2	0	11	0	10
Stops and talks (%)	4	0.5	100	78	100	90
Mean number of questions answered (out of 6)	*	*	6	3.8	4.8	4.5
Respondents (No.)	13	47	14	18	15	10
Attempts (No.)	185	1283	14	18	15	10

* Not applicable.

to try to locate "Fish Annex," or to discuss with her the possibilities of being admitted to the university.

Similar data, also shown in Table 16.1 (columns 4, 5, and 6), were obtained in the hospital. Here too, the young lady came prepared with six questions. After the first question, however, she remarked to 18 of her respondents (column 4), "I'm looking for a psychiatrist," and to 15 others (column 5), "I'm looking for an internist." Ten other respondents received no inserted comment (column 6). The general degree of cooperative responses is considerably higher for these university groups than it was for pseudopatients in psychiatric hospitals. Even so, differences are apparent within the medical school setting. Once having indicated that she was looking for a psychiatrist, the degree of cooperation elicited was less than when she sought an internist.

powerlessness and depersonalization

Eye contact and verbal contact reflect concern and individualization; their absence, avoidance and depersonalization. The data I have presented do not do justice to the rich daily encounters that grew up around matters of depersonalization and avoidance. I have records of patients who were beaten by staff for the sin of having initiated verbal contact. During my own experience, for example, one patient was beaten in the presence of other patients for having approached an attendant and told him, "I like you." Occasionally, punishment meted out to patients for misdemeanors seemed so excessive that it could not be justified by the most radical interpretations of psychiatric canon. Nevertheless, they appeared to go unquestioned. Tempers were often short. A patient who had not heard a call for medication would be roundly excoriated, and the morning attendants would often wake patients with, "Come on, you m-----f-----s, out of bed!"

Neither anecdotal nor "hard" data can convey the overwhelming sense of powerlessness which invades the individual as he is continually exposed to the depersonalization of the psychiatric hospital. It hardly matters *which* psychiatric hospital—the excellent public ones and the very plush private hospital were better than the rural and shabby ones in this regard, but, again, the features that psychiatric hospitals had in common overwhelmed by far their apparent differences.

Powerlessness was evident everywhere. The patient is deprived of many of his legal rights by dint of his phychiatric commitment (21). He is shorn of credibility by virtue of his psychiatric label. His freedom of movement is restricted. He cannot initiate contact with the staff, but may only respond to such overtures as they make. Personal privacy is minimal. Patient quarters and possessions can be entered and examined by any staff member, for whatever reason. His personal history and anguish is available to any staff member (often including the "grey lady" and "candy striper" volunteer) who chooses to read his folder, regardless of their therapeutic relationship to him. His personal hygiene and waste evacuation are often monitored. The water closets may have no doors.

At times, depersonalization reached such proportions that pseudopatients had the sense that they were invisible, or at least unworthy of account. Upon being admitted, I and other pseudopatients took the initial physical examinations in a semipublic room, where staff members went about their own business as if we were not there.

On the ward, attendants delivered verbal and occasionally serious physical abuse to patients in the presence of other observing patients, some of whom (the pseudopatients) were writing it all down. Abusive behavior, on the other hand, terminated quite abruptly when other staff members were known to be coming. Staff are credible witnesses. Patients are not.

A nurse unbuttoned her uniform to adjust her brassiere in the presence of an entire ward of viewing men. One did not have the sense that she was being seductive. Rather, she didn't notice us. A group of staff persons might point to a patient in the dayroom and discuss him animatedly, as if he were not there.

One illuminating instance of depersonalization and invisibility occurred with regard to medications. All told, the pseudopatients were administered nearly 2100 pills, including Elavil, Stelazine, Compazine, and Thorazine, to name but a few. (That such a variety of medications should have been administered to patients presenting identical symptoms is itself worthy of note.) Only two were swallowed. The rest were either pocketed or deposited in the toilet. The pseudopatients were not alone in this. Although I have no precise records on how many patients rejected their medications, the pseudopatients frequently found the medications of other patients in the toilet before they deposited their own. As long as they were cooperative, their behavior and the pseudopatients' own in this matter, as in other important matters, went unnoticed throughout.

Reactions to such depersonalization among pseudopatients were intense. Although they had come to the hospital as participant observers and were fully aware that they did not "belong," they nevertheless found themselves caught up in and fighting the process of depersonalization. Some examples: a graduate student in psychology asked his wife to bring his textbooks to the hospital so he could "catch up on his homework"—this despite the elaborate precautions taken to conceal his professional association. The same student, who had trained for quite some time to get into the hospital, and who had looked forward to the experience, "remembered" some drag races that he had wanted to see on the weekend and insisted that he be discharged by that time. Another pseudopatient attempted a romance with a nurse. Subsequently, he informed the staff that he was applying for admission to graduate school in psychology and was very likely to be admitted, since a graduate professor was one of his regular hospital visitors. The same person began to engage in psychotherapy with other patients—all of this as a way of becoming a person in an impersonal environment.

the sources of depersonalization

What are the origins of depersonalization? I have already mentioned two. First are attitudes held by all of us toward the mentally ill—including those who treat them—attitudes characterized by fear, distrust, and horrible expectations on the one hand, and benevolent intentions on the other. Our ambivalence leads, in this instance as in others, to avoidance.

Second, and not entirely separate, the hierarchical structure of the psychiatric hospital facilitates depersonalization. Those who are at the top have least to do with patients, and their behavior inspires the rest of the staff. Average daily contact with psychiatrists, psychologists, residents, and physicians combined ranged from 3.9 to 25.1 minutes, with an overall mean of 6.8 (six pseudopatients over a total of 129 days of hospitalization). Included in this average are time spent in the admissions interview, ward meetings in the presence of a senior staff member, group and individual psychotherapy contacts, case presentation conferences, and discharge meetings. Clearly, patients do not spend much time in interpersonal contact with doctoral staff. And doctoral staff serve as models for nurses and attendants.

There are probably other sources. Psychiatric installations are presently in serious financial straits. Staff shortages are pervasive, staff time at a premium. Something has to give, and that something is patient contact. Yet, while financial stresses are realities, too much can be made of them. I have the impression that the psychological forces that result in depersonalization are much stronger than the fiscal ones and that the addition of more staff would not correspondingly improve patient care in this regard. The incidence of staff meetings and the enormous amount of record-keeping on patients, for example, have not been as substantially reduced as has patient contact. Priorities exist, even during hard times. Patient contact is not a significant priority in the traditional psychiatric hospital, and fiscal pressures do not account for this. Avoidance and depersonalization may.

Heavy reliance upon psychotropic medication tacitly contributes to depersonalization by convincing staff that treatment is indeed being conducted and that further patient contact may not be necessary. Even here, however, caution needs to be exercised in understanding the role of psychotropic drugs. If patients were powerful rather than powerless, if they were viewed as interesting individuals rather than diagnostic entities, if they were socially significant rather than social lepers, if their anguish truly and wholly compelled our sympathies and concerns, would we not *seek* contact with them, despite the availability of medications? Perhaps for the pleasure of it all?

the consequences of labeling and depersonalization

Whenever the ratio of what is known to what needs to be known approaches zero, we tend to invent "knowledge" and assume that we understand more than we actually do. We seem unable to acknowledge that we simply don't know. The needs for diagnosis and remediation of behavioral and emotional problems are enormous. But rather than acknowledge that we are just embarking on understanding, we continue to label patients "schizophrenic," "manic-depressive," and "insane," as if in those words we had captured the essence of understanding. The facts of the matter are that we have known for a long time that diagnoses are often not useful or reliable, but we have nevertheless continued to use them. We now know that we cannot distinguish insanity from sanity. It is depressing to consider how that information will be used.

Not merely depressing, but frightening. How many people, one wonders, are sane but not recognized as such in our psychiatric institutions? How many have been needlessly stripped of their privileges of citizenship, from the right to vote and drive to that of handling their own accounts? How many have feigned insanity in order to avoid the criminal consequences of their behavior, and, conversely, how many would rather stand trial than live interminably in a psychiatric hospital—but are wrongly thought to be mentally ill? How many have been stigmatized by well-intentioned, but nevertheless erroneous, diagnoses? On the last point, recall again that a "type 2 error" in psychiatric diagnosis does not have the same consequences it does in medical diagnosis. A diagnosis of cancer that has been found to be in error is cause for celebration. But psychiatric diagnoses are rarely found to be in error. The label sticks, a mark of inadequacy forever.

Finally, how many patients might be "sane" outside the psychiatric hospital but seem insane in it—not because craziness resides in them, as it were, but because they are responding to a bizarre setting, one that may be unique to institutions which harbor nether people? Goffman (4) calls the process of socialization to such institutions "mortification"—an apt metaphor that includes the processes of depersonalization that have been described here. And while it is impossible to know whether the pseudopatients' responses to these processes are characteristic of all inmates—they were, after all, not real patients—it is difficult to believe that these processes of socialization to a psychiatric hospital provide useful attitudes or habits of response for living in the "real world."

summary and conclusions

It is clear that we cannot distinguish the sane from the insane in psychiatric hospitals. The hospital itself imposes a special environment in which the meanings of behavior can easily be misunderstood. The consequences to patients hospitalized in such an environment—the powerlessness, depersonalization, segregation, mortification, and self-labeling—seem undoubtedly countertherapeutic.

I do not, even now, understand this problem well enough to perceive solutions. But two matters seem to have some promise. The first concerns the proliferation of community mental health facilities, of crisis intervention centers, of the human potential movement, and of behavior therapies that, for all of their own problems, tend to avoid psychiatric labels, to focus on specific problems and behaviors, and to retain the individual in a relatively nonpejorative environment. Clearly, to the extent that we refrain from sending the distressed to insane places, our impressions of them are less likely to be distorted. (The risk of distorted perceptions, it seems to me, is always present, since we are much more sensitive to an individual's behaviors and verbalizations than we are to the subtle contextual stimuli that often promote them. At issue here is a matter of magnitude. And, as I have shown, the magnitude of distortion is exceedingly high in the extreme context that is a psychiatric hospital.)

The second matter that might prove promising speaks to the need to increase the sensitivity of mental health workers and researchers to the *Catch 22* position of psychiatric patients. Simply reading materials in this area will be of help to some such workers and researchers. For others, directly experiencing the impact of psychiatric hospitalization will be of enormous use. Clearly, further research into the social psychology of such total institutions will both facilitate treatment and deepen understanding.

I and the other pseudopatients in the psychiatric setting had distinctly negative reactions. We do not pretend to describe the subjective experiences of true patients. Theirs may be different from ours, particularly with the passage of time and the necessary process of adaptation to one's environment. But we can and do speak to the relatively more objective indices of treatment within the hospital. It could be a mistake, and a very unfortunate one, to consider that what happened to us derived from malice or stupidity on the part of the staff. Quite the contrary, our overwhelming impression of them was of people who really cared, who were committed and who were uncommonly intelligent. Where they failed, as they sometimes did painfully, it would be more accurate to attribute those failures to the environment in which they, too, found themselves than to personal callousness. Their perceptions and behavior were controlled by the situation, rather than being motivated by a malicious disposition. In a more benign environment, one that was less attached to global diagnosis, their behaviors and judgments might have been more benign and effective.

references and notes

1. P. Ash, *J. Abnorm. Soc. Psychol.* 44, 272 (1949); A. T. Beck, *Amer. J. Psychiat.* 119, 210 (1962); A. T. Boisen, *Psychiatry* 2, 233 (1938); N. Kreitman, *J. Ment. Sci.* 107, 876 (1961); N. Kreitman, P. Sainsbury, J. Morrisey, J. Towers, J. Scrivener, *ibid.*, p. 887; H. O. Schmitt and C. P. Fonda, *J. Abnorm. Soc. Psychol.* 52, 262 (1956); W. Seeman, *J. Nerv. Ment. Dis.* 118, 541 (1953). For an analysis of these artifacts and summaries of the disputes, see J. Zubin, *Annu. Rev. Psychol.* 18, 373 (1967); L. Phillips and J. G. Draguns, *ibid.* 22, 447 (1971).

2. R. Benedict, *J. Gen. Psychol.* 10, 59 (1934).

3. See in this regard H. Becker, *Outsiders: Studies in the Sociology of Deviance* (Free Press, New York, 1963); B. M. Braginsky, D. D. Braginsky, K. Ring, *Methods of Madness: The Mental Hospital as a Last Resort* (Holt, Rinehart & Winston, New York, 1969); G. M. Crocetti and P. V. Lemkau, *Amer. Sociol. Rev.* 30, 577 (1965); E. Goffman, *Behavior in Public Places* (Free Press, New York, 1964): R. D. Laing, *The Divided Self: A Study of Sanity and Madness* (Quadrangle, Chicago, 1960); D. L. Phillips, *Amer. Sociol. Rev.* 28, 963 (1963); T. R. Sarbin, *Psychol. Today* 6, 18 (1972); E. Schur, *Amer. J. Sociol.* 75, 309 (1969); T. Szasz, *Law, Liberty and Psychiatry* (Macmillan, New York, 1963); *The Myth of Mental Illness: Foundations of a Theory of Mental Illness* (Hoeber-Harper, New York, 1963). For a critique of some of these views, see W. R. Gove, *Amer. Social. Rev.* 35, 873 (1970).

4. E. Goffman, *Asylums* (Doubleday, Garden City, N.Y., 1961).

5. T. J. Scheff, *Being Mentally Ill: A Sociological Theory* (Aldine, Chicago, 1966).

6. Data from a ninth pseudopatient are not incorporated in this report because, although his sanity went undetected, he falsified aspects of his personal history, including his marital status and parental relationships. His experimental behaviors therefore were not identical to those of the other pseudopatients.

7. A. Barry, *Bellevue Is a State of Mind* (Harcourt Brace Jovanovich, New York, 1971); I. Belknap, *Human Problems of a State Mental Hospital* (McGraw-Hill, New York, 1956); W. Caudill, F. C. Redlich, H. R. Gilmore, E. B. Brody, *Amer. J. Orthopsychiat.* 22, 314 (1952); A. R. Goldman, R. H. Bohr, T. A. Steinberg, *Prof. Psychol.* 1, 427 (1970); unauthored, *Roche Report 1* (No. 13), 8 (1971).

8. Beyond the personal difficulties that the pseudopatient is likely to experience in the hospital, there are legal and social ones that, combined, require considerable attention before entry. For example, once admitted to a psychiatric institution, it is difficult, if not impossible, to be discharged on short notice, state law to the contrary notwithstanding. I was not sensitive to these difficulties at the outset of the project, nor to the personal and situational emergencies that can arise, but later a writ of habeas corpus was prepared for each of the entering pseudopatients and an attorney was kept "on call" during every hospitalization. I am grateful to John Kaplan and Robert Bartels for legal advice and assistance in these matters.

9. However distasteful such concealment is, it was a necessary first step to examining these questions. Without concealment, there would have been no way to know how valid these experiences were; nor was there any way of knowing whether whatever detections occurred were a tribute to the diagnostic acumen of the staff or to the hospital's rumor network. Obviously, since my concerns are general ones that cut across individual hospitals and staffs, I have respected their anonymity and have eliminated clues that might lead to their identification.

10. Interestingly, of the 12 admissions, 11 were diagnosed as schizophrenic and one, with the identical symptomatology, as manic-depressive psychosis. This diagnosis has a more favorable prognosis, and it was given by the only private hospital in our sample. On the relations between social class and psychiatric diagnosis, see A. deB.

Hollingshead and F. C. Redlich, *Social Class and Mental Illness: A Community Study* (Wiley, New York, 1958).

11. It is possible, of course, that patients have quite broad latitudes in diagnosis and therefore are inclined to call many people sane, even those whose behavior is patently aberrant. However, although we have no hard data on this matter, it was our distinct impression that this was not the case. In many instances, patients not only singled us out for attention, but came to imitate our behaviors and styles.

12. J. Cumming and E. Cumming, *Community Ment. Health 1*, 135 (1965); A. Farina and K. Ring, *J. Abnorm. Psychol. 70*, 47 (1965); H. E. Freeman and O. G. Simmons, *The Mental Patient Comes Home* (Wiley, New York, 1963); W. J. Johannsen, *Ment. Hygiene 53*, 218 (1969); A. S. Linsky, *Soc. Psychiat. 5*, 166 (1970).

13. S. E. Asch, *J. Abnorm. Soc. Psychol. 41*, 258 (1946); *Social Psychology* (Prentice-Hall, New York, 1952).

14. See also I. N. Mensh and J. Wishner, *J. Personality 16*, 188 (1947); J. Wishner, *Psychol. Rev. 67*, 96 (1960); J. S. Bruner and R. Tagiuri, in *Handbook of Social Psychology*, G. Lindzey, Ed. (Addison-Wesley, Cambridge, Mass., 1954), vol. 2, pp. 634–654; J. S. Bruner, D. Shapiro, R. Tagiuri, in *Person Perception and Interpersonal Behavior*, R. Tagiuri and L. Petrullo, Eds. (Stanford Univ. Press, Stanford, Calif., 1958), pp. 277–288.

15. For an example of a similar self-fulfilling prophecy, in this instance dealing with the "central" trait of intelligence, see R. Rosenthal and L. Jacobson, *Pygmalion in the Classroom* (Holt, Rinehart & Winston, New York, 1968).

16. E. Zigler and L. Phillips, *J. Abnorm. Soc. Psychol. 63*, 69 (1961). See also R. K. Freundenberg and J. P. Robertson, *A.M.A. Arch. Neurol. Psychiatr. 76*, 14 (1956).

17. W. Mischel, *Personality and Assessment* (Wiley, New York, 1968).

18. The most recent and unfortunate instance of this tenet is that of Senator Thomas Eagleton.

19. T. R. Sarbin and J. C. Mancuso, *J. Clin. Consult. Psychol. 35*, 159 (1970); T. R. Sarbin, *ibid 31*, 447 (1967); J. C. Nunnally, Jr., *Popular Conceptions of Mental Health* (Holt, Rinehart & Winston, New York, 1961).

20. A. H. Stanton and M. S. Schwartz, *The Mental Hospital: A Study of Institutional Participation in Psychiatric Illness and Treatment* (Basic, New York, 1954).

21. D. B. Wexler and S. E. Scoville, *Ariz. Law Rev. 13*, 1 (1971).

17

The Psychology of Imprisonment:

PRIVATION, POWER, AND PATHOLOGY

Philip G. Zimbardo, Craig Haney, W. Curtis Banks, and David Jaffe

In prison, those things withheld from and denied to the prisoner become precisely what he wants most of all.

Eldridge Cleaver, *Soul on Ice* (1968)

Reprinted with the permission of the authors. Unpublished manuscript.

Our sense of power is more vivid when we break a man's spirit than when we win his heart.

Eric Hofer, *The Passionate State of Mind* (1954)

Wherever any one is against his will, that is to him a prison.

Epictetus, *Discourses* (2nd century)

The quiet of a Sunday morning in Palo Alto, California, was shattered by a screeching squad car siren as police swept through the city picking up college students in a surprise mass arrest. Each suspect was charged with a felony, warned of his constitutional rights, spread-eagled against the police car, searched, handcuffed, and carted off in the back seat of the squad car to the police station for booking. In some cases, curious neighbors who witnessed these arrests expressed sympathy and concern to the families of these unfortunate young men. Said one alarmed mother of an 18-year-old college sophomore arrested for armed robbery, "I felt my son must have done something; the police have come to get my son!"

After being fingerprinted and having identification forms prepared for his "jacket" (central information file), each prisoner was left isolated in a detention cell to wonder what he had done to get himself into this mess. After a while, he was blindfolded and transported to the "Stanford County Prison." Here he began the induction process of becoming a prisoner—stripped naked, skin searched, deloused, and issued a uniform, bedding, soap, towel, toothpaste and toothbrush.

The prisoner's uniform was a loosely fitting smock with an ID number on front and back. A chain was bolted around one ankle and had to be worn at all times. In place of having his head shaved, the prisoner had to wear a nylon stocking cap over his head to cover his hair. Orders were shouted at him and the prisoner was pushed around by the guards if he didn't comply quickly enough. By late afternoon, when all the arrests were completed, and each prisoner had been duly processed, the warden greeted his new charges with an impromptu welcome:

> As you probably already know I'm your Warden. All of you have shown that you are unable to function outside in the real world for one reason or another—that somehow you lack a responsibility of good citizens of this great country. We of this prison, your correctional staff, are going to help you learn what your responsibilities as citizens of this country are. Here are the rules. Sometime in the very near future there will be a copy of the rules posted in each of the cells. We expect you to know them and to be able to recite them by number. If you follow all of these rules and keep your hands clean, repent for your misdeeds and show a proper attitude of penitence, you and I will get along just fine.

There followed a reading off of the sixteen basic rules of prisoner conduct (which the warden and his staff of eleven correctional officers had compiled):

> *Rule number One:* Prisoners must remain silent during rest periods, after lights out, during meals, and whenever they are outside the prison yard. *Two:* Prisoners must eat at mealtimes and only at mealtimes. *Three:* Prisoners must not move, tamper, deface, or damage walls, ceilings, windows, doors, or other prison property . . . *Seven:* Prisoners must address each other by their ID number only. *Eight:* Prisoners must address the guards as "Mr. Correctional Officer" . . . *Sixteen:* Failure to obey any of the above rules may result in punishment.

Most of the nine prisoners, all "first-offenders," sat on the cots in their barren cells dazed and shocked by the unexpected events which had transformed their lives so suddenly.

Something out of the ordinary *was* indeed taking place. For the police, the arrests they had made were of a routine sort and had been executed with their usual efficiency. But what was unusual were the blindfolds, the ankle chains, the stocking caps, smocks—and the long-haired, hippie-looking *guards*. Just what kind of prison was this?

> We're all of us guinea pigs in the laboratory of God. Humanity is just a work in progress.
>
> Tennessee Williams, *Camino Real*

It was, in fact, a very special kind of prison—an experimental, mock prison—created specifically for the purpose of investigating the psychological effects of imprisonment upon volunteer research subjects. When we planned our two-week long simulation of prison life, we sought answers to a number of questions of social and academic interest. How do men adapt to the novel and alien situation in which those called "prisoners" lose their liberty, civil rights, and their privacy, while those called "guards" gain power and social status? What is responsible for the alleged brutality and violence in American prisons—is it the nature of the prison population (presumably filled with sociopathic criminals and sadistic guards), or is it the social psychological environment of the prison experience? Under what conditions can a role-playing simulation achieve a sufficient level of reality to become more than just a game (in this instance, one of "cops and robbers"), so that it is both a source of new self knowledge for the participants and one of socially relevant knowledge for the researchers studying it?

Our mock prison represented an attempt to simulate *functionally* some of the significant features of the psychological state of imprisonment. We did this by first making an intensive conceptual analysis of the variables involved in the prison situation after spending hundreds of hours in discussions with ex-convicts, parole officers, and correctional personnel, and after reviewing much of the existing literature on prisons and concentration camps. We then formulated a set of procedures to operationalize these variables so they would be maximally effective given the limitations and constraints of the setting available to us. We did not intend to generate a *literal* simulation of "real" prison details or standard operational practices. Rather, our primary concern was to achieve some equivalent psychological effects despite differences between the form and structure of the particular operations employed in the "Stanford County Prison" and those in "real" prisons. We did, however, try to introduce enough "mundane realism" (Aronson & Carlsmith, 1969) into the experience so that the role-playing participants might be able to go beyond the superficial demands of their assigned roles into the deep structure of the prisoner and guard mentality. This was accomplished in part through the cooperation of the local police department who made the unexpected arrests appear as part of a routine raid. A local TV station sent a cameraman to film the "arrests," which furthered the illusion of a newsworthy event actually taking place and encouraged the arresting officers to act their roles convincingly. Realism was enhanced by a visit to the prison from a Catholic priest who had been a prison chaplain, by a public defender, who discussed bail and trial procedures with the prisoners, and by parents, relatives, and friends during several scheduled visitors' hours. There were parole board meetings as well as disciplinary meetings headed by an ex-convict and staffed by "adult authorities" who were strangers to the prisoners. Small details, such as stationery imprinted with the name of the prison also helped to carry some of the burden of realism. Thus, for example, the mother of prisoner 5486 reported to the Prison Superintendent that she had felt guilty when the mailman, delivering a letter from her imprisoned son, asked her what was the charge against him and whether his case had gone to trial yet.

The prison was physically constructed in the basement of Stanford University's Psychology building which was deserted after the end of the summer school session. A long corridor was converted into the prison "Yard" by partitioning off both ends. Three 6 ft. x 9 ft. laboratory rooms opening onto this corridor were made into cells by replacing their doors with barred ones and replacing existing furniture with three cots (to a cell). A small, dark storage closet opposite the cells served as solitary confinement, and was posted with an appropriate sign, "The Hole." Adjacent offices were refurnished as guards' quarters, interview-testing rooms and bedrooms for the "Warden" (Jaffe) and the "Superintendent" (Zimbardo). Toilet facilities (without showers) were available in a nearby corridor. A concealed video camera and hidden microphones recorded much of the verbal and nonverbal interactions between and among guards and prisoners. The physical environment was one in which prisoners could always be observed by the staff, except when they were secluded in solitary confinement.

These quarters, although clean and neat, were rather small, stark, and without aesthetic appeal. No unplanned interruptions or distractions were possible, and the natural variation in sensory stimulation was minimal. The lack of windows resulted in poor air circulation and persisting odors arose from the unwashed bodies of the prisoners. After 10 P.M. lockup, toilet privileges were denied, so prisoners who had to relieve themselves would have to urinate and defecate in buckets provided by the guards. Sometimes, the guards refused permission to have them cleaned out and this made the prison smell.

We are aware of the content of experience, but unaware that it is illusion. We see the shadows, but take them for substance.

R. D. Laing, *Self and Others*

"Real" prisoners typically report feeling powerless, arbitrarily controlled, dependent, frustrated, hopeless, anonymous, dehumanized, and emasculated. It is not possible, pragmatically or ethically, to create such chronic states in volunteer subjects who realize that they are in an experiment for only a short time. Racism, physical brutality, indefinite confinement, and enforced homosexuality were not features of our mock prison (see Davis, 1968, re: sexual assaults). Instead, we created symbolic manifestations of those variables presumably fundamental to the experience of being imprisoned.

Anonymity was promoted through a variety of operations to minimize each prisoner's uniqueness and prior identity (see Zimbardo, 1970). Their uniforms, ID numbers, and caps, as well as removal of their personal effects and being housed in barren cells—all made the subjects appear similar to each other, often indistinguishable to observers, and forced upon them the situational group identity of "prisoner." Having to wear smocks, which were like dresses, without undergarments caused the prisoners to be more restrained in their physical actions and to move in ways which were more feminine than masculine. Forcing the prisoners to obtain permission from the guards for routine and simple activities such as writing letters, smoking a cigarette, or even going to the toilet elicited from them a child-like dependency.

The oppressiveness of the environment was exaggerated by the absence of clocks or windows to mark the passage of time, by the constant surveillance of the guards, the total lack of privacy, and also by the significance of having always to wear the ankle chain.

Above all, "real" prisons are time machines for playing tricks with the human conception of time. In our prison, the prisoners often did not even know whether it was day or night, or what hour it was. A few hours after falling asleep, they were rousted by shrill whistles for their "count." The ostensible purpose of the count was to provide a public test of the prisoners' knowledge of the rules and of their ID numbers. But more importantly for us, the counts which occurred at least once on each of the three different guard shifts, provided a regular occasion for the guards to relate to the prisoners under conditions where these interactions could be recorded and subsequently analyzed. Over the course of the study, the duration of the counts was gradually and spontaneously increased by the guards from their initial perfunctory ten minutes to a seemingly interminable several hours. During these interactions, guards who were bored could find ways to amuse themselves, recalcitrant prisoners could be ridiculed, arbitrary rules could be enacted, and any dissension among the prisoners could be openly exacerbated by the guards.

The experience of going to sleep after a day of continual harassment, being awakened abruptly a few hours later, going through the tedium of the count, returned to sleep, awakened in the morning to start another day of imprisonment, had the effect of stretching time out, making it pass slowly in a seemingly unending circular, rather than linear flow. Thus, for the prisoners the subjective duration of their imprisonment was much greater than that reckoned by objective, clock time which ceased to have much validity for them in this prison.

> The time slips away from me. . . . There is no rest from it even at night. . . .
> The days, even the weeks lapse into each other, endlessly into one another.
> Each day that comes and goes is exactly like the one that went before.
> George Jackson, *Soledad Brother*

The guards were also "deindividuated" by virtue of wearing identical khaki uniforms and silver reflector sunglasses which made eye contact with them impossible. Their symbols of power were billy clubs, whistles, handcuffs, and the keys to the cells and the "main gate." Although our guards received no formal training from us in how to be guards, for the most part they moved with apparent ease into their roles. Movies, TV, novels, and all of our mass media had already provided them with ample models of prison guards to emulate.

Said one of the toughest guards, "I didn't plan things out ahead of time. It was all spur of the moment, ad lib, so to speak, and well I guess there's enough information in me that was taken from plays that I've read and movies that I've seen that enabled me to come out with a lot of things. . . ." Just as "real" correctional officers subjected to these very same cultural influences, our mock guards had available to them behavioral templates of what it means to be a guard, upon which they could build their role performances. So too, with the mock prisoners.

Our guards were told that they must maintain "law and order" in this prison, that they were responsible for handling any trouble which might break out, and they were cautioned as to the seriousness and potential dangers of the situation they were about to enter. Surprisingly, in most prison systems, "real" guards are not given much more psychological preparation than this for what is one of the most difficult, demanding, and dangerous jobs imaginable. They are expected to learn how to adjust to their new employment from on-the-job experience, as documented in the Orientation Manual for correctional personnel at San Quentin Prison (July, 1970):

> The only way you really get to know San Quentin is through experience and time. Some of us take more time and must go through more experiences than others to accomplish this; some really never do get there.

The confrontation between our mock guards and prisoners was motivated initially by the desire to earn the money we were paying for their participation in this experiment—$15 per day for an eight-hour guard duty and the same amount for each twenty-four hour period of prisoner confinement. However, over time, the money became an abstraction, a remote source of extrinsic justification which was much less compelling than the intrinsic sources of motivation which evolved from the dynamics of the prisoner-guard relationship itself. For example, guards often worked overtime, never asking to be paid for it, were never late nor called in sick, nor did they demand more money after realizing how difficult, exhausting, and tedious their job was. The prisoners did not complain of the inequity between their payment and that of the guards, and by the end of the study, all but two were willing to forfeit the money they had earned working as inmates if we would parole them. There is considerable evidence from a variety of self-reports and observational measures to indicate that these subjects were deeply into the experience of being guards and prisoners, much more so than we had thought was possible in an experiment.

The symbolic interaction between guards and prisoners requires each to play his own role while also forcing the others to play their role appropriately. You cannot be a prisoner if no one will be your guard, and you cannot be a prison guard if no one takes you or your prison seriously. Therefore, over time a perverted symbiotic relationship developed. As the guards became more aggressive, prisoners became more passive; assertion by the guards led to dependency in the prisoners; self-aggrandizement was met with self-deprecation, authority with helplessness, and the counterpart of the guards' sense of mastery and control was the depression and hopelessness witnessed in the prisoners. As these differences in behavior, mood, and perception became more evident, the need for the now "righteously" powerful guards to rule the obviously inferior and powerless inmates became sufficient justification to support almost any further indignity of man against man.

Power takes as ingratitude the writhing of its victims.

Rabindranath Tagore, *Stray Birds*

Consider the following typical comments by different members of our "correctional staff" taken from their diaries, post-experimental interviews, and "critical incident report files":

GUARD: I was surprised at myself . . . I made them call each other names and clean the toilets out with their bare hands. I practically considered the prisoners cattle, and I kept thinking I have to watch out for them in case they try something.
GUARD: During the inspection, I went to cell 2 to mess up a bed which the prisoner had made and he grabbed me, screaming that he had just made it, and he wasn't going to let me mess it up. He grabbed my throat, and although he was laughing I was pretty scared. I lashed out with my stick and hit him in the chin (although not very hard) and when I freed myself I became angry.

GUARD: I was tired of seeing the prisoners in their rags and smelling the strong odors of their bodies that filled the cells. I watched them tear at each other on orders given by us.

GUARD: (Preparing for the first Visitors' Night). After warning the prisoners not to make any complaints unless they wanted the visit terminated fast, we finally brought in the first parents. I made sure I was one of the guards on the yard, because this was my first chance for the type of manipulative power that I really like—being a very noticed figure with almost complete control over what is said or not. While the parents and prisoners sat in chairs, I sat on the end of the table dangling my feet and contradicting anything I felt like. This was the first part of the experiment I was really enjoying.

GUARD: Acting authoritatively can be fun. Power can be a great pleasure.

It was not long before the guards began to demonstrate their inventiveness in the application of arbitrary power. They made the prisoners obey petty, meaningless, and often inconsistent rules, forced them to engage in tedious, useless work such as moving cartons back and forth between closets and picking thorns out of their blankets for hours on end. Not only did the prisoners have to sing songs or laugh or refrain from smiling on command, but they were also encouraged to curse and vilify each other publicly during some of the counts. They sounded off their numbers endlessly, and were repeatedly made to do push-ups, on occasion with a guard stepping on them or a prisoner sitting on them. Push-ups were the most common form of physical punishment employed by the guards for infractions of the rules or displays of improper attitudes toward them or the institution. When we observed the guards doing this, we thought it was an inappropriate form of punishment in a prison, too much like fraternity hazing. However, we have learned from the drawings and account of a former inmate (A. Kantor, 1971) that push-ups were often used in Nazi concentration camps as mass punishment for men already at the point of physical exhaustion.

Not only did the prisoners become resigned to their fate, they even behaved in ways which actually helped to justify their dehumanizing treatment at the hands of the guards. Analysis of the taperecorded private conversations between prisoners and of remarks made by them to interviewers revealed that fully half could be classified as nonsupportive of other prisoners. More dramatic is the significant finding that eighty-five percent of the evaluative statements by prisoners about their fellow prisoners, were uncomplimentary and deprecating!

PRISONER: That 2093, the rest of us use him as a scapegoat. . . . We couldn't understand how he could mentally comply with everything asked of him.

This result should be taken in the context of an even more surprising one. What do you imagine the prisoners talked about when they were alone in their cells with each other, given a temporary respite from the continual harassment and surveillance by the guards? Girl friends, career plans, hobbies, politics, home town, etc., were what we assumed would be the major topics of conversation. But instead, their concerns were almost exclusively riveted to prison topics. Their monitored conversations revealed only ten percent of the time was devoted to "outside" topics, while ninety percent of the time they discussed escape plans, the food, grievances, opinions about ingratiation tactics to use with specific guards in order to get a cigarette, permission to go to the toilet, or some other favor. Becoming obsessed with these immediate survival concerns, made talk about past and future an idle luxury. But doing so had a doubly negative effect upon the prisoners' adjustment. First, by voluntarily allowing prison topics to occupy their thoughts even when they did not have to continue playing their roles, the prisoners themselves extended the oppressiveness and reality of the experience. Secondly, since the prisoners were all strangers to each other to begin with, they could only know what the others were really like by observing how they behaved and by evaluating their stated ideas, opinions, values, past experiences, and expectations. But what each prisoner observed was his fellow prisoners allowing the guards to humiliate them, acting like compliant sheep, carrying out mindless orders with total obedience, and even being cursed by these fellow prisoners (at a guard's command). Then when they were alone, these same prisoners spent their free time complaining and planning how to best get through some imminent prison event, rather than comparing backgrounds and sharing information about their true identities. After days of living confined together in this tight environment, many of the prisoners did not even know the names of most of the others, where they came from, nor had even the most basic information about what they were like when they were not "prisoners." Under such circumstances, how could a prisoner have respect for his fellows, or any self-respect for what *he* obviously was becoming in the eyes of all those evaluating him?

> Life is the art of being well deceived; and in order that the deception may succeed it must be habitual and uninterrupted.
>
> Wm. Hazlitt, "On Pedantry," *The Round Table*

Thus, the combination of realistic and symbolic elements in this experiment fused to create a vivid illusion of imprisonment. This illusion merged inextricably with reality for at least some of the time for every individual who became part of the improvisational drama we were staging—prisoners, guards, administrative staff, experimenters, and even visitors. It was remarkable how readily we all slipped into our roles, temporarily gave up our identities, and allowed these assigned roles and the social forces in the situation to guide, shape and eventually to control our freedom of thought and action.

But precisely where does one's "identity" end and one's "role" begin? When the private self and the public role behavior clash, what direction will attempts to impose consistency take? In our simulated prison such distinctions became blurred as we reacted in ways characterized by the following comments from various participants in this simulation.

Prisoner 416, harassed for refusing to eat, which he did as an act of independence and also as an attempt to get sick so he would have to be released, reported:

> I began to feel that I was losing my identity, the person I call (*name*), the person who put me into this place, the person who volunteered to go into this prison . . . was distant from me, was remote until finally, I wasn't that. I was #416—I was really my number, and 416 was going to have to decide what to do . . .

The cruelest guard of all, nicknamed "John Wayne" by the prisoners (because of his tough, violent, domineering style) led the assault on prisoner 416 for his disobedience of Prison Rule Two: "Prisoners must eat at mealtimes, and only at mealtimes." He punished him, as well as his cell mates, forced him to sleep with the cold, dirty sausages, kept him in solitary hours longer than our imposed limit allowed, made the other prisoners choose between keeping their blankets or having him released from solitary (the majority voted to keep their blankets), and finally asserted (without conferring with the staff) that visiting privileges for everyone would be curtailed if 416 didn't eat. The prisoners reacted not by objecting to this arbitrary rule, but by verbally and almost physically attacking 416.

This guard's reaction to the situation he created was to get indignant and angry at 416 because "he was so callous to the people around him it was really shocking . . . his fellow prisoners were pleading with him and he was just thinking about his own petty reason for attempting something so foolish as starving himself." He was also disgusted with the other prisoners because they were so obedient: "This was another experiment of mine, to see if I could get them to say things against each other and really mean it, and they really meant it against 416 today. . . . I told them to say and do some pretty obscene things, and they did."

The torment experienced by our "good guard" (the one the prisoners liked most) who shared shift duties with this "bad" guard is obvious in his perceptive analysis of what it felt like to be responded to as a "guard":

> What made the experience most depressing for me was the fact that we were continually called upon to act in a way that just was contrary to what I really feel inside. I don't feel like I'm the type of person that would be a guard, just constantly giving out shit and forcing people to do things, and pushing and lying—it just didn't seem like me, and to continually to keep up and put on a face like that is just really one of the most oppressive things you can do. It's almost like a prison that you create yourself—you get into it, and it's just, it becomes almost the definition you make of yourself, it almost becomes like walls, and you want to break out and you want just to be able to tell everyone that "this isn't really me at all, and I'm not the person that's confined in there—I'm a person who wants to get out and show you that I am free, and I do have my own will, and I'm not the sadistic type of person that enjoys this kind of thing."

Not only was he a "good" guard because of the little favors he did for the prisoners when contrasted with the indifference or hostility of most other guards, he was "good" from the guards' point of view as well—he let them do their thing without ever directly intervening on behalf of the prisoners. Bruno Bettleheim, in a personal communication, reported that this pattern was common in his concentration camp experience, namely, of the "good" guard who managed to be liked by everyone, while privately dissenting yet never publicly disobeying. Indeed, it is just such "good" people who inadvertently suppress rebellion of the powerless by proffering hope which never materializes.

In another instance, prisoner 819 who had gone into a rage followed by an uncontrollable crying fit was about to be prematurely released from the prison when a guard lined up the prisoners and had them chant in unison, "819 is a bad prisoner. Because of what 819 did to prison property we all must suffer. 819 is a bad prisoner," over and over again. When the Superintendent realized 819 might be overhearing this, he rushed into the room where 819 was supposed to be resting, only to find him in tears, prepared to go back into that prison because he could not leave as long as the others thought he was a "bad prisoner." Sick as he felt, he had to prove to them he was not a "bad" prisoner. He had to be persuaded that he was not a prisoner at all, that the others were also just students, that this was just an experiment and not a prison and the Prison Superintendent and his staff were only research psychologists.

These assurances to him were necessary reminders to us as well, because we were by this time, so much into our prison roles that we were losing the distance and objectivity critical for our other role as experimental social psychologists. A report from the Warden notes, "While I believe that it was necessary for *staff* (me) ([italics] added to highlight the unconscious depersonalization) to enact the Warden role, at least some of the time, I am startled by the ease with which I could turn off my sensitivity and concern for others for 'a good cause.'"

When a former prison chaplain was invited to talk with the prisoners (in order to offer us his evaluation of the validity of our prison setting), he puzzled everyone by disparaging the inmates for not taking any constructive action in order to get released. "Don't you know you must have a lawyer in order to get bail, or to appeal the charges against you?" Several of them accepted his pastoral invitation to contact their parents in order to secure the services of an attorney. The next night one of the parents stopped at the Superintendent's office before visiting time was scheduled to begin and handed him the name and phone number of her cousin who was a public defender. A priest had called her and suggested the need for a lawyer's services! We called the lawyer. He came, interviewed the prisoners, discussed sources of bail money and promised to return again after the weekend. But at that point we realized that we had to end this experiment because it was no longer just an experiment.

> We've travelled too far, and our momentum has taken over; we move idly towards eternity, without possibility of reprieve or hope of explanation.
> Tom Stoppard, *Rosencrantz and Guildenstern Are Dead*

We were no longer dealing with an intellectual exercise in which an hypothesis was being evaluated in the dispassionate manner dictated by the canons of the scientific method. We were caught up in the passion of the present, the suffering, the need to control people not variables, the escalation of power and all of the unexpected things which were erupting around and within us. So our planned two-week simulation was aborted after only six (was it only six?) days and nights.

But even before this study was officially terminated, we had already been "forced" to release four prisoners because of extreme emotional depression or acute anxiety attacks, and in another case, because of a psychosomatic rash over the prisoner's entire body. They had not made an adequate adjustment to "prison life"! What distinguished the five subjects who endured the prison experience to the end from those who had to be released early was differences in their scores on the F-scale of authoritarianism (Adorno et al., 1950). The higher a prisoner's F-scale score, the more likely he was to remain functioning longer in the authoritarian environment of our prison ($r=.898$). Incidentally, there was *no* group difference between prisoners and guards in their mean scores on this measure of acceptance of authority and adherence to conventional values, nor was there on Machiavellianism scale scores (Christie & Geis, 1970).

The description of our prison as "authoritarian" is substantiated by a detailed analysis of the nature of the interaction between prisoners and guards as video recorded over twenty-five separate behavioral units (such as counts, meals, etc.). These data are presented in Figure 17.1. The pattern of results which emerges is remarkably analogous to that reported by White and Lippitt (1960) in their classic study comparing autocratic and democratic forms of group leadership. They found authoritarian role leaders were differentiated from others in the marked frequency with which they gave orders, commands, and information. Similarly, in our study there was a high degree of differentiation in social be-

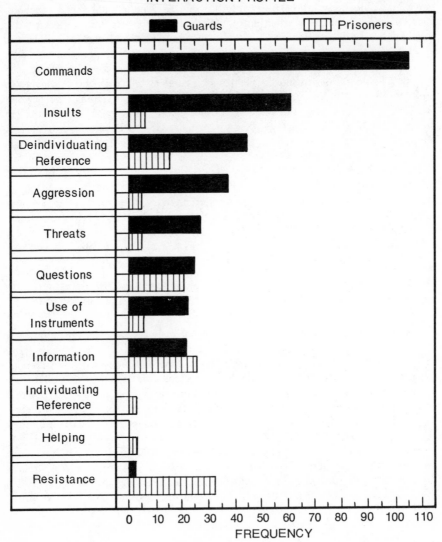

FIG. 17.1   Interaction profile of guard and prisoner behavior across twenty-five
occasions over six days in the simulated prison environment.

havior between the mock guards and prisoners. The guards' most typical mode of
response, over which they had exclusive perogative, was to give commands (which
included orders), and next most was to insult the prisoners. Their emphasis on
coercive control is further evidenced by: the relatively high frequency with which
they threatened, were physically aggressive, used instruments (night sticks, fire
extinguishers, etc.) to keep the prisoners in line, and referred to them in impersonal, anonymous, deprecating ways to reduce their individuality, such as, "Hey,
you," or "You ass hole, 5401, come here." From the first to the last day's observations there was a significant increase in the guards' use of most of these domineering, abusive tactics.

Every guard at some time engaged in these abusive, authoritarian behaviors since *power* was the major dimension on which everyone and everything was defined in this situation. To be a guard who did not take advantage of this institutionally sanctioned use of power was to appear "weak," "out of it," "wired up by the prisoners," or simply a deviant from the established norms of appropriate guard behavior. Three subgroups of guards could be distinguished. At one extreme, there were a few "good guy" guards who occasionally did little favors for the prisoners and were reluctant to punish them. About a third of the guards were "tough but fair," their orders were usually within the prescribed rules of prison operation and they made it clear to the prisoners that they were just doing their job. And finally, over a third of the guards were extremely hostile, arbitrary and cruel in the forms of degradation and humiliation they invented. They appeared to thoroughly enjoy the power they wielded whenever they put on their uniforms and were transformed from their routine everyday existence into "guards" with virtually total power over other people.

Each prisoner coped with the frustration, novel experience of being powerless, and growing sense of hopelessness in his own way after a concerted attempt to rebel was crushed by the guards on the second day. As noted, half of them reacted emotionally, breaking down, as a legitimate way of passively escaping by forcing us to release them. 416 went on his hunger strike. Some tried to be good prisoners doing whatever they were told; one of them was nicknamed "Sarge" because of his total obedience in executing all commands. One of the leaders of the prisoner revolt said:

> If we had gotten together then, I think we could have taken over the place. But when I saw the revolt wasn't working, I decided to toe the line. Everyone settled into the same pattern. From then on, we were really controlled by the guards.

Other prisoners simply withdrew into an introverted, protective shell.

From Figure 17.1 it is obvious that the prisoners *reacted* rather than acted. Initially, they resisted the guards, answered their questions and asked some. Over time, however, as they began to "toe the line," they stopped resisting, questioning, and indeed, almost ceased responding altogether. There was a general decrease in all categories of response as they learned the safest strategy to use in an unpredictable, capricious threatening environment from which there is no physical escape—do nothing, except what is required. Act not, want not, feel not and you will not get into trouble in prison-like situations.

When our mock prisoners asked questions, about half the time they got answers, but the rest of the time they got insulted and punished—and it was not possible for them to predict which would be the outcome. So, they became the human analogue of the "learned helplessness phenomenon" in animals reported by Seligman and his associates (1972). Passivity as a reaction to a traumatic, capricious environment is the result of having learned that responding bears no relationship to controlling reinforcers in that situation. Another companion response to passivity in a threatening environment, revealed in a recent study by Maslach (1973), is to avoid doing anything which might call attention to oneself. By choosing instead, to behave in ways which help de-individuate them, powerless people can at least seek the security of anonymity and non-existence in the eyes of their oppressors.

> And the only way to really make it with the bosses [in Texas prisons] is to withdraw into yourself, both mentally and physically—literally making your-

self as small as possible. It's another way they de-humanize you. They want you to make no waves in prison and they want you to make no waves when you get out.

Mike Middleton, Ex-Con, Christian Science Monitor Series

In institutions charged with the "management" of deviants and the outcasts of society—the mentally ill, the retarded, the aged, the unfit of all kinds—treatment moves from concern for humanity to "detached concern" (Lief & Fox, 1963), to indifference, and finally, to depersonalization (Rosenhan, 1972). Individuals are stripped of the attributes that have come to represent their uniqueness and singularity and even of their freedom to respond emotionally because emotions are too spontaneous, idiosyncratic, and human. Curiously, over time, the "patients" participate in their own psychological destruction firstly making themselves "small" and then, as one prisoner in Rhode Island Adult Correctional Institution told us, "by beating the system and cutting off your emotions so nothing they do to you will ever get to you and then they can't break you."

> I have made some giant steps toward acquiring the things I personally will need if I can be successful in my plans. . . . I have repressed all emotion.

George Jackson, Soledad Brother

some conclusions and implications

In this brief article we can but touch upon a few of the most salient issues and questions raised by this simulation experiment, among them: how to explain the power and pathology which merged, do the results of such a role-playing study have any meaningful generalizability, and what are the ethics of performing experiments of this kind where people are made to suffer?

who were the guards and prisoners?

Had the reactions we observed been reported as those of actual prison inmates and correctional officers, the explanation for why they occurred would probably center upon some personality characteristics peculiar to these two populations, typically, sadistic-aggression tendencies within the guards and sociopathic, defective character structures among the prisoners. To account for the observed differences between them and indeed, from our own standards of what constitutes "normal" behavior, we typically focus upon personality traits as internal dispositions for individuals to respond in particular ways.

The probability of invoking such a *dispositional hypothesis* increases as the behavior in question is more aberrant or repulsive to us, as the individuals involved are perceived as more non-comparable to us, and as the situation they are in is more unfamiliar to us. Given this orientation, the solution to social problems is always directed toward specific "problem people"—the vandals, the black militants, the revolutionaries, the underachieving school children, the welfare cheats, etc. Remedies then involve changing the people, by motivating them, isolating them, imprisoning them, committing them, executing them, cutting off aid to them, and so on. Such an analysis ignores the variation in behavior attributable to the operation of *situational*, social forces upon the individual or group.

In a real prison, it is impossible to separate out what each individual brings into the prison from what the prison brings out in each person. The research strategy we employed was designed to partial out the confounding effects of chronic personality dispositions from those attributable to the prison environment itself. Therefore, at the start of our study we made certain that every one of our objects was "normal-average" on a variety of personality dimensions and was representative of educated, Caucasian, middle-class America.

Our final sample of subjects (11 guards and 10 prisoners in all) were selected from over 75 college student volunteers recruited through newspaper ads for a study on prison life. They came from more than a dozen different colleges throughout the U.S. and Canada. After all applicants were given an intensive clinical interview and completed an extensive background questionnaire, we selected only those who were judged to be emotionally stable, physically healthy, mature, law-abiding citizens to participate. On each of eight subtests of the Comrey Personality Scale (1970) their scores fell within the middle range (40–60 percentile) of the normative male population. Then they were randomly assigned to the experimental treatment of either role-playing a prisoner or a guard. Thus, it is important to note that at the beginning of our study there were no measurable differences between those students assigned to be guards and those to be prisoners, nor for that matter, any differences between either of them and a "normal" comparison population (to which the reader probably belongs).

What is most surprising, therefore, about the outcome of this simulated role-playing experience is the relative ease with which sadistic behavior could be elicited from normal, non-sadistic people, and the extent of the emotional disturbance which emerged in young men selected precisely on the basis of their emotional stability. The pathology observed in this study cannot be attributed to any pre-existing personality differences of the subjects. Rather, their abnormal social and personal reactions were a product of their *transaction* with an environment whose norms and contingencies supported the production of behavior which would be pathological in other settings, but were "appropriate" in this prison.

Milgram's (1965) classic research has demonstrated the power of specifiable situational forces in causing good men to perform evil deeds. Mischel (1968, 1969) has convincingly argued that personality trait scores have limited predictive utility and that what we perceive as personality consistency is really consistency in the situations people voluntarily choose to enter and consistency of response imposed by others in those situations. Argyle and Little (1972) have experimentally shown that relatively little variation in a model social interaction is attributable to "person variance" (16 percent); "situation variance" accounts for most (44 percent), and the situation x person interaction next most (40 percent). Therefore, it is time psychologists stopped offering legislators, lawmen, and lay people "traits," "dispositions," and "individual differences" as reasonable solutions to existing problems in our Society.

To change behavior we must discover the institutional supports which maintain the existing undesirable behavior and then design programs to alter these environments.[1] As an instance of this principle, we learned that in our mock prison the existence of so many rules to govern prisoner behavior promoted cocercive rather than positive forms of responding by the guards. When behavior is under rule control, if the person follows and obeys the rule, he or she is behaving as expected, and naturally, there is no reward for doing what one ought to. But if the rule is broken, punishment results. The more extensive the control by rules in any situation from prison to school to home, the greater the likelihood that the dominant strategy of interpersonal control will be coercive and punitive.

reality of role-playing and significance of simulation

It was obvious to every one of us that what went wrong in this study was that it became too real, that we had to end it before the seventh day because it was working "too well." Any experienced encounter group leader can attest to the creation of "reality" out of even a relatively transient though intense role-playing situation (Aronson, 1972). When people live in a situation, eat, sleep, work there, have all their social contacts and sources of reinforcement there—it becomes a primary, present-tense reality. Janis (1971) poignantly reveals how the phenomenon of "group think" can distort existing reality and create a new reality when decision makers in the President's cabinet form an insulated, cohesive group to handle crises (such as the Cuban Bay of Pigs invasion).

The most directly relevant extension of the ideas in this prison simulation comes from a recent "mock hospital" study (Orlando, 1973). Personnel from Elgin State Hospital in Illinois role-played either mental patients or staff in a weekend simulation on a ward in the hospital. The mock mental patients soon displayed behavior indistinguishable from that which we usually associate with the chronic pathological syndromes of actual mental patients: incessant pacing, uncontrollable weeping, depression, hostility, fights, stealing from each other, complaining. Of the 29 mock patients, 93 percent reported feeling incarcerated, 89 percent felt an identity loss, and three fourths of them felt that at times nobody cared about them or treated them like a "person." A mental health specialist turned mock patient reported: "I began to feel very much like an animal, with no identity or true worth. I felt defenseless and frightened. There was no privacy, not even in the bathroom." These reactions, so similar in appearance to those of actual patients, could not easily be attributed to the internal disposition or "mental illness" of the participants since in reality they were themselves charged with the care of the patients. Many of the "mock staff" took advantage of their power to act in ways comparable to our mock guards by dehumanizing their powerless victims.

Recently, a military tribunal in Belgium heard a case of a simulated NATO army exercise in which some Belgian soldiers were taken "prisoner" by Belgian paracommandos. These mock prisoners were bound hand and foot, beaten, given electric shocks, hung from beams, and abused in other ways. Why did this occur? According to a report in *The New York Times* (11/5/72):

> During the hearing, the accused stated that they did not consider their actions to have been unusual. Said one: "I thought we had to do it. It was the only method to get needed information."

ethical considerations

The reader should be disturbed by the ethical dilemma posed in the present research—we certainly are. Some experimental subjects were made to suffer physically and mentally as prisoners, others were forced to realize that as guards they could delight in their abuse of arbitrary power and could so readily dehumanize other human beings. Moreover, these experiences were endured for nearly a week, not merely for the 50 minutes (one college class period) typical in most psychological experiments. But the potential social value of this study derives precisely from the fact that normal, healthy, educated young men could be so radically transformed under the institutional pressures of a "prison environment." The argument runs, if this could happen in so short a time, without the excesses that are possible in real prisons, in the "cream-of-the-crop" of American youth, then one can only shudder at imagining what society is doing to the actual guards and prisoners who are at this very moment participating in that unnatural "social experiment."

Prior to participating, the subjects did give their informed consent to be under surveillance, to be harassed, and to have their civil rights abridged. And everyone of the 75 applicants stated on a questionnaire that he believed with 100 percent certainty he could endure the full two-week treatment without difficulty. This common illusion of personal vulnerability, of dispositional power, caused them to underestimate the subtle power of situational forces to control and re-shape their behavior. We, too, were susceptible to this attribution error.

During a full day of debriefing sessions at the conclusion of our simula-tion (first with the ex-prisoners, then with the ex-guards, and finally, together with all participants), we all vented our strongly felt emotions, made it a time to reflect upon the moral and ethical issues each of us faced, and discussed how we might react more morally in future "real-life" analogues to this situation. Year long follow-ups via questionnaires, diaries, personal interviews, and group reun-ions indicate that the mental anguish was transient and situationally specific, but the self-knowledge gained has persisted. For every one of the subjects and re-searchers it was a profound learning experience we could not have believed pos-sible were we only observers in the audience and not actors in the drama.

We have begun to try to maximize the social value of the implications of this study by presenting the finding to a Congressional Subcommittee on Prison and Prison Reform (Zimbardo, 1971), to those in corrections, to student groups and to average citizens who continue to pay taxes to support the status quo of prison operation ignorant of the toll prisons take daily from all those inside their walls, as well as from the society in general into which ex-cons pass for a time before becoming prisoners again.

> I was recently released from "solitary confinement" after being held therein for 37 months [months!]. A silent system was imposed upon me and to even "whisper" to a man in the next cell resulted in being beaten by guards, sprayed with chemical mace, black-jacked, stomped, and thrown into a "strip-cell" naked to sleep on a concrete floor without bedding, covering, wash basin, or even a toilet. The floor served as toilet and bed, and even there the "silent system" was enforced. To let a "moan" escape your lips because of the pain and discomfort . . . resulted in another beating. I spent not days, but months there during my 37 months in solitary . . . I have filed every writ possible against the administrative acts of brutality. The State Courts have all denied the petitions. Because of my refusal to let the "things die down" and "forget" all that happened during my 37 months in solitary . . . , I am the most hated prisoner in————Penitentiary, and called a "hard-core incorrigible."
> Professor Zimbardo, maybe I am an incorrigible, but if true, it's because I would rather die than to accept being treated less than a human being. I have never complained of my prison sentence as being unjustified except through legal means of appeals. I have never put a knife on a guard's throat and demanded my release. I know that thieves must be punished and I don't justify stealing, even though I am a thief myself. But now I don't think I will be a thief when I am released. No, I'm not rehabilitated. It's just that I no longer think of becoming wealthy by stealing. I now only think of "killing." Killing those who have beaten me and treated me as if I were a dog. I hope and pray for the sake of my own soul and future life of freedom, that I am able to overcome the bitterness and hatred which eats daily at my soul, but I know to overcome it will not be easy.

conclusion

Yet, in spite of the profoundly negative characterization of prisons drawn by our results and the reports of others, there is cause for guarded optimism about the possibility of their constructive reform. If, indeed, the pathology of prisons can be isolated as a product of the power relations in the social psychological structure of the institution itself, change is conceivable. Social institutions being the creations of human beings—our experiments in social and political control—are susceptible to modification when confronted by a human consciousness protesting their inadequacy and evils, supported by an informed electorate concerned about eliminating all forms of injustice. Institutionalized prisons can be changed so that human values are promoted and celebrated rather than crushed and perverted—but "it will not be easy." [1]

note

1. We recognize, of course, that the physical institution of prison is but a concrete and steel metaphor for the existence of more pervasive, albeit less obvious, prisons of the mind which each of us daily create, populate, and perpetuate. We speak here of the prisons of racism, sexism, ageism, despair, social conventions, shyness, and the like. The social convention of marriage, as one example, becomes for many couples a state of imprisonment in which one partner agrees to be prisoner or guard, forcing or allowing the other to play the reciprocal role. Programs of social change designed to alter the environment of imprisonment must also be addressed to these less formal, more subtle social-psychological prisons.

references

Adorno, T. W., Frenkel-Brunswik, E., Levinson, D. J., & Sanford, R. N. *The Authoritarian Personality.* New York: Harper & Row, 1950.

Argyle, M., & Little, R. Do personality traits apply to social behavior? *Journal of the Theory of Social Behavior,* 1972, 2, 1–35.

Aronson, E. *The Social Animal.* San Francisco: W. H. Freeman, 1972.

Aronson, E., & Carlsmith, M. J. Experimentation in social psychology. In G. Lindzey & E. Aronson (Eds.), *Handbook of Social Psychology.* Vol. II. Reading, Mass.: Addison-Wesley, 1969, 1–79.

Christie, R., & Geis, F. L. (Eds.). *Studies in Machiavellianism.* New York: Academic Press, 1970.

Comrey, A. L. *Comrey Personality Scales.* San Diego: Educational and Industrial Testing Service, 1970.

Davis, A. J. Sexual assaults in the Philadelphia prison system and sheriff's vans. *Trans-action Magazine,* 1968, 6, 8–16.

Janis, I. J. Group think among policy makers. In N. Sanford, C. Comstock (Eds.), *Sanctions for Evil.* San Francisco: Jossey Bass, 1971.

Kantor, A. *Book of Alfred Kantor.* New York: McGraw-Hill, 1971.

Lief, H. I., & Fox, R. C. Training for "detached concern" in medical students. In Harold I. Lief and others (Eds.), *Psychological basis of medical practice.* New York: Harper & Row, 1963, 12–35.

Maslach, C. The social bases of individuation. *Journal of Personality and Social Psychology,* 1973. [In Press].

Milgram, S. Some conditions of obedience and disobedience to authority. *Human Relations,* 1965, 18 (1), 57–76.

Mischel, W. *Personality and assessment*. New York: Wiley, 1968.
———. Continuity and change in personality. *American Psychologist*. 1969, *24*, 1012–18.
New York Times. "Torture" Case in NATO weighed. November 5, 1972, p. 3.
Orlando, N. J. The mock ward: a study in simulation. In O. Milton & R. G. Wahler (Eds.), *Behavior Disorders: Perspectives and Trends*. Philadelphia: J. B. Lippincott, 1973.
Rosenhan, D. On being sane in insane places. *Science*, 1973, 179, pp. 250–258. [Reading 16]
Seligman, M. E. P. Depression and learned helplessness. In R. J. Friedman & M. M. Katz (Eds.). *The psychology of depression: contemporary theory and research*. (In Press). [Reading 11]
White, R., & Lippitt, R. *Autocracy and Democracy*. New York: Harper & Row, 1960.
Zimbardo, P. G. The Human Choice: individuation, reason, and order versus deindividuation, impulse, and chaos. In W. J. Arnold & D. Levine (Eds.). *1969 Nebraska Symposium on Motivation*. Lincoln, Nebraska: University of Nebraska Press, 1970.
———. Hearings before Subcommittee No. 3 of the Committee on the Judiciary House of Representatives Ninety-Second Congress First Session on Corrections, Part II, *Prisons, Prison Reform, and Prisoners' Rights: California*. October 25, 1971. Serial No. 15. U.S. Government Printing Office, Washington: 1971.

18

Experimental Studies of the Manipulative Tactics of Mental Patients

Benjamin M. Braginsky, Dorothea D. Braginsky,
and Kenneth Ring

So long as he remains hospitalized, the mental patient appears to suffer from a severe power disadvantage. In terms of formal power that may be exercised over him, he finds that his life, down to the most trifling aspects, can be controlled by his keepers, the hospital staff. Goffman (1961) has described in numbing detail the extraordinary range of activities for which a patient must ask staff permission before he can engage in them. There are, in addition, matters about which, even though they may and often do profoundly affect a patient's fate, he does not have even a acknowledged right to express his own opinion and have it seriously considered. A patient's life inside the hospital, then, would

From *Methods of Madness: The Mental Hospital as a Last Resort* by Benjamin M. Braginsky, Dorothea D. Braginsky and Kenneth Ring. Copyright © 1969 by Holt, Rinehart and Winston, Inc. Reprinted by permission of Holt, Rinehart and Winston, Inc.

seem to be governed almost totally by staff decisions. According to this view, a mental patient is a person whose right of choice has been formally preempted by others.

This description, though it is not inaccurate as far as it goes, is nevertheless fallaciously incomplete, for it ignores altogether the element of the patient's counterpower. . . . We argued that, as a rule, the mental patient is not a passive and helpless victim who abjectly acquiesces to the enormous power that any "total institution" (Goffman, 1961) has the authority to wield.[1] We see him, rather as a person who, within the limits of his situation, is concerned with living his life as he deems fit, just as any ordinary person of any other functioning community would be. We would expect, therefore, that a patient would attempt to control his own fate as much as possible; even when an unwelcome one is unavoidable imposed, we would anticipate that he would attempt to escape it or, that failing, resist it. If these efforts to counteract the power of the staff are at all successful, it means that the latter's control over the patient is neither so formidable nor implacable as our initial analysis implied. We are suggesting, in short, that the power of the staff can be mitigated to a considerable extent through the application of counterpower by the patients.

It is important to be clear about the nature of the power that is available to staff and patients. The power of the staff is *legitimate* power, exercised in accordance with the hospital's professed and actual standards governing the treatment and management of its residents. It is, therefore, power that is backed by the machinery of publicly constituted authority. The power that the patients can exploit and with which we are principally concerned here is fundamentally *subversive* in character. By subversive we, of course, do not mean that the patients seek to overthrow the power system, but rather that they undermine it by violating it in ways that are often not obvious or even visible to the staff. As Goffman (1959, 1961) has convincingly shown through numerous examples, a patient may indeed appear to acknowledge and even honor the power system while actually in subtle and deliberate fashion mocking the staff who enforce it as well as the system itself. (This device clearly represents a morale-boosting symbolic "turning of the tables" with little personal risk, because it involves a patient's private joke on the staff.) All of this implies that although the *form* of patient counterpower is conditioned by the legitimate power system, it acts insidiously to subvert that system.[2] The "balance of power" within a mental hospital, then, is a balance between the formal, sanctioned power of the staff and the covert, illegitimate power of the patients.

impression management as a form of patient counterpower

The manifestations of patient counterpower are surely legion, and many of them have been carefully delineated by several observers (Artiss, 1959; Goffman, 1961; Scheff, 1966; Szasz, 1961; Towbin, 1966). In the three experimental studies to be reported here, however, we focus on one general and widely used manipulative tactic that Goffman (1959) has called "impression-management." By this term Goffman means only that we can and generally do manage our expressive behavior so as to control the impressions that others form of us. Through selective disclosure of some information (it may be false information) consistent with the character we mean to sustain for the purpose of an interaction, coupled with suppression of information incompatible with that projection of self, we establish a certain definition of ourselves that we attempt to maintain throughout the interaction episode. In simple and possibly misleading terms, we act, we play roles. As a technique of interpersonal manipulation, it ought to be exploited by patients for the same reasons we use it—one can often increase the chances of achieving desirable outcomes from others by appearing to be a certain sort of person. Indeed, one may suggest that, if anything, mental patients should be even more inclined to use this tactic than we are because (1) their objective situation makes them more dependent on others for good outcomes, and (2) they are either in fact or normatively prevented from attaining the outcomes by more direct means (for example, by simply requesting permission to be allowed to go home for the weekend).

Now, the notion that mental patients can employ impression management in the service of their own motivations would be a point hardly worth mentioning, let alone emphasizing, were it not for the prevailing view that schizophrenics are for the most part incapable of executing such highly "socialized" interpersonal gestures. This mode of interaction certainly collides at any rate with the stereotype of the chronic schizophrenic as regressed and unresponsive to others. We propose, on the contrary, that not only is the mental patient capable of impression management but that also he uses it surprisingly successfully, perhaps in part because of the expectation of others that he cannot dissemble at all (or at least not without their being aware of it). If one is ready to grant at the outset that mental patients, like ordinary mortals, can manipulate and deceive for their own ends, the findings to be presented will come as no surprise. If, however, one is unaccustomed to viewing patients in this way, their experimentally induced behavior will occasion a distinct and perhaps a rude shock.

Impression management, like any other manipulative tactic, is given form by the actor's motivations and goals. It becomes necessary, therefore, in order to predict how a patient will present himself, to specify the motivations and goals that characterize him while in the hospital. Although direct evidence will be presented only in later chapters, for the time being we shall simply assert as an hypothesis that the predominant motivations of the majority of the chronic patients at any rate center around remaining in the hospital and being able to enjoy life as much as possible there. If this is so, we would expect, for at least this class of patients, that they would present themselves in such a way as to safeguard their current status. This would imply, for example, that they should be reluctant to criticize openly hospital policies and that they should try to give the impression that they are still "sick" enough not to merit discharge, but not "sick" enough to warrant being assigned to a closed ward. The typical patient, then, is assumed to be primarily motivated by a desire "not to rock the boat" and to preserve his style of life within the hospital. The form of his impression management can accordingly be anticipated to reflect these motivations.

impression management through ingratiation

Jones (1964) has suggested that *ingratiation* may be regarded as an illicit interpersonal tactic that can be used to secure benefits (or to avoid harm) from others. Jones maintains that ingratiation is illicit because it takes place within a normative framework that it appears to honor but in fact does not. Ingratiation is said to involve an attempt to increase one's attractiveness to others who have the power to reward or punish the individual; in this way, the ingratiator, if he is successful, can increase the likelihood of achieving good outcomes (or avoiding bad ones). Ingratiation, finally, may take many forms: one may flatter the target person, agree with his opinions, present oneself in an engagingly modest way, and so on.

Especially important for our purposes are the conditions under which ingratiation is likely to occur. According to Jones, they comprise a state of affairs where the potential ingratiator (1) wants some benefit, x (or wants to avoid some harm, z), (2) is dependent on somebody else, o, to provide it, and (3) believes that some action on his part will induce o to provide x (or to refrain from performing z). Presumably, a tactic that would be classified as ingratiating by an external observer (though not necessarily labeled so by the performing individual) will occur when the norms relevant to the situation preclude other more legitimate means (for example, a simple request) or when, in any case, an ingratiating maneuver promises the best or perhaps the only chance for success.

It is not difficult to see that these conditions are very often present for the mental patient. Our analysis of his power position in the hospital suggested both his dependence on others and his likely recourse to illegitimate forms of power, of which ingratiation is an obvious example, to achieve his goals. Furthermore, because ingratiation involves presenting oneself in such a way as to influence the impression others form of him, it clearly represents one instance of behavior in the service of impression management. All these considerations point to an empirically verifiable assertion: Mental patients can be expected to manage their impressions, through the use of ingratiation tactics, in their interactions with the staff. The following study, by providing patients with an opportunity to engage in ingratiation through flattery, permits a test of this hypothesis.

method

For this study (conducted by B. Braginsky, D. Ridley, D. Braginsky, and K. Ring), a thirty-item test, labeled "Hospital Opinion Inventory," was constructed. The items that were to be answered using a true-false format were of three types: (1) eleven items that expressed highly implausible but positive opinions about the mental hospital (for example, "There is nothing about the hospital that needs improvement of any kind," "Without exception, every single nurse and aide in the hospital is as good to patients as a mother or father would be to their child"); (2) nine realistic but mildly critical opinions about the hospital (for example, "There are times when I wish the hospital treated me better," "There are times when I feel that some of the hospital staff do not quite understand me"); and (3) ten unrealistically critical opinions about the hospital (for example, "The hospital always takes advantage of patients," "There is not a single good thing about being a patient in this hospital").

It seems reasonable, in view of the content of these items, to assume that patients who tend to agree with the first type and disagree with the second type are expressing exaggeratedly and unrealistically positive opinions about their institution. No mental hospital with which we are familiar comes close to meriting such encomiums. Whether such hyperbole can be taken as indicative of ingratiation or some other factor(s) plainly depends on the nature of the test-taking instructions, which are considered next.

Two experimental conditions, which differed in the instructions Ss received concerning the test, were created. In the *Public* condition, Ss were told:

> We are here today to find out how you feel about the hospital. We are interested in your opinions. On this test you will find statements which measure how you feel about this hospital. We would like you to answer them as accurately as possible. Please sign your name on the top of the first page. This is important because some of the hospital staff will review these tests later and they would like to know which patients filled out which tests. That is, they will want to identify who took the tests. This can only be done if you sign your name. Thank you.

In the *Anonymous* condition, Ss received this induction:

> We are here today to find out how you feel about the hospital. We are interested in your opinions. On this test you will find statements which measure how you feel about this hospital. We would like you to answer them as accurately as possible. Please do not sign your name to the tests. We are not interested in who takes the test. All we are interested in is how patients, as a group, feel about the hospital. So remember, do not sign your name. Thank you.

It will be obvious that of the two statements, Ss in the *Public* condition ought to be the more highly instigated to ingratiate themselves if our assumptions about their motivations . . . are sound. Only they as individuals have something to lose through endorsement of opinions critical of the hospital; only they as individuals stand to gain by praising the hospital and its staff. Ss in this condition, therefore, have a twofold motivation to ingratiate themselves: to avoid arousing the censure of the staff (prompting disagreement with the critical items) and to increase the likelihood of continued favorable treatment (prompting agreement with the positive items). Because they individually can receive neither credit for the approved response nor blame for disapproved ones, Ss in the *Anonymous* condition should show considerably less evidence of a desire to ingratiate themselves.[3]

SUBJECTS

Sixty-five male and 45 female open-ward patients served as Ss in this study. Ss were drawn from four male wards and three female wards, all of which were similar in patient characteristics such as age, education, length of hospitalization, and diagnostic category. The mean age of the patients was 43.2 years with a standard deviation of 14.1. The mean education level of the sample was 10.5 years with a standard deviation of 4.6. Their median length of hospitalization was 3.7 years. In terms of general diagnostic categories, 82 percent of the sample had been diagnosed as schizophrenic, 3 percent had been labeled as psychotic but not schizophrenic, and the remainder had been judged nonpsychotic. A comparison of males and females within each experimental condition failed to disclose any significant differences on these demographic variables.

Each experimental condition was composed of patients from two male wards and one and a half female wards. The wards were tested in groups in order to keep the patients from feeling that they had been singled out and thereby to reduce any anxiety that such an interpretation might have aroused. In addition, this procedure was adopted to make the anonymous induction more credible as well as to convey the impression that the patients were involved in a hospital opinon survey rather than an experiment.

EXPERIMENTAL DESIGN

Ss were classified according to sex and the experimental instructions they had received, thus giving us a simple two-by-two factorial design. The number of Ss in each of the conditions was unequal and ranged from 22 to 35.

results and discussion

Table 18.1 presents the mean number of items answered in an ingratiating direction. It is clear that, as expected, Ss in the *Public* condition more often respond to the test items in an ingratiating fashion ($F = 21.30$, $p < .001$). Neither the main effect for sex nor the interaction was significant, and, of course, neither was anticipated to be. Furthermore, within sex comparisons using the Newman-Keuls procedure (Winer, 1962) show a significant experimental condition effect for both males ($p < .05$) and females ($p < .01$). Finally, no significant relationships were found to exist between any of the demographic variables mentioned earlier and test scores.

TABLE 18.1   MEAN NUMBER OF INGRATIATING TEST RESPONSES ACCORDING TO EXPERIMENTAL CONDITION AND SEX

SEX	EXPERIMENTAL CONDITION	
	Public	Anonymous
Males	10.23 ($N = 35$)	7.97 ($N = 30$)
Females	11.36 ($N = 22$)	6.30 ($N = 23$)

Ten unrealistically critical items had been incorporated into the test in order to evaluate the possibility that low ingratiation scores reflected not simply realistically critical appraisals of the hospital but instead obviously unwarranted, negativistic ones. Because we found a low absolute incidence of endorsement of such items in both conditions (means of 1.91 and 2.06 for the *Public* and *Anonymous* conditions, respectively), this interpretation is effectively ruled out. Low ingratiation scores are not indicative of hypercritical attitudes toward the hospital.

In one sense the findings of this experiment are not at all remarkable—patients express more flattering (indeed absurdly flattering) opinions about their institution and its staff when their responses can be traced. If a professor reported that midway through the semester his students evaluated his course more positively when they signed their names on the evaluation form than when they did not, we would probably not jump out of our seats with astonishment. Yet we have merely documented the analogous finding for mental patients. The reader is entitled, therefore, to his "so what?"

In our view, what makes these findings noteworthy is, paradoxically, that they are so banal—imagine, mental patients respond just like anyone else! They, too, seem capable of ingratiation. This is not surprising at all perhaps until one recalls the kind of assertion mentioned in Chapter 1 that avers, for example, that schizophrenics are so different from the rest of us that they should be studied as if they were "alien creatures."

Now, it may be objected that we have not demonstrated conclusively that the clear experimental condition effect we obtained is a function of ingratiation or that, in any case, the results are at all illuminated by making reference to the construct of impression management. We agree that it would be rash to make the claim on the sole basis of the data from this study. Although some alternative interpretations can be excluded (for example, one cannot contend that the patients in the *Public* condition simply wanted to please the staff without reference to possible future self-benefit because that motivation should have been just as strong for Ss in the *Anonymous* condition), it is always possible in principle at least to suggest other parsimonious explanations. In addition, the evidence (Jones, 1964) against an ingratiator perceiving his behavior in those terms is so strong that even had we endeavored to inquire into Ss' interpretation of their own behavior or its motivation, we probably would not have been able to make a convincing case for our point of view. It seems only reasonable, then, to conclude that the data from the present experiment are consistent with the ingratiation hypothesis and with the assumption that mental patients can engage in impression management, but that there may be other interpretations of the data just as compelling.

Suppose, however, we continue to entertain our interpretation as a reasonable possibility in order to generate further research that may eventually allow us to place greater confidence in it. Viewed in this light, the data suggest that patients are quite capable of acting in their own self-interest, at least to the extent of misrepresenting their own opinions about the goodness of the hospital and its staff. We had been led to expect this outcome because we had some other evidence (still to be adduced) that made us believe that many patients were motivated to remain in the hospital, ostensibly because the life they were able to lead inside was preferred over alternatives available outside. That is, these patients appeared to us to stay in the hospital not so much because their pathology required them to, but primarily because they voluntarily chose to do so. If this assumption is correct, it would have some important implications for the kind of impressions a patient could be expected to foster.

A patient cannot remain in a mental hospital simply because he likes it (or likes it better than his available alternatives); he has to justify his being there. The justification for residing in a mental hospital is that one is mentally ill. The inference is inescapable, and even an "alien creature" such as a "mental patient" could be expected to be able to deduce it.

If patients will misrepresent their opinions concerning the mental hospital *because* of the reasons we have proposed, then they should be motivated to misrepresent their mental condition as well. If they want to remain in the hospital, they had better convince the staff that they are "sick." The next study gave them the chance.

controlling one's hospital fate
through impression management

In an experiment carried out by B. Braginsky, M. Grosse, and K. Ring (1966), we selected two classes of patients to participate who we felt (on the basis of data . . .) ought to differ substantially in their motivation to remain in the hospital. We expected that Newcomers (patients who had been hospitalized less than three months and for the first time) would be, as a group, primarily motivated to leave the hospital whereas the Old-timers (those who had been there three months or longer—the majority for over three years) would prefer to remain. We do know that as a group, Newcomers have the highest discharge rate in the hospital (80 percent are released within the first three months) while Old-timers have the lowest (only 17 percent are discharged during any one year). There are, of course, many factors which contribute to this difference, and we do not wish to deny that the nature and degree of psychopathology is one of them. What we do want to emphasize, however, is that to a very considerable extent this difference in discharge rates may perhaps be attributable to nothing more esoteric than a patient's desire to stay in or leave the hospital and his ability, through impression management, to achieve his particular goal. That, at least, was the hypothesis with which we began.

method

In this experiment we again employed a test-taking procedure, constructing for this purpose a so-called mental status test. This test consisted of 30 MMPI items all of which had received relatively neutral ratings on a social desirability scale (Dahlstrom and Welsh, 1960). We selected only such items in order to maximize the effect of the experimental manipulations, to be described later, on Ss' test responses.

Two forms of the test, differing *only* in the title printed on the test booklet, were then prepared. One version was called the "Mental Illness Test" while the other was labeled the "Self-insight Test." The items, of course, were identical.

Two experimental conditions, each using one form of the test, were next established as follows:

In the *mental illness* test condition, Ss were told, prior to taking the test:

> This test is designed to measure how severely mentally ill a patient is. We have found that the more items answered True by a patient the more severely ill a patient is and the greater are his chances of remaining in the hospital for a long period of time. Patients who answer many of the items False are less severely mentally ill and will probably remain in the hospital for a short period of time. We would like to find out how ill you are.

In the *self-insight* test condition, Ss heard these instructions:

> This test is designed to measure how much knowledge a patient has about himself. We have found that the more items answered True by a patient the more he knows about himself, the less severely ill he is and the greater are his chances of remaining in the hospital for a short period of time. Patients who answer many of the items as False know less about themselves, are more mentally ill and will probably remain in the hospital for a long period of time. We would like to find out how much you know about yourself.

It is apparent that we have deliberately provided Ss with a "script," as it were, for managing their impressions, if they desire to do so. In effect, we tell a patient that if he wants to be adjudged as mentally ill and thus deserving to remain in the hospital, he should respond True to most of the items when he takes the mental illness test, but for the most part False when the test presumably deals with self-insight. What this means, of course, is that, if patients do indeed engage in impression management, they are forced in taking one test to admit that they have the very symptoms they deny when taking the other. Conversely, if one wants to be regarded as less mentally ill, he must in general answer False to the items of the mental illness test and True to those of the self-insight test. It should be pointed out that if, instead of attempting to present himself in a particular way (that is, either as mentally ill or mentally healthy) a patient responds to the test items in terms principally of his psychopathology, he should answer the test items very much the same way, regardless of both the test title and the instructions he has received.

In addition to the two experimental treatments just described, one control condition was run. Here Ss received one or the other form of the test, but without the instructions that specified the appropriate "script." In this way, it was possible to examine the effect of the test titles alone in order to see whether they themselves were sufficient to bias patients' responses to the test.

SUBJECTS

All 60 Ss in this study were hospitalized open-ward male patients, classified as either Newcomers or Old-timers according to the criteria mentioned earlier. The mean age of the patients was 37.2 with a standard deviation of 10.6. Their mean educational level, according to years in school, was 10.2, with a standard deviation of 3.6. Not surprisingly, there were differences between the groups on both of these variables, with the Newcomers on the average younger (mean age, 31.3) and better educated (mean years of schooling, 11.0) than the Old-timers (mean age 40.0, mean years of schooling, 9.2). Diagnostically, however, there were no differences between Newcomers and Old-timers; 68 percent of all patients had been classified as schizophrenic, another 20 percent as psychotic but not schizophrenic, and the remainder were labeled neurotic. Within subject classes, there were no significant differences between conditions on any of these demographic variables.

Ss were run individually, and all were led to believe, not that they were participating in a psychological experiment, but rather that they were being given a standard clinical evaluation.

EXPERIMENTAL DESIGN AND HYPOTHESIS

Twenty Newcomers were assigned randomly and in equal numbers to the two experimental conditions; a like number of Old-timers were also allocated to each experimental condition. Because of the relative scarcity of Newcomers, only Old-timers were run in the control condition; again 20 Ss took part, divided into two equal groups. The experimental design may be summarized, then, as a two-by-three independent groups design with equal Ns.

The hypothesis under examination pertains just to the two experimental conditions and leads us to anticipate a statistical interaction of the following form: Newcomers should tend to answer False to the mental illness test but True to the self-insight test (thus conveying, so they believe, an impression of mental health), while just the opposite pattern should hold for Old-timers, (who, of course, believe that by so responding they will be regarded as mentally ill).

results and discussion

The number of True responses for each of the three conditions is presented in Table 18.2. As can be seen, the predicated interaction emerges clearly: The modal response by the Newcomers is False to the mental illness test and True to the self-insight test; the reverse is true for the Old-timers. This inter-

TABLE 18.2 MEAN NUMBER OF TRUE TEST RESPONSES ACCORDING TO TREATMENT CONDITION AND STATUS OF PATIENT

PATIENT STATUS	CONDITION	
	Mental Illness Test	Self-Insight Test
Newcomers	13.00	18.80
Old-timers	18.80	9.70
Old-timers (control)	14.60	14.30

Source: Braginsky, Grosse, and Ring (1966).

action is highly significant ($F = 15.61$, $p < .001$). Moreover, within each subject class, the difference between experimental conditions is significant ($p < .01$ for both Newcomers and Old-timers, using the Newman-Keuls procedure). Thus, the overall impression that Newcomers create by their test responses is one of considerable mental health, despite the fact that in order to do so, one set of patients must affirm symptoms that another set of comparable patients disavows.[4] Similarly, Old-timers convey an impression of mental illness by their (inconsistent) pattern of test responses. These findings are, furthermore, precisely what one would expect according to our initial contention that Newcomers are by and large motivated by a desire to leave the hospital, Old-timers, by a desire to remain, and that both classes of patients are quite capable of managing their behavior so as to influence the kind of decision made about them.

Examination of the control group means makes it evident that the test labels in themselves do not systematically bias an S's responses; a "script" in the form of a specification of the meaning and consequences of test responses appears to be necessary to produce the effect observed in the experimental conditions. A comparison of Old-timers in the experimental and control conditions reveals a near-significant interaction ($p < .10$), the form of which is clearly due to the marked divergence of the experimental group means. This effect, though only of marginal significance, is another indication of the extent to which patients can be induced to present themselves as more mentally ill than they otherwise might, as long as they know what responses will foster that impression.

We have interpreted the data from the present study as reflective of a patient's (1) desire either to leave or remain in the hospital and (2) his ability to convey either an impression of health or illness so as to (3) maximize the chances of realizing his desires. There is another cogent interpretation, however, that handles the findings just as easily and that therefore deserves to be considered. Perhaps it is simply that chronic patients are more likely to be more severely ill than newly arrived ones or, at least, believe themselves to be. Rather than responding in terms of putative motivations, then, it may be their conception of themselves, as influenced by their underlying pathology, that is affecting their test performance. A similar argument would be tenable for Newcomers.

Two points need to be made concerning this alternative interpretation before referring to data that bear on it. First, we are not asserting that it is a patient's pathology in itself that influences his test responses, for, if that were so, Old-timers, as we suggested, would be expected to score higher (that is, give more True responses) under *both* test inductions. This interpretation holds, rather, that a patient's self-conception is, in part, determined by his pathology and that his test behavior reflects that self-conception. The second point is implied in what we have just said: A patient would still be regarded as having engaged in impression management, but for different reasons from those we have proposed. Instead of a patient's stay-or-leave motivations being relevant here, we would merely have to invoke a tendency to portray oneself in a way consistent with one's self-concept.

The only difficulty with this line of reasoning is that from the results of other studies (for example, Joint Commission on Mental Illness and Health, 1961; Levinson, 1964) most mental patients do not appear to think of themselves as mentally ill. Furthermore, some opinion-survey data of our own (to be presented in detail . . .) based on 189 hospitalized patients confirm these findings: 78 percent of our sample agreed with the item "Most patients in a state mental hospital are not mentally ill." And particularly pertinent to the alternative interpretation under consideration here is the fact that agreement with this item is uncorrelated with the length of hospitalization ($r = -.11$). In short, the available evidence fails to support the view that Old-timers are more likely to think of themselves (or at least other mental patients) as mentally ill.

Assuming, then, that the findings of the present study can most plausibly be regarded as pointing to the operation of impression management tactics on the part of our Ss, a question of crucial significance for our theoretical position suddenly looms prominent: If patients do indeed use impression management in an effort to control their own fate, precisely how successful are they in doing so?

Our view, of course, has been that in the main patients are not content to leave decisions affecting their welfare entirely in the hands of others, but attempt through the use of whatever counterpower tactics that are available to them to insure that their situation in the hospital is at least moderately tolerable if not downright enjoyable. We have suggested, furthermore, that the manifestations of patient counterpower are likely to be covert, subtle, and normatively illicit and that one form that such counterpower would take is that of impression management. The question we are asking, therefore, is "Is such counterpower not only effective in principle, but effective in fact in allowing a patient to achieve his aims while in the hospital?" Let us briefly review the evidence presented thus far.

The ingratiation study demonstrated only that patients will, under circumstances where it is likely to pay off, ingratiate themselves; there was, however, no evidence from that experiment that such ingratiation did indeed lead to desirable outcomes. The experiment we have just finished recounting offered only indirect support for the efficacy of impression management tactics—there was an association, at any rate, between imputed motivation to stay in or leave the hospital and discharge rates, a relationship for which we assumed impression management was the mediating variable. That interpretation is outlined in Table 18.3.

However intriguing this interpretation may appear to be, no one could make a convincing case for the causal efficacy of impression management on the

TABLE 18.3 THE (HYPOTHETICAL) ROLE OF IMPRESSION MANAGEMENT IN MEDIATING DISCHARGE RATES FOR TWO CLASSES OF MENTAL PATIENTS

PATIENT CLASS	ASCRIBED MOTIVATION	APPROPRIATE IMPRESSION TO BE FOSTERED	TYPICAL DISCHARGE DECISION
Newcomers	I want to leave	I am mentally healthy	Discharged
Old-timers	I want to leave	I am mentally ill	Retained

basis of the data that suggested it—there are too many other explanations.[5] What we plainly need is evidence that shows in clear and unmistakable fashion that a patient's impression management can directly influence his fate in the desired way. The following experiment was designed with just this objective in mind.

effectiveness of impression management as a counterpower tactic

In the two studies already reported, patients were afforded an opportunity to manage their impressions via performance on an impersonal, paper-and-pencil test. In the experiment about to be described (B. Braginsky and D. Braginsky, 1968), we fashioned a more stringent and less artificial situation in which to test the efficacy of impression management tactics; specifically, our procedure involved requiring a patient to submit to a clinical interview conducted by a staff psychologist. Not only is such a face-to-face encounter more representative of the usual conditions under which impression management occurs but also, for mental patients particularly, this kind of evaluative interview setting is one with which they are familiar and which, because of the decisions presumably based on such interviews, ought to enlist strong motivations to engage in impression management in the service of their own personal goals.

method

Thirty male patients living on open wards were advised two days prior to the experiment that they had been scheduled for an interview with a staff psychologist. Although each patient was to be interviewed individually, all 30 were brought simultaneously to a waiting room. After each patient had been interviewed, he was not allowed to return to this room. This was done in order to prevent the patients who had completed their interviews from communicating anything about them to those who had not.

Each patient was escorted to the interview room by an assistant who casually informed the patient in a confidental tone about the purpose of the interview. According to a random procedure, patients were actually given one of three alleged purposes that constituted the independent variable of the study. The interviewer was unaware of the conditions to which Ss had been assigned, thereby eliminating interviewer bias. The three inductions were as follows: In the *Discharge* condition, patients were told, "I think the person you are going to see is interested in examining patients to see whether they might be ready for discharge." Patients in the *Open Ward* condition were informed, "I think that the person you are going to see is interested in examining patients to see whether they should be on open or closed wards."[6] Patients assigned to the *Mental Status* condition were told, "I think the person you are going to see is interested in how you are feeling and getting along in the hospital."[7]

After greeting each patient, the interviewer asked, "How are you feeling?" If a patient responded with a description of physical symptoms only, he was asked, "How do you feel mentally?" If, on the other hand, he dwelt exclusively on his mental state, he was asked, "How are you feeling physically?" All responses were tape-recorded. At the end of two minutes,[8] the interview was terminated and the real purpose of the experiment disclosed.

Three staff psychiatrists from the same hospital independently rated each of the 30 tape-recorded interviews during two 40-minute sessions. These psychiatrists had no prior knowledge of the experiment and were unfamiliar with the patients. They were told by E only that Ss were mental patients residing in the hospital and that as a group they represented a wide range of diagnostic categories.

The psychiatrists rated the patients on the following dimensions: (1) the patient's degree of psychopathology, using a five-point scale ranging from "not at all ill," scored as 1, to "extremely ill," scored as 5; (2) the amount of hospital control a patient needed, ranging on an eight-point scale from complete freedom ("discharge"), scored as 1, to maximum control ("closed ward-continual observation"), scored as 8; and (3) the structural or qualitative aspects of a patient's speech, such as pressure of speech, affect, volume, and so on. The score for each patient's speech characteristics was based on the sum of the psychiatrists' ratings of 14 Lorr scale items (Lorr, 1953). Each item was rated on an eight-point scale ranging from "not at all atypical" (1) to "extremely atypical" (8) verbal behavior.

SUBJECTS

All 30 male Ss were long-term (more than two continuous years of hospitalization) schizophrenics living on open wards who were randomly selected from ward rosters to participate in this experiment. Their mean age was 47.4 years, with a standard deviation of 8.4. The mean educational level of the sample was 8.0 years of schooling, with a standard deviation of 3.4. Their median length of hospitalization was ten years. Forty-three percent of the sample had been diagnosed as chronic, undifferentiated schizophrenics, 37 percent as paranoid schizophrenics, 10 percent as catatonic, and 10 percent as simple schizophrenics. There were no differences between the three experimental conditions on any of the aforementioned variables.

EXPERIMENTAL DESIGN AND HYPOTHESIS

The design of the present experiment is that of a simple one-way factorial with three treatments. Ten Ss were allocated to each condition.

Our experimental hypothesis is once again predicated on motivational considerations. We assume, first of all, that because all our Ss are schizophrenic Oldtimers, they, as a group, should be motivated to remain in the hospital. We assume also, however, that they want to retain the privileges of open-ward living. Because a rational strategy to achieve the former goal would seem to be to present oneself as "mentally ill" (and thus justify one's continuing to reside in the hospital) while to achieve the latter would entail that one appear moderately healthy (and thereby justify one's current ward status), we may make the following prediction: Ss in the *Discharge* condition ought to represent themselves as more mentally ill than a comparable set of Ss in the *Open Ward* condition. The test of this hypothesis and of the effectiveness of the expected mode of their impression management will be provided, of course, by the psychiatrists' ratings. Because mental status interviews are generally used to evaluate a patient's suitability for discharge, we would expect that Ss in this condition would be similar in their mode of self-representation to Ss in the *Discharge* condition. In summary, then, our predictions arrayed in terms of increasing indications, through self-presentation, of mental illness may be expressed as follows:

$$OW < D = MS$$

results and discussion

The mean interpsychiatrist reliabilities for the three variables rated were .89 for psychopathology, .74 for need for hospital control, and .65 for normality of speech characteristics—all satisfactorily high for our present purposes.

The mean ratings for the first two variables, psychopathology and hospital control, are given in Table 18.4. Both sets of ratings show very much the same pattern of differences—precisely the pattern, in fact, that was predicted. Both variables are affected significantly by experimental treatments ($F = 9.38$, $p <$ .01 for psychopathology; $F = 3.85$, $p < .05$ for hospital control) and individual comparisons for both variables disclose that the mean for the *Open Ward* condition is significantly lower than the other two ($p < .01$ for psychopathology, p $< .05$ for hospital control), which in turn are not significantly different from one another. In short, these analyses make it clear that patients in the *Open Ward* condition appear significantly less mentally ill and in less need of hospital control than patients in either the *Discharge* or *Mental Status* conditions. Obviously, the patients in these conditions are quite successful in conveying distinctly different impressions of their psychological well-being to psychiatrists despite the fact that there is no evidence of any systematic variation in psychopathology across the three conditions.

TABLE 18.4 MEAN PSYCHIATRIC RATINGS OF PATIENTS' PSYCHOPATHOLOGY AND NEED FOR HOSPITAL CONTROL ACCORDING TO EXPERIMENTAL CONDITIONS

	OW	D	MS
Psychopathology*	2.63	3.70	3.66
Hospital control†	2.83	4.20	4.10

* Range 1–5 † Range 1–8
Source: Braginsky and Braginsky (1967).

In order to ascertain the means by which patients were able to effect these different impressions, we examined three fairly obvious manipulative tactics that patients might be expected to employ (not necessarily successfully, of course). They were (1) positive self-references, (2) negative self-references, and (3) normality of speech patterns. Indexes for the first two tactics were obtained by simple counting; the counts were made by three judges independently with a mean reliability of .95. The third index was based on the psychiatrist's ratings on the 14 Lorr scale items; a score for each S was obtained by summing the ratings over the 14 items.

The first two tactics, while seemingly lacking in subtlety, were nevertheless potent determinants of psychiatrists' judgments. The more positive self-references made by a patient, the less ill he was perceived to be ($r = -.58$, $p <$ .01) and the less in need of hospital control ($r = -.41$, $p < .05$). Conversely, the more negative self-references emitted by a patient, the more ill he was perceived to be ($r = .53$, $p < .01$) and the more his judged need for hospital control ($r = .37$, $p < .05$). Congruent with our hypothesis that these patients are indeed capable of the fine art of impression management is the correlation of $-.55$ ($p < .01$) between positive and negative self-references, indicating, of course, that a patient's self-presentation tends to be internally consistent—those who make positive statements about themselves tend not to make negative ones and vice versa.

When self-references are compared by condition, we find—as we would now expect—that Ss in the *Open Ward* condition presented themselves in a significantly more positive manner than Ss in either of the other conditions. Only two patients in the *Open Ward* condition reported having any physical or mental problems, whereas 13 patients in the *Discharge* and *Mental Status* conditions made such complaints ($x^2 = 5.40$, $p < .05$).

The sheer frequency of positive or negative self-referent statements, of course, may not necessarily account for some important qualitative aspects of the impressions patients create. One patient may, for instance, indicate a single symptom but it may be a serious one (for example, hallucinations) while another may recount several trivial ailments. In order to provide a more sensitive measure of the treatment effects, therefore, all severe psychopathological symptoms (namely, reports of hallucinations or bizarre delusions) were tallied for each patient. A comparison of conditions revealed that not a single S in the *Open Ward* condition expressed such symptoms while nine Ss in the remaining conditions (that is, nearly half) did so ($x^2 = 4.46$, $p < .05$). Both in terms of number and severity of symptoms spontaneously mentioned, then, patients in the *Discharge* and *Mental Status* conditions present themselves as more mentally ill.

Concerning the last manipulative tactic to be analyzed, normality of speech patterns, no significant condition differences were found.[9] That there was a curtailed range of scores on this variable is indicated by the fact that 80 percent of the patients were judged to have relatively normal speech characteristics. Nevertheless, and consistent with our findings, there was a significant negative correlation ($r = -.35$, $p < .05$) across conditions between number of positive self-references and abnormality of speech patterns; that is, Ss whose speech was more disturbed tended to make fewer positive self-references. If anything, this concatenation of stylistic and contentual components in a patient's behavior ought to strengthen a judge's belief that the patient is mentally ill.

Altogether the results of this study strongly confirm our hypothesis as well as the set of assumptions on which it was predicated. It is clear that patients can and do act in interpersonal settings in such a way as to maximize the chances of satisfying the motivations we have attributed to them. Redlich and Freedman's (1966) assertion that the mental patient suffers from an "inability to implement future goals and present satisfactions" and that he achieves them "magically or through fantasy and delusion" would appear to stand in need of important qualification. When the self-interest of patients is at stake, they can present themselves *convincingly* as either "sick" or "healthy" depending on which mode of self-presentation is believed to increase the probability of desired outcomes.

Now, it is perfectly true that it is possible that psychiatrists might be misled and successfully deceived by patients when their evaluation is based on only a two-minute interview that is further restricted by providing psychiatrist-raters with just auditory cues. It is conceivable that actual face-to-face interaction for a longer period of time with the psychiatrist who is actually going to make important decisions concerning a patient's fate may sharply reduce a patient's ability to "con" the psychiatrist. That, we emphasize, is a possibility. Our research suggests, however, that it may instead be merely a vanity. It is equally conceivable to us at least that a patient who could fool a psychiatrist for two minutes could fool him for 30. Perhaps a patient is cleverer and a psychiatrist more fallible than we are accustomed to believe. This is no place, however, either for speculation or snideness. We need more research to settle the point, and the studies to be presented . . . will help us to do so.

conclusions

. . . We have argued that because of the nature and extent of an institutionalized mental patient's power disadvantage, he can be expected to exert counterpower that is mainly covert and subtle in form but surprisingly powerful in effect. This expectation itself is derived, of course, from the particular beliefs we hold about the sort of motivations and abilities most mental patients can be assumed to possess. . . . Mental patients, for all their pathology, are in most respects, most of the time, just like the rest of us; they want to live in a mental hospital in the same way that ordinary persons want to live in their own community— that is, they can be expected to try to satisfy their needs and, to a considerable extent, to be able to do so. But because a mental hospital, while a community of persons, is not just any community but one of a very special and potentially restrictive kind, the patient's attempts to control his own fate will often have to involve devious and indirect tactics. In this way, then, we were led to examine patients' use of one such tactic, that if impression management and several of its manifestations.

The data assembled from three separate experimental studies make it quite plain, we think, that patients do employ this tactic when given an opportunity (and one suspects that they often create their own opportunities for purposeful self-displays), that they do so with considerable skill, even finesse, and (as the third experiment demonstrated) with perhaps surprising effectiveness. It may be that any one of the reported experimental findings can be accounted for by some other factor(s) than impression management and the motivational variables we have postulated to underlie it; we doubt, however, that there is any other *single* alternative explanation that provides as satisfying and cogent an interpretation for all the data presented, considered collectively.

In each of the experiments . . . patients were placed in situations that were designed to arouse motivations leading to impression management and that furthermore often required that their impression management assume a certain modality (for example, self-presentation via a particular pattern of test responses). The question can be raised, however, whether in the absence of such experimentally induced conditions, patients would give the kind of performances observed in these studies. The answer would seem to depend on the extent to which there is a continuity between the motivations elicited in these experiments and those that govern the behavior of patients in their everyday hospital activities and interactions. There is already some reason to infer such a continuity inasmuch as our experimental settings were of course not represented as such, but rather as test or interview situations. Nevertheless, it seems important to document directly patients' hedonistic motivations that were implied, but not demonstrated, by our experiments and, once this is accomplished, to establish their consequences for patients' everyday behavior.

notes

1. Not all mental patients, of course, dwell in hospital settings that qualify as "total institutions." Nevertheless, it is frequently assumed that almost regardless of the structure and climate of the institution, it still functions as the primary determinant of the patient's in-hospital behavior (Downing, 1958; Fairweather, 1964; Goffman, 1961; Gordon and Groth, 1961; Stanton and Schwartz, 1954).

2. To allay possible misinterpretations, it should be stated that we do not mean to suggest either that the power exercised by patients is primarily symbolic in expression or that it represents only a reaction against the legitimate power enjoyed by the staff.

3. The rationale for including unrealistically critical items is not germane to the present argument and will be outlined later.

4. The ideal design for this type of study would require that each S be used as his own control; the technical problems posed by this procedure, however, made the present design more feasible.

5. For example, perhaps patients with a greater desire to leave the hospital do in fact make faster progress in dealing with their emotional problems, perhaps they are more likely to take part in formal treatment programs, perhaps the psychiatric staff is biased in favor of discharging younger persons (more likely to be Newcomers) more rapidly than older ones, and so on.

6. It may appear as if this would not be a credible induction because no patient enjoying open-ward status would believe that he could be put on a closed ward on the basis of the forthcoming interview alone. At the time this experiment was conducted, however, the hospital was in the process of a major reorganization, and the question of possible changes in one's ward status was a salient one.

7. Mental status evaluation interviews are typically conducted yearly. Patients who have been in the hospital more than a year (as had all of ours—see following) expect, therefore, to be interviewed for the purpose of determining their residency status.

8. Obviously, psychiatrists would never base such important decisions as, for example, being discharged, on a two-minute interview. Nevertheless, in order to provide an opportunity for impression management that might *influence* such decisions, two minutes was more than sufficient. Data to be presented later indicate in any case that even so brief a sample of a patient's behavior as these interviews provide is adequate to afford a basis for reliable judgments by psychiatrists. It is interesting to note, incidentally, that the typical mental status interview conducted by these psychiatrists is rarely longer than half an hour and that, according to Scheff (1966), the average in-court psychiatric interview is only about ten minutes long.

9. The failure to find evidence of differential speech disturbance among the three conditions tends to cast doubt on the possible, though somewhat implausible, alternative interpretation that Ss in the *Discharge* and *Mental Status* conditions were made more anxious by the prospect of being discharged than were *Open Ward* Ss threatened with transfer to a closed ward. If this had been so, one could easily account for Ss in the former two conditions appearing more mentally ill—they were more upset. Although our speech disturbance data do not conclusively eliminate this interpretation, they render it even more unlikely.

references

Artiss, K. *The symptom as communication in schizophrenia.* New York: Grune & Stratton, 1959.

Braginsky, B., & Braginsky, D. Schizophrenic patients in the psychiatric interview: An experimental study of their effectiveness at manipulation. *Journal of Consulting Psychology,* 1967, *21,* 543–547.

Braginsky, B., Grosse, M., & Ring, K. Controlling outcomes through impression-management: An experimental study of the manipulative tactics of mental patients. *Journal of Consulting Psychology*, 1966, *30*, 295–300.

Dahlstrom, W., & Welsh, G. *An MMPI handbook*. Minneapolis, University of Minnesota Press, 1960.

Downing, J. Chronic mental hospital dependency as a character defense. *Psychiatric Quarterly*, 1958, *32*, 489–499.

Fairweather, G. *Social psychology in treating mental illness: An experimental approach*. New York: John Wiley & Sons, 1964.

Goffman, E. *The presentation of self in everyday life*. New York: Doubleday, 1959.

Goffman, E. *Asylums*. New York: Doubleday, 1961.

Gordon, H., & Groth, L. Mental patients wanting to stay in the hospital. *American Medical Association Archives of General Psychiatry*, 1961, *4*, 124–130.

Joint Commission on Mental Illness and Health. *Action for mental health*. New York: Basic Books, 1961.

Jones, E. *Ingratiation*. New York: Appleton-Century-Crofts, 1964.

Levinson, D., & Gallagher, E. *Patienthood in the mental hospital*. Boston: Houghton-Mifflin, 1964.

Lorr, M. Multidimensional scale for rating psychiatric patients. *Veterans Administration Technical Bulletin*, 1953, *51*, 119–127.

Redlich, F., & Freedman, D. *The theory and practice of psychiatry*. New York: Basic Books, 1966.

Scheff, T. J. *Being mentally ill: A sociological theory*. Chicago: Aldine, 1966.

Stanton, A., & Schwartz, M. *The mental hospital*. New York: Basic Books, 1954.

Szasz, T. *The myth of mental illness*. New York: Paul B. Hoeber, 1961.

Towbin, A. Understanding the mentally deranged. *Journal of Existentialism*, 1966, *7*, 63–83.

Winer, B. *Statistical principles in experimental design*. New York: McGraw-Hill, 1962.

19

Failure of a Moral Enterprise:

ATTITUDES OF THE PUBLIC TOWARD MENTAL ILLNESS

Theodore R. Sarbin and James C. Mancuso

For several decades, workers in the mental health movement have engaged in a moral crusade to induce the general public to adopt the proposition that "mental illness is just like any other illness." The underlying assumption of this moral credo is that the nonstigmatizing attitudes held toward somatic illness would transfer to "mental" illness. Mental health professionals have worked as-

Reprinted from the *Journal of Consulting and Clinical Psychology*, 1970, Vol. 35, No. 2, pp. 159–173. Copyright 1970 by the American Psychological Association. Reprinted by permission.

siduously to convince the public to look at certain behaviors as manifestations of "illness," with the expectation that the sympathetic, nonrejecting valuations usually declared on physical illness would then be automatically declared on conduct deviations.

The authors employ the term *moral crusade* intentionally. Becker (1963) has described a moral crusade as the enterprise of persons who see the need for a particular rule of conduct and who become committed to a social movement that aims to establish the rule. A predictable by-product of such crusading is a professional apparatus first to "sell" the rule, then to implement it. The history of the mental health movement in America provides abundant data to confirm the authors' adopting this colorful metaphor. Psychiatry, the semiofficial authority behind the mental health crusade, has handed us the rule: unacceptable deviants are mentally ill. The implications of this history, beginning with the nineteenth-century reformer, Dorothea Dix, suggest that we regard the leaders of the movement as "moral entrepreneurs."

Entrepreneurs of morality, like entrepreneurs of commerce, may achieve success, or they may fail. Moral enterprise may be judged as having successfully achieved its goal when the rule of conduct at issue becomes a part of the moral ideology of the public, and is widely enforced through officially designated agents.

A review of the studies of the public's attitudes toward mental illness and mental health demonstrates that the moral enterprise of promoting the "mental illness" metaphor has failed (e.g., Cumming & Cumming, 1957; Nunnally, 1961; Philips, 1963). The general public has not been persuaded that illness is an appropriate metaphor for deviant behavior. In spite of extensive public relations and propaganda programs, the man in the street is not ready to use the label "mentally ill" to categorize people whose behavior would lead a professional diagnoser to apply a psychiatric label. Further, the man in the street does not advocate the use of a special cognitive category to isolate (and to segregate socially) persons whose performances motivate a professional to employ the diagnosis mentally ill. On the other hand, if the man in the street is told authoritatively that the actor is mentally ill, he will tend to place the deviantly behaving person in the "reject" category. In effect, the public tends to tolerate and to accommodate to the overt conduct that professionals label as mental illness, but tends to see persons who are branded by the label mentally ill as stigmatized.[1]

It is important to note that the authors of books and articles on the public's attitudes toward mental illness are, by and large, professional mental health workers—psychiatrists, psychologists, and social workers. These are the moral authorities who declare that the public is "misinformed," that the public holds "incorrect attitudes," and that the public has not acquired a "scientific orientation," etc. They frequently recommend "public psychotherapy" in the form of better public education about mental illness, psychodynamics, and similar topics, even reaching into the secondary schools. These observations constrain us to raise the question: Precisely what should the public be taught about deviant behavior? The systematic attitude studies lead to the inference that if the public were to classify deviant behavior as mental illness, then the deviantly behaving person would be stigmatized and rejected. Obviously, the stigmatization and rejection would be an unintended consequence. A second question is pertinent: Could a sustained, powerful propaganda effort succeed in validating the mental illness metaphor, so that the label mental illness would produce the same neutral (non-stigmatizing) valuational responses as are called forth by the labels pneumonia, cardiac failure, myopia, or indigestion? Even if a convention of mental health professionals, jurists, linguists, and educators could resolve the communication problems contained in the multiplicity of definitions (Scott, 1958), would it be possible to design an educational campaign that could detach the moral, legal, and ethical connotations from the mental illness categorization of deviant behavior? Could mental health organizations, aided and abetted by Madison Avenue, influence the public to regard mental illness judgments as having the same moral force as judgments about somatic illness? Is the detachment of morality from mental illness a worthy goal?

In the succeeding pages, the authors review the studies that warrant the conclusion that professional campaigns to promote the mental illness metaphor have failed. Further, because of the mythic status of mental illness, the campaign was foredoomed to failure. At one time, mental illness was a potentially useful metaphor. Like so many other metaphors of mentalism, it was illicitly transformed into a myth—a guide to action without empirical supports. Once such a transformation occurred, the moral valuational components could not be detached from the mythical concept.

Contrary to the pronouncements of some medical authorities, deviant conduct is by definition the application of moral, legal, and ethical percepts and rules. To partition deviant conduct from the abstraction "health" is to violate logical canons as well as common sense.

The contradictions and logical faults within the mental illness myth have been critically discussed by a number of writers (Hartung, 1965; Sarbin, 1967, 1969; Szasz, 1961). These critics have presented cogent arguments for their views that the concept of mental illness is scientifically arid and humanistically alien; its continued employment borders on the futile, if not the perilous. Hartung consistently demonstrated the logical fallacies and social injustices that follow from attempting to regard criminal behavior as an expression of mental illness. Szasz (1961, 1963) has pursued an attack on the mythology of mental illness, arguing that an attempt to regard unacceptable behavior as "diagnosable" mental illness has led to a series of socially and scientifically perilous conditions. Psychiatric labeling, he argued, leads to the false impression that one is identifying a homogeneous condition. One who holds this belief is left with the comfortable feeling that he has an "explain-all," and his attention is unfortunately diverted from "more limited, and socially and methodologically better defined, plans of attack on specific problems [Szasz, 1957, p. 412]."

The evidence of the failure to convince the public to adopt the mental illness myth, together with the logical and humanistic arguments against the myth, demand a reevaluation of the whole enterprise concerned with informing the public on the issue of inappropriate and improper behavior. The following review of studies on attitudes of the public toward mental illness summarizes evidence to support the validity of three major propositions: (a) The ordinary citizen is willing to tolerate and to accommodate to extensive behavior deviations; (b) the public is hesitant about using the mental illness label for those behavior deviations and unusual solutions to life's problems which psychiatrically oriented diagnosers would unhesitatingly label mental illness; (c) if the semantic tag, mental illness, is attached to a particular behavior, the public will tend to reject and to advocate isolation of the person whose behaviors are thus labeled.

The purpose of this review is to illuminate some of the consequences of continuing to persuade the public to employ the illness metaphor to describe improprieties in social and personal behavior.

review of systematic studies

A large number of investigations have been published on the attitudes of the public toward mental illness and health. Invariably, the studies have been conducted with the explicit or implicit purpose of assessing the success of the continuing campaign to have the public develop constructs which place deviant behavior within the mental illness paradigm. The authors of these campaigns are unanimous in their objectives that the public be encouraged to grant more power and responsibility to the mental health professions for larger and larger segments of unwanted behavior.

Available studies of the public's attitudes have varied around three general approaches. A first set of studies is characterized by the technique of inquiring about mental illness. A second approach is characterized by asking the general public about deviant behaviors (which professionals would, in general, consider to be manifestations of mental illness). A third tactic has explored the public view of mental health and illness through inquiring about how people construe their happiness, which is assumed to reflect their own mental health status.

direct inquiries into attitudes of the public
toward mental illness and health

Nunnally's (1961) study of public conceptions of mental illness and health provided a pattern which has been used by numerous other investigators. He asked his respondents to indicate the extent of their agreement with a variety of statements which purportedly described the nature of mental illness. His questionnaire included items such as the following: Women have no more emotional problems than men do; mental illness can usually be helped by a vacation or change of scene; the insane laugh more than do normal people; most suicides occur because of rejection in love; physical exhaustion does not lead to a nervous breakdown.

Nunnally subjected his data to a factor analysis. Ten factors emerged that represent a set of generalized attitudes toward mental illness. They were described as follows:

1. The mentally ill are characterized by identifiable actions and appearances.
2. Will power is the basis of one's personal adjustment.
3. Women are more prone to mental ill-health than are men.
4. If one can avoid morbid thoughts he can avoid mental illness.
5. If one can obtain support and guidance from stronger persons he can avoid mental illness.
6. One who is mentally ill is in a hopeless condition.
7. Mental disorders are caused by immediate environmental pressures.
8. Emotional difficulties are not a matter of great concern.
9. Older people are more susceptible to mental illness.
10. Mental illness is attributable to organic factors [p. 17].

The lay public, in contrast to professional mental health workers, responds more in the direction of agreeing with these 10 general statements, though the average lay person's responses are not markedly different from the average expert's responses. Nunnally further found that persons of higher education tend to show more agreement with the mental health experts, this being particularly the case when the higher educated persons are more youthful.

To extend the picture of how the public conceptualizes mental health, Nunnally used a form of Osgood's semantic differential scale (see Osgood, Suci, & Tannenbaum, 1957). A sample of 250 persons rated terms such as neurotic man, old man, insane man, etc., on a series of 7-point scales such as foolish—wise, unpredictable—predictable, bad—good, etc. The prime conclusion derived from analysis of these ratings was that "public attitudes are relatively negative toward persons with mental health problems [p. 46]." Generally, the public assigns valuations to the mentally ill as worthless, dirty, dangerous, cold, unpredictable, insincere, etc., relative to normal persons.

Further, semantic analysis showed that the public views mental health professionals in favorable terms, but less favorably than professionals who treat somatic illness. Nurses, for example, were rated more favorably than were psychiatrists on scales such as dangerous—safe and ineffective—effective. Nunnally's data also showed that a sample of high school students regard mental institutions and treatment approaches to be less valuable and trustworthy than are physical treatment centers and methods.

The public and the professionals did not differ greatly on the nature of their agreement with the 10 factors which summarized the 50-item questionnaire. Nunnally concluded, however, that the man in the street's responses to the semantic differential showed that the public was not as well informed as it might be. He devoted considerable space to the means by which the public could be "better informed" on mental health matters. Nunnally also proposed an explanation for the basis of the public's "misinformation." In keeping with the mental illness ambience, he turned to the psychodynamics of the layman and employed the mentalistic construct "anxiety." He suggested that the unpredictability of the mentally ill causes anxiety, which accounts for why "people are very uncomfortable in the presence of someone who is, or is purported to be, mentally ill [p. 233]."

Cumming and Cumming (1957) produced another study which is regularly regarded as a prime source of information on the public's attitudes toward mental illness and health. In addition to direct inquiry into how the public responds to identified mental illness, Cumming and Cumming also investigated reactions to behavioral descriptions. These two different approaches produced data which suggested an important but neglected discrepancy in attitudes. Like Nunnally, they concluded that the man in the street places a negative valuation on identified mental illness. At the same time, he tends to reflect a lack of concern, a neutral valuation, to unlabeled "case" descriptions.

Cumming and Cumming (1957) carried out their study as they tried to assess the effectiveness of a mental health education program in a small town in Canada. Using Guttman's scaling methods, they determined the social distance at which mentally ill people were held. They concluded that, in general, the public has a marked tendency to reject people who are described as being mentally ill. Further, the general public is not willing to assume responsibility for the condition of mental illness in others. Cumming and Cumming were primarily interested in achieving a shift in public attitudes, to induce the public to take a mental health attitude toward unusual conduct. Their effort to "educate" the public proved to have had little effect in producing greater acceptance of the mentally ill. Interestingly, the one clear result of the effort was that the mental health "educators" became the targets of hostile actions from the members of the community. Their study left them with two perturbing observations: (a) the expected attitudinal shift on the issue of mental illness did not occur and (b) the development of hostility toward members of the mental health team. (These issues are discussed later.)

Freeman and Kassebaum (1960), working with an original scale, asked respondents questions such as the following (a) Do you believe that people who have mental disorders get well again? and (b) Do you believe that it is possible to prevent mental disorders? They also collected data on a number of demographic variables. They found that educational level had little effect on responses to questions about the nature of mental illness. There tended to be a stronger relationship between S's knowledge of the current usage of psychiatric terminology and the opinions held toward mental illness. As one would expect, the study showed high positive relationships between knowledge of psychiatric terms and the level of education of the respondents.

Selected samples have been directly asked their views of mental illness. Using the semantic differential, Crumpton, Weinstein, Acker, and Annis (1967) compared mental patients and normals on their views toward mental patients. They summarize their findings by observing that "ratings of the concept 'mental patient' are more likely to resemble ratings of 'sick person' and 'dangerous person' when made by normals, and to resemble ratings of 'criminal' and 'sinner' when made by patients [p. 49]." Mental patients tended to report a more sympathetic, but still unfavorable, view of the status they were then occupying. It must be pointed out that the respondents in the Crumpton et al. study were indicating their reactions to the terms *mental patient* and *normal person*. If the term in the scale had been *insane man*, as it was in a study by Giovannoni and Ullmann (1963), the valuational ratings would undoubtedly have been more negative.

Other studies have made cross-cultural comparisons of views toward mental illness. Hes (1966) compared Afro-Asians and Poles who had immigrated to Israel. The Polish immigrants tended to reflect more concern over themselves or their relatives being diagnosed as mentally ill. Hes suggests that this might reflect the greater demand among Europeans that one demonstrate control over his own destiny.

Kahn, Lee, Jones, and Jin (1966) compared Korean and American mental patients on their respective attitudes toward mental illness. After asking Korean patients to indicate their position on such statements as "The best place to get hold of yourself is a psychiatric hospital" and "This hospital is like a prison for keeping people locked up," the investigators factor analyzed the total scale. Kahn, Jones, MacDonald, Conners, and Binchard (1963) had already carried out this procedure on American patients. Having available the major factors which had been extracted from both the American and Korean patients' responses, Kahn and his coworkers proceeded to contrast the two groups on their views toward mental illness and "patienthood." The American attitudes about hospitalization reflected primary concerns about the penal quality of hospitalization and external management. In contrast, the Koreans expressed views that focused on the condition of the hospital as a living situation which had pleasant or unpleasant characteristics. To the Korean the hospital was generally a place where one went in order to be "cured." American patients regarded their stay at the hospital as a form of incarceration.

These studies lead to a firm conclusion: The general public declares a negative valuation on behavior that has been identified as mental illness. If the educational campaigns of mental health professionals sought to promote an acceptance and tolerance of persons who are diagnosed mentally ill, such campaigns have made little headway toward their goals.

inquiries into the public view
of abnormal behavior

Instead of asking the respondent to give his view of mental illness, other investigators describe a set of behaviors (that are sometimes thought to be characteristic of mentally ill persons), and the respondent is asked to give reactions to the descriptions. These studies have used behavior descriptions of the type developed by Star (1955). These descriptions were patterns of behavior which would each fit a series of standard psychiatric classifications. They were meant to illustrate the diagnostic syndromes of paranoid schizophrenia, simple schizophrenia, anxiety neurosis, alcoholism, compulsive-phobic behavior, and juvenile character disorder.

Two articles (Maisel, 1951; Woodward, 1951) report a pioneering study into the public's view of mental illness. These reports warrant the conclusion that the sampled population was not inclined to think in psychiatric terms about behavior which the investigators regarded as pathological, but expressed alarm about the amount of mental illness in their community. Some of the data which led to this conclusion were as follows: When the respondents were given a description of a woman who would almost certainly be diagnosed by professionals as a paranoid schizophrenic, only about 28% recommended a form of psychiatric-medical care, whereas 26% advised consultation with a clergyman, and 34% recommended that the woman's husband take a common sense approach to allaying his wife's suspicions. When reacting to the case of a depressive man, under circumstances where consulting a clergyman was not an allowable recommendation, psychiatric-medical care was still advocated by only 30% of the respondents. Woodward's (1951) report of this study suggests some of the confusion about the public's view of the place of psychiatry in working with moral matters. When asked to make on-the-spot recommendations for disposal of a case of a juvenile character disorder, the most frequent prescription was a form of repressive action. When given a list of possible recommendations, the respondents suggested psychiatric consultation more frequently than they recommended punitive approaches. Despite the general reluctance to recommend psychiatric referral for the described cases, Maisel reported that about 75% of the population of the city under study held the opinion that there was a shortage of psychiatric facilities. At the same time, data were reported which suggest that the study population held beliefs that psychiatric knowledge is inadequate (Maisel, 1951; Woodward, 1951).

That the public is more concerned about disruption of interpersonal relationships than about the "pathology" of a behavioral syndrome is demonstrated in two studies reported by Phillips (1963, 1964). His measurement of rejection or acceptance was based on the concept of social distance. Phillips used case descriptions patterned after the Star (1955) cases, but varied them by indicating a help-source used by the target person. For example, different groups of respondents were told that the target person was visiting a psychiatrist, or that he was consulting a physician, etc. This variation allowed some assessment of which variable, the behavior deviation or the help-source, influences acceptance or rejection of the target person. Phillips (1963) showed that the social distance between a respondent and a person described in a "case" abstract was in part a function of the case being identifiable as mentally ill. For example, respondents were asked to indicate their willingness to tolerate contact with a "simple schizophrenic" for whom no help source was indicated. Such a case would be more generally tolerated than would a "normal case" described as being in a mental hospital. No matter what the nature of the case, respondents decreased their tolerance for the target person on learning that he was in consultation with psychiatric personnel.

Phillips (1964) warranted similar conclusions. Respondents indicated relatively less desire for social contact with a person said to be using psychiatric resources. A clear relationship is noted between the disruptive quality of the behavior and rejection. An example of this connection is evident in the trend in Phillips' data, which indicates that the same behavior pattern evokes a different degree of rejection depending on whether the target person is a male or a female. The male role is assumed to call for greater stability and predictability. When, for example, a male's behavior reflects depression, it is regarded as more disruptive (and thus the man is more strongly rejected) than is the same behavior in a female.[2]

Dohrenwend and Chin-Shong (1967), using similar case descriptions, demonstrated a high public tolerance for "pathological behavior." They asked their respondents first to indicate whether or not they regarded the behavior as a sign of something being wrong. If a person answered affirmatively, he was then asked whether he thought of the described person as being mentally ill. A third question was intended to reveal whether the respondent thought the situation was a serious matter. If we can assume that a person who views a "serious" condition as one to be avoided (an assumption not made by Dohrenwend & Chin-Shong, 1967), then we can use their data as indicating rejection of the behaviors that would be regarded as signs of mental illness. Of the respondents, 87% regarded the description of paranoid schizophrenic behavior as that of serious illness. This case, however, was the only behavioral description which evoked this degree of concern. Few respondents looked upon the other cases as being serious, or mentally ill, or a combination of serious and mentally ill. The public is particularly reluctant to regard behavior as serious or as mental illness if the behavior does not threaten others. If we assume that the assessment serious would precede rejection of specified conduct, then Dohrenwend and Chin-Shong's data would allow the reference that the public would tend not to reject a person whose conduct would probably be characterized by a professional as being symptomatic of mental illness.

Yamamoto and Dizney (1967) concentrated their attention on attitudes toward the mentally ill as expressed by future teachers. The Ss were student teachers who were taking a course in educational psychology. They were asked to indicate their tolerance for the hypothetical target persons whose behaviors were described by Star. The target persons were described as paranoid schizophrenic, depressed neurotic, simple schizophrenic, phobic compulsive, and normal healthy. A significant statistical difference existed in the tolerance toward the "normal healthy," as compared to all other cases. No other statistically significant differences were noted. When the future teachers recommended help for the cases, they showed more concern for the case described as experiencing greater personal distress (the depressed neurotic) than for the other cases. None of the student-teachers recommended institutionalization for any of the cases. Yamamoto and Dizney conclude their report with the familiar call for a reconsideration of our current practices of educating teachers to the psychiatric model to sharpen their skill in recognizing mental illness.

Whereas Yamamoto and Dizney express some concern about the ways in which student-teachers view mental illness, Rabkin and Suchoski (1967) report that "compared with the attitudes held by the general public, teachers express more favorable attitudes and appear to understand these concepts somewhat better [p. 39]." Rabkin and Suchoski used Nunnally's (1961) approach, asking their teachers to indicate agreement or disagreement with direct statements about mental illness and mental health. Like Nunnally, they also used the semantic differential technique of assessing meanings of mental illness. A surprising result extracted from the Nunnally scale of attitudes was that teachers tend to hold attitudes toward mental illness that are even more "correct" than are the attitudes held by experts. Rabkin and Suchoski were heartened by the implications of their results and were led to "suppose that teachers do indeed, at least on a relative basis, have more positive attitudes toward the mentally ill [p. 41]."[3]

Lemkau and Crocetti, since their first paper in 1962, have consistently produced data and interpretations which on the surface have tended to contradict the entire chain of findings on the rejection of the mentally ill. In their 1962 paper, Lemkau and Crocetti report data for a representative sample in Baltimore. They used three of Star's (1955) cases: the paranoid, the simple schizophrenic, and the alcoholic. Fifty percent of their sample identified all three cases as mental illness. Only 4% saw none of the cases as mental illness. They further report that

> age, race, marital status, and urban or rural birth were not significantly correlated with the tendency to make the identification. Educational level attained and family income did make a difference in this tendency; the more educated or the higher the income, the greater the likelihood that the case stories would be considered as presenting mental illness [p. 695].

Furthermore, Lemkau and Crocetti do not regard the social distance placed between respondents and mentally ill persons to be highly significant. Fifty percent of the sample indicated that they "could imagine themselves falling in love with someone who had been mentally ill," or that they "would be willing to room with someone who had been a patient in a mental hospital." Eighty-five percent of the sample chose home care, rather than hospital care, for cases which could be diagnosed as schizophrenic, mild senile psychotic, or depressive middle-aged breadwinner. Lemkau and Crocetti take issue with the persistently reported public rejection of mental illness. They feel that the public has been responsive to the professional leadership on the question of mental illness, and are critical of the sociological hypothesis that the public rejects persons who are diagnosed as mentally ill.

Lemkau and Crocetti's work suffers from a lack of attention to the distinction between rejection of mental illness as differentiated from rejection of behaviors that might be diagnosed as mental illness. Their data can readily be interpreted within the structure of the present argument, that the public is somewhat distrustful of mentally ill persons, but that the public is not particularly aroused by behaviors that psychiatric personnel would regard as signs of mental illness.

inquiries into attitudes toward one's own mental health

A third approach to the public view of mental illness and health is one which involves inquiring into the "happiness level" of the population. It can be cogently argued that subjective happiness, despite its frequent use as a criterion of mental health, is not an appropriate indicator (Jahoda, 1958). Nevertheless, the present authors found several studies that investigated views of mental health through analysis of responses to one's own happiness levels.

Bradburn and Caplovitz (1965), aware of the arguments against the ascription of synonymity to the terms mental health and happiness (Jahoda, 1958), believe that a gain in conceptual clarity can be derived from the data on happiness. The underlying assumption of their work is that one can identify a dimension variously labeled as mental health, subjective adjustment, happiness, etc., and that individuals can be described as being high or low with regard to this dimension. Following this assumption, one can infer that Bradburn and Caplovitz intend their data on happiness to reflect (at least in part) the public's views on its own mental health.

As a part of the work of the Joint Commission on Mental Illness and Health, Gurin, Veroff, and Feld (1960) also gave extensive attention to subjective reports on happiness. Reports of happiness and unhappiness were used as measures of general adjustment, and relationships of other variables to the measures of happiness and unhappiness were uncovered. Taking into account Jahoda's objection to the happiness concept as a suitable mental health synonym, these investigators justified their study in terms of multiple criteria for mental health and adjustment.

What does the man in the street think about his state of happiness? What does he do about his unhappiness? Does he agree with the investigators on their assumptions that his state of happiness is related to his mental health? The review of three studies (Bradburn & Caplovitz, 1965; Elinson, Padilla, & Perkins, 1967; Gurin et al., 1960) on the topic of the public's view of its own mental health leads the present authors to believe that few people conceptualize their happiness in terms of mental health constructs.

As a general rule, about 10%–15% of the population report that they are "not too happy," about 25% report that are "very happy," and the remaining 60%–65% say that they are "pretty happy." It is no surprise that in the United States, a larger portion of the not too happy respondents are from the low-socio-economic groups, whereas the very happy respondents are more likely to be those persons whose occupations are prestigeful and financially rewarding.

Reports of happiness are more a matter of positive feelings than they are a matter of absence of negative feelings. Bradburn and Caplovitz (1965) concluded that when a man's positive feelings are more prevalent than his negative feelings, he is more likely to report that he is happy. When negative feelings exceed positive feelings, the percentage of persons responding that they are not too happy is found to increase. Gurin et al. (1960) report that 24% of their very happy respondents also tell that they worry more than "a lot." These investigations conclude that although worrying and unhappiness are similar, in that they may reflect a large number of frustrating experiences, unhappiness is differentiated from worry by the absence of positive areas of satisfaction. This conclusion would readily fit into the position reached by Bradburn and Caplovitz: In spite of many negative experiences or worries, a person can report that he is very happy, particularly if the positive feelings exceed negative feelings.

If we made a direct translation of happiness into mental health, what conclusions might we draw from the reported findings? Generally, we could conclude that most of the public would see themselves as being in a satisfactory state of mental health, and 10%–15% of the public would use the category, mentally unhealthy. A person of higher educational and income level would be more likely to report that he is mentally healthy. Further, a person reporting that his positive experiences exceed his negative experiences would more likely report that he is happy than if his positive experiences do not outweigh his negative experiences.

Having taken these interpretational liberties, can we make any statements about the public's view of how it attains its mental health and how it can regain it if lost? Gurin et al. made an extensive analysis of the perceived help sources for solving their problems. About 50% of the population considers the possibility of seeking outside help from a quasi-mental-health agency, regardless of the state of their happiness or the source of their problems. People who worry a lot, who are not too happy, or who feel the possibility of a "nervous breakdown" are more likely to have already sought help from such agencies. Persons whose problems are centered around interpersonal relationships are more likely to have made use of outside help than when problems appear to originate from other sources. Again, educational level was an indicator of whether a person has actually sought help from some sort of mental health agency. Young, college-educated persons used outside help more frequently than their lesser educated contemporaries. Social and occupational status, however, were not variables which relate to help seeking.

Gurin et al. (1960, p. 288) assume that the seeking or desiring of help from professionals, including clergymen and physicians, can be the criterion for determining whether a person has accepted a mental health definition of his "unhappiness." Such an assumptive leap is untenable. Seventy-one percent of those who actually sought professional help turned to clergymen and physicians. Eighty-eight percent of the people who feel they can use help with their problems do not report that they should consult psychiatrists, psychologists, social workers, etc. The present authors note that as income and education rise, a person is more likely to seek help from a psychiatrist. Forty-seven percent of help-seeking persons earning more than $10,000 per year (in 1958) had used the services of a psychiatrist, and 29% of this group went to clergymen; 5% of those whose income was under $2,000 (in 1958) went to psychiatrists, and 48% to clergymen.

Elinson et al. (1967) report data that deviate slightly from the Gurin et al. study. About 35% of the Elinson et al. New York City sample cited the use of strictly psychiatric agencies as a possible help source, along with other sources they might use. Twenty-one percent recommended consulting a physician, while only 16% recommended a clergyman. About 28% said they would use nonprofessional sources, and about 41% said they would engage in self-help or would seek no help.

It would appear, then, that most of the general public agree that their problems in living—their sources of unhappiness—are not made more understandable by using mental health metaphors. To be sure, if one is wealthy and well educated, he is likely to impute a relationship between his problems and psychiatric causal entities. Even in this group, however, large numbers turn to their clergymen for help in solving problems in living.[4]

explanations of public negativism
toward mental illness

It is not surprising that the mental health campaigners take the public to task for its rejection of the mental illness metaphor. Disappointed with the results of their public health efforts, they offered various explanations for their lack of success.

Earlier, the authors mentioned the hostility generated in the community by mental health researchers (Cumming & Cumming, 1957). "The ranks had closed against us; the town of Blackfoot had responded as if to a threat to its integrity as a functioning community [Cumming & Cumming, 1957, p. 44]." "Generally speaking, we believe Blackfoot's response to our mental health educational program was that of anxiety [p. 46]." "We do not believe that the hostile reaction of the Blackfoot citizens was caused by our *method* of entering the community or of presenting our materials [p. 106]."

Cumming and Cumming explained the hostility which was engendered by their "mental health education campaign." They concluded that they were perceived as agents who threatened to destroy the established social response to deviance. The exposure of the community's use of "denial" as a reaction to mental illness was perceived as a threat, which in turn produced the "closed ranks" which provided the title for their study. In the same vein, the Joint Commission on Mental Illness and Health (1961) declared that the public does "not feel as sorry as they do relieved to have out of the way persons whose behavior disturbs and offends them [p. 58]."

Gilbert and Levinson (1956) attempted to show that "humanistic" approaches to mental illness are one facet of an egalitarian approach to social interaction. They used the California F Scale (Adorno, Frenkel-Brunswick, Levinson, & Sanford, 1950) as a measure of the authoritarian-egalitarian dimension and a scale of "custodial ideology" as a gauge of humanistic attitudes toward the mentally ill. They reported a strong positive relationship between authoritarianism and a custodial ideology.

Thus, the man in the street does not fare well in the hands of the psychiatrically oriented professionals who try to explain his refusal to adopt the mental illness mythology. He is judged as callous, as resorting to defense mechanisms such as denial, and as inhumane and illiberal.

conclusions

What conclusions are warranted after reviewing and synthesizing this body of research? The present conclusions do not precisely fit all the data, but they reflect the major findings. First, the public is not sympathetic toward persons who are labeled mentally ill. They look upon such persons with disrespect and are willing to relegate them to a childlike, nonperson role. An exemplar of the general public would place a sizable social distance between himself and those persons who are labeled mentally ill.

A second general conclusion is that the public does not share the professional's propensity for labeling deviant behavior as mental illness. The survey data have shown repeatedly that only persons who exhibit the most exaggerated deviations will be regarded as mentally ill, and even when this is done, the general public only infrequently makes the recommendation that such persons be hospitalized. (Lemkau & Crocetti's, 1962, findings caution against the unqualified acceptance of this conclusion. They report that high percentages of their sample classify descriptions as mental illness. The same sample, however, tended to reject the suggestion of hospitalization for persons who would be deemed psychiatric cases by professionals.)

The juxtaposition of these two conclusions has persistently presented investigators with an apparent paradox. On one hand, the researchers have been alarmed about the public rejection of the mentally ill. On the other hand, writers express concern about the public rejection of a mental illness interpretation of deviant behavior. When the public is asked how it regards mentally ill persons, the response represents a negative valuation. When asked to react to descriptions of persons that professionals would diagnose as mentally ill, the public does not define this behavior as mental illness, nor does it show an exaggerated degree of concern about unusual behavior.

A concise statement of the reaction to this paradox is found in the report of Cumming and Cumming (1957):

> Our interviewers were shocked at the respondents' denial of pathological conditions in the case histories, because they assumed that lay people could accept less behavior as normal. But a very wide spectrum of behavior appears to be tolerated by the laity—at least verbally—as reasonably close to normal . . . [p. 101].

The results of the studies which have asked people to give their impressions of those who were clearly labeled as mentally ill seem to have led investigators to expect that the general public would be quite intolerant of the people described in Star's (1955) case histories. As the authors can gather from the present review of studies which ask directly about reactions to mental illness, there is generally low tolerance of people who are thus diagnosed. It is something of a surprise, then, when the public simply does not become alarmed about a person whose conduct would motivate a professional diagnoser to employ the label, simple schizophrenic.

A third conclusion emerges from studies of happiness. The public rejects the synonymity of unhappiness and mental illness. People tend to regard their unhappiness as a response to concrete problems, interpersonal friction being one of the more frequent sources of these problems. They consider seeking help for their problems, particularly those problems which involve interpersonal relationships. When they seek help they use nonpsychiatric professionals, particularly clergymen, far more frequently than they use psychiatrically oriented professionals.

The generality of each of these three conclusions is tempered by variations in expressed attitudes associated with educational and socioeconomic status (SES). More financially secure and higher educated persons are more likely to use a mental illness orientation toward deviant behavior and unhappiness. They are more likely to think of Star's (1955) case descriptions as being cases of mental illness, and they have more of the "right" information about mental illness. When they seek help, they are inclined to consult professional psychiatric personnel. It is a fact that higher SES groups tend to hold beliefs that the locus of control of one's destiny is not exclusively "external." A well-educated person might reason as follows: "If the causes of my troubles are internal, then I shall consult a specialist on internal structures (mind, psyche), namely, a psychiatrist."

A fourth conclusion relates to the public's view of mental health personnel. The public appears to agree with the professionals on the demand for more mental health professionals. Like the professionals, the public believes there is a shortage of psychiatrically oriented personnel. The perceived lower quality of mental health professionals is reflected in the relative placement of psychiatric professionals in the status hierarchy. In addition, the public has a low opinion of the efficacy of psychiatric treatment, and expresses little confidence in the state of knowledge on psychiatric matters.

As was stated earlier, Lemkau and Crocetti (1962) interpret their data as leading to inferences that are not congruent with the results of other studies. The present analysis suggests that their results are not highly divergent from those of other researchers. They report, for example, that 50% of their sample could imagine themselves falling in love with someone who had been mentally ill. Obviously, this leaves 50% who might have responded negatively to this statement. Furthermore, their findings of 50% positive response is not startlingly different from the 32% positive responses found by Cumming and Cumming. Further, Lemkau and Crocetti found that large segments of the sample were willing to have persons who could be classified as mentally ill remain in the community. They interpret this as a sign that the mentally ill were not rejected. This interpretation hinges on the public "recognition" that the described persons were mentally ill. The description used by Lemkau and Crocetti in the part of the study directed to the question of who should be hospitalized did not identify the persons as being mentally ill. Their findings in fact offer support for the second conclusion as stated before: The public does not find it necessary to refer to deviant conduct as mental illness.

From these four specific conclusions, the present authors propose a general interpretive statement about the public's attitudes toward mental illness and health: The general public persists in seeing its own major recurring problems as deriving from matters of physical health, economics, morality, interpersonal relations, and other social issues. When people are unable to define their personal relationship to these problems, and when the strain from this lack of definition becomes particularly troublesome, the majority of persons profess a readiness to turn to professionals who are sanctioned by society to help define these problems. Most frequently, people seek help on problems involving interpersonal relationships, and the help source may be anyone who is willing to act as an intermediary. The public, in other words, has not "bought the mental health story" as applicable to itself. They feel there are "sick" people, and they should have help, but these are "other" people and not those persons within one's immediate world. They are not sure about how one identifies a mentally ill person. The man in the street will not use this category as freely as do professionals. Nevertheless, the public asserts that mentally ill people should have help available, and in fact, it is a good idea to move them out of the community when they are labeled as mentally ill.

reassessing mental health education

Even though the man in the street is not willing to look upon behavior deviation as mental illness, mental health professionals continue to promote the mental illness metaphor. A direct declaration of this position is found in *Action for Mental Health*, the final report of a many volumed series of reports issued by the Joint Commission on Mental Illness and Health (1961)—"the last word of the mental health establishment." In a section entitled "Rejection of the Mentally Ill," the Commission asserts its view of the current state of affairs:

> The principle of *sameness* as applied to the mentally sick versus the physically sick and the mentally sick versus the mentally well has become a cardinal tenet of mental health education. But this principle has largely fallen on deaf ears . . . [p. 59].

Despite the Joint Commission's general willingness to berate the public for its failure to adopt the mental illness metaphor, the Commission does make the following declaration.

Psychiatry has tried diligently *to make society see the mentally ill in its way*, and has railed at the public's antipathy or indifference. Wise men long have counseled that when a problem cannot be attacked frontally with good results *it should be turned around and viewed from the opposite side* [pp. 77–78, italics added].

None of the other studies in this review suggested the possibility that the mental illness concept might be unacceptable. Every investigator took a confident stand toward the "truth" that the public should "see the mentally ill in the psychiatric way." It is now time to turn the problem around. The viewpoint of the man in the street deserves a serious hearing. On what moral grounds should his viewpoint be regarded as less valid than that of the mental health professional?

The mental illness concept embodies a series of logical absurdities which forestall efforts to subsume certain classes of deviant behavior under the category of mental illness. As an example, let us consider the following circumstances: A wife begins to look upon her husband as having become a philanderer. No other person would agree with her that this is an "objective" event. The psychiatric, mental health ethos would require the man in the street to regard this woman as being mentally ill. If a psychiatrist were pressed to describe the features of her behavior which would allow this classification, he would undoubtedly say she is "out of touch with reality," or some other ontologically footless psychiatric conception. This troubled woman, together with the alcoholic and the juvenile character disorder (as portrayed in Star's, 1955, descriptions) are to be lumped together as cases of mental illness. What classification rules allow the behavior of these cases to be construed so that they become in some way synonymous with the suspicious wife? Are they, too, out of touch with reality? How can all these persons who behave deviantly, but in different ways, be regarded as exemplars of one inclusive category, mental illness? We can say that all three are behaving deviantly, and further, that their deviant behavior is disapproved. From the posture of the mental health propagandist, such disapproved although variegated deviant behaviors would all qualify as mental illness.

Although the investigators of the public's attitudes toward mental illness have held implicit expectations that the man in the street should be able to recognize his own mentally ill behavior, psychiatric personnel do not unequivocally inform us of how they themselves separate mental illness from any other unacceptable behavior. The writings on the topic of attitudes toward mental illness represent another example of a too easy acceptance of the illness metaphor, a metaphor that was originally intended to mollify the moralists who demanded the burning at the stake for those who behaved unacceptably. The writers about public attitudes have lost sight of the fact that they have been speaking metaphorically, and that there are no definitive criteria for separating mentally ill behavior from any other unacceptable behavior.

The confusion produced by this pursuit of an inapplicable metaphor is reflected in the public's attitude. The man in the street is reluctant to look upon deviant solutions to life's problems as mental illness. He might see deviant behaviors as unwise solutions, but a psychiatrist's help is not required in order for the deviant person to evolve a more acceptable solution. Psychiatrists, after all, are experts who work with sick people, patients with diseased minds. The man in the street is reluctant to be associated with mentally sick people. When a person is mentally diseased, he had better be isolated. Furthermore, when the layman recognizes personal problems in living, he knows that he is not sick. He is likely to indicate that he could use help, just as he could use help in solving any problem. He is unlikely, however, to consult a mental health professional.

He knows, after all, that most of his problems are matters of finances, physical ill health, and interpersonal frictions. He is likely to believe that he would not be helped, even if he were sick. In addition, he knows that he will lose status if he is known to be in the care of psychiatric personnel.

In their incisive summation of investigations into the incidence of mental illness, Dohrenwend and Dohrenwend (1965) further demonstrate the scientific weaknesses of the mental illness concept. They first bring together data that demonstrate a strong relationship between the percentage of the population judged to be psychiatrically disordered and the recency of the study. If the investigation were recently completed, it would more likely reveal a higher incidence of disorder. One could argue, among other things, that the techniques of diagnosis and investigation have improved, and that these improvements account for the rise in "discovered" incidence. Dohrenwend and Dohrenwend carefully lay this point aside, arguing that professionals have yet to produce valid measures of psychological disorder. They show that epidemiological studies have demonstrated one incontestable point: The lowest socioeconomic groups constantly are judged to have the highest rate of psychopathology. Dohrenwend and Dohrenwend are led to suggest "that the high level of symptomology in the lowest socioeconomic stratum represents, at least in part, . . . transient responses to stressors [p. 64]." They agree with the respondents in the happiness studies. The man in the street, particularly the occupant of a low SES, has told us that his unhappiness originates in identifiable problems. The mental health professional insists on disordered minds as the cause of the slum dweller's conduct; the public has not been willing to apply the myth of the professionals.

Mental health workers, themselves, provide another reason for public rejection of the mentally ill role. Despite professional protestations to the contrary, the prevailing academic view of mental illness is implicitly a negative one. Sarbin (1969) has already argued that a mentally ill person is relegated to a degraded status, to the social identity of a nonperson. The development of a professional lexicon (psychosis, mental illness, patients, etc.) only temporarily ameliorates this strongly negative evaluation. The euphemistic component of such labels fails to conceal the underlying reference: nonperson. The nonperson cannot manage his own affairs; he cannot deal with "reality," he must be "treated and cured." Other people must decide when he is well enough to face a bar of justice, and this is all done "for the good of the patient," who is obviously not capable of self-determination. When patienthood is construed in such fashion by professionals, how can the lay public (the ultimate targets of degradation) be expected to look upon mental illness as an appropriate designation for one's social identity? To work toward public acceptance of the professional definition of mental illness, with its attendant degraded status, is to be oblivious to a bare fact: To call any item of behavior a manifestation of mental illness means that the behaving person is then regarded as being incapable of personally bringing about a change in that behavior. He must, therefore, rely on others to implement the change, and moreover, he is incapable of deciding when a "proper" change has been achieved. Can we legitimately ask the man in the street to accept this nonperson status for himself and his friends?

The foregoing analysis gives charter to the present conclusion: the moral enterprise embodied in the well-intentioned work of mental health professionals has failed. Students of social science might explore the suggestion to look at "the other side." Our first job would be to answer the ontological question about mental illness. We would find that like so many other metaphors once useful, the metaphor of mental illness has been transformed into a myth. The arguments that mental illness meets all the criteria of myth are not repeated here (see Sarbin, 1967). Suffice it to say that insofar as mental illness stands for a set of dysfunctional fictions, the label becomes improper and futile. We are left with a far-reaching problem in jurisprudence, law enforcement, education, social engineering, and morality. The attitudes of the man in the street might be invoked to help find solutions to these problems. Rather than dressing him in the straight-jacket of a myth that has outlived its usefulness, we should consider accommodating our practices to his potentially useful metaphors.

The man in the street has too long been rejected as a contributor to official morality. Perhaps we can enlist his collaboration in a new moral enterprise—to set rules in regard to deviant or perplexing conduct. From the data at hand, the authors would predict his favoring a set of rules that would make obsolete the potentially derogating and disparaging employment of mental illness and mental health and the complicated medicolegal apparatus of psychiatric commitment, diagnosis, and hospitalization.

notes

1. To document this assertion, the authors refer to the midtown Manhattan study (Srole, Langner, Michael, Opeler, & Rennie, 1962) and the Stirling County study (Leighton, Harding, Macklin, Macmillan, & Leighton, 1963), both of which uncovered large numbers of cases who were residing in their communities, undiagnosed and unhospitalized, and deprived of the opportunity to acquire the status of a mental hospital patient.

2. The study cannot, in finality, tell us that a case is rejected. Phillips (1964) uses a "rejection" scale, but this gives no evidence that the highest score, 4.73, is really a rejecting score. This score, earned by the person whom professionals would diagnose as a paranoid schizophrenic male, is apparently higher than the rejection score earned by the normal male; but would the public refuse to accommodate to a person who receives a score of 4.73? Phillips used a Guttman-type scale, and these are, indeed, "high" scores in that they approach the greatest possible score of six. Nevertheless, as Crocetti and Lemkau (1965) point out, a score of 4.73 could well reflect *less* social distance than that which most whites place between themselves and members of defined ethnic minority groups.

3. On analysis, the findings of Yamamoto and Dizney (1967) and those of Rabkin and Suchoski (1967) are not contradictory. The differences derive from the conclusions drawn from the different sets of findings. The student-teachers in the study by Yamamoto and Dizney reflect the recurrent finding that persons who do not take a psychiatric orientation are able to envision a societal accommodation to behaviors that a mental health professional would wish to regard as being signs of mental illness. This leads Yamamoto and Dizney to advocate that the student teachers be "better educated." Rabkin and Suchoski, on the other hand, drew their conclusions from considering results on the Nunnally questionnaire. As Nunnally had already demonstrated, the general public does not differ radically from professionals on their view of the nature of mental illness. We would hardly expect that teachers, who might already have had extensive exposure to mental hygiene ideas, would be less well "informed" about mental illness than is the general public. The different conclusions from these two studies merely reflect the investigator's willingness to accept different indications of what reflects proper mental health education.

4. In the Elinson et al. (1967) study, one conclusion is not congruent with our general proposition. Respondents who reported that they had problems were asked to indicate where they had gone to seek help. About 79% had gone to mental health agencies, while 41% had used other professionals exclusively or in addition to mental health professionals.

references

Adorno, T. W., Frenkel-Brunswick, E., Levinson, D. J., & Sanford, R. N. *The authoritarian personality.* New York: Harper, 1950.

Becker, H. S. *Outsiders.* New York: Free Press, 1963.

Bradburn, N. M., & Caplovitz, D. *Reports on happiness.* Chicago: Aldine, 1965.

Crocetti, G. M., & Lemkau, P. V. On rejection of the mentally ill. *American Sociological Review,* 1965, *30,* 577–588.

Crumpton, E., Weinstein, A. D., Acker, C. W., & Annis, A. P. How patients and normals see the mental patient. *Journal of Clinical Psychology,* 1967, *23,* 46–49.

Cumming, E., & Cumming, J. *Closed ranks.* Cambridge: Harvard University Press, 1957.

Dohrenwend, B. P., & Chin-Shong, E. Social status and attitudes toward psychological disorder: The problem of tolerance of deviance. *American Sociological Review,* 1967, *32,* 417–433.

Dohrenwend, B. P., & Dohrenwend, B. S. The problem of validity in field studies of psychological disorder. *Journal of Abnormal and Social Psychology,* 1965, *70,* 52–69.

Elinson, J., Padilla, E., & Perkins, M. E. *Public image of mental health services.* New York: Mental Health Materials Center, 1967.

Freeman, H. E., & Kassebaum, G. E. Relationship of education and knowledge to opinions about mental illness. *Mental Hygiene,* 1960, *44,* 43–47.

Gilbert, D. C., & Levinson, D. J. Ideology, personality, and institutional policy in the mental hospital. *Journal of Abnormal and Social Psychology,* 1956, *53,* 263–271.

Giovannoni, J. M., & Ullmann, L. P. Conceptions of mental health held by psychiatric patients. *Journal of Clinical Psychology,* 1963, *19,* 398–400.

Gurin, G., Veroff, J., & Feld, S. *Americans view their mental health.* New York: Basic Books, 1960.

Hartung, F. E. *Crime, law and society.* Detroit: Wayne State University Press, 1965.

Hes, J. P. From native healer to modern psychiatrist. *Social Psychiatry,* 1966, *1,* 117–120.

Jahoda, M. *Current concepts of positive mental health.* New York: Basic Books, 1958.

Joint Commission on Mental Illness and Health. *Action for mental health.* New York: Basic Books, 1961.

Kahn, M. W., Jones, N. F., MacDonald, J. M., Conners, C. K., & Binchard, J. A factorial study of patient attitudes toward mental illness and psychiatric hospitalization. *Journal of Clinical Psychology,* 1963, *29,* 235–241.

Kahn, M. W., Lee, H., Jones, N. F., & Jin, S. K. A comparison of Korean and American mental patients' attitudes towards mental illness and hospitalization. *International Journal of Social Psychiatry,* 1966–1967, *13,* 14–20.

Leighton, D. C., Harding, J. S., Macklin, D. B., Macmillan, A. M., & Leighton, A. H. *The character of danger.* New York: Basic Books, 1963.

Lemkau, P. V., & Crocetti, G. M. An urban population's opinion and knowledge about mental illness. *American Journal of Psychiatry,* 1962, *118,* 692–700.

Maisel, A. Q. When would you consult a psychiatrist? *Colliers',* 1951, May 12, 13–15, 72–75.

Nunnally, J. *Popular conceptions of mental health.* New York: Holt, Rinehart & Winston, 1961.

Osgood, C. E., Suci, G. S., & Tannenbaum, P. H. *The measurement of meaning.* Urbana: University of Illinois Press, 1957.

Phillips, D. L. Rejection: A possible consequence of seeking help for mental disorders. *American Sociological Review,* 1963, *28,* 963–972.

Phillips, D. L. Rejection of the mentally ill: The influence of behavior and sex. *American Sociological Review*, 1964, *29*, 679–686.

Rabkin, L. Y., & Suchoski, J. F. Teachers' views of mental illness: A study of attitudes and information. *Journal of Teacher Education*, 1967, *18*, 36–41.

Sarbin, T. R. On the futility of the proposition that some people be labelled "mentally ill." *Journal of Consulting Psychology*, 1967, *31*, 447–453.

Sarbin, T. R. The scientific status of the mental illness metaphor. In S. C. Plog & R. B. Edgerton (Eds.), *Changing perspectives in mental illness*. New York: Holt, Rinehart & Winston, 1969.

Scott, W. A. Research definitions of mental health and mental illness. *Psychological Bulletin*, 1958, *55*, 29–45.

Srole, L., Langner, T. S., Michael, S. T., Opler, M. K., & Rennie, T. A. C. *Mental health in the metropolis: The midtown Manhattan study.* New York: McGraw-Hill, 1962.

Star, S. A. The public's ideas about mental illness. National Opinion Research Center, University of Chicago, 1955. (Mimeo)

Szasz, T. S. The problems of psychiatric nosology. *American Journal of Psychiatry*, 1957, *114*, 405–413.

Szasz, T. S. *The myth of mental illness.* New York: Hoeber, 1961.

Szasz, T. S. *Law, liberty, and psychiatry.* New York: Macmillan, 1963.

Woodward, J. L. Changing ideas on mental illness and its treatment. *American Sociological Review*, 1951, *16*, 443–454.

Yamamoto, K., & Dizney, H. F. Rejection of the mentally ill: A study of attitudes of student teachers. *Journal of Counseling Psychology*, 1967, *14*, 264–268.

THINK

1. Rosenhan and Zimbardo describe the deleterious situational effects that inhere in prisons and mental hospitals. To what extent are these psychological environments similar, and to what extent are they different? Does your answer suggest anything about the differences between hospitalized mental patients and convicts?

2. There seems to be no doubt that pseudopatients, such as graduate students, psychologists, and housewives, find the experience of psychiatric hospitalization intolerably dull. But Braginsky's study seems to suggest that in time, mental patients adopt the typical traits of institutional passivity and dependency. Even when given the opportunity to present themselves as less mentally ill and ready to be released, old timers appear to adopt the "sick role" and continue their hospitalizations. Is it possible that true psychiatric patients perceive the hospital differently than pseudopatients?

3. If there is a common thread that runs through all of the articles in the section, it is a thread that suggests that psychiatric hospitals and prisons are harmful places, and not the helpful places they were intended to be. Look through those articles again and see whether you can design environments that would be more therapeutic for psychiatric patients, environments that would be conducive to appropriate behavior change. Some of the ingredients concern altering the status of psychiatric patients themselves by giving them more power and making the staff more responsive to them. How might this be done?

4. Sarbin and Mancuso conclude that the public is not at all sympathetic towards persons who are labeled mentally ill. Their review of survey data shows that only persons who exhibit the most exaggerated deviations will be regarded as mentally ill, and even when they are so regarded the general public rarely makes the recommendation that such persons should be hospitalized. Professionals conclude from these data that the public needs to be educated toward greater tolerance for and understanding of mental illness, and that it needs to be desensitized of its fear and distrust of mental patients. Do you concur? Or is it possible that it is not the public that needs to be reeducated so much as it is the professionals who need to revise their labeling procedures for behavioral aberrations. Consider the study by Zigler and Philips in this context. Finally, assuming that both the public and the profession need to be reeducated, how might you initiate that process?

VI

The Rights of Psychiatric Patients

Throughout most of its history, abnormal psychology has been concerned with the diagnosis and treatment of disordered behavior, and nothing more. Certainly, that is a large enough problem, one that continues to defeat our best minds and finest research. But recently, we have come to realize that the problems of abnormal psychology extend beyond those narrow bounds, to the societies that treat troubled individuals and to the laws that protect those individuals even in their treatment.

Consider the person who has been entrusted to the care of a hospital against his will. He might have been committed because he was viewed as dangerous to himself, or dangerous to others. Or he might have been committed because it was alleged that he had performed a crime but, because of his psychological distress, was unable to advise his attorney. In so committing him to a hospital, society deprives him of many of his rights. He cannot move about freely. Often enough, he is denied the right to handle his own finances, to retain his driver's license—in short, to control his own affairs. Ostensibly, this is done for his protection. He is obviously troubled, so much so that he might make irreversible errors in the conduct of his affairs.

Depriving a person of his rights is, however, a serious matter. At the very least, it could be argued that society is obligated to restore those rights as quickly as possible by affording the person proper psychological treatment. After all, it was because he required treatment, not passive storage, that society committed him in the first place! Is there such a right as the "right to treatment" for people who are in psychiatric hospitals? And if such a right exists, how is it to be implemented? *Wyatt v. Stickney* (Reading 20) is an early, landmark "right to treatment" case, in which the court decided that patients have a legitimate right to active care. In the appendix to that decision the court went further and stipulated precisely how that right to treatment was to be implemented (Reading 21). It is an exciting verdict, one that is likely to form the basis for subsequent court battles in this area.

Social concerns with the treatment of the psychologically disordered are not limited merely to *whether* they should be treated, but also to *how* that treatment should be conducted. Consider behavior modification. Imagine a situation where, in order to induce behavioral change, you have to deprive an individual of powerful reinforcers, such as food; or one in which you have to apply aversive treatments such as painful shock. Is that permitted? What are the limits to which we can go in the name of treatment? These issues are taken up by David Wexler (Reading 22) and prove thorny indeed. The entire potential conflict between the requirements of treatment and the rights of patients come to a head in this article. Read it with care.

20
Wyatt v. Stickney

IN THE UNITED STATES DISTRICT COURT FOR
THE MIDDLE DISTRICT OF ALABAMA,
NORTHERN DIVISION

CIVIL ACTION NO. 3195-N
(Bryce Hospital and Searcy Hospital)

Ricky Wyatt, *et al.*,

Plaintiffs,

vs.

Dr. Stonewall B. Stickney, *et al.*,

Defendants,

United States of America, the American Psychological Association; the American Orthopsychiatric Association; the American Civil Liberties Union, and the American Association on Mental Deficiency,

Amici Curiae.

order and decree

This class action originally was filed on October 23, 1970, in behalf of patients involuntarily confined for mental treatment purposes at Bryce Hospital, Tuscaloosa, Alabama. On March 12, 1971, in a formal opinion and decree, this Court held that these involuntarily committed patients "unquestionably have a constituted right to receive such individual treatment as will give each of them a realistic opportunity to be cured or to improve his or her mental condition." The Court further held that patients at Bryce were being denied their right to treatment and that defendants, per their request, would be allowed six months in which to raise the level of care at Bryce to the constitutionally required minimum. *Wyatt v. Stickney*, 325 F.Supp. 781 (M.D. Ala. 1971). In this decree, the Court ordered defendants to file reports defining the mission and functions of Bryce Hospital, specifying the objective and subjective standards required to furnish adequate care to the treatable mentally ill and detailing the hospital's progress toward the implementation of minimum constitutional standards. Subsequent to this order, plaintiffs, by motion to amend granted August 12, 1971, enlarged their class to include patients involuntarily confined for mental treatment at Searcy Hospital[1] and at Partlow State School and Hospital for the mentally retarded.[2]

On September 23, 1971, defendants filed their final report, from which this Court concluded on December 10, 1971, that defendants had failed to promulgate and implement a treatment program satisfying minimum medical and constitutional requisites. Generally, the Court found that defendants' treatment program was deficient in three fundamental areas. It failed to provide: (1) a humane psychological and physical environment, (2) qualified staff in numbers sufficient to administer adequate treatment, and (3) individualized treatment plans. More specifically, the Court found that many conditions, such as nontherapeutic, uncompensated work assignments, and the absence of any semblance of privacy, constituted dehumanizing factors contributing to the degeneration of the patients' self-esteem. The physical facilities at Bryce were overcrowded and plagued by fire and other emergency hazards. The Court found also that most staff members were poorly trained and that staffing ratios were so inadequate as to render the administration of effective treatment impossible. The Court concluded, therefore, that whatever treatment was provided at Bryce was grossly deficient and failed to satisfy minimum medical and constitutional standards. Based upon this conclusion, the Court ordered that a formal hearing be held at which the parties and amici[3] would have the opportunity to submit proposed standards for constitutionally adequate treatment and to present expert testimony in support of their proposals.

Pursuant to this order, a hearing was held at which the foremost authorities on mental health in the United States appeared and testified as to the minimum medical and constitutional requisites for public institutions, such as Bryce and Searcy, designed to treat the mentally ill. At this hearing, the parties and amici submitted their proposed standards, and now have filed briefs in support of them.[4] Moreover, the parties and amici have stipulated to a broad spectrum of conditions they feel are mandatory for a constitutionally acceptable minimum treatment program. This Court, having considered the evidence in the case, as well as the briefs, proposed standards and stipulations of the parties, has concluded that the standards set out in Appendix A to this decree are medical and constitutional minimums. Consequently, the Court will order their implementation.[5] In so ordering, however, the Court emphasizes that these standards are, indeed, both medical and constitutional minimums and should be viewed as such. The Court urges that once this order is effectuated, defendants not become complacent and self-satisfied. Rather, they should dedicate themselves to providing physical conditions and treatment programs at Alabama's mental institutions that substantially exceed medical and constitutional minimums.

In addition to asking that their proposed standards be effectuated, plaintiffs and amici have requested other relief designed to guarantee the provision of constitutional and humane treatment. Pursuant to one such request for relief, this Court has determined that it is appropriate to order the initiation of human rights committees to function as standing committees of the Bryce and Searcy facilities. The Court will appoint the members of these committees who shall have review of all research proposals and all rehabilitation programs, to ensure that the dignity and the human rights of patients are preserved. The committees also shall advise and assist patients who allege that their legal rights have been infringed or that the Mental Health Board has failed to comply with judicially ordered guidelines. At its discretion, the committees may consult appropriate, independent specialists who shall be compensated by the defendant Board. Seven members shall comprise the human rights committee for each institution, the names and addresses of whom are set forth in Appendix B to this decree. Those who serve on the committees shall be paid on a per diem basis and be reimbursed for travel expenses at the same rate as members of the Alabama Board of Mental Health.

This Court will reserve ruling upon other forms of relief advocated by plaintiffs and amici, including their prayer for the appointment of a master and a professional advisory committee to oversee the implementation of the court-ordered minimum constitutional standards.[6] Federal courts are reluctant to assume control of any organization, but especially one operated by a state. This reluctance, combined with defendants' expressed intent that this order will be implemented forthwith and in good faith, causes the Court to withhold its decision on these appointments. Nevertheless, defendants, as well the other parties and amici in this case, are placed on notice that unless defendants do comply satisfactorily with this order, the Court will be obligated to appoint a master.

Because the availability of financing may bear upon the implementation of this order, the Court is constrained to emphasize at this juncture that a failure by defendants to comply with this decree cannot be justified by a lack of operating funds. As previously established by this Court:

> "There can be no legal (or moral) justification for the State of Alabama's failing to afford treatment—and adequate treatment from a medical standpoint—to the several thousand patients who have been civilly committed to Bryce's for treatment purposes. To deprive any citizen of his or her liberty upon the altruistic theory that the confinement is for humane therapeutic reasons and then fail to provide adequate treatment violates the very fundamentals of due process." Wyatt v. Stickney, 325 F. Supp. at 785.

From the above, it follows consistently, of course, that the unavailability of neither funds, nor staff and facilities, will justify a default by defendants in the provision of suitable treatment for the mentally ill.

Despite the possibility that defendants will encounter financial difficulties in the implementation of this order, this Court has decided to reserve ruling also upon plaintiffs' motion that defendant Mental Health Board be directed to sell or encumber portions of its land holdings in order to raise funds.[7] Similarly, this Court will reserve ruling on plaintiffs' motion seeking an injunction against the treasurer and the comptroller of the State authorizing expenditures for nonessential State functions, and on other aspects of plaintiffs' requested relief designed to ameliorate the financial problems incident to the implementation of this order. The Court stresses, however, the extreme importance and the grave immediacy of the need for proper funding of the State's public mental health facilities. The responsibility for appropriate funding ultimately must fall, of course, upon the State Legislature and, to a lesser degree, upon the defendant Mental Health Board of Alabama. For the present time, the Court will defer to those bodies in hopes that they will proceed with the realization and understanding that what is involved in this case is not representative of ordinary governmental functions such as paving roads and maintaining buildings. Rather, what is so inextricably intertwined with how the Legislature and Mental Health Board respond to the revelations of this litigation is the very preservation of human life and dignity. Not only are the lives of the patients currently confined at Bryce and Searcy at stake, but also at issue are the well-being and security of every citizen of Alabama. As is true in the case of any disease, no one is immune from the peril of mental illness. The problem, therefore, cannot be overemphasized and a prompt response from the Legislature, the Mental Health Board and other responsible State officials, is imperative.

In the event, though, that the Legislature fails to satisfy its well-defined constitutional obligation, and the Mental Health Board, because of lack of funding or any other legally insufficient reason, fails to implement fully the standards herein ordered, it will be necessary for the Court to take affirmative steps, including appointing a master, to ensure that proper funding is realized[8] and that adequate treatment is available for the mentally ill of Alabama.

This Court now must consider that aspect of plaintiffs' motion of March 15, 1972, seeking an injunction against further commitments to Bryce and Searcy until such time as adequate treatment is supplied in those hospitals. Indisputably, the evidence in this case reflects that no treatment program at the Bryce-Searcy facilities approaches constitutional standards. Nevertheless, because of the alternatives to commitment commonly utilized in Alabama, as well as in other states, the Court is fearful that granting plaintiffs' request at the present time would serve only to punish and further deprive Alabama's mentally ill.

Finally, the Court has determined that this case requires the awarding of a reasonable attorneys' fee to plaintiffs' counsel. The basis for the award and the amount thereof will be considered and treated in a separate order. The fee will be charged against the defendants as a part of the court costs in this case.

To assist the Court in its determination of how to proceed henceforth, defendants will be directed to prepare and file a report within six months from the date of this decree detailing the implementation of each standard herein ordered. This report shall be comprehensive and shall include a statement of the progress made on each standard not yet completely implemented, specifying the reasons for incomplete performance. The report shall include also a statement of the financing secured since the issuance of this decree and of defendants' plans for procuring whatever additional financing might be required. Upon the basis of this report and other available information, the Court will evaluate defendants' work and, in due course, determine the appropriateness of appointing a master and of granting other requested relief.

Accordingly, it is the ORDER, JUDGMENT, and DECREE of this Court:

1. That defendants be and they are hereby enjoined from failing to implement fully and with dispatch each of the standards set forth in Appendix A attached hereto and incorporated as a part of this decree;
2. That human rights committees be and are hereby designated and appointed. The members thereof are listed in Appendix B attached hereto and incorporated herein. These committees shall have the purposes, functions, and spheres of operation previously set forth in this order. The members of the committees shall be paid on a per diem basis and be reimbursed for travel expenses at the same rate as members of the Alabama Board of Mental Health;
3. That defendants, within six months from this date, prepare and file with this Court a report reflecting in detail the progress on the implementation of this order. This report shall be comprehensive and precise, and shall explain the reasons for incomplete performance in the event defendants have not met a standard in its entirety. The report also shall include a financial statement and up-to-date timetable for full compliance.
4. That the court costs incurred in this proceeding, including a reasonable attorneys' fee for plantiffs' lawyers, be and they are hereby taxed against the defendants;
5. That jurisdiction of this cause be and the same is hereby specifically retained.

It is further ORDERED that ruling on plaintiffs' motion for further relief, including the appointment of a master, filed March 15, 1972, be and the same is hereby reserved.

Done, this the 13th day of April, 1972.

/s/ Frank Johnson
UNITED STATES DISTRICT JUDGE

notes

1. Searcy Hospital, located in Mount Vernon, Alabama, is also a State institution designed to treat the mentally ill. On September 2, 1971, defendants answered plaintiffs' amended complaint, as it related to Searcy, with the following language:

Defendants agree to be bound by the objective and subjective standards ultimately ordered by this Honorable Court in this cause at both Bryce and Searcy.

This answer obviated the necessity for this Court's holding a formal hearing on the conditions currently existing at Searcy. Nevertheless, the evidence in the record relative to Searcy reflects that the conditions at that institution are no better than those at Bryce.

2. The aspect of the case relating to Partlow State School and Hospital for the mentally retarded will be considered by the Court in a decree separate from the present one.

3. The amici in this case, including the United States of America, the American Orthopsychiatric Association, the American Psychological Association, the American Civil Liberties Union, and the American Association on Mental Deficiency, have performed exemplary service for which this Court is indeed grateful.

4. On March 15, 1972, after the hearing in this case, plaintiffs filed a motion for further relief. This motion served, among other things, to renew an earlier motion, filed by plaintiffs on September 1, 1971, and subsequently denied by the Court, to add additional parties. That earlier motion asked that the Court add:

Agnes Baggett, as Treasurer of the State of Alabama; Roy W. Sanders, as Comptroller of the State of Alabama; Ruben King, as Commissioner of the Alabama Department of Pensions and Security, George C. Wallace as Chairman of the Alabama State Board of Pensions and Security, and James J. Bailey as a member of the Alabama State Board of Pensions and Security and as representative of all other members of the Alabama State Board of Pensions and Security; J. Stanley Frazer, as Director of the Alabama State Personnel Board and Ralph W. Adams, as a member of the Alabama State Personnel Board and as representative of all other members of the Alabama State Personnel Board.

The motion of September 1, 1971, also sought an injunction against the treasurer and the comptroller of the State paying out State funds for "non-essential functions" of the State until enough funds were available to provide adequately for the financial needs of the Alabama State Mental Health Board.

In their motion of March 15, 1972, plaintiffs asked that, in addition to the above-named State officials and agencies, the Court add as parties to this litigation Dr. LeRoy Brown, State Superintendent of Education and Lt. Governor Jere Beasley, State Senator Pierre Pelham and State Representative Sage Lyons, as representatives of the Alabama Legislature. The motion of March 15, 1972, also requested the Court to appoint a master, to appoint a human rights committee and a professional advisory committee, to order the sale of defendant Mental Health Board's land holdings and other assets to raise funds for the operation of Alabama's mental health institutions, to enjoin the construction of any physical facilities by the Mental Health Board and to enjoin the commitment of any more patients to Bryce and Searcy until such time as adequate treatment is supplied in those hospitals.

5. In addition to the standards detailed in this order, it is appropriate that defendants comply also with the conditions, applicable to mental health institutions, necessary to qualify Alabama's facilities for participation in the various programs, such as Medicare and Medicaid, funded by the United States Government. Because many of these conditions of participation have not yet been finally drafted and published, however, this Court will not at this time order that specific Government standards be implemented.

6. The Court's decision to reserve its ruling on the appointment of a master necessitates the reservation also of the Court's appointing a professional advisory committee to aid the master. Nevertheless, the Court notes that the professional mental

health community in the United States has responded with enthusiasm to the proposed initiation of such a committee to assist in the upgrading of Alabama's mental health facilities. Consequently, this Court strongly recommends to defendants that they develop a professional advisory committee comprised of amenable professionals from throughout the country who are able to provide the expertise the evidence reflects is important to the successful implementation of this order.

7. See n. 4, supra. The evidence presented in this case reflects that the land holdings and other assets of the defendant Board are extensive.

8. The Court understands and appreciates that the Legislature is not due back in regular session until May, 1973. Nevertheless, special sessions of the Legislature are frequent occurrences in Alabama, and there has never been a time when such a session was more urgently required. If the Legislature does not act promptly to appropriate the necessary funding for mental health, the Court will be compelled to grant plaintiffs' motion to add various State officials and agencies as additional parties to this litigation, and to utilize other avenues of fund raising.

21
Minimum Constitutional Standards for Adequate Treatment of the Mentally Ill

I. definitions:

a. "Hospital"—Bryce and Searcy Hospitals.

b. "Patients"—all persons who are now confined and all persons who may in the future be confined at Bryce and Searcy Hospitals pursuant to an involuntary civil commitment procedure.

c. "Qualified Mental Health Professional"—

(1) a psychiatrist with three years of residency training in psychiatry;

(2) a psychologist with a doctoral degree from an accredited program;

(3) a social worker with a master's degree from an accredited program and two years of clinical experience under the supervision of a Qualified Mental Health Professional;

(4) a registered nurse with a graduate degree in psychiatric nursing and two years of clinical experience under the supervision of a Qualified Mental Health Professional.

d. "Non-Professional Staff Member"—an employee of the hospital, other than a Qualified Mental Health Professional, whose duties require contact with or supervision of patients.

II. humane psychological and physical environment:

1. Patients have a right to privacy and dignity.

2. Patients have a right to the least restrictive conditions necessary to achieve the purposes of commitment.

3. No person shall be deemed incompetent to manage his affairs, to contract, to hold professional or occupational or vehicle operator's licenses, to marry

Addendum to Wyatt v. Stickney.

and obtain a divorce, to register and vote, or to make a will *solely* by reason of his admission or commitment to the hospital.

4. Patients shall have the same rights to visitation and telephone communications as patients at other public hospitals, except to the extent that the Qualified Mental Health Professional responsible for formulation of a particular patient's treatment plan writes an order imposing special restrictions. The written order must be renewed after each periodic review of the treatment plan if any restrictions are to be continued. Patients shall have an unrestricted right to visitation with attorneys and with private physicians and other health professionals.

5. Patients shall have an unrestricted right to send sealed mail. Patients shall have an unrestricted right to receive sealed mail from their attorneys, private physicians, and other mental health professionals, from courts, and government officials. Patients shall have a right to receive sealed mail from others, except to the extent that the Qualified Mental Health Professional responsible for formulation of a particular patient's treatment plan writes an order imposing special restrictions on receipt of sealed mail. The written order must be renewed after each periodic review of the treatment plan if any restrictions are to be continued.

6. Patients have a right to be free from unnecessary or excessive medication. No medication shall be administered unless at the written order of a physician. The superintendent of the hospital and the attending physician shall be responsible for all medication given or administered to a patient. The use of medication shall not exceed standards of use that are advocated by the United States Food and Drug Administration. Notation of each individual's medication shall be kept in his medical records. At least weekly the attending physician shall review the drug regimen of each patient under his care. All prescriptions shall be written with a termination date, which shall not exceed 30 days. Medication shall not be used as punishment, for the convenience of staff, as a substitute for program, or in quantities that interfere with the patient's treatment program.

7. Patients have a right to be free from physical restraint and isolation. Except for emergency situations, in which it is likely that patients could harm themselves or others and in which less restrictive means of restraint are not feasible, patients may be physically restrained or placed in isolation only on a Qualified Mental Health Professional's written order which explains the rationale for such action. The written order may be entered only after the Qualified Mental Health Professional has personally seen the patient concerned and evaluated whatever episode or situation is said to call for restraint or isolation. Emergency use of restraints or isolation shall be for no more than one hour, by which time a Qualified Mental Health Professional shall have been consulted and shall have entered an appropriate order in writing. Such written order shall be effective for no more than 24 hours and must be renewed if restraint and isolation are to be continued. While in restraint or isolation the patient must be seen by qualified ward personnel who will chart the patient's physical condition (if it is compromised) and psychiatric condition every hour. The patient must have bathroom privileges every hour and must be bathed every 12 hours.

8. Patients shall have a right not to be subjected to experimental research without the express and informed consent of the patient, if the patient is able to give such consent, and of his guardian or next of kin, after opportunities for consultation with independent specialists and with legal counsel. Such proposed research shall first have been reviewed and approved by the institution's Human Rights Committee before such consent shall be sought. Prior to such approval the Committee shall determine that such research complies with the principles of the Statement on the Use of Human Subjects for Research of the American Associa-

tion on Mental Deficiency and with the principles for research involving human subjects required by the United States Department of Health, Education and Welfare for projects supported by that agency.

9. Patients have a right not to be subjected to treatment procedures such as lobotomy, electro-convulsive treatment, adversive reinforcement conditioning or other unusual or hazardous treatment procedures without their express and informed consent after consultation with counsel or interested party of the patient's choice.

10. Patients have a right to receive prompt and adequate medical treatment for any physical ailments.

11. Patients have a right to wear their own clothes and to keep and use their own personal possessions except insofar as such clothes or personal possessions may be determined by a Qualified Mental Health Professional to be dangerous or otherwise inappropriate to the treatment regimen.

12. The hospital has an obligation to supply an adequate allowance of clothing to any patients who do not have suitable clothing of their own. Patients shall have the opportunity to select from various types of neat, clean, and seasonable clothing. Such clothing shall be considered the patient's throughout his stay in the hospital.

13. The hospital shall make provision for the laundering of patient clothing.

14. Patients have a right to regular physical exercise several times a week. Moreover, it shall be the duty of the hospital to provide facilities and equipment for such exercise.

15. Patients have a right to be outdoors at regular and frequent intervals, in the absence of medical considerations.

16. The right to religious worship shall be accorded to each patient who desires such opportunities. Provisions for such worship shall be made available to all patients on a nondiscriminatory basis. No individual shall be coerced into engaging in any religious activities.

17. The institution shall provide, with adequate supervision, suitable opportunities for the patient's interaction with members of the opposite sex.

18. The following rules shall govern patient labor:

A. *Hospital Maintenance.* No patient shall be required to perform labor which involves the operation and maintenance of the hospital or for which the hospital is under contract with an outside organization. Privileges or release from the hospital shall not be conditioned upon the performance of labor covered by this provision. Patients may voluntarily engage in such labor if the labor is compensated in accordance with the minimum wage laws of the Fair Labor Standards Act, 29 U.S.C. § 206 as amended, 1966.

B. *Therapeutic Tasks and Therapeutic Labor.* (1) Patients may be required to perform therapeutic tasks which do not involve the operation and maintenance of the hospital, provided the specific task or any change in assignment is:

(a) An integrated part of the patient's treatment plan and approved as a therapeutic activity by a Qualified Mental Health Professional responsible for supervising the patient's treatment; and

(b) supervised by a staff member to oversee the therapeutic aspects of the activity.

(2) Patients may voluntarily engage in therapeutic labor for which the hospital would otherwise have to pay an employee, provided the specific labor or any change in labor assignment is:

(a) An integrated part of the patient's treatment plan and approved as a therapeutic activity by a Qualified Mental Health Professional responsible for supervising the patient's treatment; and

(b) supervised by a staff member to oversee the therapeutic aspects of the activity; and

(c) compensated in accordance with the minimum wage laws of the Fair Labor Standards Act, 29 U.S.C. § 206 as amended, 1966.

C. *Personal Housekeeping.* Patients may be required to perform tasks of a personal housekeeping nature such as the making of one's own bed.

D. Payment to patients pursuant to these paragraphs shall not be applied to the costs of hospitalization.

19. *Physical Facilities.* A patient has a right to humane psychological and physical environment within the hospital facilities. These facilities shall be designed to afford patients with comfort and safety, promote dignity, and ensure privacy. The facilities shall be designed to make a positive contribution to the efficient attainment of the treatment goals of the hospital.

A. *Resident Unit.* The number of patients in a multi-patient room shall not exceed six persons. There shall be allocated a minimum of 80 square feet of floor space per patient in a multi-patient room. Screens or curtains shall be provided to ensure privacy within the resident unit. Single rooms shall have a minimum of 100 square feet of floor space. Each patient will be furnished with a comfortable bed with adequate changes of linen, a closet or locker for his personal belongings, a chair, and a bedside table.

B. *Toilets and Lavatories.* There will be one toilet provided for each eight patients and one lavatory for each six patients. A lavatory will be provided with each toilet facility. The toilets will be installed in separate stalls to ensure privacy, will be clean and free of odor, and will be equipped with appropriate safety devices for the physically handicapped.

C. *Showers.* There will be one tub or shower for each 15 patients. If a central bathing area is provided, each shower area will be divided by curtains to ensure privacy. Showers and tubs will be equipped with adequate safety accessories.

D. *Day Room.* The minimum day room area shall be 40 square feet per patient. Day rooms will be attractive and adequately furnished with reading lamps, tables, chairs, television and other recreational facilities. They will be conveniently located to patients' bedrooms and shall have outside windows. There shall be at least one day room area on each bedroom floor in a multi-story hospital. Areas used for corridor traffic cannot be counted as day room space; nor can a chapel with fixed pews be counted as a day room area.

E. *Dining Facilities.* The minimum dining room area shall be ten square feet per patient. The dining room shall be separate from the kitchen and will be furnished with comfortable chairs and tables with hard, washable surfaces.

F. *Linen Servicing and Handling.* The hospital shall provide adequate facilities and equipment for handling clean and soiled bedding and other linen. There must be frequent changes of bedding and other linen, no less than every seven days, to assure patient comfort.

G. *Housekeeping.* Regular housekeeping and maintenance procedures which will ensure that the hospital is maintained in a safe, clean, and attractive condition will be developed and implemented.

H. *Geriatric and Other Nonambulatory Mental Patients.* There must be special facilities for geriatric and other nonambulatory patients to assure their safety and comfort, including special fittings on toilets and wheel chairs. Appropriate provision shall be made to permit nonambulatory patients to communicate their needs to staff.

I. *Physical Plant.* (1) Pursuant to an established routine maintenance and repair program, the physical plant shall be kept in a continuous state of good repair and operation in accordance with the needs of the health, comfort, safety and well-being of the patients. (2) Adequate heating, air conditioning and ventilation systems and equipment shall be afforded to maintain temperatures and air changes which are required for the comfort of patients at all times and the removal of undesired heat, steam and offensive odors. Such facilities shall ensure that the temperature in the hospital shall not exceed 83°F nor fall below 68°F. (3) Thermostatically controlled hot water shall be provided in adequate quantities and maintained at the required temperature for patient or resident use (110°F at the fixture) and for mechanical dishwashing and laundry use (180°F at the equipment). (4) Adequate refuse facilities will be provided so that solid waste, rubbish and other refuse will be collected and disposed of in a manner which will prohibit transmission of disease and not create a nuisance or fire hazard or provide a breeding place for rodents and insects. (5) The physical facilities must meet all fire and safety standards established by the state and locality. In addition, the hospital shall meet such provisions of the Life Safety Code of the National Fire Protection Association (21st edition, 1967) as are applicable to hospitals.

19A. The hospital shall meet all standards established by the state for general hospitals, insofar as they are relevant to psychiatric facilities.

20. *Nutritional Standards.* Patients, except for the nonmobile, shall eat or be fed in dining rooms. The diet for patients will provide at a minimum the Recommended Daily Dietary Allowances as developed by the National Academy of Sciences. Menus shall be satisfying and nutritionally adequate to provide the Recommended Daily Dietary Allowances. In developing such menus, the hospital will utilize the Low Cost Food Plan of the Department of Agriculture. The hospital will not spend less per patient for raw food, including the value of donated food, than the most recent per person costs of the Low Cost Food Plan for the Southern Region of the United States, as compiled by the United States Department of Agriculture, for appropriate groupings of patients, discounted for any savings which might result from institutional procurement of such food. Provisions shall be made for special therapeutic diets and for substitutes at the request of the patient, or his guardian or next of kin, in accordance with the religious requirements of any patient's faith. Denial of a nutritionally adequate diet shall not be used as punishment.

III. qualified staff in numbers sufficient to administer adequate treatment

21. Each Qualified Mental Health Professional shall meet all licensing and certification requirements promulgated by the State of Alabama for persons engaged in private practice of the same profession elsewhere in Alabama. Other staff members shall meet the same licensing and certification requirements as persons who engage in private practice of their speciality elsewhere in Alabama.

22. (a) All Non-Professional Staff Members who have not had prior clinical experience in a mental institution shall have a substantial orientation training. (b) Staff members on all levels shall have regularly scheduled in-service training.

23. Each Non-Professional Staff Member shall be under the direct supervision of a Qualified Mental Health Professional.

24. *Staffing Ratios.* The hospital shall have the following minimum numbers of treatment personnel per 250 patients. Qualified Mental Health Professionals trained in particular disciplines may in appropriate situations perform services or functions traditionally performed by members of other disciplines. Changes in staff deployment may be made with prior approval of this Court upon a clear and convincing demonstration that the proposed deviation from this staffing structure will enhance the treatment of the patients.

CLASSIFICATION	NUMBER OF EMPLOYEES
Unit Director	1
Psychiatrist (3 years' residency training in psychiatry)	2
MD (Registered physicians)	4
Nurses (RN)	12
Licensed Practical Nurses	6
Aide III	6
Aide II	16
Aide I	70
Hospital Orderly	10
Clerk Stenographer II	3
Clerk Typist II	3
Unit Administrator	1
Administrative Clerk	1
Psychologist (Ph.D.) (doctoral degree from accredited program)	1
Psychologist (M.A.)	1
Psychologist (B.S.)	2
Social Worker (MSW) (from accredited program)	2
Social Worker (B.A.)	5
Patient Activity Therapist (M.S.)	1
Patient Activity Aide	10
Mental Health Technician	10
Dental Hygienist	1
Chaplain	.5
Vocational Rehabilitation Counselor	1
Volunteer Services Worker	1
Mental Health Field Representative	1
Dietitian	1
Food Service Supervisor	1
Cook II	2
Cook I	3
Food Service Worker	15
Vehicle Driver	1
Housekeeper	10
Messenger	1
Maintenance Repairman	2

IV. individualized treatment plans

25. Each patient shall have a comprehensive physical and mental examination and review of behavioral status within 48 hours after admission to the hospital.

26. Each patient shall have an individualized treatment plan. This plan shall be developed by appropriate Qualified Mental Health Professionals, including a psychiatrist, and implemented as soon as possible—in any event no later than five days after the patient's admission. Each individualized treatment plan shall contain:

(a) a statement of the nature of the specific problems and specific needs of the patient;

(b) a statement of the least restrictive treatment conditions necessary to achieve the purposes of commitment;

(c) a description of intermediate and long-range treatment goals, with a projected timetable for their attainment;

(d) a statement and rationale for the plan of treatment for achieving these intermediate and long-range goals;

(e) a specification of staff responsibility and a description of proposed staff involvement with the patient in order to attain these treatment goals;

(f) criteria for release to less restrictive treatment conditions, and criteria for discharge;

(g) a notation of any therapeutic tasks and labor to be performed by the patient in accordance with Standard 18.

27. As part of his treatment plan, each patient shall have an individualized post-hospitalization plan. This plan shall be developed by a Qualified Mental Health Professional as soon as practicable after the patient's admission to the hospital.

28. In the interests of continuity of care, whenever possible, one Qualified Mental Health Professional (who need not have been involved with the development of the treatment plan) shall be responsible for supervising the implementation of the treatment plan, integrating the various aspects of the treatment program and recording the patient's progress. This Qualified Mental Health Professional shall also be responsible for ensuring that the patient is released, where appropriate, into a less restrictive form of treatment.

29. The treatment plan shall be continuously reviewed by the Qualified Mental Health Professional responsible for supervising the implementation of the plan and shall be modified if necessary. Moreover, at least every 90 days, each patient shall receive a mental examination from, and his treatment plan shall be reviewed by, a Qualified Mental Health Professional other than the professional responsible for supervising the implementation of the plan.

30. In addition to treatment for mental disorders, patients confined at mental health institutions also are entitled to and shall receive appropriate treatment for physical illnesses such as tuberculosis.[1] In providing medical care, the State Board of Mental Health shall take advantage of whatever community-based facilities are appropriate and available and shall coordinate the patient's treatment for mental illness with his medical treatment.

31. Complete patient records shall be kept on the ward in which the patient is placed and shall be available to anyone properly authorized in writing by the patient. These records shall include:

(a) Identification data, including the patient's legal status;

(b) A patient history, including but not limited to:

(1) family data, educational background, and employment record;

(2) prior medical history, both physical and mental, including prior hospitalization;

(c) The chief complaints of the patient and the chief complaints of others regarding the patient;

(d) An evaluation which notes the onset of illness, the circumstances leading to admission, attitudes, behavior, estimate of intellectual functioning, memory functioning, orientation, and an inventory of the patient's assets in descriptive, not interpretative, fashion;

(e) A summary of each physical examination, which describes the results of the examination;

(f) A copy of the individual treatment plan and any modifications thereto;

(g) A detailed summary of the findings made by the reviewing Qualified Mental Health Professional after each periodic review of the treatment plan which analyzes the successes and failures of the treatment program and directs whatever modifications are necessary;

(h) A copy of the individualized post-hospitalization plan and any modifications thereto, and a summary of the steps that have been taken to implement that plan;

(i) A medication history and status, which includes the signed orders of the prescribing physician. Nurses shall indicate by signature that orders have been carried out;

(j) A detailed summary of each significant contact by a Qualified Mental Health Professional with the patient;

(k) A detailed summary on at least a weekly basis by a Qualified Mental Health Professional involved in the patient's treatment of the patient's progress along the treatment plan;

(l) A weekly summary of the extent and nature of the patient's work activities described in Standard 18, *supra*, and the effect of such activity upon the patient's progress along the treatment plan;

(m) A signed order by a Qualified Mental Health Professional for any restrictions on visitations and communication, as provided in Standards 4 and 5, *supra*;

(n) A signed order by a Qualified Mental Health Professional for any physical restraints and isolation, as provided in Standard 7, *supra*;

(o) A detailed summary of any extraordinary incident in the hospital involving the patient to be entered by a staff member noting that he has personal knowledge of the incident or specifying his other source of information, and initialed within 24 hours by a Qualified Mental Health Professional;

(p) A summary by the superintendent of the hospital or his appointed agent of his findings after the 15-day review provided for in Standard 33 *infra*.

32. In additional to complying with all the other standards herein, a hospital shall make special provisions for the treatment of patients who are children and young adults. These provisions shall include but are not limited to:

(a) Opportunities for publicly supported education suitable to the educational needs of the patient. This program of education must, in the opinion of the attending Qualified Mental Health Professional, be compatible with the patient's mental condition and his treatment program, and otherwise be in the patient's best interest.

(b) A treatment plan which considers the chronological, maturational, and development level of the patient;

(c) Sufficient Qualified Mental Health Professionals, teachers, and staff members with specialized skills in the care and treatment of children and young adults;

(d) Recreational and play opportunities in the open air where possible and appropriate residential facilities;

(c) Arrangements for contact between the hospital and the family of the patient.

33. No later than 15 days after a patient is committed to the hospital, the superintendent of the hospital or his appointed, professionally qualified agent shall examine the committed patient and shall determine whether the patient continues to require hospitalization and whether a treatment plan complying with Standard 26 has been implemented. If the patient no longer requires hospitalization in accordance with the standards for commitment, or if a treatment plan has not been implemented, he must be released immediately unless he agrees to continue with treatment on a voluntary basis.

34. The Mental Health Board and its agents have an affirmative duty to provide adequate transitional treatment and care for all patients released after a period of involuntary confinement. Transitional care and treatment possibilities include, but are not limited to, psychiatric day care, treatment in the home by a visiting therapist, nursing home or extended care, out-patient treatment, and treatment in the psychiatric ward of a general hospital.

V. miscellaneous

35. Each patient and his family, guardian or next friend shall promptly upon the patient's admission receive written notice, in language he understands, of all the above standards for adequate treatment. In addition a copy of all the above standards shall be posted in each ward.

note

1. Approximately 50 patients at Bryce-Searcy are tubercular as also are approximately four residents at Partlow.

22
Token and Taboo:
BEHAVIOR MODIFICATION, TOKEN ECONOMIES,
AND THE LAW

David B. Wexler

Not surprisingly, legal concepts from the prisoners' rights movement have begun to spill over into the area of the rights of the institutionalized mentally ill. Since the mental patient movement is free of the law and order backlash that re-

Reprinted with permission from *California Law Review*, v.61:81, pp. 81–108.

strains the legal battles of prisoners, it may evoke considerable sympathy from the public, the legislatures, and the courts.

Commentators and authorities have recently directed attention to important procedural problems in the administration of psychiatric justice[1] and the legal issues presented by various methods of therapy. Legal restrictions on a hospital's right to subject unwilling patients to electroconvulsive therapy[2] and psychosurgery[3] are developing rapidly, and close scrutiny is now being given to "aversive" techniques of behavior modification and control[4]—such as procedures for suppressing transvestitism by administering painful electric shocks to the patient while dressed in women's clothing, and procedures for controlling alcoholism or narcotics addiction by arranging medically for severe nausea or even temporary paralysis (including respiratory arrest) to follow ingestion of the habituating substance.[5] It is likely that certain treatments may be deemed so offensive, frightening, or risky that the law may eventually preclude them altogether,[6] or at least restrict them by requiring the patient's informed consent.[7]

Though aversive therapeutic techniques are receiving close attention, schemes of "positive" behavior control[8]—whereby appropriate, non-deviant behavioral responses are encouraged by rewarding their occurrence—have not been subjected to any careful study. It is perhaps assumed that when rewards rather than punishments are employed, no grave legal, social or ethical questions are involved.[9] To a great extent, that is unquestionably true: few would have their ire aroused, for example, by praising a child and offering him candy for correctly spelling or reading a word,[10] nor would many be upset over a scheme that encouraged scholastic achievement of institutionalized juvenile delinquents by offering them, contingent upon academic success, private rooms, a wider choice of food, and selections of items from a mail-order catalogue.[11] But, as will be seen in the following section, many techniques of positive control are far more troubling. Most troubling of all seem to be the use of token economies with chronic psychotic mental patients.

token economies

I. psychology and token economies

A. GENERAL CONSIDERATIONS

Many behavior modification practitioners apply clinically the learning theory principles of Skinnerian operant conditioning. Operant theory is bottomed on the principle, amply demonstrated by empirical data, that behavior is strengthened or weakened by its consequences.[12] The frequency of a behavior increases if it is followed by desirable consequences, whereas it will be extinguished if the positive consequences are discontinued or if the consequences are aversive.[13]

The application of operant conditioning to humans has come a long way since 1949, when a severely regressed person was taught to raise his arm by a procedure that rewarded appropriate arm motions by the subsequent squirting of a sugar-milk solution into his mouth.[14] Now, a multitude of therapeutic behavior modification systems are in operation on ward-wide and institution-wide scales. By and large, these programs seek to shape[15] and maintain appropriate behavior patterns—designated as "target behaviors" or "target responses"—by rewarding or "reinforcing" the desired responses. Usually, rewards are dispensed in the form of tokens or points—known as "secondary" or "generalized" reinforcers—which can then be converted, pursuant to a specific economic schedule, to "primary reinforcers" such as snacks, mail-order catalogue items, and the like.

These "token economies" have flourished since their development in the sixties[16] and are currently employed in a variety of clinical settings.[17] This Article will be confined almost exclusively to a discussion of the application of the token system to chronic psychotics.

There are two reasons for this limitation in scope: first, despite mammoth advances in psychopharmacology[18] and a burgeoning community psychiatry movement[19] which have combined to reduce drastically mental hospital enrollment, almost all chronic psychotics are still hospitalized.[20] If other clinical categories are increasingly diverted from institutions while the chronics continue to accumulate, the treatment of the chronic psychotic may soon consitute the major therapeutic concern of mental hospitals. Second, because the behavior patterns of chronic psychotics are by definition particularly resistant to therapy, more drastic methods of behavior modification have been applied to them. These therapeutic methods will raise important legal questions.

B. TOKEN ECONOMIES

Teodoro Ayllon and Nathan Azrin pioneered the token economy concept on a ward of chronically psychotic female patients at the Anna State Hospital in Illinois.[21] Because of their adaptation to long periods of stagnant hospitalization, chronic patients typically suffer from extreme apathy and dependency. This condition, known as institutionalization,[22] impedes the chronic's chances for improvement or release. To overcome this problem, Ayllon and Azrin rewarded target behaviors that would reverse the institutionalization syndrome. Work assignments within the hospital and various self-care behaviors were rewarded with tokens. The self-care category included grooming, bathing, toothbrushing, bed making, and the like.[23] Work assignments included kitchen chores, serving in the dining room, assisting in the laundry, janitorial work, and related tasks.[24]

For the token economy to succeed, it is necessary to insure that the items or events purchasable with the tokens are effective reinforcers—in lay terms, that they would in fact be desired by the patients. To solve this problem, the Anna State Hospital psychologists applied the "Premack Principle":[25] if certain behaviors occur naturally with a high frequency, then the opportunity to engage in those behaviors can be used as an effective reinforcer to strengthen a low-frequency behavior. The psychologists determined the high frequency-behaviors empirically:

> It was noted that certain patients often hoarded various items under their mattresses. The activity in this case, in a general sense, consisted of concealing private property in such a manner that it would be inaccessible to other patients and the staff. Since this event seemed to be highly probable, it was formally scheduled as a reinforcer. Keys to a locked cabinet in which they could conceal their private possessions just as they had been doing with the mattresses were made available to patients.
>
> Another activity that was observed to be highly probable was the attempt of patients to conceal themselves in several locations on the ward in an effort to enjoy some degree of privacy. A procedure was therefore instituted whereby a patient could obtain a portable screen to put in front of her bed or access to a bedroom with a door. Another event that had a high probability of occurrence for some patients was a visit with the social worker or psychologist. This was used as a reinforcer by arranging appointments with either of these staff members.[26]

Ground privileges and supervised walks by the staff were also established as reinforcers by application of the Premack Principle, since patients were frequently observed to "stay at the exit to the ward and try to leave."[27] The opportunity to attend religious services was also used as a reinforcer since several patients attended frequently when they were allowed to freely.[28]

Thus, personal cabinets, room dividers, visits with the professional staff, ground privileges, supervised walks, and religious services were all made contingently available to the patients: they could be purchased if the patient had performed a sufficient number of target responses to have earned the requisite tokens to purchase the reinforcers. They were otherwise unavailable. Other reinforcers in the Anna State Hospital program included a personal chair, writing materials and stationery, movies, television programs, and various commissary items.[29]

By using these "strong, albeit untapped"[30] sources of motivation, the Ayllon and Azrin economy produced rather impressive results when measured by standards of work performance. They compared the work output of their patients during a specified period of the token economy with a subsequent experimental period during which the various reinforcers were freely available without tokens —a situation which "approximated the usual conduct of a mental hospital ward."[31] Ayllon and Azrin found that patient performance during the experimental period plummeted to less than one-fourth the token economy level. Hence, they concluded that "the performance on a usual ward would be increased fourfold by instituting this motivating environment."[32]

Nonetheless, the Anna State Hospital program did not change the behavior of 8 out of the 44 patients[33] involved:

> Eight patients, who expended fewer than 50 tokens within 20 days, all earned by self-care rather than from job assignments, were relatively unaffected by the reinforcement procedure. Statistical comparison of them with the other patients revealed no difference in diagnosis or age. It appears that their failure to modify behavior appreciably stemmed from the relative absence of any strong behavior patterns that could be used as reinforcers. The only two behaviors that existed in strength were sleeping and eating. The present program did not attempt to control the availability of food. This action may have to be considered in future research in order to rehabilitate patients with such an extreme loss of behavior.[34]

Many token economy programs have been patterned after the Ayllon and Azrin model.[35] In Atthowe's program for chronic patients at the Palo Alto Veterans Administration Hospital, for example, patients earned points not only for their industrial therapy job assignments, but also for participating in group activities, in recreational therapy, and for attending weekend movies.[36] And reinforcers in various programs include later wake-up times,[37] passes,[38] clothing,[39] clothing maintenance,[40] reading materials,[41] dances,[42] and even release.[43] Moreover, several programs have taken the step recommended but not taken by Ayllon and Azrin and have made food and beds available only on a contingent basis.[44] Indeed, those programs have exceeded the Ayllon and Azrin recommendation by using beds and meals as reinforcers on a ward-wide basis, and thus even for patients who have not failed under a system where food and sleeping facilities were noncontingently available.

One of the token economies that hinges food and beds on appropriate behavioral responses—a chronic ward at the Patton State Hospital in San Bernardino, California—is "willing to let a patient go for as long as five days without food, or until he has been reduced to 80% of his previous body weight."[45] The Patton program is one of several token economies[46] that follows a "phase" or "tier" system, where at least certain privileges are dependent upon the patient's place in the hierarchy of tiers.

At Patton, for example, newly admitted patients are placed in the orientation group, where living conditions are exceedingly drab, and where the subsistence-level existence can be purchased for a small number of tokens. After a patient has adapted well to the orientation group, he is elevated to the middle group, where conditions are better but are considerably more expensive. Patients in the middle group are given five months to be promoted to the rather luxurious ready-to-leave group, but if after three months in the middle group a patient is not adequately facing the eventual prospect of life on the outside, he will be returned to the orientation group.[47] Margaret Bruce, a psychiatric technician at the Patton State Hospital, described the orientation group in these words:

> This group sleeps in a relatively unattractive dormitory which conforms to bare minimums set by the state department of mental hygiene. There are no draperies at the windows or spreads on the beds, and the beds themselves are of the simplest kind. In the dining room the patient sits with many other patients at a long table, crowded in somewhat uncomfortably. The only eating utensil given him is a large spoon. The food is served in unattractive, sectioned plastic dishes. So long as he is in this group, he is not allowed to wear his own clothes and cannot go to activities which other patients are free to attend off the unit. He may not have permission for off-the-ground visits, and the number of visitors who can see him is restricted.
>
> During this time, the patient learns that his meals, his bed, his toilet articles, and his clothes no longer are freely given him. He must pay for these with tokens. These tokens pay for all those things normally furnished and often taken for granted. In the orientation group most of the things the patient wants are cheap; for example, it costs one token to be permitted to go to bed, one token for a meal. Patients find it easy enough to earn the few tokens necessary for bare subsistence.[48]

Before leaving a description of token economies, it will be instructive to discuss in some detail a token environment established at the Richmond State Hospital in Indiana.[49] This particular system, although involving a population of civilly committed alcoholics rather than chronic psychotics, is particularly worthy of note because it suggests just how easily the Ayllon and Azrin token economy model can be extended to other clinical categories of patients.[50]

Prior to the inception of the token economy, legally committed alcoholics at Richmond State were first admitted to the Receiving Unit, where they were provided with rest and medical care. Within one or two weeks the patient was usually assigned to an open ward, with a work assignment within the hospital and all the available privileges.[51] When the token system was introduced, certain alcoholic patients without intellectual, organic or psychotic impairments were inducted into the program.[52] Work in the hospital labor force, compensated by points, was deemed the target behavior. The reinforcers included a broad range of patient needs and privileges:

> The motivational power of the points was derived from allowing their exchange for every possible purchase within the hospital; thus, room and board, clothing maintenance, canteen purchases, Alcoholics Anonymous meetings, short leaves of absence, disulfiram treatment, different kinds of psychotherapy, and special instruction could all be freely selected, if paid for out of earnings.[53]

Points were also needed to purchase advancement through the five tier system used at Richmond. The five tiers consisted of two closed wards, a semi-closed ward where ground privileges were available by purchase, and two open wards with pass privileges. Patients could purchase promotion only at weekly intervals.

The program was considered aversive by prospective members,[54] as well as by the inducted members who requested weekly group meetings which became, mainly, "a grievance session centering around project rules."[55] No doubt the grievances were in part attributable to the fact that "a deprivation situation was established by starting patients in a closed ward of low status, substandard material and social comfort, and curtailed freedom, relative to other wards in the hospital."[56] The legal issues raised by the token economies may be apparent by now and they will be considered in the next section. An analytical examination of some of the more difficult competing psychological and legal considerations will, however, be deferred until section III.

II. law and token economies

To speak at the moment of a specific "law of token economies" is of course out of the question, for at this date there is scarcely a handful of statutory and judicial pronouncements dealing even generally with the rights of the institutionalized mentally ill. Until very recently, the judicially manufactured "hands-off" doctrine enabled the courts to duck important questions regarding the limits of administrative discretion in the operation of prisons and mental insitutions.[57] Accordingly, the correctional and therapeutic establishments were in effect given, by default, the legal nod to manage their institutions—and to conduct their therapy[58]—as they saw fit. But the last few years have witnessed a remarkable turnabout in the willingness of courts to scrutinize living conditions in total institutions. Though the activity has thus far been slower in the mental health area than it has been with regard to prisons, the successful legal penetration of mental hospitals appears to be a more promising prospect than in the analogous prison movement. Already, some bold and far-reaching decisions have been rendered,[59] and there is the further possibility of widespread legislative action.[60] From the sparse legal precedents, one can detect a rather clear trend, and the emerging law bears rather directly on the rights of patients subjected to a token economy.

The encouragement of certain target responses—such as proper personal hygiene and self-care—surely seems beyond legal question,[61] but it will be recalled that the principle target response of most token economies is adequate functioning on an institutional work assignment. Many persons both within and without the legal profession, however, find it objectionable in effect to require patients—especially involuntarily committed patients—to work for mental institutions, particularly without standard compensation. Though the work assignments are often cast in therapeutic terms, such as overcoming apathy and institutionalization, the critics view the jobs as simple laborsaving devices which exploit patients[62] and, indeed, which sometimes make hospital retention of particular patients almost indispensable to the functioning of the institution.[63]

That patient job assignments are in fact often laborsaving is beyond question, as is the fact that work output will increase substantially when work is contingently reinforced by the standard reinforcers employed by token economies. Indeed, it will be recalled that at Anna State Hospital in Illinois, Ayllon and Azrin concluded that ward efficiency soared astronomically—fourfold[64]—because of a token system involving job performance, and they noted further that unsatisfactory job performance resulted in administrative disruption.[65] During a patient vacation period "the additional work required to keep the ward functioning . . . had to be made up by paid employees whose hours almost doubled."[66]

It seems clear that the law will not tolerate forced patient labor that is devoid of therapeutic purpose and which is required solely as a laborsaving technique. The Second Circuit, invoking a Thirteenth Amendment involuntary servitude rationale, so held in 1966.[67] Since then, recognition that there is not always a sharp line dividing therapeutic and non-therapeutic assignments has led to varying legal theories for dealing with—or for avoiding—the problem.

One rule is suggested by Bruce Ennis, a leading mental health lawyer who is keenly aware of the disparate per diem cost between private and state hospitalization and of the cost-saving devices resorted to by state hospitals. He would adopt the following as a legal rule of thumb in deciding whether work assignments have therapeutic value: "If a given type of labor *is* therapeutic, we would expect to find patients in private facilities performing that type of labor. Conversely, labor which is not generally performed in private facilities should be presumed . . . to be cost-saving rather than therapeutic."[68]

The "avoidance" approach is exemplified by the elaborate decision in *Wyatt v. Stickney*,[69] in which the court barred all involuntary patient labor involving hospital operation and maintenance—whether therapeutic or not—but permitted voluntary institutional work of either a therapeutic or a non-therapeutic nature, so long as the labor is compensated pursuant to the federal minimum wage law.[70] To insure the voluntary nature of any institutional work assignment undertaken, the *Wyatt* court specified further that "privileges or release from the hospital shall not be conditioned upon the performance of labor"[71] involving hospital maintenance.[72]

The approach taken by the landmark *Wyatt* decision, if widely followed, would have an immense impact on traditional token economies. Patients could not be forced in any way to perform institutional labor assignments—and the force could not legitimately be exerted indirectly by making basic reinforcers "contingent" upon appropriate performance. Further, if patients should decide voluntarily to undertake institutional tasks, the minimum wage is the legally required "reinforcer." Under *Wyatt*, therapeutic assignments unrelated to hospital operations can constitute legitimate target responses that can be rewarded without regard to the minimum wage. But, perhaps most significant for token economies, *Wyatt* and related legal developments seem to have a great deal to say regarding the definition of legally acceptable reinforcers. *Wyatt*, together with an occasional piece of proposed[73] or enacted[74] legislation, has begun the process of enumerating the rights guaranteed to hospitalized mental patients. The crux of the problem, from the viewpoint of behavior modification, is that the items and activities that are emerging as absolute rights are the very same items and activities that the behavioral psychologists would employ as reinforcers—that is, as "contingent rights."

According to the *Wyatt* court, a residence unit with screens or curtains to insure privacy, together with "a comfortable bed, . . . a closet or locker for [the patient's] personal belongings, a chair, and a bedside table are all constitutionally required."[75] Under *Wyatt*, patients are also insured nutritionally adequate meals with a diet that will provide "at a minimum the Recommended Daily Dietary Allowances as developed by the National Academy of Sciences."[76] *Wyatt* further enunciates a general right to have visitors,[77] to attend religious services,[78] to wear one's own clothes[79] (or, for those without adequate clothes, to be provided with a selection of suitable clothing), and to have clothing laundered.[80] With respect to recreation, *Wyatt* speaks of a right to exercise physically several times weekly and to be outdoors regularly and frequently,[81] a right to interact with members of the other sex,[82] and a right to have a television set in the day room.[83] Finally, apparently borrowing from Judge Bazelon's opinion for the District of Columbia Circuit in *Covington v. Harris*,[84] Judge Johnson in *Wyatt* recognized that "patients have a right to the least restrictive conditions necessary to achieve the purposes of commitment"[85]—presumably including, if clinically acceptable, ground privileges and an open ward.

Thus, the usual target behaviors for token economies would be disallowed and the usual reinforcers will be legally unavailable. The emerging law appears to vindicate the assertions of the patients who, at the inception of the Patton State Hospital token economy, "pointed out to the nurses that the state had an obligation to feed them and that the nurses were acting illegally in denying them entrance to the dining room."[86] Chronic patients at Anna State Hospital who had to work for screens and personal lockers to insure privacy would, under *Wyatt*, have those items provided noncontingently. According to the "least restrictive conditions" rationale of *Covington* and *Wyatt*, it would seemingly be impermissible to house on closed wards those patients clinically capable of exercising ground privileges, such as Richmond State Hospital's admittedly non-psychotic alcoholic patients who, before the onset of the token economy program, would have quickly been placed on an open ward.[87] The identical "least restrictive conditions" rationale would presumably also invalidate programs, such as the one at Anna State Hospital,[88] in which ground privileges or supervised walks are available only by purchase, and programs in which outright release from the institution is conditioned upon the accumulation of a set number of tokens or points.[89]

Wyatt is obviously a decision of extraordinary detail and specification, perhaps because of comprehensive stipulation among the parties and amici.[90] Nonetheless, the case[91] is fully consistent with the trend of legal thought.[92] Because the distinct direction of legal thinking bears so heavily on traditional tactics for the behavior modification of chronically psychotic behavior, it is important to examine closely certain particulars of the psycho-legal conflict and their implications and to point, if possible, to a proper path for future legal and therapeutic development.

III. analysis and implications

The important question of the therapeutic or non-therapeutic nature of institutional labor is unfortunately far more complex than would be indicated by the black or white treatment it has received from both legal and psychological quarters. For instance, Ennis's initially attractive and easy-to-apply rule of thumb —that types of patient labor performed at public but not at private hospitals should be presumed cost-saving rather than therapeutic[93]—simply cannot withstand close scrutiny. Ennis's formula is undermined by the clinical and socioeconomic differences between private and public hospital patients. Private hospital patients are typically skilled, of adequate means, and in the hospital for a short stay. Chronic psychotics at state institutions are almost invariably persons who have been hospitalized and unemployed for long periods of time; they are overwhelmingly poor, unskilled, of advanced age, and likely to suffer considerable stigmatization upon release from the hospital.[94]

Given this characterization of chronic mental patients, combined of course with apathy, dependency, and institutionalization, ambitious employment opportunities for released chronics are virtually out of the question.[95] Indeed, when viewed from that perspective, together with the fact that work of almost any kind is probably superior to idleness in offsetting apathy, a wide range of institutional work activities have both therapeutic value and realistically approximate future employment goals. For example, Ayllon and Azrin noted about their patients at Anna State Hospital:

> Almost all of the patients in the programmed environment were from rural or lower-class communities. They were all females. Most were housewives prior to admission and presumably would continue to be so after discharge. Their advanced age and their limited formal education indicated that if they were to be employed, they could hold only non-skilled positions. The target behaviors for these individuals seemed, therefore, to be the various performances involved in housekeeping and in unskilled employment.[96]

Further evidence that the motivation behind establishing such target behaviors is indeed therapeutic rather than simply cost-saving can be gleaned from several facts and from examples where cost-saving was not in issue. One Veterans Administration program for discharged chronics, for instance, provides patients with token-earning formal classes in shopping, washing, ironing and mending clothing, and related tasks.[97] Moreover, in one of the few reported instances where released chronics managed to adjust successfully to a form of community life and to remain employed—George Fairweather's project where released patients lived and worked together in a semiautonomous community lodge[98]—the nature of the employment was perfectly consistent with training provided by standard institutional tasks.

When the group of patients in Fairweather's project was about to leave the hospital for the community, for example, it originally planned on opening a restaurant, the bulk of positions to consist of "cook, assistant cook, dishwasher, busboys, waiters and cashier."[99] Eventually, however, the men settled on janitorial work and gardening as their source of income, but even those jobs were performed inadequately[100] until the men received specific training for the work.[101] And in a successful project conducted by one of Fairweather's associates and patterned after that model, but involving both sexes of chronic patients, community employment followed a strikingly similar course: "Men worked at golf courses and other such places in teams doing gardening, landscaping, and groundskeeping work. The women worked in groups at several nursing homes, as well as in motels and restaurants in the local area."[102]

From these examples, it should be apparent that many forms of institutional labor, even though concededly cost-saving, prevent apathy and prepare patients for life, however marginal,[103] on the outside. If the performance of therapeutic institutional labor by patients is to be encouraged, however, certain safeguards should perhaps be required to insure that no patient becomes indispensable to his supervisor, a possibility which might result in the patient's continuation on the job becoming more important to the staff than his welfare, his treatment, or even his discharge. Administrative precautions taken in the Anna State Hospital program may prove instructive as legal guidelines: Ayllon and Azrin insisted upon periodic job rotation[104] and, moreover, established a firm rule that "no patient was ever allowed to obtain a position for which she alone was qualified."[105] Instead, "a position was established only when several patients were known to be capable of filling that position."[106]

If, given certain safeguards, voluntary[107] institutional labor by chronic patients is to be encouraged, what of *Wyatt's* minimum wage mandate? Such a mandate, besides vitiating any cost-saving benefits of patient performance, might cause serious complications. First, it will inevitably divert scarce legislative appropriations away from other hospital and therapeutic uses. Second, a minimum wage requirement may encourage the hospital—and indeed the encouragement may be compounded by union and community pressure—to fill its institutional positions with permanent outsiders instead of with patients, perhaps leaving the patients to pursue less therapeutic activities.[108] In other words, a minimum wage requirement may possibly result in greater expenditures for less effective therapy.

Thus, although compensating all institutional tasks with the minmum wage appears to be an attractive goal, it is clear that several major problems might be created by that requirement.[109] It is clear, too, that various safeguards short of the minimum wage can be invoked to prevent patient peonage, and that voluntary patient labor can probably be encouraged either by monetary rewards somewhat below the minimum wage or by whatever other reinforcers satisfy the *Wyatt* test.

But in many respects the work and wage question is secondary to the question of legally acceptable and psychologically effective reinforcers. If adequate appropriations were available, if community residents did not threaten to displace patients in the institutional labor force, and if certain other kinks could be ironed out,[110] few objections would be raised to specifying the minimum wage as a legally required reinforcer for patient-performed hospital work assignments. Indeed, if monetary rewards, whether of minimum wage proportions or not, were sufficient to induce patient work performance, that would be a small price to pay to strengthen target behaviors.

The major problem faced by the token economy is the current trend towards expansion of the category of protected inmate interests. The law, relying on concepts such as freedom and dignity, would require, for example, that all patients be accorded minimal levels of privacy and comfort. To the behavioral psychologist, who operates from the premise of determinism, philosophical notions of "freedom" and "dignity" are irrelevant.[111] Rather, the psychologist views privacy or comfort as no more than useful tools which he can manipulate to make a psychotic's behavior more appropriate and socially adaptive—a goal which presumably all agree is in the best interest of both the patient and the society. In the psychologist's view it would surely be an ironic tragedy if, in the name of an illusory ideal such as freedom, the law were to deny the therapist the only effective tools he has to restore the chronic psychotic to his health—and his place in the community.

Wyatt thus poses a painful dilemma. The behavior modifier suggests that chronic psychotics respond initially to only the most primitive reinforcers, and, therefore, only their contingent availability can motivate development of socially adaptive behavior.[112] It follows, the behaviorists claim, that if the basics are made freely available as rights rather than as reinforcers, chronic psychotics may be destined to spend their lives functioning poorly in an institutional setting, whereas if those basic rights are converted into contingent reinforcers, there may be a real prospect of clinical improvement and discharge.[113]

If the empirical evidence supported the claim that token economies relying on primitive reinforcers worked very well with chronic patients—that, for example, virtually all patients improved dramatically and were able to earn the reinforcers required for a decent existence or if the evidence demonstrated that no less drastic means could accomplish similar results—a re-evaluation of the emerging law might very well be in order. But a review of the pertinent literature suggests that behavior modification proponents may have difficulty sustaining a burden of proof with respect to those matters.

First of all, while most token economy outcome studies report favorable results,[114] the successes are far from overwhelming. Even in a project as dramatic as the Anna State Hospital study, eight of the 44 subject patients were basically unresponsive to the program,[115] and success for the remaining patients was measured solely by their work output.[116] When judged by release data rather than by measures of work output, decreased apathy,[117] or improved clinical state,[118] results of token economy systems with chronic psychotics have not been encouraging. Even in the Atthowe and Krasner project at the Palo Alto Veterans Administration Hospital, which reported a doubling of the discharge rate, 11 of the 24 released patients returned to the hospital within 9 months,[119] a more rapid relapse than is normally found in studies of chronic patients.[120]

We must also consider whether the results achieved by token economies —whatever they may be—could be matched or surpassed by less drastic means.[121] Information is wanting, perhaps in part because behavior modifiers have not employed reinforcers other than the basics in standard use. It may be, for example, that creative observation of patient behavior preferences would reveal frequent behavior patterns, other than basic behaviors, which could be utilized as reinforcers. Also, although it is an impure technique according to orthodox behaviorism, another practical approach is simply to ask the patients what they would like to possess or to do.[122]

By exploring creatively for reinforcers, it is likely that therapists could construct a list of idiosyncratic objects and activities—mail order catalogue items,[123] soft-boiled rather than standard hard-boiled eggs,[124] and feeding kittens[125] are actual clinical examples—that could be made available contingently in order to strengthen appropriate target responses. Moreover, to the extent that effective reinforcers are in fact idiosyncratic, it follows almost by definition that their contingent availability could not conflict with the legally emerging absolute general rights of patients.

A system of positive behavior modification based heavily on idiosyncratic reinforcers might be clinically as well as legally superior. Psychologists employing such systems[126] have been able to devise individual treatment plans assuring each patient independent diagnostic and therapeutic attention.[127]

But individualized treatment plans, required by *Wyatt*[128] and perhaps part of the emerging right to treatment,[129] are not incompatible with the operation of ward-wide or hospital-wide general treatment systems designed to overcome general patient problems such as indecisiveness, dependency, or apathy. In fact, the most fruitful combination might be to combine individualized treatment programs with an efficient, easy-to-administer general therapeutic system.[130] If, however, the criteria for a successful system is efficacy with the least drastic deprivations possible, it appears that token economies for chronic psychotics may well finish no better than second best.[131]

Specifically, although it may not be determinative, the work of George Fairweather is highly relevant here.[132] Though he speaks the language of social psychology and of small group theory rather than the language of behaviorism and learning theory, Fairweather relies in part on principles of behavior modification, and his work is discussed prominently in texts on that subject.[133] But his study was bottomed on the belief that chronics, to survive outside, must acquire problem-solving and decision-making skills, and on the knowledge that small cohesive groups can effectively control the behavior of their members.[134] Patients were divided into small task groups with monetary and pass privileges awarded according to the level of responsibility each individual attained. The money privileges for the most part came from personal funds of the patients who participated in the programs. The amounts of money and number of passes were set up in advance for each of four progressive levels of achievement. The task group as a unit became responsible for the progress of its individual members through the four designated steps. Step one involved personal care, punctuality on assignments, and cooperation in the orientation of new members. Step two required, in addition, acceptable work on the job assignment. Requirements in step three were individualized, with patients responsible for recommending the level of their own rewards. In step four the patient had responsibility for his departure plans, and had unlimited rights to withdrawal of money and passes. In step one the patient received ten dollars and a one day pass each week; in step two he received fifteen dollars per week and an overnight pass every other week.[135]

The task group was responsible for dealing with patient problems and for recommending to the staff the level of pass and monetary privileges deserved by each patient member. Patient task group recommendations were considered weekly by a staff committee.[136] To establish cohesive and well-functioning groups, Fairweather would at times advance or demote the group as a unit.[137]

Fairweather found that over time pride in group achievement appeared to become a more important motivator than money or passes.[138] Leaders emerged in the chronic psychotic groups as well as in other clinical categories,[139] and the program was a therapeutic success: As compared with a control group subjected to traditional hospital therapy (not a token economy), the small group patients showed significantly less pathological behavior,[140] greater social interaction,[141] and greater participation during meetings.[142] Moreover, the small group program substantially reduced hospitalization.[143] When combined with an after-care program involving a voluntary living arrangement in a semiautonomous (and eventually autonomous) community lodge, the Fairweather system achieved the long-awaited goal of adequate employment and community adjustment for discharged chronic psychotics.[144] Fairweather thus produced impressive results with chronic psychotics in an environment clearly "less drastic" in deprivation than any of the traditional token economies. Obviously, Fairweather's patients were provided with food and beds. Further, the ward was open and patients had complete access to the hospital grounds.[145] The ward was equipped with a television set, table games, magazines and the like,[146] and freely available activities included library reading, movies, dances and bowling.[147]

Most of these privileges were available only by purchase in the token economy programs. Yet a patient at the bottom of Fairweather's hierarchy was provided, without a work assignment, not only with these privileges, but also with ten dollars and a one day pass each week. Indeed, life at the lowest level of Fairweather's ladder compares favorably with the conditions at advanced levels in some token systems.[148]

Fairweather's approach, then, seems preferable to token economics on several counts. First and foremost, his small group system has yielded impressive results which are unmatched by token systems. Second, while token systems deprive patients of basic comforts in their reliance on primitive reinforcers, Fairweather employs only money and passes.[149] Third, Fairweather's approach is thoroughly oriented toward release and community adjustment, and he recognizes that once cohesive groups have been formed in the hospital, "an immediate move to the community is essential."[150] Finally, Fairweather's behavior modification model emphasizes the development of confidence and decision-making ability rather than performance of assignments. For whatever it is worth, Fairweather's system may be ethically or at least emotionally more palatable than the manipulative techniques of the token economies.

conclusion

Fairweather's small group model, with its rich results and rather minor deprivations, poses a serious threat to token economies. If further studies continue to indicate that, except in extreme circumstances, token economies for chronic psychotics resort to more drastic deprivations than other therapies without producing better results,[151] it is likely that token systems will soon find themselves subject to both legal and behavioral extinction.

Indeed, if the law's general direction in the patient rights area proceeds uninterrupted, token economies may well become legally unavailable even if they are therapeutically *superior* to other approaches. That is because the developing law is creating new patient rights unaware that these rights will undermine a basic behavior modification technique. On the other hand, the behavior modifiers seem busy constructing token economies unaware that legal developments may soon call for their demolition.

Forcing these disparate disciplines to take note of each other—obviously the principle object of this Article—should be helpful to both of them. Behavior modification proponents, convinced of the therapeutic indispensability of token economies for chronic patients, may have reservations about the Fairweather model. But unless systematic comparative studies of alternative therapies are performed soon,[152] the law will be unable to incorporate the results in developing a sensible package of patient rights, and expected legal developments may ultimately preclude such studies.

notes

1. *See; e.g.*, Wexler, Scoville *et al*, The Administration of Psychiatric Justice: Theory and Practice in Arizona, 13 *Ariz. L. Rev.* 1 (1971) [hereinafter cited as *Psychiatric Justice Project*].

2. N.Y. Times, July 15, 1972, at 7, col. 3. In California, section 5325(f) of the Welfare and Institutions Code gives a patient the right to refuse shock treatment, but the following section allows the professional person in charge of the institution, or his designee, to deny the right "for good cause." Cal. Welf. & Inst'ns Code § 5326 (West Supp. 1971).

3. Breggin, The Return of Lobotomy and Psychosurgery, 118 Cong. Rec. E1602 (daily ed. Feb. 24, 1972). Possible neurological bases of deviant and violent behavior are discussed in V. Mark & F. Ervin, *Violence and the Brain* (1970). Sociolegal implications of the Mark & Ervin work are explored in Wexler, Book Review, 85 *Harv. L. Rev.* 1489 (1972).

4. R. Schwitzgebel, *Development and Legal Regulation of Coercive Behavior Modification Techniques with Offenders* (1971). Schwitzgebel's work has been condensed to article form in Schwitzgebel, Limitations on the Coercive Treatment of Offenders, 8 *Crim. L. Bull.*, 267 (1972). On aversion therapy generally, see S. Rachman & J. Teasdale, *Aversion Therapy and Behavior Disorders* (1969); A. Bandura, *Principles of Behavior Modification* 293–354 (1969) [hereinafter cited as Bandura].

5. See Schwitzgebel, Limitations on the Coercive Treatment of Offenders, 8 *Crim. L. Bull.* 267, 285–86 (1972). Anectine, a drug that induces temporary paralysis and respiratory arrest, has been used for behavior control in some California institutions.

See Note, Conditioning and Other Technologies Used to "Treat?" "Rehabilitate?" "Demolish?" Prisoners and Mental Patients, 45 *So. Calif. L. Rev.* 616, 633–40 (1972).

6. Dr. Peter Breggin argues that psychosurgery should be precluded on these grounds. *See generally* Breggin, *supra* note 3.

7. "Patients have a right not to be subjected to treatment procedures such as lobotomy, electro-convulsive treatment, adversive [sic] reinforcement conditioning or other unusual or hazardous treatment procedures without their express and informed consent after consultation with counsel or interested party of the patient's choice," Wyatt v. Stickney, 344 F. Supp. 373, 380 (M.D. Ala. 1972), (dealing with Bryce and Searcy Hospitals for the mentally ill). *See also* Wyatt v. Stickney, 344 F. Supp. 387, 400 (M.D. Ala. 1972), (dealing with Partlow State School and Hospital for the mentally retarded). These two cases will hereinafter be distinguished by bracketed indication of the hospital they dealt with.

8. Bandura, *supra* note 4, at 217–92.

9. *Cf.* McIntire, Spare the Rod, Use Behavior Mod, *Psychology Today*, Dec. 1970, at 42. Considerable controversy is, of course, generated by calls for behavioral engineering on a society-wide scale, such as is advocated in B.F. Skinner, *Beyond Freedom and Dignity* (1971). *See, e.g.,* Ramsey, Book Review, 7 *Issues in Crim.* 131 (1972) (reviewing Skinner's book).

10. *Cf.* Bandura, *supra* note 4, at 249–50 (positive reinforcement as a technique for improving reading skills).

11. *Cf.* Bandura, 278–79.

12. A good introductory text on operant conditioning is J. R. Millenson, *Principles of Behavioral Analysis* (1967). Chapters Two and Three deal with Classical or Pavlovian Conditioning, which is to be distinguished from operant conditioning; the latter provides the basis of the token economy. *See also* Note, 45 *So. Calif. L. Rev.* 616, 627–28 (1972).

13. Note that the behavioral psychologist explains both normal and abnormal behavior by the same principles, in an approach which differs fundamentally from "dynamic" psychology, of which the Freudian system of psychoanalysis is probably the most familiar to laymen. The dynamic psychologists, who follow a "medical model," explain abnormal behavior as the product of "inner conflicts" and the like. For a good introduction to behavior modification and how it contrasts with traditional dynamic concepts, see L. Ullmann & L. Krasner, *Case Studies in Behavior Modification*, 1–65 (1965). *See also* Bandura, 1–69. For more recent accounts of the application of behavioral psychology to clinical settings, see any recent issue of the *Journal of Applied Behavior Analysis*.

Technically, the term extinction is reserved for the process of reducing the frequency of a behavior by discontinuing the "reinforcing" [rewarding] consequences.

14. Fuller, Operant Conditioning of a Vegetative Human Organism, 62 *Am. J. Psychology* 587 (1949). For somewhat more recent studies, see Ullmann & Krasner, *supra* note 13, and R. Ulrich, T. Stachnik, J. Mabry, *Control of Human Behavior* (1966).

15. "Shape" is a technical term used by operant psychologists to describe the process of gradually building a new behavior by rewarding closer and closer approximations to it.

16. Ayllon & Azrin, The Measurement and Reinforcement of Behavior of Psychotics, 8 *J. of the Experimental Analysis of Behavior* 357 (1965); T. Ayllon & N. Azrin, *The Token Economy: A Motivational System for Therapy and Rehabilitation* (1968) [hereinafter cited as *Token Economy*] (report of a project begun in 1961). In part, the flourishing is no doubt due to the fact that much behavior therapy can be conducted by psychiatric nurses, attendants, and paraprofessional personnel. *See* Ayllon & Michael, The Psychiatric Nurse as a Behavioral Engineer, 2 *J. of the Experimental Analysis of Behavior* 323 (1959). The rationale behind emphasizing the development of constructive behavior rather than emphasizing the elimination per se of so-called "pathological" behavior appears to be that pathological traits in an otherwise well-functioning individual may well be dismissed as mere idiosyncracies, and, moreover, that pathological traits may not be able to coexist with functional behavior. *Token Economy* 23.

17. These include populations of juvenile delinquents, newly admitted and chronic psychotics, mentally retarded patients, etc. *Token Economy* 217. For various descriptions, see Bandura 261–82; Davison, Appraisal of Behavior Modification Techniques with Adults in Institutional Settings, in *Behavior Therapy: Appraisal and Status* 250 (C. Franks ed. 1969); Krasner, Token Economy As an Illustration of Operant Conditioning Procedures with the Aged, with Youth, and with Society, in *Learning Approaches to Therapeutic Behavior Change* 74 (D. Levis ed. 1970). *See generally* Kazdin & Bootzin, The Token Economy: An Evaluative Review, 5 *J. of Applied Behavior Analysis* 343 (1972).

18. Jarvik, The Psychopharmacological Revolution, in *Readings in Clinical Psychology Today* 93 (1970).

19. *Psychiatric Justice Project, supra* note 1, at 118–27.

20. *E.g.,* Bruce, Tokens for Recovery, 66 *Am. J. Nursing* 1799 (1966).

21. *Token Economy, supra* note 16.

22. *See generally* E. Goffman, *Asylums* (Anchor ed. 1961). *See also Psychiatric Justice Project* 237–38: "The depressing surroundings, the idleness, the loss of ordinary privileges, the isolation from family, friends and developments in the outside world— these and many other aspects of institutional life, which are almost inherent characteristics of state hospitals, lead to a loss of motivation, to withdrawal and regression, and to apathy, submissiveness and an inability to make decisions. In short, hospitalization itself produces a distinct functional pathology, appropriately dubbed 'institutional neurosis.'" (citations omitted).

23. *Token Economy, supra* note 16, at 250.

24. *Id.* at 134-35.

25. *Id.* at 60. *See* Premack, Toward Empirical Behavior Laws: I. Positive Reinforcement, 66 *Psychological Rev.* 219 (1959).

26. *Token Economy,* 61.

27. *Id.* at 221. *See also id.* at 64–65.

28. *Id.* at 62–63.

29. *Id.* at 226.

30. *Id.* at 269.

31. *Id.* at 188.

32. *Id. See also id.* at 256–61.

33. *Id.* at 239.

34. *Id.* at 269. *But see* the remarks of Davison directed at Ayllon & Azrin's conclusion: "I believe that Ayllon and Azrin would do well to break set and at least consider the possibility that the behavior (both overt and covert) of some chronic hospital patients is regulated by processes which have little, if anything, to do with operant conditioning." Davison, *supra note* 17, at 250.

35. *E.g.,* Atthowe & Krasner, Preliminary Report on the Application of Contingent Reinforcement Procedures (Token Economy) on a "Chronic" Psychiatric Ward, 73 *J. Abnormal Psychology* 37 (1968).

36. Atthowe, Ward 113 Program: Incentives and Costs—A Manual for Patients 7–8 (Veterans Ad., Palo Alto, Calif., Oct. 1, 1964).

37. *Id.* at 4. The present author also visited a token economy where naps were available for five tokens per hour.

38. *Id.* at 5.

39. Lloyd & Abel, Performance on a Token Economy Psychiatric Ward: A Two Year Summary, 8 *Behav. Res. & Therapy* 1, 6 (1970).

40. Narrol, Experimental Application of Reinforcement Principles to the Analysis and Treatment of Hospitalized Alcoholics, 28 *Q. J. of Studies on Alcohol* 105, 108 (1967).

41. Gripp & Magaro, A Token Economy Program Evaluation with Untreated Control Ward Comparisons, 9 *Behav. Res. & Therapy,* 137, 141 (1971).

42. *Id.*

43. Glicksman, Ottomanelli & Cutler, The Earn-Your-Way Credit System: Use

of a Token Economy in Narcotic Rehabilitation, 6 *Int'l. J. of the Addictions,* 525 (1971). *Cf.* Lloyd & Abel, *supra* note 39, at 5.

44. *E.g.,* Schaefer, Investigations in Operant Conditioning Procedures in a Mental Hospital, in *Reinforcement Theory in Psychological Treatment—A Symposium* 25, 26 (J. Fisher & R. Harris eds. 1966) (Calif. Ment. Health Res. Monog. No. 8); Bruce, Tokens for Recovery, 66 *Am. J. Nursing* 1799, 1801 (1966); Gripp & Magaro, *supra* note 41, at 141; Lloyd & Abel, *supra* note 39 at 6.

45. Schaefer, *supra note* 44, at 33–34. Actually, the quoted remark was made in the context of overcoming refusal-to-eat problems exhibited by some of the patients, but if the hospital is medically willing to allow those patients to miss five consecutive days of meals, it seems reasonable to assume that the same medical standard would be applied to patients who presumably desire to eat but who have not earned a sufficient number of tokens to pay for meals.

46. *E.g.,* Lloyd & Abel, *supra* note 39; Narrol, *supra* note 39. *Cf.* Atthowe & Krasner, *supra* note 35.

47. Bruce, Tokens for Recovery, 66 *Am. J. Nursing,* 1799, 1802 (1966).

48. *Id.* at 1800–01. The Patton system seems to carry to the extreme the position often advocated by behaviorists that noncontingent rewards ought to be provided at an "adequate but relatively low level," with preferred reinforcers being available "contingent upon the occurrence of desired response patterns." Bandura, *supra* note 4, at 231. Under such an approach, therapy can be managed chiefly by positive reinforcement, without resort to punishment, and patients, the argument continues, have only themselves to blame if their privileges seem inadequate. Indeed, several programs have noted the benefits of an earn-your-way system, in notable contrast to more traditional approaches where "mandating educational or group therapy participation by threatening loss of visiting and other privileges or delayed release appeared to stimulate the social defiance and self-defeating traits of the population, and rebellion against the regulations of the institution provided an increase in prestige and enhanced status in the eyes of the peer group." Glicksman. Ottomanelli & Cutler, The Earn-Your-Way Credit System: Use of a Token Economy in Narcotic Rehabilitation, 6 *Int'l J. of the Addictions,* 525 (1971). Some commentators have criticized our peno-correctional system for giving inmates non-contingently whatever benefits may be available, and then denying some of the benefits as punishment for wrongful behavior—a system where "the staff members are cast in the unenviable role of punitive agents, and the [inmates] can move only in a downward direction," Bandura 230. To the same effect, see Hindelang, A Learning Theory Analysis of the Correctional Process, 4 *Issues in Criminology,* 43, 44-45 (1969). *See also* M. Hindelang, Social Learning Theory and Social Problems: The Case of Prisons 9 (unpublished manuscript on file with author): "At the same time that a noncontingent system of rewards is operating a contingent system of punishments is attempted; the result is that inmates come to view the rewards as rights rather than privileges and when they are threatened with the denial of those rewards they become justifiably embittered." (citations omitted). It has been suggested that when contingencies are so managed, "the majority of the participants comply half-heartedly with the minimum demands of the institution in order to avoid penalties for any breach of the rules," and that, in a psychiatric setting, "patients can best maximize their rewards by merely adopting a passive patient role." Bandura 230. If the legal system wishes to accept the advice of the behaviorists, the crucial question for the law, of course, will be to define, for various clinical populations, just where the line of non-contingent rewards at an "adequate but relatively low level" ought to be drawn.

49. Narrol, Experimental Application of Reinforcement Principles to the Analysis and Treatment of Hospitalized Alcoholics, 28 *Q. J. of Studies on Alcohol* 105 (1967).

50. As will be apparent, it also raises certain serious questions about the ethical propriety of the type of psychological research involved. *See also* Rubin, Jokers Wild in the Lab, *Psychology Today,* Dec., 1970, at 18.

51. Narrol, Experimental Application of Reinforcement Principles to the Analysis and Treatment of Hospitalized Alcoholics, 28 *Q. J. of Studies on Alcohol* 105, 107 (1967).

52. *Id.*

53. *Id.* at 108. With respect to the right to treatment, the same author states: "The obligation to treat the patient need not be neglected, since purchase of all the available therapeutic services may be permitted." *Id.* at 106–07.

54. *Id.* at 109.

55. *Id.*

56. *Id.* at 108. Of particular concern, from the viewpoint of the ethics of research, is that "work was made the target behavior for the purposes of simple demonstration of reinforcement technique." *Id.* at 107–08. In other words, "the project had no therapeutic purpose, but demonstrated that behavior can be controlled in a simulated economy." *Id.* at 107. The study proved simply that project patients worked 8-hour days as opposed to the 4-hour days worked by non-project alcoholic patients. *Id.* at 109. But that is hardly a startling finding, particularly since the project was based on the Ayllon & Azrin study, which had already established the point. Indeed, the author was himself hardly surprised by the outcome: "Definite evidence of increased work output was obtained, as might be expected." *Id.*

57. *E.g.*, Note, Beyond the Ken of Courts: A Critique of the Judicial Refusal to Review the Complaints of Convicts, 72 *Yale L. J.* 506 (1963).

58. *E.g.*, N. Kittrie, *The Right to be Different: Deviance and Enforced Therapy* 307–08 (1971). *Cf.* O'Donoghue v. Riggs, 73 Wash. 2d 814, 820 n.2, 440 P.2d 823, 828 n.2 (1968): "One who enters a hospital as a mentally ill person either as a voluntary or involuntary patient, impliedly consents to the use of such force as may be reasonably necessary to the proper care of the patient . . ."

59. Covington v. Harris, 491 F.2d 617 (D.C. Cir. 1969); Wyatt v. Stickney, 344 F. Supp. 373 (M.D. Ala. 1972) (Bryce and Searcy Hospitals).

60. *E.g., Cal. Welf. & Inst'ns Code* § 5325 (West Supp. 1971).

61. Ironically, however, an experiment conducted by Ayllon and Azrin seems to demonstrate that "although the reinforcement for self-care was initiated to maintain a minimum standard of cleanliness and personal hygiene, changes in the reinforcement contingencies produced no appreciable difference in self-care practices." *Token Economy, supra* note 16, at 255.

62. *E.g.*, Ennis, Civil Liberties and Mental Illness, 7 *Crim. L. Bull.* 101, 122–23 (1971). At Anna State Hospital, because the token value of jobs is set by factors of supply and demand, "some jobs that were fairly demanding physically and that required about three hours through the day for completion, such as sweeping the floors, earned only about five tokens. . . ." *Token Economy* 204.

63. *Token Economy, supra* note 16, at 201.

64. *Id.* 188.

65. *Id.* at 201–02.

66. *Id.* at 210.

67. Jobson v. Henne, 355 F.2d 129, 132 n.3 (2d Cir. 1966). The court also noted that if concededly involuntary labor is non-therapeutic, even compensation for the work will not necessarily satisfy Thirteenth Amendment requirements, for "the mere payment of a compensation, unless the receipt of the compensation induces consent to the performance of the work, cannot serve to justify forced labor." *Id.*

68. Ennis, Civil Liberties and Mental Illness, 7 *Crim. L. Bull.* 101, 123 (1971) (emphasis in original).

69. Wyatt v. Stickney, 344 F. Supp. 373 (M.D. Ala. 1972) (Bryce and Searcy Hospitals).

70. *Id.* at 381. The minimum wage law is the Fair Labor Standards Act, 29 U.S.C. § 206 (1971). Judge Johnson in *Wyatt* further ordered that payment to patients for such work shall not be applied to offset hospitalization costs. *Id.* at 13.

71. 344 F. Supp. at 381.

72. Under *Wyatt*, the only type of work that can seemingly be "required," and the only type of work exempt from minimum wage coverage, is therapeutic work unrelated to hospital functioning. Further, according to *Wyatt*, patients may also be required "to perform tasks of a personal housekeeping nature such as the making of one's bed." *Id.*

73. Ralph Nader's Center for Study of Responsive Law has produced a suggested statute covering rights of committed patients. The proposal is reproduced in *Psychiatric Justice Project, supra* note 1, at 225–26.

74. *E.g.,* The Lanterman-Petris-Short-Act, Cal. Welf. & Inst'ns Code § 5325 (West Supp. 1971).

75. Wyatt v. Stickney, 344 F. Supp. 373, 381–82 (M.D. Ala. 1972) (Bryce and Searcy Hospitals).

76. *Id.* at 383.

77. *Id.* at 379. *See also* Cal. Welf. & Inst'ns Code § 5325(c) (West Supp. 1971).

78. 344 F. Supp. at 381.

79. *Id.* at 380. *See also* Cal. Welf. & Inst'ns Code § 5325(a) (West Supp. 1971).

80. 344 F. Supp. at 381.

81. *Id.*

82. *Id.*

83. *Id.* at 382.

84. 419 F.2d 617 (D.C. Cir. 1969).

85. Wyatt v. Stickney, 344 F. Supp. 373, 379 (M.D. Ala. 1972) (Bryce and Searcy Hospitals). The "least restrictive alternative" or "less drastic means" rationale was first applied in the mental health law area in Lake v. Cameron, 364 F.2d 657 (D.C. Cir. 1966), an opinion authored by Judge Bazelon, which held that commitment itself should be ordered only if no suitable but less drastic alternatives to commitment could be located. For a discussion of the constitutional doctrine of "less drastic means" in the commitment context, see *Psychiatric Justice Project, supra* note 1, at 140–46. *See also* Chambers, Alternatives to Civil Commitment of the Mentally Ill: Practical Guides and Constitutional Imperatives, 70 *Mich. L. Rev.* 1107 (1972). In Covington v. Harris, 419 F.2d 617 (D.C. Cir. 1969), Judge Bazelon simply extended the doctrine to life within the confines of the hospital environment.

86. Schaefer, *supra* note 44, at 29.

87. A similar problem seems to be present in the token economy system of State Hospital North, Orofino, Idaho, as described in Lloyd & Abel, Performance on a Token Economy Psychiatric Ward: A Two Year Summary, 8 *Behav. Res. & Therapy* 1 (1970). In addition to using tokens for "standard" reinforcers, the State Hospital North program has a phase system which requires the accumulation of tokens for phase promotion. Group C, for example, is a closed ward, and promotion to Group B, which has ground privileges, requires earning 2,000 tokens in a three week period. Further, failure to earn substantial tokens while in Group B or A may result in demotion to Group C. *Id.* at 5. To the extent that certain Group C patients could clinically manage ground privileges— which, given the system, seems almost beyond doubt—this program and many others devised along similar patterns seem to offend the "less drastic means" test of *Covington* and *Wyatt.*

88. *Token Economy, supra* note 16, at 226. Ayllon and Azrin do not specify the percentage of patients on their ward clinically capable of exercising ground privileges, but Atthowe and Krasner, in their report on a token economy for chronic psychotics at the Palo Alto Veterans Administration Hospital, estimate that fully 40% of their patients could, without difficulty, leave the ward unescorted. Atthowe & Krasner, Preliminary Report on the Application of Contingent Reinforcement Procedures (Token Economy) on a "Chronic" Psychiatric Ward, 73 *J. of Abnormal Psychology* 37, 38 (1968). Any scheme that required such patients to purchase ground privileges would presumably run afoul of *Covington* and *Wyatt.*

89. A token economy program in New York which involves civilly committed narcotic addicts presumably hinges release—or at least eligibility for release consideration—upon the accumulation of 936 points. Glicksman, Ottomanelli & Cutler, The Earn-Your-Way Credit System: Use of a Token Economy in Narcotic Rehabilitation, 6 *Int'l J. of the Addictions* 525–27 (1971). To the extent that the point accumulation system does not mesh squarely with statutory or clinical criteria for release, such a system presents serious questions regarding the unwarranted deprivation of liberty. The only saving grace for the described program seems to be that its patients are released after

an average stay of 4 months, whereas committed addicts not on the earn-your-way token system are confined for an average of 7.5 months. *Id.* at 528. *See also* Atthowe, Ward 113 Program: Incentives and Costs—A Manual For Patients 5, 10 (Veterans Ad., Palo Alto 1964) (before patient can be eligible for 90-day trial visit, must be in Group A for 30 days, and it costs 120 tokens to enter Group A, assuming there is an opening).

90. Wyatt v. Stickney, 344 F. Supp. 373, 375–76 (M.D. Ala. 1972) (Bryce and Searcy Hospitals).

91. Another, somewhat less precise, legal problem facing token economies may exist in the confusion between activities that constitute target responses and those that constitute reinforcers. More specifically, different token economies may classify the same activity differently. For example, chronic patients at the Palo Alto Veterans Administration Hospital *earned* tokens for attending group activities, recreational events, and movies (which were viewed as target behaviors), whereas Anna State Hospital patients had to *expend* tokens to attend similar activities (which were viewed as reinforcers). *Compare* Atthowe, *supra* note 89, at 7, *with* Token Economy, *supra* note 16, at 226. In view of the emerging constitutional right to treatment [see Wyatt v. Stickney, 325 F. Supp. 781 (M.D. Ala. 1971)], it seems problematic at best to *charge* for psychotherapy sessions, as at Anna State Hospital and Richmond State Hospital, particularly when so few patients seem willing to expend tokens to attend such sessions. *E.g.,* Token Economy 66–67, 226, 234; Narrol, *supra* note 51, at 108–09. Indeed, even the previously mentioned activities—such as recreational events and movies—may have significant therapeutic value (and may fall within the scope of the right to treatment) in reducing boredom, increasing interaction and, in the case of movies, in providing a vicarious experience for learning or modeling appropriate social behavior. *See* Bandura, *supra* note 4, at 179–82.

It can be easily contended, therefore, that therapy sessions, recreational events, movies, writing materials (to increase contact with the world outside) and other items and events ought to be provided, as part and parcel of the right to treatment, on an absolute, noncontingent basis. *Cf.* Covington v. Harris, 419 F.2d 617, 625–26 (D.C. Cir. 1969). Interestingly, however, even the noncontingent ready availability of such therapeutic items and events may be insufficient to arouse interest in them on the part of a highly apathetic patient population. A possible solution is to convert important therapeutic activities into token-earning target responses, as Atthowe did in Palo Alto. In psychological terms, such a course of action requires "considering the selection of a reinforcer as a response to be strengthened." Ayllon & Azrin, Reinforcer Sampling: A Technique for Increasing the Behavior of Mental Patients, 1 *J. of Applied Behavior Analysis* 13, 14 (1968). In legal terms, we seem to have developed a new category of "reinforced rights."

Those with Hohfeldian hangups might wish to construct a spectrum of patient rights—and correlative hospital obligations—along the line of privileges (dispensed or withheld by hospital discretion), contingent rights (legitimate primary reinforcers mandatorily available by token purchase), rights (available absolutely and noncontingently), and reinforced rights (target responses which can be engaged in as a matter of right and which will be reinforced by tokens)!

92. *E.g.,* Ennis, Civil Liberties and Mental Illness, 7 *Crim. L. Bull.* 101 (1971). *See* Cal. Welf. & Inst'ns Code § 5325 (West Supp. 1971). *See also* Psychiatric Justice Project, *supra* note 1, at 225–26 (draft legislation prepared by Center for Study of Responsive Law). The legislative developments occasionally cover ground not touched by *Wyatt.* The California statute, for example, gives patients the right "to have ready access to letter writing materials, including stamps . . .", Cal. Welf. & Inst'ns Code § 5325(e), and the statutory proposal of the Center for Study of Responsive Law states, explicitly, that patients are "to be given adequate writing paper, pencils, envelopes and stamps." *See* Psychiatric Justice Project 225. Indeed, the failure of these detailed statutes to cover some of the more basic rights—such as food and beds—must be attributed to an assumption on behalf of the draftsmen that such rights were beyond dispute or beyond denial in practice.

93. Ennis, Civil Liberties and Mental Illness, 7 *Crim. L. Bull.* 101, 123 (1971).

94. *E.g.,* Token Economy, *supra* note 16, at 54; Bandura, *supra* note 4, at 278.

See also Lloyd & Abel, Performance on a Token Economy Psychiatric Ward: A Two Year Summary, 8 *Behav. Res. & Therapy* 1, 8 (1970); Spiegler, The Use of a School Model and Contingency Management in a Day Treatment Program for Psychiatric Outpatients 6 (paper presented at Rocky Mountain Psychological Association Convention, Denver, Colorado, May 1971).

95. *E.g.,* G. Fairweather, D. Sanders, H. Maynard, D. Cressler, & D. Bleck, *Community Life for the Mentally Ill: An Alternative to Institutional Care* 207 (1969) [hereinafter cited as *Community Life*]. Indeed, the relapse rate for released chronics is so high and employment prospects are so dim that some commentators have questioned hospital release as an appropriate therapeutic goal. *See* Lloyd & Abel, *supra* note 94, at 8.

96. *Token Economy, supra* note 16, at 54.

97. Spiegler, *supra* note 94, at 4.

98. *Community Life.* Cf. B. Pasamanick, F. Scarpitti & S. Dinitz, *Schizophrenics in the Community: An Experimental Study in the Preventions of Hospitalization* (1967).

99. *Community Life* 46.

100. *Id.* at 5.

101. *Id.* at 50–51, 54.

102. *Id.* at 332. That cost-saving and therapeutic labor are not necessarily mutually exclusive concepts was recognized in Jobson v. Henne, 355 F.2d 129 (2d Cir. 1966). Note that the therapeutic or non-therapeutic nature of particular institutional work assignments may well vary among clinical groups. Just as those tasks may be therapeutic from the perspective of public hospital chronic patients but not for private hospital patients, see text accompanying note 97 *supra*, so too the work may be therapeutic for chronic state hospital patients but not necessarily for prisoners or, particularly, for juvenile delinquents—who seemingly need academic proficiency to achieve vocational success in their long lives ahead far more than they need training in janitorial work. *Cf.* Bandura, *supra* note 4, at 278. In fact, the entire legal analysis of token economies should probably vary with different clinical populations. For instance, the law would probably view the privacy claim that a room-divider screen ought to be provided as an absolute right (rather than merely be available as a contingent reinforcer) far differently in the context of dormitory-style living for the adult mentally ill than in the context of a juvenile institution. *But see* Wyatt v. Stickney, 344 F. Supp. 387, 404 (M.D. Ala. 1972) (Partlow Hospital) (screens or curtains mandated in an institution for mentally retarded children and adults). Further, resort to certain reinforcers may be arguably necessary to encourage appropriate behavior among one clinical group, but be unnecessary to induce the target behavior among a different clinical category. Consider, in that connection, the Richmond State Hospital scheme of treating nonpsychotic alcoholics in a manner very similar to the way other token economy programs treat chronic psychotics.

103. *Cf. Community Life, supra* note 95, at 337. In view of the traditionally astounding speedy relapse rates for the great majority of discharged chronic patients, Bandura, *supra* note 4, at 269, marginality in the outside community seems, at least for the near future, to be an acceptable goal.

104. *Token Economy, supra* note 16, at 202.

105. *Id.* at 201.

106. *Id.*

107. Truly voluntary work would assume, of course, that no basic rights—food, beds, ground privileges, privacy—were made contingent upon performance.

108. Activities are less therapeutic if the skills they train are not marketable in the outside community. There is no point in using the hospital setting to build up socially adaptive behaviors if one can expect that the environment the patient is placed in after release does not also reward those behaviors. *See generally, Token Economy, supra* note 16, at 49–54.

109. Another possible difficulty with mandating a minimum wage is that it imposes an external force on the token economy and may upset the system's delicate economic balance, its incentive system, etc. Winkler, who has studied the economics of token economies, has concluded that token systems constitute subtle and intricate eco-

nomic models which parallel remarkably the economic system of the outside world. Winkler, The Relevance of Economic Theory and Technology to Token Reinforcement Systems, 9 *Behav. Res. & Therapy* 81 (1971). In the Ayllon and Azrin token economy, for example, the token values of the various positions were set by concepts of supply and demand. *Token Economy* 204. A minimum wage reinforcer for all hospital positions, even if appended to a token system with different numbers of tokens available for different assignments, would surely have a profound influence on the pre-existing incentive system. *See also* Kagel & Winkler, Behavioral Economics: Areas of Cooperative Research Between Economics and Applied Behavioral Analysis, 5 *J. of Applied Behavior Analysis* 335 (1972).

110. Such as the impact of a minimum wage requirement on the economic incentive system of the hospital. *See* discussion in note 109 *supra*.

111. *See* B. F. Skinner, *Beyond Freedom and Dignity* (1971).

112. *E.g.*, Bandura 227; *Token Economy* 269.

113. At first blush, the behaviorist position seems to clash with the data provided by J. K. Wing, who found that the clinical states of schizophrenic patients at three different hospitals correlated closely—and positively—with the respective hospital policies on patient rights and liberty. Wing, Evaluating Community Care for Schizophrenic Patients in the United Kingdom, in *Community Psychiatry*, 138, 147–57 (Anchor ed., L. Roberts, S. Halleck & M. Loeb, eds. 1969). Wing's analysis may possibly be reconciled with the behaviorist contention. First, it is not entirely clear from Wing's study that patients were assigned to the three hospitals on a random basis, and if they were not, a causal connection between patient rights and clinical states could not conclusively be inferred. And even if it could, the connection could well be limited to instances where contingency management systems are absent. In other words, it may be that it is far more therapeutic to provide patients with certain privileges absolutely than it is to deny them those privileges absolutely, but that it is better still to provide the privileges on a contingent basis.

114. *See, e.g.*, Gripp & Magaro, A Token Economy Program Evaluation with Untreated Control Ward Comparisons, 9 *Behav. Res. & Therapy* 137 (1971) (summarizing results achieved by other researchers).

115. *Token Economy, supra* note 16, at 269. *See also* Lloyd & Abel, Performance on a Token Economy Psychiatric Ward: A Two Year Summary, 8 *Behav. Res. & Therapy* 1, 7 (1970) (at least 10 of 52 patients remained predominantly in the lowest group, which was a closed ward, throughout the course of the study).

116. Even the drastic deprivations at Patton State did not produce spectacular results. Schaefer, *supra* note 44, at 32. Schaefer did, however, claim some spectacular results in an *individualized* positive reinforcement program, where a behavior modification plan is tailored to each patient's particular problems. *Id.* at 33–36. Individualization will be discussed further in text *infra*.

117. Schaefer & Martin, Behavioral Therapy for "Apathy" of Hospitalized Schizophrenics, 19 *Psychological Reports* 1147 (1966).

118. Gripp & Magaro, *supra* note 114.

119. Atthowe & Krasner, Preliminary Report on the Application of Contingent Reinforcement Procedures (Token Economy) on a "Chronic" Psychiatric Ward, 73 *J. Abnormal Psych.* 37, 40 (1968).

120. "Results based on follow-up studies disclose that approximately 70 percent of chronic patients who are discharged from mental hospitals return within 18 months regardless of the type of treatment received during the period of hospitalization." Bandura, *Supra* note 4, at 269.

121. In fact, token economy programs differ considerably among themselves with regard to the nature of deprivations and contingent reinforcers resorted to. For instance, food and beds were subject to purchase at Patton State Hospital but were non-contingently available at Anna State Hospital. Further, patients in certain programs are able to earn tokens for engaging in activities which would cost tokens in other programs. See discussion in note 91, *supra*. Unfortunately, however, because reports of token economy programs are often inadequate in their description of reinforcers, and because

they often measure success according to different criteria, inferences of comparative efficacy are difficult to draw, leaving our knowledge rather incomplete with respect to the therapeutic necessity of resorting to the more drastic reinforcers.

122. This technique is "impure" because, unlike the Premack principle, it relies on verbal expressions of intention to ascertain preferred behavior, and the match is not always a perfect one. Ayllon and Azrin resorted to the technique to a limited extent. *Token Economy,* 67–72. To help insure that a patient will refrain from requesting items that he does not in fact deeply desire, a down payment of a specified number of tokens can be required at the time of the request. *Id.* at 71–72.

123. *Token Economy, supra* note 16, at 69.

124. *Id.* at 68.

125. Atthowe & Krasner, *supra* note 119, at 38.

126. *E.g.,* Schaefer, *supra* note 44, at 33–36 (Patton State Hospital individualized behavior modification program far more spectacular than its general token economy program); Spiegler, *supra* note 94.

127. In the Patton State Hospital program, individualized problem areas included eating problems, grooming habits, and hallucinatory behavior. Schaefer, *supra* note 44, at 33–36. Note that under an individualized program, it would not be unusual to have "some people paying while others are paid to play table games. . . ." Spiegler, *supra* note 94, at 8. Such an individualized approach may solve the legal problem posed by the fact that some token economies treat as reinforcers activities which others treat as target responses. *See* discussion of the problem in note 91 *supra. Cf. Token Economy,* 10–11 (visitors, ground privileges, recreational activities not desired by certain chronic patients).

128. Wyatt v. Stickney, 344 F. Supp. 373, 384 (M.D. Ala. 1972) (Bryce and Searcy Hospitals).

129. *E.g.,* Birnbaum, The Right to Treatment, 46 *A.B.A.J.* 499 (1960); Rouse v. Cameron, 373 F.2d 451 (D.C. Cir. 1966).

130. *See* Davison, Appraisal of Behavior Modification Techniques with Adults in Institutional Settings, in *Behavior Therapy: Appraisal and Status* 257 (C. Franks ed. 1969); Atthowe & Krasner, *supra* note 119, at 41.

131. The empirical evidence is convincing. *See Community Life, supra* note 95; *Social Psychology in Treating Mental Illness: An Experimental Approach* (G. Fairweather ed. 1964) [hereinafter cited as *Social Psychology*].

132. *See* references in note 131 *supra.*

133. *E.g.,* Bandura, *supra* note 4, at 269–71, 275–78.

134. In this connection, Bandura cites an interesting unpublished report where the researchers "studied the amount of disruptive classroom behavior displayed by a child in the absence of any special reinforcement and during subsequent periods when either she alone earned five points, or she and her immediate peers each earned one point for her commendable behavior. It is interesting to note that the child's activities were more effectively controlled under the peer contingency even though it produced only one-fifth of the amount of reinforcement provided on the individual basis. Apparently, through the group reward, change agents were able to enlist the peers' aid in modifying the behavior of their companion." Bandura 281.

135. *Social Psychology,* 30. Fairweather's project was conducted at a Veterans Administration Hospital, and the patients were presumably drawing psychiatric disability benefits, which is where the monetary rewards utilized in the experiment came from. Note, however, that even if this money were provided by the hospital, rather than from the patients' own sources, the total expenditure would probably be far less than if the patient labor were mandatorily compensated by the minimum wage. For comments on the possible disincentives to recovery provided by disability compensation—surely a fruitful topic for psycho-legal investigation—see Spiegler, *supra* note 94, at 6; Davison, *supra* note 130, at 257.

136. *Social Psychology, supra* note 31, at 40–41. The staff committee could of course amend or reject the suggestions. *Id.*

137. *Id.* at 173.

138. *Id.* at 189.

139. *Id.* at 181, 283. The patients in Fairweather's study constituted a heterogeneous population and varied considerably in degree of chronicity, but the various task groups surely had their share of chronic psychotics. *Id.* at 33. And Fairweather's follow-up community adjustment project involved almost exclusively chronic patients. *Community Life, supra* note 95, at 32, 238. It seems, then, that a comment made by Davison that Fairweather's study did not involve chronic psychotics, is simply erroneous. Davison, *supra* note 130, at 257. As an aside, it should be noted that Fairweather's study of heterogeneous groups yielded fascinating findings regarding tl e ideal clinical mixture required in small groups to produce first-rate decision-making. *Social Psychology, supra note* 131, at 193, 209.

140. *Social Psychology, supra* note 131, at 61.

141. *Id.* at 70, 283.

142. *Id.* at 89.

143. *Id.* at 168.

144. *Community Life.* When unaccompanied by a cohesive-group aftercare arrangement, however, chronic patients who had participated in the small group program prior to discharge had a high relapse rate, as do chronics generally. *Social Psychology* 168.

145. *Social Psychology* 32.

146. *Id.* at 46.

147. *Id.* at 153. It is not clear whether Fairweather's patients were provided with such items as screens or personal lockers, but it is clear that those items were either available or unavailable *noncontingently;* that is, it is not the case, as was true at Anna State Hospital, that they were available only to those able to purchase them. Because Fairweather did not employ those items as reinforcers, his therapeutic system would seemingly be unaffected by a requirement, such as enunciated in *Wyatt,* that all patients be given those items as a matter of absolute right.

148. *E.g.,* Bruce, Tokens for Recovery, 66 *Am. J. Nursing* 1799, 1802 (1966) (discussing conditions for the "middle group" at Patton State Hospital); Lloyd & Abel, Performance on a Token Economy Psychiatric Ward: A Two Year Summary, 8 *Behav. Res. & Therapy* 1, 5 (1970) (discussing conditions for "Group B" at Idaho's State Hospital North); Narrol, Experimental Application of Reinforcement Principles to the Analysis and Treatment of Hospitalized Alcoholics, 28 *Q. J. of Studies on Alcohol* 105, 108 (1967) (discussing steps 3 and 4 at Richmond State Hospital). *See also* text accompanying notes 52–54 *supra.*

149. Fairweather's contingent pass device may pose a question in light of the requirement of Covington v. Harris, 419 F.2d 617 (D.C. Cir. 1969), that patients be provided with as much liberty as is clinically appropriate. But the fact that even lowest level patients are entitled in the Fairweather system to one day pass per week may alleviate *Covington* objections, especially if the contingent availability of passes above and beyond one per week are shown empirically to constitute powerful motivators. But whatever *Covington* problem may exist could, of course, be vitiated entirely if monetary rewards alone were found to be sufficient reinforcers, as future research might indeed show.

150. *Social Psychology, supra* note 131, at 9.

151. One possible exception is the most extremely regressed cases who fail under all other techniques. Even under Fairweather's system, for example, it is probably true, as he admits, *Social Psychology* 172, that some patients may be unresponsive, and it is certainly possible that, for those patients, idiosyncratic reinforcers will be undiscoverable or unworkable. For them, the fields of law and psychology must face the issue whether, in the hopes of therapeutic success, basic and primitive items and activities should be used as reinforcers. If the answer is affirmative, certain safeguards should be built into the legal structure to insure that decisions to invoke the traditional token economy model are made only after full consideration and only in rare instances. For

example, demonstrated ineffectiveness of the Fairweather and idiosyncratic systems could be a legal prerequisite to reliance on the traditional token technique. Such an approach, which may create an additional incentive for patients to succeed within the Fairweather scheme and accordingly avoid the more distasteful ordeal of a standard token system, would insure that basic rights are not converted to contingent reinforcers for the bulk of chronic psychotics for whom that appears unnecessary and, *a fortiori*, for other clinical categories, such as juvenile delinquents and non-psychotic alcoholics, who presumably can be motivated by non-primitive reinforcers which fall without the prohibitions of *Wyatt* and related legal mandates. In effect, if reliance on reinforcers falling below the *Wyatt*-type baseline are to be resorted to, such a drastic scheme of positive token reinforcement should be properly deemed "aversive" for legal purposes and should follow, as closely as possible, emerging legal restrictions on aversive therapy. Hopefully, one such restriction will be the "less drastic means" rationale. *Cf*. Bandura, *supra* note 4, at 551 (complaining that "exceedingly noxious procedures are occasionally employed even though they produce no greater changes than stimuli in much weaker intensities"); Schwitzgebel, *supra* note 2, at 279 (alcoholics have been treated with drastic drugs causing respiratory arrest, even though "[t]he results . . . are not clearly better than with emetics."). A requirement of informed consent is also emerging in the aversive therapy area, [*e.g.*, Wyatt v. Stickney, 344 F. Supp. 373, 380 (M.D. Ala. 1972) (Bryce and Searcy Hospital)], but that requirement may have an awkward application in the token economy area: it is easy to imagine homosexual or alcoholic patients consenting to aversive techniques in hopes of securing desired behavioral improvement, but it is far more difficult to imagine an apathetic long-term patient, almost by definition unconcerned about his clinical state and his future, voluntarily consenting to forego the standard benefits of hospital life in favor of treatment under which those benefits would be available only by purchase. Surely, even if informed consent were given by such a patient, it might soon be revoked. *Cf*. Ex parte Lloyd, 13 F. Supp. 1005 (E.D. Ky. 1936) (addict who volunteered for treatment and contracted to remain in hospital for specified time period but later changed his mind could not be compelled to remain hospitalized for the specified period); *contra*, Oretga v. Rasor, 291 F. Supp. 748 (S.D. Fla. 1968). Arguably, informed consent in a token economy setting could be replaced by an alternative protective device, such as the informed approval of a judicially selected human rights committee chosen from outside the hospital. *See, e.g.*, Wyatt v. Stickney, 344 F. Supp. 387, 400 (M.D. Ala. 1972) (Partlow Hospital) (requirement that aversive behavior modification programs involving the mentally retarded "shall be reviewed and approved by the institution's Human Rights Committee and shall be conducted only with the express and informed consent of the affected resident, if the resident is able to give such consent, and of his guardian or next of kin, after opportunities for consultation with independent specialists and with legal counsel"). Further, a time limit should probably be set on the length of time the token procedure could be invoked, with provision for a return to the noncontingent availability of basic benefits for patients seemingly unresponsive to even the token system. But clear-cut answers on the extent to which traditional token economies should be treated legally as an aversive technique must await further development in the law of aversive therapy itself—an area which, as noted in the Introduction to this Article, is receiving an ever-increasing amount of attention from the courts and the commentators. The use of aversive techniques raises squarely one of the perennial problems of law and research: society will obviously want to forbid aversive practices unless they have been demonstrated to be efficacious, but *research*—rather than legal prohibition—is needed to demonstrate whether the practices are in fact efficacious. To the extent that many aversive therapies are obviously experimental in nature, the emerging legal and ethical restrictions regarding experimentation with human subjects ought to be pertinent in devising a balanced but protective regulatory framework for their application. *See generally Experimentation with Human Subjects* (P. Freund ed. 1970); J. Katz, *Experimentation with Human Beings* (1972).

152. The desirability of such studies has been repeatedly noted. *See, e.g.*, Bandura, *supra* note 4, at 274.

THINK

1. In this landmark case, the court emphasized that the standards that were required for Bryce and Searcy were minimal medical and constitutional ones. In light of Rosenhan's observations (Reading 16), what additional provisions might have been added to provide a humane psychological and physical environment?

2. If psychiatric patients are social lepers, then you might expect state governments and even hospital administrations to be distressed by the expenses that the court orders are likely to generate. There will be further court battles on this matter, no doubt, as states attempt to minimize the resources they must allocate to the psychiatrically distressed. But even if the *Wyatt* v. *Stickney* decision is upheld, it is likely that there will be attempts to circumvent it. How might that be done?

3. You know from your other courses in psychology, and perhaps also from this one, that attitude change often follows behavior change. If you can get people to change their behavior, their attitudes will fall in line with their behavior—even though they seem "unalterably opposed" right now. For example, when the United States Supreme Court ruled in 1954 that separate school facilities for black and white children were illegal, people's attitudes toward integrated schools gradually became more favorable. But before integration became reality in schools, many of these same people were very much opposed to it. Behavior change, wrought this time through law, bred attitude change.

    You recall that Mosher and Gunderson (Reading 12) observed that the initial reaction of townspeople to the closing of California's Modesto State Hospital was negative. But over time, and especially since the hospital remained closed, the attitude became more positive toward the closing.

    In light of *Wyatt* v. *Stickney*, what changes in public attitudes toward the mentally ill themselves, and toward their treatment, are likely to occur if the minimal standards recommended by the court are implemented?

4. Imagine that you are responsible for the treatment of a particularly unresponsive hospitalized patient. Nothing you do seems to "work." You read a paper that asserts that such difficult patients are often responsive to "deprivation schedules." If you take away these patients' food and privileges contingent on their engaging in a therapeutic regimen that is known to be good for them, they seem to improve. You are tempted to institute that kind of treatment for your patient. What kinds of considerations should cross your mind? Should you, in the final analysis, use such treatments? Under what conditions?

The Nature and Effects of Psychotherapy

During the past decade, there has been such a burgeoning of therapies that it is hard to know where and how to begin to describe them, and it is even harder to describe the scientific trends that promote them. This has not always been the case. Thirty years ago, there really was only one kind of psychotherapy that was worth writing about: psychoanalysis. Even so, things were pretty complicated. Freud had his supporters and detractors. Psychoanalysis had its offshoots. There were questions about how analysis should be implemented, how long it should continue, and even rumblings about its effectiveness. But compared to what we have today, things in those days were quite simple.

A decade ago, a description of psychotherapies would have been larger than it was forty years earlier, but still manageable. It would have included, in addition to the psychoanalytic approaches, client-centered therapies, crisis interventions, educational therapies, and behavior modification. Inspired by the experimental psychology of learning, behavior modification was most promising for human welfare, most interesting scientifically, and attracted most debate.

But for reasons that are not clear, today the field of psychotherapy is exploding with novelty. Hardly a year goes by without several therapies being born, all of them widely heralded. In fact, last year's psychotherapeutic fashions are old hat this year. Just take a look at a partial list of the currently available "therapies":

Encounter groups of all kinds
Gestalt therapy
Sex therapy
Arica
Attribution therapy
Primal therapy
Relaxation therapies
Desensitization
Implosion
Hypnotherapy
Psychoanalysis
Existential analysis
Client-centered therapy
Family therapy
Job therapy
Marathons
Identity therapy
Rational-emotive therapy
Massage
Psychocybernetics
Rolfing
Psychodrama
Reichian sensitivity therapy
Reinforcement therapies
Self-instructional therapies

We know a good deal about some of these therapies. However, about most of them, we know very little. We don't know whether they work, and if they work how they work, who benefits and who gets hurt. (Yes, "therapy" does sometimes *hurt* some people.) We don't know these things because the therapies are too new to have been much researched, and because it is easier to invent the therapy (at least to judge by the number of inventions) than it is to assess its effectiveness.

In this section, we want to give you a sense of where the action has been, and where it is likely to be in the field of psychotherapy. That is not quite as easy to do as it seems. In the first place, you have to select from all that has been called psychotherapy that which seems to have genuine substance. And secondly, you want to predict what will happen in psychotherapy—where it is likely to move, what new directions therapy will take, and where the frontiers are likely to be five years from now. Not an easy task, it clearly is one about which there will be considerable debate. After you read these selections, you may very well want to add your own voice to the clamor.

Long before the therapy explosion, in the days when there were only insight therapies, there was nevertheless considerable debate about the nature of those therapies: Which was better, how did they operate, why did they seem to do what they did. Many of these debates were acrimonious, but as Perry London points out (Reading 23), for all their apparent differences, these therapies had much in common. Client-centered therapy, for example, shares a great deal with psychoanalysis, however much the practitioners of each insist on seeing them as quite different.

With the invention of behavior therapies, which were inspired by principles of learning, the debates and acrimony between behavior therapists and psychoanalytically oriented ones increased by orders of magnitude. Again, the possibilities of similarity were overlooked, and with them the possibilities of rapprochement. In fact, there are marked theoretical similarities between these forms of treatments, and these similarities raise the possibility that a cognitive psychology of behavior change might embrace the findings of both the insight and the action therapists.

Behavior therapy itself is undergoing enormous and rapid change. Originally inspired by Pavlov and Watson, it very early took an experimental approach to behavior change. More than therapists of other persuasions, behavior therapists insisted on evidence that their methods worked. Such an insistence is found in the paper by Mary Cover Jones (Reading 24) which was published in 1924. She compared several different methods of eliminating children's fears, and found that two of them seemed to work best. Her findings still hold true today.

Self-control is a central personality process upon which much of socialization and the gratifications of maturity depend. The development of self-control is likely to become one of the central concerns in psychotherapy. Because self-control is a covert process, it is only recently that the problems that inhere in self-control have become amenable to scientific analysis. But there is already a flourishing literature in that area, some of which was summarized earlier by Goldfried and Merbaum (Reading 5). Donald Meichenbaum and Joseph Goodman (Reading 25) seek to train impulsive children to control themselves. Rather than using reward and punishment for these purposes, they turn to cognitive procedures and, in this case, to having children talk to themselves, covertly and overtly, in order to control themselves. Compared to other procedures, cognitive self-instructions are quite successful. The notion that what we say to ourselves is valuable not only for personality change but also for the maintenance of that change will attract considerably more attention in the coming decade.

Much as the last decade saw of the growth of the behavior therapies, the present one is likely to witness the growth of cognitive treatments, and especially treatments that implicate social psychology. The tendency of people to seek causes for the things that happen to them, and perhaps especially to attribute causes to their upsets, is used by Michael Storms and Richard Nisbett to treat insomnia (Reading 26). Basing some of their effort on the earlier work by Schachter (Reading 3), Storms and Nisbett find that pills that are alleged to keep you awake will put you to sleep *faster* than pills that are supposed to induce sleep. This is a fascinating "reverse prediction," which is directly derivable from theory and seems to have lots of promise for therapeutic application.

Perry London closes this section with a plea for an end to useless conflict among psychotherapists and theorists of behavior change (Reading 27). Not only is there less to argue about than we once believed, but there seems yet to be much work to be done before we have invented all of the treatments that are necessary to alleviate psychological distress, and to give people some happiness. London points to some of the things that need to be done to facilitate these developments. Whether anyone troubles to take his advice seriously will be known when the next edition of this book is published!

23
The Secrets of the Heart:
INSIGHT THERAPY
Perry London

Magazines, movies, plays, television programs, novels, short stories, and learned texts have all told much about Insight psychotherapy, often very accurately. Artists, poets, composers, and movie scenarists have all borrowed from it for their work, and if their renderings are less than clear expositions of it, still

From *The Modes and Morals of Psychotherapy* by Perry London. Copyright © 1964 by Holt, Rinehart and Winston, Inc. Reprinted by permission of Holt, Rinehart and Winston, Inc.

they are illustrations of its pervasiveness in this culture. It is unnecessary, to say the least, to introduce sophisticated readers to this discipline, for they have been introduced almost endlessly to one or another aspect of it in education, in entertainments, in cultural pursuits, in social relationships, and perhaps in their personal lives. This is even more true in metropolitan than in rural areas, for large cities have the resources to sustain formal societies of psychotherapists, and in such settings the educated public is likely to learn a good deal about the different trademarks of different psychotherapeutic denominations. The less initiated, on the other hand, are more likely simply to equate psychotherapy with psychoanalysis, a confusion which is given unwitting support by the many Insight therapists who simultaneously affirm and deny that they are psychoanalysts, usually by calling themselves "psychoanalytically oriented."

Far from belittling this equivalence, however, I shall argue that the apparently ignorant gathering of many psychotherapeutic sheep into a single fold is more justified than not, and that the many different Insight schools of therapy, instead of differing vitally from each other, as they allege, in practice are united by more significant commonalities than they are separated by discords. The areas of disagreement are worth some attention because, among other reasons, they have been sources of intense personal argument among psychotherapists and have given rise historically to a large number of schools, some of which feel so strongly about their differences that they avoid contact or interaction with members of rival camps.[1] These differences have also consumed considerable space in the psychotherapeutic literature. But they are here regarded chiefly as curiosa, and one purpose in citing them will be to discount them.

The progenitor of all modern types of Insight therapy, if not of all psychotherapy, is Sigmund Freud's psychoanalysis, and as prototype, it has continued to this day to serve both as bible and whipping boy to all the subsequent developments in this field. It will do as much for this characterization of Insight psychotherapies, for the most vital attributes of psychoanalysis apply equally well to its progeny, justifying the allegation that they are all "psychoanalytically oriented" whether they say so or not.

Insight therapists vary considerably both in the degree of and the reasons for their divorcement from Freudian psychoanalysis. Disciples of the American psychiatrist Harry Stack Sullivan, for example, himself only a vicarious disciple of Freud, are likely to say that they differ radically from Freudians because of their different theory of personality, which asserts a cultural rather than biological origin of neurosis. But they also claim to differ on the technical grounds that the patients of Freudians have to lie down where they cannot see the therapist during their appointments while their own patients are permitted both to sit upright and to face their doctor.

Perhaps the Insight school which claims the greatest difference from psychoanalysis and for the most reasons is that founded by the psychologist Carl Rogers. It is variously known as Rogerian, nondirective, or client-centered therapy, and not only does it fail to specify any origins in psychoanalysis, but it also identifies the most critical aspects of its operations as critically different from psychoanalysis. Like the Sullivan school, it is an American product.

Existential analysis, on the other hand, originates in Europe and has become widely known in the United States only within the past few years. This movement, as its name implies, tries to blend the insights of psychoanalysis with the insights of existential philosophy to elicit insights from troubled people. Without totally disavowing psychoanalysis, it claims to be and do more than analysis.

the technical equivalence of insight therapies

To begin with their operations, there are two gross commonalities among all the Insight therapies, one positive and one negative, which dwarf both their many differences and all their other likenesses:

1. The single allowable instrument of the therapy is talk, and the therapeutic sessions are deliberately conducted in such a way that, from start to finish, the patient, client, analysand, or counselee does most of the talking and most of the deciding of what will be talked about.
2. The therapist operates with a conservative bias against communicating to the patient important or detailed information about his own life, that is to say, the therapist tends to hide his personal life from the patient.

There are considerable differences in the rationale of these procedures among different schools, just as there are differences between them in the actual conduct of many details of therapy. But the foregoing characteristics are still sufficiently vital to determine the general appearance of all Insight therapy sessions, and even a superficial description of them does not require very many qualifications to incorporate the differences from one school to another.

The actual conduct of an Insight therapy session might proceed as follows:

The patient and doctor greet each other and take positions in the doctor's office. If the patient lies down on a couch (classical psychoanalysis), the doctor generally sits behind his head towards the side, in order to see him without being seen. If the patient sits (client-centered, Sullivanian, and so on), the doctor usually sits facing him. In either case, the positions tend to be fixed and constant for all sessions; neither party will ordinarily get up or move around the room during the session, nor will there ordinarily be any physical contact between them. Talk is the legal tender of expression and communication here, talk and not motion; there are therapists who say one must never take notes, but listen in rapt attention, motionless. For some even, talk means only speech and no other kind of words, as with therapists who discourage or forbid patients to make agendas or other notes about themselves or read them during the session; notes are words, but not talk.

As physical positions are established, and patient and doctor get "set," there may be some brief exchange of a conventional social kind, though many therapists frown on this. In any case, it is always desultory and impersonal, about the weather, the traffic, and so forth, a part of the preparatory activity. It is usually introduced by the patient, not the therapist, who probably makes no more response to it than necessary, partly because of its baldly social character, with its implications for his role in the relationship, but more because it is plainly not the *res gestae* of the therapy session. Some talk is worth more than other talk. Thus, if the patient begins the therapy session with irrelevant pleasantries rather than diving headlong into serious things, the casual conversation is as likely to die off into silence as to blossom into more momentous talk.

And the silence is likely to be maintained until and unless the patient begins talking, for it is the rule that, in the ordinary course of Insight therapy, all possible options on decisions belong to the patient. Once the decision to undergo therapy is made, along with arrangements for the business of its conduct, such as hours and fees, there is nothing left to opt except the decision to talk and the content of the talk. The explicit responsibility for both of these is never assumed by the therapist,[2] though he may appear to prod the patient into talking by comments or reflections upon his silence.

Even after the patient has begun to talk, the therapist is unlikely to make very explicit evaluations of his remarks, such as indicating that one thing is important and another not. Nor is he likely to assume even such passive responsibility for the interchange as directly answering most direct questions. Should the client hestitate, for example, to choose between two things to talk about, the therapist would not choose either one—and if the client named the things and asked him outright which to speak of first, the therapist would almost certainly not say. On the contrary, Insight therapists devote a good deal of their energy, particularly in the early part of treatment, to subtly turning the patient's attention in upon himself and to accustoming him to become completely self-responsible for the entire flow of his consciousness. And this is done by practice rather than precept, for the therapist accomplishes this end by taking on himself essentially the reverse of that role he wishes the patient to adopt, leaving the patient with only the alternatives of carrying the ball himself or having no interaction. The therapist does not discourse or lecture; he merely responds suggestively.

If the foregoing description applies more literally to classical psychoanalysis than to other forms of Insight therapy, it is only because analysis is practiced more consistently and lasts longer than other Insight therapies. The procedural bias of them all lies in this direction, and it has long since been shown that the operations of trained therapists of different Insight schools are relatively hard to tell apart.

Fiedler's study is now more than fifteen years old, and its result apparently still stands, but the practical similarity in therapeutic work of different schools still comes as a surprise to many Insight therapists, the more so as they have been schooled in the comparison of differences. It might be useful therefore, at this point, assuming some general knowledge on the reader's part of individual Insight schools, to explore the semantics of technique they employ and see how critical their differences really are.

psychoanalysis and client-centered therapy

The extremes of technical difference among the Insight schools are represented by the systems of Freud and Rogers respectively. Their differences in technique are mainly concerned with the therapist's instrument of response, his remarks, and the kind of material to which they should be addressed. Rogerians place primary reliance on the technique called "reflection," while Freudians give similar weight to one called "interpretation." Reflection is a therapist's remark which tries to communicate that the patient has been thoroughly understood, while interpretation is one which, in addition to understanding, implies some elaboration, explanation, or assessment of meaning by the therapist. When a therapist reflects a remark, he might repeat the patient's very words or synonyms for them, whereas in interpreting a remark he would be freer to say things whose meaning was less obvious from the patient's words.

The distinction between reflection and interpretation is more apparent than real, however, when they are both considered in the context to which Rogerians and Freudians respectively recommend that psychotherapists apply themselves. Rogerians limit the therapeutic attack to the exposure of feelings in whatever connection they are presented to the therapist, while Freudians, though similarly interested in dealing with feelings, are concerned with identifying their sources as well. This difference may seem great, but its significance depends entirely on the extent to which reflections and interpretations can be distinguished from each other and can be seen to have different consequences. Neither is easy to do.

Since feelings are the pivotal contents of client-centered therapy, reflection is meaningfully directed towards feelings alone. The impact of the therapist's reflection of feelings is likely always to be greatest when the relevant feelings are implied rather than spoken, for it is in such situations that the reflective response can be most clearly seen to contain more empathy than mimicry. But to the extent that it addresses the implicit rather than the explicit, the reflection is itself interpretive, for it both assesses and elaborates upon the actual content which has been presented.

Even when the feeling is explicit though, reflection may still be seen as nothing more than a relatively restricted response on precisely the same continuum where interpretation lies—both are counter-remarks or responses of the therapist to something the patient has elected to say. The difference between them would then be quantitative only, and since reflection is quantitatively more restricted than interpretation, its consequences might differ simply by being less effective in communicating the very messages of "acceptance," "empathy," and so on, for the facilitation of which it is specifically prescribed. In effect then, the risk of failing to communicate empathy may be no greater for an interpretation that says too much than for a reflection that says too little. In either case, moreover, the therapeutic effectiveness of the remark will depend upon the interpretation lent it by the patient, not the intention of the therapist. The peculiar emphasis that the Rogerians lay on reflection may thus have no operational significance.

But what of the importance of interpretation, the equivalent cornerstone of psychoanalytic responses? It involves a somewhat greater latitude of content on the part of therapists, but does it have any greater significance than reflection? Perhaps not, especially if interpretation eventuates as a communication from the Freudian therapist of meanings equivalent to those the Rogerian conveys by reflection. The difference between them would then be a function only of the difference between the theories on which they were based. My contention is that these distinctions of devices serve to satisfy some theoretical preferences of the therapists who use them, but without much difference in effects on patients.

The Freudian scheme of things is more complicated than the Rogerian, which suggests that it requires a more complicated approach for its implementation. Since the source of feelings may involve the examination of an individual's history, and since some people find history a less than obvious subject for discussion, the Freudian therapist permits himself greater latitude for comment than does the Rogerian. It takes more to direct the patient's attention where he wants it to go. The Rogerian, on the other hand, theoretically does not want to make the patient's attention go anywhere, which is one reason his therapy is called nondirective. Consequently, he neither requires nor permits himself the same latitude of deliberate interpretation. Of course, he does want the client's attention to be focused on his own feelings, but he regards his part in getting it there as a mirroring function only.

The difference in usage is then a matter of exposing feelings in the proper context. The Freudian requires more interpretive latitude in order to get them to appear in the context of history, while the Rogerian can afford merely to reflect because he will in any case interpret the exposed feelings with no reference to time. These different techniques are, then, both equally closely related to the different theories of the Freudians and Rogerians respectively. And therefore, to the extent that the theories have similar objectives in therapy, the techniques will mean the same thing. Both Freudians and Rogerians would argue that the differences in therapy theories are of cardinal importance, but there are some grounds for questioning this.

In the first place, the Freudian emphasis on history in the development of neurosis is not challenged by the Rogerian scheme; on the contrary, the latter simply does not consider it important to deal with history in the course of therapy, attending instead to phenomenology. Any contradictions between them must then be sought in the present tense, where the sum of the differences seems to be that the Freudians claim to know a great deal about the structure and content of neurosis and the Rogerians claim that they do not. On the basis of what they believe to be their knowledge of neurotic development, the Freudians deduce a rather plausible scheme of treatment to unravel the neurosis. The Rogerians challenge the psychoanalytic genetics of personality as involving both unknowns and unknowables, but rather than contradicting it as wrong, they seem to believe simply that analytic therapy involves procedures which are unnecessary. The Rogerians then describe a treatment strategy of their own, which limits the therapist to doing only that minimum which is indispensably necessary for treatment to succeed. Their scheme thus ends up as a distillation of the Freudian, which does no real violence either to the theory of psychoanalysis or to the essence of its technique.

The single differences on which the whole technical controversy hinges may be seen as a dispute over the extent to which it is cricket for the therapist to cue the patient, and the difference here is not all that great. Freudians, for example, regard dreams as rich sources of therapeutically useful information and are therefore eager to hear their patients' dreams. But they do not prod the patient to produce them; they are much less likely to ask for dreams in the first place than they are simply to respond in a reinforcing way if a patient spontaneously brings up the subject. Similarly, they believe that the therapy sessions, to be completely effective, must involve a microcosmic repetition by the patient of important emotional experiences of earlier life, with the therapist placed in the same light as were the loved and hated figures of childhood. But the therapist hardly lectures to the patient about this expected transference of feeling, nor does he ask the patient to watch for it and let him know when some such mental spots appear. Essentially, the therapist simply waits for signs of its occurrence, and when they appear, he responds to them in such a manner as to support their exposure without demanding it. The Rogerian may accuse him of wasting time on irrelevancies by fiddling with dreams or history, but of little else, for he himself uses precisely the same general technique: he responds selectively to those unsolicited remarks of the patient that are most critically important for his treatment. The Rogerian tries to limit himself to selecting feeling tones and responding only to them, while the Freudian permits himself to respond to other things as well and to look for connections between things; but both regard the feelings as centrally important, however complicated they may be to untangle.

the personal reticence of therapists

From the preceding discussion, it is clear that Insight psychotherapists of all kinds will go to some lengths to avoid giving information about their own personal lives to their patients. From the purely tactical side, this practice seems to be corollary to the rule that patient-opted talk be the focus of therapy. In other words, if the patient must do all the talking, then the therapist had better not, and if the patient is to be encouraged to talk about his most private feelings, then it might be ill advised for the therapist to talk about himself in any terms.

But it is not simply relevance that dictates this procedure, and it is anything but corollary—for by and large, the therapist masks himself from the patient outside the therapy session as well as within it, avoiding even casual social relationships. If that is plainly impossible to begin with, he will probably not accept the patient for treatment, and if social contacts later occur unavoidably, he will limit them and probably discuss them at length as part of the therapy. At all events, it is considered extremely improper by all Insight schools for therapists deliberately to undertake or even permit social relationships with their patients or clients.[3] However personal this relationship may be in some sense, it is not in any social sense—for to make it so would be to make it an extension of that ordinary existence in which people are mostly preoccupied by their engagements with other people and with objects, and the recipient of Insight therapy must be permitted to engage with nothing but himself. His interest in the therapist as a person must be transmuted into transference projections for the Freudian and deflected away from himself and onto others who, by virtue of their physical absence, are no more than extensions of the patient's thoughts. And for the Rogerian, this interest must be reflected back onto the patient from a therapist who, operating at his best, is suffused with *empathy*, that is, who feels the patient's feelings proper, not mere sympathetic kinship with them, and who, to the extent that he succeeds, is himself the patient's self in kindly form, so that the patient may learn to see himself in the image of this beautifying mirror.

To summarize the techniques of Insight Therapy: The patient initiates all critical talking and assumes responsibility for it, while the therapist reinforces that talk which is of the most personal and feeling kind, always maintaining himself as an object but never subject of what has its meaning ultimately as an elaborate monologue. He guides the patient, as it were, by following his lead, always without letting his own identity be fully known, and without forewarning the patient where the path will lead, however many times the therapist has earlier guided others over similar paths through similar forests.

But where does the path lead? Curiously enough, for the Insight therapist this is a very secondary question to that which asks from where it originates, for the former is inexorably tied to the latter, and it is towards the clarification of that tie in the patient's mind that the therapist directs his functioning. This takes us to the examination of the theory that underlies the Insight techniques.

the motives of behavior

If "insight" is the critical term that incorporates the technical objectives of the psychotherapy system we are discussing, then "motive" is the parallel term to caption the theory of personality it employs. For the cardinal assumption which unites all dissidents among the Insight schools is that the significant problems or behaviors which are the target of psychotherapy are the products of some equally significant motives, and that the solution to those problems and changes of behavior must result primarily from changes in the motives producing them. This same proposition can be put in several different ways, and it may be well to state them, for there is no overstating its importance to the understanding of Insight therapy:

In common parlance, it says that there are compelling reasons for everything one does, that these reasons are the sources or causes of one's acts, and that the only effective way of changing the acts in question is by changing the reasons which compel them.

Yet again, this theory says that people behave in whatever ways they do because they are driven to behave so, and they cannot be persuaded or induced to behave otherwise unless they are otherwise driven or their energies reduced.

What motivates a man, what drives him, what his needs are, or his tensions, what gratifies him, what his reasons are, or goals, or objectives—all these terms mean essentially the same thing, and all may be employed equally aptly in the basic formula of motivation theory, that motives determine and dictate acts. In the order of behavioral events, motives seem to occur prior to the acts they motivate. Their priority in sequence is taken as a basis by the Insight therapist, from which, adding on some secondary postulates, he builds an intellectual structure in which motives are prior in significance as well. At the extreme of this position, acts are left dangling as helplessly from their motives as puppets from their strings.

There is a biological basis to this argument which is so familiar to the experience of everyone that it seems like the most elementary common sense: We eat because we are hungry, sleep because we are tired, evacuate because our bowels are full, and so forth. In each case, these acts, which we may plainly observe in another person, are driven or compelled or motivated by things within him which we cannot see, but none can doubt that such acts are a consequence of their motives. And if this is the case in biology, it hardly strains credibility to extend it to psychology, proposing that more refined and less vital drives develop from fundamental ones, so that general hunger may eventually result in a specific craving for meat or bread or ice cream or even for money with which they can be procured. By such reasoning, one may finally reach the point of arguing that all behaviors may be explained by some motives which underlie them, and that all acts seek ultimately to satisfy unseen drives.

If this idea is applied to the symptoms that cause people to undergo psychotherapy, then all such symptoms can be properly understood as attempts to satisfy some need, as expressions of some drive, revelations of some longing or some fear. Far from being pointless, accidental, automated things irrelevant to the essence of one's life, as measles, broken legs, and staph infections are irrelevant, these symptoms are replete with meaning, derivatives of unseen needs, immeasurably significant of causes whose content may be vague, but that lurk beneath the symptom as surely as the symptom can itself be seen.

This view of symptoms bespeaks some hope or confidence that the world is a rational place in which results do not take place without causes, nor consequences without antecedents, and this suggests a strategy for treatment. Not only should the symptom be relieved, but tracing back its course to find its origin may make it possible to quell the flood of misery at its source—while failing to do so, and attacking the symptom alone, runs the risk of damming up one outlet only to leave the torrent free to break through at another point, in another symptom.

The implication for treatment is more ambiguous and has been less important, however, to Insight therapy than the model of disorder implied by this doctrine, for the suggestion that there is no such thing as a meaningless symptom, and that all symptoms have reference to ideas or feelings or impulses which go to the core of a man's being, intimates as well that all of his experiences are somehow important and worthy of his attention. And if he does not engage in any truly incidental behavior, then he must operate entirely on some pay-off principle that directs every motion, however minute, to the satisfaction of some need. But if that is the case, then the definition of a symptom is now clearly reduced to "that behavior which tries to gratify some need and fails to do so." Then the problem of understanding the nature of the disorder is one of tracing, in detective story fashion, the need whose satisfaction is the symptom's futile aim, and insofar as treatment involves the removal of symptoms, it becomes a matter of trying to do away with the need, which is generally unlikely, or more realistically, of finding and using means other than the symptom by which it can be satisfied. At all events, the belief that acts are essentially the consequences of their underlying motives forces one's attention to a consideration of the "meaning" of any act, for meaning means the pattern of events and circumstances which antecede, surround, and "cause" events. The motive of an act thus is its meaning, and this consideration ultimately demands, as we shall see, that as therapeutic discourse involves motives of increasing significance, the therapeutic situation itself evolves into an exploration of the meaning of one's life. This is least deliberately true, historically, of Freudian psychoanalysis, which is even today "classically" articulated as a system aimed at facilitating personal adjustment, in other words, at reducing psychological distress so that people may conduct their affairs without undue susceptibility to feelings of anxiety and guilt. The search for meaning is fostered more strongly, albeit passively, in the Rogerian system, which is built entirely on a concern with a capitalized, concretized entity called the Self, whose very definition must incorporate the meaning systems people use to judge themselves. But the search culminates actively, explicitly, and deliberately in the writing of the existential analysts, who identify psychological distress as a loss of meaning and treatment as the effort to discover or construct a meaning in life, regardless of the fate of the symptoms themselves. This is the situation which describes the patient who, when therapy is done, says that his tics and headaches are still there, but that his attitude has changed for the better, so that they no longer bother him. However ironical, this is a logical development in a system which posits, as its first principle, that the most apparent behavior is peripheral and less important than some unseen thing that lies behind it. It says in effect that the "real problem" is never what it seems to be.

The assumption of the prepotent effects of motivation lends an aura of indirection to the operations of Insight therapists. Symptoms must be flanked rather than attacked outright, not because they cannot be assaulted directly, nor even because symptomatic changes, when induced, might be unstable in and of themselves, but for another reason: The vital task is, to begin with, the discovery of the complex of motives from which the symptoms spring. And this is no simple matter, for not only are motives less than evident to others, but they are also often hidden from the sufferer himself. The significance of consciousness, or rather unconsciousness, is second in importance in the theories of Insight systems only to that of motivation. The main reason why people continue to manifest their symptoms over long periods of time despite their efforts to change is that their motives are hidden from themselves. The task of therapy is to expose those motives, not so much to the therapist as to the patient himself. The techniques of therapy are then systems for facilitating this exposure, for producing consciousness. And the occurrence in one's awareness of things of which he was previously unaware defines insight.

Insight is thus synonymous with consciousness, and the expansion of consciousness is indeed the productive goal of all Insight therapies. What then is the significance of the widely touted phenomena called unconscious processes? With the exception of classical psychoanalysis, this is a moot point. The Freudian system has assumed that motives were effective in producing neurotic symptoms somewhat in proportion to how thoroughly out of awareness they were, and a large scholarly industry has developed within psychotherapeutic writing and research on personality, as well as in practice itself, for analyzing, exploring, elaborating, elucidating, and otherwise inquiring into Unconsciousness and the mental mechanisms which sustain it. But the secondary position of such processes in Insight systems is clear enough if we keep in mind that unconscious contents are never dealt with directly; they are always inferred, never measured, and thus far, are not clearly measurable.[4] Most important, they are inferred primarily from that material which occurs in consciousness, whether free associations, dreams, or straightforward reports of experience. The very assumption of the existence of unconscious processes can be seen as a means of facilitating the expansion of consciousness, for it suggests that there is an endless supply of content within the mind of the patient which can be coaxed into awareness.

The minimum assumptions of Insight therapists about personality are that symptoms, like all behaviors, are significantly motivated and that their operations are sustained and their removal impeded by a relative dearth of consciousness. The activities of all Insight therapists must therefore involve some kind of insight-producing sequence of (1) exposure, whether by requiring free association or passively letting people say what they wish; (2) therapist operation on the exposed material, whether by analytic interpretation or empathic reflection; and (3) consciousness or insight within the patient, whether intellectual, a greater understanding of himself, or emotional, a feeling of awareness of himself.

But what is insight supposed to do in turn? How is it supposed to change anything? We find in Insight therapy a body of techniques of practice and assumptions about personality that are reasonably consistent with each other, and we are returned once more to the question of where the system is supposed to go.

the uses of consciousness

To be fair and accurate, I believe that this question must be properly answered at two different levels, a *scientific* one, whose value now appears chiefly historical, and a *moralistic* one, which may finally propose more questions than it answers. The scientific answer is that insight is supposed to produce relief from the symptoms which have been troubling the person and to provide him with a greater degree of control over himself than he has previously felt. The moralistic answer is that insight is not supposed to do anything, that it is a quantum desirable in maximum amounts and sufficient unto itself, and that its achievement in proper measure represents the point in therapy at which the doctor has fulfilled his responsibility and may discharge his patient as cured. Cured of what? Of ignorance of self.

science and insight therapy

Insight therapy began as a thoroughly scientific enterprise in the work of Breuer and Freud, both at that time practicing physicians deeply concerned with finding means for treating neurotic symptoms. The discovery of the techniques from which psychoanalysis evolved, and the later elaboration of those techniques into a formal system of treatment, was directed primarily at an attack on a limited set of symptoms. Even the intricate personality theory that Freud's genius constructed out of a medley of clinical observations, personal experiences, and literary acumen was intended primarily as a means for deducing how neurotic symptoms arose and for predicting the course that psychoanalytic therapy might take towards their relief. In other words, the system started with the technical problem of the existence of neurotic symptoms and worked itself both backwards to a theory explaining their origins and forwards towards a means of hastening their end; but theory of any kind was, for a long time, entirely adjunct and subsidiary to a concern with curing symptoms, and success or failure of the therapy could be judged entirely in those simple but eminently scientific terms.

Insight came to be regarded as a curative agent because early Freudians viewed the development of symptoms as an immediate consequence of an unconsciousness-producing mental mechanism—repression. Repression prevented its victim from recognizing his motivations, which, continuing to operate sub rosa, eventually expressed themselves in the unhappy form of neuroses. Lifting the repression, permitting consciousness, or eliciting insight, might therefore be expected to relieve the pressure of the motive, so that it would not force its expression any longer in the form of symptoms. Once insight occurred, the symptom might go away by itself, as it were, without further attempts at decision. If not that, the occurrence of insight still meant that the patient would recognize his motives clearly, and this done, he would be able to find ways of fulfilling or handling them which would make the symptoms superfluous, thus atrophying them.[5]

As stated, the foregoing scientific rationale for Insight therapy remains a basic tenet to this day of all those schools of therapy that orient themselves towards psychoanalysis, whether "neoFreudian" or "classical," for it is just this rationale that justifies the therapy of searching for underlying motives. But there are probably few adherents of this system who nowadays would state its doctrine in such an elementary form, for in that form it is, by and large, invalid. For most of the problems of most people, it seems generally to be the case that the achievement of insight, however detailed and precise, into their motivations, however unconscious, does not by itself solve their problems, reduce their symptoms, or change their lives in any but a gross intellectual or economic sense—they have an enormous body of information for talking about themselves at cocktail parties, and they are out so much and so much in analytic fees.

It is possible, of course, that whenever insight does not produce relief, it is false insight, with the true motives still remaining hidden, or that the insights achieved are valid but incomplete, with their motivations actually more complicated than was thought. Puristic adherents of insight make precisely such claims, and analysts who keep patients in treatment for ten or fifteen or twenty years are implicitly making them.[6] The concept of "interminable analysis," a problem of some currency among psychoanalysts even during Freud's life, can be sustained by this argument. But if this idea is not false just because it is logically circular, it is still terribly wasteful; in scientific matters, merely reasonable arguments, which this one is, rarely succeed as explanations in competition with parsimonious ones, and a parsimonious argument here would be that insight is just not very effective by itself in solving most therapeutic problems.

Most modern Insight therapists have had too much experience with this situation to insist any longer that the achievement of insight spontaneously melts away all other problems, but they are still prone to approach therapeutic problems by asking about the underlying complexes of motives which produce them and by assuming, in the first instance, that these problems can be treated by insight methods. They are likely to rationalize the use of insight more in terms of somewhat indirect effects mentioned earlier. "True, achieving insight will not necessarily solve all problems or remove all symptoms," they say, "but what it will do is put the patient in a position where he can now control his behavior if he is sufficiently motivated to do so." To some extent, this position suffers from the same circularity as the previous one, for the only obvious index of whether the patient is sufficiently motivated is whether or not the relief of symptoms occurs. If it does not, then it becomes possible to say that the patient's claim was untrue that he wanted an end put to his symptoms, and the plea was itself the result of hidden motives which require exploration. We are then back where we started, but this kind of risk is inherent in any argument that puts much emphasis or credence on the efficacy of unseen and essentially invisible and unmeasurable factors—there is no clear-cut point at which they can be logically excluded as explanations of events.

The importance of the second argument is not in any logical superiority it may have over the first one, but rather in its implication that psychotherapy is a more limited or less specific endeavor than one might otherwise guess it to be. The idea that insight facilitates control rather than removes symptoms reduces the responsibility of the therapist—he is no longer required to seek to cure the patient, but rather to put the patient in a position where, if he so wishes, he will now be able to cure himself!

In one sense, this position is more consistent with the actual techniques of Insight therapists than is the argument that success is defined by relief. Throughout the actual course of treatment, initiative is left to the patient and the responsibility for what is done in the sessions must be assumed by him. Then why not responsibility for the cure as well?

The scientific difficulty with this position is brought on, not by making the patient responsible for the removal of his own symptoms, but by exempting symptom-removal itself from the requirements of cure, for this removes the most clearly measurable means of assessing what psychotherapy has accomplished. When the connection between insight and symptoms is loosened, as it is here, it may be proper to "successfully" terminate treatment with symptoms still present, or conversely, to say that treatment is a failure even with all the symptoms gone unless insight has somehow been achieved. The first case is akin to saying that the treatment cured everything except what bothered the patient in the first place, while the second says that it does not matter if the patient is well unless he is also educated. Finally, since insight is itself applied to hidden motives whose precise quantity is made unsure by the very fact that they are hidden, how does one know how much insight is enough? The scientific status of the therapy depends upon its success or failure in terms of some measurable relationships between the insight it produces and the object towards which that insight is directed, and no object is more obvious than symptoms.

morals and insight therapy

Despite these difficulties, the divorce of insight from such practical effects as symptom removal is not altogether senseless. It does not necessarily follow that, since the existence of symptoms is what starts the search for motives going in the first place, the discoveries which result will ipso facto satisfy the impetus for the search. The fact that Columbus failed to find a new route to India did not make the discovery of America less real or less important. The Insight therapist, by the same token, may propose to start on the motivational path suggested by the symptoms which confront him without prejudice as to where it will lead, with only the faith that it will lead somewhere worth going. But in so doing, he effectively abandons the elementary notions of treatment and cure that are common to patients and doctors alike for most ailments; for all practical purposes, he makes of insight an end unto itself, which, insofar as it does not relate to symptoms, forces a redefinition of his work; this new definition is one that casts him in the mold of a secular moralist. As long as the prescription of insight is rationalized in terms of its effect on some demonstrable set of symptoms, the therapist can claim that his is a technical operation, more or less scientifically conceived and directed at some measurable end. But the more the concrete ends are attenuated, the less is this possible, till even the idea that treatment is a preventive against some future chain of events which can act on a person to produce some specific symptoms is a weakened claim to practice. And when the justification of insight no longer bears on its effect upon some known distress, but on different ends, then the fitness of its dispensation is more a moral than a scientific matter.

The plainest moral problem in its dispensation is seen if we think of insight as having some moving effect upon one's life in every way except in its ability to cure symptoms, for the fact that the doctor is then trying to sell something other than what the patient intended to buy is morally questionable. The same question might apply almost as well, however, if insight cured symptoms too, for so long as it did more than that, it would do other than that; but in such events, it is usually easy to overlook the other effects. In any case, the point here is not so much one of establishing professional ethics, which are often no more than fair trade laws, as of assessing the very nature of the profession. It does not propose that Insight therapists, by doing something other than curing symptoms, are immoral rather than moral, but that they are thereby moralists rather than scientists. It is the generality of their efforts, not their efficacy, which forces this conclusion.

What is the morality they promote? By precept, it is the virtue of insight, or consciousness, or self-knowledge. By example, it is the necessity for each man to assume his own initiatives in the quest for insight and to be alone responsible for its achievement. By implication, it is the right of individuals above all else to live as they choose.

For the Freudian, the unknown self that needs knowing is ultimately one of violent and lustful impulses, denied as one's own, attributed only to the foulest parts of others, filled with the antitheses of the domestic or heroic virtues decreed by the culture and ordered to be exalted by the individual. For the Rogerian, it is a self of discrepancy, where exalted ideals and aspirations are masks for fear, and where deprecation of self is a false and unworthy treatment of an immeasurably acceptable, lovable person. For the existentialist, it is a self alone in a hostile universe who, to become capable of knowledge, must recognize its inevitable aloneness as the first step towards the imposition of meaning upon chaos. Regardless of the content to be exhumed, the supposition of all the Insight theorists is the same: that the self is valuable, that it is worthy of being known, and that its title to explication and intelligibility is its very existence rather than any behavior it undertakes or performance it sets in motion.

That one must in therapy assume initiative himself for the discovery of self is a technicality based partly on the assumption that he will refuse to hear or understand the meanings of self if they are delivered from outside. But it is also a means of reinforcing the moral doctrine of selfhood, by making the patient be alone even within the therapy sessions, by enforcing independence. And the moral goal this tactic finally serves—autonomy, freedom to experience the self, to enhance it, to gratify it, to unbind it, to give it rein to palpate itself and, so doing, to be fulfilled. What concrete acts subserve this end and constitute some therapeutic deeds? Exactly none, or any, or all—what serves the self, or fairly represents it to itself, can qualify.

The virtues of this moral are so popular among educated people in democratic countries that it would be redundant to recount them in any detail. It exonerates the individualism of the Protestant ethic in a more plausible context than could any believing Christian; it grounds the search for the justification of political autonomy in lawful biology; it poses man's right to independence in more elementary and final terms than could the best of eighteenth-century rationalists, offering in drive reduction theory a more "natural" order of things than Encyclopedists or natural theologians ever dreamed; it frees the artist from suspicion of perversity, both by assigning the same perversity to all mankind and by casting on conformism the shadow both of perversity and hypocrisy. It offers the ultimate justification of the individual, and so it has since its earliest, most conservative exposition at Freud's hand; his theory, for example, of the original bisexuality of man can be seen as an attempt to deny the biologicial sociality of humankind, and to assert the unique right of the individual to survive alone.

In its most modern and extreme form, culminating in existential analysis, Insight therapy strives to establish or restore meaning, not function, to life. This is as much as to say that the object of treatment here is not so much surcease of pain as the establishment of a context of meaning in life of which the pain is an intelligible part. This of course, is what religions have long since tried to do; and it is what, when they failed to maintain enough credibility for the intelligentsia of any age, philosophies tried to replace. Thus Stoicism and Epicureanism in the ancient world when the mystery religions gave up their strength. Now Zen Buddhism and such in the West, nonprofessional counterparts of existential analysis, all alike striving to replace the meanings that were lost with the loss of the extrinsic morality of Judaism and Christianity.

the problems of insight morality

The extent to which Insight therapy fails to restore function is the extent to which we must discount its scientific pretensions as an applied healing art, and any such scientific failure raises moral questions in its own right. But the evaluation of function is the bête noire of the Action therapists anyhow, so it is not necessary to look closely at it here. It is precisely to the meanings which are implicit in Insight therapy that the most significant moral questions must be addressed, and these questions, centering around the implications of hidden motives and the status of individualism, must be examined for more than their positive contributions to social philosophy. Insight therapies, particularly psychoanalysis, have become the psychological orthodoxies of our time, and like all orthodoxies, their moral orders have such a familiar ring that, at their worst, they may appear more comfortably familiar than repulsive.

The system proposes, for example, to operate by lending all initiatives to the patient. But does it really do so, or is the proposal itself part of a massive seduction that culminates when the patient voluntarily exercises the therapist's preferences? If the latter, then the seduction may become even more effective when the therapist shares the myth of his own psychological midwifery. By this idea, Insight therapists insulate themselves from all assaults—if they fail to relieve symptoms, they fail only passively, and are not much responsible for a condition whose cure resides within the patient alone to begin with; but if they succeed in changing him otherwise, and in ways that are opprobrious to the patient, or the therapist, or the society, they are not culpable there either—for all they have done is put him in contact with himself by catalyzing his own behavior, and the choices he makes are his, not theirs.

But are the choices really his either according to this system? The seeming endless chain of underlying motives, especially those *unseen* (and thus demanding *insight*), suggests that he is finally free of choice, or will, or all executive capacities. As Anna Balakian suggests, does not "the preoccupation with the subconscious . . . anesthetize the sensitivities of that faculty which used to be called 'conscience'?" That is, perhaps any moral sense must be attenuated beyond repair by introspection of a causal sequence that puts events so far in time and space from their inception that it makes the notion of responsibility absurd, literally *ab-surd*, rootless, unanchored in any recognizable self.

And if so, then the doctrine which espouses a search for some self hidden beneath the surface of behavior sustains this very rootlessness by claiming that there is a "real self" somehow different from what is seen. The assumption of massive complexity, the mental iceberg that Freud describes, by its denial of the relevance of parsimony and the possibility of measurement, will always witness in defense of nonresponsibility, leaving the individual free to see his self as unsullied and inviolable.

Perhaps the heart of the problem lies here, not in the question of whether the Insight therapist really can confer freedom of choice or even of whether he should want to, but rather that the outcome of his most successful efforts might be a person who, schooled in all the erstwhile hidden references to self, could be best described as a well-adjusted psychopath. This is not to say that such a person necessarily would be, except in the most conventional terms, amoral, but rather that his would be a moral order whose referents lay all within himself. If so, then the core question is whether the broad facilitation of this doctrine would create individuals who could support a social order. If the methods of Insight therapy are effective in making a person cognizant of his self as an entity, then may he not see it ultimately in isolation? In this sense, the existentialists are quite correct in speaking of "the ultimate aloneness of man." Such a self is, at best, asocial, and its possessor could presumably be as antisocial as might serve his purposes at any time.

If sociality meant crude conformity to mindless automata or to the brutal dicta of aloof tyrannies, then nurturing the lonely self would preserve humanity. But this is not the usual case, and it is least so in societies where psychotherapies all flourish best and individuals are most secure from harm. For those individuals, C. P. Snow puts the problem clearly: "Most of our fellow human beings . . . are underfed and die before their time. In the crudest terms, *that* is the social condition. There is a moral trap which comes through the insight into man's loneliness: it tempts one to sit back, complacent in one's unique tragedy, and let the others go without a meal" (*The Two Cultures*, p. 7).

The asocial implications of Insight therapy have disturbed its adherents as well as its critics, and they have made many attempts, both formally and casually, to incorporate sociality within one or another rationale of Insight therapy. Arguments in this direction sometimes take the form that real selves are discovered finally in interpersonal relationships such as love, or that, since in the therapy situation the self is discovered through the medium of a social relation, a generalized need develops for fulfillment through relationships. Sophisticated theories, like those of H. S. Sullivan, offer these principles as more than articles of faith, and offer plausible descriptions of how the self comes into being in the first place in a social context, implying that its existence must be maintained in one. But none of these answers satisfy the question, for they say simply that the self can make use of sociality—we are asking whether it can be used for society.

In some ways, this question is tangential to the purposes of Insight therapy. For societies exploit people in terms of functions, and this system is ultimately directed at meanings. A man's social functions are things outside his self, but his existence is finally meaningful only with reference to his self. This argument is, I believe, common to all Insight therapies, and since they tend only to discuss self, not social functions, it commits all of them equally to a moral order in which individuals, pitted against societies, have prior right. But it is a right without mandatory commitment or responsibility, and in this, it differs not only from classical social theory, which, as Phillip Rieff so eloquently describes it, sees society as the true therapeutic agent and good citizenship as the final mental prophylactic. It differs too from classical definitions of virtue, both religious and secular, which hinge human dignity, or worthiness, or finally even meaning, to moral codes that lie outside the self, whether revealed in thunder and inscribed in stone, or elected into law by common counsel among peers.

If the latter have no more claim to truth than Insight, and surely age alone can give them none, they at least have the qualities of being represented in functions that are identifiable, and measurable, and—relative to insight doctrines—simple. And this suggests a final question of the moral force of Insight therapy.

The essence of this system is that it rationalizes behaviors in terms of the motives which precede or underlie them. But when the behaviors under study are weak or stupid or vile, representative of some *malfunction*, the distinction between explanation and excuse becomes confused and arbitrary in fact, if not in theory. There is a danger then, since this system must in any case proceed this way, that the wholesale quest for insight into self which occupies so much of intellect in these times, is not so much a quest for truth at large, or even for control of self, as a grand apology for impotence in fact, which makes the search for meaning but a final desperate substitute for functions which were long since lost.

conclusion

The earliest efforts of Insight therapists, as described here, were directed at the alleviation of symptoms. Later, more attention was paid to making it possible for the patient to increase control of his behavior, including control of some kinds of symptoms. Most recently, effort has been made to help people to discover meanings in their existence that would make life more worthwhile even if their symptoms were quite unchanged. In the first category, symptoms included things such as phobias and hysterical paralyses; the second class expanded the concept of symptoms, or at least of disorders amenable to psychotherapy, to things such as uncontrollable impulses, sexual perversions, and so-called disorders of character; and the third class expanded the scope of the Insight therapist to things such as a general concern with happiness, or death, or security. The last category clearly refers to matters of a traditionally moralistic rather than scientific nature, but it is the second category, with its obvious problems of perspective and of the social consequences of behavior, which requires that the finest distinctions be made between the roles of moralist and applied scientist. If Insight therapists have failed to concern themselves with this distinction, it is at least as much because they operate in a society basically sympathetic to individual liberty and rich and powerful enough to tolerate a great deal of deviation within it as because they have generally wished to reject the role of moralist. The latter is nonetheless true, as should be partly apparent from the very neutrality of their procedures. At all events, it seems plain that their theoretical positions are such that they would be thoroughly committed to a morality of individualism were they to specify their moral role. The single qualifier of importance currently popular among Insight therapists is that people, in doing what they please, should not hurt others. Adherents of Western religions and utopian social visions would, by and large, view this as an inadequate morality, however therapeutic for individuals. Opponents of Insight therapy among professional members of the therapeutic disciplines may see it as antitherapeutic for individuals, however moral.

The opponents of Insight therapy among psychotherapists are, if anything, even less concerned with morals than are Insight therapists. But they are, by their own lights, more concerned with science. Their indictment of Insight therapy has nothing to do with the category of problems of meaning, which they sometimes see as a meaningless concept, and not much more with the moral implications of the second category, problems of character. It is to the problem of symptom removal that they address themselves, proposing stridently that Insight therapy is, in the first place, generally incapable of relieving symptoms, that it is grossly uneconomical when it is successful, and that in those instances where successes are recorded, they have nothing to do with the achievement of insight, but are either accidental or the result of specific *actions* which can be identified and measured.

notes

1. They sometimes try to protect patients from them too, as when a Freudian therapist told a patient to make his wife stop seeing a Jungian because "we can't have two kinds of therapy going on in the same family."

2. Freudian psychoanalysts are kind enough to try to remove this responsibility from the patient as well by their "cardinal rule of analysis," which is to say whatever comes to mind. Analytic hypnotherapists may go even further by suggesting not only that the patient assume no responsibility for what he says, but also that he does not have to listen to it or remember it afterwards.

3. This analysis pays no attention to those mundane reasons which have nothing to do with either technique or theory of therapy, but may still be important, such as the fact that therapist and patient may both be embarrassed by a tea party relationship after the intense interactions of their sessions, or that therapists in particular would just as soon not be bothered with the same people after hours, or that neurotics may be unpleasant company.

4. There may be important exceptions to this with respect to some physiological and psychological changes that unconsciously accompany some psychological states and

may be controlled by them (see Blum and Razran), and certainly a great deal of routine performance in everyday life is unconscious (Eriksen). The argument does apply to unconscious "content" that is inferred from verbal reports, however, and is therefore applicable to virtually everything that happens in Insight therapy.

5. The language of classical psychoanalysis is enormously more complicated than my statement suggests, but I do not think its ideas really are. Very many terms are used to describe the prevention of consciousness, such as "defenses," "denial," and "projection," but these are all variants of repression. Similarly, many terms describe the facilitation of consciousness—"abreaction," "working through," "screening," and so on but these all concern variations in the situations, processes, and experiences that culminate in insight.

6. The figures used here are not literary but literal ones: a colleague recently brought to my attention that the analytic consultant to a distinguished mental hospital urged the psychotherapists there not to give up "too easily" on their cases. To illustrate, he told how he was now in the sixteenth year of treating a homosexual, though intensive treatment had been going on only for ten. He was pleased to report that the man was finally making such progress that "in another four years he should be able to make a heterosexual adjustment."

24

The Elimination of Children's Fears

Mary Cover Jones

The investigation of children's fears leads directly to a number of important problems in the genetic study of emotion. At the Johns Hopkins laboratory Dr. John B. Watson has analyzed the process by which fears are acquired in infancy, and has shown that the conditioned reflex formula may apply to the transfer of emotional reactions from original stimuli (pain, loud noises, or loss of bodily support) to various substitute fear objects in the child's environment. This process has been further demonstrated by the author in the case of children from one to four years of age. A study of how children's fears may be reduced or eradicated would seem to be the next point for an experimental attack. Such a study should include an attempt to evaluate, objectively, the various possible methods which laboratory experience has suggested.

The present research, an approach to this problem, was conducted with the advice of Dr. Watson, by means of a subvention granted by the Laura Spelman Rockefeller Memorial to the Institute of Educational Research of Teachers College.

The subjects, 70 children from 3 months to 7 years of age, were maintained in an institution for the temporary care of children. Admission to this institution depended as a rule upon conditions which made it difficult or impos-

Reprinted from the *Journal of Experimental Psychology*, 1924, Vol. 7, No. 5, pp. 382–390. Copyright 1924 by the American Psychological Association. Reprinted by permission.

sible to keep the children at home: a case of illness in the family, the separation of father and mother, or an occupation which kept the mother away from home for a part of the day. As there was a charge for weekly care, those homes which were in actual poverty were not represented; the economic and social status of the parents, as well as the results of our intelligence tests (Kuhlmann and Terman) would indicate that this group of children was normal, and superior to the average for orphan asylums and similar institutions. As the danger of contagion is great in a group so constantly changing, a very thorough medical examination eliminated all those with symptoms of infection, and even those decidedly below normal in nutrition or general development. Our laboratory could not determine the admission and discharge of children, nor interfere in the prescribed routine of eating, sleeping and play. It was possible however for the experimenter to live in the building with the children in order to become acquainted with them in their usual environment, to observe them continuously for days at a time, and to take them daily, or oftener if desirable, to the laboratory where observations could be made under specifically controlled conditions.

In our selection of children from this group, we attempted to find those who would show a marked degree of fear under conditions normally evoking positive (pleasant) or mildly negative (unpleasant) responses. A wide range of situations were presented in a fairly standardized way to all of the children: such as being left alone, being in a dark room, being with other children who showed fear, the sudden presentation of a snake, a white rat, a rabbit, a frog, false faces, loud sounds, etc. This procedure served to expose fear trends if they were already present; it was not designed as a conditioning process, but merely as a method of revealing prior conditionings. In the majority of the children tested, our standard situations failed to arouse observable negative responses. This survey of children's fears is reported in another article.

When specific fears were demonstrated, our next step was to attempt their removal. By what devices could we eliminate these harmful reactions, which in many cases were subject to diffusion, and were interfering with the formation of useful attitudes and necessary habits? Our method or combination of methods depended upon the type of case presented and the manner in which treatment was received, as well as upon such external circumstances as quarantines, and the length of time the child was likely to remain in the institution.

the method of elimination through disuse

A common assumption with regard to children's fears is that they will die out if left alone, i.e., if the child is carefully shielded from stimuli which would tend to re-arouse the fear. "Elimination through disuse" is the name given to this process. The following cases from our records provide suggestive material:

case 1.—Rose D., age 21 months

General situation: sitting in play-pen with other children, none of whom showed specific fears. A rabbit was introduced from behind a screen.

Jan. 19 At sight of the rabbit, Rose burst into tears, her crying lessened when the experimenter picked up the rabbit, but again increased when the rabbit was put back on the floor. At the removal of the rabbit she quieted down, accepted a cracker, and presently returned to her blocks.

Feb. 5   After 2 weeks the situation was repeated. She cried and trembled upon seeing the rabbit. E. (the experimenter) sat on the floor between Rose and the rabbit; she continued to cry for several minutes. E. tried to divert her attention with the peg-board; she finally stopped crying, but continued to watch the rabbit and would not attempt to play.

case 8.——Bobby G., age 30 months

Dec. 6   Bobby showed a slight fear response when a rat was presented in a box. He looked at it from a distance of several feet, drew back and cried. A 3-day period of training followed bringing Bobby to the point where he tolerated a rat in the open pen in which he was playing, and even touched it without overt fear indications. No further stimulation with the rat occurred until

Jan. 30   After nearly two months of no experience with the specific stimulus, Bobby was again brought into the laboratory. While he was playing in the pen, E. appeared, with a rat held in her hand. Bobby jumped up, ran outside the pen, and cried. The rat having been returned to its box, Bobby ran to E., held her hand, and showed marked disturbance.

case 33.——Eleanor J., age 21 months

Jan. 17   While playing in the pen, a frog was introduced from behind her. She watched, came nearer, and finally touched it. The frog jumped. She withdrew and when later presented with the frog, shook her head and pushed the experimenter's hand away violently.

March 26   After two months of no further experience with animals, Eleanor was taken to the laboratory and offered the frog. When the frog hopped she drew back, ran from the pen and cried.

These and similar cases show that an interval of "disuse," extending over a period of weeks or months, may not result in eliminating a fear response, and that when other conditions are approximately constant there may be no diminution in the degree of fear manifested. From our experience, it would appear to be an unsafe method to attempt the cure of a fear trend by ignoring it.

the method of verbal appeal

As most of our subjects were under four years of age, the possibilities of verbal analysis and control were very limited. We attempted to find how much we could accomplish toward breaking down a negative reaction by merely talking about the fear-object, endeavoring to keep it in the child's attention, and connecting it verbally with pleasant experiences. This method showed no applicability except in the case of one subject, Jean E., a girl in her fifth year. At the initial presentation of the rabbit a marked fear response was registered. This was followed by ten minutes daily conversation about the rabbit; to hold her interest the experimenter introduced such devices as the picture book of "Peter Rabbit," toy rabbits, and rabbits drawn or modelled from plastocene. Brief stories were used, and there was always a reference to the "real" rabbit as well. On such occasions she would say, "Where is your rabbit?" or "Show me your rabbit," or once

"I touched your rabbit, and stroked it, and it never cried." (This latter was pure make-believe, and an interesting example of projection.) However, when the rabbit was actually presented again, at the end of a week, her reaction was practically the same as at the first encounter. She jumped up from her play and retreated; when coaxed, she reluctantly touched the rabbit while the experimenter held it; when the animal was put down on the floor she sobbed "Put it away," "Take it," and ran about the room frightened and distracted. She had learned to speak freely of rabbits, but this altered verbalization apparently was not accompanied by any change in her response to the rabbit itself. The experiment was interrupted after another three days of the same procedure, at the end of which time Jean left the institution with her initial fear patterns intact, so far as we could tell. It seems likely that many hours of training in the toleration of symbols may have little or no modifying effect on a mass reaction to the primary stimulus.

the method of negative adaptation

This method is based on the theory that familiarity breeds indifference: if the stimulation is repeated often enough, monotonously, the subject finally becomes used to it and tempers his response accordingly.

case 17.—Godfried W., age 3 years

A white rat was introduced from behind a screen. Godfried sat quietly for a few minutes, watching the rat with close attention. He then began to cry, made avertive movements with his hands and feet, and finally withdrew as far as possible from the animal. At the next presentation of the rat, Godfried did not cry; he advanced cautiously, making quick startled withdrawals whenever the animal moved.

A few days later when the same situation was presented, Godfried smiled and said, "Put it down on the floor." After three hours the rat was again brought in and allowed to run free in the pen. It scurried about and occasionally came very near him, but Godfried made no attempt to withdraw even when the animal advanced and touched him.

In this case, with practically no reëducative measures except repeated stimulation, Godfried conquered his specific fear. The experiment was not carried to the point where he showed a distinct positive reaction to rats, but he had developed a socially satisfactory attitude. As a strictly non-verbal approach, the method of negative adaptation is undoubtedly useful with infants and animals. In actual practice, however, we find very few fears in children of the pre-language period, and with the older children it is inefficient to eliminate the degree of control, however slight, which language may afford.

Furthermore, with all but a few of our fear-objects the aim was not indifference, which negative adaptation implies, but something farther along the scale toward an acceptance reaction.

From our experience in general, it would appear that the repeated presentation of a feared object, with no auxiliary attempt to eliminate the fear, is more likely to produce a summation effect than an adaptation. With Godfried (the case just quoted) the loss of his resistance was possibly due to the fact that he had been afraid the animal would bite him. This fear, unrealized, was gradually overcome.

the method of repression

In the home, as well as in the school and playground, social repression is perhaps the simplest and most common method of dealing with fear symptoms . . . a method, which, we may commonly note, often fails to remove the roots of the fear. As there are already too many examples of the maladaptive results of repression, we shall not attempt to add to their number. In our laboratory we used no repressive punishment, but within a group of children the familiar situations of ridicule, social teasing and scolding frequently appeared. Because of shame, a child might try to contain his fears without overt expression, but after a certain point had been reached, the reaction appeared nothwithstanding.

case 41.—Arthur G., age 4 years

Arthur was shown the frogs in an aquarium, no other children being present. He cried, said "they bite," and ran out of the play-pen. Later, however, he was brought into the room with four other boys; he swaggered up to the aquarium, pressing ahead of the others who were with him. When one of his companions picked up a frog and turned to him with it, he screamed and fled; at this he was chased and made fun of, but with naturally no lessening of the fear on this particular occasion.

Three boys standing around the aquarium each cried "Give me one," holding out their hands for a frog. But when the frog was offered they all precipitously withdrew. When two girls (4 years old) sang out to Sidney (age 3) "Sidney is afraid, Sidney is afraid," Sidney nodded his head in assent . . . illustrating what often happens in the use of social ridicule: the emotion is re-suggested and entrenched, rather than stamped out.

the method of distraction

A convenient method, used frequently and with fair results, involves offering the subject a substitute activity. In order to capture a safety pin from the baby's hand and still preserve peace, its attention may be distracted with another toy, while you steal away the pin. Such a device, known to every mother, may be applied to the problem of eliminating fear responses. Arthur, whose fear of frogs had received some attention from us, wished to play with a set of crayons kept in the laboratory. We placed the crayons close to a frog on the table. Arthur stepped forward cautiously; keeping his gaze on the frog, he grabbed paper and crayons and showed alacrity in darting out of the danger zone. The experience, however, seemed to reassure him. "I ran over there and got it," he told us, "He didn't bite me. Tomorrow I'll put it in a little box and bring it home." At one stage of his fear of the rabbit, Sidney would whine whenever the rabbit was brought near, but he could readily be diverted by conversation about the rabbit's name, or some innocuous detail. For verbal distraction the constant presence of a grown-up is of course necessary; this introduces factors which are not always advantageous (such as reliance upon adult protection). Essentially, distraction soothes a fear response by inducing the child temporarily to forget the fear-object. (Substitution of an alternate stimulus-response system.) This may fail to result in any permanent reduction of the fear trend. Where the situation is properly managed, however, distraction passes over into a method which we have found distinctly useful, and which will now be described.

the method of direct conditioning

It is probable that each of our methods involves conditioning in one form or another. Under this heading, however, we include all specific attempts to associate with the fear-object a definite stimulus, capable of arousing a positive (pleasant) reaction. The hunger motive appears to be the most effective for use in this connection. During a period of craving for food, the child is placed in a high chair and given something to eat. The fear-object is brought in, starting a negative response. It is then moved away gradually until it is at a sufficient distance not to interfere with the child's eating. The relative strength of the fear impulse and the hunger impulse may be gauged by the distance to which it is necessary to remove the fear-object. While the child is eating, the object is slowly brought nearer to the table, then placed upon the table, and finally as the tolerance increases it is brought close enough to be touched. Since we could not interfere with the regular schedule of meals, we chose the time of the mid-morning lunch for the experiment. This usually assured some degree of interest in the food, and corresponding success in our treatment. The effectiveness of this method increases greatly as the hunger grows, at least up to a certain point. The case of Peter (reported in detail elsewhere) illustrates our procedure; one of our most serious problem cases, he was treated by the method daily or twice daily for a period of two months. The laboratory notes for the first and the last days of the training period show an improvement which we were able to attribute specifically to the training measures used.

case 30.—Peter, age 2 years, 10 months

March 10, 10:15 A.M. Peter sitting in high chair, eating candy. Experimenter entered room with a rabbit in an open meshed wire cage. The rabbit was placed on the table 4 feet from Peter who immediately began to cry, insisting that the rabbit be taken away. Continued crying until the rabbit was put down 20 feet away. He then started again on the candy, but continued to fuss, "I want you to put Bunny outside." After three minutes he once more burst into tears; the rabbit was removed.

April 29, 9:55 A.M. Peter standing in high chair, looking out of the window. He inquired, "Where is the rabbit?" The rabbit was put down on the chair at Peter's feet. Peter patted him, tried to pick him up, but finding the rabbit too heavy asked the experimenter to help in lifting him to the window sill, where he played with him for several minutes.

This method obviously requires delicate handling. Two response systems are being dealt with: food leading to a positive reaction, and fear-object leading to a negative reaction. The desired conditioning should result in transforming the fear-object into a source of positive response (substitute stimulus). But a careless manipulator could readily produce the reverse result, attaching a fear reaction to the sight of food.

the method of social imitation

We have used this method extensively, as it was one of the first to show signs of yielding results.

case 8.——Bobby G., age 30 months

Bobby was playing in the pen with Mary and Laurel. The rabbit was introduced in a basket. Bobby cried "No, no," and motioned for the experimenter to remove it. The two girls, however, ran up readily enough, looked in at the rabbit and talked excitedly. Bobby became promptly interested, said "What? Me see," and ran forward, his curiosity and assertiveness in the social situation overmastering other impulses.

case 54.——Vincent W., age 21 months

Jan. 19   Vincent showed no fear of the rabbit, even when it was pushed against his hands or face. His only response was to laugh and reach for the rabbit's fur. On the same day he was taken into the pen with Rosey, who cried at the sight of the rabbit. Vincent immediately developed a fear response; in the ordinary playroom situation he would pay no attention to her crying, but in connection with the rabbit, her distress had a marked suggestion value. The fear transferred in this way persisted for over two weeks.

Feb. 6   Eli and Herbert were in the play-pen with the rabbit. When Vincent was brought in, he remained cautiously standing at some distance. Eli led Vincent over to the rabbit, and induced him to touch the animal. Vincent laughed.

The second case illustrated a fear socially induced (this is perhaps the most common source of maladjustive fear trends) and the later removal of the fear by social suggestion. Many of the fears we studied pointed to an origin in a specific traumatic experience; it would probably have been a valuable aid in our procedure, had we been able to trace the developmental history of each of these fears. It was usually impossible to do this, however, in view of the institutional life of our subjects, and the fact that parents, even when they could be reached and consulted, were as a rule ignorant of their children's emotional mishaps.

summary

In our study of methods for removing fear responses, we found unqualified success with only two. By the method of direct conditioning we associated the fear-object with a craving-object, and replaced the fear by a positive response. By the method of social imitation we allowed the subject to share, under controlled conditions, the social activity of a group of children especially chosen with a view to prestige effect. Verbal appeal, elimination through disuse, negative adaptation, "repression," and "distraction" were methods which proved sometimes effective but were not to be relied upon unless used in combination with other methods. It should be remarked that apart from laboratory analysis we have rarely used any of the above procedures in pure form. Our aim has been to cure the fear, by the group of devices most appropriate at any given stage of treatment.

25
Training Impulsive Children to Talk to Themselves:
A MEANS OF DEVELOPING SELF-CONTROL
Donald H. Meichenbaum and Joseph Goodman

The development of the functional interaction between self-verbalization and nonverbal behavior has received much attention (Luria, 1961; Piaget, 1947; Reese, 1962; and see especially a review by Kohlberg, Yaeger, & Hjertholm, 1968). Two general research strategies have been employed to assess the influence of self-verbalizations on behavior. The first strategy is characterized by S's performance on a task and E's subsequent inference as to the presence or absence of specific cognitive activities. In general, this approach has used the concept of "deficiency" to explain poor performance. Reese (1962) has suggested a mediation deficiency hypothesis; Flavell and his co-workers (Flavell, Beach, & Chinsky, 1966; Moely, Olson, Halwes, & Flavell, 1967) have offered a production deficiency hypothesis, and most recently Bem (1970) has suggested a comprehension deficiency hypothesis. The developing child is characterized as going through stages during which he (a) does not mediate or regulate his overt behavior verbally; (b) does not spontaneously produce relevant mediators; and (c) does not comprehend the nature of the problem in order to discover what mediators to produce. Thus, problem solving is viewed as a three-stage process of comprehension, production, and mediation, and poor performance can result from a "deficiency" at any one of these stages. The deficiency literature suggests that a training program designed to improve task performance and engender self-control should provide explicit training in the comprehension of the task, the spontaneous production of mediators, and the use of such mediators to control nonverbal behavior. The present cognitive self-guidance treatment program was designed to provide such training for a group of "impulsive" children.

The other strategy, which is designed to assess the functional role of private speech in task performance, directly manipulates the child's verbalizations and examines resulting changes in nonverbal behavior. Vygotsky (1962) has suggested that internalization of verbal commands is the critical step in the child's development of voluntary control of his behavior. Data from a wide range of studies (Bem, 1967; Klein, 1963; Kohlberg et al., 1968; Lovaas, 1964; Luria, 1959, 1961; Meichenbaum & Goodman, 1969a, 1969b) provide support for the age increase in cognitive self-guiding private speech, and the increase in internalization with age. These results suggest a progression from external to internal control.

Reprinted from the *Journal of Abnormal Psychology*, 1971, Vol. 77, No. 2, pp. 115–126. Copyright 1971 by the American Psychological Association. Reprinted by permission.

Early in development, the speech of others, usually adults, mainly controls and directs a child's behavior; somewhat later, the child's own overt speech becomes an effective regulator of his behavior; and still later, the child's covert or inner speech can assume a regulatory role. The present studies were designed to examine the efficacy of a cognitive self-guidance treatment program which followed the developmental sequence by which overt verbalizations of an adult or E, followed by the child's overt self-verbalizations, followed by covert self-verbalization would result in the child's own verbal control of his nonverbal behavior. By using this fading procedure, we hoped to (a) train impulsive Ss to provide themselves with internally originated verbal commands or self-instructions and to respond to them appropriately; (b) strengthen the mediational properties of the children's inner speech in order to bring their behavior under their own verbal or discriminative control; (c) overcome any possible "comprehension, production, or mediational deficiencies"; and finally (d) encourage the children to appropriately self-reinforce their behavior. We hoped to have the child's private speech gain a new functional significance, to have the child develop a new cognitive style or "learning set" and thus to engender self-control.

Two studies are reported which apply the cognitive self-guidance treatment regimen to impulsive school children. The first study, using second-grade children who had been assigned to an "opportunity remedial class," provided four ½-hr. individual training sessions over a 2-wk. period. The effects of training on performance measures and classroom behavior is reported. The second study examines the modification value of a particular component of the treatment regimen, namely modeling, which is designed to alter the child's impulsive cognitive style in one treatment session as assessed on Kagan's (1966) Matching Familiar Figures (MFF) Test. The impulsive Ss in the second study have been selected from kindergarten and first-grade classes as assessed by their failure to follow an instruction to "go slower" on a preassessment of the MFF test. Both studies indicate the general treatment regimen designed to train impulsive children to talk to themselves, a possible means of developing self-control.

study I

method

SUBJECTS

The Ss were 15 second-grade children (8 females, 7 males) whose ages ranged from 7 to 9 yr. with a mean of 8 yr., 2 mo. and who had been placed in an "opportunity remedial class" in a public elementary school. The children were placed into the opportunity class because of behavioral problems such as hyperactivity and poor self-control, and/or they had low IQs on one of a variety of school-administered intelligence tests. The cutoff point on the IQ measures was 85, but for several Ss the last assessment was several years prior to the present research project. The children's behavior both in class and on performance measures was measured before and after treatment as well as in a 1-mo. follow-up assessment described below. Following the pretreatment assessment, Ss were assigned to one of three groups. One group comprised the cognitive self-guidance treatment group (N = 5). The remaining two groups included in the study were control groups. One control group met with E with the same regularity as did the cognitively trained Ss. This attention control group (N = 5) afforded an index of behavioral change due to factors of attention, exposure to training materials, and any demand characteristics inherent in our measures of improvement. In addition, an assessment control group of Ss who received no treatment was included. The assessment control group ($N = 5$) provided an index of the contribution of intercurrent life experiences to any behavioral change (e.g., being a member of the opportunity remedial class). Assignment to these three groups was done randomly, subject to the two constraints of (a) equating the groups on sex composition and (b) matching the groups on their prorated WISC IQ performance scores taken prior to treatment.

TREATMENTS

Cognitive training group. The Ss in this group were seen individually for four ½-hr. treatment sessions over a 2-wk. period. The cognitive training technique proceeded as follows: First, E performed a task talking aloud while S observed (E acted as a model); then S performed the same task while E instructed S aloud; then S was asked to perform the task again while instructing himself aloud; then S performed the task while whispering to himself (lip movements); and finally S performed the task covertly (without lip movements). The verbalizations which E modeled and S subsequently used included: (a) questions about the nature and demands of the task so as to compensate for a possible comprehension deficiency; (b) answers to these questions in the form of cognitive rehearsal and planning in order to overcome any possible production deficiency; (c) self-instructions in the form of self-guidance while performing the task in order to overcome any possible mediation deficiency; and (d) self-reinforcement. The following is an example of E's modeled verbalizations which S subsequently used (initially overtly, then covertly):

> Okay, what is it I have to do? You want me to copy the picture with the different lines. I have to go slow and be careful. Okay, draw the line down, down, good; then to the right, that's it; now down some more and to the left. Good, I'm doing fine so far. Remember go slow. Now back up again. No, I was supposed to go down. That's okay. Just erase the line carefully. . . . Good. Even if I make an error I can go on slowly and carefully. Okay, I have to go down now. Finished. I did it.

Note in this example an error in performance was included and E appropriately accommodated. In prior research with impulsive children, Meichenbaum and Goodman (1969b) observed a marked deterioration in their performance following errors. The E's verbalizations varied with the demands of each task, but the general treatment format remained the same throughout. The treatment sequence was also individually adapted to the capabilities of the S and the difficulties of the task.

A variety of tasks was employed to train the child to use self-instructions to control his nonverbal behavior. The tasks varied along a dimension from simple sensorimotor abilities to more complex problem-solving abilities. The sensorimotor tasks, such as copying line patterns and coloring figures within certain boundaries, provided S with an opportunity to produce a narrative description of his behavior, both preceding and accompanying his performance. Over the course of a training session, the child's overt self-statements on a particular task were faded to the covert level, what Luria (1961) has called "interiorization of language." The difficulty level of the training tasks was increased over the four training sessions requiring more cognitively demanding activities. Such tasks as reproducing designs and following sequential instructions taken from the Stanford-Binet intelligence test, completing pictorial series as on the Primary Mental Abilities test, and solving conceptual tasks as on the Ravens Matrices test, required S to verbalize the demands of the task and problem-solving strategies. The E modeled appropriate self-verbalizations for each of these tasks and then had the child follow the fading procedure. Although the present tasks assess many of the same cognitive abilities required by our dependent measures, there are significant differences between the training tasks and the performance and behavioral indexes used to assess improvement. It should be noted that the attentional control group received the same opportunities to perform on each of the training tasks, but without cognitive self-guidance training.

One can imagine a similar training sequence in the learning of a new motor skill such as driving a car. Initially the driver actively goes through a mental checklist, sometimes aloud, which includes verbal rehearsal, self-guidance, and sometimes appropriate self-reinforcement, especially when driving a stick-shift car. Only with repetition does the sequence become automatic and the cognitions become short-circuited. This sequence is also seen in the way children learn to tie shoelaces and in the development of many other skills. If this observation has any merit, then a training procedure which makes these steps explicit should facilitate the development of self-control.

In summary, the goals of the training procedure were to develop for the impulsive child a cognitive style or learning set in which the child could "size up" the demands of a task, cognitively rehearse, and then guide his performance by means of self-instructions, and when appropriate reinforce himself.

Attention control group. The children in this untutored group had the same number of sessions with E as did the cognitive training Ss. During this time, the child was exposed to identical materials and engaged in the same general activities, but did not receive any self-instructional training. For example, these attentional control Ss received the same number of trials on a task as did the cognitively trained Ss, but they did not receive self-instructional training. An attempt was made to provide both the experimental and attention control groups with equal amounts of social reinforcement for behavioral performance on the tasks.

Assessment control group. This untreated control group received only the same pretreatment, posttreatment, and follow-up assessments as the cognitive treatment and attention control groups.

INSTRUMENTS

Two general classes of dependent measures were used to assess the efficacy of the cognitive self-guidance treatment regimen to improve performance and engender self-control. The first class of measures involved performance on a variety of psychometric instruments which have been previously used to differentiate impulsive from nonimpulsive children. The second class of measures assessed the generalizability of the treatment effects to the classroom situation. The female E who performed the pretreatment, posttreatment, and follow-up assessments on the performance measures and the two female E's who made classroom observations during pretreatment and posttreatment periods were completely unaware of which children received which treatment.

Performance measures. Three different psychometric tests were used to assess changes in behavioral and cognitive impulsivity during the pretreatment, posttreatment, and follow-up periods. Several investigators (Anthony, 1959; Eysenck, 1955; Foulds, 1951; Porteus, 1942) have demonstrated that the Porteus Maze test, especially the qualitative score which is based upon errors in style and quality of execution, distinguishes between individuals differing in impulsiveness. Most recently, Palkes, Stewart, and Kahana (1968) have reported that hyperactive boys significantly improved on Porteus Maze performance following training in self-directed verbal commands. Thus, the Porteus Maze performance provided one indicant of behavioral change. Because of the length of the assessment (some 45 min.), only years 8–11 of the Porteus Maze test were used. On the posttest the Vineland Revision form of the Porteus Maze test was used.

A second measure which has been used to assess cognitive impulsivity is Kagan's (1966) MFF test. The S's task on the MFF test is to select from an array of variants one picture which is identical to a standard picture. The tendency toward fast or slow decision times and the number of errors are used to identify the degree of conceptual impulsivity. Further support for the use of the MFF test in the present study comes from research by Meichenbaum and Goodman (1969a), who have reported a positive relationship between a child's relative inability to verbally control his motor behavior by means of covert self-instructions and an impulsive conceptual tempo on the MFF test. Parallel forms of the MFF test were developed by using six alternate items in the pretreatment and posttreatment assessments, with the pretreatment MFF test being readministered on the follow-up assessment.

The final set of performance measures was derived from three performance subtests of the WISC. The three subtests selected were Picture Arrangement, Block Design, and Coding. Respectively, these subtests are designed to assess (a) the ability to comprehend and size up a total situation requiring anticipation and planning; (b) the ability to analyze and form abstract designs as illustrated by S's performance and approach to the problems; and (c) the child's motor speed and activity level (Kitzinger & Blumberg, 1957; Lutey, 1966; Wechsler, 1949). The results from the WISC subtests are reported in scaled scores and as a prorated IQ performance estimate.

In summary, the performance measures were designed to assess the range of abilities from sensorimotor, as indicated by qualitative scores on Porteus Maze and Coding tasks on the WISC, to more cognitively demanding tasks such as the MFF test, Block Design, and Picture Arrangement subtests.

Classroom measures. Two measures were used to ascertain whether any of the expected changes would extend into the classroom. The first measure behaviorally assessed the 15 children on their appropriateness and attentiveness within the classroom setting. We used a time-sampling observational technique (10 sec. observe, 10 sec. record) which was developed by Meichenbaum, Bowers, and Ross (1968, 1969) to rate inappropriate classroom behavior. Inappropriate classroom behavior was defined as any behavior which was not consistent with the task set forth by the teacher, that is, behavior which was not task specific. The children were observed for 2 school days 1 wk. before and immediately after treatment. The second measure involved a teacher's questionnaire which was designed to assess each child's behavioral self-control, activity level, cooperativeness, likeability, etc. The questionnaire consisted of 10 incomplete statements, each of which was followed by three forced choice alternative completions. The teacher filled out the scale immediately prior to treatment and 3 wk. later at the conclusion of the posttreatment assessment.

results

The relative efficacy of the cognitive self-guidance treatment program was assessed by means of a Lindquist (1953) Type I analysis of variance which yields a treatment effect, trials effect (pretreatment and posttreatment assessments), and a Treatment × Trials interaction. The results from the 1-mo. follow-up measures were analyzed separately. Multiple *t*-test comparisons (one-tailed) were performed on the change scores for each of the dependent measures. Figure 25.1 presents the performance measures.

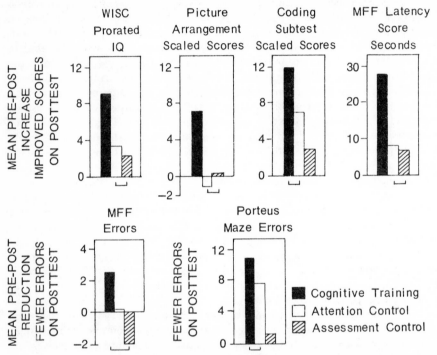

FIG. 25.1   Mean change scores from pretreatment to posttreatment on performance measures. (Groups not connected by solid line are significantly different at .05 level.)

The analyses of the three WISC subtests revealed only a significant Group × Trials interaction on the Picture Arrangement subtest ($F = 4.56$, $df = 2/12$, $p = .033$) and a strong trend towards significance on the Coding subtest (Group × Trials $F = 2.87$, $df = 2/12$, $p = .10$). The performances on the Block Design subtest did not yield any significant groups, trials, or Group × Trials interactions. When the performances on the three WISC subtests were combined to yield a prorated IQ score, the relative efficacy of the cognitive training procedure is further revealed in a significant Group × Trials interaction ($F = 3.97$, $df = 2/12$, $p = .05$). The cognitive training group improved 8.3 IQ points ($SD = 3.8$), from an IQ of 88.4 to an IQ of 96.7. In comparison, the attention control group and the assessment control group improved, respectively, 3.4 ($SD = 4.1$) and 2.2 ($SD = 3.0$) IQ points. Multiple t comparisons indicated that the cognitive training group was significantly different ($p < .05$) from the attentional and assessment control groups on the Picture Arrangement and Coding subtests, and on the prorated IQ scores, whereas the two control groups did not significantly differ from each other on the WISC measures.

Further evidence for the efficacy of the cognitive training is derived from the measure of cognitive impulsivity, namely, the MFF test. A significant Group × Trials interaction ($F = 9.49$, $df = 2/12$, $p = .004$) was found on the initial decision time or latency score on the MFF test. The cognitive training group increased its mean total decision time for the six MFF items from pretest to posttest by 27.4 sec. ($SD = 10.3$), in comparison to the attention and assessment control groups who, respectively, increased their total posttest decision times by 7.4 sec. ($SD = 3.8$) and 6.8 sec. ($SD = 9.9$). The differential increase in response time indicates that the impulsive Ss in the cognitively trained group took significantly longer before responding on the posttest. The analyses of the error scores on the MFF test did not yield any significant differences, although the trend of the results did suggest differential effectiveness for the cognitively trained Ss. The cognitively trained Ss had a group total decrease on the posttest of 8 errors in comparison to the attentional control Ss, who had a group total decrease of only 2 errors on the posttest, and the assessment control Ss, who had a group total increase of 10 errors on the posttest. The absence of statistical significance on the error scores may be due to the relative ease of the MFF test for this age level and the use of a shortened version of the test in order to develop parallel forms (i.e., 6 items were used instead of the usual 12-item test). The potential usefulness of the cognitive training procedure in altering cognitive impulsivity was examined in the second study which is described below.

An analysis of the performance on the Porteus Maze test indicated a significant Group × Trials interaction ($F = 5.52$, $df = 2/12$, $p = .02$), with the cognitive training and the attentional control groups making significantly ($p < .05$) less errors on the posttest than the assessment control group. The mean change scores indicated that (a) Ss who received cognitive training improved most with 10.8 ($SD = 4.3$) less errors on the posttest; (b) Ss in the attentional control group made 7.8 ($SD = 6.8$) less errors on the posttest; and (c) the assessment control group made 1.2 ($SD = 4.7$) more errors on the posttest. Both the cognitive training group and the attentional control group decreased errors on the posttest by cutting fewer corners, crossing over fewer lines, lifting their pencils less frequently, and producing fewer irregular lines. Palkes et al. (1968) have reported a significant improvement on the Porteus Maze test for a self-directed verbal command group relative to an assessment or no-treatment control group, but they did not include an attentional control group. The present results indicated that an attentional control group which received only practice on a variety of sensorimotor and cognitive tasks also significantly improved their performance on the Porteus Maze test. The inclusion of such an attentional control group is thus necessary in order to exclude alternative hypotheses.

The analyses of the Ss' classroom behavior by means of time-sampling observations and by teachers' ratings did not yield any significant differences. The absence of a significant treatment effect in the classroom may be due to a lack of generalization because of the limited number of training sessions and/or the lack of sensitivity of the assessment measures. The analyses of the 4-wk. follow-up assessment revealed that the cognitive training group maintained their improved performance on the test battery, relative to the attentional and assessment control groups. The analyses of the follow-up test performances relative to the pretreatment performance indicated that on the Picture Arrangement sub-test, the WISC prorated IQ score, and the decision time on the MFF, the cognitive training group was significantly different ($p < .05$) from the two control groups. The analysis of the qualitative performance on the Porteus Maze test indicated that both the cognitive training group and the attentional control group maintained their improved performance relative to the assessment control group.

The results of the first study proved most encouraging and suggested that a cognitive self-guidance training program can significantly alter behavior of impulsive children. The purpose of the second study was to examine the differential contribution of the various components of the treatment program in modifying impulsive behavior. The cognitive training procedure involved both modeling by E and subsequent self-instructional training by S. In this study a comparison is made between the relative efficacy of modeling alone versus modeling plus self-instructional training in modifying cognitive impulsivity as measured by the MFF test. Kagan (1965) has defined cognitive impulsivity as a conceptual tempo or decision-time variable representing the time S takes to consider alternate solutions before committing himself to one of them in a situation with high response uncertainty. Kagan and his associates (Kagan, 1965, 1966; Kagan, Rosman, Day, Albert, & Phillips, 1964) have shown that performance on the MFF test has high stability and intertest generality and is related to performance on visual discrimination tasks, inductive reasoning, serial recall, and reading skills. Most recently, investigators have been interested in the modification of cognitive impulsivity. Kagan, Person, and Welsh (1966) have attempted to train, in three individual sessions, inhibition of impulsive responding by requiring the child to defer his answer for a fixed period of 10 to 15 sec. During this period the child was encouraged to study the stimuli in the task and to think about his answer, but he did *not* receive training in more efficient procedures to emit during this interval. Significant changes in latency or decision time occurred, but no corresponding significant change in errors was evident. Debus (1970) examined the usefulness of filmed modeling of reflective behavior and found a decrease only in decision time, and, like Kagan, Pearson, and Welch (1966), no corresponding change in errors. The studies by Kagan et al. (1966) and Debus (1970) have concentrated on increasing latency times without paying sufficient attention to inducing improved cognitive and/or scanning strategies in the impulsive child. Siegelman (1969) and Drake (1970) have demonstrated that different attentional and cognitive strategies seem to underlie the performance of impulsive and reflective Ss. The data from Siegelman and Drake indicate that the impulsive child on the MFF test (*a*) displays a greater biasing of attention both in extent of scanning and in number of alternatives ignored; (*b*) is simply in search of some variant that globally resembles the standard and is not very discriminating or analytic in his viewing. In comparison, the reflective child seems to follow a strategy designed to find explicit differences among alternatives and then to check the standard for verification. The impulsive child's approach or strategy on the MFF task results in many errors and quick decision times. The purpose of the present study was to examine the usefulness of the cognitive self-guidance training procedure in altering the attentional strategy of the impulsive child on the MFF test. The efficacy of the self-instructional training procedure in modifying cognitive impulsivity is compared with a modeling-alone procedure. An attentional control group which received exposure to the practice materials but no explicit training was included for comparative purposes.

study II

method

SUBJECT

The 15 impulsive children who received training were selected from a larger group of kindergarten ($N = 30$) and first-grade ($N = 30$) public school children on the basis of two behavioral criteria. All of the children were individually tested on parallel forms of six items each of the MFF test. Interspersed between the two MFF forms the instruction "You don't have to hurry. You should go slowly and carefully" was given to all Ss. The 15 impulsive Ss (4 male and 4 female kindergarteners and 4 male and 3 female first graders) were selected on the basis of the S's initial performance on Form I of the MFF test and the absence of any appreciable improvement in performance on Form II of the MFF test. Thus, the selected impulsive children were initially cognitively impulsive, and they did not significantly alter their style of responding even though they were instructed to do so. The use of an instructional manipulation to select Ss is consistent with Vygotsky's (1962) suggestion that a child's capabilities are best reflected by his response to instructions.

Following Session 1, the 15 selected impulsive Ss were randomly assigned to one of the treatment groups (viz., modeling alone or modeling plus self-instructional training) or to the attentional control group, subject to the constraint of comparable age and sex representation in each group. One week later in a second session, each of the impulsive Ss was individually seen by a different E (female), who conducted the treatment, afer which Ss were tested on a third form of the six-item MFF test by the first E (male) who had conducted the testing in Session 1. The E who administered the three forms of the MFF test was thus unaware into which group S had been placed. The training materials consisted of the Picture Matching subtest from the Primary Mental Abilities (PMA) test and items from the Ravens' Matrices test. These materials elicit similar task abilities to the MFF test and provide a useful format for modeling reflective behaviors. The training procedure which lasted some 20 min. consisted of E performing or modeling behavior on one item of the practice material and then S doing an item. There were in all eight practice trials.

TREATMENTS

Cognitive modeling group. The Ss in this group ($N = 5$) initially observed the E who modeled a set of verbalizations and behaviors which characterizes the reflective child's proposed strategy on the MFF test. The following is an example of E's modeled verbalizations on the PMA Picture Matching test:

> I have to remember to go slowly to get it right. Look carefully at this one (the standard), now look at these carefully (the variants). Is this one different? Yes, it has an extra leaf. Good, I can eliminate this one. Now, let's look at this one (another variant). I think it's this one, but let me first check the others. Good, I'm going slow and carefully. Okay, I think it's this one.

The impulsive child was exposed to a model which demonstrated the strategy to search for differences that would allow him successively to eliminate as incorrect all variants but one. The E modeled verbal statements or a strategy to make detailed comparisons across figures, looking at all variants before offering an answer.

As in the first study, E also modeled errors and then how to cope with errors and improve upon them. For example, following an error E would model the following verbalizations:

> It's okay, Just be careful. I should have looked more carefully. Follow the plan to check each one. Good, I'm going slowly.

After E modeled on an item, S was given an opportunity to perform on a similar practice item. The S was encouraged and socially reinforced for using the strategy E had just modeled, but did not receive explicit practice in self-instructing. This modeling-alone group was designed to indicate the degree of behavioral change from exposure to an adult model.

Cognitive modeling plus self-instructional training group. The Ss in this group were exposed to the same modeling behavior by E as were Ss in the modeling-alone group, but in addition they were explicitly trained to produce the self-instructions E emitted while performing the task. After E modeled on an item, S was instructed to perform the task while talking aloud to himself as E had done. Over the course of the eight practice trials, the child's self-verbalizations were faded from initially an overt level to a covert level, as in Study I.

Attentional control groups. The Ss in this group observed the E perform the task and were given an opportunity to perform on each of the practice items. The E's verbalizations consisted only of general statements to "go slow, be careful, look carefully," but did not include the explicit modeling of verbalizations dealing with scanning strategies as did the two treatment groups. The Ss were encouraged and socially reinforced to go slow and be careful, but were not trained to self-instruct. In many ways this group approximates the methods teachers and parents use to demonstrate a task in which they make general prohibitions, but do not explicate the strategies or details involved in solving the task. This group can be considered a minimal modeling condition or an attentional control group for exposure to E and practice on task materials.

An attempt was made to provide all three groups with equal amounts of social reinforcement for their performance. At the completion of the modeling session, all Ss were told, "Can you remember to do just like I did whenever you play games like this? Remember to go slowly and carefully." The E who conducted the training departed, and the first E then administered Form III of the MFF test.

results

SELECTIONS OF Ss

Table 25.1 presents the performance of reflective and impulsive Ss on the initial MFF test (Form I) and on the MFF test (Form II) which was administered immediately after the instructions to "go slower." Of the original 60 Ss tested, 45 were classified into either the reflective or impulsive groups, based on the S's response time and errors relative to the performance of the same age and sex peer group. The instructions to go slower resulted in a significant ($p < .05$) increase in the mean total response time on initial decisions for reflective Ss (i.e., from 99.8 to 123.8 sec.), but no comparable change in errors. The latter finding may be due to a "ceiling effect" and/or a slight decrement in performance resulting from anxiety. Several reflective Ss indicated that they interpreted E's instruction to go slower as an indicant that they were not performing adequately. Ward (1968) has reported that anxiety over failure played a greater role in the performance of reflective children than it did in the performance of impulsive

TABLE 25.1 IMPULSIVE AND REFLECTIVE ss' PERFORMANCE ON INITIAL MFF TEST (FORM I) AND ON THE MFF TEST (FORM II) ADMINISTERED AFTER INSTRUCTIONS TO "GO SLOWER"

ss	MFF PERFORMANCE			
	FORM I		FORM II	
	$\overline{X}$	SD	$\overline{X}$	SD
Reflectives ($N = 20$)				
Total errors	6.3	3.5	7.7	4.0
Total decision time	99.8	6.5	123.8	10.5
Impulsives ($N = 25$)				
Total errors	16.4	3.8	11.4	7.0
Total decision time	42.9	5.5	58.1	7.6

children. The impulsive Ss demonstrated a marked variability in how their performance changed as a result of the instructional manipulation. This variability permitted selection of the 15 most impulsive Ss whose performance changed minimally. In a second session, these impulsive Ss were provided with treatment. Table 25.2 presents the performance scores for the impulsive Ss who were selected for treatment and those impulsive Ss who significantly improved their performance from the minimal instructional manipulation.

In summary, from a group of 60 kindergarten and first-grade children, 15 Ss were selected who were most cognitively impulsive on initial testing and who minimally altered their response style when explicitly given the instruction to do so.

ANALYSIS OF TREATMENT EFFICACY

Figure 25.2 presents the performance of the modeling group, modeling plus self-instructional group, and the attentional control group for the three six-item forms of the MFF test. The analyses of the decision times and error scores

TABLE 25.2 A BREAKDOWN OF IMPULSIVE ss' PERFORMANCE ON FORMS I AND II OF THE MFF TEST

ss	MFF PERFORMANCE			
	FORM I		FORM II	
	$\overline{X}$	SD	$\overline{X}$	SD
Impulsive Ss selected for treatment ($N = 15$)				
Total errors	15.2	3.5	12.2	4.6
Total decision time	42.8	5.3	51.2	5.9
Impulsive Ss *not* selected for treatment ($N = 10$)				
Total errors	17.6	4.2	10.5	5.4
Total decision time	43.0	6.0	65.0	8.3

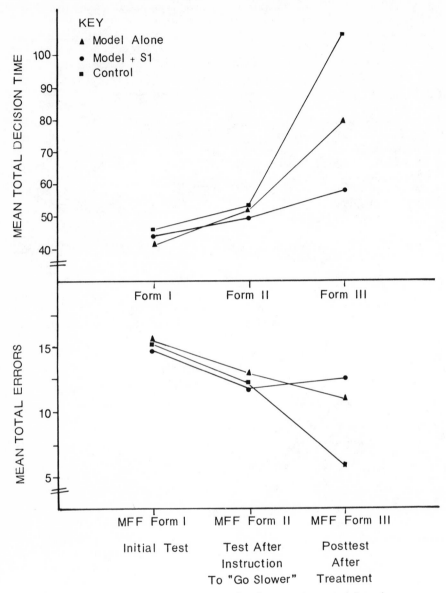

FIG. 25.2   MFF performances of impulsive Ss who were in a modeling-alone group, a modeling plus self-instructional training group, and an additional control group.

on Forms I and II of the MFF test yielded no significant group, trials, or Group × Trials interaction, indicating that prior to treatment the three groups performed comparably on initial performance and in response to instructions to go slower. The differential efficacy of the treatment procedures is indicated in the analysis of Form III of the MFF test which was administered immediately after treatment. On the decision time measure, the two treatment groups significantly ($p < .05$)

slowed down their decision time on Form III relative to their own prior perform-ances on Forms I and II and relative to the control groups' performance on Form III. The modeling plus self-instructional training group which slowed down the most was significantly different ($t = 8.10$, $df = 8$, $p < .001$) from the modeling-alone group on Form III. The analyses of the error scores indicated that *only* Ss who received modeling plus self-instructional training significantly ($p < .05$) improved their performance relative to the other two groups and rela-tive to their own prior performances.

In summary, the results indicated that the cognitive modeling plus self-instructional group was most effective in altering decision time and in reducing errors. The modeling-alone group significantly decreased decision time, but did not significantly reduce errors. The efficacy of the self-instructional component of the training procedure in fostering behavioral change is underscored by the fact that three of the five Ss in the self-instruction group spontaneously self-verbalized on Form III of the MFF test, whereas none did so in the other two groups. Simi-larly in Study I, several Ss in the self-instructional training group spontaneously self-verbalized in the posttest and follow-up sessions. It does appear that self-instructional training can bring an impulsive child's overt behavior under his own verbal discriminative control. At a macroscopic level, the impulsive children, after self-instructional training, do seem to be approaching psychometric tasks dif-ferently, taking their time, talking to themselves, and improving their perform-ance. Research is now underway to explore the generality, persistence, and behavioral changes that result from self-instructional training.

discussion

The results of the two studies indicate that a cognitive self-guidance pro-gram which trains impulsive children to talk to themselves is effective in modi-fying their behavior on a variety of psychometric tests which assess cognitive im-pulsivity, Performance IQ, and motor ability. The results of Study II indicate that the addition of explicit self-instructional training to modeling procedures sig-nificantly alters the attentional strategies of the impulsive children and facilitates behavioral change. The impulsive children were taught to use their private speech for orienting, organizing, regulating, and self-rewarding functions with the con-sequences of greater self-control. The present self-instructional procedure seems applicable to the culturally deprived child, who has been described by Bereiter and Engelmann (1966) and Blank and Solomon (1968, 1969) as having a "cen-tral language deficit," namely, the inability to relate what he says to what he does. The deprived child does not spontaneously use language to direct his problem-solving behavior, especially when specific demands to do so are removed, nor does he exhibit normal capacities for self-control. An examination of the usefulness of the present self-instructional training procedures over a prolonged period of time with such deprived children is now underway.

The present studies indicate that the therapist can now attempt to modify not only the patient's overt behavioral response, but also the antecedent and/or accompanying cognitions. For example, cognitive self-guidance training proce-dures may be used to influence the attentional and cognitive strategies patients emit in a variety of situations. The possibilities of using self-instructional training procedures to alter (*a*) the "attentional deficit" in schizophrenics (Lang & Buss, 1965); (*b*) psychophysiological reactions of psychiatric patients (Grings, 1965;

Schachter, 1966); and (c) cognitive styles in general (Ellis, 1963) are most promising. The application of the self-instructional procedure to operant conditioning programs with human Ss, especially children, also seems worthwhile. We suggest that having S self-verbalize, initially aloud and subsequently covertly, the contingencies of reinforcement will result in greater change and more generalization. Reinforcement can be made contingent upon not only the emission of the desired behavior, but also S's self-verbalization of what he must do to secure reinforcement. The literature on awareness (see review by Bandura, 1969) provides further support for the possible efficacy of having S learn to self-verbalize the correct reinforcement rules which influence his subsequent responding.

With the cognitive training procedure, the response chain to be modified is broadened and may thus be subjected to such modification techniques as modeling, reinforcement, and aversive consequences. We have explored in a series of studies the use of behavior modification techniques to alter the self-verbalizations of such patients as phobics, schizophrenics, smokers, speech- and test-anxious Ss, as well as impulsive children (Meichenbaum, 1970, 1971; Meichenbaum, Gilmore, & Fedoravicius, 1971, in press; Steffy, Meichenbaum, & Best, 1970). In each case, therapeutically attending to the patient's self-verbalizations, as well as his overt maladaptive behavior, has led to greater behavioral change, greater generalization, and greater persistence of treatment effects. In each of these therapy studies the goal has been to bring S's overt behavior under his own discriminative control, a means of developing the self-regulatory function of private speech.

In conclusion, a *heuristic* assumption underlying the present line of investigation has been that symbolic activities obey the same psychological laws as do overt behaviors and that private speech is teachable. Thus, behavior modification techniques which have been used to modify overt behaviors may be applied to cognitive processes. Only future research will indicate the validity of this assumption, but the by-products, in terms of the development of new treatment techniques, will be sizable.

references

Anthony, A. Normal and neurotic qualitative Porteus Maze performance under stress and non-stress. Unpublished PhD thesis, Columbia University, 1959.

Bandura, A. *Principles of behavior modification.* New York: Holt, Rinehart and Winston, 1969.

Bem, S. Verbal self-control: The establishment of effective self-instruction. *Journal of Experimental Psychology,* 1967, 74, 485–491.

Bem, S. The role of comprehension in children's problem-solving. *Developmental Psychology,* 1970, 2, 351–358.

Bereiter, C., & Engelmann, S. *Teaching disadvantaged children in the preschool.* Englewood-Cliffs, N. J.: Prentice-Hall, 1966.

Blank, M., & Solomon, F. A tutorial language program to develop abstract thinking in socially disadvantaged preschool children. *Child Development,* 1968, 39, 379–389.

Blank, M., & Solomon, F. How should the disadvantaged child be taught? *Child Development,* 1969, 40, 47–61.

Debus, R. L. Effects of brief observation of model behavior on conceptual tempo of impulsive children. *Developmental Psychology,* 1970, 2, 22–32.

Drake, D. M. Perceptual correlates of impulsive and reflective behavior. *Developmental Psychology,* 1970, 2, 202–214.

Ellis, A. *Reason and emotion in psychotherapy.* New York: Holt, Rinehart and Winston, 1962.

Eysenck, A. J. A dynamic theory of anxiety and hysteria. *Journal of Mental Science,* 1955, *101,* 128–151.

Flavell, J. H., Beach, D. R., & Chinsky, J. M. Spontaneous verbal rehearsal in a memory task as a function of age. *Child Development,* 1966, *37,* 283–299.

Foulds, G. A. Temperamental differences in maze performance. *British Journal of Psychology,* 1951, *42,* 209–217.

Grings, W. W. Verbal-perceptual factors in the conditioning of autonomic responses. In W. F. Prokasy (Ed.,) *Classical conditioning: A symposium.* New York: Appleton-Century-Crofts, 1965.

Kagan, J. Impulsive and reflective children: Significance of conceptual tempo. In J. D. Krumboltz (Ed.), *Learning and the educational process.* Chicago: Rand McNally, 1965.

Kagan, J. Reflection-impulsivity: The generality and dynamics of conceptual tempo. *Journal of Abnormal Psychology,* 1966, *71,* 17–24.

Kagan, J., Pearson, L., & Welch, L. The modifiability of an impulsive tempo. *Journal of Educational Psychology,* 1966, *57,* 359–365.

Kagan, J., Rosman, B. L., Day, D., Albert, J., & Phillips, W. Information processing in the child: Significance of analytic and reflective attitudes. *Psychological Monographs,* 1964, *78* (1, Whole No. 578).

Kitzinger, H., & Blumberg, E. Supplementary guide for administering and scoring the Wechsler-Bellevue. Intelligence Scale (Form I). *Psychological Monographs,* 1951, *65,* (10, Whole No. 319).

Klein, W. L. An investigation of the spontaneous speech of children during problem solving. Unpublished doctoral dissertation, University of Rochester, 1963.

Kohlberg, L., Yaeger, J., & Hjertholm, E. Private speech: Four studies and a review of theories. *Child Development,* 1968, *39,* 691–736.

Lang, P. J., & Buss, A. H. Psychological deficit in schizophrenia: Interference activation. *Journal of Abnormal Psychology,* 1965, *70,* 77–106.

Lindquist, E. F. *Design and analysis of experiments in psychology and education.* Boston: Houghton Mifflin, 1953.

Lovaas, O. I. Cue properties of words: The control of operant responding by rate and content of verbal operants. *Child Development,* 1964, *35,* 245–256.

Luria, A. R. The directive function of speech in development. *Word,* 1959, *15,* 341–352.

Luria, A. R. *The role of speech in the regulation of normal and abnormal behavior.* New York: Liveright, 1961.

Lutey, C. *Individual intelligence testing: A manual.* Greeley, Colo.: Executary, 1966.

Meichenbaum, D. Cognitive factors in behavior modification: Modifying what people say to themselves. Unpublished manuscript, University of Waterloo, 1970.

Meichenbaum, D. Examination of model characteristics in reducing avoidance behavior. *Journal of Personality and Social Psychology,* 1971, *17,* 298–307.

Meichenbaum, D., Bowers, K., & Ross, R. Modification of classroom behavior of institutionalized female adolescent offenders. *Behaviour Research and Therapy,* 1968, *6,* 343–353.

Meichenbaum, D., Bowers, K., & Ross, R. A behavioral analysis of teacher expectancy effect. *Journal of Personality and Social Psychology,* 1969, *13,* 306–316.

Meichenbaum, D., Gilmore, J. B., & Fedoravicius, A. Group insight versus group desensitization in treating speech anxiety. *Journal of Consulting and Clinical Psychology,* 1971, *36,* 410–421.

Meichenbaum, D., & Goodman, J. The developmental control of operant motor responding by verbal operants. *Journal of Experimental Child Psychology,* 1969, 7, 553–565. (a)

Meichenbaum, D., & Goodman, J. Reflection-impulsivity and verbal control of motor behavior. *Child Development,* 1969, 40, 785–797. (b)

Moely, B., Olson, F., Halwes, T., & Flavell, J. Production deficiency in young children's recall. *Developmental Psychology,* 1969, 1, 26–34.

Palkes, H., Stewart, W., & Kahana, B. Porteus Maze performance of hyperactive boys after training in self-directed verbal commands. *Child Development,* 1968, 39, 817–826.

Piaget, J. *The psychology of intelligence.* London: Routledge & Kegan Paul, 1947.

Porteus, S. E. *Qualitative performance in the maze test.* Vineland, N. J.: Smith, 1942.

Reese, H. W. Verbal mediation as a function of age level. *Psychological Bulletin,* 1962, 59, 502–509.

Schachter, S. The interaction of cognitive and physiological determinants of emotional state. In C. D. Speilberger (Ed.), *Anxiety and behavior.* New York: Academic Press, 1966.

Siegelman, E. Reflective and impulsive observing behavior. *Child Development,* 1969, 40, 1213–1222.

Steffy, R., Meichenbaum, D., & Best, A. Aversive and cognitive factors in the modification of smoking behavior. *Behavior Research and Therapy,* 1970, 8, 115–125.

Vygotsky, L. S. *Thought and language.* New York: Wiley, 1962.

Ward, W. C. Reflection-impulsivity in kindergarten children. *Child Development,* 1968, 39, 867–874.

Wechsler, D. *Manual: Wechsler Intelligence Scale for Children.* New York: Psychological Corporation, 1949.

26

Insomnia and the Attribution Process

Michael D. Storms and Richard E. Nisbett

In an important experiment on emotion published in 1962, Schachter and Singer exposed subjects to situations designed to elicit either anger or euphoria. Prior to their exposure to these situations, subjects were injected with adrenalin, a drug which produces autonomic arousal. Some of the subjects were told that they were being injected with a drug which would cause autonomic arousal, while other subjects were given no information about the arousal effects which the injection would produce. The uninformed subjects were far more emotional—either euphoric or angry, depending on the experimental condition—than were informed subjects. The experiment has been taken as evidence of the emotional plasticity of the state of autonomic arousal. Individuals in a state of arousal may

Reprinted from the *Journal of Personality and Social Psychology,* 1970, Vol. 16, No. 2, pp. 319–328. Copyright 1970 by the American Psychological Association. Reprinted by permission.

experience very disparate emotional states or no emotional state at all, depending on the cognitions which attend the arousal. A perhaps equally important implication of the experiment has received little attention. Not only were informed subjects less emotional than uninformed subjects, they were also less emotional than control subjects who received a placebo. This trend, though statistically not significant, suggests that informed subjects overcompensated for the injection. They perhaps attributed not only adrenalin-produced arousal to the injection, but naturally occurring arousal as well. As a consequence, informed subjects were less emotional than they "should" have been, given the emotion-eliciting situations in which they were placed.

In order to determine whether people can be induced to believe that part of their naturally occurring arousal is due to an artificial, external source, Nisbett and Schachter (1966) gave sugar pill placebos to subjects who were about to undergo a series of electric shocks. Some of their subjects were told that the pill would produce palpitation, breathing rate increase, and "butterflies in the stomach." Other subjects were told that the pill would produce a variety of symptoms which were not autonomic in nature. Those subjects who believed themselves to be in a state of drug-produced arousal found the shocks less painful than did other subjects, and were willing to tolerate higher shock intensities. Furthermore, an internal analysis revealed that toleration of shock was a direct function of the extent to which subjects ascribed their arousal to the pill. The experiment indicates that it is indeed possible to persuade subjects that their naturally occurring arousal has an external origin. As a consequence, such subjects lower their estimation of the intensity of the stimulus which actually produced the arousal.

It is useful to discuss this research in the context of the attribution theory of Kelley (1967) stemming from Heider's (1958) work. Briefly, Kelley proposes that many cognitive and motivational phenomena are the result of the individual's perception of causes for the psychological effects which he observes in himself. In this process of causal attribution, the individual can make mistakes, that is, attribute an effect to the wrong cause. Such errors may have pronounced effects on his subsequent motives and beliefs. Thus, the subjects in Schachter and Singer's (1962) experiment may be viewed as victims of an experimentally produced attribution error. Uninformed subjects in that experiment who were injected with adrenalin mistakenly attributed their arousal to the situation in which they found themselves, rather than to the injection. As a consequence, they became emotional. Similarly, subjects in Nisbett and Schachter's (1966) experiment, who were told that their placebo pills would produce arousal, mistakenly attributed shock-produced arousal to the pills, and as a consequence found the shock to be less aversive than it "really" was.

Ross, Rodin, and Zimbardo (1969) have proposed that the reattribution of arousal symptoms may be of use in alleviating maladaptive emotional states. Ross et al. conducted an experiment similar to that of Nisbett and Schachter. Their subjects were encouraged to attribute the arousal symptoms accompanying fear of electric shock to a loud noise piped in over a headset. Such subjects were shown to be less fearful than subjects who could only attribute their arousal symptoms to fear of electric shock. Following Valins' (Valins, 1966; Valins & Ray, 1967) suggestion that cognitive manipulations of perceived *level* of arousal may have therapeutic applications, Ross et al. proposed that manipulations of the perceived *source* of autonomic arousal may also have therapeutic uses. The present experiment was an attempt to produce such a therapeutic lessening of a maladaptive emotional state by means of a reattribution of arousal symptoms.

The state of insomnia seems a promising candidate for a first attempt at a therapeutic intervention using the reattribution technique. Emotionality at bedtime can be a chief proximal cause of insomnia. The high level of mental activity and the alertness produced by an emotion are incompatible with sleep and could delay sleep onset. The present line of theorizing would suggest that to the extent that an insomniac goes to bed in a state of autonomic arousal and associates that arousal with cognitions which are emotionally toned, he should become more emotional and have greater difficulty getting to sleep. However, if the insomniac were to take a "drug" which he believed to be capable of producing arousal symptoms, he might attribute part of his arousal to the drug, and might perceive the emotionally toned cognitions to be less intense. As a consequence, such a subject might become less emotional. Insomniac subjects given a placebo which they believe to be an arousal agent might therefore paradoxically get to sleep more quickly than usual.

Such an experiment also provides a framework within which to test a second hypothesis of theoretical and practical interest. If the belief that arousal has been produced by a drug leads to lowered emotionality, then the belief that arousal has been reduced by a drug should lead to increased emotionality. The subjects who mistakenly believe themselves to be under the influence of an arousal-decreasing agent should become highly emotional. Such subjects should say to themselves, in effect, "If I feel as aroused as I do now, when a drug is operating to lower my arousal, then I must be very aroused indeed." More formally, such subjects should perceive any arousal which they experience to be an under-representation of the intensity of their emotionally toned cognitions. If such a subject experiences normal arousal, but thinks it has been "drug reduced," he will infer that his cognitions are unusually powerful. Emotionality should thus be increased, and the state of insomnia should become worse for such subjects.

Thus, it was hypothesized that (a) insomniacs given placebo pills, which they believe capable of arousing them, will attribute their naturally occurring arousal to the pill, will therefore experience less intense emotions, and will fall asleep more quickly than usual; and (b) insomniacs given placebo pills, which they believe capable of calming them, will attribute more than their naturally occurring arousal to emotionally toned cognitions, will therefore experience more intense emotions, and will fall asleep less quickly than usual.

method

The experimental test of the hypotheses required (a) recruiting subjects who suffer from insomnia; (b) leading some subjects to believe that a pill would increase their arousal at bedtime, and leading others to believe that a pill would decrease it; and (c) measuring changes in the delay of sleep onset.

subjects

Forty-two subjects were recruited by signs posted on the campus of Yale University. The signs were headed "Insomniacs wanted for psychological research on dreams." Attached to the posters were cards which volunteers completed and mailed in. The experiment was described to volunteers over the telephone as one on dream-content analysis which would take two ½-hour sessions and pay $3.00. Subjects were told that "light sleepers" were being recruited because "they tend to have more dreams and to remember them better than deep sleepers."

Ages of the subjects ranged from 19 to 26 years, with a mean age of 22.1 years. Thirty-three of the 42 subjects were male, and all but 2 were undergraduates or graduate students. As a group, the subjects appeared to be people who had considerable difficulty in getting to sleep. They reported taking 42.56 minutes, on the average, to get to sleep on the 2 nights preceding the first experimental session. This is comparable to the 59.06 minutes characteristic of the "poor" sleepers in Monroe's (1967) study of insomnia and very much more than the 7.18 minutes reported by his "good" sleepers.

procedure

Subjects were seen individually in two 30-minute sessions, the first session on a Wednesday and the second on Friday of the same week. On Wednesday, subjects answered questions about their sleep on the 2 previous nights, Monday and Tuesday. The experimenter then explained the alleged purpose of the study. "I am interested in the possible effects of level of bodily activity on dream content. I think there might be some relationship between how active your body is internally, during sleep, and what you dream about."

Subjects were then told that they would be given a drug in the experiment:

> In order to find out the effects of bodily activity, I'm going to give you a drug to take tonight and tomorrow night. Of course, the drug is harmless; it's a nonprescription drug. It will have no effect on your ability to work or study.

Possible side effects of the drug, which constituted the experimental manipulation, were then described. While the experimenter excused himself to get the pills, subjects answered a bogus questionnaire about the frequency and type of dreams they usually experienced. When this was completed, subjects were given two sugar pill placebos, with instructions to take one that night, Wednesday, and the other on the next night, Thursday, about 15 minutes before going to bed. Subjects were instructed to continue taking any other medications as usual.[1] The drug side effects were then reiterated. To complete the cover story, subjects were given short dream-report forms which they were told to take home and complete whenever they awoke on the next 2 mornings. Finally, subjects answered a questionnaire designed to check whether they knew what symptoms the experimenter had told them to expect from the pill. The experimenter was prepared to correct any mistakes, but all subjects were aware of the appropriate side effects, and correction was never necessary.

Subjects returned on Friday of the same week for a session scheduled at the same time as the Wednesday session, and answered questions about their sleep on Wednesday and Thursday nights. Additional questions were asked about the experimental manipulation and the effects of the pills. Subjects were then interviewed, debriefed, and paid $3.

manipulating attribution

Arousal condition. The subjects' attribution of arousal was manipulated by varying the described side effects of the placebo pills. The pill was described to one group of subjects, those in the arousal condition, as a drug which would increase their level of arousal.

> This drug will increase your bodily activity. It works on the sympathetic nervous system, which is the system that arouses you and sends adrenalin

through your system. The pill will increase your heart rate and it will increase your body temperature. You may feel a little like your mind is racing. In general it may arouse you.

These side effects were selected from arousal symptoms which pretest subjects reported as being typical of a night with insomnia. When subjects who have received this side-effect description go to bed, they should believe themselves to be under the influence of an arousal-producing drug. To the extent that they experience arousal symptoms, they should attribute them to the pill, rather than to emotional cues. This attribution should result in lowered emotionality, with a consequent decrease in the time needed to fall asleep.

Relaxation condition. For subjects in the other experimental group, those in the relaxation condition, the pill was described as one which would decrease arousal.

This drug will lower your bodily activity. It works on the parasympathetic nervous system, which is the system that relaxes you. The pill will lower your heart rate. It will decrease your body temperature so that you will feel a little cooler. And it will calm down your mind. In general, it will relax you.

When subjects who have received this side-effect description go to bed, they should believe themselves to be under the influence of an arousal-reducing drug. Any arousal which they experience should be perceived as an underrepresentation of their true level of arousal. Such subjects should therefore attribute greater intensity to emotional cues than would otherwise be the case. This should result in heightened emotional states and a consequent increase in the time needed to fall asleep.

Control condition. As a control on any possible variations in sleep behavior from the earlier to the later part of the week, and as a check on any possible effects of simply being in an experiment, a control group was included. These subjects were not given pills, and were asked just to report on their dreams. They were given the same cover story about the experimenter's interest in the relation between bodily activity and dream content, but were told: "You have been placed in a control group. We want to see what kind of dreams you report on your own, without me giving you a drug." The control group and each of the experimental groups contained 14 subjects.[2]

measurement

Sleep onset. In order to avoid possible suspicion as to the true nature of the experiment, the subjects were never directly asked how long it took them to fall asleep. Instead, subjects were asked to estimate for each of the 4 nights of the experiment, (a) when they went to bed and (b) when they fell asleep. The time it took each subject to fall asleep was computed by subtracting the time he reported going to bed from the time he reported falling asleep. This measure of sleep onset constituted the chief dependent variable.

Arousal symptoms. In order to determine the extent to which arousal symptoms were experienced at bedtime and were attributed to the pills, subjects were asked to report on arousal symptoms for the 2 preexperimental nights and the 2 experimental nights. All questions were answered on either 5- or 7-point scales. In order to measure the level of experienced arousal, the following were asked: "How warm or cold did you feel?" and "How much did your mind race?" In order to determine the extent to which arousal was attributed to the pills, subjects were asked how much the pills affected their body temperature, mental activity, and alertness.

In addition, subjects were asked how much they suffered from insomnia on each night, what drug they thought the pills actually contained, and what medications they had taken during the week. Finally, subjects were asked in an open-ended interview how the manipulation had affected them and whether they had suspected the true purpose of the experiment.

results

Subjects who were encouraged to attribute their arousal to the placebo (arousal condition) should have attributed less arousal to emotional cues, should consequently have experienced less intense emotional states, and should have gotten to sleep more quickly than usual. Subjects who were encouraged to believe that the placebos had calming properties (relaxation condition) should have assumed that the arousal they experienced was an underrepresentation of that produced by emotional cues, should consequently have experienced more intense emotional states, and should have gotten to sleep less quickly than usual. If arousal subjects are to attribute less arousal to their cognitions than relaxation subjects, it is essential that they attribute more of their arousal to the pill. For preexperimental and experimental nights, subjects were asked how much arousal they experienced (how much their minds raced and how warm or cold they felt); and for experimental nights, subjects were asked how much arousal the pill produced (how drowsy or alert the pills made them feel, how much the pills made their minds race, and how warm or cold the pill made them feel). Differences in reported arousal for preexperimental and experimental nights were slight and nonsignificant. Arousal subjects reported trivially more arousal on experimental than on preexperimental nights ($+ .25$, on a 12-point scale consisting of the sum of the two arousal items), and relaxation subjects reported trivially less arousal ($- .57$, on the scale). Differences in attribution of arousal to the pill were quite marked, however. On each of the items which assessed beliefs about pill effects, arousal subjects reported more arousal as a consequence of having taken the pill than did relaxation subjects. The difference between the sum of the three items was highly significant ($t = 4.36$, $p < .001$).[3]

The differential attribution of arousal was associated with substantial differences in the time it took for subjects to fall asleep. Table 26.1 presents subjects' reports of the amount of time it took to fall asleep on preexperimental

TABLE 26.1 MEAN TIME TO GET TO SLEEP PER NIGHT, IN MINUTES, AS A FUNCTION OF EXPERIMENTAL CONDITION

STATISTIC	AROUSAL	CONTROL	SEDATION
Average of preexperimental nights	53.22	38.40	36.09
Average of experimental nights	41.52	36.96	51.24
Mean change	11.70	1.44	−15.15
t	2.25	.27	2.16
p	<.05	ns	<.05

Note.—$n = 14$ in each condition.

nights (Monday and Tuesday), and on experimental nights (Wednesday and Thursday), reported as mean number of minutes per night. It may be seen that changes were in the predicted direction. The analysis of variance of the changes in sleep-onset time was significant at the .02 level ($F = 5.03$, $df = 2/39$). Moreover, the individual treatment effects were significant. The change of nearly 12 minutes in time to get to sleep reported by subjects in the arousal condition was a significant improvement. The 15-minute change in time to get to sleep reported by subjects in the relaxation condition was a significant worsening. Subjects in the control condition reported only a trivial improvement of less than 2 minutes. Both of the hypotheses were therefore confirmed.

Examination of the sleep-onset means for the preexperimental nights showed that the arousal group took longer to get to sleep on those nights than the other groups. It therefore is important to demonstrate that the improvement shown by the arousal group was not simply due to regression. That the improvement was not due to regression is indicated by the following facts: (*a*) The difference in the highly variable sleep-onset times for preexperimental nights was not significant ($F = 1.45$, $df = 2/39$). (*b*) The elevated mean for the arousal group was entirely due to the presence in this group of two individuals who took an extremely long time to get to sleep on preexperimental nights. When these subjects were excluded from consideration, the experimental effect was still present. Eight of the remaining 12 subjects fell asleep more quickly on experimental nights, and only 2 feel asleep less quickly ($p = .05$). (*c*) Most importantly, an analysis of covariance of the change scores with preexperimental sleep onset as the covariate quite clearly indicated that regression did not account for the experimental effects. With all of the subjects included in this analysis, the F ratio was 5.38 ($df = 2/38$, $p < .01$). The fact that the covariance F was slightly higher than the F for the simple analysis of variance indicates that the experimental effects actually counteracted, to a degree, the effects of regression.

It is noteworthy that the experimental effects occurred only for subjects who believed the pill descriptions. In this first attempt at a therapeutic intervention, the experimenters were not uniformly successful in persuading the subjects that they were being given a real drug. At the final session, subjects were asked if they had believed that the pills they took were arousers, relaxers, or something else, such as a placebo. Two of the subjects in the arousal condition and six of the subjects in the relaxation condition indicated that they had not believed that either of their pills contained a drug with the properties described by the experimenter. Table 26.2 presents sleep-onset times for believing and disbelieving subjects in the arousal and relaxation conditions. It may be seen that disbelieving

TABLE 26.2   CHANGE IN SLEEP-ONSET TIME, IN MINUTES, AS A FUNCTION OF EXPERIMENTAL CONDITION AND BELIEF OR DISBELIEF IN PILL DESCRIPTIONS

GROUP	AROUSAL	RELAXATION
Believers	14.28	−29.40
	(12)	(8)
Disbelievers	−3.72	3.78
	(2)	(6)

Note.—Numbers in parentheses indicate number of subjects.

arousal subjects took slightly longer to get to sleep on experimental nights than on preexperimental nights, and disbelieving relaxation subjects fell asleep somewhat more quickly on experimental nights. This suggests that the experimental effects occurred only when subjects reinterpreted the meaning of their symptoms in lights of the "knowledge" that they had taken a drug with effects on arousal state.

It will be recalled that subjects were asked how much they suffered from insomnia on each of the preexperimental and experimental nights. The data for reported suffering do not at all resemble the data for sleep onset. Arousal subjects actually reported a trivial increase in suffering on experimental nights (.214 points on a 7-point scale), and relaxation subjects reported a trivial decrease (.071 points). Subjects apparently did not base their reports of suffering on the relative amount of time it took them to get to sleep. The correlation between the change in reported time to get to sleep and change in reported suffering was only .07.

Why is it that reports of suffering do not reflect the same patterns as reports of sleep onset? It may be that this result is merely another instance of a general, rather paradoxical finding common to studies employing cognitive manipulations of feeling states. Differences in verbal reports of feelings in these studies are usually much weaker than differences in physiological, behavioral, or behavioroid measures (Davison & Valins, 1969; Nisbett & Schachter, 1966; Valins & Ray, 1967; Zimbardo, 1966). This does not explain the present pattern of results, since the general pattern in studies of this type is itself unexplained. However, it is important to note that this is not the first study to obtain such a discrepancy.

Whatever the reason for the discrepancy, the data on reported suffering are comforting in one respect. They serve to reduce the likelihood that the data on sleep onset were produced by possible demand characteristics inherent in the design. Demand characteristics are at work if subjects, sensing what results the experimenter expects or would like to obtain, behave in such a way as to yield those results. Demand characteristics could have produced the data in the present experiment if subjects in the arousal condition sensed that the experimenter expected their insomnia to improve, and if subjects in the relaxation condition sensed that the experimenter expected their insomnia would become worse. If such biases were at work, it seems likely that they would have been reflected in subjects' answers to the straightforward question, "How much did you suffer from insomnia?" The fact that subjects did not respond in the predicted ways to such a direct question makes it appear unlikely that their reports of sleep onset were produced by a desire to please the experimenter.[4]

discussion

therapeutic applications

Insomniac subjects were led to believe that a pill produced their arousal symptoms at bedtime and were consequently able to fall asleep more quickly than usual. The goal of demonstrating the potential usefulness of reattribution therapy has therefore been realized. It would be premature, however, to propose that the reattribution technique has widespread therapeutic implications. The present study represents only a single therapeutic attempt, using only one technique, to achieve moderate improvement of unknown duration in a rather mild pathological condition. Moreover, the failure to obtain improvement in subjects' self-report of suffering must temper the authors' enthusiasm. One should demand of a therapeutic technique that it produce improvement in subjective state, not merely improvement of behavior. Nevertheless, the present findings are encouraging for a first attempt. It is hoped that the present investigation will prompt the study of other applications of the reattribution technique. To that end, the authors speculate briefly on extensions and improvements of the present method.

One undesirable aspect of the technique used in the present study, from the standpoint of producing lasting improvement, was the reliance on pills and deception. More permanent and less "gimmicky" techniques for achieving reattribution may be possible, however. For example, insomnia sufferers could be told that their arousal at bedtime is due to a general condition of high base-line autonomic arousal. (There is evidence that insomniacs do in fact have higher baseline arousal; Monroe, 1967). Just as some people have high metabolic rates, insomniacs might be told, others have a high rate of autonomic functioning. This technique, like the pills, might offer a nonemotional attribution for naturally occurring bedtime arousal, yet at the same time would eliminate the need for the patient's continuing belief in placebos.

A second extrapolation of the present method might allow for temporary use of the pill technique. Let us consider what would happen to a patient whose condition improved through the use of placebos, and who then discovered that he had been hoaxed. An experimental model of such a situation has been examined by Davison and Valins (1969). Their subjects were given a series of electric shocks and were then given placebos which, they were told, might affect their sensitivity to shock. This was followed by a series of shocks surreptitiously decreased in intensity. At this point half of the subjects were told that their pills were really placebos, and the other half were told that the drug was wearing off. In a third set of shocks, "dehoaxed" subjects were able to tolerate shocks of greater intensity. This experiment suggests that dehoaxed subjects benefited from the belief that they themselves, instead of a drug, were responsible for their behavioral improvement. Similarly, insomniacs might also benefit from learning that a mere reattribution of arousal had caused improvement. This might make it apparent to such individuals that their suffering is not inevitable and that their attitudes toward their symptoms exert an influence on the symptoms.

the attribution process

In addition to demonstrating that reattribution techniques are of potential therapeutic value, the present study was concerned with shedding more light on the attribution process itself. It should be admitted at the outset of a discussion of process that we have no definitive means of showing that the sleep-onset changes were produced by the differential attribution of arousal symptoms to the pills. Sleep-onset changes may have been produced by a variety of processes which are theoretically less interesting. It is conceivable, for example, that before going to bed, the arousal subjects were worried about the possibility that the pill would make them uncomfortably aroused, and were relieved to find that it did not have this effect. This feeling of relief might have made it easier for arousal subjects to get to sleep. Similarly, relaxation subjects might have been happily anticipating a state of relaxation at bedtime. Their disappointment (and/or resentment) upon realizing that they were not in such a state might have prevented them from going to sleep. It is also possible that there were attention shifts which made it easier for arousal subjects to fall asleep and harder for relaxation subjects to fall asleep. For example, arousal subjects may have concentrated on their symptoms rather than their worries. Or it is possible that there were differences in behavior before bedtime which made it easier for arousal subjects to fall asleep and harder for relaxation subjects to fall asleep.

The scope of the present experiment was such as to make it impractical to control for all possible alternative explanations. Thus, there is little which can be said to counter these alternatives, except to point out that they detract little from the practical interest of the present research, and to note that there was nothing in the formal or informal comments of the subjects to lend plausibility to any of these alternatives. There is, however, a remaining alternative mechanism which is wholly consistent with the attribution-theory framework and highly plausible in view of some of the comments made by subjects.

Sleep-onset changes may have been produced not by an alteration in the perceived intensity of emotionally toned cognitions, as was proposed in the introduction, but by another consequence of the initial attribution error. Informal conversations with subjects revealed that many of them appeared to worry about the fact that they were insomniacs—about their inability to control such a basic function as sleep and about the state of insomnia as evidence of more general pathology. There is good reason to believe that the experimental manipulations would have had an effect on worries such as these. Arousal subjects were told, in effect, that on experimental nights their insomnia would be caused by a drug. On experimental nights, therefore, arousal subjects did not have to view their symptoms as evidence of inadequacy or pathology. They may have worried less about their condition and may have gotten to sleep more quickly for this reason. Similarly, relaxation subjects were told, in effect, that on experimental nights they should experience fewer insomnia symptoms than usual. On experimental nights, therefore, relaxation subjects would have had to view anything less than a noticeable reduction in their symptoms as evidence of a particularly bad bout with insomnia. Upon failing to experience such a reduction, they might have worried more than usual about their condition and consequently have gotten to sleep less quickly. The attribution error may not have resulted in a change in emotionality across the board, then, but only in a change in degree of worry about the condition of insomnia. To the extent that worry about insomnia further interferes with sleep, such changes could have produced the experimental results.

Whether or not such processes occurred in the present experiment, it seems likely that there are pathologies involving a vicious cycle of the following type: (a) occurrence of symptoms, (b) worry about symptoms, and (c) consequent exacerbation of symptoms. For example, males with problems of impotence probably respond with alarm to signs of detumescence in the sexual situation. Alarm, of course, would increase the likelihood of continued loss of erection. If it were possible to change the meaning which detumescence has for the individual, alarm and consequent impotence might be prevented. Such an individual might be given a drug, for example, and told that it might occasionally produce momentary detumescence; or he might be assured that occasional detumescence in the sexual situation was characteristic of most normal males, or even that it was characteristic of particularly virile males. A cycle of symptoms, worry about symptoms, and intensified symptoms might be expected to occur with a number of other behaviors as well, including perhaps stuttering, extreme shyness, and excessive awkwardness in athletic situations. With each such condition, an externalization of the symptoms or a reinterpretation of the symptoms in nonpathological terms might help to break the cycle.[5]

suggestion and attribution

A striking aspect of the present findings is their apparent contradiction of the body of thought and research dealing with the concept of suggestion effect. On the surface, the present experiment resembles a conventional study of suggestion or placebo effects, for example, an experiment showing that administration of a "pain killer" placebo produces a reduction of pain symptoms. Yet the predictions and the obtained results of the present study were exactly opposite to those which would be indicated by suggestion theory. Subjects given a "stimulant" actually got to sleep more quickly, and subjects given a "relaxant" got to sleep less quickly. How can the present results be reconciled with the characteristic findings in the area of suggestion effects? The answer probably lies in the fact that subjects in the present experiment were quite familiar with the symptoms of insomnia. Thus, subjects had two items of information, the first supplied by the experimenter's suggestion, and the second supplied by the subject's own past experience with insomnia symptoms: (a) Subjects knew that they had taken a drug which was supposed to affect insomnia symptoms, and (b) subjects knew that their actual experience of insomnia symptoms was about the same as it usually was. Subjects should have inferred from these facts that the arousal produced by their emotions was of a different magnitude than usual. Arousal subjects should have assumed that the magnitude of emotion-produced arousal was less than usual, and relaxation subjects should have assumed the magnitude was greater. Such an additional implication, stemming from an awareness of typical symptom level, is not characteristic of most suggestion experiments, with the following notable and very instructive exception.

Experiments designed to test the effectiveness of tranquilizers must have a control condition in which subjects are given placebos which they believe to be tranquilizers. Such a placebo control condition closely resembles the relaxation condition in the present experiment. The present line of reasoning leads to the expectation that such subjects would become more anxious upon realizing that their arousal level is still rather high, despite the "fact" that they are taking tranquilizers. Work done by Rickels and his colleagues (Rickels, Baumm, Raab, Taylor, & Moore, 1965; Rickels & Downing, 1963; Rickels, Lipman, & Raab, 1966) shows that this is often the case and indicates that the subjects who get worse are precisely those with the greatest awareness of typical symptom level.

A study by Rickels et al. (1966) shows that both prolonged experience with the anxiety state and extensive experience with tranquilizing drugs increase the likelihood that treatment with placebos will produce a worsening of anxiety state. Both experience with anxiety and experience with drugs would of course serve to give the patient a more accurate base line against which to judge the effectiveness of the placebo. Patients with a chronic, long-standing illness or patients who have previously experienced anxiety relief from drugs would readily perceive that the placebo is having little effect. If such patients infer from this fact that their symptoms are unusually severe, they should get worse. This is apparently the case. The results reported by Rickels et al. (1966) are particularly striking for patients whose experience both with drugs and with their illness is extensive. Whereas almost 80% of such patients improved when treated with tranquilizers, fewer than 30% improved on placebos. Although it is not completely clear from the presentation of the data, it seems likely that the majority of the placebo-treated patients got worse. In contrast, over 70% of the acutely ill patients with no previous experience with tranquilizers actually improved on placebo. Other work, by Rickels and Downing (1967) and Rickels et al. (1965), indicates that the higher the anxiety level of the patient, the more likely it is that his condition will worsen when placed on placebo. Patients with the highest anxiety levels would of course be expected to have the greatest awareness of their predrug symptom level. It should be particularly clear to these patients that the drug is having little effect, and they should therefore be particularly likely to infer that they are getting worse.

The findings of Rickels and his colleagues lend considerable support to the present theoretical framework. Their evidence indicates that some patients do indeed get worse when given placebos which they believe to be tranquilizers. The patients who get worse are precisely the ones who would be expected to do so in terms of the present framework. Rickels et al. (1966) professed themselves to be surprised at their findings, as well they might, since theory in the area of suggestion effects is not equipped to deal with the kinds of reversal effects which attribution theory leads us to expect. A clear implication of the present findings and framework is that clinical workers should beware the use of placebos and suggestion. Before resorting to placebos or suggestion, clinicians should probably ask themselves: "Is there a further implication of the suggestion I am making to the patient? If he fails to experience the effects I suggest, can he infer something damaging about himself?"

notes

1. Only three subjects, all in the control condition, were taking sleeping pills, and they all took equal doses of their drug on each of the 4 nights of the experiment.

2. The first four subjects in the control condition were given pills "to change bodily activity level," but were told that they would not perceive any side effects. These subjects behaved like the other control subjects, and the two groups are combined for purposes of analysis.

3. All probability values are based on two-tailed tests.

4. One further artifactual possibility deserves some mention. It may have occurred to the reader that relaxation subjects might have gone to bed earlier than their usual bedtime, in the expectation that the pill would help to put them to sleep. If so, relaxation subjects might have been less tired than other subjects and might have gotten to sleep less quickly for this reason. Actually, there was a slightly greater tendency for relaxation subjects to go to bed earlier on experimental nights than there was for arousal subjects ($t = 1.57$, $p < .15$). However, the two groups reported almost identical degrees of tiredness at bedtime on experimental nights (5.32 for relaxation subjects; 5.31 for arousal subjects). Moreover, there was no correlation between the tendency to go to bed earlier on experimental nights and the tendency to take longer to get to sleep on experimental nights ($r = .12$ for relaxation subjects; $r = .04$ for arousal subjects). Thus, it seems unlikely that the tendency of relaxation subjects to go to bed earlier was responsible for the worsening in sleep-onset time.

5. The authors are indebted to Stanley Milgram for pointing out that this exacerbation cycle is probably characteristic of a number of pathologies.

references

Davison, G., & Valins, S. Maintenance of self-attributed and drug-attributed behavior change. *Journal of Personality and Social Psychology*, 1969, *11*, 25–33.

Heider, F. *The psychology of interpersonal relations.* New York: Wiley, 1958.

Kelley, H. Attribution theory in social psychology. *Nebraska Symposium on Motivation,* 1967, *15,* 192–240.

Monroe, L. J. Psychological and physiological differences between good and poor sleepers. *Journal of Abnormal Psychology,* 1967, *72,* 255–264.

Nisbett, R. E., & Schachter, S. Cognitive manipulation of pain. *Journal of Experimental Social Psychology,* 1966, *2,* 227–236.

Rickels, K., Baumm, C., Raab, E., Taylor, W., & Moore, E. A psychopharmacological evaluation of chlordiazepoxide, LA-1 and placebo, carried out with anxious, neurotic medical clinic patients. *Medical Times,* 1965, *93,* 238–242.

Rickels, K., & Downing, R. Drug- and placebo-treated neurotic outpatients. *Archives of General Psychiatry,* 1967, *16,* 369–372.

Rickels, K., Lipman, R., & Raab, E. Previous medication, duration of illness and placebo response. *Journal of Nervous and Mental Disease,* 1966, *142,* 548–554.

Ross, L., Rodin, J., & Zimbardo, P. G. Toward an attribution therapy: The reduction of fear through induced cognitive-emotional misattribution. *Journal of Personality and Social Psychology,* 1969, *12,* 279–288.

Schachter, S., & Singer, J. E. Cognitive, social and physiological determinants of emotional state. *Psychological Review,* 1962, *69,* 379–399.

Valins, S. Cognitive effects of false heart-rate feedback. *Journal of Personality and Social Psychology,* 1966, *4,* 400–408.

Valins, S., & Ray, A. Effects of cognitive desensitization on avoidance behavior. *Journal of Personality and Social Psychology,* 1967, *7,* 345–350.

Zimbardo, P. G. The cognitive control of motivation. *Transactions of the New York Academy of Sciences,* 1966, *28,* 902–922.

27

The End of Ideology in Behavior Modification

Perry London

When little "behavior modifiers" sit at their professional daddys' knees and ask, "Where did I come from?" they are usually told a story about the "principles of learning" that spawned them, the evil clinicians who left them to perish on a hillside, and the kindly shepherd doctors who found them, raised them as their own, and eventually restored them to their rightful position as the benefactors of behavior. When they grow up, confer their own benefits, and spawn their own little behavior modifiers, they become disabused of the myth. But not entirely— there remains, at the very least, a tradition of deferring to the principles of learning as the ultimate source of all good modifications and a parallel ritual of knocking psychoanalysts, Rogerians, existentialists, and general psychiatrists who have not yet mastered or endorsed the jargon of respondents, operants, and reinforcements.

Reprinted from the *American Psychologist,* 1972, Vol. 27, No. 10, pp. 913–920. Copyright 1972 by the American Psychological Association. Reprinted by permission.

Like most myths, this tale has been based on some true events and has proved useful for the promotion of behavioristic patriotism and for extending the frontiers of experimentation and the clinical and technical growth of the field. And it makes a good story. But enough is enough. The borders are secure now, the settlers are thriving, the dark untrammeled forests are trammeled and cut down, the stumps blown, the fields plowed. It is time now to build this domain, not defend it.

Building it requires three things: first, abandoning strife with other modalities and developing peaceful commerce to see what they have to offer and exchange; second, examining the constructs that underlie modifying operations and that give clues for the design of new ones; and finally, devoting ourselves to "criterion validity," that is, to building treatment methods that work. The entire field has been moving in these directions during the past few years, but only partly I think, as a result of the intelligent pressures of people making these recommendations. The shift results also from technological changes in related disciplines and from attitude changes in the entire society that supports them. New equipment brings new possibilities for use and a new social readiness to use it, and the speed with which it gets advertised and talked about pushes advances in practice that no theory is likely to keep up with. This article argues that it is probably just as well.

For public purposes, behavior modifiers of the 1960s usually described their activities as logically inevitable corollaries of theorems or principles of learning and of ongoing discoveries about how they applied to disordered human behavior. Actually, there were only about three principles that they ever referred to, all of which can be reduced to one or one and a half principles—namely, that learning depends on the connections in time, space, and attention between what you do and what happens to you subsequently (Franks, 1969; Lazarus, 1971). In addition, the special application to human behavior was predicated less on ongoing scientific discoveries about learning or about people than on the idea that human neuroses are probably about the same as animal neuroses (Wolpe, 1958). The critical principles of learning involved had all been spelled out rather elaborately between 1898 and 1938, and the business about animal neuroses was posited by Pavlov in the same period. During that period, in fact, Pavlov, Watson, Jones, Mowrer, and Guthrie pretty much spelled out all of the major behavior therapy methods that became popular for treating people since 1958, with the possible exception of desensitization and operant behavior shaping (London, 1964). And they are exceptions only because the former is not derived from the usual learning principles, and cannot be, and because the latter is something everybody knew about anyhow but never applied ingeniously until Skinner laboriously spelled out its monumental implications.

evolution of behavior modification

The early growth of behavior modification as a professional specialty was largely polemical and political, not theoretical, and most of its scientific hoopla evolved to serve the polemical needs of the people who made it up—not all of it, however, and not only polemical needs.

The study of learning for behavior therapists, in fact, was always more for the purpose of metaphor, paradigm, and analogy than for strict guidance about how to operate or about what it all means. Whatever value theory may have for dictating laboratory procedures, therapeutic operations have been essentially seat-of-the-pants affairs, and still are, because they address immediate practical problems that require solutions in fact, not in principle. The disregarding of principles to see what really works, in this connection, reflects the intelligence and scientific good sense of therapists. The search for principles to explain what works, on the other hand, reflects their integrity and their anxiety—integrity because only fools would accept their own results without question, anxiety because therapists seek principles as much to increase their confidence as to reduce their ignorance. People also look for principles to help fight intellectual battles. Conventional therapies could be assaulted for their ineffectiveness, but the basis for offering new ones had to be more than complaints about the old ones. And in the case of behavior modification, it had to be more than a simplistic appeal to "what works." Of all popular therapies, psychoanalysis in particular was based on a pretentious, respectable, and smart *theory*. It could not be challenged with less than a theory.

Learning theory was an obvious choice: first, because there is a history of suggested therapeutic applications of learning principles, from Thorndike and Pavlov through Mowrer and Guthrie; and second, because the heart of any *psychotherapy* is changing people's behavior without changing their body structure or gross functions—which means, in plain language, teaching them and getting them to learn.

Even so, the evolution of behavior modification did not go so neatly. It could not make much use of learning theory, except for the broadest principles of learning, because most of the principles either do not yet have any really systematic application to disorders, or because they are much more in dispute than naive students realize.

The polemics actually used attacked evident flaws in psychoanalytic and other psychiatric formulations, sometimes also getting a little professional jealousy of psychologists for doctors into the act. Their main points were (*a*) an attack on "the medical model"; (*b*) the insistence that the origins of disorder were in *learning* instead of biochemical or genetic events; (*c*) the proposition that effective therapeutics should treat symptoms instead of their causes, that is, that disorders are identical with their symptoms; and finally, (*d*) the demand that even the name of the game should be changed from psychotherapy to behavior therapy, so no one thinks we are mentalistic or unscientific, as other therapies obviously are (sic).

This description is not exaggerated at all. Eysenck's (1959) tabulation of "the more important differences between Freudian Psychotherapy and Behavior Therapy," for instance, says that Freudian therapy is "based on inconsisent theory never properly formulated in postulate form," while behavior therapy is "based on consistent, properly formulated theory leading to testable deductions." Similarly, Freudian practice is "derived from clinical observations made without necessary control, observation or experiment," while behavior therapy is "derived from experimental studies specifically designed to test basic theory and deductions made therefrom [p. 67]." Franks (1969) is kinder than Eysenck, but even he says, a decade later, "for most behavior therapists, the preferred sequence of events is from experimental observation to clinical practice. This may be contrasted with the approach of traditional psychotherapists, in which the sequence is often reversed [p. 3]."

These arguments are not entirely pointless, but they are not entirely apropos of anything either, except who is smart and who will get the last word. What makes them largely irrelevant is that explanatory concepts are only necessary to explain what is going on—and until you know that, you do not need a theory, at least not much of one. Such theory, at this point in this enterprise, has to be stretched to fit facts rather than tailored to them. And it is damaging in the long run because people may start believing it and making up nonsense to plead silly cases that confuse everybody and enlighten no one. Enormous time and space have been wasted in pious debates on irrelevant aspects of most of the popular polemic issues of psychotherapy.

Discussions of "the medical model," for instance, often contrast "learning theory" approaches to "psychodynamic" approaches. There is a real question about the relative utility of *organic* versus *dynamic* perspectives on some behavior disorders, but all learning theory formulations are, in fact, dynamic ones. Also, there are many medical models, and the general attack on "the" medical model is only applicable to the *infectious disease* model, and only usable against psychoanalysis by lamely borrowing against Freud's (1961) unfortunate statement about putting demonology inside peoples' heads. Medical *epidemiological* models should have some appeal to Skinnerians, in fact, with their emphasis on environmental determinants of disorder, just as psychological models of habit formation are good for understanding the course of some developmental or degenerative medical conditions like heart disease.

The controversy about (learned versus structural) origins of disorder is mostly pointless because it is mostly irrelevant to treatment. The behaviorist attack commonly assumes that a genetic or biochemical view of etiology is bad because if disorder is learned, then treatment must be a learning process. This is nonsense. Etiology and treatment have no logical connection in either direction. Anxiety, for example, may be the result of prior experience, but can be alleviated chemically; or it may be aroused by essentially chemical circumstances (like fatigue plus mild arousal to danger), but can be soothed physically or verbally (Davison, 1968).

The only treatment question of relevance is that of the functional relationship between the problem and its solution. The process is what matters and nothing else.

The biggest polemic, of course, about treating symptoms versus causes has occurred largely because of the uncertain danger of symptom return or symptom substitution. Everywhere, much confusion has occurred, mostly because of confusion about the "medical model"—in this instance, about the exact meaning of symptom. If symptom means trouble, surely it should be treated. If not, maybe not. The polemic has been around the question of symptoms as "the main trouble"; this is because of the widespread belief, largely from psychoanalysis, in symptom return or substitution. (Buchwald and Young [1969] point out, incidentally, that some analysts, such as Fenichel and, later, Alexander, thought that symptoms should be treated directly.)

The real issue, in any case, is the consequence of the treatment for the person's condition—or his life. Sometimes too, the issue is prophylactic or preventive rather than ameliorative. This becomes clear by comparing the infectious disease and chronic ailment models in medicine. Behavior disorders are more like chronic ailments, where medical treatment generally aims at the symptoms only. The control of diabetes, on the other hand, is not treatment of symptoms, but their prevention. Is the shaping of behavior likewise? For changing the table manners of psychotics' ward behavior, maybe not; for molding children's manners, maybe so. The same question may be addressed to assertive training or to aversion training. Is teaching someone to talk back to his mother-in-law "reducing his anxiety" or preventing it from happening? Is teaching a homosexual man to attend to women when aroused and to feel repugnance for sex with men relieving his symptom or preventing a disorder (which does not exist legally until he "goes for" the man), teaching a habit pattern or unteaching one, changing a life style, altering a phenomenological field, shifting ego boundaries, redirecting id impulses or superego functions, or cathexis? And if he "feels" different or thinks about it differently, is it still behavior therapy?

These are silly questions. The change in the homosexual is all those things, depending on how you want to talk about them. Understanding the process is what matters, not belaboring the different styles of talking about it. The only important question about systematic treatment is that of the simultaneous relevance of the treatment technique to the person's manifest trouble and to the rest of his life.

Sometimes it accounts for both at once—as when he is suicidal. Sometimes it accounts for the rest of his life but not for the symptom—which is the behavior modifier's claim against insight types' preoccupation with motivation. Sometimes it accounts for only the manifest trouble—which is the insight therapists' accusation against behavior modifiers, based on the specious presumption that everything in a person's life is integral to it.

All of these polemics were not so much meaningless as overdone. The assault on psychoanalysts and existentialists was too extreme; the scientific claims on learning were too grandiose (Buchwald & Young, 1969; Franks, 1969). Changing from psychotherapy to behavior therapy may have been useful for people brought up on mind-body dualism, but for those of us who always thought the mind hung around the brain and that behavior meant "what happened," the distinction was graceless and gratuitous.

When you eliminate the polemics and politics and gratuities, however, what remains of theory to define the field and to tell you what it is about? Not a whole lot. The definition of the field either becomes very inclusive (Lazarus, 1971; Marks, 1971; Marston, 1970; Paul, 1969; Skinner, 1971) or very narrow (Eysenck, 1960; Skinner, 1963; Wolpe, 1968). This probably makes no serious difference to anything. As Kuhn (1962) said, "Can a definition tell a man whether he is a scientist or not [p. 160]?"

But what about theory? If behavior modification lacks theory, then is it not reduced to a technology rather than a science? Yes it is, and I believe that is what it should be, just as medicine is technology rather than science.

There is some dispute in the field about this point. The sides are well represented by Lazarus, who agrees with my view, and Franks, who does not. Lazarus (1971) said, in his latest book:

> The emphasis of the volume is upon techniques rather than upon theories. . . . Methods of therapy are often effective for reasons which are at variance with the views of their inventors or discoverers. Technical eclecticism (Lazarus, 1967) does not imply a random melange of techniques taken haphazardly out of the air. It is an approach which urges therapists to experiment with empirically useful methods instead of using their theories as a priori predictors of what will and will not succeed in therapy (Eysenck, 1957, p. 271). The rationale behind the methods described in this book is predicated upon London's (1964) observation that: "However interesting, plausible, and appealing a theory may be, it is techniques, not theories, that are actually used on people. Study of the effect of psychotherapy, therefore, is always the study of the effectiveness of techniques" [p. 33].

Franks (1969) argued, to the contrary:

> It would seem to be highly desirable for the therapist to aspire to be a scientist even if this goal were difficult to realize. To function as a scientist, it is necessary to espouse some theoretical framework. For reasons too obvious to detail here, this is true of the behavioral therapist. . . . How the behavior therapist practices (including his choice of technique, his approach to the problems of general strategy, and his specific relationships with his patient) thus depending both upon his explicit theoretical orientation and upon his implicit philosophical and cultural milieu [p. 21].

The argument that behavior modification should view itself as technology rather than as science is not meant to denigrate the importance of theory, either scientifically or heuristically. Scientifically, theory is valuable because it directs the systematic search for new information by interpreting and integrating what is already known. Heuristically, theory is valuable because it lays our biases out in the open and, by explicating them, makes it easier for us to disavow them when they are found to be inadequate.

The question with respect to behavior modification is twofold: First, is current theory very good (scientifically) in this case? Second, is any theory very useful for the current development of this field at this time? I think the answer to both questions is no.

In reality, behavior therapists never did have so much a theory as an "ideology"; in my own paraphrase of Bell (1960) and Tomkins (1964), "Ideology does not mean just ideas, but ideas to be acted on . . . [London, 1969]." What behavior therapists called theory actually served as bases for commitment or a rallying point for talking about disorder and treatment in a certain way and, more important, about acting on it within particular sets of limited operations, that is, technical limits. In this case, the commitment is to the *functional analysis of problems.* And it is for this reason that the domain incorporated within the legitimate purview of the field becomes broader and broader and the polemics milder and milder—as it is recognized that even Rogerians and humanists and psychoanalysts may analyze some things functionally and act on them accordingly.

What results from the increasing functional analysis of problems is an increasing number of plausible methods for coping with them—until the proliferation of methods is tested and found to work, no theory is really very necessary to explain *why* they work. For practitioners, none may be needed even then, if they work well. In any case, theory will largely grow from practice (Lazarus & Davison, 1971) and practice from instrumentation, in the broadest sense; this will happen to behavior modification just like it did to psychoanalysis, but with two generations' more experience, the results, hopefully, will be more scientific.

The status of theory comes largely from the belief that technique develops out of theory, that is, that science underlies engineering. But this is only partly true even among very "hard" sciences, less so among "soft" sciences, like the social and behavioral sciences, and not at all true for many endeavors where the existence of the technological capacity and the practical need is what produces the technical application and, indeed, what "nourishes" much of the theoretical development itself (Oppenheimer, 1956).

This does not mean that the alternative to rude theory is rude empiricism; rather, it suggests a close-to-the-situation functional analysis instead of a premature and precocious search for general principles from which to get overextended, or for a professional ideology to which to be committed. Such a development seems to be proceeding now, with practitioners using the techniques of behavior modification but declining the identity (Paul, 1969b), and scholars recommending heterodoxies like "technical eclecticism" without shame (Lazarus, 1971). The rest of this article spells out what this development means, so we will see clearly what we are doing, with the view to doing it better.

By deducing the intellectual condition of behavior modification from the technology it uses, there seem to be two kinds of conceptual schemes which characterize it. Borrowing from Price's (1971) book, *Abnormal Psychology: Perspectives in Conflict*, in turn derived from Kuhn's (1962) *Structure of Scientific Revolutions*, these are first, *metaphors* or analogies, and second, *paradigms* or models.

In the conventional classification of how much we seem to know what we are talking about in science, these concepts fit the lower end of the scale of certainty whose upper rungs are called "theories" and "laws." A scientific law, in other words, is an idea that seems absolutely to comprehend all of the facts it talks about; a theory is one that hopes to do so, but is not so compellingly known to do so. The activities involved in behavior modification are a good distance below both those points on the same continuum. A few are paradigms or models, that is, ideas that seem to explain a group of facts pretty precisely; most are metaphors or analogies, that is, ideas that look like they might fit a group of facts, where there is no clear evidence that they really do.

In general, the treatment methods derived from speculations about conditioning studies of animals are metaphorical or analogous, especially desensitization and implosion, or flooding. In general, the treatment methods that fall under the heading of education or training or, in jargon, of instrumental learning are paradigmatic or exemplary, including modeling, shaping, and possibly aversion techniques.

The difference between the metaphoric and the paradigmatic treatments is not in how well they work, but only in how well their workings are understood. This, in turn, reduces to how much of the mechanics involved can be predicted or explained with what degree of precision, which reduces still further to how many of the details are visible or can be inferred with different degrees of correlation. For practical purposes, the difference is simply one of the extent to which you can see what is going on enough to figure out how variations in your approach will affect it. The more you can peer intellectually into the "black box" in other words, and the prediction proves correct, the more you are dealing with a paradigm rather than a metaphor. A paradigm, in other words, is an attempt to construct a direct model or example of how something works. A metaphor is a more oblique comparison, in which the flaws in the analogy are obvious, but the similarities are still big enough to allow us to ask whether the comparison might "work."[1]

Desensitization is only a metaphor or analogy to conditioning: first, because it involves a specific cognitive process (the use of language) that classical conditioning does not; second, because it involves a mechanism of sequential imagination that can only be guessed at from conditioning studies; and third, because it is subject to a variety of successful variations that could not be predicted from the situations from which the metaphor was derived in the first place. Finally, desensitization does the same thing that implosion or flooding does, though it appears to be an opposite method.

Implosion is a better analogy than desensitization because Stampfl's original experiment (London, 1964) seems to parallel both Mowrer's (1950) theoretical statement, Solomon, Kamin, and Wynne's (1953), and Black's (1958) animal experiments more closely than Wolpe fits Masserman's cats or Pavlov's dogs. Also, implosion technique does predict all of its own variants—including Watson, Gaind, and Marks' (1971) finding that practice helps to extinguish phobic reactions and that using real objects instead of imagination as fearful stimuli also is helpful—but it is metaphorical nonetheless because it is between people, and because it is administered in social situations where the pressure *not* to escape is obviously coming from the thoughts that the patient has about the situation, not from physical restraints on his action.

Shaping is more exemplary or paradigmatic than conditioning treatments because it presumes less, in the first place, on the black box—modeling, likewise. Stated differently, both shaping and modeling methods can aim for precision in establishing the conditions that will work the desired effects without having to worry much about what is going on in the person that makes them work. *Aversion* treatment is more paradigmatic than metaphoric because its critical stimulus is not cognitive; that is, it hurts the patient physically. Giving a person an electric shock is much more like shocking a dog than telling scary stories to a person is like blowing air up a rat's behind; ergo, it is more paradigmatic than metaphoric.

Neither metaphors nor paradigms are scientific theories by some distance, but both of them are useful intellectual tools. *Metaphor* and *analogy* are good heuristically—they help to turn images into thoughts and inchoate hunches into articulate propositions. *Paradigms* are more literally useful—they model to scale what you need to do, or give a mathematical formula into which you can put specific quanta.

Notice, however, that none of this has anything to do with whether anything works for any practical problem. Desensitization may be a poor deduction from conditioning, but it is a fine treatment for phobias. Behavior shaping may be an excellent paradigm for getting autistic children to hug people, but it does not teach them syntactical speech.

Whatever scientific concern people have about the intellectual status of the field, at this point in the development of this enterprise, none of this material is yet very important to practitioners, and it is barely important to clinical research. What *is* important, at this juncture, is the development of systematic practice and of a technology to sustain it. My thesis is that, in the long run, scientific understanding will derive from them.

The practitioner tries to figure out what will work, for the most part, and then, if he is scientifically inclined, looks for a way to rationalize it if it does. The technologist devises machinery to support him. This is not a bad idea, even if it doesn't add up to test-tube-pure, white-coat science. Systematic desensitization is a good example of this process because, by "working" in the first place, it has given rise to technological refinements of itself that also work and that still leave the reasons unexplained. In the long run, this must force better and better logical and experimental confrontations with the reasons for the phenomenon—which success alone would not have done.

New equipment, new drugs, new gimmickry and gadgetry should now be the basis for systematically developing new methods of behavior modification and for streamlining the established techniques with controlled experimental testing. Instead of looking for new principles, or justifying worn-out ones, we should look for new applications: What could we do to treat such-and-such if we had such-and-such machinery? What would be required to build it? To test it? And then, finally, to determine what it means?

The critical point is that *good technology always undermines bad theory*.

"Bad" is not meant to be pejorative here; it means metaphoric. Precise technology reveals the empirical error in metaphoric reasoning and in the operations that result from it. So Lang's (1969a, 1969b) on-line computer removes the therapist from the desensitization process; Quirk's (1970) machine removes the imagining and the relevance of the phobic subject matter; and Wolpin's (Jacobs & Wolpin, 1971; Wolpin, 1969; Wolpin & Raines, 1966) removes the need for hypnosis, for the fear hierarchy, and, indeed, for relaxation. Since the method still works, the need for explanation becomes more and more apparent (Davison, 1969), as does the inadequacy of the very plausible metaphor that launched Wolpe (1958) on the whole business.

Technology promises, in fact, more and more to turn metaphor to paradigm, if not paradigm to theory, by going directly into the black box and doing funny things to it and, increasingly, by bringing the black box out into the open where we can see more and more what has been happening in it. For the former, I refer to drug research and to the work in progress on electrical stimulation of the brain (Cohen, 1969; Delgado, 1969; London, 1969). These activities undercut specious distinctions between learned and unlearned patterns, either by manipulating the patterns out of hand or by potentiating learning so effectively that the issue of its importance disappears.

Bringing the black box out into the open is one of the main results likely to accrue from *biofeedback* research, and it is probably the best illustration one can find of technology feeding sciences with one hand as it enhances practice with the other. All of the biofeedback methods work on a single principle, whether they teach people to ring buzzers from a switch in their heads or to alter their blood pressure or heartbeat or skin resistance by monitoring lights and gauges. The principle is finding a means of accurately externally recording some internal process, then of projecting that record into the person's consciousness so that he can literally see or hear what his blood vessels or brain waves or heart muscles are doing. Then let him learn to manipulate his conscious sensory experience in whatever way people learn to do anything consciously—something about which we really know next to nothing.

The clinical value of biofeedback methods remains to be seen and will certainly not be what alpha-machine hucksters seem to wish—instant cool for overheated psyches. Its clinical utility is not yet the point, only its technological sophistication and the scientific potential that comes from that.

To turn the point around, I am saying that theory has worn itself out in behavior modification and that technology, essentially of treatment, should now be a primary focus, perhaps, in the long range, even for serving scientific purposes. What began with the Mowrers' quilted pad in 1938 is extending now into therapeutic on-line computers, electric pottie chairs, electronic skin braille, and an almost self-generating brace of valuable hardware for therapeutic purposes. A summary of much of it will appear soon in a book by Robert and Ralph Schwitzgebel [1973] entitled *Psychotechnology*.

But the proper development that I am suggesting is not limited to hardware and is not self-generating, but reaches to the systematic exploration of all kinds of therapeutic things without inhibition or concern as to whether they fit ostensible *principles* of learning, or reinforcement, or whatever, but with a singular focus on whether they fit the *facts* of human experience. No one has been more forthright or resourceful in this connection than Lazarus (1971), whose latest work, *Behavior Therapy and Beyond*, goes into such things as imagery exercises for depression; thought control, straight out, for whatever it works for;

hypnosis for all kinds of things; exaggerated role taking à la the late George Kelly; differential relaxation; covert sensitization for aversive imaging; and Masters and Johnson's penis squeezing for premature ejaculation. It would take a genius or a madman to shelter this whole array of techniques under the intellectual umbrella of conditioning, or learning, or any other single psychological theory. It would take a fool to want to. The first issue, scientifically as well as clinically, is the factual one—Do they work? On whom? When? The how and why come later.

With the era of polemics virtually ended, and Skinner (1971) citing Freud over and over again in his latest work, and the American Psychoanalytic Association at a recent convention casually incorporating behavior modification into its discourses on psychotherapy, the political utility of learning theory, so called for the definition of the field, is ended. It was never really theory anyhow, as we used it, but ideology for professional purposes and mostly metaphor for clinical ones. It is time now, I think, for the remedial branch of this business to stop worrying about its scientific pretensions, in the theoretical sense, as long as it keeps its functional nose clean, and to devise a kind of engineering subsidiary, or more precisely, a systems analysis approach to its own operations. We have gotten about as much mileage as we are going to out of old principles, even correct ones, but we have barely begun to work the new technology.

note

1. Oppenheimer (1956) distinguished analogy from metaphor because the "structural similarity" of analogous events implies more precision in their comparison than is ordinarily true of metaphoric comparisons. I am putting them together here, however, to distinguish them both from paradigm.

references

Bell, D. *End of ideology: Exhaustion of political ideas in the fifties.* Glencoe, Ill.: Free Press, 1960.

Black, A. H. The extinction of avoidance responses under curare. *Journal of Comparative and Physiological Psychology*, 1958, *51*, 519–524

Buchwald, A. M., & Young, R. D. Some comments on the foundations of behavior therapy. In C. M. Franks (Ed.), *Behavior therapy: Appraisal and status.* New York: McGraw-Hill, 1969.

Cohen, S. I. Neurobiological considerations for behavior therapy. In C. M. Franks (Ed.), *Behavior therapy: Appraisal and status.* New York: McGraw-Hill, 1969.

Davison, G. C. Systematic desensitization as a counter-conditioning process. *Journal of Abnormal Psychology*, 1968, *73*, 91–99.

Davison, G. C. A procedural critique of "desensitization and the experimental reduction of threat." *Journal of Abnormal Psychology*, 1969, *74*, 86–87.

Delgado, J. M. R. *Physical control of the mind.* New York: Harper & Row, 1969.

Eysenck, H. J. Learning theory and behavior therapy. *Journal of Mental Science*, 1959, *105*, 61–75.

Eysenck, H. J. (Ed.) *Behavior therapy and neuroses.* London: Pergamon Press, 1960.

Franks, C. M. *Behavior therapy: Appraisal and status.* New York: McGraw-Hill, 1969.

Freud, S. *The standard edition of the complete psychological works of Sigmund Freud.* London: Hogarth Press, 1961.

Jacobs, A., & Wolpin, M. A second look at systematic desensitization. In, *Psychology of private events*. New York: Academic Press, 1971.

Kuhn, T. S. *The structure of scientific revolutions*. Chicago: University of Chicago Press, 1962.

Lang, P. J. The mechanics of desensitization and the laboratory study of human fear. In C. M. Franks (Ed.), *Behavior therapy*. New York: McGraw-Hill, 1969. (a)

Lang, P. J. The on-line computer in behavior therapy research. *American Psychologist*, 1969, *24*, 236–239. (b)

Lazarus, A. A. *Behavior therapy and beyond*. New York: McGraw-Hill, 1971.

Lazarus, A. A., & Davison, G. C. Clinical innovation in research and practice. In A. E. Bergin & S. L. Garfield (Eds.), *Handbook of psychotherapy and behavior change*. New York: Wiley, 1971.

London, P. *The modes and morals of psychotherapy*. New York: Holt, Rinehart & Winston, 1964.

London, P. *Behavior control*. New York: Harper & Row, 1969.

Marks, I. M. The future of the psychotherapies. *British Journal of Psychiatry*, 1971, *118*, 69–73.

Marston, A. Parables for behavior therapists. Address given to Southern California Behavior Modification Conference, Los Angeles, October 1970.

Mowrer, O. H. *Learning theory and personality dynamics*. New York: Ronald Press, 1950.

Oppenheimer, R. Analogy in science. *American Psychologist*, 1956, *11*, 127–135.

Paul, G. L. Behavior modification research: Design and tactics. In C. M. Franks (Ed.), *Behavior therapy: Appraisal and status*. New York: McGraw-Hill, 1969. (a)

Paul, G. L. Outcome of systematic desensitization: II. Controlled investigations of individual treatment, technique variations and current status. In C. M. Franks (Ed.), *Behavior therapy*. New York: McGraw-Hill, 1969. (b)

Price, R. *Abnormal psychology: Positions in perspective*. New York: Holt, Rinehart & Winston, 1972.

Quirk, D. A. *Stimulus conditioned autonomic response suppression: A behavioral therapy*. Toronto: University of Toronto, Clarke Institute of Psychiatry, 1970.

Schwitzgebel, R. L., & Schwitzgebel, R. K. *Psychotechnology*. New York: Holt, Rinehart & Winston, 1973.

Skinner, B. F. Behaviorism at fifty. *Science*, 1963, *140*, 951–958.

Skinner, B. F. *Beyond freedom and dignity*. New York: Knopf, 1971.

Solomon, R. L., Kamin, L. J., & Wynne, L. C. Traumatic avoidance learning: The outcomes of several extinction procedures with dogs. *Journal of Abnormal and Social Psychology*, 1953, *48*, 291–302.

Tomkins, S. The psychology of knowledge. Invited address to Division 8 presented at the meeting of the American Psychological Association, Los Angeles, September 7, 1964.

Watson, J. P., Gaind, R., & Marks, I. M. Prolonged exposure: A rapid treatment for phobias. *British Medical Journal*, 1971, *1*, 13–15.

Wolpe, J. *Psychotherapy by reciprocal inhibition*. Stanford: Stanford University Press, 1958.

Wolpin, M. Guided imagining to reduce avoidance behavior. *Psychotherapy: Theory, Research and Practice*, 1969, *6*, 122–124.

Wolpin, M., & Raines, J. Visual imagery, expected roles and extinction as possible factors in reducing fear and avoidance behavior. *Behavior Research and Therapy*, 1966, *4*, 25–37.

THINK

1. In "The Secrets of the Heart," London contends that insight therapists offer insight for its own sake. Moreover, they appear not to take responsibility for the cure or absence of cure in their patients. His arguments seem very different from those offered by insight therapists themselves. Is London correct? Does insight have any therapeutic function? If so, what might it be?
2. When does a recently invented psychotherapy become a genuine treatment? Does the invention alone guarantee effectiveness? Or do we have to obtain some data on the effectiveness of the psychotherapy before we call it a treatment? If so, how much data should we obtain before we certify that the treatment is effective? And do you think we should certify treatments through a federal agency, much as we certify drugs for their effectiveness and their potential harm?
3. Imagine yourself doing attribution therapy in the manner of Storms and Nisbett. How might you function with a person who is excessively shy? What would you suggest?

   Are there any dangers involved in this kind of therapy? There clearly is some deception involved in it. What happens if the client discovers the deception? How does one later maintain his trust?
4. In "The End of Ideology in Behavior Modification," London argues that technology and techniques of behavior modification can develop without the aid of theory. Do you agree with his position? How can such development occur except on a hit and miss basis? Doesn't one need theory in order to know where to look and how to invent techniques and technologies?

Name Index

Subject Index